LAROUSSE
WINE

English text copyright © 2011 by Octopus Publishing Group Ltd.

All rights reserved.
Published in the United States by Clarkson Potter/Publishers, an imprint of
the Crown Publishing Group, a division of Random House, Inc., New York.
www.crownpublishing.com
www.clarksonpotter.com

CLARKSON POTTER is a trademark and POTTER with colophon is a
registered trademark of Random House, Inc.

Originally published in France as *Grand Larousse du Vin* by Editions
Larousse, Paris, in 2010. Copyright © 2010 by Larousse, Paris. This
English translation was originally published in Great Britain by Hamlyn,
a division of Octopus Publishing Group Ltd., a Hachette UK Company,
London, in 2011.

Library of Congress Cataloging-in-Publication Data is available upon request.

ISBN 978-0-307-95222-6

Printed in China

Endpaper photograph (top right): Andrew Gunners/Digital Vision/Getty
Images

10 9 8 7 6 5 4 3 2 1

First American Edition

LAROUSSE

WINE

THE WORLD'S GREATEST

VINES, ESTATES, AND REGIONS

CLARKSON POTTER/PUBLISHERS
NEW YORK

CONTRIBUTORS

The following have contributed to this edition:

Georges Lepré, Master Sommelier, technical consultant for the entire book

and:

Guy Bonnefoit, wine expert and author of books on wine
Pierrick Bourgault, agronomist, journalist, and photographer
Jean-Moïse Braitberg, journalist and author of books on wine
David Cobbold, journalist and critic, author of articles and books on wine
Jean-Michel Deluc, Master Sommelier, international consultant, and lecturer
Michel Dovaz, oenologist, professor at the Académie du Vin in Paris
Sébastien Durand-Viel, journalist and critic, author of articles and books on wine
Benoît Grandin, wine journalist
Mathilde Hulot, journalist and author of books on wine
Egmont Labadie, journalist and author on gastronomy and wine
Valérie de Lescure, journalist and critic, author of books on wine
Evelyne Malnic, journalist and author of books on wine
Antoine Petrus, Best Young Sommelier in France 2007

The publisher is also grateful to the following for their assistance: Myriam Huet for *Vers une agriculture plus écologique* (*Toward greener wine production*), *Des techniques qui font polémique* (*Techniques that are controversial*), and *Les idées fausses autour du vin* (*False beliefs about wine*); Hélène Piot for *Sommelier, l'ambassadeur des vins* (*The Sommelier as wine ambassador*); and Véronique Raisin for *Le marché mondial du vin* (*World of wine*).

Contents

PREFACE

Wine is an invitation to go on a journey. This book bears witness to that trip. The road begins with discovery of the extraordinary diversity of grape varieties and *terroirs* that exist all over the world. It then introduces you to the people involved and the work they accomplish in countless vineyards and wine cellars. Finally, it takes you into the world of wine tasting and reveals the incredible variety of wines on every continent.

I am dedicated to learning about the wines of the world. I have spent a good part of my life in this pursuit, and I continue to study the development of the many, diverse vineyards with immense curiosity. Driven by a quest for new *terroirs* and grape varieties, I have visited several regions and on every occasion have learned a great deal, both on a cultural and a personal level. Today, I am aware that every continent displays a desire, even an obsession, to produce the finest wines.

There is no doubt that the traditional vineyards of Europe, represented in particular by France, but also by Italy and Spain, still occupy a leading position as a result of their history, culture, traditions, and scale. However, many of us have yet to discover the fascinating diversity of vineyards in Central and Eastern Europe. Some countries in the Middle East also show good potential, with the emergence of small, ambitious wineries. And what about all the New World wines that arrived on the shelves of our supermarkets and our wine shops starting 25 years ago, transforming the economic landscape of wine production? There are beautiful estates to explore, whether in Chile or California, and each embarked on the hunt for new *terroirs* suitable for producing ever more concentrated, balanced wines. Lastly, we watch with interest as India and China develop significant wine projects. The fact that Asia is as interested in producing wine as it is tea represents a real sea change. But wine inspires aspirations everywhere. New countries are introducing viticulture, and a huge variety of wines are out there for us to investigate. This book will help you discover the diversity and richness of wines produced throughout the world. I also hope it will inspire you to rediscover familiar wines as well as to explore those with unexpected aromas and flavors.

Olivier Poussier
World's leading sommelier

DISCOVERING VINES AND WINE

THE ORIGINS
OF WINE

HOW WINE BEGAN

Who made the first wine? Where was the first vineyard located? So many questions remain unanswered. However, the fact remains that wine has been intimately linked to world culture for 7,000 years and continues to influence it today.

The first vineyard

The accidental production of wine probably occurred in those places where wild vines and human habitats overlapped. The step from wild vines to the cultivation of wine was significantly greater. Archaeologists can determine whether seeds found at inhabited sites came from wild or cultivated grapes that are 7,000 years old; and seeds from cultivated vines have been uncovered in the Caucasus, to the east of the Black Sea. It seems, therefore, that the first vineyard was planted somewhere between the countries known today as Turkey, Georgia, and Armenia. Wild vines were already present in this region, in which both the climate and terrain are suited to their cultivation.

WINE, A MAJOR PART OF CIVILIZATION. When looking at the early period of wine's history, it is vital to take into account the key role it played in the daily lives of the Ancient Greeks and, later, the Romans. This and, importantly, its use in religious events and rituals, made wine a major factor in early western civilization. At the time of the Ancient Greeks, the inhabitants of China also were aware of wine, but did little to

The Babylonians evoked a magical vineyard made of precious stones in the epic poem of Gilgamesh (18th century BC), the earliest written work.

exploit it. The growing of vines also touched towns in Persia and India, but without huge significance. The cultivation of vines was never part of pre-Columbian America despite the presence of wild vines and the existence of quite sophisticated civilizations.

Dionysus, Bacchus, and the wine of the early Christians

GREECE. The role of wine in Christian practices descended in a direct line from Ancient Greek and Roman rituals. Its use in the sacramental rites has links with Judaism; but it is with the Greek cult of Dionysus, the god of wine, and of Bacchus, his Roman equivalent, that the greatest similarities are found. According to legend, Dionysus brought wine to Greece from Asia Minor, which is now Turkey. As the son of Zeus, he was born twice: once as a mortal human and once as divine. His first birth was to a simple mortal mother, Semele. He was the vine and the wine was his blood.

THE ROMAN EMPIRE. The Romans adopted the Greek gods and added them to their own. Dionysus became Bacchus, the name by which he was already known in the Greek cities of Lydia, in Asia Minor. Bacchus was transformed from the god of wine into a savior. His cult spread among women, slaves, and the poor. The Emperors tried to forbid it, but without much success. Christianity, the development of which is inseparable from that of the Roman Empire, adopted many of the rites associated with Bacchus and attracted, in its early stages, the same categories of the faithful: women, slaves, and the poor. The significance of the Eucharist is too complex a subject to be dealt with in just a few lines, but suffice it to say that the presence of wine at communion was as important to a Christian congregation as that of the priest. As a result of the vital role it played in religious practices, wine survived even during the Dark Ages of the barbarian invasions that followed the decline of Rome.

> Greek ceramic representing Dionysus.

DID YOU KNOW...?

For people in the Middle Ages, wine and beer were not luxuries but necessities. Water supplied in towns was impure and often dangerous. The antiseptic role played by wine made it a part of the rudimentary medicine of the era. Mixed with wine, water became drinkable, if not palatable. Water was rarely consumed on its own, at least in cities. "Water is not wholesome, sole by its self, for an Englishman," wrote the erudite Englishman Andrew Borde, in 1542.

> Harvesting, crushing grapes, and filling barrels, represented by a miniature in a Book of Hours used in Paris.

The English were very fond of Bordeaux wines

In the 14th century, considerable amounts of wine were exported to England from Bordeaux; enough that the average annual consumption for that time was surpassed only in 1979. King Edward II of England ordered the equivalent of more than a million bottles for the occasion of his marriage to Isabel of France in 1308. During the reign of Elizabeth I, almost three centuries later, the English drank more than 40 million bottles of wine per year, with a population of just 6.1 million inhabitants.

The conquest of Northern Europe

Wine was linked to the Mediterranean way of life. North of the Alps, more sedentary activities such as winemaking were endangered by the threat of ferocious invaders. It was only the church, which needed wine and managed to maintain a continuous supply, that facilitated the survival of vineyards. So after Europe emerged from its turbulence, most vineyards were located near monasteries and cathedrals.

MONKS AND WINE. The monks were not content simply to make wine; they wanted to improve it. In the Middle Ages, the Cistercians of Burgundy were the first to study the soil of the Côte d'Or region and transform local vineyards by selecting better plants, experimenting with pruning, and choosing the areas least exposed to frost in order to produce the ripest grapes. They built walls around the best vineyards; those enclosed areas that remain, if only in name (Clos Vougeot, Clos des Pucelles…), bear witness to the insight of these wine-producing monks. The Cistercians of Kloster Eberbach did the same in the Rhine district, which is today one of the most famous wine regions of Germany (*see* p.408). Their goal was not just to produce wine for Mass, but also for sale. As a result, the monks played a key role in the commercial wine trade in the Middle Ages.

Trading in wine

When European life became more peaceful again, vineyards spread and trade resumed. However, wine had never wholly abandoned its role as a tradable commodity: during the High Middle Ages (circa the 5th to 10th centuries), merchant ships slipped discreetly out of Bordeaux or the mouth of the Rhine into pirate-infested western seas and headed for what is now the United Kingdom, Ireland, and further north. Even the least powerful barbarian chiefs felt obliged to celebrate festive occasions with wine, and the most remote hermitage still needed communion wine.

With the revival of trade, great fleets carrying wine appeared and hundreds of ships headed for London and the Hanseatic ports. Rivers also became important trade routes; barrels filled with wine were heavy and cumbersome, so ships were the most practical transportation.

WINE AS PORTRAYED IN ANCIENT MINIATURES

Illuminations in several books from the Middle Ages represent the various labors undertaken in the vineyards—evidence of the presence of wine in medieval society.

1. Pruning the vines, the *Book of Hours* of Charles of Angouleme (14th century).
2. Harvesting and crushing the grapes, *Breviary d'Amor* (14th-century encyclopedia).
3. September labors, the Duke of Berry's *Très Riches Heures*, the Book of Very Rich Hours (15th century).
4. Pruning the vines in March, Roman missal used at Tours (early 16th century).
5. Scenes of trading life (14th century).
6. A treatise on hygiene (15th century).
7. Monk tasting wine, *Book of Health* (13th century).
8. The Marriage at Cana, *Très Belles Heures* Book of Very Beautiful Hours of Notre Dame (15th century).

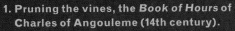

REVOLUTIONS IN WINE

For many centuries, wine producers and wine merchants worked to satisfy the demand for ordinary wines for "everyday" drinking; but toward the end of the 17th century there was a new development: a wealthy public wanting to enjoy wines with distinctive class.

Lovers of good wines

Ancient Romans had already recognized the best wines in their empire. Kings and abbots during the Middle Ages also demanded high quality. However, a new pheno-menon took place in France and, of course, England: the emergence of a social class equipped with both money and a sense of taste that was prepared to pay extra for good wines. In France, the Regency courtesans (1715–1723) demanded—and obtained—large quantities of the best quality, most effervescent Champagne. Simultaneously, the most influential people in England, with Prime Minister Robert Walpole at the fore, were demanding the best red wines from Bordeaux.

It is to this generation that we owe the concept of great wines as we appreciate them today. Until their influence, wine was consumed during the year in which it was made; and at the approach of the harvest the price of "old" wine dropped. However, in 1714, a Parisian wine merchant asked his supplier in Bordeaux for "some good wine, old, dark and velvety." And from this point, ways were found to mature and improve wine. The age of quality wines had begun.

Around 1865, the extent of French vineyards reached its peak: 6.25 million acres (2.5 million ha), despite measures—from planting limits to actually grubbing up vineyards—undertaken by different governments over the centuries to curb wine production.

The great Bordeaux wines

Arnaud de Pontac, president of the Bordeaux parliament around 1660, has often been credited with launching the search for quality. Owner of Château Haut-Brion, he set to producing a new type of wine, applying methods that later would become common practice: small yields, careful selection, and strict attention to the winemaking process and maturation. The aim, of course, was to create a reputation that justified charging high prices. In London, Haut-Brion wines reached three times the price of other good wines. Within one generation, other estates in the Bordeaux region—Latour, Lafite, and Margaux, in particular—had followed Haut-Brion's lead.

Such refinements were successful: selection of the best grape varieties, draining of the vineyards, and increasing precision in maturation and care in the cellars. Fine wines began to be made in great quantities.

France had to wait for the Industrial Revolution for the volume of ordinary wine to increase at a similarly significant rate. The development of towns, and their steadily increasing numbers of workers, multiplied the demand for cheap wine. The railroads

> During the 18th century, wine became an essential part of a sophisticated menu.

The grandfather of oenologists

Production had long been based on empiricism, with the result that winemaking had not been subjected to serious investigation by scientists. From 1854, however, the scientist Pasteur changed this by making a study of the three types of fermentation that produce vinegar, beer, and wine. The results of his research were not put into practice until the 20th century, and they were not implemented by wineries until 1945 or even later. From then forward, oenologists were trained in universities and laboratories. They were charged with directing wine production at single estates as well as for cooperatives. Wine progressed from empiricism to science.

> Loading of casks of wine on the quays at the port of Bordeaux (around 1890).

made it possible to supply this need by shipping wine from the vast vineyards in the south.

THE NEW WINES OF THE 17TH AND 18TH CENTURIES. From the 17th century and throughout the 18th century, the development of vineyards matched that of Paris itself. Wine consumption increased and wines from the Orleans region were introduced to meet the demand. Toward the end of the 18th century, the production of Beaujolais—the most recent of the French vineyard areas—was developed to satisfy demand from Paris. But the joint requirements of England and Paris outstripped the capacity of the merchants. So, rather than buying from the estates, they began to purchase grapes from growers, giving rise to a new business: wine producers making wine without vines. They made, bottled, corked, and finally delivered their own wines—the first "brands" or "labels" of wine.

DID YOU KNOW...?

Champagne was the direct result of the union of bottle and cork. Regional wine production had stagnated during the 16th century. Effervescence was a problem when the Champagne was transported long distances. It caused explosions within the barrels, the only form of container authorized by royal regulations.

The bottle (which the English were the first to use for the transportation of wine) and Portuguese cork came together to solve this problem. Dom Pérignon provided Champagne's other stroke of good fortune. The Benedictine monk, cellar man at the Abbey of Hautvilliers, rediscovered cork's excellent properties for sealing bottles at the same time as perfecting the art of blending. The cork stopper was born, and its use continues to the present day (see also pp.88–9).

IN THE 19TH CENTURY. Members of parliament and clerks of the court drank "bourgeois" wines that were seen as eminently acceptable at even the best tables, in Bordeaux in particular. During the 19th century, wine merchants developed their marketing methods and began selling wine in bottles; previously wine had been sold only in barrels. Wine became one of France's major industries, largely due to industrialization and the advent of railroads. In Languedoc-Roussillon, the vineyards were planted with new grape varieties which produced vast quantities of wine for everyday consumption.

TRUE OR FALSE?

Banning the drinking of wine in the Islamic world goes back to the era of the prophet Muhammad.

FALSE. *The ban dates from two or three centuries later and was dictated by the threat of famine. After a series of victories, Islam was able to live on the profits of war; but eventually its resources were exhausted, and the cultivation of wheat and rice replaced that of grapes. This was one of the measures that permitted Muslim countries to feed their populace.*

The scourge of the vine

It was in 1863, in the south of France, that the most devastating scourge of the vine appeared. The hugely destructive phylloxera is a member of the aphid family. It is no larger than the head of a pin, but it slowly kills the vine by feeding on the sap of its roots. It arrived by accident from North America, when steamboats began crossing the ocean at sufficient speed for the parasite, living on imported plants, to survive the journey. The whole of Europe was affected and hardly a vine escaped. After 40 years of havoc, the solution—that of grafting vines onto American rootstocks, which were immune to the aphid—was finally found (see p.34).

Phylloxera, however, was not the only problem; two other cryptogamic diseases—mildew and powdery mildew—hit the vines of Europe at the same time. In France, as in other European regions, many affected vineyards were never replanted.

THE NEW WORLD OF WINE

In many respects, it took most of the 20th century for the world of wine to recover from the phylloxera crisis. However, a more recent decade—the 1980s—heralded a key turning point in wine history. New players on the stage began to up their game and match the quality of European producers.

The French *appellations d'origine* (designations of origin)

At the end of the 19th century, the reputation of French wine production was in ruinous decline. Baron Leroy de Boiseaumarié, the leader of Châteauneuf-du-Pape, arrived on the scene in time to steady this fall. In an attempt to rescue the vineyards, he decided to abandon the commercial methods employed during the previous century: mediocre grape varieties giving poor yields, inadequate land, inadequate and excessive fertilization, haphazard watering, etc. He advocated certain grape varieties and sought the banning of others, as well as fixing the percentage of alcohol content and the maximum yield per acre. His struggle lasted almost a dozen years. Finally, in 1930, the law on *appellations d'origine* became the charter of all Châteauneuf-du-Pape wine producers. Champagne adopted it in 1935; Arbois and the Val de Loire, Bordeaux, and Burgundy in 1936; and Beaujolais in 1937. All other French regions followed, and the system of *appellations* was put in place progressively. Today it is the basis of all legislation for wine production in Europe, despite successive regulatory adaptions, the latest of which was passed in 2009. (*See box p.95.*)

> *Many wine-producing areas have emerged in New World countries since the 1980s. Players on the world's "chessboard of wine" change constantly, and wines from new producers now rub shoulders with those of European vineyards at the tables of wine lovers.*

Vineyards of the world: the most closely controlled products

After 1945, science began to play an important role in viniculture; programs on vines, fermentation, and maturing in cellars were developed. Along with new knowledge came control, and yields became higher and more predictable. At the same time, the consumption of wine became a worldwide phenomenon. The famous vineyard regions were able to meet the demand thanks to excellent and abundant harvests—1980 and 1990 were particularly successful. In addition, the best New World wines began to rival the top European *grands crus* in quality. The end of the 20th century proved a very prosperous period for producers. For wine lovers it was a golden age, with many more good wines at relatively reasonable prices on the market. The victims of these developments were the producers of cheaper wines.

In the United States

Most current North American wine producers did not exist before 1966. At least 70 percent of California wine companies were started after this date; in New York State, at least 80

Wine production on a grand scale

Vines are grown in half of the French political regions or departments. Some 2.2 million acres (890,000 ha) of vines delivered nearly 1.1 billion gallons (42.6 million hl) in 2008, the equivalent of circa 5.6 billion bottles. In the league of wine producers, France ranks second to Italy (in volume of wine produced). Today, much less wine is consumed in France than 30 years ago. The average annual consumption per capita was 42 gallons (160 l) in 1965, but is now about 14 gallons (54 l) per year, though of better quality wine.

> A "map" showing the California vineyards during the 1940s.

Grape varieties in New Zealand

The hybrids dominant in New Zealand until the 1960s were replaced by European varieties. German grape varieties were planted first, but they gave way to varieties from central France (Sauvignon Blanc in 1970 and Chardonnay in 1980) that were better adapted to the climate. Among the red varieties, only Cabernet Sauvignon has a long history of use in New Zealand, but it has largely been overtaken by Merlot and Pinot Noir.

> During the period of Prohibition in America (1919–1933), banned wine was seized and poured down the drain.

percent were launched after 1976. During the 1970s and 1980s, new producers managed to get costly local regulations rescinded, along with the fiscal measures imposed at the end of Prohibition. Until the mid-1980s, wines produced in the United States were not intended for export; but in 1991, America became the fourth-largest wine producer in the world, after Italy, France, and Spain and ahead of Argentina—a position it has retained to this day.

In South America

As the political and economic conditions of South America countries began to stabilize after the 1980s, foreign investors started to express greater interest in land that might be suitable for vineyards. Most of the big exporters have modernized their installations and developed new styles of wines and wine-making techniques.

Since the early 1990s, Chilean wines have been unbeatable in many markets, especially those where the demand for quality is matched by that for value. Argentina embarked on this course later than its neighbor Chile, but many observers consider its potential greater. The other South American countries are not in the same category, but Uruguay produces some interesting wines and Brazilian production could be stimulated in the future by its internal market.

In South Africa

Following the abolition of apartheid in 1991, South Africa's isolated wine industry embarked on the conversion of its production, then largely devoted to brandy, to grapes for wine-making. Farmers had previously concentrated on quantity, but now had to switch their focus to quality. Vineyards that grew grape varieties intended for bulk production and destined for distillation were now converted to "noble varieties" (Chardonnay, Sauvignon Blanc, Cabernet Sauvignon, Merlot, Syrah, Pinotage) more suited to international tastes. These varieties represented 43 percent of total plantings in 2003, and

they have greatly eroded the monopoly of Chenin Blanc, South Africa's emblematic grape. The growth of red varieties, formerly very much in the minority, has continued to increase: reaching 50 percent of the vineyards in 2005 versus 18 percent in 1996. This rapid conversion allowed South Africa to offer very good quality wines. Progress meant the export of South African wines doubled between 1998 and 2003. Greater political stability also attracted foreign investors, including the Swiss, Germans, Belgians, Italians, Americans, and the French.

Grape varieties in Australia

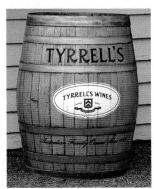

In 1970, Riesling and Semillon were the only quality white grape varieties grown in any great quantity in Australia. It was not until 2003 that they were overtaken by Chardonnay. Syrah (known as "Shiraz" in Australia) was formerly used for making fortified wines. It is now extremely fashionable and forms the base of a large number of the country's most successful wines: whether as a single grape variety or blended with Cabernet, or with Grenache and Mourvèdre, known as "Mataro." It is followed by Cabernet, which has gained ground in a very short time. Merlot serves as a blender, and Pinot Noir is used mostly in sparkling wines.

FALSE BELIEFS ABOUT WINE

Wine long remained the exclusive domain of connoisseurs, those who possessed specialized knowledge and did their best not to share it. In the absence of clear explanations, a new enthusiast trying to access information could sometimes come to the wrong conclusions.

The older a wine, the better it is.

Rosé: a mixture of red and white wines?

" A wine for laying down is a wine that will improve with time. It deserves to wait for a few years before it is consumed. This applies particularly to tannic red wines, which are rough on the tongue and gums when young. With time, the tannins soften and the flavor develops; but if kept too long wine loses its body and dries out. One must monitor its development, since there is nothing worse than uncorking a bottle and finding that it must once have been good, but not anymore. Much better to uncork a bottle too soon than open a dozen too late!"

" It almost happened! Some European countries hoped to obtain authorization to mix white and red wines to produce rosé table wines (as was current practice in certain New World countries). Fortunately, France and Italy prevailed. Making rosé wine (see p.66) requires red grapes. The color is contained in the skins; and the exact intensity required is extracted, either by the same process used for red wine (the juice is left in contact with the skins for just a few hours, known as the bleeding method) or by that used for making white wine (the grapes are squeezed lightly to extract a small amount of color and this lightly colored juice is simply fermented, the direct pressure method). Mixing red and white wine is only permitted in France during production of pink Champagne."

Crystals in the wine! Has the winemaker added sugar?

" These crystals, transparent in white wine, sometimes colored in reds, are potassium bitartrate, or just tartrates, which tend to form more quickly under the influence of lower temperatures. To prevent this happening in the bottle, it is sometimes caused deliberately by cooling the wine in tank. These tartrates in no way affect the quality of the wine. Don't worry if you find these little crystals in your wine. They are not sugar and have no adverse effects on the taste of the wine or on your health!"

Vines must suffer to produce great wines.

66 The soil of a good vineyard should never be very fertile. In fact, when grape vines are planted in rich soil, they become too vigorous and their yield too high. They produce grapes that are diluted and make wine that is too light. However, in order for the grapes to ripen, the vine must not be unbalanced or suffer deprivation. A lack of iron, for example, can prevent photosynthesis and slow the growth of the fruit. The same applies to water: when the vines are overwatered, the fruit becomes saturated, diluted, and lacking in sugar. If it gets too dry, the vine becomes dormant and the grapes fail to ripen. Vines, therefore, must feed regularly, without stress or irregularity, and certainly without abuse."

Tears in a wine are glycerin.

66 Those transparent drops that slide slowly down the side of the glass are called "tears" (or "legs"). They are caused by the difference in the rate of evaporation and the capillary tension between water and alcohol, and are that much larger when the alcohol content is high. Glycerol is one of the alcohols contained in wine, but in lesser concentration than ethanol. The term "glycerin" is therefore incorrect. It is often believed that tears are a guarantee of quality or keeping potential. This is wholly false: the tears simply give an idea of the wine's richness in alcohol (see also p.209)."

Red wines are consumed chambré!

66 The term chambré dates from the end of the 19th century, when the temperature in homes rarely exceeded 68°F (20°C). When bringing red wine up to temperature, care must be taken not to go above 64°F (18°C) or the alcohol comes to the fore and dominates the flavor. Never hesitate to cool a red wine that is too warm by plunging it into a bucket of cold water and even adding a few ice cubes (to the water) to lower its temperature by two or three degrees. Be careful not to make it too cool. A robust red wine becomes very hard and its tannins will seem rough if it is served too cold (see also pp.186–7)."

Beef blood used to be added to wine to color it.

66 Wine contains many proteins. To eliminate them, an unrelated outside protein is added to the vat or cask. This attaches to the proteins and causes them to settle at the bottom. The wine, now clear, can then be transferred to another container. The importance of this procedure is that it eliminates anything that has been added to the wine. Nothing could be more natural! Egg albumin is most frequently used, either in the form of fresh egg whites or freeze-dried powder. Bentonite is not a protein but a type of clay with the same properties and is an alternative product for this process. At one time, albumin from beef blood was employed for the task but this has been banned since the mad cow disease crisis. The blood was never used to color the wine."

THE WINE-PRODUCING *TERROIRS*

The word terroir *covers a number of factors that influence the character of the wine.*
While natural conditions can be modified, it is the choice of site that remains key to
the final qualities of the wine.

The concept of *terroir*

Originally conceived with reference to wine production in France, the concept of *terroir* is now universally known. It covers all the natural and climatic elements linked to a particular vineyard area. The *terroir* is the primary influence on the character of the wine, though the grape variety and the methods used by the wine producer remain important factors.

A FEW PARAMETERS. *Terroir*, contrary to commonly held beliefs, does not simply refer to the soil and what lies beneath the vines (granite, limestone, etc.). It also includes other local factors, such as the slope (hillsides or plain), altitude, exposure, environment (proximity to a forest, lake, etc.), and of course the climate. The *terroir* is the combination of all these factors and it gives each wine-producing site its unique identity.

TERROIRS IN OTHER PARTS OF THE WORLD. Today, the *terroirs* of certain vineyard regions in the New World are clearly identified. They are capable of producing great quantities of wines that compare favorably with the *grands crus* of Bordeaux or top quality Spanish and Italian wines. When compared with wines such as Château Latour, Sassicaia, Vega Sicilia, and Scharzhofberger wines, they can hold their own. Opus One from the Napa Valley in California, Cuvée Almaviva from the Maipo Valley in Chile, or Penfolds Grange from Australia are just some of these.

Wine derives its "nobility" from the terroir *in which the vines are grown. The key elements of light, temperature, and water combine with the soil to determine its quality and characteristics.*

Some areas are more favorable than others

Vines do not always produce good wine. Wet or humid regions do not suit vines; and while they will still grow in cold countries, the fruit fails to ripen properly. For the most part, they produce the best quality wine when grown in less fertile soil; on rich, alluvial plains their large grapes can make fairly tasteless wine. The best *terroirs* are those of poor soil on well-drained hillsides where excess water is avoided, and the vines enjoy good exposure to sunlight in order for their fruit to ripen effectively. As a result, the best wines are often grown in gravelly, sandy or stony soil, and on a hillside rather than on a plain. In northern vineyards, they also enjoy a southeast aspect, affording lengthy exposure to the sun. These are the key characteristics and features of a quality *terroir* that encourages the growth of the vine and the production of ripe, concentrated grapes.

Good climatic conditions

Globally, the best areas for vines are generally between 35° and 50° latitude, north or south. Europe, with its temperate climates, has a privileged location. The seasons alternate, with fairly long and dry summers, in which the grapes mature slowly, followed by long, cold winters that allow the vines to rest. These conditions are essential, even if in some cases growers can compensate for less favorable locations: for example, through irrigation in very dry climes, as in the case of Australia.

THE BASIC REQUIREMENTS. Vines require good sunlight, moderate rain (between 20 and 28 in/500 and 700 mm *per annum*) and moderate temperatures (between 50° and 77°F/10° and 25°C). If temperatures are too high or too low, growth is halted; excessive rain produces, at best, enormous grapes saturated with water and lacking sweetness and flavor (*see* p.48).

Is this the end of French distinction?

European countries, and France in particular, are very attached to the concept of *terroir*. It forms the basis of all regulations on *appellations d'origine* (see pp.94–5). Until the mid-20th century, wine producers the world over always felt that quality wines could only be produced in the "traditional" countries. The increase in international trade and the opening up of many countries, combined with the extraordinary economic success of the wine industry in the 1980s to encourage wine producers to produce ever greater quantities of wine and, in some cases, to make quality wines outside the usual "recognized" areas. Today, every vineyard has the potential to produce quality wines.

TRUE OR FALSE?

Vines grow well at high altitude.

TRUE. *High-altitude plateaus are much sought-after* terroirs *in Australia, in southern Italy, and in all regions with very hot summers. The cool nights and sunny days in such areas result in a temperature range that encourages the grapes to develop their full aromatic potential. The reverse is true of mountainous areas, where temperatures drop too low and strong winds dry out the plants.*

> At Châteauneuf-du-Pape, the presence of round pebbles helps with soil drainage. The vines benefit from the release at night of the warmth accumulated during the day in the stones.

MICROCLIMATE. In addition to the regional climate, the natural environment can, in subtle ways, produce a microclimate that favors the cultivation of vines. A nearby forest can offer a natural barrier to wind; the presence of a body of water will mitigate changes in temperature and enhance light radiation; passing air currents will influence the ripening of the grapes by drying the atmosphere, etc. In countries like Switzerland, where one might think it would be too cold for vines, producers choose areas with beneficial microclimates.

ANNUAL VARIATIONS. In countries with fairly stable climates, such as Chile or Australia, wines tend to be of a similar quality year after year. On the other hand, in France and other European countries, extreme climatic conditions (frost, drought, torrential rain, etc.) can damage the quality of the wine in a given *terroir*. It is a good idea, therefore, to take note of vintages (or the year of the harvest) for European wines that sell at higher prices.

The effects of global warming

Early studies of the consequences of climate change reveal that a rise in temperature has been globally beneficial for the quality of wine. However, while a hot summer is often associated with a *grand millésime*, excessive warming between now and the end of the century could have detrimental effects on wine production in certain southern regions. Problems include drought, the development of disease, or the potential erosion of the soil due to repeated flooding.

NEW AREAS OF PRODUCTION AND THREATENED REGIONS. Logically, the regions most in danger are those with the hottest climates, such as southern Europe and California. By 2100, if nothing is done, only the coastal zones of the American West, cooled by the Pacific Ocean, will still be able to cultivate vines. We are already seeing vineyards above the 50th parallel, in Sweden and Denmark.

POSSIBLE SOLUTIONS? In an attempt to anticipate or counteract the effects of climate change, it has been suggested that vines should be planted at ground level in order to retain humidity and afford grapes protection from the sun. The development of controlled irrigation has also been put forward as a solution. In southern hemisphere locations, such as Australia, vineyards could be planted in cooler zones (*see box p.473*).

Water: neither too much nor too little

Generally speaking, the water content of a good *terroir* is either poor or very low; vine roots and water do not go well together. Freely draining soil is ideal for cultivating vines, unlike very compact earth with very fine granulation that impedes the flow of water. Poor natural drainage can be improved by the laying of drains; the best *crus* in the Bordeaux region use this method. However, the vines must never be short of water or they risk becoming dormant. A constant and uninterrupted water supply is the ideal.

Scientists are already working on ways of adapting the roots of certain vine varieties to support higher temperatures, while also seeking to counteract the detrimental effects of excessively high temperatures on the taste of the wine (for example, high sugar and alcohol content). And lastly, replanting grape varieties from southern regions in more northerly areas is an option under consideration.

What types of soil do vines prefer?

Poor and stony soil, shale, granite, sandstone, and a variety of other forms of soil are suitable for vine cultivation. The soil must perform four key functions: to serve as a support system, to provide moisture, to give warmth (different soils warm and cool at different speeds), and to feed the vines.

WHY LOW FERTILITY? The vine is one of the least demanding plants in terms of nutritive elements. Traditionally, vines were cultivated on land that was insufficiently fertile for other crops. In fact, if the land is too rich it can produce an excessive yield, and yield and quality do not always make a happy marriage: the juice of the grapes is too diluted, the flavor less concentrated, and the wine less impressive. The vine must "suffer" in a sense, from the poor quality of the soil, in order to deliver a wine of quality. Its roots go deeper in search of nutrition, resulting in wines that express the mineral quality of their *terroir* more effectively.

PERMEABLE OR DENSE? It is not enough to define soil in terms of fertility. Each soil has its own structure. Aerated and permeable soils heat up very quickly, helping to ripen the grapes properly. Examples include the sandy soil of the St-Émilion area, the limestone soil of Champagne, or the gravelly soil in the Médoc. Others are heavy, moist, and cool, like the clay of the Alsatian plain or at the foot of the Burgundy hillsides. The best *grands crus*, such as Château Haut-Brion, come from permeable soil made up of gravel on a limestone base. Dense, moist soils, such as the marshy area in the Dordogne Valley (fertile alluvial soil) are doubly inconvenient: they encourage rot and are slow to heat up. While various factors need to be taken into account, there are still exceptions to these basic rules. The famous Château Paveil de Luze from the Margaux appellation produces wine from vines grown on rich and fertile marshy land that is cool and allows the fruit's essential qualities to be retained.

Does a *terroir* have a taste?

The soil plays a key role in the quality, aroma, and taste of wines, particularly in France. This concept has led to the demarcation of the *appellations d'origine contrôlées*, now extended throughout all European Union countries.

A FEW EXAMPLES. According to some specialists, substances present in the subsoil are very important for the flavor of the wine. Château Pétrus, in the *terroir* of Pomerol, has a rich and concentrated taste as a result of iron in the subsoil. The Burgundy *grand cru* Chevalier-Montrachet is lighter than its neighbor Montrachet because it is grown on more stony soil. The opulence and fleshiness of Château Cheval Blanc is due to the sandy, gravelly soil on clay subsoil (but also to a higher proportion of Cabernet Franc compared with other *crus* from St-Émilion). The brown, calcareous soil of the Burgundy *grand cru* La Tâche, which is very clay-rich and not very substantial, gives the wine greater aromatic fullness and elegance, compared with the austere Romanée-Conti. Most specialized French and Italian wine reference books mention the way in which the various minerals, the clay, or limestone of a soil affect the aromas and thus the taste of the wine.

WHAT ROLE DOES THE *TERROIR* PLAY IN THE MAKING OF A GREAT WINE?

Oliver Poussier's opinion, *as The Best Sommelier in the World in 2000, is as follows:*

"A great wine is a combination of complexity, finesse, balance, and persistence, which give enormous pleasure to those who taste it. With time, its flavor and aromas should improve. The fullness of its expression comes more from its terroir than from the grape variety or the year in which it was grown. There can be no great wine without a man who, through an intimate understanding of the terroir, knows how to reveal its very quintessence."

In the opinion of Michel Rolland, *an oenologist from Bordeaux who offers wine advice throughout the world:*

"A great wine is the sum of a number of factors, the most important being the terroir, which gives the wine its character. Man is the vital, indispensable link in the process by which a wine's qualities are revealed, through his constant work in the vineyards and wineries adapted to their conditions and circumstances. The age of the vineyard, its balance, and yield are also important."

The artists of *terroir*

The 20th and early 21st centuries saw the emergence of a generation of wine-makers who changed the face of the world of wine. While earlier great names in oenology—Emile Peynaud, Pascal Ribéreau-Gayon—had focused on the removal of faults, following as they did the best traditions of Pasteur, the new-comers' priority was to create a style. Whereas the Bordeaux producers, inclu-ding the famous Michel Rolland, favored a concentrated, fruity style that has so often served as the modern model, other winemakers were more modest in their goals and content to focus on getting the best out of their small-holdings. However, through their skill at revealing the quintessential nature of their own *terroir*, they all managed to raise wine up to the rank of work of art.

DENIS DUBOURDIEU, MAGICIAN OF THE HAPPY MEDIUM

Oenologist, wine producer, and acade-mic, **Denis Dubourdieu** takes his place in the line-up of the great winemakers of Bordeaux. Owner of several estates in the Sauternes region and the Bordeaux hills, this native of Barsac built his reputation on the search for a compromise between a style accessible to a wider public and respect for the *terroir*. A great specialist in white wines, and a consultant to numerous French and other vineyards, he promotes the development of grape varieties right up to the northern limit of where they are grown. His art lies in revealing the aromas of the grapes to make fruity, fresh, and ele-gant wines. The Dubourdieu style, as he says himself, is his ability to arrange for the "goodness" of a wine to be its best quality.

ANNE-CLAUDE LEFLAIVE, WINEMAKER THROUGH AND THROUGH

When dynamic, innovative, pragmatic **Anne-Claude Leflaive** from Burgundy took over the family estate in Puligny-Montrachet, she wanted to imprint her own style on it by venturing into organic growing. Quickly convinced by conclusive results, she decided to convert all 57.5 acres (23 ha) to biodynamic cultivation in order to produce *grands crus* in keeping with her philosophy. Today, she is convinced that she has given the vines renewed vigor to maximize their expression of the *terroirs*. Indeed, even the most skeptical observers admit that the Leflaive style, reflected in the body and mineral content of the wines, is synonymous with excellent keeping qualities and good evolution.

1. Anne-Claude Leflaive
2. Denis Dubourdieu
3. Paul-Vincent Avril
4. Paul Draper
5. Egon Müller
6. Michel Rolland

PAUL-VINCENT AVRIL, THE EXCELLENCE OF SIMPLICITY

The American magazine *Wine Spectator* described the 2005 Châteauneuf-du-Pape from Clos des Papes as the best wine in the world in 2007. This came as a surprise for the neophytes, but not for those wine-lovers familiar with the excellent work achieved by Paul-Vincent Avril in his 87.5-acre (35-ha) vineyard. The small yields produced by organic methods—no more than five bunches of grapes per vine—and rigorous selection of very ripe Grenache are his apparently quite simple rules for success. However, the essence of Paul-Vincent Avril's skill lies in the actual winemaking process, which avoids overly frequent *remontage* ("pumping over" during fermentation) and results in wines, albeit with a high alcohol content, that are supple and velvety, and further refined during a long period of ageing in the vat.

EGON MÜLLER, HEIR TO A CHARACTER

Egon Müller, owner of the Scharzhof estate in the Ruwer Valley, is the fourth bearer of the same name since 1887. His father, Egon Müller III, who died in 2001, took this vineyard, planted with Riesling, to the top of the league of German wines—if one is to judge by the price of his *selection de grains nobles* (Trockenbeerenauslese) sold at the Trèves wine auction. "The quality of our wines is 100 percent due to the vines, 101 percent if we add the cellar work," joked Egon Müller IV. Indeed, part of his recipe for success seems to be a combination of good fortune in owning an exceptional *terroir* and the use of only well-ripened, meticulously hand-picked grapes. The balance lies in his character and personal philosophy—the most secret and most powerful of ingredients.

PAUL DRAPER, THE CALIFORNIA VISIONARY

Paul Draper settled at Ridge Vineyards in the Santa Cruz Mountains, southwest of San Francisco Bay, in 1967, having spent some time in Chile. Over the years, this doctor of philosophy and atypical wine producer has become one of the great visionaries of California winemaking, producing excellent red wines that have often been placed ahead of Bordeaux *grands crus* in blind tastings. On the one hand, his art lies in the identification of the best Cabernet Sauvignon *terroirs*, and on the other, in a collection of the oldest Zinfandel vines. A well-judged amount of French and American oak barrels for the maturation process lends a final touch to his wines, which are considered exceptional, the *cuvée* Ridge Monte Bello in particular (*see also* box p.447).

THOUSANDS OF GRAPE VARIETIES

There are more than 5,000 different grape varieties in the world, but only a few dozen of them are cultivated over large areas. Each of these types of vine has its own distinct features, and it is these that influence the character of the wine.

What is a *cépage*?

A *cépage*, broadly speaking, is a variety of vine. However, this term is not strictly correct from a botanical point of view. A variety is technically produced from seed, which is not so in the case of vines. *Vitis vinifera*, a type of domesticated vine that originated in Asia Minor, is the source of almost all modern cultivated grape varieties. As a result of natural mutation, cross-breeding, and selection engineered by people, the original type has diversified into several thousand grape varieties with names such as Cabernet, Chardonnay, Pinot, Riesling, etc. Today, just a few dozen varieties provide the bulk of wine production. Some are now famous across the globe, such as Cabernet Sauvignon and Chardonnay.

"Lambrusque" is a form of wild vine (liana) that grows around trees in woodland. It is the distant ancestor of cultivated vines and can still be found in a few regions of Europe and Asia: Austria, the Balkans, the Caucasus, Afghanistan.

Each one has distinctive characteristics

There are several types of grape variety: those intended for eating, which produce attractive fruit; those for drying, providing us with raisins; and those intended for winemaking. Some have multiple usages. Muscat of Alexandria grapes, for instance, can be used for raisins or Muscat wine.

In botanical terms, grape varieties are distinguished by morphological characteristics (their color, shape, number of fruit bunches, the way the leaves are notched) and by physiological features (their flowering, ripening time, susceptibility to disease, yields, etc.) The winemaker will choose a variety according to the quality of wine required and, at least in Europe, according to the *terroir* in which it is to be planted. (All grape varieties are likely to produce the best results in certain soils and/or in a particular climate.)

THE ROLE OF TASTE. Each grape variety has distinct traits that give the wine its character. For example, a given vine will produce fruit in which the sugar or tannin content is of greater or lesser significance, or with aromas of more or less pronounced intensity. A wine made from the Sauvignon Blanc grape has certain characteristic flavors—fruity, floral, or herbaceous notes—common to all Sauvignon Blanc wines the world over. However, according to the *terroir*—meaning the latitude, the date of the harvest, the climate, and winemaking methods used—there will be variations in their aromatic make-up. Thus, a Sauvignon Blanc wine made in Sancerre, France, will be dry, frank, fruity, and typical of the grape; if produced in the Marlborough region in New Zealand, its substance will be more mineral, spicier, and more exotic.

> The indentation of the leaves is one of the morphological characteristics that helps in the identification of a grape variety.

DID YOU KNOW...?

There are no fewer than 40,000 different names given to grape varieties around the world. However, many of these refer to the same variety—the names vary according to the country and even from one region to another. Taking into account different synonyms and translations, the varieties cultivated across the planet number about 5,000. Experts are still a long way from achieving a truly accurate number.

How many grape varieties in one wine?

In the early days of winemaking, it was often normal to mix two or three varieties with somewhat different characteristics: one to give color and tannins; another for delicacy and bouquet; and a third, possibly high-yielding variety, was added to the final mix to ensure some degree of consistency in the production. Today, many wines are still a mixture of two or three grape varieties that complement each other in terms of quality and yield. However, some wines are produced from a single grape variety, and are known (in French) as *monocépages* or varietals.

SOME EXAMPLES: Chablis is made exclusively from Chardonnay; Beaujolais is made solely from Gamay; Vouvray comes from Chenin Blanc; Sancerre from Sauvignon Blanc. On the other hand, red Bordeaux wines contain, in varying proportions, Cabernet Sauvignon, Cabernet Franc, Merlot, and a few secondary varieties that give the wine many nuances. Some mixes are even more complex: Châteauneuf-du-Pape, for example, can contain as many as 13 different grape varieties.

Grape varieties: a free choice or imposed?

Over the course of time, in each region, certain varieties became dominant. This may have occurred through mutation or local selection, or when the environment was found to be favorable to imported varieties and those varieties eventually became native to that area. In most European countries, when the regulation of wine production is firmly established, the varieties were ratified and the types of wine represented by their grape varieties were sanctioned by *appellations d'origines*.

LEGISLATION INFLUENCES CHOICE IN EUROPE. Until 2009, it was not permitted to simply plant a grape variety anywhere you chose, and each region had a precise list of "recommended" and "authorized" varieties. Today, every member state of the European Union has an official catalog of grape varieties that are authorized to be planted–for eating or for winemaking. In France, this covers 200 varieties for winemaking. The choice of grape varieties available for the production of specific appellation wines is set out in a precise list that distinguishes between three categories of grape variety: principal, complementary, and accessory (*see* box p.43). The regulation is more flexible in the case of a *vin de pays* (or wine with a protected geographic indication [GI], or a *vin de table* (wine without a GI).

AND IN THE REST OF THE WORLD? On the American continents, in Australia, and in New Zealand, wine producers in a given region are not required to use any particular variety. They also have the right to include the name of the grape variety on the label, which is only permitted in France in certain cases (*see* below). The New World, with its vineyards planted for the most part with varieties imported from Europe, may still be discovering the ideal character for wines coming from a particular *terroir*.

Printing the grape variety on the label

Labels of European *appellation controlée* (AOC) wines rarely specify the name of the grape variety from which they are made. The label on a red Burgundy, for example, does not mention that the wine is made solely from Pinot Noir. California winemakers were among the first to distribute wines under the name of their grape variety, encouraging consumers to identify, for example, Chardonnay as a wine as well as a type of vine.

In France, regulations banned any mention of the grape variety on the label of AOC wines. The exception is Alsatian wines, such as Riesling, which is the name both of the grape variety and the wine. Varietal names are tolerated, however, for *vins de pays*, which is why some wine producers prefer their wines to be classified in that category rather than as an AOC. They feel mentioning the name of the grape variety on the label gives the wine a greater chance of being identified and appreciated by the consumer. The *L'Institut National de l'Origine et de la Qualité* (or National Institute of Origin and Quality) (INAO), disapproves of this practice, and does not officially recognize *vins de cépage*, or wines bearing the name of the grape variety.

International and indigenous grape varieties

The Chardonnay and Cabernet Sauvignon wines of California, Chile's wines from Merlot, and the Syrah or Shiraz wines of Australia are some of the grape varieties originally associated with classic French wines that have crossed borders. When wine production developed in the New World, winemakers naturally made use of the most prestigious European grape varieties. Some of them proved unsatisfactory, but others adapted well. Grown on vast areas of land, they produced new wines that enjoyed rapid success. Demand increased, confirming their popularity to the detriment of other, often more local varieties. With this said, the greater part of world production still comes from little-known or non-classic grape varieties. These may be grown because of local tradition, for their yield, or because they are well adapted to local soils and climate. But it is not only the classic varieties that produce good wine. And the tendency the world over to promote a handful of grape varieties endangers indigenous ones. With their particular characteristics, indigenous varieties represent a precious source of genetic material and produce wines that have a distinctive identity. Many wines that are little known outside their own region rank as very good wines.

The effects of the phylloxera crisis

Between 1860 and 1880, an aphid called phylloxera, accidentally introduced to Europe from the United States, wreaked havoc on European vineyards (*see* p.21). The larvae of this parasite attack the young roots of the vines, biting into the plant tissue with their projecting mouthpieces. For American varieties, their impact was very limited; but the aphids swarmed in huge quantities over the roots of the less resistant European *Vitis vinifera*. Their bites caused disruption in the cells of the plant until the circulation of the sap was finally blocked. The vines then weakened and died over the course of three to ten years.

GRAFTING SAVES THE DAY. Determined to save the grape varieties of *Vitis vinifera*, European growers found the solution was to graft them onto the roots of wild American vines, which were resistant to the parasite. Since then, vine stocks have been composed of a graft (the part of the plant that grows above ground) attached to a rootstock. The former is always a *Vitis vinifera*, while the rootstock is nearly always from another species.

SEVERAL TYPES OF ROOTSTOCK. The rootstock that supports the graft must fulfill a number of conditions: it must be resistant to phylloxera, suited to the *terroir* in which it is to be planted, and compatible with the graft. Also its vegetative properties must conform to the needs of the grower. These days, every member

> After grafting, the part of the plant that will remain above ground is coated with a wax mixture.

TRUE OR FALSE?

Ungrafted vines have all disappeared.

FALSE. *Even though most of the vineyards in the world are planted with grafted vines, there are exceptions. In France, for instance, the Marionnet vineyard in Touraine contains a plot planted with vines that are 120 to 150 years old, therefore from the pre-phylloxera era. One part of that estate has also been planted* franche de pied, *which is to say with ungrafted vines, and they are still resistant to phylloxera. But it is the vineyards of Washington State in the USA and also in Chile that have the most ungrafted vines.*

country of the European Union has a list of rootstocks recommended for grafting. (All others are banned.) In France, several dozen among those available have been selected for their resistance to drought, as well as to soil lime (which causes chlorosis, a disease resulting in yellowing of the leaves), and for their fast rate of growth. Unfortunately, the latter encourages high yields to the detriment of quality and hardiness. These rootstocks are all of American origin (*Vitis riparia*, *V. rupestris*, or *V. berlandieri*).

Constant improvement of grape varieties

The improvement of grape varieties, which aims to obtain better quality fruit and make the plants more resistant to different vine

---

Small differences rather than similarities

The long-term survival of vineyards presupposes the eradication of diseases and the use of clonal selection. There are, however, disadvantages to the use of clones. The quality of a wine does not, in fact, depend on the vines being exactly the same as each other, but rather on the very slight differences that exist between members of the same variety. Clonal selection, however, produces plants with one genetic identity. To remedy this, nurseries have begun to offer several cloned versions of the same variety. There are, for example, 26 registered clones of Cabernet Franc, all with slightly different characteristics.

diseases, depends essentially on two kinds of selection: massal selection and clonal selection. A number of big estates, especially in the Bordeaux region, prefer to rely on local genetic diversity and the use of massal selection. But it is perfectly possible to use both kinds of selection, actually planting vine stock selected by both processes in the vineyards of the same estate.

MASSAL SELECTION. This has been used in agriculture for centuries. It entails choosing the most appropriate plants for a given purpose: fruit appearance or taste. In the case of grape vines, plants are selected for propagation according to foliage density or the strongest wood, or for bearing the most fruit or the largest–or smallest–grapes, depending on the type of production required. Massal selection favors local genetic heritage, but offers no guarantee that the plants will be healthy.

CLONAL SELECTION. Practiced by nurseries since 1960, clonal selection responds to the potential of health deficiencies in massal selection. A particularly suitable vine plant is selected, its health is checked (through virological tests), and its characteristics are improved as required (with thermotherapy or heat treatments). The results are then approved by an authorizing agency before the nursery proceeds to make identical copies by cloning (taking cuttings or grafting) from this basic plant material for certified sale and distribution.

The creation of new varieties

Research centers in every country breed different varieties of *Vitis vinifera* to create crossbreeds. (These are not hybrids, which are the result of crossing two different *Vitis* species.) They are tested for many years before being recognized as new varieties. In France, however, they are not used to make AOC wines.

BASIC CROSSBREEDING. The only human intervention involved in basic crossbreeding is the choice of the parent plants. A Riesling can be crossed with a Traminer a dozen times and obtain a dozen different crossbreeds, just as a man and a woman can have a dozen children who are different from each other. In the future, once the genetic code of grape varieties has been mapped, crossbreeds will no doubt be selected according to their genes.

The failure of "direct producers"

When phylloxera destroyed European vineyards, grape growers tried to replace old vines with "direct producers." These plants, produced by crossing the European species (*Vitis vinifera*) with American species, were supposed to combine the qualities of French vines with the resistance to disease of the American grape varieties. The resistance to phylloxera was, indeed, excellent; but the resulting fruit was coarse. The flavor was "foxy," making the wines unattractive and even toxic. Such crossbreeding is now banned, and hybrids of European with American species are only used as vine rootstocks.

THE GERMAN EXAMPLE. The most active center of vine research is in Geisenheim, in the Rhine region. Its activities date back many years, including responsibility for the creation of Müller-Thurgau in 1883 (a cross between Riesling and the Madeleine Angevine), which is the most cultivated white variety in Germany. Other, very aromatic, white varieties that have been very successful since their early- to mid-20th-century creation include the Scheurebe (Sylvaner and Riesling), the Huxelrebe (Chasselas and Muscat), and the Kerner (a cross between Trollinger and Riesling).

Recourse to genetic engineering?

Microbiologists are interested in manipulating the genetic codes of grape varieties to strengthen the vine's defenses, or, more ambitiously, to obtain better tasting fruit. French researchers, for example, have succeeded in isolating the gene responsible for the immunity of American vines against fan-leaf, a serious virus that causes degeneration of the vine. At present, if a plot of land is infected, the only remedy is to treat the soil and then wait seven years before replanting, using American vine stocks. With genetically modified vines, the alternative rootstock would no longer be needed; and it would be possible to replant immediately, even in infected soil. However, before venturing into the realm of genetically modified crops, researchers and producers must make sure that such interventions present no risks to the health of the environment and guarantee that the character of the modified grape variety will remain unchanged. At the moment, no studies are being made of genetically modified grapes or of wine made from them.

> One of the pre-phylloxera vines preserved in the Domaine La Charmoise belonging to the Marionnet brothers.

THE GREAT RED GRAPE VARIETIES

From among the vast number of red grape varieties, some have been selected for their distinctive characteristics and some, such as Cabernet Sauvignon, Merlot, and Syrah, have become international stars. But good wine can be made entirely from less well-known varieties.

Cabernet Sauvignon

This grape variety was derived from crossbreeding a Sauvignon Blanc and a Cabernet Franc. The cross-fertilization took place three centuries ago, somewhere in the Gironde area of Bordeaux, France.

THE PRINCIPAL *TERROIRS*. Cabernet Sauvignon has long been a traditional grape variety in the Medoc of Bordeaux. The poor, gravelly soil of this *terroir* seems to offer the ideal conditions for its cultivation; but it can adapt to various conditions and is planted all over the world in vineyards that receive a minimum of 1,500 hours of sunlight per year. It is found, for instance, in most of the countries north of the Mediterranean Sea as well as in North America and across the southern hemisphere.

THE CHARACTERISTICS. Dark red in color, it has aromas of blackcurrant when young. Wine made from this grape variety becomes brick red, with cedar wood aromas, as it develops. When the yield is controlled, the wine producer can draw a great wine from this grape: fine, tannic, spicy, which both can and must be aged. Cabernet Sauvignon is often blended with other varieties. It is the major ingredient of Bordeaux blends sourced from the left bank of the Gironde. It gives structure to wines to lay down: a great red Bordeaux from a good year will continue improving for decades.

> *White wine can be made from red grape varieties. It is achieved by simply preventing the grape juice, which is colorless, from macerating with the skins. Wine color comes from the pigment in the skins.*

Cabernet Franc

This grape variety is similar to Cabernet Sauvignon, but without its panache. It may have already been present in the Bordeaux region in the 4th century, but under the name "Vidure."

THE PRINCIPAL *TERROIRS*. Cultivated in the Bordeaux region, Cabernet Franc is also grown in certain regions of the Loire Valley of France. Its early maturing qualities mean it can be planted further north than Cabernet Sauvignon. Apart from northern Italy and, in smaller quantities, California, this grape variety is grown in very few places outside France.

CHARACTERISTICS. This variety produces wines with fresh, fruity aromas, and with a characteristic flavor of ripe red or black fruits. In the Bordeaux area, when blended with Merlot or Cabernet Sauvignon, this variety is almost always the minor component. On the other hand, in the wines of the Loire Valley, such as Saumur, Bourgueil, and Chinon, it dominates other

> Cabernet Sauvignon

> Cabernet Franc

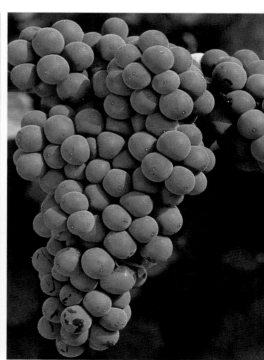

> Gamay

varieties. A wine made solely from Cabernet Franc is generally relatively light and not for keeping.

Gamay

The precise origin of this grape variety is not known, but it was undoubtedly pre-13th century and probably in the Beaujolais region of France. Although this grape variety doesn't produce great wines, it makes a light style of red, which is enjoyed worldwide.

THE PRINCIPAL *TERROIRS*. Gamay likes granitic soil. It is the only grape variety used in the production of red Beaujolais, though it has also been grown in the Loire Valley (particularly Touraine), in some vineyards in central France, and in Switzerland.

CHARACTERISTICS. Wine made from Gamay is light, rich in primary aromas, and has the flavor of ripe red fruit. It has little tannin and is often acidic. This grape variety became popular in the late 20th century due to the popularity of Beaujolais Nouveau. But the Beaujolais *crus* made in the traditional way give more prominence to the floral fruitiness of the grape.

Grenache

Spanish in origin and brought to France around the 14th century, this grape variety arrived in the Rhône Valley, at Châteauneuf-du-Pape, three centuries later.

THE PRINCIPAL *TERROIRS*. It is grown across southern France, from Provence through the Languedoc. It gives the best results on dry and stony hillsides, like those of Rivesaltes or Châteauneuf-du-Pape. It is the main red grape variety in Spain and is often used as a complement to Syrah in Australia and the USA.

CHARACTERISTICS. Wine made with Grenache is rich in alcohol, heady, and with low acidity. Its oxidizing qualities are valuable in the production of natural sweet wines (Banyuls, Maury, and Rivesaltes). In France, Grenache is often blended with Mourvèdre and Syrah in the production of wine to lay down. In Spain, it produces light wines in Rioja and more substantial ones in the Valladolid region.

Merlot

Merlot, which possibly originated in the Bordeaux region, was only recorded in the 19th century.

THE PRINCIPAL *TERROIRS*. The *terroir* of choice for Merlot is on the right bank of the Garonne in Bordeaux, at St-Émilion and Pomerol, on a cool mix of limestone and clay. But it is also grown in the south of France, the north of Italy, and, for several years now, in California and Washington State.

CHARACTERISTICS. Wine made from Merlot is supple and fruity, with aromas of blackcurrant and plums. It is generally for early drinking, but when blended with other grape varieties, notably Cabernets Sauvignon or Franc, it can produce a wine that takes on a splendid complexity. Indeed, Merlot plays an essential role in such illustrious *crus* as Pétrus.

Nebbiolo

Nebbiolo was probably already being cultivated in the Piedmont region by the time of the Romans. It is Italy's major contribution to the classic grape varieties.

THE PRINCIPAL *TERROIRS*. Nebbiolo is hardly grown at all outside the Piedmont region of Italy—the area that suits it best—apart from a minimal presence on the American continent.

CHARACTERISTICS. This classic Italian grape variety produces the two great acidic and tannic wines, Barolo and Barbaresco. With legendary longevity, they need to spend a certain length of time in bottle to allow their bouquet to develop.

> Grenache

> Merlot

> Nebbiolo

Pinot(s)

This ancient plant almost certainly originated in Burgundy and was described by Columelle at the beginning of the 1st century. Genetically unstable, Pinot is the origin of a large family of grape varieties, including both red and white: Pinot Noir, Meunier (red), Gris or Beurot (grayish pink, white, etc.).

PINOT NOIR. Fairly delicate, among all the grape varieties it has the special feature of being the most refined and the most sensitive to *terroir*. This is the reason why Pinot Noir in Burgundy can produce a different (always great) wine every 500 yards or so. Apart from Burgundy, it also makes great wines in Champagne, where it is often blended with Pinot Meunier or Chardonnay. On the other hand, the wine produced from Pinot Noir in Oregon, Australia, and New Zealand varies in quality.

PINOT MEUNIER. This is grown mostly in Champagne and gives supple, fruity red wines.

Syrah

For many years, it was thought that Syrah originated in Persia, but the discovery that its genome revealed Mondeuse—a variety from Savoie, France—among its antecedents, eventually put an end to that theory. With its small yields, this grape variety makes high-class wines when grown on the *terroirs* to which it is most suited.

THE PRINCIPAL *TERROIRS*. Syrah is most notably the grape variety of the Rhône Valley and forms the base of famous great wines such as Hermitage and Côte-Rôtie. Nevertheless, it is also cultivated in Australia, under the name Shiraz, where it produces good results.

CHARACTERISTICS. Syrah produces a *vin noir*, a peppery, structured wine with violet aromas. It is used as a single variety in some of the great Côtes du Rhône wines from the northern part of that area. It is also used to improve blended wines from Mediterranean regions, to which it brings spicy notes.

Tempranillo

Tempranillo is considered the most prestigious of the Spanish grape varieties. It owes its name to its early-ripening qualities,

> Pinot Noir

> Syrah

as *temprano* is the Spanish word for "early."

THE PRINCIPAL *TERROIRS*. Tempranillo is grown most notably in Spain, where it has become the leading red grape variety. It is found only in limited quantities elsewhere in the world, with Portugal and Argentina being the only places where it is grown extensively.

CHARACTERISTICS. It is the key grape variety of the powerful and harmonious great Spanish wines of Rioja and Ribera del Duero. Its aroma is somewhat reminiscent of Burgundy's Pinot Noir. In Portugal, where it is called *Tinta Roriz* or *Aragonês*, it is one of the five recommended varieties in the production of red port.

Zinfandel

The only wine that is considered typically American is made from Zinfandel—known as "Zin" in the United States. This grape variety was introduced to the USA around 1850 and came from Primitivo, which has been grown in the Apuglia region of Italy since the end of the 18th century.

THE PRINCIPAL *TERROIRS*. Zinfandel is cultivated in several American states, but most notably in California. It is also grown in northern Mexico and in Australia.

CHARACTERISTICS. This excellent grape variety is rich in sugar and fruity aromas. It is a multipurpose grape, producing white wines (from black grapes), rosé wines (called "blush"), and table wine, as well as wines for ageing. Generally, it is used as a single variety, but it can also be blended with other reds.

Other important red grape varieties

The varieties listed below are of varying importance. Some are linked exclusively to an appellation.

BARBERA. Very widespread in Italy (Piedmont) and in California, Barbera produces generous, nicely crisp wines.

BLAUFRÄNKISCH. Called Lemberger in Germany, this Austrian grape variety produces fruity wines, full of freshness in the style of those from Beaujolais.

CARIGNAN. This variety is most commonly grown in the south of France and in Mediterranean countries. It produces wines that are robust, full-bodied, tannic, crisp, and of variable quality.

CARMENÈRE. Originally from Bordeaux, this variety is still used in the AOC wines of Bordeaux, Medoc, and St-Émilion. It is the signature grape of Chile, where it produces wines of great depth.

CINSAUT (OR CINSAULT). A medium-quality grape variety that is happy in hot climates, it is used for blending (in the south of France, Lebanon, and North Africa), as it brings suppleness and lightness.

GROLLEAU. Grown mostly in the Loire Valley of France, it produces light wines with low alcohol content, including rosés. It is most used in the Anjou, Touraine, and Rosé de Loire AOCs.

KADARKA. This Hungarian grape variety, introduced many years ago by the Turks, is considered promising, but currently produces wines that often have bitterness and flavors reminiscent of semi-sweet wines.

LAMBRUSCO. A grape variety grown in Emilia-Romagna in Italy, it goes into making several sweet, light, and slightly sparkling wines that are produced for rapid consumption.

MALBEC (OR CÔT, OR AUXERROIS). The principal grape variety used to make Cahors AOC wines, it has supple fruit character. It is the signature variety in Argentina and produces robust wines to lay down. **MONDEUSE.** Related to Syrah, this grape variety is most characteristic of the Savoie region of France. The wine that is produced from it is structured and tannic.

MONTEPULCIANO. One of the principal Italian grape varieties, it produces vigorous red wines in central Italy and is often blended with Sangiovese.

MOURVÈDRE. This variety is used for producing blends in the Rhône Valley, in Provence, and in the Languedoc to produce tannic, full-bodied, spicy wines with good keeping qualities.

NÉGRETTE. Because it is fragile, this grape variety is becoming increasingly rare. Mainly found in the Haute-Garonne of southwest France, at Fronton, it brings violet and licorice aromas to wines with a medium lifespan.

Rediscovered grape varieties

Grape varieties don't escape the influence of production methods. One such example is Mourvèdre. Its future seemed uncertain after the Second World War, when new grafts took badly, but it is now being grown in increasing quantities. Viognier is also a "miracle" grape variety. Reduced to a few dozen acres in the 1950s, due to poor conditions that affected the health of the vines, its production was irregular. But today, in the Rhône and the Midi, large amounts of Viognier wines are produced and a piece of previously forgotten wine heritage is slowly being rediscovered. Wines are also made from pre-phylloxera vineyards and labeled "Forgotten Vines."

NIELLUCIO. This grape variety is grown in northern Corsica, where it forms part of the blend for the Patrimonio AOC.

PETIT VERDOT. Grown more in Bordeaux than elsewhere, it is used in making the AOCs Medoc and Graves. It produces rich and tannic wines that improve with age.

POULSARD. Grown especially in the Jura region of France, Poulsard produces very light-colored wines with a particularly delicate aroma. It is often used alone in Arbois wines.

SANGIOVESE. This grape variety produces fruity, balanced wines, the most famous being Chianti, which contains 75 to 100 percent Sangiovese.

TANNAT. Rich in tannin, this grape variety is the principal component of many Pyrenean wines, notably those from Bearne, France. It is also very well adapted to the climate and soil in Uruguay, where it is the signature variety.

> Tempranillo

> Zinfandel

> Petit Verdot

THE GREAT WHITE GRAPE VARIETIES

White grape varieties, used alone or in conjunction with others, produce a wide variety of wines: dry, off-dry, aromatic, and sweet. Among the best known, Chardonnay, Riesling, Chenin Blanc, and Sauvignon Blanc are now cultivated all over the world.

Chardonnay

Chardonnay is a grape variety that has "gone global." While exactly when it came into being is unknown, its "parents" have been identified as Gouais Blanc, a mediocre variety from the Jura and Franche-Comté regions of France, and Pinot Noir.

THE PRINCIPAL *TERROIRS*. The wine regions most notable for growing the Chardonnay grape are Burgundy and Champagne. This prestigious grape variety is used in Montrachet and all the great white Burgundy appellations, as well as in the Champagne *blancs de blancs*. It has great resilience, being able to adapt to varying soils and climates.

CHARACTERISTICS. Chardonnay is capable of producing powerful aromas: the aromas of brioche, fresh butter, hazelnuts, and toast found in the Chardonnays of Burgundy give way to those of citrus fruits, pineapple, and exotic fruits in hotter regions. The greatest Chardonnay wines, such as white Burgundies, age well. Others, especially those not aged in wood, are intended for early consumption.

The skins of white grapes contain no anthocyanins, the pigment that is present in red varieties. They are translucent, with a color that varies from pale green to yellow-gold, and can even sometimes be slightly pink.

Chenin Blanc

By the ninth century, Chenin Blanc was already being cultivated at Glanfeuil Abbey in the Anjou district of the Loire Valley.

THE PRINCIPAL *TERROIRS*. Chenin Blanc is still widespread in the Loire, where it originated, and is one of the components of Vouvray, Savennières, Bonnezeaux, and some wines from appellations in Anjou. It is also grown widely outside France, in South Africa in particular, under the name Steen. This all-purpose grape variety adapts well to all soils and all climates.

CHARACTERISTICS. Depending on the *terroir*, Chenin can produce wines that differ greatly, from *crémant* to natural sweet wine, from dry to sweet wines, from crisp to those lacking in character, and from the very ordinary to exceptional. In the heart of Chenin territory, in the Layon Valley and the Vouvray region, it can produce white wines for ageing, the crispness of its youth evolving in maturity to a voluptuous sweetness. In South Africa, in California, and in other countries, it produces demi-sec wines of a neutral nature—with no particular vices or virtues.

> Chardonnay

> Chenin Blanc

> Gewurztraminer

Gewurztraminer

The aromatic Traminer (*gewürz* is the German word for spice,) was imported from the Palatinate, and has been grown in Alsace since 1870. Traminer, which is in fact Savagnin Blanc, a grape variety from the Jura region, is made up of two pink versions. One is not aromatic (Klevener from Heiligenstein) and the other is very much so, the Traminer Musqué or Gewurztraminer.

THE PRINCIPAL *TERROIRS*. The variety is at home growing on both sides of the Rhine, in Alsace and in southern Germany, as well as in northern Italy and in Austria. Outside the central European vineyards, it is grown with only limited success. It is nevertheless also cultivated in California.

CHARACTERISTICS. Gewurztraminer produces a wine that is very fruity, with pronounced spicy notes and an aroma of roses. Good wines from Alsace or Baden (Germany) have an intense presence on the palate, despite being almost always weak in acidity. Harvested late, this wine becomes voluptuous and rich.

Muscat(s)

Probably originally from Asia Minor, Muscat was cultivated in Ancient Greece and is one of the oldest grape varieties in the world. It constitutes a vast family of at least 200 varieties, including black, red, and white.

THE BEST KNOWN MUSCATS AND THEIR *TERROIRS*. The Muscat of Alexandria is the most extensively grown, with the Muscat Blanc à Petits Grains being judged the best. The Muscat Ottonel—a product of crossbreeding Muscat with Chasselas, which took place in the Loire during the 19th century and was carried out by Moreau-Robert—found refuge in Alsace, Austria, and Eastern Europe. Aleatico, a black Muscat grape cultivated in many regions of Italy, is undoubtedly a parent of the Muscats.

CHARACTERISTICS. Anyone who has tasted a Muscat grape will have no difficulty in recognizing a wine made from this variety. The wines are very varied and range from a sparkling white to the rich, dense, fortified wines of Australia. Dry wines are made from Muscats in Alsace. There are very aromatic, naturally sweet and heady wines at Frontignan, as well as sparkling wine at Die, and so on.

Riesling

This ancient grape variety is of German origin, but according to certain specialists, it was introduced by Roman legions.

THE PRINCIPAL *TERROIRS*. For some oenophiles, Riesling rivals Chardonnay in quality. But it doesn't have the same resilience and is restricted to shale and the limestone clay soils in northern Europe, on well-exposed hillsides. Widespread in Germany, where it occupies the finest *terroirs*, it is also grown in Austria and northern Italy, and also in France (in Alsace only). In the New World, it produces good results in California, Washington State, New Zealand, and Australia. The crisp acidity of the

> Muscat de Beaumes-de-Venise

> Muscat de Frontignan

> Riesling

German Rieslings can, however, be lacking when this variety is cultivated in hotter climates.

CHARACTERISTICS. Riesling produces wines with a good balance of acidity and sweetness. They can be dry, fine, elegant, lemony, and for early drinking. But this grape variety also makes great sweet wines and wines to lay down; vigorous and complex, they will keep for decades. Generally speaking, the French wines are drier and higher in alcohol than the German ones.

Sauvignon Blanc

Grown for centuries in the Loire and Bordeaux regions of France, this grape variety is now cultivated all over the world.

THE PRINCIPAL *TERROIRS*. Sauvignon Blanc likes the limestone soil and cool climate it finds in the Loire and Bordeaux regions; it loses a little of its character in hot climates. It is nevertheless cultivated in every region and especially in New Zealand.

CHARACTERISTICS. This grape variety produces a dry white wine for early drinking. It is direct, sometimes simple, with characteristic gooseberry, box hedge, even "cat's pee" aromas. Used on its own without other varieties, it holds the reputation of the wines of Sancerre, Pouilly, and Quincy, all in the Loire Valley. In the Bordeaux region, it is often blended with Sémillon, whether in dry or sweet wines, and is used in the making of white Graves and Sauternes.

Sémillon

> Sauvignon Blanc

> Sémillon

Other important white grape varieties

The following grape varieties are of varying importance. Some are exclusively linked to an appellation.

ALBARIÑO. This Spanish grape variety produces interesting dry white wines, including Rías Baixas, which is a DO (*denominación de origien*—equivalent to the French *appellation d'origine*).

ALIGOTÉ. This variety produces the dry, fairly crisp, white AOCs Bourgogne Aligoté and Bouzeron.

BOURBOULENC. Grown in Provence and Languedoc, this grape forms part of many AOCs (Bandol, Cassis, Minervois, etc.).

CATARRATTO. This Sicilian grape variety goes into the production of Marsala, and also table wines.

CHASSELAS. Both a dessert and a wine grape variety, it is used in winemaking at Pouilly-sur-Loire, in Alsace, in Savoie, in Germany (Gutedel), and in Switzerland. It produces a fruity wine.

CLAIRETTE. An ancient grape variety from the Midi, where it is used to make a dry, floral, slightly flabby wine.

COLOMBARD. A native of southwest France, it is also grown in California and South Africa. The wines produced from it are fresh and crisp. It is also used in the production of brandy.

FOLLE BLANCHE. These grapes are used to make Gros-Plant and the finest Armagnac brandies.

FRIULANO. The principal grape variety in northwest Italy, Friulano produces a straw-colored wine with almond aromas.

Sémillon is subtle and restrained, needing time to assert itself, and is therefore not a very fashionable wine.

THE PRINCIPAL *TERROIRS*. Apart from the Gironde of Bordeaux, the *terroir* in which it thrives best, it is only in the Hunter Valley of Australia that this grape variety has made a name for itself. Despite this, there are plantings of Sémillon in Chile, Argentina, and South Africa.

CHARACTERISTICS. Sémillon takes on *pourriture noble* (botrytis, or "noble rot") well and gives fleshiness and body to sweet wines, particularly Sauternes. It is also used in blends for dry white wines and is present, notably, in the great white Graves. The Australians use Sémillon on its own to produce superb dry wines for ageing.

FURMINT. A Hungarian grape variety, it goes into the making of the sweet, very aromatic wine Tokay.

JACQUÈRE. Mainly cultivated in Savoie, this variety produces a wine that is low in alcohol and crisp. It is used in the AOC wines Vin de Savoie and Vin de Bugey.

MACCABEU. This is one of the principal grape varieties used in the production of French natural sweet wines.

MALVOISIE (VERMENTINO). This ancient Mediterranean grape variety has given its name to some of the sweetest Madeiras. Cultivated in Italy and Corsica, it produces a rich, rounded wine.

MARSANNE. From the northern Rhône region, this grape variety is similar to a Rousanne, but produces a more supple wine with less finesse.

The grape varieties benefiting from a wine *appellation d'origine* in France

The specifications for French *appellation d'origine* wines restrict the choice of grape varieties in order to preserve the traditional character or typicity of regional wines. Included is a hierarchy that distinguishes between the "main" grape variety, which is an obligatory component of the wine, always used in sizeable proportions; the "complementary" varieties, present in lesser amounts; and the "accessory" varieties, which must not exceed 10 percent of the whole. Any modification to the mix of grape varieties in an appellation wine is subjected to prior experimentation. Each new grape variety that is accepted will have the status of "accessory" variety.

MAUZAC. This grows only in Limoux (Blanquette de Limoux), in the Aude region of France, and in Gaillac in southwest France. It has a characteristic flavor of apples.

MELON DE BOURGOGNE. Called Muscadet in the Nantes region, it produces a dry, easy-to-drink wine.

MÜLLER-THURGAU. Grown in Germany, this grape variety produces a robust, slightly musky wine.

MUSCADELLE. This fragile grape variety brings an aromatic touch to some of the sweet wines of southwest France.

PALOMINO. This vine bears moderately sweet white grapes, with only slight acidity, that go into the making of sherry. Outside Spain, it is grown in California, Australia, and South Africa.

PEDRO XIMÉNEZ. This very sweet white grape variety is used to make sherry, and Montilla-Moriles in particular.

PETIT MANSENG. This variety from Gascony, France, is used to make the medium-sweet wines of Jurançon.

PINOTS. Pinot Gris (pink to bluish-gray fruit) is used in producing the rich, fleshy, white wines of Alsace and Germany. Pinot Blanc, highly valued in Italy and California, produces a straightforward, and often quite simple, wine.

ROUSSANNE. An aromatic variety from the northern Rhône region and Savoie, it produces a fine, balanced wine to lay down.

SAVAGNIN. A grape variety from the Jura region of France, it is made into Vin Jaune or sometimes a very distinctive white wine. Blended with other grape varieties, it brings to the wine an element of quality and a capacity for ageing.

SEYVAL BLANC. This hybrid, very crisp grape produces a neutral, dry white wine in the state of New York and in Canada.

SYLVANER. Widely planted in Alsatian and German vineyards, this high-yielding grape variety is made into simple, floral, and vigorous wines.

TORRONTÉS. Grown in Spain, it is also one of the most interesting white grape varieties of Latin America. It produces lively, aromatic wines that are often pleasantly spicy.

UGNI BLANC (TREBBIANO). Used to make Cognac brandy, this grape variety also goes into the making of crisp, fairly neutral white wines from Provence and Languedoc. In Italy it is known as Trebbiano.

VERDEJO. Considered one of the best white grape varieties of Castille-León, Spain, it is a notable presence in several of the Rueda DO (*Denominación de Origen*) wines.

VERDELHO. Known as one of the principal grape varieties that go into the making of Madeira wines, it is also part of the blend used in several Australian whites.

VIOGNIER. Grown in the south of France and in the Pyrénées-Orientales at Vaucluse, it can produce high quality, strongly perfumed wines (Condrieu and Château-Grillet AOCs).

WELSCHRIESLING. This grape variety is made into light, fruity wines in Austria, northern Italy, and southeastern Europe.

> Riesling vines in the Schoenenbourg *terroir*, a *grand cru* of Alsace (Domaine Hugel & Fils).

GRAPE VARIETIES AND *TERROIRS*:
FAMOUS COMBINATIONS

The combination of terroir *and grape variety strongly influences a wine's personality. In some vineyards, the factors affecting quality—climate, exposure, soil—combine to transform the "expression" of the grape variety and result in a unique wine.*

Cabernet Sauvignon in Bordeaux

A classic or noble red grape variety, Cabernet Sauvignon is harvested late. It is resistant to rot and is completely happy in poor soil, so long as it is well drained.

The Cabernet Sauvignon grape is grown all over the world, but the Bordeaux region provides the ideal *terroir*. This is especially so on the left bank of the Gironde, where the majority of the soil is a stony and gravelly mix and where the ocean climate dominates.

In this region, where the vineyards of Haut-Medoc and Graves are found, it is the dominant grape variety of the *grands crus classes* or great growth wines, blended with Cabernet Franc and Merlot. Cabernet Sauvignon produces wines with a

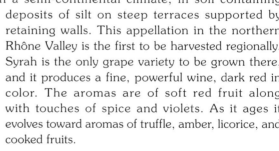

The grape grower can improve the wines that a terroir *produces by making the right choices, such as choosing an appropriate grape variety or the best way to manage the vines. The grapes must be able to ripen satisfactorily and express their original, characteristic features.*

tight tannic fabric, especially in a young wine, which ensures a longevity that is sometimes exceptional. As they age, they take on the body, elegance, and finesse of a great wine.

Syrah in Cornas

Syrah is a tannic red grape variety that produces wines that age well. It grows best in granitic terrain—the *terroir* of the northern Rhône Valley is ideal, in appellations such as Côte-Rôtie, Hermitage, Crozes-Hermitage, and St-Joseph. But it is the Cornas *terroir* that provides the very best conditions.

The vines that produce Cornas are grown in a semi-continental climate, in soil containing deposits of silt on steep terraces supported by retaining walls. This appellation in the northern Rhône Valley is the first to be harvested regionally. Syrah is the only grape variety to be grown there, and it produces a fine, powerful wine, dark red in color. The aromas are of soft red fruit along with touches of spice and violets. As it ages it evolves toward aromas of truffle, amber, licorice, and cooked fruits.

Viognier in Condrieu

Viognier is a capricious and fragile white grape variety that gives only low yields. It is the exclusive variety used in two French AOC wines, Château-Grillet and Condrieu. The latter appellation, with a moderate continental climate, extends over steep hillsides arranged in terraces on pebbly sand or granitic soil. This is where Viognier produces its best results: a superb white wine, pale yellow in color with golden glints, and generous aromas, both floral (violet, iris, wild flowers) and fruity (white peach, apricot). A supple, unctuous, and heady mouth-feel, is matched with great freshness and good length on the palate. It is a rare, expensive, and sought-after wine for early drinking.

Two recent innovations have proven to be controversial for some wine-lovers, while being acclaimed by others: increasing the length of time the wine spends in new oak barrels and producing it as a late harvested, dessert wine.

> Cabernet Sauvignon grapes in Graves, Bordeaux.

Chardonnay in Puligny-Montrachet

A white grape variety of quality when held to a low yield, Chardonnay produces fine wines that age well. While it is grown more or less everywhere in the world, with more or less satisfactory results, in Burgundy it produces the greatest dry white wines in France.

Chardonnay produces the best results on stony, limestone clay soils that grow wines of great finesse. This is the case in the appellation of Puligny-Montrachet, in Côte de Beaune. The climate is temperate, tending toward continental. The soil lies in banks of marly limestone clay; and the exposure is east-southeast, giving the perfect amount of sunshine. Grown in this *terroir*, Chardonnay produces fairly small grapes. Their sugar content can reach high levels, while still retaining a significant acidity, resulting in particularly well-balanced, powerful, pleasant wines. They are mouth-filling and fleshy, notably with regard to the four *grands crus* (Montrachet, Chevalier-Montrachet, Bienvenues-Bâtard-Montrachet, and Bâtard-Montrachet) that are found in Puligny.

Tempranillo in Rioja

Tempranillo is the Spanish answer to Cabernet Sauvignon. Its name is derived from *temprano*, the Spanish word for "early," since it is an early-ripening variety. The fact that it ripens quickly means it can be grown in cooler regions. It produces the best results in Rioja, in northern Spain. This is particularly true west of the town of Logroño in Rioja Alta, the highest part of the region (between 1,300 and 1,600 ft [400 and 500 m]), open to the Atlantic. It prospers on arid and stony soil, made up of solidified sediments and rocks that centuries of erosion have uncovered. The resulting wines are reputed for their finesse, structure, and their excellent ageing properties.

> Viognier grapes in France's Condrieu vineyards.

Sangiovese in Chianti

Seventy to 80 percent or more of the grapes grown in the Chianti appellation are of this Italian red variety. Sensitive to external factors such as the soil and the climate, it ripens at different times in different vineyards. Grown in the sandy clay of the Colli Aretini, the wines are tender; while in the limestone clay of the Rufina crus, they become full-bodied; and they are rich and strong from the Colli Senesi. Under a generous sun, ripening is often tempered by the proximity to the cool sea and the general whims of the climate. To favor the balance and consistency of the wines, the grapes are often harvested as late as the end of October, which is surprising in a Mediterranean region. Sangiovese produces Chianti wines that are supple, perfumed, fruity, and of the great quality that is famous throughout the world.

> A Tempranillo vine in Rioja, Spain.

Qualified specialists in *terroir*

Claude and Lydia Bourguignon have been studying soils for more than 20 years; not only their physical and chemical composition but also their microbiological properties. They have discovered the role played by small creatures, from insects to microorganisms, which enable the plant to successfully assimilate the soil's mineral elements and help develop the expression of a *terroir* in the wine. They also demonstrated that clay plays a vital role in storing these elements. Thanks to these studies, the Bourguignons have been able to draw up a register classifying the soil's capacity to produce great wines.

FROM VINE TO BOTTLE

THE GROWTH CYCLE OF THE VINE

The vine is both a hardy perennial and a fruit tree. Hence it has an annual cycle of fruit production and its own particular life cycle: first it is a cutting; then it becomes a young vine before reaching full maturity and maximum production.

The needs of the vine

Above all, the vine needs light. However, direct sunlight is not essential; daylight alone is adequate. The average temperatures required for its development are quite specific: 50°F to 77°F (10°C to 25°C). Above 82°F (28°C), its water content evaporates and its leaves wither. Growth also stops when it becomes too cold. It only needs water intermittently and does not require an excessive amount (20 to 27.5 inches or 500 to 700 mm per year). If the climate is too wet, the vine may be attacked by diseases or produce huge berries that contain far too much water, causing the skin to burst. Rain has a negative effect, especially during flowering.

The vine and vine leaf

THE VINE. Vines consist of a number of organs, including the fruiting branches or arms that grow on the sizeable wooden stem or trunk. These branches are arranged in a succession of internodes (*mérithalles*), separated by nodes that have swollen to varying degrees and from which the leaves, buds, tendrils, and inflorescences emerge. During the summer, a branch matures and its color changes from green to brown. This is known as lignification or *aoûtement*, and at this stage the branch becomes a cane.

In vineyards all over the world, the vine's growth cycle resumes in the same way. Dormant at the beginning of winter, the vine starts to grow in the spring to produce ripe clusters in autumn. That is, if the climate is mild, and the wine-producer is careful...

VINE LEAVES. Positioned alternately on the nodes, leaves have five main veins. The enormous variability of other characteristics—lobes, serrations, villosity (presence of a surface fuzz), and pigmentation—is a reminder that the leaves are a key element in differentiating grape varieties.

Flower buds

BUDDING. This stage of the annual cycle of the vine is when the buds open in spring (March to April for the northern hemisphere and September to October for the southern hemisphere). After a long period of dormancy in winter, branches and leaves grow and the sap begins to flow.

THE PROMPT BUD AND LATENT BUD. The prompt bud develops in the same year it emerges; this is not the case for the latent bud, which is alongside the prompt bud. The latent bud develops into a branch only in the year after it begins to grow. The prompt bud produces only short secondary shoots (*entre-coeurs*), which sometimes produce small clusters of grapes. (These small bunches are almost never harvested.) In contrast, the latent bud (*œil latent*) develops the following year into branches that will bear fruit. Thus the quantity of the harvest for a particular year is in part dependent on the growth of the plant during the previous year.

> Budding

> Flower buds

> Flowers

Pests that damage vines

Fungi: Powdery mildew grows on the green sections during budding and then attacks the skin of the berries. Mildew affects the green parts of the plant. The grapes turn brown and shrivel. As for *Botrytis cinerea* (*see* box p.54), it is sometimes harmful, sometimes beneficial.

Parasites: Besides phylloxera (*see* p.21 and p.34), there are grape worms and mites (which cause *Colomerus vitis* and *Caleptrimerus vitis*), and red or yellow spiders mites.

Viruses: Transmitted by grafting, short-leaf and coil viruses, for example, are detrimental to the yield, the longevity, and sugar content of the berries.

> Having reached their maximum size, the clusters soak up the sun to reach full maturity.

FLOWERING. The inflorescences, which later become the clusters of grapes, are located at the base of branches on the opposite side to the leaves. Their number ranges from none to four per branch. Tendrils, located on higher nodes, are only budding inflorescences. Depending on variety and environmental conditions, the number of flowers that make up the inflorescences can vary from a hundred to several thousand. The time of flowering depends on the variety and especially on the weather. It is between five and ten weeks after budding (May to June for the northern hemisphere and November to December in the southern hemisphere).

From flowers to grapes

FRUIT SETTING. This stage of the cycle of the vine is when the ovaries of pollinated flowers develop into tiny berries: the inflorescences became clusters. The phenomenon of fruit setting occurs in early summer. This is the most crucial moment in the growth cycle of the vine, because it largely determines the size of the harvest.

BERRY GROWTH. This takes place in four distinct phases. Slowly for about 20 days, then it accelerates for a similar period of time, only to slow sharply again until veraison.

VERAISON. This refers to the physiological process during which the sugars in the berries begin to intensify. The berries of red grapes begin to acquire their color. It is in essence the actual beginning of the maturation of the grapes (in August for the northern hemisphere, and February in the southern). The degree of maturity, which determines the harvest date, is decided according to the type of wine required.

DORMANCY. In autumn, falling leaves indicate the end of the annual growth cycle and the beginning of winter dormancy.

> Fruit setting

> Berries growing

> Veraison

WORK IN THE VINEYARD DURING THE YEAR

Current wine production combines the expertise of centuries gone by with science and the most advanced modern techniques.

Human intervention

PREPARATION OF THE GROUND. In most large vineyards, traditional methods of cultivating the soil continue to be used: banking up the earth in the fall (to protect the vines from excessive cold and damp), plowing back the earth in the spring (to open up the base of the vines), de-earthing (removal of soil from between the vines), and hoeing. Those who follow the method of non-cultivation, which replaces this work with the effective use of herbicides, do not perform these tasks, nor do those who use cover crop planting to fight against soil erosion (*see also* p.58).

Despite advances in technology, the work of the wine producer has not changed: his task is to manage growth; to control weeds, insects, and grapevine diseases; and to harvest at the right time. The schedule of work on the vine is still the same.

FERTILIZATION. Manure may be added, along with fertilizers and various additives (organic or inorganic substances to make the soil more fertile).

TREATMENTS. Bordeaux mixture (*see* box on the following page) and other preventative pesticide treatments are applied repeatedly to the graft, stem, and branches.

PRUNING. Between December and March (in the northern hemisphere), while the sap is down, the vines undergo winter pruning (*see* p.52) using techniques specific to each individual region in order to reduce growth. Summer pruning, which consists of several operations—trimming, topping, thinning, etc. (*see* p.52)—helps to retain the sap for the berries, to aerate the vine, and to optimize the amount of sun received.

> Winter pruning

> Burning of clippings after pruning

> Tying pruned vine shoots

> Mechanical plowing

> Thinning

> Harvest

Bordeaux mixture

Mildew is a disease caused by a fungus attacking the leaves and clusters. The remedy is called Bordeaux mixture. This blue fungicide, which is prepared with copper sulfate and lime water, is sprayed on the vines. The Bordeaux mixture used today is less toxic and degrades more readily than that of earlier times. However, the general use of copper, which accumulates in the soil, has been criticized to the point that a directive was passed by the European Union in 2002 to limit its use and decrease the amount permitted every year. Laboratories are testing replacements.

> Harvest at Château Reynon, in Bordeaux.

Work in the vineyard, month by month (for the northern hemisphere)

JANUARY. The vines are pruned by hand. This delicate work has hardly been mechanized. Minimal pruning takes place in some New World vineyards. The vine cuttings that have been removed are burned.

FEBRUARY. Pruning of the vines continues.

MARCH. The vine awakes from its winter dormancy. In Champagne, as in many New World vineyards, virtually no plowing takes place: the weeds, instead of being buried, are destroyed by herbicides. With this said, today we are witnessing the return of plowing, advocated by those in favor of organic and sustainable viticulture.

APRIL. This is when new buds appear (budding). At the same time, young vines are planted and trellising takes place (repairing the posts, the wires, and then attaching the plant).

MAY. Spring frosts are a concern now. The plants are treated against disease (mildew, powdery mildew, gray rot) and animal pests (grape worms, spider mites, etc.), and these treatments continue until mid-September. They must cease between 15 days and three weeks before harvest. A second plowing is carried out. Organic wine producers do not weed.

JUNE. The vine flowers. New branches are trellised. Treatments continue.

JULY. Another plowing. Further treatments, if necessary. The vine is cut back. Branches that are too long are pollarded (or pruned): this is trimming (since, if the vine grows too extensively,

it produces under-ripe fruit) or thinning by removing some of the young clusters in order to limit the yield.

AUGUST. Second thinning. Treatment, if necessary.

SEPTEMBER. Harvest begins. Harvesting machines often replace human grape pickers, except for many top vineyards. In vineyards where it is very hot, it is common to harvest at night to take advantage of the cooler temperature.

OCTOBER. Harvesting ends. The soil is enriched with fertilizer, manure, or waste.

NOVEMBER. If the year is a good one, the last few grapes are harvested; this is the late harvest. The large shoots are pruned. Anti-mildew treatment is applied. Plowing takes place. If appropriate, old vines are uprooted.

DECEMBER. The drains are cleared. Roads, terraces, and walls are repaired. Pruning work begins.

DID YOU KNOW...?

Horse-drawn plowing, which had abandoned for some time, is once again being used. Vineyards using biodynamic and organic farming methods have revived the popularity of this practice. Mechanical plowing also takes place; but tractors, which are often very heavy, compact the earth. Horses, by contrast, can plow more lightly. Moreover, if the vine is on a steep slope, it is easier to plow with a horse rather than with a machine.

PRUNING AND YIELD
OF THE VINE

*Since the beginning of viticulture, growers have found that when vines are pruned—
when they are prevented from achieving full natural growth—they yield better quality
fruit and thus better wine.*

The principles of pruning

To achieve the same aims, the wine producers of Europe and the New World have distinct patterns of pruning. These differences illustrate how the soil determines not only the choice of grape variety to grow, but also cultivation practices.

IN EUROPE. European wine producers prune their vines in winter to control the growth of the plant and reduce yields: the shorter the vine is cut, the fewer the grapes. In summer, the vine develops its foliage at the expense of the fruit. So, in order to encourage cluster ripening, the vines are trimmed laterally and vertically. This ancient practice of maintaining a balance between the volume of leaves and fruit must be carried out so that the grapes ripen under the best possible conditions, with the leaves acting as a "lung" for the vine via photosynthesis, and the grapes ripening thanks to the effects of sunlight on the foliage.

IN THE NEW WORLD. Pruning has had to be adapted in the vineyards of the New World, where the vines are planted in

*Pruning allows
the vines to be
shaped as required.
Even today, it is the least
mechanized of all the
tasks performed in a
vineyard.*

more fertile soil and in a warmer climate. European techniques might produce abundant but low quality wines if used there. Californian and Australian winemakers now employ "canopy management," which involves shaping the leaf mass to reduce yields and thus ensure better concentration of juice in the grape. In addition, since the late 1980s in California and Australia, new vineyards are planted at higher altitude locations, on less fertile land.

A technique for every season

WINTER PRUNING. Winter pruning shapes the vine (*i.e.* determining the growth path it takes), which will maintain its shape through the years, and stabilizes production. In the first two or three years, the structure is pruned. Then the pruning is just of the fruit-bearing parts, intended to leave on the vine a number of fruit-bearing buds compatible with the desired output and the plant's capabilities. This concerns only the shoots (the shoots of that year). Short pruning means leaving only the shoot bases with a very small number of eyes. The short shoots are designated by different terms: *court-bois*, *coursons*, *cots*, etc. When fruiting branches of a certain length are left on the stock, this is called long pruning. The vine shoots are then called *longs-bois*, *baguettes*, or *astes*.

SPRING PRUNING. In the spring, barren branches, called suckers, which have developed at the base or the trunk of the vines, are removed.

SUMMER PRUNING. During the summer, leaf stripping (which is leaf removal near the cluster to expose it to sunlight), the topping of branches (the removal of the top of the

> Winter pruning at the Champagne Roederer estate in France.

branches), and thinning (trimming of summer growth) are carried out. The parts of the plant that have grown are identified and trained to the trellising system (the supporting set of posts and wires). Depending on whether this is done prudently or too severely, this thinning process will have a positive or negative effect on the quality of the harvest.

Yield

To produce quality wines, it is essential to limit the yield of vines.

IN THE PAST. The old methods of viticulture were laborious and often doomed to failure: rot, mildew, insects, rain, wind, hail, and frost damaged the grapes and man could not prevent this effectively. Those who could afford it sent workers to remove the insects by hand, but others lost their crops. A wet summer meant the grapes rotted because there were no anti-rot treatments. However, traditional methods produced low yields per acre of vines, so the grape juice was concentrated and had good flavor potential.

TODAY. One acre (0.4 ha) of vines may contain 600 to 4,800 vines. Each foot can produce a single grape cluster or a full basket of them. These choices fall to the wine producer, who is constrained by any regulations governing the vineyards. French and Italian laws are based on a maximum yield of a certain volume of wine per acre. Germany sets no upper limit to production, but requires a classification of wines according to the amount of sugar in the musts. As for the New World, they have no regulations and do not impose restrictions on yields. Only the best vineyards limit their yields in the same way as in Europe.

> Summer pruning at the Michel Juillot estate in Côte Chalonnaise, France.

WHAT WORK NEEDS TO BE DONE? Minimal enrichment is required, but other work is needed. Winter pruning can control the growth of the plant. Summer pruning promotes the concentration and maturity of the grapes. Similarly, de-budding, de-suckering (removing unwanted young shoots) at the end of spring, and the "green harvest" (removing some of the clusters) during the summer contribute to reduction of the yield.

Two worlds, two schools of thought

The wine authorities of Europe believe that low yields are a good thing. Vines that face poor soil, high plant density, short pruning, and minimal soil enrichment produce a better wine. Even if, in the New World, very drinkable wines are produced from impressive yields, many experts agree that quality wines are synonymous with low yields.

A level of 3.5 tons per acre (50 hl/ha) appears to be a reasonable yield for grands vins (2,670 bottles per acre, or 6,600 bottles per hectare), beyond which the wine producer is taking risks with the quality of the wine.

Finally, the weather must be factored into account. In a year when the weather is perfect, a yield of 4 tons per acre (70 hl/ha) could provide an excellent wine; but in a tough year, even a yield of 2 tons per acre (35 hl/ha) may produce mediocre wines.

TRUE OR FALSE?

The more vines per acre, the greater the yield.

FALSE. A vineyard planted with 2,400 to 3,200 vines per acre (6,000 to 8,000 vines per hectare, which is the average density in France) will have a lower yield than one planted with 1,000 to 2,000 vines per acre (2,500 to 5,000 vines per hectare, the average in New World countries).

Three ways of guiding vine growth

Goblet: The "cup" looks like a small tree with a rather short trunk and arms heading in opposite directions, each terminated by a spur cut out with two eyes.

Cordon: Cordon trellising involves bending the trunk and placing it horizontally at the desired height along a wire.

Guyot: Guyot trellising comprises a vertical trunk and one or two very short arms. During pruning, the long fruit-bearing branches and a spur are kept. The latter offers a shoot to be retained for the next year.

THE HARVEST

Harvest is the vital link that connects the work in the vineyard to the production of wine. This is an opportunity for growers to see their efforts rewarded in the quality of the crop. Each cluster contains a record of the past year within its berries.

A perfect grape

The decision to begin the harvest, by assessing exactly when the grapes are at their optimum level of maturity, is always difficult. Different varieties reach their respective maturity at different times. In addition, grapes from the same variety that are planted in different places in a vineyard do not always ripen at the same time.

PHYSIOLOGICAL MATURITY. When grapes ripen, sugar builds up in the berries. During maturation, the sugar level rises steadily until it stabilizes at a specific point. At the same time, the acidity of the grapes gradually decreases and then stabilizes as well. At that stage the grapes are ripe, and this is called "alcoholic maturity." Measurement of maturity, based on the sugar/acid ratio, may be taken by state laboratories—especially in Europe. The wine producer also takes individual measurements. After pressing the first berries that have been picked, the juice or must is measured using a hydrometer (to check its sugar content) or a refractometer (to measure the potential alcohol content).

In a week, a single machine can do the same amount of work as 50 people in three weeks. Mechanization of harvesting has reduced the operating costs of many vineyards.

PHENOLIC MATURITY. This is another test of maturity for red or black grapes, which takes into consideration the color of the skins and taste of the seeds. A good level of phenolic maturity allows production of red wines with ripe and pleasant tannins, as opposed to herbaceous and rough ones. The faults of the latter are excused by saying that they were "consumed too soon."

Unknowns in the harvest

THE SHORT YEARS. It may happen that wine producers bring forward the harvest date, either by choice or because they have been forced to do so. In the event of deteriorating berry health or disastrous weather conditions, they will opt for less than perfect maturity, rather than losing their crop. This will be a "short year." Similarly, in the case of a very hot year, if the acidity of white grapes, which is essential for the balance of the wine, is falling too quickly, it may be necessary to harvest earlier than expected.

SELECTIVE HARVESTING. On the other hand, if production of a sweet white wine is being considered, their over-ripeness, or their transformation resulting from the action of the botrytis, is desired. To this end, skilled grape pickers gather only clusters or berries that have reached the necessary stage. They must make several passes around the vineyard, and this is called selective harvesting.

> The ripe grapes can be harvested individually in several passes.

Botrytis cinerea and gray rot

Botrytis cinerea is a fungus that grows on grape skins that have swollen during maturation. This condition is responsible for the gray rot that changes the color of the wine and gives it a musty taste. One particular form of *Botrytis cinerea* leads to the formation of brown rot, or so-called "noble rot." In this case, the fungus attacks the berry without harming it. It produces "scorched" grapes, which are dried out and have high concentrations of sugar and acidity. This botrytis is sought for the sweet white wines of Bordeaux and southwest France (Sauternes, Monbazillac), the sweet wines from the Loire Valley (Vouvray, for example) and from Alsace, as well as for some wines from Germany and Hungary (Tokay).

> Manual harvesting in the vineyards of the Médoc.

Manual harvesting

HARVESTING THE GRAPES. There are generally two grape pickers, or cutters, and they pick the grapes on each side of the row. Pruning knives have been replaced by *épinettes* (pruning shears with straight blades) and *vendangettes* (shears with curved blades), and sometimes by a pair of scissors with rounded points.
STORING THE GRAPES. The harvested grapes are traditionally placed in wicker (*vendangerots*, *vendangeois*) or wooden (*baillots*, *bastiots*) containers. Wooden (*seilles*), metal, or plastic buckets are also used now, with the same capacity of 13–22 lbs (6–10 kg). Plastic lugs may also be used.

DID YOU KNOW...?

The harvest is an occasion for many festivals. The proclamation of the harvest, the earliest legal date on which it is permitted to harvest (in Europe), is often announced in a solemn fashion. But the grape harvest begins and ends with festivities ranging from a simple banquet to large traditional festivals. The custom of holding a banquet was once very common, with La Paulée in Burgundy and Gerber in southwest France among those that have survived to the present day. Some festivals, such as Les Acabailles in Sauternes, include a floral procession. Finally, there is a French tradition on the last day of the harvest that the grape pickers accompany the last cart to the place where the wine is to be produced.

REMOVING THEM FROM THE ROWS. Baskets or buckets are emptied into larger containers supported by carriers. They take their load to the edge of the vineyard where they tip it into a bin or transport container. There are three to five cutters for each carrier, depending on the harvest in the particular vineyard.
PROTECTING THE GRAPES. Some wine producers prefer wooden or plastic boxes, which serve to transport the grapes as well as pick them. This reduces handling, keeping the grapes whole and intact until they reach the place where the wine will be produced.

TRUE OR FALSE?

Mechanical harvesting alters the taste of the wine.

FALSE. Since the 1970s, mechanized harvesting has increased steadily. The berries are harvested by shaking, and the leaves are removed by a fan. With these advances in technology, it is virtually impossible to distinguish between wines that have been manually or mechanically harvested, at least in years when the climate has been mild. Even so, harvesting in prestigious vineyards is mostly done by hand.

Mechanical harvesting

Today, virtually all vineyard regions use mechanized harvesting. The rows must be accessible regardless of weather conditions, which implies chemical weeding or mowing. To produce a quality wine, the vineyard must be in perfect health at the time of harvesting. The development of rot, for example, causes significant losses from the heavy release of juice during picking and during the transfer of the crop. Two types of machine exist: those that are self-propelled and those that are towed. In most cases, picking the berries from the stalk is done via a series of alternate crosswise movements.

TOWARD GREENER WINE PRODUCTION

It was during the 1960s that the use of weedkillers and other artificial aids became commonplace in agriculture, in order to make work easier and reduce production costs. Since the turn of the millennium, more concern is being shown for the impact of this method on the environment.

Sustainable agriculture

This branch of agriculture will use all products at its disposal to fight against diseases and pests. It is sustainable in that it acts with a sense of proportion, using treatments only when appropriate. To qualify as sustainable, an estate must meet many specific criteria, consisting of "good practices that are objectively environmentally friendly," including those specific to viticulture. Some certifying bodies specify allowing grass to grow in the vineyard to combat soil erosion, and maintaining hedges and ditches in order to preserve fauna and flora.

Organic farming

According to statistics from Agence Bio, a public interest group responsible for the promotion of organic farming, organic wine production in France has increased from fewer than 500 estates and 11,775 acres (4,765 ha) in 1998 to more than 1,900 and 55,616 acres (22,507 ha) in 2007 (including 19,464 acres, or 7,877 ha, in conversion). Although this represents only 2.8 percent of French vineyards, the area of land used has quadrupled in 10 years!

Today, France is the third-largest consumer of pesticides; its vineyards, which occupy only 3 percent of agricultural land, account for more than 20 percent of these chemicals.

Proponents of organic farming refuse to use any conventional chemicals, relying instead on natural treatments or the prevention of disease through better maintenance of the vineyard. Since 1991, European regulations on organic farming have concentrated solely on farming techniques, forbidding any synthetic chemicals, fungicides, pesticides, or fertilizers. It will soon include organic wine production, allowing just 15 additives (as opposed to 40 in conventionally produced wines) with much lower maximum doses, a ban on GM products, and outlawing corrective practices.

NO PESTICIDES. This stance allows the fauna in the soil to develop, transform, and regenerate. All pesticides are banned to safeguard biodiversity. Sulfur and copper are used to combat insects, while seaweed is used to repair the damage caused by botrytis. There are also modern techniques of biological control, such as mating disruption, which can reduce insects attacking the grape cluster. However, organic agriculture does not have a solution for everything, and it still has not found a way to combat serious diseases that cause vine death.

NO ARTIFICIAL CHEMICAL FERTILIZERS. Organic viticulture is not looking to feed the plant directly, but to ensure

"Natural" wines?

Some wine producers go further than the organic or biodynamic process, and actually ban the use of any additives, such as lyophilized yeast, sugar (chaptalization), and even sulfur dioxide, an antioxidant and antibacterial that prevents the wine from turning to vinegar.

Some areas like Gramenon (in the Rhône Valley) or Marionnet (in Touraine) can produce wines with great purity of fruit. But winemaking can be difficult to control. A "natural" wine may hold some surprises (such as the taste of rotten eggs), masking what was being sought at the outset: the pure expression of *terroir*.

> Horse-drawn plowing at a vineyard on the Coulée de Serrant estate, in the Loire Valley.

> Agriculture that respects the natural environment and encourages biodiversity in the vineyard.

soil fertility by maintaining biological activity within it. This is done with compost or green manure (clover or rye), or with mineral fertilizers (bone meal for phosphorus, fertilizer for potash, etc.).

NO WEEDKILLERS. Weeds are removed by plowing, or cover planting is practiced.

Biodynamics

In 1924, Rudolf Steiner, the Austrian philosopher and scientist, produced guidelines for this discipline, which studies the link between humans, plants, the earth, and the entire universe. Regarded as a branch of organic farming, biodynamics goes much further than simply excluding the use of artificial chemicals. It uses basic products (*see* box right), based on silica or cow dung.

THE PRINCIPLE OF HOMEOPATHY. All of these preparations are diluted in water, according to the principle of homeopathy, then "energized" by mixing, first in one direction, then the other, for a set period of time. Next, the energized solution is spread in droplets on the ground, in place of dung and compost, or on leaves, instead of silica. It also uses plants, such as nettles, valerian, horsetail, or cedar in the form of homeopathic tinctures or dilutions, to avoid disease.

THE CALENDAR. Implementation of biodynamics requires knowing the position of the stars and constellations on a daily basis. Its followers consider that plant growth depends on cosmic influences that act in a certain pattern, directly linked to the positions of the Moon and the Sun in relation to the constellations of the zodiac. Hence, depending on the day, the plant stimulates its roots, leaves, flowers, or fruit. Work and treatment on the vines are governed by this timetable. Consequently, it is best to plant during "root days" or "fruit days." To improve the quality of the grapes, cultivation and treatment should take place on "fruit days."

AN IRRATIONAL APPROACH? This may seem strange to rational minds. Steiner, however, always asked that his theory be believed only on the basis of what was experimentally verified. Today, this method is very effective on the ground. Is this due to the level of care taken by wine producers or to these specific formulations? Biodynamic wine producers are convinced by this method. Although some practitioners are not believers, the results are there to be seen.

Preparations that harness energy

Biodynamic preparations are employed to stimulate the life forces at work inside the plant.

Horn dung: A cow horn filled with manure is buried in the soil from the fall equinox until the spring so that it is almost like humus. Its main action is to make the vine roots go deeper into the soil, resulting in a greater resistance to drought.

Horn silica: Composed of finely ground quartz mixed with a little water, it is put into a cow horn, buried from the early summer until Christmas, and subsequently exposed to the sun. It is supposed to stimulate the development of fruit.

Dung compost: This consists primarily of cow dung, silica, limestone, and various preparations made from plants (yarrow, camomile, nettle, oak bark, dandelion). These composts, which are rich in bacteria, enhance the decomposition process of organic matter and help damaged ground to recover its vitality.

FERMENTATION

It is through alcoholic fermentation that grape juice becomes wine. This fermentation is the conversion of natural sugars (glucose and fructose) into alcohol, under the action of yeasts (tiny microorganisms). Carbon dioxide is also produced. A second (malolactic) fermentation, which occurs later, gives the wine softness.

Alcoholic fermentation

Fermentation is both a complex chemical reaction and a totally natural process. The grapes ferment once the skin of the berries is broken: the sugars inside the ripe fruit then come into contact with yeasts present on the thin film that covers each berry, and fermentation begins. The wine producer simply provides the container (a vat) that contains the juice and crushes the grapes.

THE PROCESS. Under the action of the yeasts, which consist of very small organisms, fermentation produces carbon dioxide initially and then ethanol, which is the alcohol in wine. Other substances result from this process: there is glycerol, which makes the wine rich; esters or aromatic compounds; higher alcohols used as flavor carriers; aldehydes; and acids. By-products from the fermentation contribute significantly to the flavor of the wine and are particularly responsible for so-called "secondary" aromas (*see* p.211).

> *Fermentation is a perfectly natural phenomenon. People have used this process from the earliest times to create wine to quench thirst and provide the greatest possible pleasure.*

Young wine

When the yeast has converted all of the sugar into alcohol, fermentation stops. Sometimes the sugar content is so high that the alcohol reaches a level that inhibits the action of the yeast: it produces a powerful yet sweet wine, still containing residual (unfermented) sugar. Also, if the ambient temperature is insufficient, the yeast may stop working before the sugar has been transformed: the wine will thus have an alcohol content lower than would have been possible in terms of the maturity of the grapes. Alcoholic fermentation usually ends after one to three weeks. The young wine is then very cloudy, because of the lees (dead yeast cells), pulp, and seeds in the vat.

Yeasts

Fermentation is caused by the action of yeasts present on the skin of the grapes or in the air, or added to the vat. Among the former two, only the most widespread variety, *Saccharomyces cerevisiae*, can react with the grape sugars to produce alcohol. Each kind of yeast has special features as regards the production of alcohol, functional temperature range, the formation of flavoring substances, the rate of fermentation, etc.

> Throughout fermentation, the wine producer regularly monitors the temperature of the must.

DID YOU KNOW...?

Fermentation is different for red and white wines. For red wines (see pp.68–9), the crushed grapes and juice are put into a vat and we wait for fermentation to start. The length of time this takes is variable. For white wine (see pp.64–6), the grapes are first pressed to extract the juice, which is then fermented on its own in vats or barrels. Hence, the difference in flavor and structure between reds and whites. Only red wines are fermented with their skins and seeds; these pass on not only color but also tannins and additional ingredients that provide flavor. After fermentation comes the maturation phase (see pp.76–9).

Chaptalization and reverse osmosis

Described in 1801 by Jean-Antoine Chaptal in his *Treatise on making wines*, chaptalization consists of adding sugar to a must to increase the alcoholic strength. By adding 2.27 oz of sugar per gallon of must (17 g/l), an extra percent of alcohol is produced. Enrichment with sugar is carefully controlled in France. Banned in the south, it is allowed further north to a limited extent, but cannot add more than two percent of alcohol to the wine. It does not add any quality to the wine in terms of taste or bouquet. The novel feature of chaptalization lies in the possibility of measuring the amount of sugar added (*see also* p.63). Chaptalization is sometimes replaced by self-enrichment techniques, the most common of which is reverse osmosis. This involves subtracting a certain amount of water from the must (*see also* p.62), which results in an increase in the concentration of other ingredients (including sugar). The addition of must with concentrated sugar is also permitted.

> *Cuvier* is the French word for the place where winemaking vats are located in a winery.

NATURAL OR SELECTED YEASTS. To better control the fermentation, some wine producers, particularly in the New World, prefer to employ selected yeasts (or yeast cultures). This practice, which is permitted, nonetheless goes against the idea of respect for *terroir*. Producers of fine wines have understood this, deciding that nothing beats the natural or indigenous yeasts for greater complexity and flavor.

Temperature control

When the temperature exceeds 54°F (12°C), the must begins to ferment. Once engaged, the process generates heat and proceeds automatically. The must warms and fermentation starts bubbling under the action of the carbon dioxide. Around 95–99°F (35–37°C), yeasts will be killed by the heat and fermentation stops. Today, steel tanks are equipped with a system for cooling and, if necessary, heating the must. Regulating the temperature of the tanks is one of the great advances in wine production. The gain in quality is important, and the deterioration caused by breaks during fermentation is avoided.

Malolactic fermentation

Malic acid, which can exist in high concentrations in grapes, has a distinctive green apple taste. After fermentation, the action of lactic bacteria transforms malic acid into lactic acid and carbon dioxide (thus a malolactic or secondary fermentation). Lactic acid is less bitter than malic acid, so the wine becomes softer. This degradation of malic acid into lactic acid is always sought in a quality red wine (and in some white wines). For it to happen, a certain level of heat (68°F/20°C) is required. The winery is heated if necessary, or hot water is circulated in the pipes normally used for cooling the tanks. Sometimes it is necessary to resort to culturing (adding lactic bacteria).

TRUE OR FALSE?

Wine cannot be sweetened.

FALSE. In Germany, for the QmP category of wine (*see* p.98), as in Italy too, a method of adding unfermented must is used. It must come from the same vineyard and be of the same expected level of quality as the wine. It is added after fermentation, and before bottling, to produce a sweeter style.

TECHNIQUES THAT ARE CONTROVERSIAL

Scientific research has helped to improve wine quality. Yet some oenological practices may worry the consumer, who does not always understand what they involve.

CRYOEXTRACTION OR EXTRACTION USING COLD TEMPERATURES

66 Sweet wines are generally made from grapes concentrated by botrytis or by over-ripening. With cryoextraction, grapes that are insufficient in sugar are enriched by freezing them. The grapes are placed in cold storage at a temperature between 23°F and 18°F (-5°C to -8°C) for 20 or more hours. During pressing, which takes place soon after, only the sweetest (not frozen) grapes have their juice extracted. Those that are not sufficiently concentrated remain frozen and are eliminated.

- **FOR.** Cryoextraction may be regarded as a system of selection, since it eliminates the insufficiently concentrated grapes. It can also remove water from a recent rainfall.

- **AGAINST.** Using these methods makes things artificially easier, say many wine producers. To make a great sweet wine means accepting the restrictions imposed by nature."

REVERSE OSMOSIS OR CROSS-FLOW FILTRATION

66 Another way to concentrate the must is to eliminate some of the water from the grapes by very fine filtration carried out at high pressure. The filter lets the water through, but not other substances whose molecules are larger.

- **FOR.** In difficult years, this may be a solution that saves the wine.

- **AGAINST.** Concentrating the must will never replace true levels of ripeness. It is even more shocking that these devices, which are very expensive, are sometimes used by those producers classified as *grands crus*."

OAK SHAVINGS TO REPLACE BARRELS

66 Oak shavings come in the form of chips that are cut, dried and heated in the oven. In the fermenting wine, they produce flavors of coconut, toast, or smoke, depending on the extent to which they are heated. They are used in vats as a kind of infusion. In South America, they have been used since the 1980s; the European Union has authorized their use since 2006.

- **FOR.** Oak flavors without any disadvantages: this technique is much cheaper and much easier to use! A Bordeaux barrel of 59 gal. (225 l), used for three years, costs $3.65 per gal. (€74 per hl) of wine produced. The shavings, used at a dose of 0.67 oz per gal. (5 g/l), cost just 25 cents per gal. (€5 per hl).

- **AGAINST.** The flavor produced by this technique does not compare to the complexity of barrel ageing."

THE USE OF SULFUR

66 Sulfur dioxide (SO_2) is used to protect the must and wine against oxidation. It also has an antiseptic role against microorganisms. At low doses, it is put into the must before fermentation starts, as it prevents the development of bacteria for a short time, while allowing the growth of the yeast. A higher dose is added after fermentation to stabilize the wine. (*see also* p.65 and p.78)

• **FOR.** An oxidized wine is not good; a vinegary wine is not good either. The doses of sulfur dioxide are now very low and are no longer likely to cause any much-maligned headaches!

• **AGAINST.** Some brave souls produce wine without sulfur dioxide. The few who manage to avoid faults (oxidation, fermentation problems, bacterial invasions) produce wines with exceptional purity of fruit. The rest produce wine with significant faults. Is it worth doing?"

CHAPTALIZATION OR ADDING SUGAR

66 When the grapes are not ripe enough, you can add sugar to the must at the start of fermentation. This is called chaptalization. Using 2.27 oz of sugar per gal. (17 g/l) of must produces one degree of additional alcohol. In France, the doses added must be less than two degrees, in other words 4.54 oz per gal. (34 g/l). In southern French regions, this method is not allowed; but you can enrich the must with rectified must concentrate, solutions of almost pure sugar obtained from grapes (*see also* p.61).

• **FOR.** Used in moderate doses and to correct a slight lack of maturity due to weather conditions, chaptalization can improve the balance of the wine. In addition, nuclear magnetic resonance can now accurately measure the added sugar in the must and prevent any harm being done.

• **AGAINST.** Used excessively, it produces poor wines, unbalanced by too much alcohol. Furthermore, with reasonable yields and well-maintained vineyards, chaptalization is not necessary except in cold and rainy years!"

THE ADDITION OF YEASTS DURING FERMENTATION

66 Even if fermentation is a spontaneous phenomenon, it is sometimes slow to start and it is hard to finish with musts that are very high in sugar. Hence, the wine producer adds dehydrated, commercially purchased yeasts to the must (*see also* p.61).

• **FOR.** Some strains of yeast, selected for their resistance to high levels of alcohol, are very useful when fermentation is difficult to complete. The addition of yeast also helps prevent the development of certain organisms naturally present on the skin of berries or in the winery, which can be harmful (*e.g.* Brettanomyces produces a rustic odor reminiscent of horse sweat).

• **AGAINST.** More and more growers, particularly those who practice organic farming, refuse to use these yeasts because they are afraid of standardization. They prefer indigenous yeasts, as they feel that these are better able to retain the character of the *terroir*. It should be noted that flavored yeast strains were misused in the 1980s, producing many flavors such as banana or pear drop, making some disgusting young wines!"

PRODUCING WHITE AND ROSÉ WINES

Despite its many variants, the production of white wine is still based on the fermentation of the grape juice alone. Making rosé wine follows the same principle, though sometimes the juice must first be colored by keeping it in brief contact with the skins.

Which grapes for which wine?

The type of wine produced (white, rosé, or red) is determined by two factors: the nature of the grape (the presence or absence of colorants) and the duration of maceration (contact between the juice, known as the must, and the solids, including the skin or film).

WHITE GRAPES. If the grapes are white, with a colorless pulp and a film, they are always used to produce white wine. In this case, it is important that only the must, separated from the solid parts of the cluster (skin, seeds, etc.), is used for fermentation, without any maceration (*see* below).

RED GRAPES WITH COLORLESS PULP. If the grapes are red, with a colored skin or film and a colorless pulp, it is possible to make a white, rosé, or red wine. If there is no contact with the skin, white wine is produced. If the contact is brief, it will be a rosé wine (*see* p.66). If it is prolonged, red wine will result (*see* pp.68–9).

RED GRAPES WITH COLORED PULP. If the grapes are red, with a colored pulp and film, only red wine may be produced, whether or not maceration takes place. These grapes, called teinturiers, are rarely used alone, but may serve to accentuate the color intensity of the wine. They are used only for *vins de table* and are currently the subject of grubbing up at the urging of the European Union.

Vinification, or wine-making, is the phase between the completion of the harvest and the end of alcoholic fermentation. It involves different stages, depending on the wine that the winemaker wants to produce.

From vine to wine press

For white wine production, it is essential that the grapes reach the winery with their skin intact, not broken, so that the yeasts on the skin do not come into contact with the pulp. The clusters are picked whole, preferably by hand if the grower is seeking optimal conditions. In the same vein, the preferred means of transportation for the grapes is in boxes rather than in large containers where they would be crushed.

CRUSHING OR DE-STEMMING. Sometimes the grapes are squeezed whole. This is the case for Champagnes and sparkling wines. But they can also be pre-crushed and de-stemmed—two operations that help facilitate the extraction of the must. The crushing is done to break the berries, without crushing the seeds. De-stemming separates the berries from the stems (the skeleton of the cluster). In both cases, once the operation is complete, the grapes are immediately transferred into the wine press by pumping. In terms of maceration, it is important to avoid the presence of stems as they give the grape juice a bitter taste.

Cold soak

In most cases, the white winemaking process does not involve maceration. But sometimes the winemaker seeks flavors present in the skins of grapes, especially for the Sémillon, Sauvignon Blanc, Muscat, Riesling, and sometimes Chardonnay varieties. To this end, a brief "cold soak" or maceration is carried out before pressing: the grapes, which have already been de-stemmed and crushed, are put in a vat for a few hours. This technique, also called "pre-fermentation maceration," may yield a deeper wine color after a few years in bottle.

> When they reach the winery, the grapes are poured into a container equipped with an endless screw or worm gear.

Different wine presses

There are many kinds of wine press, with capacities ranging from a few hundred pounds to several tons of grapes. Modern presses are completely automated, and the most common type of press is horizontal. Among them, the pneumatic press, which has an inner membrane that is inflated to press the grapes, has the gentlest action. Some winemakers prefer traditional vertical presses, however: for moderate pressure over a large area, they give a clearer juice, which is less difficult to settle.

> During de-stemming, the stalks are separated from the berries.

PRESSING. Pressing aims to extract all the juice from the grapes. This task takes a relatively short time, yet is one of the most delicate stages in white wine production because the quality of the wine depends upon it. (Also, the mass of semi-liquid pulp must be maintained at low temperature to avoid fermentation starting early. This can only take place between 54°F and 75°F [12°C to 24°C].) If the pressing is done in appropriate conditions, it results in a clear juice without crushing the seeds. If they were crushed, the wine might taste grassy. As well, this process must be done quickly to avoid oxidation.

Clarifying the must

SETTLING. After it has come from the wine press, the must can be rather cloudy. It contains solids or sedimentary material that can make wine taste bad, and must be removed. To do this, the juice may be moved to the centrifugal extractor, which is quick and efficient, although some allege that this reduces the quality of the resulting wine. This technique is mostly used by producers of very large volumes of *vin ordinaire*. The other method, stabilization by cold (at almost 32°F or 0°C) is better, as the juice is prevented from starting fermentation while the sediment naturally falls to the bottom of the tank.

ADDING SULFUR. Whatever the method used for settling, sulfur is added at this stage. This means adding sulfur dioxide (SO_2) to the juice to prevent oxidation and to neutralize development of any microorganisms. The doses depend on the health of the juice and the ambient temperature. Used in excess, sulfur dioxide can mask all the wine's flavors. Dosage is tightly regulated and adjusted for each wine (*see also* p.78).

Alcoholic fermentation

The juice is then poured into vats where it will ferment slowly for one to four weeks. Fermentation can be stimulated by an injection of cultured yeasts or by inoculation with fermenting juice from another vat. The temperature determines the extent of fermentation and hence the style of wine desired. The lower the temperature, the more time the wines will take to ferment. This enables more sediment to be extracted and results in higher quality wines. The higher the temperature, the quicker the fermentation, but also often lower quality and an increased possibility of an inferior taste, that is to say, a "cooked" flavor.

FERMENTATION VATS. To make wine, the wine producer can choose vats made of wood, stainless steel, concrete, or plastic. Each has its advantages and drawbacks. Stainless steel is very common, as it is easier to clean and cool. But temperature can also be regulated in wooden vats, which have a thermal inertia that steel lacks. To make great wine for ageing, Burgundian

TRUE OR FALSE?

Additives used are always mentioned on the label.

FALSE. In France, several consumer groups, and some winemakers, would like the label to list any additives that are not from the grape. Only sulfur dioxide has to be mentioned right now. If used in excessive quantities, this is likely to cause headaches for some people.

Wine produced in barrels

Throughout history, the Burgundians made great white wines, including Chardonnay, in casks designed for long ageing. The capacity of the cask, about 60 gal. (228 l), is ideal for white wine production without temperature control: the liquid rises to 77°F (25°C) and is maintained at this level through fermentation. The wine acquires a special flavor, related to its contact with the wood. Finally, the wine remains in contact with its lees (the deposit resulting from fermentation), which protects it from oxidation and enriches it at the same time. The winemaker mixes the lees into the wine regularly using a stick, in order to make it complex and rich. That is what we call *batonnage* (see also p.77).

winemakers use oak barrels (*see* box above). More generally, many great châteaux have reverted to wooden vats after embracing the modern trend of stainless steel.

Final stages

NO MALOLACTIC FERMENTATION. Naturally occurring after alcoholic fermentation, malolactic fermentation (*see* p.61) helps to round out acidic wines, but it may degrade fruity wines from warm regions. In general, the white winemaker seeks to prevent "malo" and treat the wine to remove the bacteria that can cause it. Doing so calls for dosing the wine slightly with sulfite again, passing it through a centrifuge, or using microfiltration followed by bottling under sterile conditions.

DECANTING. Fermentation and wine production are now complete. Yet the wine still needs to be clarified. It contains sediment, a deposit consisting primarily of yeast that has completed its task. The wine is therefore carefully poured out of the vat while the sediment remains at the bottom. This operation is called racking. It will be repeated several times during the maturation process (*see* p.76). For the development of certain wines, such as Muscadet in Nantes, France, the sediment is left in the wine until it is bottled, which results in certain flavor characteristics, such as the presence of gas bubbles that give the wine extra freshness.

The case of sweet wines

Sweet wines are made from grapes so sweet that fermentation cannot transform all the sugar into alcohol. For sweet wines, wine producers leave the grapes on the vine until they are too ripe, hoping that *botrytis cinerea* (or "noble rot") will appear. The fungus dries the grapes, whose already sweet juice is concentrated into very rich droplets. The wine will then go through the same production as for dry white wines. However, in an environment high in sugar, yeast works more slowly and is exhausted after a few days. Fermentation stops and some of the sugar will not be transformed into alcohol, hence the sweet taste. This applies to wines such as Sauternes in France,

Trockenbeerenauslese in Germany, Tokaj aszú in Hungary, and several New World wines. We may also use desiccated grapes, that is to say, grapes dried on racks. This is the case for *vin de paille* in France (*see* box below) or Italian Vin Santo.

Rosé wine production

There are three ways to produce rosé wines: pressing, *saignée* ("bleeding"), and blending (which, in France, applies only to Champagne). Direct pressing results in subtle and fine wines, while *saignée* produces more "winey" and full-bodied ones. Without exception, a rosé is always consumed in a year or two of bottling. Its aromas and flavors are most often richer versions of white wines.

PRESSING. Some rosés, made from grapes that are deep in coloration and sufficiently ripe, can be obtained by direct pressing. This is the case with the rosés of Anjou and Touraine in France. The must is then processed with techniques used for producing white wine. A slight maceration before pressing is often necessary to imbue the wine with a deep color. White wines are produced in the same way but using grapes with little or no color, like Grenache Gris. In those instances, even if you leave the skins to soak in the juice, there is very little change in color.

SAIGNÉE. This involves draining off a certain proportion of juice from a red wine vat after only a few hours of maceration (and before filling the vat again). The majority of the rosé wines from Provence and Tavel in France are produced in this way. The must that is "bled," and which has not yet begun to ferment, is made into wine in accordance with the principles of white winemaking.

BLENDING. Permitted only in Champagne in France, it involves adding to white wine, before its second, sparkling fermentation, a percentage of red wine from Champagne grapes. About 95 percent of rosé Champagnes are produced in this way.

TRUE OR FALSE?

Rosé wine can be produced by mixing red and white wine.

TRUE. But in France, only Champagne can blend wines in this way (*see* below). In other countries, blending is allowed to produce table wines.

DID YOU KNOW...?

Producing **vin de paille** *can take up to four years. A product of Jura, France, this very special wine is made from grapes left on a bed of straw (now more often on racks) from October to January, which results in desiccation of the berries to produce a richer and more concentrated juice. While 220 lbs (100 kg) of grapes normally produces 18–20 gal. (70–75 l) of must, the equivalent volume for* **vin de paille** *is no more than 5 or 6 gal. (20–25 l). Fermentation in small casks is very slow and may take up to four years. Produced in limited quantities, this wine has an amber color and a rich flavor with a hint of nuts.*

MAKING RED WINE

It may be easier to make red wine than white wine. The work of the winemaker is to oversee the development of a natural process that is very simple in principle. However, the production of red wines still requires careful handling and a great deal of skill.

Basic principles

As with white wines, winemaking involves transforming the sugary must into alcohol. The distinctive feature of making red wine is its maceration. During this infusion stage, the coloring matter, tannins, and aromatic compounds contained in the solid parts of the grape (skin and pulp) are dissolved in the juice, giving the wine its color and character. The techniques employed all follow the same principle, although they vary depending on the grape variety, climate, and local traditions.

Classic maceration

The maceration process described here is broadly used in France and around the world. Red grapes are first crushed and de-stemmed. They are burst, releasing their juices, and detached from the skeleton of the cluster (the stalk). Then the must, the juicy mass of crushed grapes, is transferred into thermo-regulated stainless steel or wooden vats.

A long period of maceration gives the wine its color and tannic structure, but any excessive extraction of substances in the solids may yield vegetal or bitter flavors that are sometimes unpleasant.

The duration of fermentation, involving maceration and fermentation, can range from a few days to three weeks, depending on the style of wine.

CAP FORMATION. Once in the tank, the solids of the berries rise to the top and come together to form the "cap." Gradually, the colorants and all the constituent parts of the cap will transfer to the juice. This operation, called "extraction," is encouraged by the heat of fermentation, with the winemaker restricting the temperature to around 86°F (30°C).

PUNCHING DOWN, *REMONTAGE*, OR USE OF A ROTARY VAT. Some techniques can facilitate the extraction process. Punching down involves pushing the cap into the must with a stirrer, a wooden paddle, hydraulic cylinders, or even feet.

Remontage, or "pumping over," is immersing the cap by pumping the juice gently from the bottom of the vat to soak over it.

There also are vats equipped with rotary blades that re-suspend the solids in the liquid. Whatever method is used, the operation is delicate, because the goal is to extract the colors and flavors, but not to excess.

LENGTH OF MACERATION. For the production of many wines, only a very partial extraction from the solids is required because the emphasis is on primary flavors (*see* p.211). The time spent in a maceration vat is therefore relatively short. However, for a wine like Chinon from the Loire Valley, berries can be macerated for a month or more to extract the maximum character. The wine will be rich in tannins and so will be aged for some time before drinking.

> Crushing grapes at Château Lascombes in Margaux, France.

TRUE OR FALSE?

The winemaker constantly checks the thermometer.

TRUE. Monitoring the temperature during fermentation is critical. The must should be kept in a desired temperature range and, if necessary, a cooling system used. Fruit flavor and finesse are extracted via fermentation at a relatively low temperature of around 75°F (24°C). With higher temperatures, 86–97°F (30–36°C), even for a very short period of time, maximum color and intensity of flavor are produced.

Carbonic maceration

The greatest difference between carbonic maceration and the previous method is the use of uncrushed grapes. Fairly widespread in Beaujolais, France, this technique places whole berries in a closed vessel, which is filled with carbon dioxide. Under the effect of this gas, a peculiar phenomenon called "intracellular fermentation" occurs. It

> Racking the wine during wine production.

> Wine is also racked during the maturation stage.

leads, inside each berry, to the formation of a small amount of alcohol and malic acid degradation. This fermentation-in-a-berry is accompanied by the production of bright, primary flavors. A short fermentation period of four to six days produces a very floral wine, with an immediate softness. Subsequently, carbon dioxide is released and the fermentation continues normally. Carbonic maceration is well established for wines produced from Gamay grapes and sold young, like much Beaujolais. It is also now widely applied to certain varieties, where a portion is blended with wines made using traditional maceration to produce a softer result, especially in Mediterranean regions.

Running off and pressing

Whatever the method of maceration, it is necessary at some point to drain the liquid in the vat. When the winemaker considers the optimal maceration time complete, whether alcoholic fermentation is complete or not, the wine is "run off." A valve is opened at the bottom of the tank to flush out the liquid, permanently separating it from the solids. This completes the maceration phase.

FREE-RUN WINE AND PRESS WINE. The juice that is run off, which is of the finest and highest quality, is called free-run. Next, the grape skins and lees (solids still containing liquid) are pressed to extract any remaining juice—called "press wine." This represents 8 to 15 percent of the total volume of a tank. At a later stage, possible blending of the free-run and press wine will depend on various criteria.

FINAL FERMENTATION. The free-run and press wines are then placed in separate tanks. At this stage, winemakers conduct a comprehensive analysis, including the alcohol and acidity levels. Fermenting of the juice then will be completed if the process was not completed at the time of running off. Following alcoholic fermentation, malolactic fermentation will take place in all cases (see p.61). The wine is then clarified during the maturation phase (see p.76).

Vins de garage

The term *vins de garage* is unofficial. It relates to small vats that could fit into the garage of a private home. This style of wine is produced from small vineyards with a deliberately reduced yield of fully ripened grapes. Leaving aside the hype that has made their prices soar, *vins de garage* are often excellent wines, especially from St-Émilion in Bordeaux, although neighboring Médoc is also starting to produce these wines. Making the wine requires extreme care: removal of the stalks by hand, followed by long fermentation in stainless steel vats, punching down the must, placing in new oak barrels for malolactic fermentation, and ageing for two years.

MAKING SPARKLING WINES

All fermentation produces carbon dioxide gas that escapes into the open air. If trapped in a bottle, the gas creates a sparkling wine. Champagnes and sparkling wines are produced on the basis of this principle.

Basic principles

THE ANCESTRAL METHOD. Historically, sparkling wines were produced using what we call the "ancestral" method, also known as the "rustic," "Dioise," or "Gaillacoise" method. This method is still practiced by some producers in the French regions of Die, Limoux, and Gaillac. It involves putting the wine into bottles during fermentation, before all the sugar has been transformed into alcohol. The method is tricky, and sometimes the bottles explode under the pressure of the gas after being sealed. Following a year in the cellar, they are ready for sale. The wines produced in this way in France are all official AOC. These are from Die; Clairette de Die Tradition (Muscat-based); from Limoux, the Blanquette traditional method; and from Gaillac, wine produced by the *methode gaillacoise* (both based on Mauzac).

Production of sparkling wines always follows the same principle, which is to allow the wine to ferment in a closed bottle (or sometimes a closed vat), so that the carbon dioxide produced by fermentation cannot escape and is dissolved into the wine.

THE CHAMPAGNE METHOD. Later, producers in Champagne developed what is called the Champagne method, also known as the traditional method. Safer than the ancestral approach, it was the first to let the must ferment in vats to produce a still *premier vin* between 9 and 9.5 percent alcohol. Then a second fermentation is generated in sealed bottles, by adding wine sugar and yeast at the bottling stage. This technique is now used in many areas of France: in the Loire (Vouvray, Saumur, Crémant de Loire), in Burgundy (Crémant de Bourgogne), in Bordeaux (Crémant de Bordeaux), in Alsace (Crémant d'Alsace), in the Rhône (Clairette de Die, sparkling Saint-Péray), in the South (Blanquette and Crémant de Limoux), etc. Around the world, among the most well-known sparkling wines, some Spanish Cava, German Sekt, Italian Prosecco, and sparkling wines from California and Australia are also prepared in this way.

> Traditional presses at the Louis Roederer house at Aÿ in Champagne.

> Mechanical *remuage* of bottles (gyropalette) at Château Moncontour in the Loire Valley.

Harvesting for blending

The complex stages involved in the production of Champagne make it an unparalleled wine of consistent quality. The selection of grapes is essential. These consist of red grapes (Pinot Noir and Pinot Meunier) and white (Chardonnay, but also Arban, Petit Meslier, and Pinot Blanc), grown in a named and clearly defined area, with the maximum possible yield.

PRESSING AND FERMENTATION. Soon after picking the grapes, pressing is carefully performed in order to obtain clear juice, whose brief contact with the skin of the berry extract has resulted in only a little tannin and no color. The first fermentation takes place in wooden vats or stainless steel tanks.

BLENDING. Blending then takes place: at each stage of the operation officials taste wines from each vintage–from different soils, grape varieties, and plots. The goal is to assemble a wine that reflects the style of the house and achieves the same character and quality from one year to the next. Wines from previous years, so-called reserve wines, may form part of the blending. The final result is called a *cuvée*.

Second fermentation

THE PRISE DE MOUSSE ("formation of bubbles"). Once the blending of the wine is complete, a mixture of sugar and yeast—the *liqueur de tirage*—is added during bottling. The whole mixture is then bottled into thick glass bottles, sealed with metal caps. The bottles are stored horizontally in the darkest and coolest cellars. Second fermentation starts, including the production of carbon dioxide to form the bubbles or *prise de mousse*. This takes about a month.

REMUAGE. The wine is then stored in the cool cellars that are typical of the Champagne region. Ageing here, which has a legal minimum term of at least 15 months following bottling (and at least three years for vintage wines), leaves a deposit of dead yeast. To remove this deposit, the bottles are placed neck down on special tilted racks called *pupitres*. For two or three months, the tilt of the bottles is progressively increased. The bottles are maneuvered or "riddled," two by two, by experienced cellar workers (*remuers*) or processed en masse by a mechanical device known as a gyropalette.

From disgorgement to corking

The next step, disgorgement, involves removing the residue that has been deposited in the neck of the bottles. This is accomplished by soaking the bottle neck in a liquid refrigerant that freezes the sediment in an ice cube. Then the bottle is opened and, under pressure from the gas inside, the ice is ejected with the deposit. It is quickly replaced by *liqueur d'expédition*, a mixture of Champagne and sugar cane. This stage, called *dosage*, determines the future character of the Champagne: brut, extra dry, sec, demi-sec, or doux/sweet. At corking, the bottles are closed with the traditional cork stopper, held in place by a metal wire cage. Generally, they are not sold immediately, but stored for a few weeks by the producer so that this dosage can blend with the wine.

Charmat method and gasification

Other sparkling wines are produced by different methods. With the Charmat process, the second fermentation, following the addition of the *liqueur de tirage*, takes place not in the bottle but in a closed tank. The wine is then cooled, filtered, and transferred under pressure into a second tank, sweetened with *liqueur d'expédition*, and bottled. These wines lack finesse and complexity. As for gasification (or carbonation), it is a primitive method by which carbon dioxide is injected into the wine before bottling. The sparkling wines produced in this way have no right to any official appellation.

MAKING FORTIFIED WINE

Fortified wines are rich in sugar, flavor, and alcohol. Making wine of this kind involves the addition of alcohol, called mutage or fortification, which stops the action of the yeast and prevents complete fermentation, thus preserving some of the sugar from the grapes.

The basic principles

Fortified wines are produced in the same way as other wines, the difference being the addition of alcohol in the form of rectified spirit or *eau-de-vie*. Sherry, port, and Madeira from the Iberian peninsular nations, French *vins doux naturels*, French *vins de liqueur*, and Marsala from Sicily are all fortified wines. They differ in the grape varieties from which they are made, in terms of the moment at which the alcohol is added, and the amount involved. There are two main methods of fortification: during fermentation (port) or after (sherry). Historically, wine was fortified so that it could be readily shipped elsewhere without spoilage. When the processes of fermentation were poorly understood, it often restarted in wine casks and damaged the wine during transport. Over time, this practice became established to the point of representing an entire family of wines.

Fortification can highlight the specific flavors of the grapes from which the wines are made. Depending on the alcohol used, the type of maturation, and the ageing time, very different styles can be produced.

Port

Today, port is made using modern techniques. After being separated from the cluster and crushed, the berries are poured into vats where the fermentation will start. There, giant drums use rotation to mix the juice and skins. The aim of this process is to extract the pigments in the film surrounding the berry in a short period of time. It is important to not extract harsh flavors from the solid parts, but lots of color for the wine. More traditional methods here include crushing the grapes by trampling on them. Finally, the winemaker stops the fermentation by adding alcohol.

THE ADDITION OF *EAU-DE-VIE*. When fermentation has reached the required level of alcohol (about 9% ABV), the new wine is poured into tanks and an *aguardiente* (grape brandy) is added. The amount of alcohol in the addition is 25 percent, and it brings the level of alcohol in the port to about 18–20 percent, depending on the extent to which the action of the yeast is neutralized. The sugar not converted into alcohol remains in the wine, which is now port. The result is a dark red color and a pleasant sweetness with a strong raisiny flavor. (Though there are also white ports.) Ports need time for the alcohol to blend into the wine. During the first spring, the winemaker tastes the wine and classifies it according to its qualities.

> At cellars in Oporto, the winemaker takes a sample using a pipette.

Sherry

This fortified white wine is easier to produce than port. It is created like any other white wine, with the new wine being poured into a wooden barrel that it is not completely filled. A few months later, a special regional mold called *flor* appears in some barrels. The sherry is then fortified with grape brandy depending on its style: a small amount for *finos* (up to about 15.5 percent alcohol) affected by the *flor*, more for *olorosos* (up 18 percent), which come from barrels where *flor* has not developed. The wines are then aged in *soleras*, rows of barrels laid out at three or four different

> Barrels of sherry in the
Bodega González Byass
cellars, in Jerez, Spain.

*The grapes for some ports are still pressed by
being foot trampled. After being crushed and
removed from the cluster, the grapes are put into
large open stone containers, called* lagares, *where
they are trampled under foot. Although laborious,
this traditional method is considered the best way
to extract the color of grapes without the risk of
crushing the seeds. The juice then ferments in
the* lagares *for between 24 and 36 hours before
the addition of* eau-de-vie
*distilled from grapes. The
cost of labor, however, means
that these techniques are used
to produce only the very best
wines in Oporto, Portugal.*

heights, with the oldest wines on the lowest level (*see also*
p.77). The blending and ageing of sherry give it its complexity,
with each bottle containing wine from different barrels and of
different ages.

Vins doux naturels

Vins doux naturels of France are significantly distinct in color and
flavor (*see* pp.160–1). Produced mainly in Roussillon (Banyuls,
Rivesaltes, Maury, Roussillon, Muscat de Mireval, de Rivesaltes,
de St-Jean-de-Minervois, de Lunel, and de Frontignan), in the
Rhône Valley (Muscat de Beaumes-de-Venise, Rasteau), and

in Corsica (Muscat du Cap Corse), they are fortified with a
96 percent alcohol spirit, amounting to 5 to 10 percent of the
volume of the must during fermentation.

For red wines, a short maceration (two or three days) is
followed by adding the alcohol to the fermenting juice. However,
in some cases, in Banyuls and Maurys especially, fortification is
practiced on the marc, that is to say, the solid parts of the grape
(skin, seeds, etc.). The marc alcohol mixture is then macerated
for 10 to 15 days, which produces wines that are rich in color,
tannin, and flavors. Whites and Muscats are produced in the way
of regular white wines, with the fortification also taking place
during fermentation.

Vins de liqueur

Production of *vins de liqueur* is much more limited than for
vins doux naturels. Their alcohol content is between 16 and 22
percent. These wines are made by mixing grape juice prior to
fermentation with neutral alcohol (brandy distilled from wine,
grape must concentrate, or a mixture). This is the case, for
example, with Pineau des Charentes, a blend of Cognac and
grape juice from the same area; Floc de Gascogne, which is
fortified with Armagnac; and Macvin du Jura, which is fortified
with marc.

Finos and olorosos,
two families of sherry

Sherry has a range of styles, from dry (*manzanilla*)
to sweet (cream). It is divided into two families: *finos*,
which are dry and light; and *olorosos*, which are
deep-colored and powerful. *Fino* should be drunk
very young and not aged in bottle. *Manzanilla*,
the driest and lightest sherry of all, is particularly
appreciated for its slightly iodized taste; and
amontillados are aged in cask for at least eight years.
Olorosos can also be stored for several years. These
are medium-dry, rich, and concentrated wines.

> Some wines such
as Maury are aged
outdoors in demijohns.

THE ART OF MATURATION

Vinification, in the strict sense of the term, is complete when the must has been transformed into wine by fermentation. Maturation then begins, and comes to an end at the point of bottling.

The aims and duration of maturation

The term "maturation" describes the slow work required to refine and develop the qualities of a wine. When maturing a wine, a winemaker has two objectives. The first aim is technical, namely to clarify the wine. The second is sensory, to allow the wine to develop perfectly and acquire complex flavors.

The maturation period can be very short for simple wines, a few weeks or even days, though for most wines it is no more than a few months. For high quality wines, maturation can take about two years or more—such as for some Champagnes, for *grands crus* from Bordeaux or Burgundy—and for some ports and sherries it takes at least seven years. Depending on the type of wine that the winemaker expects, maturation can take place on a large scale in tanks, or in small volumes in oak barrels. In recent decades, the use of barrel ageing has increased considerably—preferably in new oak barrels, especially for fine wines (*see* pp.80–1).

The length of time for maturation varies according to the type of wine being produced. Young wines are bottled immediately after being made, while red vins de garde *are aged for 6 to 18 months, sometimes up to 24 months.*

Clarifying the wine

After the wine has been made, it still has tiny particles of grape material, yeast, and bacteria suspended in the liquid. These lees, which would likely produce a second fermentation on contact with any residual sugars, are generally removed. If racking, fining, and filtering are the most common methods used, there are also other practices such as centrifugation (where the wine is placed in a rotating drum which spins the solids toward the edge) or pasteurization (in which the wine is briefly heated to very high temperatures).

RACKING. This is the most common method. It is generally used for quality wines, and complemented by filtration before bottling. Racking means separating the wine from the lees by carefully pouring it from one container to another. This operation eliminates the lees that had settled naturally at the bottom of the tank or barrel and, optionally, oxygenates and softens the wine (*see also* p.66). It also releases residual carbon dioxide produced during fermentation. When the wine must be stored in tanks or barrels for a long time, racking is done two to four times per year. But this frequency may greatly increase when the maturation period is short or after fining.

FINING. This method is often used before bottling, whether or not racking has already taken place. It takes advantage of colloid flocculation. The fining agent, once in contact with the wine, forms sediment by binding with any microscopic impurities. All that remains is to eliminate, by successive racking, the sediment that has precipitated to the bottom in about 10 days. The best agent for red wines is beaten egg white (six eggs per barrel), while for white wines casein is best. Another popular material is bentonite clay. After fining, red wines lose some of the roughness caused by tannins, and gain softness and finesse.

FILTERING. This sometimes complements the racking carried out during maturation. But more often it takes place before bottling. The plate or membrane filters used here have smaller or larger pores. When they are tiny (less than one thousandth of a millimeter), the wine not only has the lees removed, but is also sterilized because bacteria too are unable to pass through the very tiny holes.

Maturation *sur lie*

When the lees are retained during the wine's development, it is called maturation *sur lie* (on the lees). Muscadet in the Pays Nantais of France is matured in this way, and the wine retains

> New barrels in a Bordeaux barrel cellar.

> The Château de Beaune winery in Burgundy is home to the prestigious wines of Bouchard Père & Fils.

a little residual carbon dioxide, which creates a slight tingling sensation on the tongue. Similarly, some Bordeaux wines (red *vins de garage*, *see* p.69; Pessac-Leognan whites) or white *grands vins* from Burgundy are matured on the lees. In the latter cases, the practice of stirring occurs, which is to re-suspend in the liquid the lees that have settled to the bottom of the barrel or tank. These sediments are stirred with a stick, or by a machine for large volumes. The aim here is to increase interaction between the solids and the liquid so that the wine becomes more complex, soft, and rich. Fining and a light filtration are often carried out before bottling.

Hygiene issues

In the past, many wines were spoiled as a result of poor hygiene, since the mechanisms of oxidation and proliferation of bacteria were little known. Today, wine producers pay special attention to the cleanliness of their cellars and equipment. Tanks, for example, must be cleaned and scaled regularly to avoid bacteria. For barrels, the perfect hygienic solution would be for the container always to be full; otherwise the most frequently adopted solution is "wicking," which involves burning sulfur in the empty barrel before sealing it tightly.

Blending, an optional step

Blending is a difficult technique. It relates to the harmonious combination of wines sourced to offer different characteristics. In Bordeaux, for example, it entails combining a certain number of tanks from various vineyards, and different grape varieties, from vines of different ages, harvested at different times. In regions where ageing in barrels is normal practice, the decision involves selecting various barrels for final blending, depending on the appellation criteria (grape varieties, geographic location).

AT WHAT STAGE? For many white or red wines, including some fortified wines, blending can occur throughout the maturation process up to the final bottling. For Champagne, it is done before maturation, just after fermentation, sometimes involving up to 50 or 60 selected vats. In Bordeaux, blending takes place between November and March, before a tasting of the young wines, which occurs in April. Nevertheless, a final adjustment may be made just before bottling.

THE CASE OF SHERRY. Sherry is aged in barrels arranged in pyramids, at three or four different heights, the lowest level (*solera*) containing the oldest wines, and the top level (*criadera*), the youngest. At bottling, a small amount of wine in the *solera* alone is removed and replaced with wine drawn from the next highest level, which is younger, and so on until the top is reached. Because of this unique method of fractional blending, each bottle contains wine from several *soleras*, but also wines of different ages from within a single *solera*.

TRUE OR FALSE?

The period of maturation continues until the wine is consumed.

FALSE. Also known as "bringing up the wine," maturation takes place between the end of fermentation and bottling. It is done in steel tank or a wooden container (or barrel). Once the wine is bottled, ageing takes over.

> Piping

> Racking

> Stirring

Aerating the wine, but avoiding oxidation

In general, red wines, but also some white wines, need aeration when starting to mature. This is provided either by the racking, by slow diffusion of oxygen through the seams of the barrel, or by micro-oxygenation or *microbullage* (*see* box below). But the amount of oxygen should remain minimal. Except in rare cases, such as wines fortified with alcohol, the producer always avoids direct and prolonged contact between wine and air. Oxygen promotes the growth of bacteria such as acetobacter, which can turn the alcohol into vinegar. It also alters the color and taste of wine. To avoid all these pitfalls, the wine producer generally adds sulfur and/or carries out "topping up" or filling barrels.

Microbullage

Intentional oxygenation requires much skill. Even the use of "natural" micro-oxygenation, obtained by simply maturing wine in barrels, has risks. To achieve an ideal level of micro-oxygenation, and not leave it to chance, Patrick Ducournau, a Madiran (France) winemaker, has introduced a new device: a *microbullage* generator installed at the bottom of a neutral tank. It is a small piece of equipment common in laboratories, and the amount of bubbles produced can be adjusted. This system works well, and it has been approved for use by European wine authorities.

TOPPING UP. To avoid oxidation, containers of wine must be completely filled, without any air pockets. Some evaporation of liquid occurs naturally in the tanks or barrels used for maturation. The speed of this process varies, depending on the humidity and temperature of the winery. But to compensate for this loss, topping up must take place; that is to say the container needs to be filled up regularly, using a large pipette called an *ouillette*. The quality of wine used for the topping up must be equivalent to that of the wine being aged, and from the same source, if it is a wine with an appellation. In France, only the *vin jaune* of Jura (*see also* p.307) and some *vins doux naturels* are aged without topping up. The wine is therefore reduced by evaporation and a thin film of yeast known as a *voile*, is formed on its surface. The slow subsequent oxidation produces distinct flavors.

ADDING SULFUR. Sulfur, in the form of sulfurous anhydride (or sulfur dioxide), is used during the production and maturation of wine. An antioxidant and antibacterial, it is, in the correct doses, a panacea to protect the wine and combat certain problems. Unfortunately, this product also has many disadvantages: it helps cause ferric and copper casse disorders, it is responsible for various defects (reduced mercaptan odor, *see* box next page), and in particular it causes discomfort and headaches in some people. Its use is restricted by French and European regulations, and chemists are looking for alternatives. Until now, nothing has replaced it, although various products or practices (rigorous hygiene, filtering, etc.) have reduced its use. Some producers are trying to make wine without sulfur, but very few manage to produce bottles that do not contain some faults (*see* p.58).

> Topping up

> Taking a sample

> Barrels in the winery

Faults in wine

We no longer produce wine on a purely empirical basis, as we did in the past, but now know what to do and why, so very few wines should have faults.

MINOR FAULTS. There may be a slight smell of staleness, fermentation gas, or sulfur. In most cases, these defects disappear with time. If they are found, it is possible to oxygenate the wine by pouring it into a carafe, or "decanting" as it is known, when tasting (see p.193). The stale smell is the result of prolonged deprivation of oxygen. The fermentation gas should have disappeared if the wine was aerated before bottling. As for the smell of sulfur, which is caused by a dosing error, this lingers mostly in white wines, which are very sensitive to oxidation and protected by more sulfur anhydride.

MAJOR FAULTS. Serious faults are unacceptable and irreparable. These are mercaptan, oxidation, or acetification. Mercaptan, caused by a reaction of the fermentation yeast with sulfur in the lees, produces an unpleasant smell of rotten eggs. Oxidation, resulting in a deterioration of the bouquet, is caused by prolonged contact with air and an insufficient dosage of sulfur dioxide during ageing. Acetification, or acetic spoilage, is caused by a bacterium (acetobacter) and produces an "acetic" wine (which tastes of vinegar). The sale of such wine is prohibited once such volatile acidity exceeds a certain level.

DID YOU KNOW...?

Even organic wines may contain sulfur. However, the specifications followed by organic wine producers impose much lower levels of sulfur anhydride than in conventional viticulture. Some producers have totally banned its use. This is not without its risks because there are two potential dangers with an untreated wine: either premature ageing, even maderization (this is especially the case for white wines, displaying the yellow color and taste similar to Madeira); or an instability making them unsuitable for shipping, exposure to light, and heat. This can lead to re-fermentation or the serious fault in wine called acetification.

The maturation of *vins doux naturels*

During maturation especially, the specific characteristics of different fortified wines become clear. There are two categories of *vins doux naturels*.

MUSCATS. They must be protected from oxidation to preserve their fruity flavors.

OTHER WINES. Rivesaltes, Maury, Banyuls, and Rasteau reach their peak after an ageing process in which oxidation plays an important part. They develop mostly in demijohns or in wood. The slow oxidation alters them completely and gives them hints of cocoa, plum, and coffee. These wines, when they are very old, are known as a *rancio*, which means "rancid" in Spanish. They have an amber color with green hues and distinctive flavors of walnuts, raisins, and prunes.

THE ROLE OF BARREL AGEING

In Bordeaux and Burgundy, the properties of new oak are used both for red wines and, to a lesser extent, for white wines from Chardonnay. The wine gains spicy and toasted or grilled flavors from the casks. But there could be other reasons for barrel ageing...

A fairly recent fashion

Maturation in oak barrels is common for wines that need to be aged for a long period. In the great châteaux of Bordeaux (Latour, Haut-Brion, etc.), the wine was once sold in barrel to *négociants* who were responsible for maturation. It was only in the 20th century that the idea of wine being "estate bottled" developed. Since the 1970s, the use of new wood has become widespread. "Oaky" wine, or more accurately oaky flavors, became fashionable. This distinct aroma, for that is what it really is, became even more pronounced since the famous American critic Robert Parker popularized it. Other reasons, however, can make the wine producer decide to age wine in cask (*see* below).

Today, it would be difficult to find a wine region where no one ages wine in new oak barrels, including in Australia, New Zealand, and California.

The size and age of the barrels

The word "barrel" is a generic term for all wooden containers used to house wine. The best-known today are the Bordeaux barrel, containing 59 gal. (225 l), and the Burgundy barrel, which holds 60 gal. (228 l). The latter is also known as a *pièce*.

THE STANDARD SIZE. The ideal size for a barrel was gradually determined by trial and error. Without detailed discussion, an average capacity of between 53 and 61 gal. (200 and 230 l) became accepted. The Bordeaux barrel has become a standard, and is thought to provide the most suitable surface area of wood to enrich the wine with its aromas. Smaller barrels provide a proportionally greater ratio of contact area between the wine and

the wood, but they are less economical. Larger barrels, such as *pipes*, holding 166 gal. (630 l) and used for ageing port wine, reduce the ratio of contact area between the wood and the wine.

THE IMPORTANCE OF NEW BARRELS. A new wooden barrel will provide the wine with the most aroma and flavor. When used for the first time, tannins and other substances are transferred to the wine, and tartar crystals, even a portion of wine, are deposited into the wood. Year after year, fewer constituent elements are exchanged back and forth: the thicker the tartaric layer, the less effect the wood will have.

THE USE OF OLDER BARRELS. A barrel that is no longer new (a barrel that has held several vintages of wine) does not provide the wine with wood tannins, but it does offer slow oxygenation. Air enters via the bunghole and some seams (and not through the pores of the wood). This slow oxygenation is very favorable to the development of the wine, helping to blend the flavors and soften the tannins. For some fortified wines such as Banyuls, port, and Maury, maturation of this kind produces so-called *rancio* flavors.

> Carved stopper in a barrel from Alsace.

DID YOU KNOW...?

A wine with oak-like flavors has not always been aged in wooden barrels. It is possible to obtain such flavors with oak chips placed into stainless steel vats of wine. To reduce production costs and compete with overseas producers, France has allowed the use of oak chips since 2006. Indeed, some estates in the New World (Chile, New Zealand, etc.) have been using this technique for a long time. Similarly, the famous Greek Retsina has a resiny flavor because small pieces of Aleppo pine resin are added to the must (see box p.427).

How long in the barrel?

The length of time a wine matures in barrel varies from 12 to 18 months for wines from Bordeaux or Burgundy to more than two years for Spanish Gran Reservas. It depends mainly on the constitution of wine, its ability to "take the wood" and resist drying out. All wines would end up "dried out" and lose their richness if they remain in a wooden container for too long. Some experts believe that we can assist the contact between the wine and wood by filtering the wine before putting it into barrels, thereby preventing the lees from being deposited on the sides of the barrel.

Oak flavors

Although some barrels are made of chestnut, oak is universally appreciated for its physical properties and its flavor contributions. Its wood is rich in components that enhance the flavor of wine. To date, more than 60 polyphenols have been identified in its cells, including 18 different phenols—the most significant being vanillin. Wine tasters can distinguish, in addition to notes of vanilla, various aromas: coconut, pepper, carnations, smoke, etc. The oak also provides the wine with types of tannin (known as "noble" tannins) other than those transmitted by the skin and

> At the Michel Juillot estate in Mercurey (France), Clos des Barraults wine spends 18 months in barrels.

The source of the oak for wine barrels

It takes about 180 years for an oak tree to mature sufficiently. To meet the ever-increasing needs of the coopers, who export worldwide, French oak is no longer sufficient. Supplies now come from diverse sources: oaks from Poland, Slovenia, and Russia, all of high quality, are also employed. American oak, for its part, provides very pleasant vanilla flavors; but it is not particularly compatible with *grands crus* that need a long period of ageing.

stalks of the grapes (so-called "vegetable" tannins). These strengthen the structure of the wine.

CHOOSING A SUITABLE OAK. When choosing a barrel, winemakers always consider the source of the wood. Oak of the Limousin forest of France, which has a "coarse grain" from a wide tree, produces a strong, firm wood, with powerful tannins that are well suited to *eaux-de-vie* such as Cognac. Sessile or patraean oak provides a "fine grained" wood. This produces softer tannins, which will be released more slowly, and is considered ideal for maturing wines such as the *grands crus* of Bordeaux and Burgundy.

TRUE OR FALSE?

An ordinary wine will gain character by being aged in oak barrels.

FALSE. Maturation in new oak is not a universal panacea. The belief that a meager wine can be rescued by "improving" it with a rich wood is an illusion, and even an error. Experience shows that for a successful interaction between the wood and the wine, the wine must be able to integrate the wood; it must be substantial, or have a strong "body." Far from hiding the characteristics of the wine, the wood must actually play a modest part and only increase its complexity of flavor.

MAKING A BARREL

Practiced since ancient times, the sequence of tasks that a cooper undertakes has barely changed through the centuries. Some steps are now carried out using machines, but making barrels remains a skilled craft.

The key steps

A barrel is always composed of pieces of wood called staves, held together by iron or chestnut hoops, and ends called heads. Several tasks are necessary to manufacture a barrel: taking measurements; producing the staves; assembling and shaping them; arching them over fire; trimming; preparing the ends; their production, drilling, and binding together; then finishing off and testing their strength.

MANUFACTURE. The first step is creating the pieces of wood, namely the staves (28 to 32 on average) and head pieces (12 to 16 of these). This was traditionally done by hand, but nowadays is usually done using a machine.

SHAPING. The cooper then creates the shape of the barrel for the first time, by assembling the staves together one by one in a rough circle. They are then gradually tightened and balanced.

A cooper can give a new lease of life to a barrel. To do so, he takes it apart, planes the staves, then reassembles the whole thing. The newly revealed surface of the wood will now have qualities similar to those of new oak.

ARCHING OVER FIRE. This is generally done over a wood fire placed inside the assembled staves. This operation in particular determines how long the barrel will last. If this heating process is not carried out properly, the staves may break at the bilge (the widest part of the barrel) after a few years of use, because of constant play in the wood.

FROM TRIMMING TO BINDING. Trimming is to prepare the heads of the barrel in order to embed the two lids (sinking). Once these are in place, it only remains to make the final hoop.

FINISHING TOUCHES. The barrel has now been assembled. Finishing touches include sanding the heads and bevels; piercing the bunghole; noting the origins of the wood, the degree of heating, and the name of the manufacturer. Then there is a final check that everything looks and feels fine before the barrels are sold.

> Preparing the staves

> Assembling the staves roughly in a circle

> Arching over a fire

> Bordeaux barrels made at the Darnajou cooperage.

SIGNATURE. Every barrel that is ready for use is signed off by the craftsman on the two heads. This signature indicates their expertise and provides information about the origin of the barrel.

The effect of heat on the barrel

Arching over a fire, a crucial step in manu-facturing a barrel, has the effect of toasting its inner walls. Experience has shown that a greater or lesser level of toasting results in differences to the wine being matured. A high level of toast carbonizes the barrel and produces a charcoal layer between the wine and the wood: it generates strong flavors and a wide variety of phenolic compounds. (When the grilled or smoked character of a wine is very strong, we say that it is "toasted.") A gentle toast, by contrast, will better display those components of the wood with slightly more nuance.

TRUE OR FALSE?

The barrel was invented by the Gauls.

FALSE. Though the Gauls actually made barrels as we know them today, historians believe that the origins of the barrel are much older. The first wooden containers, from around 2000 BC, were probably composed of slats held together by links, and the whole thing was coated with a resinous substance. They were first used to contain solids, before being improved, much later, so that they could also hold liquids.

DID YOU KNOW...?

The best oak trees are from the French forest of Tronçais in the département of Nièvre. Jean-Baptiste Colbert, the busy minister of Louis XIV, who planted this forest, never imagined that he would contribute to the production of the finest wines. His aim was to have a source of the oak that was essential for the construction of royal ships.

> Final binding using a press

> Smoothing off with a plane

> Stamped signature

SOME BEAUTIFUL BARRELS

Cask, barrel, vat... These wooden containers, made of oak or chestnut, are used to age or to store wines. Sometimes they are also works of art.

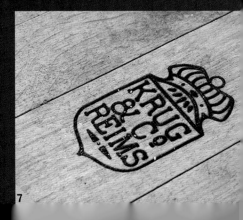

1. Barrel with stamp (Bouchard Père & Fils, Beaune).
2. Carved stopper on a vat (Domaine Marcel Deiss, Bergheim).
3. and 4. Carved stoppers (Domaine Hugel & Fils, Riquewihr).
5. Carved stopper on a barrel (Château de Pommard).
6. A Die stamp with Château Latour emblem (Pauillac).
7. Krug estate stamp (Reims).
8. and 12. Carved vats (Louis Roederer, Reims).
9. and 10. Painted vats (Château de Pommard).
11. Carved vat (Domaine Hugel & Fils, Riquewihr).

BOTTLING

It is impossible to discuss wine without mentioning its inseparable companion, the bottle. Once ageing is complete, the wine is bottled—a complex and difficult task. In its glass case, it then leaves the estate winery or the cellar of the négociant *to be sold to the consumer.*

Preparing the wine

FINAL PROCEDURES. Most wine lovers will not tolerate particles or deposits in a bottle. In most cases, the producer completely clarifies the wine before it is bottled. This involves two procedures before bottling: fining and filtration (*see* p.76). They may be combined, but will affect the flavor of wine.

A CONTROLLED ENVIRONMENT. At this stage, the wine, which is perfectly clear and stable, must be bottled. Again, careful attention to detail and cleanliness are required because poor bottling can jeopardize the quality of the wine. There is a significant risk of contamination by the bottling equipment and glass. Furthermore, aeration of the wine, if too extensive, can harm it. Finally, care must be taken to ensure an effective closure.

The choice of the bottle

Glass remains the perfect material for storing and ageing wine. The international standard bottle is 750 ml. Almost all of the great wines of the world are sold in bottles of this capacity or a multiple of this volume.

THE COLOR OF THE GLASS. The color of glass used for the bottle is far from irrelevant. It varies according to region and wine, but must be dark enough to protect the wine from light. It has been found that the wine develops faster in a clear bottle, even if the wine cellar is dark.

PREPARATION OF THE BOTTLE. Cleanliness of the bottles is essential. The rinsing method most often used with new

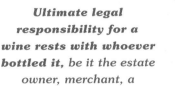

Ultimate legal responsibility for a wine rests with whoever bottled it, be it the estate owner, merchant, a cooperative, or a bottling company.

bottles is injecting hot water. The use of second-hand bottles is risky, even if the cleaning is done scrupulously. The bottles are immersed in hot water with detergent added, brushed, and rinsed under pressure.

Bottling

BOTTLING THE WINE. One challenge of bottling is to fill the bottle with a specific volume of wine, while leaving enough room for the closure and making allowances for increased volume due to changes in the temperature of the liquid. At some small estates, bottles are still filled directly from the tap of the barrel; but this results in a compromise to the speed and quality of the bottling. That is why bottling machines have become widespread.

SEALING THE BOTTLE. Adding the traditional bottle closure is carried out by a method based on a simple principle. The cork (*see also* pp.88–9), which is new, of good quality, and of a "relaxed" composition, is compressed by "jaws" or "clamps" in order to be smaller than the bottle neck, and then rapidly pushed into it by a vertical piston.

Capacity of bottles

Major wine regions offer many traditional sizes other than the standard 750 ml. Thus, a magnum is 1.5 liters (or 2 bottles), a Jeroboam is 3 liters (or 4 bottles), a Rehoboam is 4.5 liters (6 bottles), a Methuselah (or Imperial) is 6 liters (8 bottles), a Salmanazar is 9 liters (12 bottles), a Balthazar is 12 liters (16 bottles), and a Nebuchadnezzar is 15 liters (20 bottles). Sweet "late harvest" wines or wines made from grapes that have been dried on the vine (*vin de paille*, Italian Recioto di Soave) are often sold in 500 ml bottles.

"Bordeaux"

"Burgundy"

> Today the bottling process at wineries is very often completely automated.

Bottles and their shapes

Different regions or countries have adopted specific bottle shapes to distinguish their wines.

THE THREE MOST COMMON SHAPES. These are the "Bordeaux," the "Burgundy," and the "flute." The Bordeaux is straight with a high "shoulder." It is green in color for red wines and dry white wines, and semi-clear for sweet wines. It is often also used outside of Bordeaux, as well as for some New World Cabernet Sauvignons. The Burgundy is the main bottle for the French regions stretching from Chablis to Lyon. Almost all red wines and many white wines from Burgundy are bottled in bottles of this type, as well as some Chardonnays and Pinot Noirs from

the New World. The main color is a muted green. The third format commonly used is the tall "flute" of the Rhine and Moselle of Germany. Rhine flutes are made of brown glass, while those from Moselle and Alsace (France) are green.

TRADITIONAL SHAPES. These are less universally used, but restricted to wines produced in certain areas, whether in France or elsewhere. Jura has a special shape and size for *vin jaune*: a 1.3 pint (62 cl) *clavelin* is used to show what is left of a liter after six years of evaporation in barrel. Champagnes and sparkling wines are housed in thick glass bottles that can withstand the pressure of carbon dioxide. Other bottle shapes include the *quille* used in Provence and a similar bottle for Verdicchio in Italy. The Franconia region of Germany uses a *bocksbeutel*, a bulging and flattened bottle. Vintage port comes in a straight bottle with a tall shoulder and a slight swelling at the neck.

BOTTLES FOR MARKETING PURPOSES. Today, the size and shape of bottles are increasingly seen as marketing vehicles. In Italy, for example, new wines are remarkable for their heavy and expensive glass as well as original shapes and colors.

"Flute" from Alsace

"Quille" from Provence

"Clavelin"

"Champagne"

CLOSURES

The choice of the bottle stopper is a complex task, but it is very important for the longevity of wine. Although new materials exist, cork is unquestionably the principal material used for sealing wine bottles.

The bark of the cork oak

A UNIQUE MATERIAL. Cork has unique physical properties and is ideal for sealing a glass bottle. Its cells form microscopic "suckers" that grip the bottle neck. It is inert and impervious to liquids, does not react with wine, and does not rot. Only weevils and fungi are likely to affect it, but these problems can be avoided. Despite every effort, its reliability is not completely guaranteed and occasionally some bottles will have a "corked" or tainted aroma and flavor.

A UNIQUE TREE. The cork oak (*Quercus suber*) grows only in the western Mediterranean and Portugal. A cork oak is stripped—they call it "extracted"—of bark every 12 years; but only the fourth, fifth, and sixth extractions provide highest quality cork. You can expect yields a quarter of the time across the lifetime of a tree (from 150 to 200 years).

Preparation of the cork

DRYING. Planks of cork bark are removed from the tree, stacked, and dried in the open air. They must be subject to the sun, rain, and cold for two winters and one summer before being used. During this drying, they lose their sap and their tissues are tightened.

BOILING. After drying, the planks are boiled in water at 212°F (100°C) for 30 to 60 minutes. The cork then expands by about 20 percent and acquires its maximum elasticity. In addition, when the planks emerge from this bath, they are sterile and can be smoothed out. They are then rested for two or three weeks before being cut. At this stage, an initial selection takes place on the basis of two criteria: thickness and quality. This is made easier by straightening the four sides of the raw plank.

Production of corks

CUTTING. When the planks have an ideal level of moisture, they are cut into strips of the same width as the length of the corks they will become. To produce a cork just under an inch (24 mm) in diameter, which is the most common size, you need planks with a thickness of 1.1 to 1.2 inches (28 to 30 mm). The strips are then passed onto a punch. This work is done manually—so as to avoid defects, many of which can occur—to produce a good percentage of quality corks. The final yield is about 33–55 lbs of stoppers (15–25 kg) per 220 lbs (100 kg) of raw cork.

SHAPING. The plugs cut from the punch are sanded with emery to obtain a regular and smooth surface and cross-section. They are then washed to remove the dust and residue in the lenticels (as the small holes visible on the surface are called). Often, their appearance is improved by passing them through a dye bath.

FINAL SELECTION. There then follows a second screening stage. This sorting can be partially automated with machines capable of counting the number of lenticels flush with the surface of the cork. It is, however, carried out largely by hand because green spots, dry cork, or cracks might not be spotted by mechanical processing.

FINISHING TOUCHES. Sometimes the lenticel pores are clogged with powdered cork paste, which improves the mechanical properties of the cork.

If well kept in the cellar, a good cork can protect a wine for several decades; but to be safe, the leading estates re-cork their wines every 25 years.

Other closures

Some wine producers are considering abandoning cork, a material used for more than 2,000 years, in favor of alternatives. Manufacturers are using either screwcaps or corks that look like traditional corks in terms of shape and appearance. For the latter, they use plastic foam, the surface of which has a high friction coefficient and can be pulled with a standard corkscrew. However, these advantages are confirmed only for wines that are consumed quickly (young whites or reds that will be consumed within three years). It is too early to determine the effect of these stoppers in the long term and therefore whether they are suitable for *vins de garde*. It will take several more years to know.

A closure for every kind of wine

There are several types of closure, each designed for different wines. From a standard diameter of just under an inch (24 mm), they are compressed by a machine into a 0.73 inch (18.5 mm) neck. Champagne corks, which are wider, at 1.2 inches (31 mm), are compressed even more, because they must withstand pressurized carbon dioxide. Except in the case of Champagne, labeling corks is not compulsory in France. When done, it generally includes the vintage, the place of bottling, and the name of the producer or wine.

LONG CORKS. Estates generally use these closures to protect their high quality wines as they age over decades; their reserve wines may be re-corked every 25 years.

SHORT CORKS. These are made of cork and are used for wines with a shorter lifespan.

AGGLOMERATED CORKS. Made of many combined cork pieces, they are commonly used for *vins courants* and some Champagne corks.

> When opening wine, popping the cork announces the imminent pleasure of drinking it.

SYNTHETIC CORKS. Plastic foam or colored closures, these are suitable for wine that needs to be kept for a moderate amount of time, and they are increasingly used for this purpose.

CHAMPAGNE CORKS. Agglomerated cork onto which one to three layers of solid cork are adhered. They are driven halfway into the bottle, so only the part driven into the bottle is compressed (hence the mushroom shape). They must be labeled with the word "Champagne" and the relevant vintage, if applicable.

SCREWCAPS. While the idea has been accepted by some professionals, it has not been enthusiastically received by everyone. According to their supporters, a screwcap removes the risk of the flavors being corrupted by natural cork and premature oxidation. In some countries (Switzerland, New Zealand), the use of the screwcap is very common.

A restricted area of production

The cork oak tree grows in a restricted geographical area: the Iberian peninsula, southern France, southern Italy, Corsica, Sardinia, and North Africa. With its thick bark, it is more resistant than other species to heat and extreme cold. Trials to see whether the tree will grow in the southern hemisphere, North America, or Asia continue to be inconclusive, something which is not without economic consequences for the various countries in those regions.

CHOOSING, STORING, AND TASTING WINE

HOW CAN YOU IDENTIFY A WINE?

APPELLATION SYSTEMS

Geographical origin is regarded as an index of quality, and the provenance of a wine is guaranteed by the appellation system, which is supervised in France by the INAO (Institut National de l'Origine et de la Qualité) and by similar organizations in other European countries.

Appellations in Europe

Every bottle of European wine carries a label indicating its geographic provenance, and this acts as a guarantee of its source and its regional characteristics. The approach was developed in France during the first half of the 20th century, and its broad principles have been adopted by a number of countries. The European Union established a system intended to integrate these various jurisdictions in August 2009. Though each country retains its specific nomenclature, you will find throughout the world a hierarchy that runs from wines with no other mention of their origins, other than their country of production to wines with specific local or regional place names.

French AOC wines

In France, there are more than 470 *appellations d'origine contrôlée* (AOC) classifications. Under the

One of the tasks that the European Union's new system of appellations has set itself in the face of competition from the New World is to make wine classification clearer.

newly revised European appellation system (*see* box on next page), these refer to wines in the *appellation d'origine protégée* (AOP) category (wines whose provenance is a registered trademark) but may also include those with a protected geographic indication (PGI). Although the approval procedure has now changed and the specifications are more restricted, the heart of the AOC remains unchanged; each is delimited according to a region's "local, loyal, and constant usages." An AOC is primarily defined by its geographic extent, but other rules play a part as well.

THE GEOGRAPHIC AREA. This may be regional—Burgundy, Alsace, Bordeaux— or tied to a village—St-Estèphe in Bordeaux, Gigondas in the Rhône Valley, Morgon in Beaujolais. It may even cover only a very small location—a *cru* or a *grand cru* vineyard, such as Zinnkoepflé in Alsace. In Burgundy, it is common for a wine to be marketed under three appellation names that may overlap, such as: *Grand Vin de Bourgogne*

Why are there now more AOC wines?

The number of French AOC wines has increased over the last four decades, and this process may follow several routes. Some villages in the Rhône valley, for example, have been able to add their name to the Côtes-du-Rhône regional appellation. These specified areas—such as Gigondas, Cairanne, Vacqueyras—have then later achieved independence or become AOC wines in their own right. Viré-Clessé in the Mâconnais sub-region has undergone a similar process. Elsewhere, the name of a cru has been systematically added to a regional appellation; in Alsace, the AOC Alsace Grand Cru includes 51 separate designations. There are also many vineyards whose names are linked with the Alsace regional appellation. In Languedoc, the regional appellation of Coteaux-du-Languedoc is often augmented with a local geographical designation such as Coteaux-du-Languedoc Pic-St-Loup, Terrasses de Béziers, St-Saturnin, etc.

> The 124 acres (50 ha) that produce the Burgundy *grand cru* of Clos de Vougeot are shared by more than 70 owners.

New European regulations

The reformed appellation regulations that came into force in August 2009 provide for two categories of wine.

Table wine (wine without geographic designation): This category corresponds to the French vin de table and is now allowed to indicate grape variety and year, details that were not previously permitted. The wine also is allowed to contain up to 15 percent of another vintage. The wine is obliged to indicate its country of origin, or, in the case of a blend, the denomination vin de la communauté européenne (VCE) or "European Table Wine." Yields are not limited and certain winemaking techniques such as adding aroma through wood shavings or producing low alcohol variants are permitted.

Quality wines produced in specified regions: These correspond to the French appellation d'origine protégée (AOP) and protected geographic indication (PGI) classifications. AOP wine specifications were drawn up by an organisme de défense et de gestion (ODG) representing the wine trade. They are subject to production and wine reviews by professionals and carried out by an independent inspection body (known as the OI). PGI wines also are obliged to institute similar specifications under inspection by an independent organization. The addition to a given blend of up to 15 percent from another year or grape variety will be permitted, with some exceptions.

> The Schlumberger estate at Guebwiller produces Alsace and Alsace Grand Cru wines.

(a regional appellation), *Chablis Grand Cru* (the local appellation), and *Bougros* (the *climat,* or vineyard sub-division). In Bordeaux, a "village" appellation such as Margaux may include five actual villages. The wines might also bear the regional designation of "Bordeaux." Specific descriptions such as *cru bourgeois* do not fall under AOC regulation—their attribution is overseen by the *Bureau Veritas*, an independent organization, at the request of the trade—although designations such as *cru classé*, *premier cru*, and *grand cru* depend on it. There are even some appellations that cover only a single estate, such as Château-Grillet in the Rhône Valley or Romanée-Conti (*see* pp.288–9) in Burgundy, for example.

GRAPE VARIETY. The grape variety or varieties authorized for a given appellation are strictly defined in Europe. It might be a single grape per wine—Gamay for Beaujolais—or a blend of varieties—Cabernet Sauvignon, Cabernet Franc, and Merlot for Bordeaux reds, for example (*see also* pp.32–5).

YIELD. Each AOC has a set maximum yield expressed in hectoliters of wine per hectare (hl/ha) or tons per acre (ton/acre), or by weight of grapes in Champagne. This amount varies widely: 4 tons per acre (66 hl/ha) in Alsace, 1.8 tons per acre (30 hl/ha) for Banyuls wines.

TECHNIQUES. Regulations even control the number of vines per acre, harvesting methods, pruning techniques, chaptalization, vinification, the date it goes to market, and the amounts to be sold. Controlling this last point causes the authorities the most trouble, even though every quantity produced is registered and checks are made to ensure that this corresponds with the yield of the wine producer who has made it. In certain regions, the production methods are actually part of the AOC designation:

> An advertisement for Tio Pepe, a sherry produced by Gonzáles Byass in Spain.

in Champagne, for example, there are strict rules governing the processes of *cueillette* (picking by hand), grape-pressing, and maturing the wine.

Other French wine classifications

In addition to the AOC designation, the classification of French wines also used to include the designations AOVDQS (*appellation d'origine vin délimité de qualité supérieure*) and *vins de pays*. This changed in 2009, and AOVDQS wines are due to disappear by the end of 2011; their producers may choose between joining the AOP and submitting to additional restrictions, or taking on a PGI designation, which is

TRUE OR FALSE?

The French system was the inspiration for Portugal, Greece, and Switzerland.

TRUE. Apart from Italy, most other European countries have adopted the French classification system. The highest quality wine, corresponding to France's AOC, is known as DOC (*denominação de origem controlada*) in Portugal, OPAP (*onomasia proeléfseos anotréras piotitos*) in Greece, and in Switzerland they have stayed with AOC, although the definition varies by canton and anyone but a specialist is likely to get lost in a maze of village appellations. (There are, for example, 19 AOC designations for the canton of Neuchâtel alone.)

more flexible. *Vins de pays* are to become PGI wines. The new definition tightens up the rules governing their vinification, but leaves more latitude in authorizing blends of grape varieties and years. The old designations (about 150 in number) are to be retained, but larger appellation areas are being created.

Italian regulations

The new European regulations apply in Italy with a few differences, since Italian wine producers relaxed their rules some time ago.

THE HIERARCHY OF QUALITY. The basic Italian classification equivalent to the French *appellation d'origine contrôlée* is known as the *denominazione di origine controllata* (DOC). To distinguish themselves from this level, certain producers requested the creation of a "superdenomination," the DOCG (*denominazione di origine controllata e garantita*), which is subject to even stricter standards than a DOC. The category beneath DOC, corresponding to *vin de pays*, is known as *indicazione geografica tipica* (IGT). At the bottom of the scale is simple *vino da tavola* (table wine). On occasion, producers of the best wines wishing either to distance themselves from certain appellations that are too large or insufficiently supervised, or to escape the constraints of authorized grape varieties, have been known to choose an IGT label or even a *vino da tavola* designation.

Spanish regulations

The new regulations allow Spain to retain its classification system, which is based on the wine's age and maturation (*see* box below).

QUALITY LEVELS. Wines with no geographic designation are known as *vinos de mesa* (table wine). *Vinos de la tierra*, which correspond to French *vins de pays* and which have a regional designation, are of the same order as the new PGI wines, and *vinos de calidad producidos en regiones determinadas* (VCPRD, quality wines with a regional designation) are equal in quality to the new AOP and have been sub-divided into four levels since 2003.

Wine age on Spanish labels

Vino joven (young wine): wine bottled as soon as possible after clarification; also known as vino del año (this year's wine).

Vino de crianza (matured wine): wine that has been matured for at least two years, with a minimum of six months in barricas (oak barrels).

Reserva: red wine with three years maturation in a bodega (cellar), of which at least one year is in barricas. Rosé and white wine must have two years, with six months in barrels.

Gran reserva: red wine that has matured for five years, with a minimum of 18 months in barrels. There are few whites or rosés in this category, but these require four years of maturation, of which six months must be in barrels.

THE FOUR LEVELS OF QUALITY. *Vino de pago*, which can be traced to a very precise origin (specific valley or slope, single estate, etc.; *see also* p.379) is to be found at the top of the list, followed by DOC wines (*denominación de origen calificada*), and then DO (*denominación de origen*). DO corresponds very closely to France's AOC, and DOC is a sort of "super-DO" conforming to very precise criteria of quality. Currently, only Rioja and Priorat are entitled to call themselves DOC. The final place is occupied by the *vinos de calidad con indicación geográfica*, which on occasion may be wines produced in zones straddling several DO appellations or uniting several *vinos de pago* but not qualifying for a DO of their own.

German regulations

While conforming to new European regulations, the German system retains its own classification with respect to white wines, based on geographical origins, quality, and sugar content of the grape juice.
THE FOUR LEVELS OF QUALITY. *Tafelwein* with no geographic designation is table wine. If the label specifies *Deutscher* ("German"), then the wine was produced by a German grower; if not, it will be a wine from some other EU country that has been bottled by a German merchant. The term *landwein*, corresponding to *vin de pays* (PGI), denotes the best table wine with a geographic designation. Quality wine from a specified area is known as QbA (*qualitätswein bestimmter anbaugebiete*), and at the top rank there is QmP (*qualitätswein mit prädikat*), "quality wine of distinction."
CLASSIFICATION BY SUGAR CONTENT. *Qualitätswein mit prädikat* (QmP) is made from grapes with a sugar content sufficient to require no chaptalization. Such wines are further divided into six sub-categories according to the sugar content of the original must. These are, in ascending order: *kabinett* (the basic QmP wine), *spätlese* (a sweet or dry wine), *auslese* (an aromatic sweet or dry wine), *beerenauslese* (a sweet wine made from over-ripened grapes), *trockenbeerenauslese* (TBA; a very sweet wine,

---

Change on the way for Hungary

Hungary has 22 geographic wine designations. As a member of the European Union, the country has received considerable grants that were mainly devoted to tearing out old vines, although these were not always replaced. The new European wine legislation will apply to Hungary's geographic appellations, and the country also will be obliged to regulate and limit planting rights and put an end to chaptalization; though enriching wines with concentrated musts will be allowed.

---

made from botrytized grapes), and *eiswein* ("ice wine" made from an extremely concentrated must where the grapes have been subject to frost on the vine). This official classification might be misleading for non-German wine lovers, but it reflects a desire to produce quality wines with the emphasis on the ripest grapes.

> A decorative signpost surrounded by vines in Baden, Germany.

DID YOU KNOW...?

Austria has the strictest wine laws of any European country.
As in Germany, wine quality is determined by the sugar content of the must. In 2003, however, the category of DAC (Districtus Austria Controllatus) was created. It guarantees the distinctive character of certain wines made from selected grape varieties, much like AOC, thus allowing each regional wine producer's association to choose a type of wine that is typical for that area. Implementation of the new European regulations, which draw a distinction between PGI and AOP wines, will not change these national requirements.

A comparative table of European appellations

The appellation system was originally introduced in France to protect quality wines made in certain traditional regions. Since the 1960s, other European countries have adopted the system for the same reasons. The European Union usually recognizes four grades of quality, and the following table shows a comparison of these four grades in various countries.

	TABLE WINE (WINE WITHOUT GEOGRAPHIC DESIGNATION)		QUALITY WINES PRODUCED IN SPECIFIED REGIONS	
	European table wine/Vin de la communauté européenne (VCE)	Protected geographic indication (PGI)	Protected appellation/ Appellation d'origine protégée (AOP)	
France	Vin de table	Vin de pays (VDP), Indication géographique protégée (IGP)	Appellation d'origine contrôlée (AOC)	
Italy	Vino da tavola (VDT)	Indicazione geografica tipica (IGT)	Denominazione di origine controllata (DOC) Denominazione di origine controllata e garantita (DOCG)	
Germany	Deutscher Tafelwein	Landwein	Qualitätswein bestimmter anbaugebiete (QbA) Qualitätswein mit prädikat[1] (QmP)	
Spain	Vino de mesa	Vino de la tierra	Denominación de origen (DO) Denominación de origen calificada (DOC)	
Portugal	Vinho de mesa	Vinho regional	Indicação de proveniência regulamentada (IPR) Denominação de origem controlada (DOC)	
Great Britain	Table wine	Regional wine	English/Welsh vineyards quality wine	
Hungary	Asztali bor	Tájbor	Minöségi bor Különleges Minöségü bor	
Greece	Epitrapezios inos	Topikos inos	Onomasia Proeléfseos Anotréras Piotitos (OPAP) Onomasia Proeléfseos Eleghomeni (OPE)	
Austria	Tafelwein	Landwein	Qualitätswein Kabinett Prädikatswein[2] Vinea Wachau[3]	
Switzerland	Grape variety with no indication of origin	Wine with cantonal designation	Appellation of specified geographic origin, listing canton, village, and/or grape variety	

1. *Prädikat* (distinction) includes six grades of maturation and quality: *kabinett, spätlese, auslese, beerenauslese, trockenbeerenauslese, eiswein.*

2. *Prädikat* (distinction) includes eight grades of maturation and quality: *spätlese, auslese, beerenauslese, trockenbeerenauslese, eiswein, ausbruch, strohwein, bergwein.*

3. The best wines from the Vinea Wachau region have their own indications of maturity and quality: *steinfeder, federspiel, smaragd.*

APPELLATIONS FROM OTHER COUNTRIES

The countries of the New World grade their wines more by grape variety and brand than by provenance. The idea of appellation as it is understood in Europe is nonetheless gaining ground.

Fewer restrictions than Europe

Many New World countries—in the southern hemisphere and the United States, for example—are more concerned with factors other than geography; it is grape variety and brand (or the name of the wine producer), rather than place of origin that lead and dictate consumer choice. Detailing geographic appellations that are more or less regulated is a recent development. Up until 1994, for example, it was possible for an Australian wine producer to use any geographic name he chose, with no regard to where his grapes actually originated; and things were not so different in most of the United States (with local "Chablis or "Burgundy"). Most of the countries of the New World have since begun to regulate geographic designations, but with far fewer constraints than in Europe.

Wine production rules in New World countries are extremely relaxed. If they include the idea of terroir (local character), this is often interpreted liberally—a wine from one region may be made in part with grapes from another region.

America

American wine labels may mention the state, the county, and—since the 1980s—the AVA (American viticultural area). However, in contrast to the European system, any such geographic designation is not linked to constraints on grape variety, yield, or production techniques, nor is there any system of grading wines by tasting (*see also* p.435).

REGULATION. When a wine bears the name of a state (California, Texas, etc.), it is required that at least 75 percent of the grapes used to produce that wine were cultivated in that state. (Bear in mind, though, that California grows 35 grape varieties for white wine and 65 for red.) If the label mentions the name of a county, the same 75 percent rule applies. (The exception is Oregon, which stipulates 90 percent.) A wine listing an AVA must contain at least 85 percent of its grapes from the place mentioned (again, 90 percent in Oregon). AVAs are defined according to natural climatic frontiers, topographic regions, or specific soil types, and give a better idea of the style of the wine. Regulations are much more

> Entry sign at the Fetzer Vineyards in Mendocino County, California.

Grape varieties in the New World

If a wine contains a certain percentage of a grape variety, that variety may be mentioned on the label; for wines exported to the European Union, the content must be at least 85 percent. If two varieties feature on the label, they together must make up 100 percent of the blend. The rules are sometimes more flexible for wines intended for domestic consumption. In New Zealand, Argentina, Australia, South Africa, and the United States (with the exception of Oregon, which has a stricter regime), it is enough for the wine to consist of between 75 and 85 percent of the variety mentioned on the label.

Sonoma Valley
Vintners & Growers Alliance
BLACKSTONE WINERY
ARROWOOD
B.R. COHN
WELLINGTON
KUNDE
FAMILY WINERIES
SL CELLARS
BENZIGER
LANDMARK
LEDSON
2 MI
ST FRANCIS
VJB VINEYARDS & CELLARS
1 MILES
KENWOOD VINEYARDS
SCHUG
Valley of the Moon
MAYO FAMILY WINERY
CASTLE

> The Errazuriz estate in Aconcagua, Chile.

TWO CATEGORIES. VQA requirements state that wines must come from grape varieties cultivated in their province and they must be bottled there. There are two kinds of appellation: provincial and geographic. Provincial appellations allow for the use of hybrid grapes and *vinifera* varieties (European vines). The grape variety mentioned on the label should make up at least 75 percent of the contents of the bottle, and the label must be stamped "product of Ontario" or "product of British Columbia." Geographic appellations denote precise growing regions. Only *vinifera* varieties are permitted in such cases, with at least 85 percent of contents being the variety stated. Vintage wines must contain at least 95 percent wine from the same year.

Chile

The DO (*denominación de origen*) designation has existed here only since 2002. Five large regions have been recognized, divided into sub-regions that correspond to particular valleys. The notion of named places of origin as an index of wine style is still in its infancy, as most Chilean wines are produced as blends of different sub-regions. Nonetheless, named regions, sometimes of great size, such as Colchagua, are beginning to emerge.

Argentina

Argentina produced national wine legislation in 1999 and again in 2004 to regulate production under the supervision of the *Instituto nacional de vitivinicultura*. Even bearing in mind the considerable economic clout wielded by the large companies that dominate national wine production, the system is extremely flexible and subject to few restrictions—there are no regulations limiting yield, for example. Three kinds of origin may appear on the label: *indicación de procedencia* (indication of provenance); *indicación geografica* (geographic designation) for wines vinified and bottled in a region; *denominación de origen controlada* (a denomination corresponding to France's AOC) for wines of superior quality. An indication of origin may be included on the label if 100 percent of the wine originates from the place mentioned. Grape variety may be indicated if this represents at least 85 percent of the wine produced. Vintages are required to contain 85 percent wine from the year in question.

relaxed as far as the idea of an "estate" is concerned; it is often the case that estate wines are produced with grapes from vineyards owned by others growers in the same area, without this being indicated on the label. Only "control" over viticultural decisions is required.

Canada

Regulations here vary by region. The Vintners' Quality Alliance (VQA) bases its requirements on the French appellation system; these apply only in British Columbia and Ontario, but almost all Canadian wine is produced there. VQA wines are evaluated by a group of professional tasters who judge their style and quality. Approved wines receive a black VQA stamp; wines scoring more than 15 out of a possible 20 points receive a superior appellation and a gold stamp.

Australia

Most Australian wines indicate the name of the grape variety, although a tendency has been noted to give brand names or estate names to the most prestigious wines, such as Penfolds Grange (*see* p.479) or Henschkes Hill of Grace (*see* p.480). It is becoming more and more common to include the name of the region on the label beside the name of the producer.

While a very scaled-down system of appellations exists, a great innovation in recent years has been that every detail on the label, from year and grape variety to region, should be correct and verifiable (*see also* p.473).

Producers are now obliged to include their address on the label, but are not required to reveal the origins of the grapes; if they choose to do so, 85 percent of the grapes must come from the place indicated. The same is true of the grape variety. If several regions or varieties are indicated, they are to be listed in descending order of importance. It is common practice for entry-level wines to be blends from various regions.

New Zealand

New Zealand producers have used French and German names to identify their style of wines for many years; the most popular modern approach is to list the name of the grape variety. A registration system established in 1994 delimits growing areas by setting out the borders of recognized regions, sub-regions, and even of individual estates; but wines detailing their region of origin tend to be exported. A regional name may be featured on the label if 100 percent of the wine originates from there (with the grapes both grown and processed locally): Marlborough and Hawke's Bay are the regions most often noted (*see* p.486).

The district of Wairapara, including the town of Martinborough, which has imposed its own rules, features a small adhesive label carrying the legend "100% Martinborough Terrace Appellation Committee," certifying that the wine is 100 percent from that region.

South Africa

The "Wine of Origin" system (WO) introduced in 1973 divides winemakers across several regions, sub-regions (districts), and areas (wards), in decreasing order of size (*see also* p.467). The most concentrated production area, known as the Coastal Region, is situated in a 60-mile (100-km) strip around Cape Town. The WO system certifies a wine's origins, and the delimitation of the zones is determined by geographic, topologic, and geologic factors. Any winery wishing to benefit from a WO appellation must subject wines to constant sensory tests and chemical analysis from harvesting to bottling, and the number of wines submitting to these checks is growing all the time. Most national wine producers adhere to an environmental program with 15 rules.

> Vines belonging to Drayton's Family Wines in the Hunter Valley, Australia.

HOW TO "DECODE" A WINE LABEL

If you can read a label, it is like looking at a wine's passport or identity card. For the producer, the label should tempt someone to buy the bottle as well as provide a certain amount of information required by law. For the consumer, the label should provide enough information to make an informed choice.

A wine's passport

Wine labelling, which is subject to strict regulation by public authorities working in conjunction with professional bodies, addresses one chief concern: providing the consumer with the best information possible about the product's origins and its principal characteristics. Some of the details included also serve to provide the authorities with data for fiscal use.

The label's first duty is to certify the authenticity of the wine, ensuring that it was produced according to the winemaking regulations in force for a given producer and category of wine. In France, the *direction générale de la concurrence, de la consommation et de la répression des fraudes* (DGCCRF, the Serious Fraud Office) and the customs and excise authorities are entitled to check whether a wine matches the details provided on its label, and if the label itself conforms to regulations.

The label "speaks" to the buyer, who is often faced with multiple shelves of bottles. It guarantees the authenticity of the wine and allows government authorities to check its conformity with current regulations.

Useful information

Reading the front label, and the back one, where present (*see* p.109), will provide the consumer with certain information. Apart from the origins of the wine, it may provide details of the year of harvest. It also will show the name of the producer or bottler, or whether it comes from a cooperative, etc. It is worth remembering that only certain phrases, such as *mis en bouteille au château* (estate-bottled), are legally protected. Others, such as *vieilles vignes* (old vines), are terms specific to the producer who made the wine and are really no more than marketing devices.

Regulations governing wine labels are in constant flux, as is shown by recent declarations of the European Union with respect to appellations (*see* p.95). The possible introduction of regulations for organic wine is similarly under review (*see* p.58).

The capsule and the cork

Most bottles carry a capsule, also known as a "foil." In France, they are marked with an excise stamp indicating the registered winemaker and region of production, and confirming that the wine is licensed for distribution by the excise authorities. French bottles without a capsule must feature a paper excise stamp (see p.127). To combat fraud, a number of winemakers have resorted to stamping their corks, which will feature the origins of the wine (either the name of the winery or appellation) and the year. Sparkling appellation wines such as Champagne and the crémants are obliged to include their appellation on the cork. Some countries (South Africa, Austria, and Portugal) feature a "ribbon" supplied by the government, which is attached over the cork or capsule.

> The capsule, known as the *capsule représentative des droits* (CRD) in France, proves that the wine may be legally distributed.

> Wine labels can be sparse in detail, creatively laid out, or signed works of art.

Mandatory details

CATEGORY. In France, wine belongs to one of two categories: wine without geographic designation, in other words *vin de table* (table wine); and quality wine produced in specified regions, *i.e. vin de pays* (listed as IGP since August 2009) and protected appellations (AOP; *see also* p.95).

The old AOVDQS (*appellations d'origine vin délimité de qualité supérieure*) appellations for wine quality are disappearing and being integrated into one of these two categories. In the case of table wine, the label will feature either the terms *vin de France* or *vin de la communauté européenne* (European Community wine).

The term *vin de pays* followed by a geographic area, such as *vin de pays charentais*, for example, is now optional and will vary by region; *vins de pays d'Oc,* for example, now styles itself *Pays d'Oc* followed by the designation *indication géographique protégée* (IGP). AOP wines must include their appellation on labels; and this may be a region, such as Alsace or Champagne, or a more specific area. In Burgundy, the appellations will first list the region, then the villages located within the region, and then, like the last in a series of Russian dolls, the individual estate, which may be very small indeed (*see* p.276). In such cases, the consumer is expected to know that Échézeaux, for example, is a small but prestigious estate in Burgundy.

BOTTLER'S NAME AND ADDRESS. The label generally shows if the wine was bottled where it was made; in such cases it is legally entitled to bear the inscription *mis en bouteille à* (or *de*) *la propriété* (or possibly either *au/du domaine* or *au/du château*), all of which mean the same thing. It is worth bearing in mind that French law considers a cooperative as an extension of a producer; if an individual producer's wine is made individually but bottled by a local cooperative, the

producer will still have the right to print *mis en bouteille à la propriété* on the label. If a wine is bottled outside the estate by a third party, the label must bear the inscription *mis en bouteille par...* (bottled by...) followed by the bottler's name and postal code. Inscriptions such as *mis en bouteille dans nos chais* (or *par nos soins*) generally indicate that it is a wine blended from multiple sources.

NOMINAL VOLUME. Detailed in liters, centiliters, or milliliters. The most common value is 750 ml, although the half-bottle (375 ml) and the magnum (1.5 liters) are ubiquitous. Sweet wines (straw wines, late-harvested wines, etc.) are sometimes sold in 330 ml or 500 ml bottles. The *clavelin* (620 ml) is used only for Jura *vin jaune* ("yellow wine," *see* p.307). Bordeaux and Champagne wines are also to be found in bottles sizes up to 15 liters, known in Champagne as a "nebuchadnezzar" (*see also* box on p.86).

ALCOHOLIC STRENGTH. Expressed in percentage of alcohol by volume (ABV). Most wines have an alcohol content of between 11 and 14% ABV, but some may have a lower strength, such as Italy's Moscato d'Asti at

> Château Le Bon Pasteur is a Pomerol appellation made by Michel Rolland, a leading winery consultant.

was not permitted for many years in France, but is now legal. If the vintage is specified, at least 85 percent of the wine, whatever its category, must come from the year indicated.

TRADEMARK. This may be a simple logo (a proper name followed by the ® sign, for example) or something more complex (winery name and location, such as *Domaine X, Château Y,* etc.). The terms *château, clos,* and *abbaye* may be used only for AOP wines and must refer to an actual place that exists on a survey map. The terms *domaine* and *mas* cannot be applied to table wine. Only the phrase *mis en bouteille au château* or its various equivalents will guarantee that the wine is estate-produced.

TRADITIONAL EXPRESSIONS. Terms such as *cru classé, premier cru, grand cru,* and *cru* are traditional monikers associated with a limited number of wines and defined by appropriate legislation. Bordeaux *crus classés* refer to a hierarchical grading of estates (*see* pp.250–1). Burgundy's *premiers crus* and *grands crus,* much like the *grand cru* of Alsace, denote a classification by place and local character (*see.* pp.279 and 305). In Champagne, the monikers refer to the villages (*see* box, p.298). Provence's *crus classés* date back to the 1950s when they were instituted by the Côtes-de-Provence appellation (*see* p.348).

GRAPE VARIETY. The inclusion of grape variety for AOC wines in France varies by appellation. Always included in Alsace, it appears on rare occasions in Bordeaux (for wines made with Sauvignon Blanc) and occasionally in Burgundy (for wines made with Pinot Noir). A *vin de pays* is required to be made 100 percent from the grape variety indicated on the label. If it is a blend, the various varieties used are generally listed on the back label. Inclusion

6% ABV, or be considerably more potent, such as natural sweet wines. (Banyuls can be more than 20% ABV.)

THE COUNTRY OF PRODUCTION, *e.g.* "Product of France." This category was once reserved for wines intended for export, but is now obligatory for all wines.

HEALTH WARNINGS. An indication of the presence of sulfites, *i.e.* sulfur compounds used as preservatives, was initially required on labels of bottles destined for English-speaking countries, but is now required on the front or rear label of all wine sold in Europe. Similarly, a graphic warns against consumption of alcohol for pregnant women. It is possible in the future that the presence of allergens such as albumin, which is used to clarify wine, will also be indicated.

LOT NUMBER. Added to the label or printed directly onto the bottle as required by the producer or the merchant to make the specific bottle identifiable and traceable.

The main optional items

Optional details allow producers to include additional information about the nature of the wine, making the consumer's choice easier.

VINTAGE. Inclusion of the year of production, which sometimes features on a collar around the neck of the bottle, is optional for both AOC wines and *vins de pays,* but almost all producers will mention it. Including the year for *vin de table*

What is "retreat"?

In order to benefit from a registered appellation of origin in France, a wine must combine certain recognized qualities when tasted and analyzed. If it fails to live up to the appellation's criteria, but is wine of a "sound and sellable" quality, the producer may request for the wine to replier (literally, to "retreat") into a larger and less demanding appellation in the same area. A Pauillac, for example, may "retreat" to a Médoc or a Bordeaux, and a Chablis to a Burgundy. This said, surplus wine that exceeds authorized yields is never subjected to such a "retreat" and so-called déclassé (declassified) wine is best avoided since it is never what it claims to be.

of grape variety is optional for table wine. In the great majority of the world's wine-producing countries, more emphasis is often placed on the name of the grape or grapes than on the appellation, and this features systematically on the label. Legislation in European countries prescribes a minimum percentage (between 75 and 100 percent of the grape variety indicated).

VINEYARD TERMS. Words such as "owner," "grower," etc. may optionally be included (for Champagne, *see* box on p.301).

PRODUCTION METHODS. When a wine has been produced organically, the winemaker may indicate this on the label (in France) with the logo AB (*see* image above). In such cases, it is also required to detail the name of the certificating organization (usually Ecocert in France). Terms such as *agriculture raisonnée* or *vin naturel* are merely terms from the producer. Agriculture conforming to biodynamic standards may be certified by an organization (Demeter); but, in contrast to organic farming, such certification is not compulsory and the term "biodynamic" is not protected.

Other optional details

VENDANGES MANUELLES (handpicked). To include this on the label, the winemaker must have had the wine grapes harvested manually.

CUVÉE NON FILTRÉE (unfiltered). This term means that the wine has been fined, but not filtered (*see* p.76). The larger deposit thrown by an unfiltered wine is never detrimental to its taste.

ÉLEVAGE SUR LIES (or similar; matured on the lees). In regions such as Nantes in the Loire Valley, the lees are not removed (by racking). Instead, the wine is left "on the lees" until it is bottled (*see* p.76). The wine thus retains residual carbon dioxide created during fermentation, which accentuates its lively texture.

VIEILLI EN FÛT (DE CHÊNE). Aged in (oak) casks; these are usually *vins de garde* (wines for laying down). This maturation gives the wine vanilla, woody, or toasted notes. Often more expensive, such wines are not always of a

better quality, as the notes introduced by the wood can "drown out" other aromas.

OFFICIAL DISTINCTIONS. If a wine has won awards or competitions, these distinctions may legally be recorded on the label, although the wine should be from the vintage recognized. Such distinctions are reserved in France for appellation wines and *vins de pays*. For the merit of such awards, *see* p.121.

ILLUSTRATION ON THE LABEL. In France, the image of an *estate* building or the residence of the proprietor featured on a label must be of an actual structure, even if it is a reproduction of a work of art. In either case, a representation of any *château* other than the one whose name the wine bears is not permitted.

RESIDUAL SUGAR LEVEL. Inclusion of terms such as *sec, demi-sec, moelleux,* or *liquoreux* (dry, medium dry, medium sweet, sweet) is not obligatory. This can lead to occasional surprises, notably with Alsace wines in which sugar content is never certain, except when identified as botrytized or late harvest. Nonetheless, if the term is mentioned on the label, it must correspond to a precise residual sugar level defined in regulations.

> A wine's vintage may be listed on a label placed on the shoulder of the wine bottle.

> Bugey-Cerdon wines are *pétillant*, and they are often rosé.

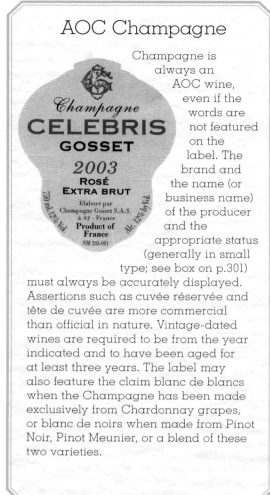

Champagne is always an AOC wine, even if the words are not featured on the label. The brand and the name (or business name) of the producer and the appropriate status (generally in small type; see box on p.301) must always be accurately displayed. Assertions such as cuvée réservée and tête de cuvée are more commercial than official in nature. Vintage-dated wines are required to be from the year indicated and to have been aged for at least three years. The label may also feature the claim blanc de blancs when the Champagne has been made exclusively from Chardonnay grapes, or blanc de noirs when made from Pinot Noir, Pinot Meunier, or a blend of these two varieties.

Non-regulated features

These are details that convey information the authority of which is based on nothing beyond the good faith of the claimant.

VIEILLES VIGNES (old vines). Old vines generally yield a more concentrated wine in that it is made from a smaller, and thus better, yield. But since the consumer is unable to determine the age of the vines, such a detail is of no real use.

CUVÉE SPÉCIALE, RÉSERVE EXCEPTIONNELLE, GRANDE CUVÉE, ETC. These terms imply that the wine represents the best quality (and highest price) from a given producer, either because the wine is from an exceptional location or from especially mature vines. In either case, such assertions are founded only on the good faith of the winery.

CRÈME DE TÊTE. This term is applied to Sauternes wines made using the first selection of fruit from the harvest. The wines are made only with overripe grapes and are extremely sweet.

GRAND VIN DE (followed by the name of a region). Such claims are largely advertising. This should not to be confused with a *grand vin* of a *cru classé* Bordeaux château, which denotes a wine of great quality. In such cases, the phrase *grand vin* must be followed by the name of the region concerned, e.g. *Grand Vin de Bordeaux*.

SERIAL NUMBER. Its presence on the label implies a certain rarity for the wine, but this may be relative.

Sparkling wines

The term "sparkling wine" denotes a wine containing carbon dioxide under pressure, which is released and effervesces when the wine is opened. French sparkling wines are divided into *vins perlants*, *vins pétillants*, and *vins mousseux*, in ascending order of effervescence. The lattermost category includes Champagnes

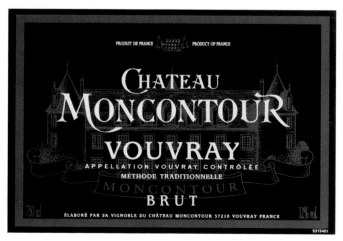

> The label for a sparkling Vouvray.

Classification varies by country

The information contained on wine labels produced in most countries is now more or less the same: appellation name, nominal container volume, grape variety, the name of the producer or seller, the alcohol content by volume, any health warnings, and country of origin. That said, while European regulations—even those determining the size of the lettering on the labels—are gradually converging, the hierarchy of the information detailed on the label is very different from country to country. On Spanish, Portuguese, and Greek labels, for example, the name of the seller or of the individual wine may feature more prominently than the appellation. In most New World countries, the appellation often takes second place to the grape variety.

and other *crémant* styles. The labels of *vins perlants* and *vins pétillants* are not subject to any particular regulations.

DOSAGE. This term refers to the residual sugar level (expressed in grams per liter). In other words, it is the sucrose content of the sugar-and-yeast mixture that is added before final bottling and that gives the wines a more or less sweet taste. Depending on the residual sugar level, the wine may be classified as: *doux* (more than 50 g/l), *demi-sec* (between 33 and 50 g/l), *sec* (between 17 and 35 g/l), "*extra-dry*" (between 12 and 20 g/l), *brut* (less than 15 g/l), or *extra-brut* (less than 6 g/l). Levels of less than 3 g/l may be classified as *brut nature*, *non dosé*, or *dosage zéro* (all meaning "no added sugar").

PRODUCTION METHOD. The vast majority of quality sparkling wines are produced using the secondary fermentation method first used in Champagne. The label may thus read *méthode traditionnelle*, a term that has replaced *méthode champenoise*.

Some French wine regions, such as Gaillac, Limoux (Blanquette), and Savoie prefer another method that achieves sweeter wine with fewer bubbles: Young wines are bottled before all the residual sugar has turned into alcohol, and fermentation continues in the bottle, releasing carbon dioxide. Labels here may mention *méthode ancestrale* or *méthode rurale*. A slight variation on this method is used for Clairette de Die sparkling wine from the Rhône, and has become known as the *méthode dioise*.

CRÉMANT. First applied to semi-sparkling (*demi-mousse*) Champagne, the term *crémant* has been used since 1992 in France to identify sparkling wines with a geographic appellation and a traditional production method. The foremost French appellations are the *crémants* de Bourgogne, d'Alsace, du Jura, de Bordeaux, de Die, and de Limoux. Further afield in Europe you will also find Crémant du Luxembourg, Cava in Spain, Sekt in Germany, and various wines labelled *metodo classico* in Italy.

Back label

Although it is not a compulsory feature, the back label is often the wine's true passport, with the main label serving more as a simple business card. Placed on the opposite side of the bottle, and sometimes of an even larger size, it conveys information as varied as the grape variety, the characteristics of the parcel of land from which the wine was sourced, the manner and length of its maturation, the ideal serving temperature, and even some serving suggestions for food that the wine will complement. The back label is an extremely common feature in English-speaking countries and is catching on more and more in France.

TRUE OR FALSE?

No obligatory or optional details are included on the back label.

FALSE. Some winemakers use the back label to include both required and optional information, while the front label is used to attract consumer attention with an image such as a reproduction of a painting or a branded wine name. That approach is also used for basic table wine in order to hide its modest origins or its perceived poor image.

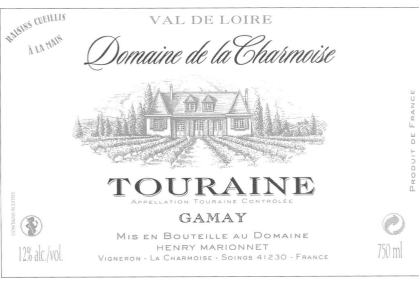

> The label...

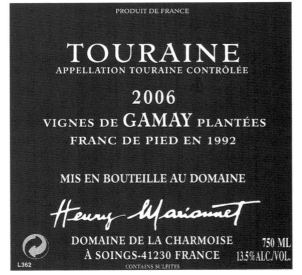

> ... and the back label.

SOME EXAMPLES OF DIFFERENT LABELS

The label, the wine's passport, has evolved in significant ways. Required information, optional details—which are still regulated—and inscriptions that amount to little more than marketing leave almost no more room on the classic label. As a result, many bottles now bear a back label featuring ever more information aimed at promoting or helping the consumer understand the product.

BORDEAUX WINE

Optional detail

Estate name, compulsory

Regulated optional detail

Appellation name, optional but regulated

Regulated detail, indicating that the wine was bottled at the place of production

Compulsory

Indication of year, optional but regulated

Optional design

Owner's name, compulsory

Alcoholic content, compulsory

Volume content, compulsory

BURGUNDY

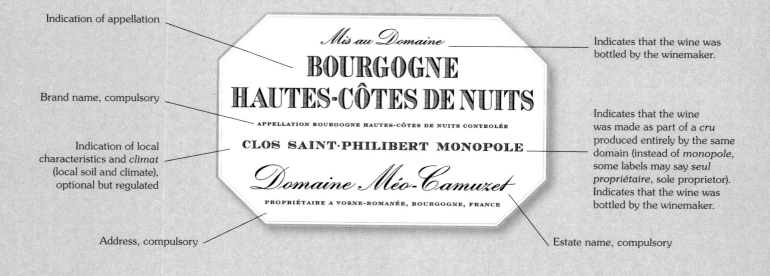

Indication of appellation

Indicates that the wine was bottled by the winemaker.

Brand name, compulsory

Indicates that the wine was made as part of a *cru* produced entirely by the same domain (instead of *monopole*, some labels may say *seul propriétaire*, sole proprietor). Indicates that the wine was bottled by the winemaker.

Indication of local characteristics and *climat* (local soil and climate), optional but regulated

Address, compulsory

Estate name, compulsory

CHAMPAGNE

Optional design

Optional but regulated

Compulsory. AOC is understood, as all Champagne is AOC

Brand name, compulsory

Optional; in Champagne, *grand cru* indicates a village where the price of the grapes agreed between the growers and the producers is the highest possible because of the quality of the local soil

Style of the wine, compulsory. A *demi-sec* contains between 33 and 50 grams per liter of sugar

Nominal volume, compulsory

Alcoholic content, compulsory

Maker's name and address, compulsory

CM indicates *coopérative de manipulation* (trade cooperative) followed by an identification number; this Champagne was therefore made by a cooperative

ALSACE

Indication of quality, optional but regulated; this indicates that the wine was made exclusively with botrytized grapes harvested in successive sortings

Estate name, compulsory

Optional detail

Appellation name, regulated, compulsory if followed by *Appellation Alsace Contrôlée*

Name and address of bottler, compulsory

Grape variety, compulsory if preceded by *Appellation Alsace Contrôlée*. Here, the producer has associated his name with the grape variety as a registered trademark

All other compulsory details appear on the back label.

VIN DE PAYS
(Indication géographique protégée)

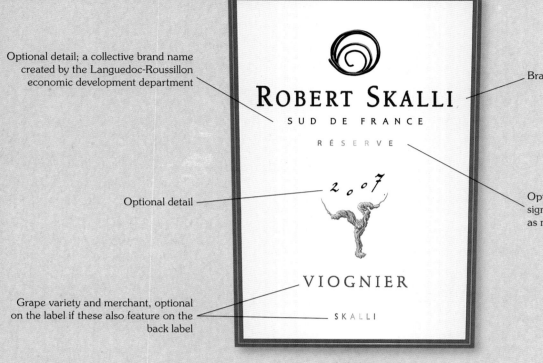

Optional detail; a collective brand name created by the Languedoc-Roussillon economic development department

Brand name, compulsory

Optional detail

Optional detail; of no particular significance in France other than as marketing

Grape variety and merchant, optional on the label if these also feature on the back label

Label

Grape variety; compulsory if more than 85 percent is of the same variety

Health warning, compulsory

Indications of quality, optional but regulated

Origin, compulsory, as provided in the European Union regulations of 2009

Name and address of distributor, compulsory

Compulsory for the domestic market since 2009

Alcoholic content by volume, compulsory

Optional

Back label

SPANISH WINE
· · · · · · · · · · · · · · · · · · · ·

Optional design

Name of the wine

Appellation, compulsory

Regulated, indicating that the wine is at least three years old, of which six months were spent in barrels

Denominación de origen calificada, compulsory, indicating that the wine corresponds in category to an AOC

Brand name

Regulated, indicating that the wine was made, matured, and bottled at the estate (even if the grapes may have come from other estates)

All other compulsory details are included on the back label

ITALIAN WINE
· · · · · · · · · · · · · · · · · · · ·

Optional design; should generally represent an existing building or site

Name of a line of wines, regulated

Optional but regulated; generally indicates that the wine has been matured for two years, of which three months were in the bottle (this period may vary by appellation)

Indication of origin, optional but regulated, as it must be followed by *Denominazione di origine controllata et garantita* (DOCG). "Classico" indicates that the wine is from the appellation's historic heartland

Producer's name, compulsory, and also the brand name, optional

All other compulsory details are included on the back label

GERMAN WINE

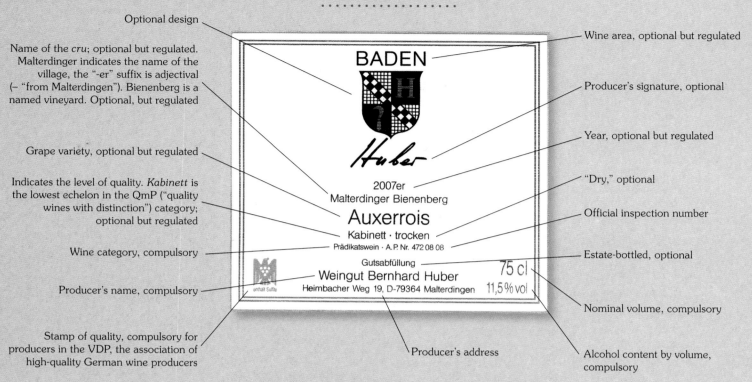

Optional design

Name of the *cru*; optional but regulated. Malterdinger indicates the name of the village, the "-er" suffix is adjectival (– "from Malterdingen"). Bienenberg is a named vineyard. Optional, but regulated

Grape variety, optional but regulated

Indicates the level of quality. *Kabinett* is the lowest echelon in the QmP ("quality wines with distinction") category; optional but regulated

Wine category, compulsory

Producer's name, compulsory

Stamp of quality, compulsory for producers in the VDP, the association of high-quality German wine producers

Wine area, optional but regulated

Producer's signature, optional

Year, optional but regulated

"Dry," optional

Official inspection number

Estate-bottled, optional

Nominal volume, compulsory

Alcohol content by volume, compulsory

Producer's address

BADEN

Huber

2007er
Malterdinger Bienenberg
Auxerrois
Kabinett · trocken
Prädikatswein · A.P. Nr. 472 08 08
Gutsabfüllung
Weingut Bernhard Huber
Heimbacher Weg 19, D-79364 Malterdingen
75 cl
11,5 % vol

AUSTRALIAN WINE

Wine name, optional

Year, optional

Nominal volume, compulsory

Brand name, compulsory

Region of origin, optional

Grape variety, optional

KILIKANOON
CLARE VALLEY
Mort's Reserve
WATERVALE
RIESLING
2 0 0 9
750 mL

All other compulsory details feature on the back label

CHILEAN WINE

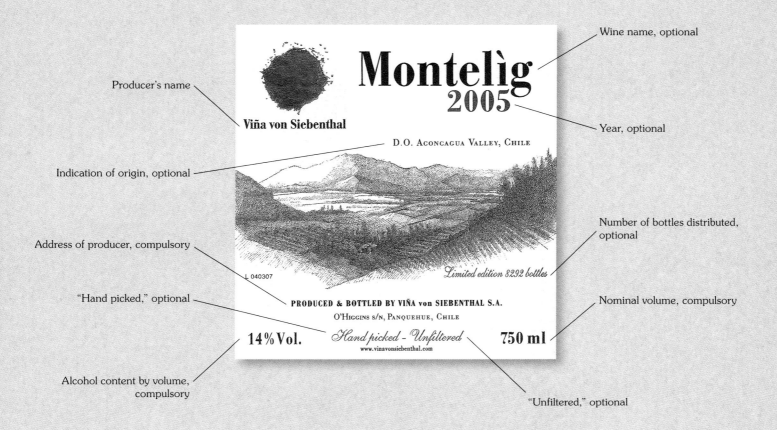

Wine name, optional

Producer's name

Year, optional

Indication of origin, optional

Number of bottles distributed, optional

Address of producer, compulsory

"Hand picked," optional

Nominal volume, compulsory

Alcohol content by volume, compulsory

"Unfiltered," optional

AMERICAN WINE

Year, optional

Estate name

Indicates that the wine was made and bottled at the estate, optional

Grape variety, optional but regulated; the wine must consist of at least 75 percent of the variety mentioned

AVA (American viticultural area), specific area of production, regulated

Alcohol content by volume, compulsory

All other compulsory details are featured on the back label

LABELS OLD AND NEW

Understated, classic and modern, original labels are as diverse as the wines they represent.
Some of the most beautiful specimens are even collector's items.

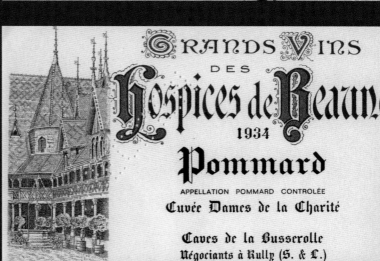

Château Leyritz-Moncassin

Rosé

Vincent DELMOTTE
Propriétaire
SCEA SOVIMON
47700 LEYRITZ MONCASSIN
FRANCE

BUZET
APPELLATION BUZET CONTRÔLÉE

12% vol.   750 ml
MIS EN BOUTEILLE AU CHATEAU
PRODUIT DE FRANCE   CONTAINS SULPHITES

Cuvée du Poilu

CÔTES DU RHÔNE
1918

APPELLATION CONTRÔLÉE
1988

MIS EN BOUTEILLE PAR LES PRODUCTEURS RÉUNIS A F 26790-357

CAVE LA ROMAINE
84110 VAISON · LA · ROMAINE

75 cl   12,5 % Vol.
          PRODUIT DE FRANCE

CUVÉE SAINT-VALENTIN

SAINT · AMOUR
APPELLATION SAINT-AMOUR CONTRÔLÉE

MIS EN BOUTEILLE PAR
LOUIS TÊTE À 69430 BEAUJEU - FRANCE
PRODUIT DE FRANCE

13% vol   75 cl

VIN des AMPHORES

SYRAH

VIN DE PAYS D'OC
Les Coteaux de Saint-Cyr

12% vol.   75 cl
MIS EN BOUTEILLE
PAR LA S.C.V. SALLELES D'AUDE
PRODUIT DE FRANCE

CUVÉE PASTEUR

ARBOIS
APPELLATION ARBOIS CONTRÔLÉE

12,5%Vol.   75cl e
PRODUIT ET MIS EN BOUTEILLE PAR
HENRI MAIRE AU CHATEAU BOICHAILLES 39600 ARBOIS JURA FRANCE

HOW TO
BUY WINE

TOOLS FOR BUYING WINE

In order to choose from the huge range of wines available, wine enthusiasts may turn to expert media and buying guides. While these are useful, you should remember that, ultimately, the opinions presented depend on the writers' own preferences.

Buying guides

Every year, buying guides are published with a view to helping consumers find the best value for their money. Some aim to outline the best estates or the best wines for each appellation or *terroir*, others focus on low-priced wines or wines available in supermarkets. The guides differ primarily in their presentation. For some, tasting notes are a priority, while others focus on regions and producers. One guide may be based on the opinions of famous critics, while another relies on blind tastings carried out by a panel of sommeliers or wine experts.

Are their recommendations reliable?

All guides judge samples that they receive from producers, which leaves the door open to potential variability, in that producers will be sure to send only their best wines. However, the tastings are taken very seriously and these experts will have judged the wine that was sent to them as objectively they can. But the fact remains that any assessment of a wine involves the subjective element of a taster's personal preferences. Moreover, no general review can claim to be exhaustive. If a wine is not listed in relevant guides, this does not necessarily mean that it is of poor quality. However, it is rare for an excellent wine to pass completely unnoticed.

Accepting these reservations, buying guides remain valuable tools for the variety that they offer and the practical information that they provide. They also are a useful indicator of general trends in prices and other developments in the wine world, such

Wines that have been praised as being excellent value often disappear quickly from winery inventories. Wine enthusiasts may then be able to find them at wine retailers or in restaurants, but it will be at a higher price.

as the emergence of interesting new producers, or changes in fashions or winemaking practices that affect the styles of wines in a particular area.

Some leading wine guides

ANDREA ROBINSON'S WINE BUYING GUIDE FOR EVERYONE (Andrea Robinson). This annual reference title from a high-profile master sommelier and television host offers lively, practical advice on successful wine buying and food pairing. Learn more at her fun, constantly updated website: Andreawine.com.

EXPLORING WINE (Steven Kolpan, et al.). The wine textbook for the prestigious Culinary Institute of America. It's a weighty tome with all the basics, but also amazing reference material on the art and science of matching food and wine.

HUGH JOHNSON'S POCKET WINE BOOK (Hugh Johnson, et al.) The world's most popular quick reference for wine has been published annually for 35 years. A stable of top contributors from around the planet makes it authoritative and up-to-date with definitions, vintage ratings, and more.

> A wine that you don't like is too expensive, no matter what its price. But there are good wines in every price category.

The mainstream press and the wine press

In France, there is now an annual publishing ritual. Every fall, when the supermarkets run big wine promotions, most mainstream weekly and monthly titles distribute special issues devoted to wine. Since they are aimed at the general public, the articles are usually written for novices. Serious wine enthusiasts will prefer the specialized wine press, such as the *Revue du Vin de France* (even though the articles are frequently penned by the same authors who put out those mainstream supplements).

OLDMAN'S GUIDE TO OUTSMARTING WINE (Mark Oldman). This very popular title presents wine know-how in just over 100 very short chapters. While full of solid information, it's also presented in a fun, lighthearted style—with "cheat sheet" summaries, recommendations, and pronunciations.

THE OXFORD COMPANION TO WINE (Jancis Robinson). More than 800 pages of erudite entries covering everything from fundamentals to esoterica, this is widely regarded as the leading encyclopedia on wine. An essential reference for members of the trade studying for advanced qualifications.

SECRETS OF THE SOMMELIERS (Raj Parr and Jordan Mackay). Industry experts Parr and Mackay employ anecdotes and stories to weave together practical advice on wine from the realm of elite sommeliers. As the subtitle indicates, they show readers how to think and drink like a pro.

WINDOWS ON THE WORLD COMPLETE WINE COURSE (Kevin Zraly). A 25-year bestseller developed from 35 years of teaching at New York City's number-one wine school. Beyond the expected basics, Zraly's work on interpreting labels is particularly helpful, and a series of end-of-chapter quizzes help readers retain what they learn.

THE WINE BIBLE (Karen MacNeil). Journalist, television host, and educator MacNeil has assembled nearly 1,000 pages of comprehensive yet readable wine reference material on all key topics for both novice and expert alike. Skillfully done: very clear and appealing.

WINE FOR DUMMIES (Ed McCarthy and Mary Ewing-Mulligan). Master of Wine Ewing-Mulligan and her husband apply the wildly popular "Dummies" format to demystify wine for the masses. Twenty quick chapters bring even the most nervous newbie up to speed.

WORLD ATLAS OF WINE (Hugh Johnson and Jancis Robinson). Dozens of colorful maps detailing the world's leading wine regions are accompanied by statistics on local terroir—latitudes, elevations, annual rainfall, etc—and excellent explanatory comments. Another top resource for serious students of wine.

The merits of tasting

To "understand" a wine, nothing beats tasting (*see* pp.203–25). It is very difficult to obtain an accurate idea of the style of a wine purely from its description. We therefore cannot recommend

> Tasting wines allows you to judge them on the basis of your own preferences and to make better purchases.

enough that enthusiasts take advantage of the many opportunities that are available for tasting.

Where can wines be tasted? Tasting events are organized across the country by regional wine associations and promotional bodies. Plus, there are several great events produced by leading wine publications. Tastings are also offered by wine retailers, and there are wine clubs that provide beginners with a general introduction or serious wine lovers with a deeper understanding of specific wines. Tastings at winery tasting rooms can be an excellent education. But note that, while they are a good opportunity to sample a wine and learn about how it is made, you are politely expected to buy at least one bottle. Finally, it's also a good idea to get into the habit of making notes during each tasting: this will enable you to gain maximum benefit from the thousands of recommendations and comments from experts such as buying guide authors, sommeliers…and friends.

Some simple criteria for choosing wine

Wine enthusiasts need to choose on the basis of their own criteria, from the vast number of wines listed in guides. Which kinds of wines capture their interest (*see* pp.154–61)? In what price range? Are they looking for a wine to drink immediately, as part of their regular consumption? Or is it a wine to lay down in the cellar, which will be saved for a special occasion? Taking these factors into account will help in making a choice.

THE PRICE OF WINE

While the price of a bottle is supposed to reflect the quality of the wine, it also depends on its reputation, reviews in guides and, most of all, demand.

The wine hierarchy

There is a hierarchy in France and across Europe, which goes, starting at the bottom, from table wines with no indication of origin and sold at the lowest prices, to prestigious appellations, such as the classified growths, which can reach hundreds of dollars. Generally, a long-standing reputation equates to a higher price. *Vins de pays* are table wines that qualify for protected geographical indication (PGI). They are theoretically less expensive than AOC wines, because yields are higher; but sometimes *vins de pays* that have gained a reputation for quality will be sold at similar or even higher prices than wines with appellation status.

The value of an appellation

Each European appellation, or wine-producing area, has a benchmark price set by demand. This is the price per barrel or hectoliter (approximately 26 gallons) at which negotiations are carried out between producers and merchants or negociants. The system is particularly relevant in regions in which production is high (such

as Bordeaux, Languedoc, and the Rhône Valley) and where a substantial proportion of the wine goes through *négociants*. The appellation prices are less important in areas where most of the production is sold in bottles at the estate, such as in Alsace. Displayed in the local newspaper, an appellation's average price is based on its reputation, its previous prices, the quantity of wine available, the quality of the vintage, and demand.

Various other factors also contribute to determining the retail prices of wines, such as the vagaries of fashion and the wine producer's reputation. Lastly, the price of a wine can depend on the way it is sold (direct, via supermarkets, etc.).

Prices by wine-producing area

The following table offers guideline prices for a range of appellations in France and other countries, arranged by "wine family" (*see* pp.154–61). These prices are for single bottles sold at the estate. These prices have been converted from the native currency into US dollars and pounds Sterling, but please note that prices will fluctuate according to exchange rates.

LIGHT, FRUITY RED WINES					
Coteaux-du-Lyonnais	< $7 (£4)	Vin de Savoie	< $14 (£9)	Arbois	< $20 (£14)
Beaujolais	< $14 (£9)	Hautes-Côtes-de-Beaune	< $17 (£10)	Alsace Pinot Noir	< $20 (£14)
Anjou	< $20 (£14)	Côtes-du-Jura	< $18 (£11)	Hautes-Côtes-de-Nuits	< $20 (£14)
Navarre	< $14 (£9)	St-Nicolas-de-Bourgueil	< $18 (£11)	Burgundy	< $28 (£17)
Malbec from Argentina	< $14 (£9)	Bourgueil	< $17 (£10)	Sancerre	< $28 (£17)
FULL-BODIED, FRUITY RED WINES					
Chianti	< $14 (£9)	Côtes-du-Rhône-Villages	< $17 (£10)	Chinon	< $19 (£12)
Valpolicella	< $14 (£9)	Gaillac	< $17 (£10)	Côtes-de-Bourg	< $20 (£14)
Bordeaux	< $20 (£14)	Bergerac	< $20 (£14)	Castillon-Côtes-de-Bordeaux	< $28 (£17)
Buzet	< $14 (£9)	Bordeaux Supérieur	< $20 (£14)	Crozes-Hermitage	< $28 (£17)
Côtes-du-Frontonnais	< $14 (£9)	Australian Shiraz	< $11 (£7)	Saint-Joseph	< $28 (£17)
Côtes-de-Provence	< $14 (£9)	Bierzos	< $14 (£9)	Coteaux-d'Aix-en-Provence	< $28 (£17)
Touraine	< $14 (£9)	St-Nicolas-de-Bourgueil	< $18 (£11)	Coteaux-Champenois	> $28 (£17)
GENEROUS, POWERFUL, COMPLEX RED WINES					
Pomerol	> $7 (£4)	Red Rioja	< $28 (£17)	Barbaresco	< $40 (£25)
Côtes-du-Roussillon-Villages	< $14 (£9)	Vacqueyras	< $20 (£14)	Valpolicella Amarone	> $20 (£14)
Minervois	< $17 (£10)	Madiran	< $20 (£14)	Sonoma Valley California Pinot Noir	< $35 (£22)
Cahors	< $7 (£4)	Pécharmant	< $20 (£14)		
Minervois-la-Livinière	< $18 (£11)	Languedoc	< $28 (£17)	Châteauneuf-du-Pape	> $28 (£17)
Corbières	< $20 (£14)	Gigondas	< $28 (£17)	Great Argentinian wines from Mendoza	> $40 (£25)
St-Chinian	< $20 (£14)	St-Émilion	< $35 (£22)		
SLEEK, TANNIC, COMPLEX RED WINES					
South African Pinotage	< $14 (£9)	Cornas	> $17 (£10)	Barbera d'Asti	< $28 (£17)
Graves	< $28 (£17)	Pauillac	> $17 (£10)	Saint-Julien	> $19 (£12)
Haut-Médoc	< $28 (£17)	Pessac-Léognan	> $17 (£10)	Côte-Rôtie	> $28 (£17)
Bandol	> $14 (£9)	Saint-Estèphe	> $17 (£10)	Hermitage	> $28 (£17)
Médoc	> $14 (£9)	Saint-Émilion Grand Cru	> $18 (£11)	Barolo	< $55 (£35)

SLEEK, ELEGANT, COMPLEX RED WINES

Mercurey	< $28 (£17)	Vosne-Romanée	> $35 (£22)	Gevrey-Chambertin	> $40 (£25)
Pommard	> $20 (£14)	Corton	> $40 (£25)	Great reds from Ribera del Duero	> $55 (£35)
Volnay	> $20 (£14)	Great reds from the Napa Valley	> $40 (£25)		
Chambolle-Musigny	> $35 (£22)			Bolgheri Sassicaia	> $140 (£90)

FRUITY, LIVELY ROSÉ WINES

Luberon	< $14 (£9)	Côtes-de-Provence	< $8 (£5)	Côtes-du-Jura	< $10 (£6)
Rosé de Loire	< $7 (£4)	Les Baux-de-Provence	< $14 (£9)	Coteaux-d'Aix-en-Provence	< $17 (£10)
Irouléguy	< $14 (£9)	Coteaux-Varois	< $17 (£10)	Bellet	< $20 (£14)

STRONGER, FULL-BODIED ROSÉ WINES

Corbières	< $7 (£4)	Languedoc	< $14 (£9)	Tavel	< $20 (£14)
Côtes-du-Rhône	< $7 (£4)	Lirac	< $14 (£9)	Bandol	< $28 (£17)
Bordeaux Clairet	< $14 (£9)	Marsanney	< $17 (£10)	Rosé des Riceys	< $28 (£17)

LIVELY, LIGHT, DRY WHITE WINES

Gros-Plant	< $11 (£7)	Bourgogne Aligoté	< $14 (£9)	Vin de Savoie	< $14 (£9)
Bergerac	< $14 (£9)	Cour-Cheverny	< $14 (£9)	Petit Chablis	< $17 (£10)
Entre-Deux-Mers	< $14 (£9)	Crépy	< $14 (£9)	Cheverny	< $8 (£5)
Saint-Pourçain	< $7 (£4)	Alsace Pinot Blanc	< $14 (£9)	Pouilly-sur-Loire	< $17 (£10)
Basque Txakoli dry white	> $7 (£4)	Alsace Sylvaner	< $14 (£9)	New Zealand Sauvignon Blanc	> $14 (£9)

FRUITY, SUPPLE, DRY WHITE WINES

Muscadet	< $14 (£9)	Corsican wines	< $17 (£10)	Jurançon sec	< $20 (£14)
Gaillac	< $14 (£9)	Arbois	< $17 (£10)	Sancerre	< $20 (£14)
Roussette du Bugey	< $14 (£9)	Graves	< $17 (£10)	Dry white from Collio	< $20 (£14)
Blaye-Côtes-de-Bordeaux	< $17 (£10)	Coteaux-d'Aix-en-Provence	< $20 (£14)	Chablis	< $28 (£17)
Côtes-de-Provence	< $14 (£9)	Montlouis sec	< $20 (£14)	Pouilly-Fumé	< $28 (£17)
Mâcon	< $14 (£9)	Quincy	< $17 (£10)	Gewurztraminer Alto Adige	< $28 (£17)
Dry white from Penedès	< $17 (£10)	Bandol	< $20 (£14)	Pouilly-Fuissé	< $35 (£22)

SLEEK, FULL-BODIED, DRY WHITE WINES

Dry white from Rías Baixas	< $14 (£9)	Pessac-Léognan	> $17 (£10)	Chassagne-Montrachet	> $28 (£17)
Savennières	< $20 (£14)	Napa Valley Chardonnay	< $35 (£22)	Hermitage	> $28 (£17)
Dry white from Rueda	< $20 (£14)	Châteauneuf-du-Pape	> $20 (£14)	Corton-Charlemagne	> $35 (£22)
Vouvray	< $28 (£17)	Meursault	> $20 (£14)	Puligny-Montrachet	> $40 (£25)
Chablis Premier Cru	< $28 (£17)	Chablis Grand Cru	> $28 (£17)	Montrachet	> $55 (£35)

VERY AROMATIC DRY WHITE WINES

Muscat d'Alsace	< $14 (£9)	Gewurztraminer d'Alsace	< $20 (£14)	Condrieu	> $28 (£17)
Alsace Pinot Gris	< $14 (£9)	Fino or Manzanilla sherry	< $20 (£14)	Vin Jaune from the Jura	> $28 (£17)
Alsace Riesling	< $14 (£9)	Château-Chalon	> $28 (£17)		

SEMI-DRY AND SWEET WHITE WINES

Pacherenc-du-Vic-Bilh	< $14 (£9)	Cérons	< $28 (£17)	Riesling SGN	> $28 (£17)
Cadillac	< $17 (£10)	Vouvray Moelleux	< $28 (£17)	Sauternes	> $28 (£17)
Coteaux-du-Layon	< $28 (£17)	Late Harvest Riesling (VT)	< $35 (£22)	Hungarian Tokaj	> $28 (£17)
Loupiac	< $28 (£17)	Passito de Pantelleria	< $55 (£35)	Gewurztraminer SGN	> $35 (£22)
Monbazillac	< $28 (£17)	Barsac	> $28 (£17)	Pinot Gris SGN	> $35 (£22)
Montlouis Moelleux	< $28 (£17)	Late Harvest Gewurztraminer (VT)	> $28 (£17)	German Trockenbeerenauslese	> $70 (£45)
Ste-Croix-du-Mont	< $28 (£17)	Quarts-de-Chaume	> $28 (£17)		

NATURAL SWEET WINES AND FORTIFIED WINES

Mireval Muscat	< $14 (£9)	Banyuls	> $14 (£9)	Muscat de Beaumes-de-Venise	< $28 (£17)
Muscat de Rivesaltes	< $14 (£9)	Rivesaltes	> $14 (£9)	Muscat de Frontignan	< $28 (£17)
Pineau des Charentes	< $20 (£14)	Macvin du Jura	< $28 (£17)	Rasteau	< $28 (£17)
Porto	< $20 (£14)	Maury	< $28 (£17)		

SPARKLING WINES

Lambrusco	< $10 (£6)	Vouvray	< $28 (£17)	Montlouis, Saumur	< $14 (£9)
Clairette de Die	< $14 (£9)	Blanquette de Limoux	< $14 (£9)	Crémant du Jura	< $14 (£9)
Crémant de Bordeaux	< $14 (£9)	Crémant d'Alsace	< $14 (£9)	Cava	< $17 (£10)
Gaillac	< $14 (£9)	Crémant de Bourgogne	< $14 (£9)	Champagne	> $18 (£11)

BUYING FROM WINE SHOPS AND SUPERMARKETS

Most wines consumed at home today are purchased in supermarkets. While the choice and prices are attractive, informative service is often lacking, except for the rare stores with dedicated wine department staff. A good wine retailer will offer sound advice and sometimes have rare wines; however, prices are usually higher than in supermarkets.

Supermarkets

STRENGTHS. The main strength is, of course, their prices. Due to centralized buying and low logistics costs, supermarkets offer very competitive prices in all wine categories. They are often lower than those of wine retailers, and sometimes even lower than those available at the winery itself. Faced with the growing demand for good wines, some supermarkets have hired highly qualified, specialized buyers, with a wine industry background. Others have entered into contracts with big wineries or even wine-producing regions in order to develop a good quality brand of their own. Significant progress has also been made regarding the display and storage of wines, especially in superstores. Bottles are generally not left on the shelves exposed to light for very long, as turnover is high. Some supermarkets have even

Today's market offers thousands of wines from all around the world. Most purchases are made in supermarkets, where prices are usually the most competitive. Wine retailers offer specialized selections and valuable advice.

created fine wine "cellar" areas where the wines are stored away from light at the correct temperature.

WEAKNESSES. Supermarkets receive the most criticism from wine producers. In order to get their wines stocked, they are forced not only to commit to large quantities, but also commercial terms that could become risky in a difficult year. The large-scale distribution market therefore favors the bigger producers and *négociants*, and wine regions with high production volumes. Another issue is that wines may be arranged on the shelves without any real respect for region. Plus, a customer might find a good wine, and then learn that it is not available a few weeks later. Finally, in the absence of a salesperson equipped to provide advice, you are left on your own to make sense of labels (*see* pp.104–15).

IN CONCLUSION. Most supermarkets today offer consumers a huge range of wines at very competitive prices. However, do not

Wine fairs and festivals at big retailers

Wine fairs or festivals organized by large retailers annually or bi-annually present some excellent opportunities. While there will always be both good and some less impressive wines on offer, genuine bargains can be found with a little searching. The best deals are usually from recent good vintages and currently popular import regions. Beware of less successful vintages and bottles from small wineries with fancy labels that may contain a very ordinary wine. It is advisable to visit these events during the first few days, as the best bargains tend to disappear very quickly. Take along a guidebook, wine supplement, a wine magazine (some of the leading magazines are *Wine Spectator*, *Wine Enthusiast*, *Wine & Spirits*, Robert Parker's *The Wine Advocate*, *Decanter*, and *The World of Fine Wine*), or an internet-enabled smart phone. They can all prove to be very useful.

> Wine retailers should always be able to help you discover interesting new wines.

> A wine merchant's shop in St-Émilion, France.

expect to discover some wonderful gem of a wine, since many producers choose, for image reasons, not to be represented in this segment of the market.

The independent wine retailer

For many wines, the wine retailer remains the main link between the producer and consumer. Some merchants have professional qualifications, although not all are officially recognized. Good wine retailers will impress you with their accessibility, and their love and knowledge of wine. They will travel to wine regions and trade tastings regularly to find new and great value wines, which they will then be pleased to offer their customers. Their range will include the classics, little-known wines, older vintages, seasonal wines, easy-drinking bottles, and wines to lay down. A wine merchant should be able to advise both the occasional buyer and the serious enthusiast.

VALUABLE ADVICE. Like a sommelier, the wine retailer's job is to help customers find the right balance between quality, price, and good food-pairing combinations. Like a personal adviser, they can help the neophyte with the mysteries of wine and offer regular tastings at their store. The services of a good wine merchant warrant slightly higher prices (between 10 and 20 percent on average) than those of the supermarkets. However, not all wine merchants possess this ideal profile.

Wine retail chains

Halfway between the independent wine retailer and the supermarket, wine chain stores (such as Binny's in Illinois and Crown in Florida) attempt to combine the services of the former with the competitive prices of the latter. While prices are kept low by centralized purchasing, the service that you receive will depend on the manager and their team. Chains are found around many large cities and offer a good selection of all styles of wine in a wide range of prices.

ADDITIONAL SERVICES. Most chains organize tastings, sales promotions, and wine fairs. Some also offer detailed catalogs and special services such as the possibility of buying "futures" or en primeur (see pp.128–9) wines for laying down (sometimes at prices lower than those available at the estate), home delivery, or express shipping of a bottle or case to friends.

DID YOU KNOW...?

Retailers often have their own brands. To meet growing demand, many large retailers have created their own labels. These are wines from various sources, produced by cooperatives or négociants and bottled directly on behalf of a retailer. The quality of certain wines is often praised by critics. (One example is the Kirkland Signature line by Costco.) But the quality of specific wines cannot be judged from the store's general policy, as this may be to offer everything from the best wines to the absolute cheapest.

BUYING FROM WINERIES

Direct purchasing has several advantages: in addition to possible discounts, it also can be an opportunity to discover little-known wines and to build a special relationship with a winemaker or a member of staff.

Buying at the property

Buying at the property is often a good way to obtain good wines that are not widely distributed, or possibly not at all. Moreover, establishing an ongoing relationship with staff at the property can sometimes lead to access to older vintages or special edition bottlings.

THE RIGHT CONDITIONS. Visiting a winery can be a great opportunity to learn. If you can take a tour, seeing a clean, well-organized cellar is a good sign. For a successful tasting, it's best to make an appointment, especially around harvest time. If you like the wine, you will be happy to buy a few bottles. If you don't, the situation can be awkward, and you may feel obliged to buy some wine in order not to offend the producer.

It can often be difficult to decide with confidence when you're there with tasting room staff, so sampling some wines from the same region before you visit can be helpful. Without that kind of prep, wines that seemed enjoyable when tasted at the vineyard or in a beautiful cellar may subsequently reveal themselves to be quite ordinary. The certainty of having made the right choice is worth the advance effort.

SOME PRECAUTIONS. For visitors to French wine regions, don't buy wine without an invoice. All bottles should be clearly labeled and have a *"capsule-congé,"* a capsule with the government seal on it, showing that the relevant tax has been paid. Alternatively, they should be accompanied by an official document called a *"congé"* (*see* box). Do not let yourself be taken in by an offer of "declassified wine," which has no real meaning, since any wine that does not comply with the appellation regulations must be thrown out. If such a purchase were inspected during your trip, you would be likely to receive a heavy fine.

WINE TASTINGS. Regional tasting events for the general public offer a very wide range of wines. The friendly atmosphere makes them a convenient and enjoyable way to meet producers, and to taste a lot of wines in comparatively little time. Many regional wine producers that you already know

Wine tourism is booming. Wine trails are becoming more established across the world. They provide guidance on exploring a wine region, over a weekend or longer. Check out promotional websites for your favorite wine regions for more information.

will be there; and if you ask them in advance, they will be able to bring you any wines that you want to buy.

Buying from a cooperative

There are more than half a million grape growers in France, and millions across Europe. Not all market their own wine; some sell their grapes to a cooperative. Cooperatives offer a service to growers without much land or without the equipment to make and store wine. They will market the grower's entire production, either by delivering it in bulk to merchants or by selling the bottled wine themselves. They generally produce wines that offer good value. The best cooperatives pay the growers according to grape quality and encourage the planting of noble grape varieties, thereby contributing to improving a region's reputation for good quality wines.

Some growers are members of a cooperative that gives them a share of their production in the form of wine bottled with

> Keeping notes and tasting wines several times helps you to make an informed choice.

Proof of "congé" (clearance) is a legal requirement in France

Transporting wine in France is strictly regulated. A "capsule-congé" with a tax stamp must be affixed to the top of each bottle, to show that duties have been paid. Wine bought in bulk or in bottles without capsules must be accompanied by a "congé" (clearance certificate), issued by the wine producer or by the nearest tax office. This document should include the name of the vendor and the wine, the volume and number of containers, the consignee, and the method and duration of transportation. Transporting wine in France without clearance constitutes tax fraud and is punishable by a fine.

> Traveling around a wine region and visiting wineries is a great way to learn about wine.

their own labels, which they can then sell. This practice is very common in Champagne, where many wines that are associated with a property are in fact produced by a cooperative, as the latter is legally considered to be an extension of the property. In such cases, it is best to go directly to the cooperative where the prices are likely to be lower for an equivalent wine.

In bottles or in bulk?

The purchase of wine "in bulk" (*i.e.* not in bottles) is now common, not only for everyday drinking but also for some higher quality wines. The Bag-in-Box system has more or less replaced the old European "Cubitainer" (rigid plastic box). The wine is prevented from coming into contact with air as the three- or five-liter bag gradually contracts as wine is consumed. (The bag is in a cardboard box equipped with a tap.) This is a good way of storing larger volumes of wine; but they should be consumed within two weeks of first opening the bag. This packaging format is now seen at wineries, wine retailers, European cooperatives, and most supermarkets. If you buy European wine in the older Cubitainer format, it should be consumed quickly. Buying in bulk generally gives you around 25 to 33 percent more wine for the same price (as bottles).

TRUE OR FALSE?

Buying from a winery is always less expensive.

FALSE. Buying directly from a winery, especially in large quantities, remains one of the most popular ways of obtaining good wine at an attractive price. However, not all producers discount like this, and some even discourage it by aligning their prices with those at wine retailers, in order to avoid unfair competition.

Transporting wine

Whether wine is white, rosé, or red, sudden changes in temperature should be avoided. When moving wine or taking delivery of wine, it is best to avoid periods of extreme heat or cold. Furthermore, wine is heavy: a case of 12 bottles weighs about 35 lbs (16 kg)—more if the cases are made of wood or if the winery uses heavier grade bottles. (Sparkling wine bottles are the heaviest.) If you are a serious shopper, it's a good idea to check your vehicle's loading capacity before filling your trunk, to avoid damaging the suspension.

Once the wine has safely arrived at its destination, the bottles should be checked and then placed directly into a cool, dark spot. Let the wine rest for one to two weeks before drinking, or several months for old vintages of fine wines. The above precautions also apply if you have the wine delivered (*see* box, p.131).

DID YOU KNOW...?

Some European producers sell a portion of their wine at depots on the outskirts of large towns. Bottles are simply displayed on pallets or in crates, and prices are often great. However, these big discount stores require a degree of caution from the wine enthusiast. It is important to be attentive to aspects such as the origin, packaging, and vintage of the wines. The words "mise en bouteilles à la propriété" ("bottled at the property") are usually a guarantee of authenticity.

1 **2**

Buying wine futures or en *primeur*

Buying wine futures or *en primeur* is to purchase wine before it has been released to the market. It usually, but not always, refers to the top wines of Bordeaux, and in most cases will prove to be a good deal; but there is a speculative side to buying wine futures that carries some risk.

THE PRINCIPLE

Wines of the most recent vintage, still being matured and not yet bottled, are sold by subscription on a preview basis. The prices can be much lower than those listed when the wines are available on the open market, that is to say 18 months to two years later. For example, a wine purchased *en primeur* in 2011 will have been made from the 2010 harvest, and will not be available in bottles until 2013. One could say that the *en primeur* system functions on a *quid pro quo* basis. The producer receives advance payment, and in return the purchaser receives a discount on the future price of the wine. The procedure is straightforward: you agree to buy a certain quantity of the latest vintage while it is still in barrels at a fixed per bottle price. You pay half the value of the order immediately, and receive a reservation certificate. The balance of payment then becomes due on delivery. The terms of sale (such as quantities, possibility of mixed orders, delivery dates, for example) depend on the producers. Subscriptions usually open during the spring or, at the latest, during the summer following the harvest, for a certain proportion of the wine. They are open for just a limited period: between two and three months. Prices are established at tastings, in Bordeaux, for example, during April. These tastings are attended by thousands of professionals from all over the world (wine merchants, sommeliers, journalists). The tastings will be covered by the media (Wine Spectator, *Revue du Vin de France*, etc.), and it is advisable to read their reports carefully before approaching producers or wine merchants. The prices of the wines vary every year depending on the quality of the vintage, the volumes produced, and demand.

1. Vines at Château Lynch-Bages in Pauillac, one of the classified growths that may be purchased *en primeur*.
2. A cellar in Burgundy.
3. Sampling in the winery at Château Bon Pasteur in Pomerol.
4 and 5. In the spring, wine professionals taste wines that have just been made, so as to form an idea of their potential.

WHICH WINES ARE INVOLVED?

Traditionally, the *en primeur* system operates in Bordeaux; but, in recent years, it has gained popularity in other wine regions such as Burgundy, the Rhône Valley, Alsace, and elsewhere. In Bordeaux, some 200 wines (the classified growths and the *cru bourgeois*) are involved. The best deals are to be found among the top *crus bourgeois* of the Médoc and Haut-Médoc, and certain outstanding châteaux in the so-called "peripheral" appellations such as Castillon-Côtes-de-Bordeaux, Côtes-de-Blaye, Côtes-de-Bourg, Listrac, Fronsac, etc.

MANY ADVANTAGES

There are many advantages to this type of purchase. Buying *en primeur* is the best way of obtaining a wine below its market price. It is possible to see savings of 20 to 30 percent on the final sale price, depending on the year. Buying this way ensures that you obtain a wine that may become very hard to find, since it provides access to highly sought-after labels and to fine wines that are produced in small volumes. It is particularly interesting if you want to build up a good cellar. Finally, speculating on the *grand crus* can be a way of generating substantial capital gains.

BUT ALSO A FEW RISKS

There are risks involved in buying *en primeur* wines, both in terms of price and quality. For example, if prices collapse, the final market price may be less than the subscription price. The wine that is eventually delivered may turn out to be not as good as you had expected. Judging a wine's potential by tasting it in its extreme youth is a difficult exercise, particularly as the final proportions of the various grape varieties and vineyard blocks may not have been determined. Plus, it is not always easy to predict how a wine will evolve. These problems can be minimized by following a few simple rules: trust the producer, look carefully at the shipping charges, as they can be very high, and, if possible, form a group in order to share costs. Lastly, give preference to average vintages, as they usually offer the best deals.

WHERE TO BUY *EN PRIMEUR*

Formerly reserved for wine merchants, the *en primeur* market is now accessible through a variety of channels that include wine shops, mail order companies, the internet (see next page for addresses of sites), and producers themselves.

BUYING THROUGH OTHER CHANNELS

The sale of wine by mail order and in particular via the internet has seen considerable growth in recent years. There are some excellent opportunities available online, as long as you deal with reputable sites. Auctions are also becoming of increasing interest to informed enthusiasts.

Buying online

The internet has almost completely replaced mail-order catalogs. Online service is mainly provided by wine merchants, who likely sell all types of wine. There are two kinds of cyber wine merchants. The first category consists of those with little or no inventories who work on a just-in-time basis. They buy their wines from wineries or merchants as a function of demand. The second category consists of the large wine merchants who already have a large inventory and can offer both *en primeur* wines (*see* pp.128–9) and older vintages. Finally, many producers also sell their wines via the internet.

HOW TO CHOOSE A WEBSITE. There are hundreds, if not thousands, of websites that sell wines online. The most interesting are those that also provide information and advice about their products, such as food-pairing suggestions, etc. When using online services, it is essential to compare offers and terms of sale, *i.e.* the quality and range of wines available; the price per bottle, which may or may not include tax; the minimum quantity that may be purchased; shipping costs, which can be very high; and the after-sales service in the event of a complaint. When an order is placed, specify the exact date of delivery; if it is a grouped order (*see* box on following page),

> A few rare bottles of fortified wine sold at auction at Sotheby's in London

Reliable sites for buying wine online

www.bbr.com Britain's oldest wine and spirit merchant, having traded from the same shop for over 300 years. The website offers an extensive and eclectic wine list and also offers *en primeur* wines.

www.brownderby.com Lots of great California wines at this mid-America retailer, with some hard-to-find gems and always low mark-ups.

www.chambersstwine.com Impressively esoteric selections by this New York merchant, with plenty from the Loire and Bordeaux.

www.directwine.co.uk An independent wine merchant located in Belfast, this website offers a comprehensive range of high quality wines. It also offers *en primeur* wines.

www.jeanmerlaut.com Operated by a large family of wine producers and wine merchants, this French site offers some of the best value for wine on the internet, particularly in the Bordeaux *en primeur* market.

www.klwines.com A serious California wine retailer for more than 30 years. Wines from around the world, and real-time inventory shown on the website.

www.laithwaites.co.uk The largest independent merchant in the UK. Laithwaites offers a broad selection of wines and also offers *en primeur* wines.

www.wine.com The largest internet wine commerce site in America. It offers a broad selection of wines and competitive prices.

www.wineandco.com A French site that has established itself as a serious contender in terms of choice, deliveries, and providing information.

www.1855.com This French site has a simple, straightforward style, and offers a selection of more than 500 wines, with a wide variety of Bordeaux classified growths, frequently at attractive prices. Single bottle purchases are possible.

Payment and shipping

Shipping costs for wines purchased online vary from one site to another. Some sites offer free shipping for orders above a certain amount. Make sure you find out in advance. Secure online payment by credit card is almost always available. Wines tend to be delivered within 5 to 10 business days. For all such sites, it is advisable to call before ordering in order to be sure of the terms of payment and delivery.

> Bids by candlelight at the Hospices de Beaune.

decide on a place where the bottles can be stored, and check the merchandise for errors or breakages on arrival.

Through wine clubs

Wine clubs, like that run by *The Wall Street Journal* or other publications, also have a solid online presence and provide an additional guarantee regarding the wines offered, advice, and tasting. Big clubs provide a very full range of services. Some offer their members wines that are selected by well-known critics and bottled under the club's own label. They also may offer courses in wine tasting. Almost all operate by home delivery, though this will depend on the alcohol laws in your state. In general, any basic wines are sold at higher prices than you will find in supermarkets. However, wine enthusiasts can find *grand*

It is possible to participate in an auction without being present, simply by communicating your maximum bid to the auctioneer at least 24 hours in advance, or by bidding by telephone, or even via the internet.

DID YOU KNOW...?

Organizing a group purchase can be worthwhile in order to qualify for prices that are usually available only to trade customers. This can be done through a wine club, or simply among friends, but in all cases it's worth taking great care in the preparation and delivery of the order (the quantities of each wine, collection of payment upon ordering, where the wines will be stored, etc.). Group purchases usually enable savings on shipping costs, and are also a good option when buying en primeur *(see pp.128–9).*

cru wines and wines from very good estates at prices below those charged by wine merchants.

Auctions

Auctions are not just for very expensive, rare bottles of famous wines. They may provide an opportunity for a collector to find wines from the vintage of their birth year. The informed wine enthusiast, assuming they can control the urge to indulge in a wild bidding spree, can acquire a case of wine from a good vintage, which may or may not be famous, but is going at a good price.

WHAT TYPES OF WINE? Most wines sold at auction are ready to drink, or soon will be; so it should not be necessary to age them in a cellar. Bargains are found by avoiding very prestigious wines (such as famous sweet wines, Bordeaux *grand crus*, etc.). To identify interesting lots, the neophyte would be well-advised to seek the help of an expert, in the form of a friend or a wine merchant. It is also worth obtaining a price list for fine wines from various years that has been drawn up by experts, in order to avoid overpaying.

PRACTICAL INFORMATION. Information on auctions in France can be found in the *Gazette Drouot*, available from newsstands, which lists all the upcoming auctions in Paris and other areas. One then contacts the auctioneers to request a detailed catalog of the lots and their estimated value, and information on the condition of the bottles, such as the label and the cork, the level of the wine in the bottle neck (*see also* pp.142–3), whether it is in the original case, and how it was stored. In addition to the auction price, there is usually commission, taxes, and shipping and insurance costs, which can add up to 20 percent to the basic price.

HOW SHOULD WINE BE STORED?

THE IDEAL ENVIRONMENT FOR STORING WINE

The romantic image of an old candlelit cellar is not necessarily the best place to store wine. If a wine is to achieve optimal ageing, then some basic principles need to be observed.

Temperature: cool and unchanging

THE EFFECT OF TEMPERATURE. Wine should be kept at a constant temperature between 46 and 64°F (8–18°C), and ideally between 50 and 54°F (10–12°C). Below these temperatures, it will not improve, although it may remain drinkable for months or even years.

High temperatures, above 68°F (20°C), are more damaging because the wine will age prematurely. More seriously, it will deteriorate, losing its color and fresh flavors. With this said, it is primarily sudden changes in temperature that should be avoided: a gradual increase in cellar temperature from 54°F (12°C) in the winter to 64°F (18°C) in the summer will not harm the wine. However, the same variation in one day—or even one week—could result in problems. As the wine expands and contracts in the bottle, unwelcome pressure is applied to the cork. Eventually, the wine seeps out around the cork, leaving a sticky deposit

If wine is to be kept for more than a few weeks, it should be stored in correct conditions. For this, a good cellar should be ventilated, dark, clean, quiet, and fairly humid.

on the capsule. The bottle has begun to "weep," which is never a good sign.

CONTROLLING THE ENVIRONMENT. When you choose a storage area, record the maximum and minimum temperatures in various locations in order to identify the coolest spots (ideally, do this over a year). If possible, locate sources of heat and reduce their effect, for example by insulating hot water pipes. Block out any sources of very cold air. Insulate doors leading to heated parts of the house with extruded polystyrene ("Stryofoam"). The goal is to obtain as constant a temperature as possible.

Wine should not be exposed to light

Light damages wine, especially white wines and sparkling wines, to which it eventually gives a rotten egg character. Make sure your storage area is dark and screen any sources of direct outside light. Install a low-power light source (25 watts) to permit

> A spacious cellar can be made into a special place to enjoy wines with friends.

> Wine needs a cool, dark, quiet environment to mature in peace.

you to move around, but avoid fluorescent and halogen lamps. Make sure you always turn the light off when leaving.

High humidity

The ideal humidity is 75 to 80 percent. Too much humidity can cause labels to peel off, and mold to grow on corks. But a lack of moisture is even more dangerous, as the corks will dry out (see p.142).

If your storage area is very dry, the humidity can be increased by covering the floor with a layer of gravel, and then sprinkling it with water on a regular basis. However, in much of the US, the natural humidity is generally sufficient. At an extreme, dehumidifiers can prevent excessive moisture. But they can be expensive, and may be worth installing only in very large cellars. In a small storage area, the ventilation can be improved and specific sources of moisture can be insulated.

Good ventilation but no drafts

Air circulation is essential, even though it can raise the temperature. A good storage area should have air vents or fans for the entry and circulation of external air. However, it also needs to be possible to seal off air inlets during very cold or very hot weather. If the cellar is north-south oriented, place fans as low as possible on the north side and as high as possible on the south side. Convection will cause warm air to exit through the high vents on the south side. This will then be replaced by cool air entering from the north side.

Hygiene: beware of bad smells!

Thoroughly clean the area before storing any wine. Use a disinfectant, preferably an odorless one, to remove mold and grime. Then, on brick or stone walls, apply whitewash. This porous paint will not prevent natural ventilation. Avoid storing your bottles next to paint or fuel, as these can generate fumes that will affect the wine, even through the cork. Vegetables, or any plant or food products, nearby can result in the appearance of fungi and insect pests.

A quiet environment: avoid vibrations

Frequent, strong vibrations can have a damaging effect on wine, whether they come from inside (from a household appliance, for example) or outside (from a road that is used by heavy vehicles, or a nearby subway or rail line). There is a risk that they can cause wines to age more quickly.

The ideal storage area

An appropriate wine storage area should meet the criteria below.

– A north-facing orientation;
– Ventilation via a door and/or small north-facing air inlet near the ground, and a south-facing static or mechanical outlet near the ceiling;
– High humidity (75 to 80 percent);
– A constant temperature, between 46 and 64°F (8–18°C);
– Darkness;
– Clean, no odors;
– Quiet;
– Damp, gravel floor;
– Stone or brick walls.

CREATING A CELLAR

When creating an area to store or age wine, the wine enthusiast should take into account the number of bottles and type of wine to be stored, and also—more importantly—the space available. Whether you live in a town or in the country, you will find options and solutions for every situation and budget.

Before starting

DEFINE THE PROJECT. Spending some time thinking about your cellar before you embark on its creation is highly recommended. Poor design can result in exorbitant costs, out of proportion to the value of the wines to be stored, or a failure to fulfill the cellar's primary purpose of providing the best conditions in which to age your wines. First, it is necessary to estimate the number and type of bottles to be stored. A hundred bottles of the same type of wine will not occupy the same space as 10 batches of wines from different wine-producing areas. Will the cellar be purely for storing wine, or also for tasting?

DETERMINE THE LOCATION. It's then necessary to check that the proposed space (basement, garage, shed, etc.) meets the requirements of a good cellar (*see* pp.134–5). The use of an unsuitable space could involve the installation of expensive equipment (*e.g.* air

Once stored, a wine should not be handled. You should not have to move one bottle to reach another. Avoid rigid layouts that cannot easily be changed.

conditioning to maintain the cellar at the right temperature) and add considerably to your electricity bill. Unless you use a cellar-installation specialist, it is best to draw up a precise specification, which should then be scrupulously respected by the person or contractor who undertakes the work.

PROTECT YOUR INVESTMENT. A large cellar should be protected in the event of a flood, fire, or burglary, especially if it is in the basement of an apartment building. Such protection can be very expensive (reinforced doors, insurance, etc.), and it is sometimes preferable to purchase a wine storage cabinet or to rent cellar space elsewhere.

Turnkey cellars

The creation of a cellar has to take into account a large number of parameters (the nature of the site, choice of materials, etc.) if it is to function correctly. If you are not a home-improvement enthusiast, it may make sense to use a specialized contractor to install either a prefabricated cellar—an underground vaulted or spiral type unit that goes into a hole in the ground—or a custom-built cellar in a garage, a basement, or even inside an apartment.

For the first solution, prices start at around $10,000 (£6,000) for a small cellar that can store about 600 bottles. A spiral cellar with capacity for 1,000 bottles should cost around $30,000 (£20,000) complete with stairs and concrete compartments. For a larger cellar, with room for 2,000 bottles, expect to spend around $50,000 (£30,000). Such models can be viewed at manufacturer showrooms; it is essential to visit them before making a purchase.

> A prefabricated underground cellar.

Renting a cellar

Residents of large cities can rent storage space. Depending on the service, the wine is stored lockers or in walk-in rooms. Current rates may be about $25 (£15) per month for a 12-case locker. Security is excellent, but renting such a space requires working around certain business hours for retrieving or depositing bottles. A short-term cellar at home is therefore advisable, where wine can be stored for a few days in appropriate conditions.

> To be completely stable, metal racks should be attached to the floor and wall.

Converting a space into a cellar

As long as proper research is carried out before starting work, the conversion of an existing space into a cellar can be an economical and convenient solution.

BASEMENT CELLARS. It is essential to check the temperature and humidity at different times of the year and ensure good ventilation (via air vents). In the event of insufficient humidity, the floor can be covered with gravel or even sand (*see* p.135). Hot water and heating pipes should be insulated. Poor thermal insulation can be improved by building a brick wall separated from the existing wall by an air gap. The installation of an air conditioner may be necessary.

GARAGE CELLARS. Whether occupying all or part of a garage, these cellars generally require very good insulation. To separate a corner cellar, it's advisable to build a concrete block wall. The walls and door will need to be insulated with extruded polystyrene ("Styrofoam"), and the ceiling with a double layer of the same material or fiberglass. In the absence of an air vent, it may be necessary to equip the space with an air conditioner and a humidifier.

Wine "fridge"

If space for a suitably protected cellar is not available, then a wine cabinet or "fridge" may prove to be the best solution, especially for modest quantities of wine (less than 200 bottles). There is a wide range of models of all sizes (starting at $350/£200 for 30 bottles). The simplest enable wines to be stored but not to be aged, while more sophisticated models offer two or three temperature zones, with different compartments for storage, chilling, or bringing wines to room temperature; the largest models can hold up to 200 bottles and cost around $3,000–$5,000 (£1,800–£3,000).

Wine cabinets may be equipped with a simple cooling system or a dual system that also provides heat if the cabinet is placed in an area that is not heated in the winter. Make sure that any model you consider is equipped with an anti-vibration system. Also, in the event of a malfunction, a good model should ensure very gradual warming or cooling.

DID YOU KNOW...?

You can install a cellar in your apartment. *A north- or east-facing room can be used as a cellar, provided the wine can be protected from light and the right conditions in terms of temperature and ventilation can be maintained. These can be difficult to achieve, and often require the installation of an air conditioner, making it an expensive operation. This kind of cellar is best used for storing bottles intended for consumption in the near future (a year at most), because the wine will not age properly. The same applies to smaller spaces, even if they are well insulated, such as a cupboard under your stairs, or a closet in a bedroom. Take care to avoid vibrations, light, heat, and poor ventilation.*

Four different wine collections

Classic or eclectic, simple or sophisticated, a wine collection will always reflect its owner's preferences. It also will depend on the available storage space and how much money you are willing to spend. For a certain number of bottles in the same style of wine, for example sparkling wines, you can choose a less prestigious appellation (Crémant de Bourgogne or Cava, for example) in the case of a modest budget; or, if the selection is not limited by price, a top quality vintage Champagne. Here are four examples of a well-balanced collection based on four different budgets.

The simple cellar

STYLE	NO.	NAME OF WINE
Light or fruity dry white wines	6	Bourgogne Aligoté, Cheverny, Entre-Deux-Mers, Pinot Blanc d'Alsace, Côtes-de-Provence, Corsican wines.
Sleek, full-bodied, dry white wines	10	Chablis Premier Cru, Meursault, Savennières, Vouvray, Gewurztraminer.
Sweet white wines	4	Ste-Croix-du-Mont, Cérons, Coteaux-de-l'Aubance, Monbazillac.
Fruity red wines	15	Beaujolais, Hautes-Côtes-de-Beaune, Anjou, Côtes-de-Forez, Coteaux-du-Lyonnais, St-Nicolas-de-Bourgueil, Bordeaux, Côtes-du-Rhône-Villages, Vins de Pays d'Oc.
Complex red wines	10	Bordeaux Supérieur, Haut-Médoc, St-Émilion, Graves, Cahors, Buzet, Minervois-La-Livinière, Pécharmant, Mercurey.
Rosé wines	4	Côtes-de-Provence, Luberon, Côtes-du-Jura, Corbières, Lirac, Tavel.
Sparkling wines	6	Blanquette de Limoux, Clairette de Die, Gaillac, Saumur, Vouvray, Crémant de Bourgogne, Crémant d'Alsace.

The convivial cellar

STYLE	NO.	NAME OF WINE
Light or fruity dry white wines	12	Muscadet, Entre-Deux-Mers, Bordeaux, Petit Chablis, Sylvaner d'Alsace, Côtes-de-Provence.
Sleek, full-bodied, dry white wines	12	Pessac-Léognan, Graves, Chablis Grand Cru, Meursault, Puligny-Montrachet, Condrieu.
Sweet white wines	6	Loupiac, Ste-Croix-du-Mont, Coteaux-du-Layon, Montlouis, Late Harvest Alsace Pinot Gris, Late Harvest Alsace Riesling, Jurançon.
Fruity red wines	12	Bordeaux, Bordeaux Supérieur, Hautes-Côtes-de-Nuits, Saumur-Champigny, Bourgueil, Vin de Savoie, Côtes-du-Rhône-Villages.
Complex red wines	12	Haut-Médoc, Médoc, Pauillac, St-Estèphe, St-Julien, St-Émilion, Pessac-Léognan, Volnay, Vosne-Romanée, Crozes-Hermitage, St-Joseph, Bandol.
Rosé wines	6	Bordeaux Clairet, Marsannay, Languedoc, Irouléguy, Palette.
Sparkling wines	6	Dry non-vintage Champagne.
Natural sweet wines	4	Banyuls, Muscat de Rivesaltes, Muscat de Beaumes-de-Venise, Port.

The refined cellar

STYLE	NO.	NAME OF WINE
Light or fruity dry white wines	12	Premières-Côtes-de-Blaye, Bordeaux, Graves, Bandol, Bellet, Cassis, Coteaux-d'Aix, St-Véran, Sancerre, Roussette de Savoie, Jurançon sec.
Sleek, full-bodied, dry white wines	18	Pessac-Léognan, Puligny-Montrachet, Chassagne-Montrachet, Meursault, Chablis Grand Cru, Savennières, Vouvray, Château-Châlon, Condrieu, Riesling d'Alsace Grand Cru.
Sweet white wines	12	Sauternes Crus Classés, Bonnezeaux, Gewurztraminer Sélection de Grains Nobles, Riesling Sélection de Grains Nobles, Vouvray, Tokaj.
	3	Loupiac, Ste-Croix-du-Mont, Coteaux-du-Layon, Montlouis, Jurançon.
Fruity red wines	12	Bordeaux, Crus du Beaujolais, Hautes-Côtes-de-Nuits, Saumur-Champigny, Bourgueil, St-Nicolas-de-Bourgueil, Vin de Savoie, Côtes-du-Rhône-Villages.
Complex red wines	18	Haut-Médoc, Médoc Crus Classés, St-Émilion Grand Cru, Pomerol, Pommard, Volnay, Chambolle-Musigny, Gevrey-Chambertin, Côte-Rôtie, Hermitage, Cornas, Bandol.
Rosé wines	6	Bordeaux Clairet, Marsannay, Coteaux-du-Languedoc, Irouléguy, Palette, Côtes-de-Provence.
Sparkling wines	6	Top brand Champagnes, vintage Champagnes.
	6	Saumur, Vouvray, Clairette de Die.
Natural sweet wines	5	Port, Rivesaltes, Banyuls, Maury, Rasteau.

The prestige cellar

STYLE	NO.	NAME OF WINE
Light or fruity dry white wines	24	Premières-Côtes-de-Blaye, Bordeaux, Graves, Bandol, Bellet, Cassis, Coteaux-d'Aix-en-Provence, St-Véran, Sancerre, Roussette de Savoie, Jurançon sec.
Sleek, full-bodied, dry white wines	24	Pessac-Léognan, Puligny-Montrachet, Chassagne-Montrachet, Meursault, Chablis Grand Cru, Savennières, Vouvray, Château-Châlon, Condrieu, Riesling d'Alsace Grand Cru.
Sweet white wines	12	Sauternes Crus Classés, Bonnezeaux, Gewurztraminer Sélection de Grains Nobles, Riesling Sélection de Grains Nobles, Vouvray, Tokaj.
	6	Loupiac, Ste-Croix-du-Mont, Coteaux-du-Layon, Montlouis, Jurançon.
Fruity red wines	24	Bordeaux, Crus du Beaujolais, Hautes-Côtes-de-Nuits, Saumur-Champigny, Bourgueil, St-Nicolas-de-Bourgueil, Vin de Savoie, Côtes-du-Rhône-Villages.
Complex red wines	30	Haut-Médoc, Médoc Crus Classés, St-Émilion Grand Cru, Pomerol, Pommard, Volnay, Chambolle-Musigny, Gevrey-Chambertin, Côte-Rôtie, Hermitage, Cornas, Bandol.
Rosé wines	12	Bordeaux Clairet, Marsannay, Languedoc, Irouléguy, Palette, Côtes-de-Provence.
Sparkling wines	12	Top brand Champagnes, vintage Champagnes.
	6	Saumur, Vouvray, Clairette de Die.
Natural sweet wines	5	Port, Rivesaltes, Banyuls, Maury, Rasteau.

IN THE SILENCE OF THE CELLAR

Wine is fragile and needs to be treated with care in order to age properly and realize its full potential. Within the dark coolness of the cellar a silent alchemy occurs.

1. Domaine Trimbach (Alsace).
2. Domaine Michel Juillot (Burgundy).
3. Domaine Hugel & Fils (Alsace).
4 and 8. Private cellars.
5. Louis Roederer Champagne.
6. Domaine Bouchard Père & Fils (Burgundy).
7. Domaine Jean-Maurice Raffault (Loire Valley).
9. Château Lascombes (Bordeaux).
10. Château L'Angélus (Bordeaux).

ORGANIZING AND MANAGING YOUR CELLAR

When all the conditions for good storage have been met, the next stage is to plan the layout. Bottles need to be properly arranged so that they age in the best conditions. And, most importantly, so that you can find them with ease when the time comes to drink them.

Storing bottles

POSITION AND LOCATION OF BOTTLES. With the exception of brandies, port, natural sweet wines, and fortified wines, which should be stored upright, bottles should be laid horizontally (so that the wine stays in contact with the cork). You can stagger the rows, if you choose, but all bottles should be easily identifiable to avoid unnecessary handling. The air is cooler near the ground, and so it is recommended that bottles are organized by style of wine as follows, from bottom to top: sparkling wines, sweet wines, dry white wines, rosé, red wines for short- to medium-term drinking, red wines for long-term drinking, and finally, prestigious red wines. A well-maintained cellar book (*see below*), or cellar management software, will enable the ageing and consumption of wines to be monitored.

STORAGE STRUCTURES. Compartments and shelves should be stable and easily accessible. They can be made of stainless steel or wood (treated against insects and moisture). When batches are small (fewer than six bottles), individual cell style storage is

> *Managing a cellar requires discipline, time, and some basic knowledge. To reap maximum benefit, it is important to check the levels of the wines and the state of the corks...and to drink the wines at the right time.*

preferable, since it protects the wine against thermal shock, humidity, and vibrations. Cardboard boxes should be avoided: due to humidity, they quickly become unusable and release odors that can harm the wine. Beware of tissue paper: it can stick to labels and stain them. Bottles can be left in their original wooden case, as long as the lid is removed to let them breathe, and the case is raised off the floor. However, wooden cases encourage insects and parasites, and make a thief's work much easier.

LABELS. They should be oriented so as to allow different batches to be easily located. Alternatively, tags can be attached to the necks of the bottles. To preserve wine labels, bottles can be covered in plastic wrap or placed in plastic bags (but the cork must be able to breathe). Labels may be removed from empty bottles by using very wide transparent tape, specially made for this purpose. Alternatively, fill the bottle with cold water and then immerse it in hot water.

Monitor the level of the wine in the bottles

It is quite normal for a little wine to evaporate through the cork as it ages. In Bordeaux, one refers to the "level" of the bottle. This level is very important when buying at auctions. For a young wine, the level should still be high in the neck. After several years in the cellar, it usually goes down to the base of the neck. A level at the top of the "shoulder" of the bottle is acceptable for wines more than 20 years old and for rare, older wines. A mid-shoulder level is typical for wines more than 30 years old; in younger wines, it would suggest a problem with the cork, due to a fault in the bottling process. If this is the level in a large number of bottles, it may be due to excessive heat or insufficient humidity. Bottles are sometimes said to "weep." When the level reaches the bottom of the shoulder, there is cause for concern about the wine's condition. It certainly will have lost some of its resale

> Wooden cases must be treated to protect against humidity and insects.

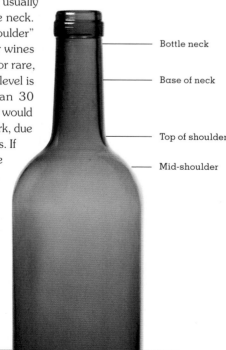

Bottle neck

Base of neck

Top of shoulder

Mid-shoulder

> In a large cellar, it is essential to label the batches carefully.

EXAMPLE OF A CELLAR RECORD

IDENTIFICATION	
WINERY NAME	Château Sociando-Mallet
APPELLATION	Médoc
REGION	Bordeaux
COLOR	Red
VINTAGE	2001
PURCHASE	en primeur the Internet
DATE	May 2002 (delivery June 2003)
PRICE	35
MERCHANT	Jean Gautreau
ADDRESS	(only en primeur purchase)

MANAGEMENT OF BOTTLES STORED	
NUMBER OF BOTTLES	one case of 12 bottles
REMAINING	10
DRINK BEFORE	2015-2020

TASTING NOTES

SERVED AT CHRISTMAS 2006: One bottle (with Michael, Sandra, Andy, and Bill). Still a little closed, tannins very noticeable, lots of power. Woodiness needs to become more integrated. The nose is not very developed. Promising, needs more time.

SERVED MARCH 30, 2008: One bottle with Eric and Sandra. Decanted one hour before the meal. Lots of substance, beginning to open up, subtle tannins and woodiness. Still very promising. Superb, showing incredible youth. Perfect with the duck breast.

value. As for below mid-shoulder level, this almost always indicates that the wine has become undrinkable.

The cellar book

A cellar book—a record with columns for wine purchased and wine consumed—will help you to keep your cellar up to date.

Storing wine in wooden cases

Wines may be stored in their original wooden cases, despite a slight risk of dry rot. Place the boxes on strips of wood rather than directly on the floor. Cardboard boxes should only be used for temporary storage, as the humidity will cause them to become moldy and develop odors. Remember to keep the original wooden cases if you plan to sell the wine later: they are reassuring for buyers at auctions and increase the value of the wine. This is particularly true for magnums and very large bottles.

However, this practice is difficult when you have a lot of single bottles, or wines in small quantities.

PRESENTATION. Use a special notebook or software to record the wines you have purchased by the case and/or those that you plan to keep for a long time (*see* table above). A good cellar book will keep track not only of incoming and outgoing wines, but also of your tasting notes, thereby helping you to monitor your wines as they age and to plan future purchases.

USE IN THE CELLAR. If necessary, make a schematic in your cellar book. Label the racks and compartments. For actual bottles, use individual labels or plastic tags. If wine is stored in wooden boxes, be sure to leave the side of the box with the wine's name visible, so that you do not have to move it.

TRUE OR FALSE?

Bottle sizes affect the wine.

TRUE. Different bottle sizes are not just a matter of varying volumes of wine: they also affect the ageing process. Wine matures more slowly in large bottles—a fact that should be remembered when making a purchase. This is due to the effect of the increased mass, and the oxidation-reduction phenomena in the maturing process, as well as a slower rate of sedimentation. Many wine enthusiasts believe that a magnum (1.5 liters or two bottles) is the optimal size for ageing.

STORING WINE: A FEW TIPS

Most wine lovers, at one stage or another, will have questions about the storage of the wines in their cellar. The answers are generally a matter of common sense, but these tips will help you make the right choices.

Should wine be stored upright or lying down?

66 There is no doubt that for storing and ageing wine, bottles should be kept in a horizontal position—at least if the closures are made of real cork, which is still usually the case. This is not an issue for synthetic closures because they do not dry out. Bottles with synthetic closures may be stored upright. During transportation, wines will be less disturbed if the bottles are upright and well secured. The best system is to wrap them in newspaper and pack them tightly in a sturdy container such as a cooler for camping or a solid old wine case."

66 In theory, your wine will be alright. The capsule and cork should be sufficient protection for a bottle, in the event that it spends a few days under water. However, you may lose the labels. If this is a risk, make sure when organizing bottles that you could identify any that had lost their "identity card." If your bottles were stored in wooden cases, you should get rid of these, as they could start to rot after being soaked and then give the wine a taste bad."

My cellar has flooded. Will the wine be OK?

How can I avoid unwanted flavors?

How can I protect my labels?

66 A good wine cellar has no odors. While a little mold might seem part of the charm of some grand old cellars, the musty, fungal odor sometimes found in fine wines may have been transmitted by mold. If you have a damp basement, it is best to clean it regularly. But avoid the use of any chemical products that could stay in the atmosphere and harm the wine. And it is well known that while cheese and wine go well together at the table, they are poor company when stored in the same cellar."

66 A moldy, indecipherable label may seem romantic, but it could prevent you from identifying the wine. The best way of protecting labels is to partially cover the bottles with plastic wrap. This will protect labels from humidity for a while, but the plastic will need to be replaced after two or three years."

Do I need to worry about noise?

" As a rule, wine likes peace and quiet. A life of movement and vibration will cause it to age more quickly and can cause certain problems. Avoid storing your bottles near a rail line or a road where heavy trucks pass. Continuous vibrations can stimulate certain bacteria and reactivate malolactic fermentation in unstable wines. This problem can be avoided by placing rubber spacers—pieces of tire, for example—under the racks, if they are mobile, which will absorb the vibrations."

I am bottling some wine. What type of cork should I use?

" We now know that the air that slowly passes through traditional corks is not essential for the ageing process. However, such corks can spoil excellent wines by giving them a "corked" taste. To avoid this problem, use synthetic corks. The air that you leave between the cork and the wine—about half of the neck—is sufficient for the wine to 'breathe'."

How long should I wait to drink a wine that has just been shipped?

How long can I keep wine purchased in bulk?

" As little time as possible, if you intend to bottle a wine that is in a Cubitainer. Allowing the wine to rest for 24 hours in a cool place is a good idea, but then bottling should not be delayed. Once bottled, it is advisable to wait a week before opening the first one. A boxed wine for everyday consumption can wait three to four months before being opened. Then, since no air enters as the bag empties, it can be kept for a few weeks in a cool place."

" Generally speaking, once wine is in bottle it should not be shaken. So after wine has been transported, it is important to allow it a period of rest, the length of which depends on several factors. For a young red, or any white wine, three or four days are usually enough. If the wine was bottled less than two months ago, it is best to wait a good week. If the wine is more than five years old, and especially if it is red, it would be advisable to wait eight to 10 days. For a fine red wine more than 10 years old, a thorough rest of at least two weeks is recommended."

KEEPING AND AGEING WINES

There are fine wines that will improve over the course of a slow maturation process, and there are others that are intended to be enjoyed in their immediate youth. Knowing the principles of how wines change as they age offers a better understanding of when they are at their peak and the best time to drink them.

Early wines were consumed young

The quality of a great wine is often gauged by its capacity to age; but this was not always the case. For centuries, it was considered best to drink wine when it was young, shortly after it had been made. Before the use of sulfur became widespread, there was a considerable risk that a wine would quickly turn into vinegar. With the help of today's scientific analyses, it is now easy to understand why wine is an unstable liquid. The presence of oxygen transforms alcohol into acetic acid, or vinegar, due to a certain bacteria called *Acetobacter aceti*. In the past, fermentation was a rather random process that took place in barrels or vats that were relatively clean, but left the wine exposed to the air. For a long time, the only way of compensating for the risks created by the poor production conditions was to make wines with a high alcohol content.

How wine ages is determined in part by the winemaker, but it depends mainly on the grape variety, the nature and age of the vines, the microclimate and soil (or terroir), and the weather during a particular year.

Wines that improved with age

Wines that lasted longer appeared only during the past few centuries, with the development of techniques such as fortification (the addition of alcohol during fermentation), the use of sulfur dioxide to combat bacterial growth, and *ouillage* (ullage, the regular topping up of the barrels with more wine in order to compensate for evaporation and thereby prevent the wine from coming into contact with air). However, once the wine was drawn from the barrel, it had to be consumed. The glass bottle and cork did not appear until the late 18th century, and they first enabled wine to be kept at home for a reasonable amount of time. Before their arrival, wine was aged in barrels stored by wine merchants or in taverns.

These new techniques also enabled certain wines that were considered undrinkable just after they had been made (because they were so tannic, acidic, and concentrated) to be kept until they softened and reached their peak—the stage at which a wine's various flavors open up—and its components (tannins, acidity, etc.) became balanced. The notion of keeping wines to let them improve was born.

Wines evolve in bottle

OXIDATION. The work of Louis Pasteur during the 19th century showed that wine deteriorates through oxidation or exposure to air. Oxidation causes red and white wines to become brown, much like an apple that has been peeled. But why does wine oxidize in the bottle, given that the cork lets in little or no air? The explanation is that oxygen dissolved in the wine continues to cause slow reactions in the anaerobic environment, resulting in the growth of bacteria, yeasts, and other chemical components in the wine: more than 400 of these have already been discovered, and the list is still growing.

CHEMICAL REACTIONS. Research has helped to explain certain changes in colors and flavors. Tannins and flavor components that come mainly from grape skins (and give wines their color), and also from the grape stalks and wooden barrels, undergo changes in time. They combine with each other (polymerization)

> The longevity of a wine depends on many factors, including the *terroir*, the type of grapes, and the winemaking processes.

and fall to the bottom of the bottle (sedimentation). A wine with a purplish color will gradually become ruby red and then lighten to an orangey brick red. The astringent acidity of young fruit will soften. The aggressiveness of an immature wine disappears, giving way to generosity and smoothness, expressed through complex flavors. All wines move through this ageing process, except for simple table wines that do not contain enough substance.

What is a wine "for laying down?"

Each type of wine develops at its own pace. Some, like Beaujolais and many white wines, should be consumed early: they quickly reach their peak and then rapidly decline. Others, like the great wines of Bordeaux, Burgundy, and the Rhône Valley, take longer to reach their peak, and then stay there for a long time, before declining slowly. These are wines for laying down (*vins de garde*). **GRAPE VARIETIES SUITED TO AGEING.** Grape varieties are a key factor in the longevity of wines. Those made from noble, austere Cabernet Sauvignon, and powerful, smooth Merlot grapes (in Bordeaux), or rich, full-bodied Pinot Noir (in Burgundy),

> Truly great wines, capable of lasting decades, are rare. To drink such a wine is a privilege and a special occasion.

are much more concentrated than the light, fruity wines produced from the Gamay grape (in Beaujolais). Among reds, wines suitable for ageing include: Cabernet Franc, Grenache, Mourvèdre, Syrah, Tannat, Petit Verdot, Carignan, Tempranillo from Spain, and Nebbiolo and Sangiovese from Italy. Among white wines, there are: Gewurztraminer, Riesling, Roussanne, Chardonnay, Grenache Blanc, Chenin, Sémillon, and Muscadelle (the last four having exceptional ageing potential when they are used to make sweet wines).

VINIFICATION AND MATURATION. The potential of a wine to improve with age also depends on how it is made. For red wines, the winemaker's goal is to extract plenty of tannins by grape skin maceration before pressing (see p.68), in order to give the wine the structure necessary for gradual ageing. The balance between free-run wine and press wine has a major impact on the final texture. Maturing wine in new barrels is another significant factor in ageing potential. With white wines, the key is to obtain a good level of acidity. For those that are not made from a grape variety with high acidity, barrel ageing (of a Chardonnay, for example) also helps ageing potential.

DID YOU KNOW...?

Whether a wine is humble or a grand cru, its life cycle in the bottle remains the same. After what is known as "bottling sickness," wines slowly regain their original flavors and lose the "rough" character of their early youth: fermentation- and maturation-related characters gradually fade, allowing the primary flavors of the fruit to come through. The ageing process then begins, often characterized by a short period of the wine being mute or "closed." Finally, the wine enters its peak period: its texture becomes softer, and its complex bouquet blends notes of fruit with spice or herbal aromas. This period can last several decades for some grand crus before they begin to decline.

TRUE OR FALSE?

A wine's development can only be monitored by tasting.

TRUE. To know when a wine has reached its peak, it is not advisable to rely on the suggestions made by the producer or wine merchant at the time of purchase, since storage conditions, which can vary from one place to another, will affect its development. The best method is to open a bottle from time to time and taste it.

Average wine longevity

While some wines should be consumed young, others need to be kept for a few years before being enjoyed when they have fully matured. Each wine should be opened within a certain period of time, which depends on the wine region, the type of wine produced, and also the quality of the vintage in question. Vintages may be rated from 1 to 10 (see pp.164–5). The time that a wine should remain in the cellar can vary, depending on whether it is from a good year (a score of 6 to 7 out of 10), a great year (a score of 8 to 9) or an exceptional year (10 out of 10).

Key:
- good vintages are ready to drink (meaning vintages scoring 6 to 7 out of 10)
- great vintages are ready to drink (scores of 8 to 9)
- exceptional vintages are ready to drink (scores of 10 out of 10)

	6 mth	1 yr	2 yrs	3 yrs	5 yrs	8 yrs	10 yrs	12 yrs	15 yrs	20 yrs	25 yrs	30 yrs	50 yrs	100 yrs
BORDEAUX														
Red wines : Médoc - Graves														
Red wines : Saint-Émilion - Pomerol														
Bordeaux and Bordeaux Supérieurs														
Dry white wines														
Sweet white wines														
BURGUNDY														
Red wines : Côte de Nuits														
Red wines : Côte de Beaune														
Red wines : Côte Chalonnaise														
Red wines : Côte d'Or grands crus														
White wines : Mâconnais														
Red wines : Pouilly-Fuissé and Chablis														
White wines : premiers crus														
White wines : grands crus														
Crémant de Bourgogne														
BEAUJOLAIS														
Beaujolais Primeur														
Beaujolais and Beaujolais-Villages														
Crus (Juliénas, Morgon, St-Amou)														
CHAMPAGNE														
Non Vintage														
Vintage														
Grandes cuvées														
ALSACE														
White wines														
Grands crus														
Late harvest														
Crémant d'Alsace														
JURA AND SAVOIE														
Red wines														
White wines														
Vin jaune														
LOIRE VALLEY														
Red wines														
Light rosé and white wines														
Full-bodied rosé and white wines														
Sweet white wines														
Sparkling wines														

	6 mth	1 yr	2 yrs	3 yrs	5 yrs	8 yrs	10 yrs	12 yrs	15 yrs	20 yrs	25 yrs	30 yrs	50 yrs	100 yrs
RHÔNE VALLEY														
Red wines			▓	▓	▓	▓	▓	▓		▓	▓			
White wines	▓	▓	▓	▓	▓	▓	▓							
Rosé wines	▓	▓	▓	▓	▓	▓								
LANGUEDOC AND ROUSSILLON														
Red wines			▓	▓	▓	▓	▓	▓						
White wines	▓	▓	▓	▓	▓	▓								
Natural sweet wines			▓	▓	▓	▓	▓	▓	▓	▓	▓	▓	▓	
PROVENCE														
Red wines			▓	▓	▓	▓	▓							
White and rosé wines	▓	▓	▓	▓										
CORSICA														
Red wines			▓	▓	▓	▓	▓	▓						
White and rosé wines	▓	▓	▓											
Sweet white wines			▓	▓	▓	▓	▓	▓						
SOUTHWEST FRANCE														
Red wines			▓	▓	▓	▓	▓	▓	▓	▓				
Dry white wines	▓	▓	▓	▓										
Sweet white wines					▓	▓	▓	▓	▓	▓	▓	▓		
ITALY : Piedmont and Tuscany														
Barolo and Brunello di Montalcino					▓	▓	▓	▓	▓	▓	▓			
SPAIN														
Rioja and Ribera del Duero red wines					▓	▓	▓	▓	▓	▓	▓			
Fino sherry					▓	▓	▓	▓	▓	▓	▓	▓		
PORTUGAL														
Vintage port					▓	▓	▓	▓	▓	▓	▓	▓	▓	
GERMANY : Mosel and Rhine regions														
Dry white wines	▓	▓	▓	▓	▓									
Sweet white wines			▓	▓	▓	▓								
Ice wines					▓	▓	▓	▓	▓	▓	▓			
SWITZERLAND, AUSTRIA, AND HUNGARY														
Red wines	▓	▓	▓	▓	▓	▓	▓							
Dry white wines	▓	▓	▓	▓	▓	▓	▓	▓						
Sweet white wines									▓	▓	▓			
MEDITERRANEAN COUNTRIES AND NORTH AFRICA														
Red wines			▓	▓	▓	▓								
Rosé wines	▓	▓												
UNITED STATES : California														
Red wines			▓	▓	▓	▓	▓	▓	▓	▓				
White wines		▓	▓	▓	▓	▓	▓							
CHILE														
Red wines			▓	▓	▓	▓	▓			▓	▓			
White wines	▓	▓	▓	▓	▓	▓	▓							
ARGENTINA														
Red wines			▓	▓	▓	▓	▓			▓	▓			
White wines	▓	▓	▓	▓	▓	▓	▓							
SOUTH AFRICA														
Red wines			▓	▓	▓	▓	▓	▓		▓	▓			
White wines	▓	▓	▓	▓	▓	▓								
AUSTRALIA														
Red wines			▓	▓	▓	▓	▓	▓						
White wines			▓	▓	▓	▓	▓							
NEW ZEALAND														
Red wines			▓	▓	▓	▓	▓	▓						
White wines			▓	▓	▓	▓	▓							

COLLECTING AND INVESTING IN WINES FOR YOUR CELLAR

At the top end of the market, wine can become not only a passion but also an investment opportunity. Purchasing such wines is a complex operation; but, once you have done so, their presence and development add to the value of a beautiful collection.

Collecting wines

Some wine enthusiasts regard their cellar as a formal collection. It might contain a wide variety of wines from the same region, all the vintages from one great château, or all the châteaux from a certain vintage.

APPROPRIATE STORAGE CONDITIONS. Collectors have to take extra care regarding storage conditions, since some wines, particularly very old ones, are fragile. Labels and wooden cases also need to be cared for, because bottles and cases are part of the collection and may be kept as souvenirs after the wine has been consumed.

BOTTLE SIZES. Unlike an ordinary cellar, a formal wine collection may include more magnums or even bigger bottles. These will not fit into standard racks, and appropriate storage space will need to be provided. Very large bottles are often kept in their original boxes.

One of the finest collections of rare wines in the world belongs to Michel Chasseuil. Now retired, he patiently assembled 20,000 bottles of fine wines throughout his working life.

Collection strategies

Wine collectors, unlike investors, are not limited to buying "safe" wines that can easily be resold. They may adopt different strategies, depending on their approach. They might, for example, collect all the Pauillac classified growths of the year of their birth, or systematically buy all the vintages of one château *en primeur* (*see also* pp.128–9), or all the labels produced by a small but prestigious appellation in Burgundy, such as Clos de Vougeot.

They will buy only perfect bottles, and, if wines are not available *en primeur*, will source them from cellars where the storage conditions are known to be reliable. Finally, every collector hopes that when the time comes to drink the wine, or to sell it, the source—their own cellar—will enhance its reputation.

How much wine should one buy?

How many bottles should be kept in a cellar? The answer is simple: as many as possible depending on the objectives of the collection. If you feel that your collection has become too large, or you want to expand or change it, then it is always possible to sell bottles at auctions or on internet sites.

THEORY. To collect fine wines that will not reach their peak for at least a decade, a large cellar is

> Bottles of Château Latour, Grand Cru Classé.

DID YOU KNOW...?

French government institutions such as the Elysée Palace, the National Assembly, and most of the ministries have their own wine cellars, often managed by a sommelier. These cellars are considerable assets, and their make-up varies depending on the origin of the wines and the tastes of the incumbent. For a long time, the best cellar was that of the Hotel de Lassay, the official residence of the president of the National Assembly. The Elysée Palace cellar, which holds the French president's wines, has had its ups and downs, but still contains treasures that are reserved for important state dinners.

> The collector Michel Chasseuil and his vintages of Pétrus.

necessary. If they are consumed at a rate of two or three bottles per year, or are being kept as a long-term investment, the quantity will inevitably multiply over time. For example, if you buy 36 bottles of a top Bordeaux every year for 10 years, and drink just two a year, you will have 340 bottles at the end of that period. A collection for drinking and a collection for investment purposes should be approached quite differently. In the first scenario, you may as well store the wines in your own cellar, especially if you have friends who share your passion. In the second scenario, it can be preferable to rent secure strorage with a professional company. **REALITY.** In practice, this difficult choice rarely comes to pass. Most collectors, unless they have an unlimited budget or are planning a career as a wine merchant, are wine enthusiasts who very often succumb to the urge to share their prized bottles with friends, rather than taking the risk of pursuing the speculative approach to its logical conclusion of selling the wine. Furthermore,

unless you plan to leave an inheritance for your descendants, it should be kept in mind that—once you yourself have reached a certain age—you may not be around to enjoy a great wine at its peak. So there is a balance to be struck between collecting two types of wine: those that one can be sure of drinking in the medium term, and great wines that will be consumed much later or which will be sold to raise funds for the collection's renewal.

Wine as an investment

When purchasing wine for speculative purposes, it is advisable to be familiar with the market and to buy at the best possible price. **WHICH WINES SHOULD I BUY?** Wines that are bought as an investment include the *grands crus* of Bordeaux, the top Burgundies and some of the wines from the Rhône Valley. Wines that start out as being expensive generally generate the highest margins. There is one golden rule: you should only buy wine with money from your savings, or, if you are a collector, from the profits from sales of other wines.

HOW SHOULD I BUY WINES? It's also necessary to be sure that you are buying a good vintage. This is why buying *en primeur* is often the best way of obtaining a good deal; regional wine fairs in Europe are another possibility.

WHAT RETURN CAN I EXPECT? Investing in wine can be very profitable. This has certainly been the case over the past 20 years for anyone who has invested in some of the great vintages of Bordeaux (1986, 1995, and 2000), whose prices have sometimes increased threefold. However, as a rule, do not expect to achieve an overall gross margin of more than 50 percent in less than 10 years. You can monitor your investment's development on relevant investment websites; but, when you choose to sell, whether it is through an auction room or online, it is best to consult an expert.

Insuring a cellar

Like all property, a cellar can be covered by a home insurance policy. However, its existence must be declared and it contents' value assessed in order to receive compensation in the event of a claim. Unless stipulated in a policy, there is no specific coverage for the contents of a cellar. In other words, if your policy does not state a precise amount for the value of the wine stored, you will be covered only for a fixed sum that depends on the type of insurance. In every case, it is strongly recommended that all possible proof of wine purchases (invoices, photographs, etc.) be carefully preserved.

HOW TO CHOOSE WINE

WINE STYLES

An inexperienced wine enthusiast may be daunted by the task of choosing from the huge variety of wines available from supermarkets or wine merchants. It helps to keep in mind the notion of the wine's style or family. Here are 14 wine styles, classified according to their sensory qualities and principal grape varieties. For each style, the most representative appellations are listed, as well as the dishes with which they pair best, and the ideal temperatures at which they should be served.

Light and fruity reds

These wines are essentially for immediate consumption and can be classified as "easy drinking." Typically, they have expressive aromas of soft fruits or flowers, and their light tannic structure is compensated by a pleasant crispness, with a simple and thirst-quenching finish.

GRAPE VARIETIES. These include Cabernet Franc, Gamay, Pinot Noir, Poulsard, Tempranillo, Trousseau, and Zinfandel. Their primary fruit and flower characters deliver a spectrum of aromatic expressions.

APPELLATIONS. A few examples in this category include, from France: Anjou, Beaujolais, generic Burgundy, Bourgueil, Côtes-du-Jura, Coteaux-du-Lyonnais, Hautes-Côtes-de-Beaune, Hautes-Côtes-de-Nuits, Pinot Noir d'Alsace, St-Nicolas-de-Bourgueil, red Sancerre, and Saumur-Champigny; Italian wines include Valpolicella; California has Zinfandel; Switzerland has Pinot Noir from the Valais; and Spain has Tempranillos of Castile.

FOOD PAIRING. These light and fruity red wines are best with simple foods. Their great adaptability means that they can be served throughout a meal; and they are good with charcuterie, quiches, pizzas, savory pastries, rabbit terrine, and creamy goat or cow's milk cheeses such as St-Marcellin.

It's easier to choose a bottle if you keep in mind that wines can be classified according to their style, their color, and their tasting personality, e.g. complex, classy reds or firm, light whites, and so on.

SERVING. Serve these wines lightly chilled, between 54 and 57°F (12–14°C); they are best when consumed young, within two years of bottling or three at most.

Medium-bodied, fruity reds

These are often simple wines, but they differ from the lighter reds in their heavier mouth-feel and more perceptible, though unaggressive, tannins. In general, they are not matured in new wood and they retain their fruity character. These wines will develop a bouquet reminiscent of red fruits, often with spicy undertones.

GRAPE VARIETIES. Cabernet Franc, Carignan, Grenache, Merlot, Mondeuse, Pinot Noir, Syrah, and Sangiovese are the most common grape varieties used in making these wines.

APPELLATIONS. These fruity wines include the French appellations Bergerac, Bordeaux Supérieur, Buzet, Chinon, Castillon-Côtes-de-Bordeaux, Côte Chalonnaise, Côtes-de-Provence, Côtes-du-Rhône-Villages, Coteaux Champenois, Fronton, and St-Joseph. In Italy, there is Chianti, and in Spain Penedès.

FOOD PAIRING. These wines go well with regional European cooking: for example, small game, country pâté, sauced meat dishes like beef bourguignon, roasted or grilled red meat, as well

DID YOU KNOW...?

The color of a red wine is a clue to its identity.
It can range from very light ruby to deepest garnet. A wine with an intense, dark appearance (or color) shows concentration. On the other hand, a paler wine suggests a lighter, less tannic palate. By simple visual observation, the taster can already get an idea of the wine's personality and even, sometimes, deduce its origin. For example, if you know it's French, a deep garnet color may indicate that the wine comes from Bordeaux or the south of France, rather than Beaujolais or Burgundy.

as pressed, uncooked cheeses such as Tomme or St-Nectaire.

SERVING. These wines are best consumed after ageing for one or two years in the bottle; they should be served at a temperature between 59 and 63°F (15–17°C).

Full-bodied, fruity reds

These wines are more pronounced and powerful, with a soft texture based on high alcohol content and plenty of tannins that will need some time to integrate. They are generally matured in oak barrels and develop a complex bouquet with spicy notes often associated with ripe, dark fruits. Initial tasting reveals a full-bodied impression, whether they are hot, sunny-climate wines (from the Languedoc, for example) or more classic appellations such as those of the Libourne region of Bordeaux. The finish is complex and long. Wines containing a high percentage of Merlot, such as those from Pomerol and St-Émilion (*see* pp.267 and 268), are particularly smooth and are the most expensive in this category.

GRAPE VARIETIES. These red wines come from varieties such as Auxerrois, Cabernet Franc, Carignan, Grenache, Malbec, Merlot, Mourvèdre, Syrah, and Tannat.

> A selection of full-bodied, fruity reds.

APPELLATIONS. These include the following French designations: Cahors, Châteauneuf-du-Pape, Corbières, Côtes-de-Bourg, Côtes-de-Blaye, Côtes-du-Roussillon-Villages, Coteaux-du-Languedoc, Fronsac, Gigondas, Madiran, Minervois, Lalande-de-Pomerol, Pomerol, and St-Émilion Grand Cru. Outside France, there are the Rioja wines of Spain, Merlots from Chile, and Shiraz from Australia.

FOOD PAIRING. These complex, powerful, and generous wines demand richly flavored, fatty dishes such as cassoulet, duck confit, mushrooms (especially truffles), foie gras escalope, dishes in red wine sauce (daubes), grilled or roasted red meat, game, *i.e.* pheasant or boar, and pressed, uncooked cheeses such as Tomme or Cantal.

SERVING. These wines need to be left for at least three years in bottle. If consumed young, they will benefit from being decanted and served at a temperature of 59–63°F (15–17°C).

Complex, tannic, "thoroughbred" reds

These classy, distinguished red wines are found in the highest price brackets. They deserve legitimate attention when tasted, and will mature in bottle for several years. Due to their significant tannin content, they will often taste rather austere when young. But over time the tannins will soften, yielding a firm, elegant, dense body with a smooth texture. Usually matured in new oak barrels, they develop toasty, spicy notes and soft red and black fruit aromas; but their full, complex flavors and long, classy finish come to the fore only on maturity.

GRAPE VARIETIES. These wines are made from grapes such as Cabernet Sauvignon, Mourvèdre, Syrah, and Nebbiolo.

APPELLATIONS. French appellations include Bandol, Cornas, Côte-Rôtie, Graves, Haut-Médoc, Hermitage, Margaux, Pauillac, Pessac-Léognan, St-Estèphe, and St-Julien. In Italy, there is Barolo; in California, Chile, and South Africa, there is Cabernet Sauvignon.

FOOD PAIRING. These complex, tannic, "thoroughbred" reds go best with full-flavored but not over-fatty dishes such as truffles, game, and roast lamb; they are also good with pressed, uncooked cheeses such as Cantal or St-Nectaire.

SERVING. These wines are best consumed no earlier than five years after bottling; they should be decanted and served at a temperature between 59 and 63°F (15–17°C).

Complex, elegant, "thoroughbred" reds

This category includes the *premier* and *grand cru* wines of Burgundy, which are rare and exceptional due to their limited production. These complex red wines are characterized by the powerful aromas of red berries or flowers such as roses. Over time, they mingle elegant notes of undergrowth or game. Their silkiness on the palate and long-lasting finish are distinctive indicators.

GRAPE VARIETIES. As with all the red wines of Burgundy, these wines are made from a single grape variety: Pinot Noir.

APPELLATIONS. How do we list the best of Burgundy? Take, for example, some of the famous *premier* and *grands crus* of the Côte d'Or, centered on the communes of Gevrey-Chambertin, Morey-St-Denis, Chambolle-Musigny, and Vougeot. To the north, the Côte de Nuits produces Vosne-Romanée; while the Côte de Beaune has Corton, Pernand-Vergelesses, Beaune, Volnay, and Pommard. In North America, the best Pinot Noir wines from Oregon deserve special mention.

FOOD PAIRING. These classy, elegant reds make a great accompaniment to slow-cooked dishes such as *coq au vin*, *œuf en meurette* (eggs poached in red wine sauce), roasts, small game, and semi-soft cheeses with a "bloomy" rind, such as Brie or Coulommiers.

SERVING. After a minimum of five years in bottle, these great wines should be served at a temperature between 61 and 63°F (16–17°C).

Fresh and fruity rosés

These easy-drinking wines should be enjoyed young. They are very refreshing, slightly crisp, decidedly fruity, and are usually made by direct pressing of red grapes.

GRAPE VARIETIES. The chief varieties include Cabernet Franc, Carignan, Cinsaut, Grenache, Poulsard, Tibouren, and Zinfandel.

APPELLATIONS. These lively, fruity wines come from many French appellations, including Bellet, Coteaux-d'Aix-en-Provence, Coteaux Varois, Côtes-du-Luberon, Côtes-de-Provence, Côtes-

> Some complex, elegant, "thoroughbred" reds.

> Several fresh and fruity rosés.

du-Jura, Irouléguy, Palette, and Rosé de Loire. In North America, there are the "blush" wines of California.

FOOD PAIRING. These wines are the perfect accompaniment to light summer cooking, especially crudités, pasta with vegetables, mixed salads, vegetable tarts, tapenade, pizzas, and fresh or slightly mature goat's cheese.

SERVING. These wines are best consumed in their first year and should be served at 46–50°F (8–10°C). They should not be over-chilled, since this will limit their fruity, floral bouquet.

Round, full-bodied rosés

While retaining rosé's refreshing quality, these wines are less crisp and offer a soft-fruit or spicy bouquet. They have a rounder, grapey mouth-feel and a light tannic structure. They are deeper in color than the wines above and are often made by the *saignée* method (*see* p.66).

GRAPE VARIETIES. Carignan, Grenache, Merlot, Mourvèdre, Négrette, Pinot Noir, Syrah.

APPELLATIONS. The rosés from the following French appellations are good examples of this category: Bandol, Bordeaux clairet, Coteaux-du-Languedoc, Côtes-du-Rhône, Lirac, Marsannay, Rosé des Riceys, and Tavel. There also are the rosés of Italy, Spain, and all around the Mediterranean basin.

FOOD PAIRING. These full-bodied, round rosés go well with full-flavored summer dishes that involve olive oil, vegetables, and fish, such as aïoli, bouillabaisse, tian of eggplant, ratatouille, and red mullet. They are also good with grills and mature goat's cheeses, as well as Middle Eastern or Asian dishes.

SERVING. These wines should be served chilled, between 46 and 50°F (8–10°C) and consumed within two years of bottling.

> A selection of light, firm, dry whites.

Light, firm, dry whites

These lively, easy-drinking, refreshing wines develop uncomplicated flowery and fruity bouquets.

GRAPE VARIETIES. The most commonly used varieties are Aligoté, Chasselas, Chardonnay, Gros Plant, Jacquère, Melon de Bourgogne (Muscadet), Pinot Blanc, Sauvignon Blanc, Sylvaner, or Albariño (Alvarinho in Portugal).

APPELLATIONS. The French appellations that best illustrate this family are Bourgogne Aligoté, Cheverny, Crépy, Entre-deux-Mers, Mâcon-Villages, Muscadet, Petit Chablis, Alsace Pinot Blanc, Alsace Sylvaner, and Apremont. Also included are Switzerland's Fendant, Portugal's Vinho Verde, the Sauvignon Blanc of Friuli (Italy), and California's Fumé Blanc.

FOOD PAIRING. These firm, light wines are best with simple cuisine and unadorned flavors: seafood such as oysters and mussels, raw or cooked vegetables, grilled and fried fish, charcuterie, and goat's cheeses.

SERVING. Drink these wines quite young (less than two years in bottle) and chilled to around 46°F (8°C).

Supple, fruity, dry whites

These wines are soft-bodied, with a very fruity bouquet. They often have a touch of citrus, and are pleasantly fresh.

GRAPE VARIETIES. These whites are produced from varieties such as Altesse, Chardonnay, Chenin Blanc, Clairette, Gros Manseng, Mauzac, Rolle, Sauvignon Blanc, Sémillon, Ugni Blanc, and Vermentino.

APPELLATIONS. French AOCs include: Bandol, Bellet, Cassis, Chablis, Côtes-de-Blaye, Coteaux-d'Aix-en-Provence, Côtes-de-Provence, Gaillac, Graves, Jurançon sec, Pouilly-Fumé, Pouilly-Fuissé, Montlouis, Roussette de Savoie, Saint-Véran, and Sancerre. Also Corsican wines and whites from Sardinia (Italy).

FOOD PAIRING. These wines go well with a variety of dishes, whether simple or more elaborate, including raw or cooked shellfish, seafood pasta, fish mousse, raw or grilled fish, charcuterie, and ripe or mature goat's cheeses.

SERVING. These white wines can be consumed up to three years after bottling. They should be served chilled, between 46 and 50°F (8–10°C).

Full-bodied, classy, dry whites

More complex than the preceding whites, these wines are notable for rich, fleshy, mouth-filling structure. They also have a pleasant crispness that makes them very refreshing. The finish is long and, in the best examples, classy. Often matured or vinified in oak barrels, these wines mingle toasty notes with a touch of vanilla creaminess. Aromas include ripe orchard fruit, aromatic herbs, and white flowers.

GRAPE VARIETIES. These distinguished whites are made with the classic or noble varieties: Chardonnay, Chenin Blanc, Marsanne, Riesling, Roussanne, Sauvignon Blanc, and Sémillon.

APPELLATIONS. These include Burgundy's greatest white wine appellations, such as Chablis Premier and Grand Cru, Corton-Charlemagne, Meursault, Chassagne-Montrachet, Puligny-Montrachet, and Montrachet; also Loire Valley appellations include Montlouis, Savennières, and Vouvray. As well, there is the Bordeaux appellation Pessac-Léognan, and the best Chardonnays from California, Chile, New Zealand, and South Africa.

FOOD PAIRING. These wines naturally accompany fine dining. They are good with Coquilles Saint-Jacques, lobster, turbot, and also with pan-fried foie gras, wild mushrooms, white meats in cream sauces, creamy cheeses such as St-Félicien or St-Marcellin, and mature goat's cheeses like Picodon.

SERVING. The full amplitude of these wines is revealed after three to five years in bottle; above all, they should not be served too cold. Somewhere between 50 and 54°F (10–12°C) is best.

Aromatic, dry whites

These wines are notable for their exuberant flavors and big personalities. Typically, their characteristic aromas make it possible to identify the grape variety simply by scent.

GRAPE VARIETIES. Such is the case with Gewurztraminer, with its notes of exotic fruits and Turkish delight; Viognier, with its scents of peach or apricot; and the grapey bouquet of Muscat; the smoky, spicy, honeyed notes of Pinot Gris; or Riesling, the mineral tones of which are sometimes reminiscent of petroleum.

> A full-bodied, classy, dry white.

The same can be said of Savagnin, used in the *vin jaune* from Jura (France), and Palomino, an Andalusian grape which is used to make sherry: it has a bouquet reminiscent of wheat, dried fruits, walnut shells, and spices.

APPELLATIONS. The most famous French appellations are the *vin jaune* and Château-Chalon from Jura or the Condrieu and Château-Grillet from the Rhône Valley. In Alsace, they simply follow the German approach, displaying the name of the grape variety, whether Gewurztraminer, Muscat, Riesling, or Pinot Gris. In Spain, the best-known appellation is fino sherry from the larger family of sherries (*see vins doux naturels*, pp.160–1).

FOOD PAIRING. These distinctive wines require special treatment; those made with Savagnin or Palomino grapes go best with aromatic dishes flavored with spices or herbs, such as meat or seafood curries, chicken with cream and morels, lobster in tomato and tarragon sauce. Rieslings and Pinots Gris are good with salmon with dill, and also with smoked fish. In terms of cheese, pressed, cooked cheeses such as Beaufort and Comté, or those with a pronounced taste like Munster, complement them particularly well.

SERVING. Wines made from Muscat and Viognier grapes should be consumed fairly young and slightly chilled, between 46 and 50°F (8–10°C); the rest need three to five years in bottle and should be served between 50 and 54°F (10–12°C).

Rich, medium-dry and sweet whites

> Some rich, medium-dry and sweet whites.

The chief characteristic of these wines is the proportion of residual sugar naturally contained in the grape juice that has not been transformed into alcohol. This can be obtained either by supermaturation (leaving the grapes to ripen longer to reduce their moisture content), which means that they are harvested late to give a very concentrated juice, or by the action of a microorganism, Botrytis cinerea, on the grapes (*see* box p.54). In the first case, the wines will be medium-dry or rich; in the second they are described as sweet as they are packed with sugars. These wines are defined by their soft, almost viscous body, balanced by good acidity (crispness) and a rich, complex bouquet of fruits and honey. They also have a long, lasting finish.

TRUE OR FALSE?

White wines don't keep.

FALSE. Great sweet whites can remain drinkable for several centuries! The secret of a long life is the combination of three elements: sugar, alcohol, and acidity. These wines come from often acidic grape varieties, such as Sémillon (for Sauternes), Chenin Blanc (for Vouvray), and Furmint (for Tokaj).

GRAPE VARIETIES. Only certain varieties are suitable for these wines. The best-known are Chenin Blanc from the Loire Valley; Petit-Manseng, Sauvignon Blanc, Sémillon, and Muscadelle in southwest France; Muscat, Gewurztraminer, Riesling, and Pinot Gris in Alsace.

APPELLATIONS. The principal appellations include: in Alsace, Gewurztraminer *vendanges tardives* and *sélection de grains nobles*, Pinot Gris *vendanges tardives* and *sélection de grains nobles*, and Riesling *vendanges tardives* and *sélection de grains nobles*; in the Loire region, Bonnezeaux, Coteaux-de-l'Aubance, Coteaux-du-Layon, Quarts-de-Chaume, Montlouis, and Vouvray. Additionally, Cérons, Jurançon, Monbazillac, Sainte-Croix-du-Mont, and Sauternes in southwest France; and the icewines of Germany (*eiswein*) and Canada.

FOOD PAIRING. As well as being splendid on their own, these white wines are traditional partners for rich dishes such as foie gras, chicken à la crème, duck à l'orange, blue cheeses like Roquefort, tarts made with yellow fruit, and cream-based desserts (sabayon, crème brûlée). Not too sugary, they also complement more exotic, spicy cuisine, and they match salty with sweet.

SERVING. These wines are best appreciated after three to five years in bottle. They should be served chilled but not iced, around 46–50°F (8–10°C).

Sparkling wines

Quintessential party drinks, sparkling wines constitute a large family in which Champagne is the most illustrious representative. However, practically all the wine-producing regions of the world produce this type of wine. Significant levels of carbon dioxide and good acidity give them a light and lively feel that makes them very refreshing. In terms of dryness, they can be *extra-brut*, *brut*, *sec*, *demi-sec,* or *doux.* Sparkling wines have delicate flavors of fruit, flowers, and sometimes bread or pastries.

GRAPE VARIETIES. The principal varieties are Cabernet Franc, Chardonnay, Chenin Blanc, Clairette, Mauzac, Merlot, Muscat, Pinot Blanc, Pinot Noir, Pinot Meunier, Sauvignon Blanc, and Savagnin.

APPELLATIONS. While Champagne gets top honors, other regions produce great sparkling wines, too. Some are crafted according to the same method of secondary fermentation in the bottle, such as the *crémants* from Alsace and Burgundy, as well as Blanquette de Limoux from the Midi, Saumur and Vouvray in the Loire Valley, Savoie's Seyssel, and some Spanish Cava. Other appellations are produced following a local method, such as Clairette de Die or some sparkling wines from Gaillac. These bubbly wines are often lighter and sometimes fruitier than Champagne. Moscato d'Asti, Asti Spumante, and Italian Prosecco are examples, as well as Germany's Sekt and most of Spain's Cava.

FOOD PAIRING. While appreciated as an aperitif, sparkling wines can also be served throughout a meal. The *brut* varieties go well with seafood; fish terrine; or fish that is grilled, smoked, or served in a light cream sauce. They are also good with semi-soft cheeses with a crust such as Camembert. *Sec* and *demi-sec* sparkling wines also go with the same cheeses, and with fruit desserts, meringues, and dishes with a light custard sauce (*crème anglaise*).

SERVING. Most sparkling wines should be consumed when young and must be served chilled, at a temperature between 46 and 50°F (8–10°C).

Vins doux naturels (VDN) and *vins de liqueur* (VDL)

This family groups together *vins d'exception* or fortified wines, strongly aromatic with a high alcohol and sugar content. They are developed by regionally specific methods.

Vins doux naturels (VDN) are produced by mutage, the process of adding neutral alcohol during fermentation in order to retain some of the grapes' natural sugars while increasing the final alcoholic strength to 14–18% ABV. These wines are produced in warm regions such as Languedoc-Roussillon, the southern Rhône

> Several sparkling wines.

DID YOU KNOW...?

To keep a sparkling wine from overflowing when uncorked, ensure that all of the wine in the bottle is at the same low temperature. Just leave it in the bottom of the refrigerator for three hours. A Champagne bucket can then be used to keep the wine chilled throughout the meal. Remember that most great white wines should be served at a temperature between 52 and 54°F (11–12°C).

Valley, Corsica, and, of course, Portugal. All have a silky, sumptuous mouth-feel with a long, aromatic finish. *Vins de liqueur* (VDL) are a blend of grape juice, very slightly fermented or not at all, with eau-de-vie (neutral spirits). Alcohol strength ranges from 16 to 22% ABV, and they have a particularly fruity flavor.

GRAPE VARIETIES. The principal varieties used in the making of French *vins doux naturels* are, for reds, Grenache Gris or Noir and Maccabeu; the whites are made with Grenache Blanc, Malvoisie, or Muscat. *Vins de liqueur* are chiefly made using Folle Blanche, Colombard, and Ugni Blanc for whites; Merlot, Cabernet Sauvignon, and Cabernet Franc for the rosés and reds. Macvin uses grape varieties from the Jura region of France. In Portugal, key varieties include Touriga Nacional and Tinta Roriz.

APPELLATIONS. Port in Portugal. In France, Banyuls, Rivesaltes, Maury, Rasteau, Muscat de Beaumes-de-Venise, Muscat du Cap-Corse, Muscat de Frontignan, Muscat de Mireval, and Muscat de Rivesaltes. Sherry, Madeira, Malaga, and Marsala also belong to this category of fortified wines, despite significant differences in the way they are made. Among the VDLs, Pineau des Charentes, Floc de Gascogne, and Macvin du Jura hold an AOC. Others include Ratafia from Champagne.

FOOD PAIRING. VDNs are excellent on their own; but they also have a place during the meal. Depending on how they are made (*see* box below), they call for different dishes. The whites made in an oxidative style (open to air), go well with foie gras, whether fresh or in a terrine. The other whites are best with fruit desserts such as apricot tart and also with blue cheeses like Roquefort. Because of their tannic strength and fruitiness, the reds that have been exposed to the open air—such as Banyuls Rimage and vintage ports—make good partners for game and sweet-savory dishes such as duck cooked with figs or cherries, or even Peking Duck. They are also good with blue cheeses. Thanks to their bouquet, the oxidative reds are natural partners for chocolate or coffee desserts or those with dried fruits. Because of their high sugar and alcohol content, VDLs are best served alone, although they can also be served with pan-fried foie gras.

SERVING. Muscat-based VDNs should be consumed while young and fruity, as should the *vins de liqueur*. However, oxidative white and red VDNs may be consumed young but also improve with keeping. The rest of these wines are worth keeping three to five years in bottle to allow their full qualities to come to the fore.

> A few *vins doux naturels* and *vins de liqueur*.

Vins doux naturels: flavors and colors!

Depending on how they are made, the color and flavor personality of these wines varies. Wines produced without an exposure to air and bottled early retain their primary aromas of fruits and flowers and, for reds, their full tannic strength. Examples include the Muscats from Beaumes-de-Venise and Frontignan in France, which have a lovely golden color and delicious notes of apricot, melon, honey, flowers, and fresh mint. The same goes for Rivesaltes wines, which retain a clear appearance and aromas of white flowers and honey. On the other hand, contact with air or oxidation develops deep colors and a maderized or *rancio* bouquet in these wines. So, for example, Rivesaltes, when matured in an oxidative environment, takes on dark tones ranging from brick red to amber. They also have pronounced notes of almonds, walnuts, hazelnuts, and candied citrus fruits.

Legendary wines

They are known as "dream wines" because they seem almost unattainable. They are very rare and—of course— expensive. These wines are more talked about than consumed.

PÉTRUS 1945

Although it was not among the *grands crus* classified in Bordeaux in 1855, Pétrus has become a legend; and its 1945 vintage a myth within a myth. Why? Because 1945 was when Edmonde Loubat gained a controlling interest in Pétrus, and lifted her vineyard to the ranks of greatness thanks to an intelligent alliance with the wine merchant Jean-Pierre Moueix. Enjoyed by Britain's Queen Elizabeth as well as the late President Kennedy, Pétrus boomed during the 1960s. It's a cult wine, and a bottle of Pétrus 1945 is valued at $2,300–$2,500 (£1,400–£1,500).

CHEVAL BLANC 1947

Classified as an A-list *premier grand cru*, the wine from Château Cheval Blanc, owned by Bernard Arnault and Albert Frère, has been established since the 19th century as one of the greatest St-Émilions. It is distinguished by a 91-acre (37-ha) vineyard planted with an unusually high proportion of Cabernet Franc grapes, in an area where Merlot is king. The legendary year of 1947 made its mark as an exceptional vintage. The wine has a still-astonishing youthfulness and jammy, spicy, coffee aromas reminiscent of a great vintage port. Estimate: $1,600–$2,300 (£1,000–£1,400) per bottle.

MOUTON-ROTHSCHILD 1945

Owned by the Rothschild family since 1853, this 208-acre (84-ha) domaine in the Pauillac appellation of Bordeaux was classified as *second cru* in 1855. Then Baron Philippe de Rothschild secured its elevation to *premier cru* in 1973. Considered legendary by many, the 1945 vintage bears a label showing V for wartime victory, the first in a long series of labels designed by artists. Appreciated as much for its quality as for its symbolism, on September 28, 2006, Mouton-Rothschild 1945 became the world's most expensive wine at an auction organized by Christie's: a lot of 12 bottles was sold for a total of $311,000 (£190,000) or almost $30,000 (£19,000) per bottle.

CHÂTEAU D'YQUEM 2001

At the time it was classified in 1855 as *premier grand cru exceptionnel*, this 247-acre (100-ha) Sauternes estate was already

1. Pétrus (Bordeaux).
2. Château Mouton-Rothschild (Bordeaux).
3. Château Cheval Blanc (Bordeaux).
4. Château d'Yquem (Bordeaux).
5. Romanée-Conti (Burgundy).
6. Scharzhofberger (Mosel).
7. Tokaj maturing in barrel.
8. Château Rayas (Châteauneuf-du-Pape).

much appreciated by the American president Thomas Jefferson, and by many of the crowned heads of Europe. Owned since the 18th century by the Lur-Saluces family, the domaine passed into the control of the LVMH luxury group in 1999. Two years later it produced one of its most famous vintages, acclaimed by all critics as exceptional and equal to the great years 1811 and 1847. Its price? Around $1,770 (£1,090) per bottle.

ROMANÉE-CONTI 1990

Covering only 4.5 acres (1.80 ha), this Burgundy "monopole" (i.e. land exclusive to a sole proprietor) produces fewer bottles than the smallest châteaux of the Bordeaux region. The critics are unanimous in considering this wine close to perfection, most notably the 1990 vintage, and describe it as the quintessence of Pinot Noir. The price of a bottle varies between $10,000 and $16,000 (£6,000-£10,000), which makes Romanée-

Conti 1990 one of the world's most expensive wines.

CHÂTEAU RAYAS 1978

Discreet, if not secret, this famous Châteauneuf-du-Pape *cru* stands out by being produced exclusively from old Grenache vines. By contrast, the reputation of this great appellations rests on the blending of many varieties. Château Rayas was taken over by Jacques Reynaud in 1978. His trial run was a masterstroke, and the 1978 vintage took the US by storm. Celebrated for its concentration and finesse, this wine—characterized by spicy, leathery overtones—requires lengthy laying down. At auction a bottle will go for more than $1,300 (£800).

TBA SCHARZHOFBERGER 1976

In Germany's Saar Valley, Egon Müller is the heir of a family whose name is associated with great Riesling. Ripening

by "noble rot" produces outstanding sweet wine, thanks to their concentration of sugars and their acidity. They also do not exceed 6% ABV. A Trockenbeerenauslese (TBA), the equivalent of a French "selection of noble grapes," from the Scharzhofberger vineyard is a remarkable wine. The 1976 vintage, considered one of the best ever, is estimated to sell for more than $1,300 (£800) per half-bottle.

TOKAJ DISZNÓKÖ 6 PUTTONYOS 1993

The rebirth of the prestigious Tokaj region in eastern Hungary was marked by the arrival of Western investors. Disznokö, the "boar's rock," whose *terroir* was classified as *grand cru* in 1772, is owned by the AXA insurance company, which has entirely restructured it. In the Aszú category (sweet wines made from individually picked grapes), the 1993 vintage signaled the true revival of the domaine.

Recent vintages

Rating the quality of each vintage (from 1 to 10) is just a general expression about a whole wine-producing region. It is important to bear in mind that this is a broad-brushstroke statement about quality and ageing potential. In fact, appreciable differences are found within the same vintage, depending on the vineyards and producers.

Key: Average year   Good year   Great year   Exceptional year

ND: data unavailable. Regarding port, the years for which there is no information were not officially declared as "vintage." For other regions (South Africa, Argentina, Chile, Switzerland), the absence of evaluation signifies that there were no wines worth laying down.

	2008	2007	2006	2005	2004	2003	2002	2001	2000	1999	1998	1997	1996	1995	1994	1993	1992	1991	1990	1989	1988	1987
Bordeaux Reds	8	7	7	10	7	8	7	7	10	7	8	6	8	8	7	6	6	7	9	9	8	6
Bordeaux Dry whites	7	7	8	9	8	6	8	7	8	6	7	6	8	8	8	6	5	6	8	9	9	7
Bordeaux Sweet whites	8	7	8	8	5	9	9	8	6	8	8	9	9	9	7	5	5	7	10	10	10	5
Burgundy Reds	6	8	7	10	7	8	8	7	7	6	8	7	8	7	7	7	7	7	9	8	8	6
Burgundy Whites	7	7	8	10	8	10	8	8	8	6	8	8	10	8	8	6	8	7	9	8	8	6
Champagne (Vintage)	8	7	8	7	8	7	9	5	8	8	7	8	10	8	5	6	6	5	9	8	9	5
Alsace	7	7	7	7	7	6	5	6	6	5	7	7	6	6	6	7	5	6	10	8	8	6
Jura, Savoie	7	7	8	9	7	8	7	5	7	7	7	7	8	7	6	4	5	6	10	8	8	5
Loire Valley	7	7	6	9	6	8	6	7	8	6	7	8	9	8	6	6	6	6	10	10	9	6
Rhône Valley	6	7	7	9	7	7	5	8	8	8	9	7	7	8	6	6	6	7	10	9	8	7
Languedoc-Roussillon	7	8	7	7	7	7	5	8	8	6	7	6	6	7	5	7	6	7	9	8	9	7
Provence	6	7	8	6	8	6	5	7	7	8	8	7	7	8	5	5	4	6	8	8	9	7
Corsica	7	8	8	7	8	8	5	8	8	8	8	5	6	6	6	6	5	5	9	7	6	7
Italy Piedmont	9	6	8	6	8	8	7	8	7	8	10	10	10	7	7	7	5	7	10	10	8	7
Italy Tuscany	9	7	9	7	8	9	7	8	10	9	8	10	10	10	8	8	7	8	10	7	10	8

	2008	2007	2006	2005	2004	2003	2002	2001	2000	1999	1998	1997	1996	1995	1994	1993	1992	1991	1990	1989	1988	1987
Spain Rioja	10	7	8	8	7	8	6	8	8	7	8	7	8	10	9	8	7	7	7	7	6	8
Portugal Vintage port	nd	7	8	10	9	9	7	8	10	–	8	9	7	–	10	–	9	9	–	–	–	7
Germany Mosel	7	8	8	7	7	7	8	7	6	7	8	8	6	7	8	7	7	7	10	7	8	6
Germany Rhine	7	8	7	8	7	8	8	8	7	7	7	7	7	7	7	8	8	6	10	8	8	7
Switzerland	9	9	8	9	9	10	8	8	9	8	10	–	–	–	–	–	–	–	–	–	–	–
Austria	7	8	9	8	8	7	9	8	8	10	8	10	9	9	8	9	–	–	–	–	–	–
Hungary Tokaj	nd	nd	7	8	6	9	5	9	10	8	5	4	5	6	4	10	4	7	4	8	4	5
United States California	8	9	7	7	7	8	9	8	7	8	7	10	8	9	9	7	9	8	8	8	7	8
Chile	8	9	9	8	9	8	9	9	8	9	–	–	–	–	–	–	–	–	–	–	–	–
Argentina	8	9	9	9	8	8	9	8	8	9	–	–	–	–	–	–	–	–	–	–	–	–
South Africa	8	8	9	9	8	9	8	9	9	8	–	–	–	–	–	–	–	–	–	–	–	–
Australia	8	7	9	10	9	9	9	9	8	8	9	8	9	8	9	8	8	8	8	8	7	7
New Zealand	8	7	9	8	8	7	8	7	9	8	9	8	8	8	8	7	8	8	8	8	7	7

Among earlier great vintages in France, the following should be mentioned: 1985, 1982, 1978, 1970, 1961, 1959, 1955, 1953, 1947, and 1945.

PRINCIPLES FOR MATCHING FOOD WITH WINES

A modest wine is an agreeable accompaniment to an unpretentious meal. However, when the cuisine is more elaborate or the ingredients rather special, a fine wine is more appropriate. Here is some advice on matching wines to dishes, depending on circumstances and on particular flavors.

Choose according to circumstances

Wine is not consumed with every meal in everyday life. But if desired for a simple meal, it can be a simple, modest bottle without the accolade of a famous appellation. However, the pleasure of more elaborate cuisine is enhanced if it is accompanied by high quality wine. Here are some suggestions, which can be adapted according to your budget, with the knowledge that you can find real flavor experiences across a wide range of prices.

A SINGLE DISH. Simplicity is normally the name of the game when you and your friends gather to share a single, convivial dish: a chili, some spaghetti, or paella. For the first two, a fresh and fruity red such as a Beaujolais-Villages or Saumur-Champigny from France will go down very well. A rosé from Provence, Côtes du Rhône, or Languedoc will also complement any of these three dishes. The same wines can

Among the terms typically used to describe the delicate match of food and wine are marriage, alliance, and harmony. For a successful pairing, it's important to take into account the texture and flavor characteristics of both.

also be enjoyed with a Camembert at the end of the meal. From the New World, consider wines such as Grenache, Tempranillo, and Zinfandel.

A FAMILY GATHERING. For family feasts, several wines from well-known appellations might be suggested. In order to suit everyone, it's best to opt for "consensus" wines. Among French whites, the wines of Alsace, Entre-deux-Mers, Muscadet, and Saint-Véran should be mentioned. Several choices are possible for red wine. If we are talking about a roast: think of *crus* from Beaujolais, Côtes-de-Bourg, Gigondas, Madiran, Minervois, Bandol, Cornas, or Saint-Nicolas-de-Bourgueil. Other crowd-pleasers are Sauvignon Blanc and Pinot Gris among whites, and Cabernet Franc and Malbec among reds.

WITH A GOURMET MENU. The more refined the cuisine the more important it is that the accompanying wines should be of indisputable quality. Among the white wines you might consider one of the Côte de Beaune *crus* or a Hermitage, Pessac-Léognan, Savennières, Condrieu, Château-Chalon, an Alsace *grand cru*, or a *vin jaune* from the Jura. Good red wines are legion, although sometimes high-priced. Worthy choices are the grand families of Pomerol or Saint-Émilion, the classified *crus* of Médoc or Graves, the Côte-Rôtie, and the *premiers* and *grands crus* of Burgundy.

In what order?

AS AN APERITIF. Cocktails or spirits actually do nothing to help prepare the palate to appreciate delicious cuisine and accompanying wines. Before embarking on a good meal, the simplest option is to serve a white wine that will also go with the first course. The most elegant choice would be a glass of "blanc de blancs" Champagne.

WITH THE FIRST COURSE. The aim is to stimulate the taste buds without overwhelming them. For example, you could choose a lively, fruity Muscadet-type wine or one made from grapes such as Sauvignon Blanc, Sylvaner, Aligoté, or Chardonnay; these wines can also be served as an aperitif.

WITH THE MAIN COURSE. The important thing is to select one or more wines that will not clash with the preceding one. In general it's advisable to serve dry white wine before red, young red wine before an older one, the lightest wine before a fuller-bodied ones, and the simplest wine before the most complex.

SUNDAY MENU

Chicken liver terrine
> *Saint-Nicolas-de-Bourgueil (or light Cabernet Franc)*

Roast guinea-fowl with mushrooms
Saint-Nectaire cheese
> *Bourgogne Hautes-Côtes-de-Nuits (or savory Pinot Noir)*

Strawberry tart
> *Sainte-Croix-du-Mont (or late-harvest Semillon)*

While not too expensive, the wines suggested to serve with this Sunday meal are of reasonable quality and sufficient flexibility to go well with the classic French dishes. Each of the red wines suggested here can be served with the first course, main course, and the cheese. The dessert will be enhanced by the agreeable softness of the sweet white wine.

Wines for snacks

Here are some ideas for enjoying a good wine with just a snack rather than a whole meal. A Beaujolais, Beaujolais-Villages, Côte-Roannaise, Côtes-du-Forez, or a Coteaux-du-Lyonnais go well with all kinds of charcuterie. The same goes for good Chianti Classico and many Rhône-style blends from the New World.

A *vin jaune* from the Jura goes well with Comté cheese; a dry amontillado sherry works with a few shelled walnuts; a Banyuls pairs nicely with a good sheep's-milk cheese accompanied by a spoonful of black-cherry jam; a Gewurztraminer can be enjoyed with a mature Munster served with country bread. Partner Clairette de Die with a simple brioche and serve gourmet biscuits with *demi-sec* Champagne or off-dry sparkling wine.

> A chilled, crisp white wine is the perfect choice to prime the appetite.

WITH CHEESE. Cheese's naturally salty, lactic character goes better with white wines, dry or sweet, than with reds. Despite tradition, there is no point in serving the best wine from your cellar; there is no need to match your selection of cheeses with one *cru* or another (*see also p.172.*).

WITH DESSERT. You could opt for a sweet wine or for a white *vin doux naturel* (such as a French Muscat from Mireval, Rivesaltes, or Beaumes-de-Venise) or a red VDN (such as Rasteau, Rivesaltes, Banyuls, or port). These whites go particularly well with fruit-based desserts, while the reds are good with chocolate in all its various forms.

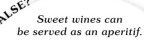

Sweet wines can be served as an aperitif.

TRUE. Although sweet wines are perfect dessert wines, they can also be enjoyed as an aperitif, especially if foie gras is to follow as a first course. For a holiday feast, choose Cérons, Coteaux-du-Layon, Jurançon, Sainte-Croix-du-Mont, or Monbazillac. For a gastronomic blowout, or for really special occasions, serve a late-harvest wine such as sweet Sauternes or rich Vouvray.

Choosing according to the season

Our food preferences are influenced, to some degree, by the weather. In cold weather, everyone appreciates rich, warming dishes; while summer heat sparks a desire for vegetables and fresh fruit. Likewise, the pleasure experienced from drinking

TRADITIONAL MENU

Oysters
> ***Chablis (or unoaked, cool-climate Chardonnay)***

Roast duck with small vegetables
> ***Saint-Émilion Grand Cru (or fine, structured Merlot)***

Roquefort
Gâteau Saint-Honoré
> ***Muscat de Beaumes-de-Venise (or any late-harvest Muscat)***

Down-to-earth, country cooking calls for the Chablis (or steely Chardonnay) served with the oysters, the comforting St-Émilion Grand Cru (or high-end Merlot) with the roast duck, and a great harmony of flavors with the perfect combination of Roquefort cheese and Muscat de Beaumes-de-Venise, which will remain on the table for the Gâteau Saint-Honoré.

This elegant menu for ten guests is one you can serve without worrying about pairing mistakes. The subtle food-wine matches are perfect: foie gras with a sweet white wine is a classic; the lamb, mushrooms, and Mimolette or Edam seem to have been made for great Médoc or a fine Cabernet. As for the chocolate cake, which everyone will enjoy, it has few wine affinities except with a vin doux naturel, such as this outstanding Banyuls.

this or that wine varies according to the seasons and the dishes featured on the menu.

CHILLED REDS AND SUMMER ROSÉS. In warm weather, lively, fruity wines are often best. The liveliness is conveyed by a sense of freshness, due to perceptible acidity and a touch of soft tannins. These quaffable reds can be served at a temperature around 57°F (14°C); they include French Beaujolais, Côtes-du-Forez, Coteaux-du-Lyonnais, Côte-Roannaise, Alsace Pinot Noir, Anjou, Bourgueil, Bordeaux, and Bordeaux Supérieur. Italian Dolcetto and Spanish Garnacha can also fit the bill.

THIRST-QUENCHING WHITES. If you want a snappy white, try a French Bourgogne Aligoté, Cheverny, Crépy, Entre-deux-Mers, Mâcon-Villages, Saint-Pourçain, Alsace Sylvaner, or a Vin de Savoie. If serving more sophisticated dishes, it's best to opt for the "blancs de

DID YOU KNOW...?

A strong, characterful wine is necessary to accompany a powerfully flavored dish. If you match a delicate dish with a really powerful wine, you risk killing the flavors of the food with those of the wine. For instance, a fish mousse should be accompanied by a dry, light wine, with good acidity, such as Muscadet or Sancerre; and a fish in sauce is best paired with a supple wine with subtle aromas, such as a Savennières or white Pessac-Léognan; while fish in meunière *sauce calls for an Alsace Riesling or a Mâcon Lugny; finally, Bouzy is a good choice for a* ris de veau *(veal sweetbreads).*

blancs," whether Champagne, Pouilly-Fumé, Sancerre, Chablis, Graves, or Alsace Riesling. Outside France, Sauvignon Blanc is generally a safe bet.

WINES FOR WINTER. Long winter evenings are made for rich, well-structured wines. The whites will be full-bodied and fleshy. To serve with good quality fish, shellfish, and white meats, try Corton-Charlemagne, Meursault, Puligny-Montrachet, Savennières, Alsace Gewurztraminer, Alsace Pinot Gris, white Châteauneuf-du-Pape, or California Chardonnay. Red wines should be robust and structured with fruit and tannins. There's no better accompaniment for roasted or sauced red meat, game stew, or other slow-cooked dishes than a red from Cahors, Madiran, Pauillac, Gevrey-Chambertin, Vacqueyras, Rioja, or Chilean Cabernet Sauvignon.

Match the dominant flavor of a dish

Taste buds are receptive to four basic flavors: sweet, salty, sour, and bitter. In food, these elements are perceived to varying degrees. In wine, it is accepted that "salty" hardly exists. For successful pairings of food and wine, it is advisable to not partner wines with dishes that have an excess of one of the four basic flavors.

WITH SALTY DISHES. Avoid overuse of salt (in cured meat, charcuterie, salty fish, etc.). It will detract from the appreciation of complex, old, mellow wines, whether red or

> Seafood's iodized flavor goes well with a simple white wine.

white. With rather salty dishes, it's best to serve very young, fruity, slightly sharp, thirst-quenching whites such as Muscadet, Saint-Véran, Vins de Savoie, or maybe red Sancerre.

WITH SWEET DISHES. Sugary dishes, including many containing fruit (peaches, cherries, prunes, figs, pineapple, coconut), will over-intensify dry wines. They make reds too astringent and whites too bitter. These dishes need very fruity wines that are soft and aromatic or very powerful. For dishes like the famous duck à l'orange, fortified wines like Banyuls or the exceptional *vin jaune* from the Jura make a perfect partnership.

WITH ACIDIC DISHES. Acidity is a threat to every tannic or mature wine. With a vinaigrette, for example, water is the only possible accompaniment. With a lightly acidic dish, serve a very young, simple white or rosé wine rather than a red, especially one that is very tannic and has been patiently aged. Otherwise a double offense will have been committed, against the wine and the dish!

WITH BITTER DISHES. Bitterness can be hidden in many ingredients, especially certain vegetables such as artichokes, asparagus, endives (chicory), and spinach. Coffee, tea, and chocolate are also bitter. Wines do not go well with bitter foods, which turn them hard and astringent. There are a few exceptions: Alsace Muscat, *vin jaune,* and sherry can be served with bitter vegetables (so long as these are not seasoned with a vinaigrette); red VDNs are fine with chocolate.

Harmonize textures and aromas

Lovers of fine food don't just appreciate a dish for its flavors, but also for its textures and aromas. In the context of a good meal, these elements should also be considered when choosing the wine.

TEXTURES. There are smooth wines (Beaujolais, Muscadet), fleshy wines (Burgundy, Côtes-du-Rhône), and astringent wines (wines from southwest France, Bordeaux). These characteristics can complement certain dishes. For instance, a beef stew is well

> A country terrine is a delicious reason for a wine tasting without having to serve a meal.

matched with a fruity, lively Beaujolais-Villages that will soften the fibrous texture of the beef and the pungent flavor of the sauce. Likewise, the cuisine of southwestern France is perfect with the well-structured wines of that region (Madiran, Cahors, Tursan, Côtes-du-Brulhois), with the tannins softened by the fleshy, full-flavored dishes. In general, dishes with a soft consistency are associated with light, low-tannin wines, while rich dishes with a fuller texture are best with a rounder wine.

AROMAS. Sometimes the food can enhance the wine, although this is not easy to achieve. Some partnerships are nevertheless well known: duck with cherries or figs intensifies the red and black fruit flavors of a Banyuls Rimage; a dish made with truffles is sublime with a mature Hermitage or a Pomerol; an orange or lemon tart enhances the bitter orange taste of an old Sauternes. The important thing to bear in mind is that the flavor of the wine should not overpower that of the dish, or vice versa.

Difficult pairings

Vinaigrettes and bitter vegetables (artichokes, asparagus, endives, spinach) kill the flavor of most good wines. Also, the natural sweetness of petits pois peas and carrots can blunt the taste of tannic reds. In the case of meats and fish, there is less chance that they will alter the taste of wine; nevertheless, take care with very spicy dishes (east Asian ones, for example) and with sweet-and-sour flavors (including Chinese). In general, this type of cuisine goes only with highly structured, aromatic white wines like Gewurztraminer, Riesling, and Pinot Gris, or rosés such as Tavel or Côtes-de-Provence, and also with the *vins doux naturels.* Few reds will suit them.

TRUE OR FALSE?

Wine suffers more from cold than heat.

FALSE. It is heat rather than cold at the point of service that can ruin the quality of a wine. White wines, rosés, and very young reds, above all, should be served chilled. It's interesting to note that a low temperature accentuates the sharper or tannic characters of these wines, enabling them to counterbalance the heaviness of certain dishes.

Proven partnerships

From a wide range of possibilities, some pairings of foods and wines have proven their worth and contributed to fine gastronomy.
WITH SEAFOOD. In the case of shellfish, the choices range from Muscadet through Entre-deux-Mers, Sancerre, Cassis, St-Véran, or perhaps a Bouzeron. For good quality fish served in sauce or with shellfish, it's better to go for the white *premiers* or *grands crus* from Burgundy or one of the rare white Hermitages. Riesling from Alsace, a region where great dry or sweet white wines proliferate, deserves fine seafood dishes or even caviar. Outside France, consider Italian Vermentino and Spanish Rueda.
WITH MEAT DISHES. There's nothing better for a grand occasion than a red Bordeaux, for instance with roast lamb. The most appropriate choices to serve with game are found among the great red Burgundies or a Côte-Rôtie, Madiran, Châteauneuf-du-Pape, or a Bandol. With a casserole, the preferred partner is a Côtes-du-Rhône-Villages or a Cahors. For a creamy chicken dish, the unctuous flavor of a white Burgundy such as Meursault makes a good choice. With grilled meat, a Médoc or a red wine from the Côte de Nuits is preferable. In the New World, good red options are Washington State Syrah, Oregon Pinot Noir, and Argentinian Malbec.
REGIONAL ALLIANCES. Many traditional European dishes have a natural affinity with the wines produced in their region. Cahors and Madiran are good partners for the rich cassoulets of southwest France. Switzerland's dry white wines are a splendid accompaniment to a fondue. In Spain, the dry white wines of Rías Baixas, made from the local Albariño grape, are served with Galician shellfish, while further inland classic red Riojas are traditionally served with roasted or grilled meat.

Wine and cheese: a delicate match

Making good partners with wine and cheese is not immediately obvious: cheese is salty, often with a pronounced flavor and a fairly dense texture. Those are tough characteristics for many wines to handle.
WITH RED WINES. Reds generally go less well with cheese than do white wines, as the salt accentuates their tannins. The custom of serving a mature red wine with cheese is often a mistake, because the subtle taste of the wine will be masked by the cheese's stronger flavor. There are a few exceptions, though: semi-soft cheeses with a "bloomy" crust (Brie, Camembert, or Coulommiers among others) go well with a Côte-de-Beaune, a Côtes-du-Rhône, a Pomerol, or a St-Émilion. Likewise, pressed, uncooked cheeses (Cantal, Gouda, Mimolette (Edam), St-Nectaire) make good partners for great, aged Bordeaux wines (Médoc, Pomerol, St-Émilion, Pessac-Léognan). In the New World, look for drier, lighter, aged styles of Pinot Noir and Merlot.
WITH WHITE WINES. Whether dry or somewhat sweeter, white wines are an easier pairing with cheese. Their sharpness brings a necessary freshness and their fruitiness counterbalances the cheese's strong flavor personality. The absence of tannins in white wines also explains this alliance. Tannin, especially in young red wines, is firmly accentuated by the salt content of cheeses.

TRUE OR FALSE?

The wine used to cook should be served at table.

TRUE. Wine features as an ingredient in many recipes. The traditional French *coq au vin* was originally made with wine from Chanturgues; it became *coq au vin jaune* in Jura, *coq au Chambertin* in Burgundy, and *coq au Riesling* in Alsace. Throughout Europe, meat is slow-cooked in wine, whether in a French *daube*, a Greek *stifado*, or an Italian *stufato*. These dishes should be served with a bottle of the same wine that was used to make them.

EXCEPTIONAL WINE CALLS FOR EXCEPTIONAL FOOD

With a top classified cru red from Bordeaux. To do a grand cru *justice*, the cooking sometimes needs a little adaptation. The many noble or fine tannins in a great Bordeaux do not go well with desserts, except for the one suggested here, where the wine can reveal its full complexity. Avoid putting too much garlic in the lamb.

> GASTRONOMIC MENU
>
> Quail stew
>
> Roast leg of lamb
>
> Pommes forestière
>
> Aged Mimolette (or Edam)
>
> Fresh fruits macerated in Bordeaux wine

> GASTRONOMIC MENU
>
> Foie gras
>
> Roast duck with peaches and spices
>
> Roquefort
>
> Puff pastries

With a Sauternes. An opulent, fleshy, dominant wine, Sauternes calls for savory, rich, spicy dishes. Its classic partners are foie gras, Roquefort, or puff pastries. In this menu, duck (which goes very well with fruit) is accompanied by peaches. Together with the Sauternes, it's a perfect partnership.

With a Banyuls. An opulent, powerful, rich wine that goes well with savory, spicy, strong-flavored dishes. Its high alcohol content is balanced by cool ingredients and fruit. The menu suggested here presents no problem.

> GASTRONOMIC MENU
>
> Duck foie gras
>
> Tajine of pigeon with almonds and raisins
>
> Stilton
>
> Gâteau Opéra

> GASTRONOMIC MENU
>
> Terrine of scallops
>
> Free-range chicken in cream and chanterelles
>
> Creamy Chaource
>
> Peach Melba

With a vintage Champagne. A "white" menu will highlight this great Champagne. The seafood, the lightness of the chicken, the cream, chanterelles, cheese, and Peach Melba all make splendid partners for this festive wine. Colors and textures come together in perfect harmony.

With a vin jaune from Jura, France. The unusual aromas (walnuts, spices, warm bread) and the dominating, persistent flavor of vin jaune will harmonize perfectly with each of the dishes suggested here; although it might be helpful to alert your guests to this wine's distinct character.

> GASTRONOMIC MENU
>
> Asparagus in sauce *mousseline*
>
> *Coq au vin jaune*
>
> Comté
>
> Walnut gâteau

Successful food and wine partnerships

The following table lists some classic or regional partnerships of foods and wines. It also suggests more surprising matches that have been discovered during tastings. However, these suggestions are only a guide; there are no fixed rules for pairings. Personal taste and culture strongly influence the appreciation of different flavors.

APPETIZERS	
Anchovies, fresh	White Banyuls, white Châteauneuf-du-Pape, Collioure rosé, Coteaux-d'Aix-en-Provence rosé, Spanish rosé, sherry.
Artichokes, stuffed (with bacon, mushroom, onion)	Coteaux-d'Aix-en-Provence rosé, Côtes-de-Provence rosé, Lirac rosé, Spanish rosé.
Asparagus, green	Viognier, dry Muscat, Alsace Muscat, Roussillon *vin de pays*, sherry.
Asparagus, white	Pinot Blanc, Alsace Muscat.
Avocado	Côtes-de-Provence rosé, Mâcon-Villages, Sancerre.
Caviar	*Blanc de blancs* Champagne, dry Alsace or German Reisling (Or iced vodka!)
Chicory (endive) and walnut salad	Savagnin-based Jura wines: Arbois, Côtes-du-Jura, L'étoile.
Eggs Mimosa (or deviled eggs)	Chinon rosé, Spanish rosé, white Côtes-de-Provence, Mâcon-Villages.
Foie gras terrine	Sweet wines such as Sauternes, Coteaux-du-Layon, Jurançon moelleux, Monbazillac, Pinot Gris *sélection de grains nobles*, Gewurztraminer *sélection de grains nobles*, or a fortified wine such as Banyuls Rimage or port.
Gazpacho	Spanish rosé, Collioure rosé, Côtes-du-Rhône-Villages rosé, Tavel.
Guacamole	Sauvignon Blanc, Spanish Rueda, unoaked Chardonnay.
Melon	*Vins doux naturels*: Muscat de Beaumes-de-Venise, Muscat de Rivesaltes, Banyuls, Rivesaltes; ruby port; sercial or bual Madeira.
Salad Auvergnate (mixed salad with sausage, and potatoes)	Beaujolais-Villages, Côtes-d'Auvergne, Côtes-du-Forez.
Salade niçoise (mixed salad with olives, tuna, anchovies)	Bandol rosé, white Bellet, white Cassis, Coteaux-d'Aix-en-Provence rosé.
Taramasalata	Pouilly Fumé, Alsace Riesling, or New World Sauvignon Blanc.

HOT FIRST COURSES	
Bacon quiche	Pinot Blanc, Pinot Gris, white wines from Savoie or light red wines (Beaujolais, lighter style Cabernet Franc, basic Pinot Noir).
Cheese soufflé	Jura wine made with Savagnin grapes, Arbois, Côtes-du-Jura, Château-Chalon.
Escargots à la bourguignonne (snails)	Bourgogne Aligoté, white Beaujolais, Chablis, Mâcon-Villages, or unoaked Chardonnay.
Fish soufflé	Chablis, white Graves, white Pessac-Léognan, Pouilly Fumé, California Fumé Blanc.
French onion soup	Beaujolais-Villages, Entre-deux-Mers, Mâcon-Villages, New World Chardonnay.
Fresh foie gras, warm	A rich, sweet wine such as Banyuls Rimage or Sauternes; full-bodied red wines (Madiran, Cahors, or other Malbecs).
Frogs' legs	Bourgogne Aligoté, Petit Chablis, Mâcon-Villages, unoaked Chardonnay.
Garbure (stew with cabbage, beans, salted duck or pork, etc.)	Cahors, Irouléguy, Madiran, or New World Malbec or Tannat.
Onion tart	Pinot Blanc or Sylvaner.
Petits farcis provençaux (zucchini or other stuffed vegetables Provençal-style)	Bandol rosé, white or rosé Bellet, red Côtes-du-Rhône-Villages, Tavel, or New World Grenache.
Pike quenelles	Chablis, Pouilly-Fuissé, Saint-Véran, Roussette de Savoie, lightly oaked Chardonnay.
Pizza	Coteaux-d'Aix-en-Provence red or rosé, Luberon red or rosé, Chianti, Valpolicella, Zinfandel.
Vol-au-vent	Jura *vin jaune*, a great Chardonnay (Corton-Charlemagne, Meursault, Montrachet, Sonoma Chardonnay).

CHARCUTERIE

Andouille (pork sausage)	Mâcon-Villages, Sancerre, Savennières, South African Chenin Blanc.
Boudin noir (black pudding)	Chinon, Crozes-Hermitage, Saint-Joseph, Saumur-Champigny, and good New World Cabernet Franc or Syrah.
Chicken liver mousse	Beaujolais *crus*, white Beaune, white Ladoix-Serrigny, Meursault, or full-bodied New World Chardonnay.
Chorizo (spicy)	Cahors, Irouléguy, Rioja, Grenache, Zinfandel.
Country pâté	Beaujolais, Chinon, Coteaux-du-Lyonnais, Côtes-du-Rhône-Villages, Crozes-Hermitage, Saint-Joseph, Saumur-Champigny, and New World Cabernet Franc or Syrah.
Dried sausage or salami	Crozes-Hermitage, Burgundy Hautes-Côtes-de-Beaune, Burgundy Hautes-Côtes-de-Nuits, Sancerre rouge, and Sonoma Pinot Noir or Washington State Syrah.
Game terrine	Bergerac, Châteauneuf-du-Pape, Mercurey, Gevrey-Chambertin, Pomerol, St-Émilion, Vacqueyras, Garrafeira from central Portugal, and many good American Rhône-style blends.
Ham, cooked	Beaujolais-Villages or Beaujolais *crus*, Mercurey, Mâcon-Villages.
Ham, cured	Collioure, Irouléguy, Pinot Grigio from Italy's Alto Adige, Soave Classico, Rheingau Riesling trocken (dry), fino or manzanilla sherry, and many young Spanish red wines.
Ham, smoked	Riesling—French *vendange tardive* style, German *spätlese* style, or New York State off-dry style.
Jambon persillé (cold ham in parsleyed gelatin)	White or red Beaujolais, Chablis, white Mercurey, Pouilly-Fuissé, white Saint-Romain, and many good unoaked Chardonnays.
Pork sausage	Buzet, Côtes-du-Rhône, Gigondas, Italian Dolcetto d'Alba, Washington State Merlot, and Spanish Rioja.
Rabbit terrine	Bourgueil, Cheverny, Cour-Cheverny, St-Nicolas-de-Bourgueil, Morgon, Moulin-à-Vent, and good New World Cabernet Franc.
Rillettes	Montlouis, Sancerre, Vouvray, as well as New World Chenin Blanc and Sauvignon Blanc.
Salami	Irouléguy, Tavel, Vin de Corse rosé; red or rosé wine Spain's Navarre; red from Italy's Barbera, Chianti Classico, Montepulciano d'Abruzzo, Rosso Conero; or dry amontillado sherry.

EGGS

Eggs in gelatin	Young, fruity wines from the Côte de Beaune (Santenay, Maranges).
Eggs poached in red wine	Beaujolais *crus*, red Mâcon, Pinot Noir from the Côte de Beaune and Côte Chalonnaise, as well as basic Pinot Noir from Oregon.
Omelette, cheese	Chardonnays and Savagnin from Jura, France; and unoaked New World Chardonnay.
Salmon eggs (red caviar)	Chablis, Alsace Riesling, Vouvray; and good South African Chenin Blanc.
Scrambled eggs	Light and fruity red wines (Beaujolais or unoaked New World Gamay).
Scrambled eggs with truffles	White Hermitage, Montrachet, and Sonoma Chardonnay.

SHELLFISH

Crab	White Cassis, Chablis, Entre-deux-Mers, Muscadet, New Zealand Sauvignon Blanc, and good American Chardonnay.
Crayfish, poached in wine or broth	Condrieu, white Châteauneuf-du-Pape, dry Riesling.
Crayfish, grilled	Chablis Premier or Grand Cru, white Hermitage, Pessac-Léognan, Riesling.
Lobster in a tomato and tarragon sauce	Good Pinot Gris, Jura *vin jaune*, medium-dry Vouvray or Chenin Blanc.
Lobster, grilled	Corton-Charlemagne, white Hermitage, Pessac-Léognan, Meursault, Alsace Riesling, Savennières, Verdicchio dei Castelli di Jesi, good Washington State or Sonoma Chardonnay.
Mussels in cream sauce	White Bergerac, white Côtes-de-Blaye, Pouilly-Fuissé, white Rully, and crisp New World Chardonnay.
Mussels in white wine	Entre-deux-Mers, Muscadet, Sauvignon Blanc, Albariño.
Oysters	Chablis, Entre-deux-Mers, Muscadet, Picpoul-de-Pinet, young Riesling.
Oysters, cooked	*Blanc de blancs* Champagne, white Graves, rich Riesling, Savennières, Vouvray, and good New World Chenin Blanc.
Paella	White Yecla (Spain), dry rosé, and generally any dry aromatic white wine, such as Sauvignon Blanc.
Prawns/langoustines in mayonnaise	Pouilly Fumé and Sancerre, or any good Sauvignon Blanc; as well as Chablis or any good unoaked Chardonnay.
Scallops	*Blanc de blancs* Champagne, white Châteauneuf-du-Pape, white Hermitage, Pessac-Léognan, good dry Riesling.
Shrimp	White Bergerac, white Cassis, Petit Chablis, Entre-deux-Mers, Muscadet, Picpoul-de-Pinet, and most crisp, unoaked whites from around the world.
Shrimp in sweet and sour sauce	Pinot Gris, Alsace Muscat, Tavel, Bellet rosé.

FISH	
Bouillabaisse	Bandol rosé, Cassis, Coteaux-d'Aix-en-Provence rosé, Tavel, as well as Spanish rosé.
Cod, salted, with aïoli	White or rosé Bandol, Cassis, white or rosé Côtes-de-Provence, rosé Collioure, Irouléguy rosé, as well as Spanish rosé.
Cod, salted, in purée	Cassis, white Hermitage, white Saint-Joseph, and good Roussanne.
Eel in Bordelaise sauce	Red Bergerac, red Bordeaux supérieur, Graves, satellite appellations of St-Émilion, and good New World Cabernet Franc.
Fish pie (with cream sauce)	Mâcon-Villages, Pouilly-Fuissé, Oregon Pinot Gris, Bianco di Custoza, Pfälz (Germany) Sylvaner, Nahe (Germany) Müller-Thurgau, and Napa Valley Chardonnay.
Fish, plain	White wines of a varying degree of crispness, depending on how fatty the fish and its garnish are: from Chilean Chardonnay to one of the *grands crus* of Burgundy or Alsace. Red wines, if not too tannic (such as Cabernet Franc, Gamay, or Pinot Noir).
Fish terrine	Bouzeron Aligoté, Chablis, white Graves, Mâcon-Villages, Muscadet, Sancerre, Alsace Sylvaner, and lightly oaked New World Chardonnay.
Freshwater fish	Chablis, Swiss Chasselas, white Graves, white Mercurey, Montlouis, white Rully, Sancerre, Vouvray, and good New World Pinot Gris and Pinot Blanc.
Fried fish	Beaujolais, Entre-deux-Mers, Gamay, Muscadet, Roussette de Savoie, Chardonnay- or Savagnin-based whites from the Jura, Pinot Grigio from Friuli (Italy), Frascati Superiore (Italy), and good Sauvignon Blanc.
Hake, cold with mayonnaise	Mâcon-Villages, Pinot Blanc, white Vin de Savoie, and Sylvaner.
Oily fish (swordfish, herring, mackerel, sardines, tuna)	Bourgogne Aligoté, Muscadet, Sancerre, Sauvignon Blanc from South Africa and New Zealand, Sylvaner, white Dão (Portugal), Vinho Verde (Portugal).
Raw fish	Chablis Premier Cru, Meursault, white Graves, New Zealand Chardonnay.
Red mullet	Red Bandol or Bandol rosé, Collioure, red or white Côtes-de-Provence.
Salmon in sorrel sauce	Condrieu, white Châteauneuf-du-Pape, and good Viognier.
Salmon, poached	Whites: white Burgundy, Sancerre, Savennières, dry Vouvray, Sicilian white wine, and good Chenin Blanc. Reds: Beaujolais-Villages, Bourgueil, and Oregon Pinot Noir.
Salmon, smoked	*Blanc de blancs* Champagne, good dry Riesling, Sancerre (or a peaty single-malt whisky).
Sardines, grilled	Côtes-de-Provence, white Côtes-du-Rhône-Villages, white Coteaux-du-Languedoc.
Sea bass (Bass), grilled	White Bellet, white Châteauneuf-du-Pape, white Côtes-de-Provence, Chablis Premier or Grand Cru, and good American Chardonnay.
Smoked fish	Chablis Premier Cru, *blanc de blancs* Champagne, Pouilly-Fumé, Sancerre, off-dry Riesling, and Pinot Gris.
Sole meunière	White Bellet, Chablis Premier or Grand Cru, Sancerre or other good Sauvginon Blanc, and Riesling.
Sushi	Mâcon, Muscadet, St-Véran, Menetou-Salon, New Zealand Sauvignon Blanc.
Tuna Basque-style (with ham and tomatoes)	Red or rosé Collioure, red or rosé Coteaux-du-Languedoc, red Côtes-du-Rhône-Villages, Irouléguy rosé, Tavel, and Spanish rosé.
Turbot in hollandaise sauce	Corton-Charlemagne, white Hermitage, Meursault, Pessac-Léognan, and good Sonoma or Washington State Chardonnay.
White fish in *beurre blanc*	*Blanc de blancs* Champagne, dry or medium-dry Vouvray, Meursault, Pessac-Léognan, Puligny-Montrachet, Savennières, Mosel (Germany) Rieslings, and good Sonoma or Washington State Chardonnay.
White fish, grilled	A dry white *grand cru*, white Coteaux-d'Aix-en-Provence, Soave (Italy), Verdicchio (Italy), white Vin de Corse, and oaked dry Semillon.
Whitebait, fried	Bourgogne Aligoté, Mâcon, Muscadet, Vinho Verde (Portugal).

LAMB	
Lamb couscous	Cahors, Côtes-du-Rhône-Villages, Madiran, Gigondas, and good New World Grenache and Rhône-style blends.
Lamb curry	Bergerac, Castillon-Côtes-de-Bordeaux, Francs-Côtes-de-Bordeaux, Lalande-de-Pomerol. (Also, good beer!)
Lamb sautéed Provence-style	Red Coteaux-d'Aix-en-Provence, red Côtes-de-Provence, Côtes-du-Rhône-Villages, and good New World Grenache and Rhône-style blends.
Lamb stew	Pinot Noir from Côte de Beaune, Côte Chalonnaise, Oregon, and New Zealand, as well as Beaujolais *crus*.
Leg of lamb with herbs and/or garlic	Generous, powerful red wines (Bandol, Châteauneuf-du-Pape, Côtes-du-Roussillon-Villages, Coteaux-du-Languedoc, St-Chinian, Vacqueyras, and good New World Syrah and Rhône-style blends).
Mechoui (spit-roasted lamb)	Red Coteaux-du-Languedoc, Bandol, red Coteaux-de-Mascara (Algeria), and good New World Syrah and Grenache.
Rack of lamb	Graves, Médoc, Pauillac, Pessac-Léognan, St-Julien, as well as California, Washington State, and Chilean Cabernet Sauvignon.
Roast lamb	Classy, complex red wines like the Bordelais *crus* (Graves, Margaux, Pauillac, Pomerol, St-Émilion), a good vintage Bandol; Spanish Rioja Reserva and Ribera del Duero; California, Washington State, Chilean Cabernet Sauvignon.
Roast shoulder of lamb	Haut-Médoc, Médoc, and California, Washington State, or Chilean Cabernet Sauvignon
Saddle of lamb	Côte-Rôtie, Hermitage, Médoc, Pomerol, St-Émilion, and good New World Cabernet, Merlot, or Syrah.
Tajine of lamb with apricots	Bonnezeaux, Coteaux-de-l'Aubance, Coteaux-du-Layon, Quarts-de-Chaume, Montlouis Moelleux, Vouvray Moelleux. Also good Oregon Pinot Gris or Pinot Blanc.
Whole leg of lamb, spit-roasted	Pinot Noir from Côte de Beaune or from Oregon; Cabernet Franc from Bourgueil, Chinon, St-Nicolas-de-Bourgueil, or Washington State.

BEEF	
Beef casserole	Cahors, Corbières, Côtes-du-Rhône-Villages, Côtes-du-Roussillon-Villages, Madiran, and a broad range of New World Malbec, Syrah and Rhône-style blends.
Beef Wellington	Reds from Bordeaux (Médoc or the Libournais) and Burgundy. Also good New World Cabernet Sauvignon and Pinot Noir.
Bœuf bourguignon	New World Cabernet Franc and Pinot Noir.
Carpaccio	Reds from the Côte Chalonnaise; Chianti Classico or Chianti Rufina; good New World Sangiovese.
Chateaubriand	Gevrey-Chambertin, Graves, Pomerol, Pommard, St-Émilion. Also good New World Merlot and Pinot Noir.
Chili con carne	Argentinian Malbec; California Zinfandel; St-Chinian, Cahors.
Couscous with meatballs	Gris de Boulaouane (Morocco), Fitou, red Coteaux-de-Mascara (Algeria), Côtes-du-Rhône, New World Rhône-style blends, Cairanne rosé, and, in general, lively, fruity or full-bodied rosés.
Entrecôte à la bordelaise	Bergerac, Bordeaux supérieur, Côtes-de-Blaye, Castillon-Côtes-de-Bordeaux, Fronsac, Graves, and good New World Cabernet France and Merlot.
Entrecôte, grilled	Cabernet Sauvignon-based wines from around the world, including a recent vintage Médoc. Also, young, generous wine Rhône-style blends (including Châteauneuf-du-Pape, Cornas, Gigondas, Vacqueyras).
Pot-au-feu (beef stew)	Red Anjou, Bourgueil, Côtes-de-Bordeaux, Saumur-Champigny, Pinot d'Alsace, red Sancerre. Also, New World Cabernet Franc and Pinot Noir.
Roast beef	Powerful, well-structured generous, red wines (from the Côte de Nuits, Margaux, Pauillac, Pomerol, and St-Émilion to Washington State Merlot and Oregon Pinot Noir).
Steak tartare	Buzet, Cahors, Crozes-Hermitage, Chilean Merlot, Australian Shiraz.
Steak with pepper sauce	Red Côtes-du-Rhône, Fronton, California Zinfandel, Australian Shiraz.
Steak, grilled	Chénas, Fronton, Cornas, Moulin-à-Vent, Chianti Classico Riserva, as well as Washington State Syrah and Argentinian Malbec.

PORK	
Andouillette à la crème (sausage made with pork chitterlings in cream sauce)	White Beaujolais, Chablis, Pouilly-Fuissé, white Rully, Saint-Véran, and good, rich, New World Chardonnay.
Andouillette, grilled	Light red wines (red Anjou, Beaujolais-Villages, Gamay, Pinot Noir, red Sancerre); dry, fruity white wines (Chablis, Gaillac, white Saumur, good New World Chardonnay).
Choucroute (dressed sauerkraut/white cabbage)	Alsace Pinot Gris, Alsace Riesling, Alsace Sylvaner.
Curried pork	Pinot Gris, Gewurztraminer, white Lirac, white Hermitage, and, in general, fragrant, dry, white wines.
Pork grill	Full-bodied, fruity wines: Bergerac, Crozes-Hermitage, Saint-Joseph, Saumur-Champigny, and good New World Cabernet Franc and Syrah.
Pork shoulder	Light white wines (white Anjou, Mâcon-Villages, Pinot Blanc, Sylvaner, dry Riesling) and light, fruity red wines (Beaujolais, Mâcon-Villages, young Pinot Noir).
Potée au chou (pork and cabbage soup/stew)	Brouilly, Mâcon-Villages, red Sancerre, and good young Pinot Noir.
Roast pork	Crozes-Hermitage, Côte-de-Beaune, Côtes-du-Rhône-Villages, Saint-Joseph, and New World Rhône-style blends.

VEAL	
Blanquette de veau (creamy veal stew)	Beaujolais-Villages, Mâcon-Villages, white Mercurey, white Givry, red Sancerre, and good, rich New World Chardonnay.
Calf's head	Beaujolais *crus*, Pouilly-Fuissé, Sancerre rosé, Tavel and other good, dry rosé.
Escalope Normande (with mushrooms, calvados, and cream sauce)	White Burgundy, Chardonnay- or Savagnin-based Jura wine, California Chardonnay, Washington State Chardonnay.
Escalope, fried	Beaujolais *crus*, red wines from Côte de Beaune, red Graves. Also Oregon and New Zealand Pinot Noir.
Osso-buco	Barbera, Barbaresco, Chianti Classico, Valpolicella.
Pan-fried veal kidneys in mustard sauce	Full-bodied, fairly young red wine (Pomerol, Saint-Émilion); Chinon, Morgon, St-Amour, Côte Chalonnaise Pinot Noir. Also good New World Cabernet Franc and Merlot.
Roast veal	Beaujolais *crus*, Côte de Beaune Pinot Noir, Oregon and New Zealand Pinot Noir.
Rolled veal	Beaujolais *crus*, Bourgueil, St-Nicolas-de-Bourgueil, New World Cabernet Franc, Burgundy Pinot Noir, Oregon and New Zealand Pinot Noir.

Veal chop	Médoc *grands crus* (Pauillac, St-Estèphe), *crus* from the Côte de Nuits (Gevrey-Chambertin, Chambolle-Musigny). Also, fine California Cabernet and Oregon Pinot Noir.
Veal liver	Chinon, Pomerol, St-Émilion, red Sancerre. Also, good New World Cabernet Franc and Merlot.
Veal Marengo (with mushrooms and red wine)	Côtes-du-Rhône-Villages, Costières-de-Nîmes, Ventoux, red wine from Dão (Portugal). Also, good New World Grenache and Rhône-style blends.
Veal Orloff (braised with mushrooms and béchamel sauce)	A great white Burgundy such as Chassagne-Montrachet, Corton-Charlemagne, Meursault; also deep, fruity red wines, *e.g.* a Burgundy from the Côte de Beaune. From the New World, try Sonoma Chardonnay or Oregon Pinot Noir.
Veal sweetbreads in cream sauce	A great white Burgundy such as Corton-Charlemagne, Meursault, Montrachet, Château-Chalon; Jura *vin jaune*, Alsace Pinot Gris, medium-dry Vouvray. Also, rich New World Chardonnay or Pinot Gris.

DUCK, GOOSE, PIGEON

Cassoulet	Cahors, Côtes-du-Brulhois, Madiran. Also New World Malbec and Rhône-style red blends.
Duck à l'orange	Young sweet wines: Cérons, Loupiac, Monbazillac, Sauternes, Jura *vin jaune*. Also, late-harvest Sémillon.
Duck confit	Bergerac, Buzet, Cahors, Châteauneuf-du-Pape, Madiran, Pécharmant. Also, New World Malbec and Rhône-style red blends.
Duck with figs or cherries	Rich, powerful wines (Bandol, Châteauneuf-du-Pape, Rhône-style red blends); young fortified wines (Banyuls, Maury, Rivesaltes).
Duck with olives	Côtes-du-Rhône-Villages, Gigondas, Vacqueyras, and New World Rhône-style blends.
Peking duck	Gewurztraminer or Pinot Gris, and Arbois, Château-Chalon, or Jura *vin jaune*.
Magret (duck breast)	Good Bordeaux vintages (Médoc and Libournais). Also good Cabernet and Merlot.
Pigeon pastilla (savory game bird pie)	Rioja or good New World Tempranillo. Also, a fortified wine (Banyuls, Muscat de Beaumes-de-Venise, Muscat de Rivesaltes, or Muscat du Cap-Corse); red Costières-de-Nîmes; Alsace Muscat; Gris de Boulaouane (Morocco).
Roast duck	Merlot-based wines: Lalande-de-Pomerol, Pomerol, Saint-Émilion; also good Pinot Noir such as *crus* from the Côte de Nuits.
Roast goose	Mature red wines from Côte-Rôtie (or Syrah), Côte-de-Nuits (or Pinot Noir), Madiran (or Tannat), Margaux (or Cabernet), St-Émilion (or Merlot), and even late-harvest Pinot Gris.
Roast pigeon	A good vintage Cabernet or Merlot from Médoc or the Libournais; or a Bandol, Châteauneuf-du-Pape, or Hermitage. Even a Chilean Merlot.
Salmis de palombes (slow-cooked pigeon breast)	Pomerol, Saint-Émilion, Chilean Merlot, Washington State Merlot.

POULTRY

Chicken Basque-style (chicken fricassee-style dish with tomatoes, peppers, and ham)	Bordeaux supérieur, Corbières, Coteaux-du-Languedoc, Fronton. Also good New World Merlot and Grenache.
Chicken with cream and mushrooms	Arbois, Château-Chalon, Jura *vin jaune*, good Pinot Noir or Chardonnay from Côte de Beaune, Sonoma, or Oregon.
Chicken with ginger	White wines that are medium-dry and rich, or sweet such as Jurançon, late-harvest Gewurztraminer, and late-harvest Pinot Gris.
Chicken with truffles	Great Chardonnays (Corton-Charlemagne, Meursault, Montrachet, Russian River California), white Hermitage, Arbois, Château-Chalon, Jura *vin jaune*.
Chicken vinaigrette	Anjou-Villages, Bourgueil, Chinon, St-Nicolas-de-Bourgueil, Saumur-Champigny, and good New World Cabernet Franc.
Chicken, roast	Good Pinot Noir from France (Côte de Beaune, Côte Chalonnaise), New Zealand, or the USA. Also Gamay (Moulin-à-Vent).
Chicken, stewed	Beaujolais, white Mâcon, Pouilly-Fuissé, white Rully, and generally good Chardonnay.
Coq au vin	Burgundy, New Zealand, or Oregon Pinot Noir. Also Gamay (Moulin-à-Vent).
Turkey with chestnuts	Côte Chalonnaise Pinot Noir (Mercurey, Givry) or Côte de Beaune (Savigny-les-Beaune, Volnay). Also New Zealand or American Pinot Noir.
Turkey, stuffed	Full-bodied wines such as Châteauneuf-du-Pape, Hermitage, Pomerol, Madiran, St-Émilion, and Washington State or Chilean Merlot. Also good Oregon or Sonoma Pinot Noir.

RABBIT

Rabbit in mustard sauce	Chénas, Chinon, Mercurey, red Sancerre, St-Joseph. Also a broad spectrum of good New World Cabernet Franc, Pinot Noir, and Syrah.
Rabbit stew	Beaujolais-Villages, Bourgueil, Côte Chalonnaise, Saumur-Champigny. Also, good New World Cabernet Franc.

Rabbit with prunes	Bergerac, Buzet, Côtes-de-St-Mont, red Gaillac, Pécharmant. Also, good New World Malbec.
Roast rabbit with thyme	Les Baux-de-Provence, Coteaux-d'Aix-en-Provence, Palette, red Vin de Corse. Also, good NewWorld Rhone-style red blends.

GAME

Game generally	In principle, serve the best red vintages at their peak: *grands crus* from Burgundy, Bordeaux, or the Rhône Valley. Also, top New World Pinot Noir, Cabernet, and Syrah.
Game, marinaded	Cahors, Châteauneuf-du-Pape, Madiran, Gigondas, Vacqueyras. Also good New World Rhone-style red blends.
Haunch of venison with huntsman's sauce	Côte-Rôtie, Hermitage, Corton, Châteauneuf-du-Pape. Also, good New World Syrah.
Jugged hare	Bandol from a great year, Côte-Rôtie, *grands crus* from Côte de Nuits, Châteauneuf-du-Pape, Hermitage, Pomerol, St-Émilion. Also, good New Zealand Pinot Noir and Washinton State Merlot or Syrah.
Roast haunch of boar	Châteauneuf-du-Pape, Côtes-du-Roussillon-Villages, Corbières, St-Chinian, and good New World Rhone-style red blends.
Small feathered game (wood-cock, pheasant, partridge)	Pinot Noir from Côte de Beaune, Côte de Nuits, New Zealand, Oregon, and Sonoma.
Small furred game (wild rabbit, hare)	Côte Chalonnaise Pinot Noir, Médoc, St-Émilion. Also good New World Pinot Noir and Merlot.

VEGETABLES (SEE ALSO APPETIZERS)

Cabbage, stuffed	Beaujolais-Villages, Gamay, South African Pinotage.
Cauliflower	Luberon, Dolcetto, Sauvignon Blanc.
Eggplant	Red Coteaux-d'Aix-en-Provence, Coteaux-du-Languedoc, and red Côtes-de-Provence; also Greek red wines (Xinomavro, Naoussa).
French green beans	White Sancerre or Sancerre rosé, Coteaux-d'Aix-en-Provence rosé, white Côtes-de-Provence. Also, good New Zealand Sauvignon Blanc.
Gratin dauphinois (gratin potatoes)	Chardonnay- or Savagnin-based white wines from the Jura, *e.g.* white Arbois; white Roussette-based wines from Savoie; good Sonoma Chardonnay.
Mushrooms	Merlot- or Pinot Noir-based wines at their peak, such as reds from the Libournais (Bordeaux) and Burgundy, or Washington State and Oregon.
Pasta	Light white, rosé, or red wines depending on the ingredients in the sauce.
Pasta with tomato and basil	Good rosés, including from Côtes-du-Rhône-Villages, Lirac, or Coteaux-d Aix-en-Provence.
Pasta with meat sauce	Beaujolais-Villages, Bourgueil, Coteaux-du-Tricastin, Mâcon-Villages, Chianti Classico, Valpolicella, and Zinfandel.
Seafood pasta	Chablis, Mâcon-Villages, Sancerre, Sauvignon Blanc, dry whites from Italy.
Raw vegetables	Dry white wines, Bourgogne Aligoté, Petit Chablis, Sauvignon Blanc, or light Gamay-based reds.
Risotto	Dry, fruity Italian white wines (Pinot Grigio, Bianco di Custoza, Trebbiano d'Abruzzo), Italian red wines (Chianti Classico), or Spanish reds (Rioja or La Mancha).
Truffles	Good Merlots such as Pomerol and St-Émilion *grands crus*; also good Syrah such as from the north Rhône Valley (Côte-Rôtie, Hermitage); and good Barolo (Italy).

DESSERTS

Chocolate-based desserts	Fortified red wines (Banyuls, Maury, Malaga, port, Rivesaltes).
Crème brûlée	Muscat-based *vins doux naturels* (Muscat de Rivesaltes, Muscat de St-Jean-de-Minervois), Jurançon, Pacherenc-du-Vic-Bilh.
Desserts with spices	Aromatic, sweet wines (late harvest Pinot Gris or Pinot Gris *sélection de grains nobles*, and Jurançon).
Entremets (between courses – palate cleanser)	Dry or medium-dry Champagne; Clairette de Die, Muscat-based *vins doux naturels*.
Floating islands(meringue with vanilla custard)	Medium-dry rosé Champagne, Muscat-based *vins doux naturels*.
Fruit Charlotte	Medium-dry Champagne, Muscat-based *vins doux naturels* (Muscat de Beaumes-de-Venise, Muscat de Rivesaltes, Moscatel de Valence).
Fruit Sabayon	Sweet, Sauternes-type wines, late harvest Pinot Gris and Gewurztraminer *sélection de grains nobles*.
Lemon tart	Sweet wines (Cérons, Jurançon, Ste-Croix-du-Mont, Sauternes).
Red berry tart	Dry or medium-dry rosé Champagne, Clairette de Die, sparkling Gaillac, Muscat-based *vins doux naturels*.
Tarte Tatin (caremalized apple tart)	Rich Loire Valley wines such as Bonnezeaux, Coteaux-du-Layon, Coteaux-de-l'Aubance, Montlouis moelleux, Quarts-de-Chaume. Also, late-harvest Semillon.

Pairing cheeses with wines

The table below lists the seven great cheese categories with their chief characteristics, the best-known examples of each category, and their classic wine pairings.

The table on page 183 presents, in alphabetical order, a selection of cheeses together with the wines that suit them best.

GREAT CHEESE CATEGORIES AND WINE MATCHES	
FROMAGE FRAIS AND WHITE CHEESES	
Examples	All fromage frais and white cheeses made with cows' or goats' milk, *e.g.* Fontainebleau, Petit-Suisse.
Characteristics	Soft consistency, strong milky taste, more or less salty, perceptibly sharp.
Complementary wines	If serving the cheese with sugar or, better still, honey, select sugar-rich wines such as Muscat-based VDNs (Muscat de Rivesaltes, Muscat de Mireval) or soft, aromatic wines (late-harvest Gewurztraminer, late-harvest Pinot Gris, Jurançon); if they are served with herbs, salt, and pepper, choose a dry, aromatic white wine (Condrieu, Pinot Gris, Viognier).
GOATS' MILK AND SHEEPS' MILK CHEESE	
Examples	Broccio, Chabichou, Charolais, Crottin de Chavignol, Pélardon, Pouligny-Saint-Pierre, Saint-Félicien, Saint-Marcellin, Selles-sur-Cher, Valençay.
Characteristics	The density of the cheese depends on how long it has been matured: whether it is fresh, semi-dry, or dry. The drier the cheese, the stronger and saltier it will taste.
Complementary wines	Select soft, fruity, dry white wines (Chablis, dry Jurançon, Pouilly-Fuissé, dry Vouvray) and lean toward Sauvignon Blanc-based wines (Sancerre and Pouilly-Fumé); alternatives are medium-dry white Chenin Blancs (Vouvrays or Montlouis) and light, low-tannic reds made from Gamay grapes (Beaujolais), Cabernet Franc (Bourgueil, St-Nicolas-de-Bourgueil), or even Pinot Noir (Hautes-Côtes-de-Beaune, Hautes-Côtes-de-Nuits, Oregon or Sonoma Pinot Noir).
SEMI-SOFT CHEESE WITH SURFACE CRUST	
Examples	Brie, Brillat-savarin, Camembert, Chaource, Coulommiers.
Characteristics	Smooth cheeses with a taste ranging from sweet and creamy to powerful or strong.
Complementary wines	Avoid young and tannic reds; it's best to go for reds that are fruity and have very little oak influence (Pinot Noir such as Burgundy from Côte Chalonnaise and Côte de Beaune, Coteaux Champenois, red Sancerre; red Côtes-du-Rhône; Pomerol, St-Émilion); also young *blanc des blancs* Champagnes.
SEMI-SOFT CHEESE WITH WASHED RIND	
Examples	Époisses, Livarot, Pont-l'Évêque, Langres, Maroilles, Mont d'Or, Munster, Reblochon, Vacherin.
Characteristics	Creamy cheeses with a pronounced, often powerful, flavors.
Complementary wines	Avoid powerful, full-bodied reds; choose aromatic white wines (Gewurztraminer, dry or late harvest; peak-condition Meursault; mature Riesling; Jura *vin jaune*; and mature Champagnes).
BLUE CHEESE	
Examples	Bleu d'Auvergne, Bleu de Bresse, Fourme d'Ambert, Roquefort, Stilton.
Characteristics	Creamy, often fatty, cheeses with a strong, salty taste.
Complementary wines	Choose sugar-rich wines such as white or red VDNs (Muscat de Beaumes-de-Venise, Banyuls, Rivesaltes), and sweet wines (Coteaux-du-Layon, Quarts-de-Chaume, Cérons, Sauternes).
PRESSED, UNCOOKED CHEESE	
Examples	Cantal, Edam, Gouda, Mimolette, Morbier, St-Nectaire, Tomme de Savoie.
Characteristics	These are often formed into balls or wheels; some have a creamy texture, others a denser body.
Complementary wines	Select mature Bordeaux or similar red wines (Médoc, Pauillac, Pomerol, St-Émilion, good New World Cabernet or Merlot) and also, for the wheels, white wines from Jura or Savoie.
PRESSED, COOKED CHEESE	
Examples	Appenzell, Comté, Emmental, Fribourg, Gruyère.
Characteristics	Hard, rather salty cheeses, often with a strong taste.
Complementary wines	Best with rather aromatic, dry, white wines, preferably from Savagnin grapes like the Jura *vin jaune*; also opulent, mature, white wines such as Meursault and Sonoma Chardonnay.

CHEESE FROM A TO Z WITH BEST WINE PAIRINGS

CHEESE	WINES	CHEESE	WINES
Abbaye de Cîteaux	Beaujolais-Villages, Côte Chalonnaise, Fleurie, Gamay.	Livarot	Late-harvest Gewurztraminer, late-harvest Pinot Gris.
Appenzell	Château-Chalon, Jura *vin jaune*.	Maroilles	Full-bodied Gewurztraminer, late-harvest Pinot Gris.
Banon	Red Côtes-du-Rhône-Villages, good New World Grenache, white Côtes-de-Provence.	Mimolette, aged	Graves, Médoc, Pomerol, St-Émilion, good New World Cabernet Sauvignon and Merlot.
Basque or Corsican sheeps' milk cheese	Dry Jurançon, Muscat du Cap-Corse.	Mont-d'Or	Mature Swiss Chasselas (Dézaley), Mâcon-Villages, Roussette de Savoie.
Beaufort	Château-Chalon, Jura *vin jaune*.	Morbier	White wine from Savoie.
Bleu d'Auvergne	Loupiac, Maury, Sainte-Croix-du-Mont, young Sauternes.	Munster	Dry or late-harvest Gewurztraminer.
Bleu de Bresse	Monbazillac, white Rivesaltes.	Neufchâtel	Hard cider, Champagne, Coteaux Champenois.
Bleu des Causses	Banyuls Vintage, Barsac.	Ossau-Iraty	Jurançon, white Irouléguy.
Bleu de Gex	Cérons, Maury, Loupiac.	Pélardon	Red or white Châteauneuf-du-Pape, Condrieu, Viognier-based whites.
Boursault	Bouzy, Coteaux Champenois, red Mâcon, Rosé des Riceys.	Pérail de Brebis	Corbières, Coteaux-du-Languedoc, Côtes-du-Roussillon, Faugères, St-Chinian, Rhône-style red blends.
Bouton-de-Culotte	Beaujolais, white or red Haute-Côte-de-Beaune or Mâcon, good Oregon Pinot Noir.	Picodon	Red Côtes-du-Rhône-Villages, red or white St-Joseph, good New World Grenache.
Brie de Meaux or de Melun	Champagne, Pomerol, St-Émilion, red Sancerre, Merlot.	Pont-l'Évêque	Chassagne-Montrachet, Meursault, good New World Chardonnay, mature Riesling.
Brillat-Savarin	*Blanc de blancs* Champagne.	Pouligny-Saint-Pierre	Cheverny, white Reuilly, white Sancerre, Sauvignon Blanc.
Brin-d'Amour	Red Vin de Corse, white or red Côtes-de-Provence.	Reblochon	Pouilly-Fuissé, Crépy, Roussette de Savoie.
Broccio de Corse	Dry Corsican white wines or Muscat.	Rocamadour	Dry Jurançon, sherry.
Camembert	Sweet (hard) cider, Champagne, Coteaux Champenois.	Roquefort	Banyuls Rimage, port, Rivesaltes *rancio*, Sauternes.
Cantal	Red Côtes-d'Auvergne, Mercurey, Pomerol, St-Émilion, Merlot.	Saint-Félicien	Red or white Beaujolais, white St-Joseph, Roussanne.
Chabichou	White Menetou-Salon, white Sancerre, Sauvignon Blanc.	Saint-Marcellin	Red Beaujolais, white Châteauneuf-du-Pape, white St-Joseph, Roussanne.
Chaource	Rosé Champagne, Coteaux Champenois.	Saint-Nectaire	Chinon, Médoc, Pauillac, good New World Cabernet Sauvignon or Cabernet Franc.
Charolais	Chablis, Mâcon-Villages, Saint-Véran, unoaked or lighly oaked Chardonnay.	Sainte-Maure	Dry or medium-dry Bourgueil, or good New World Cabernet Franc.
Chèvre, mature	Beaujolais, Mâcon-Villages, Pouilly-Fuissé, unoaked or lightly oaked Chardonnay.	Salers	Red Côtes-du-Rhône-Villages, Mercurey, Pomerol, St-Émilion, good Merlot.
Comté	Château-Chalon, mature Meursault, good Sonoma Chardonnay, Jura *vin jaune*.	Selles-sur-Cher	Pouilly-Fumé, white Sancerre, Sauvignon Blanc.
Coulommiers	Young *blanc de blancs* Champagne, Coteaux Champenois.	Stilton	Banyuls, Maury, vintage or LBV port, Rivesaltes.
Crottin de Chavignol	Pouilly Fumé, white Sancerre, Sauvignon Blanc.	Tomme d'Abondance	Swiss Chasselas, Roussette de Savoie, white St-Joseph, Roussanne.
Edam	Chinon, Médoc, Pauillac, Cabernet Franc, Cabernet Sauvignon.	Tomme d'Auvergne	Côtes-d'Auvergne, red Côtes-du-Rhône-Villages, Mâcon-Villages.
Emmental	Roussette de Savoie, white Vin de Savoie.	Tomme des Pyrénées	Mature Madiran or Tannat.
Époisses	Red Bandol, full-bodied Gewurztraminer.	Tomme de Savoie	Bourgueil, Chinon, red and white wines from Savoie including Roussette de Savoie, good Cabernet Franc.
Fontainebleau	Muscat de Beaumes-de-Venise, Muscat de Mireval.	Vacherin	Mature Swiss Chasselas (Dézaley), mature Meursault, Roussette de Savoie, good Sonoma Chardonnay.
Fourme d'Ambert	Banyuls, Rivesaltes, port.	Valençay	Quincy, white or rosé Reuilly, white Sancerre, Sauvignon Blanc.
Fribourg	Château-Chalon, mature Meursault, good Sonoma Chardonnay, Jura *vin jaune*.	Vieux-Gris de Lille	Good ale, gin.
Gouda	Médoc, Madiran, St-Estèphe, Cabernet Sauvignon.	Vieux-Pané	Red Anjou, St-Nicolas-de-Bourgueil, red Touraine, good New World Cabernet Franc.
Gruyère	Mature Swiss Chasselas, Roussette de Savoie, Roussette du Bugey.		
Laguiole	Red Bergerac, Fronton, Cabernet Franc.		
Langres	Fairly mature Champagne, Marc de Champagne.		

HOW TO SERVE WINE

SERVING TEMPERATURE

To get the most from the tasting experience, it is important to serve wines at the temperature that suits them best. A wine that is too warm or too cold cannot be fully appreciated.

Regulating the temperature

CHILLING WINE. An ice bucket is the quickest and best way to chill wine. It is essential to add water to the ice and to immerse as much of the bottle as possible so that all of the wine is at the same temperature. It will take 10–15 minutes for the temperature to drop from 68 down to 46°F (20 to 8°C). A refrigerator will take between 1.5 and 2 hours to achieve the same result, maybe more in warm weather. The time taken to cool the wine is an important factor: too short and the contents of the bottle may not all be of the same temperature, too long and the wine will be too cold. Likewise, a wine chiller sleeve may not always achieve an even cooling of the wine.

Never put a bottle of wine in the freezer or in the chill cabinet of a refrigerator, which is far too cold; moreover, the bottle may burst if it's forgotten.

When the wine has reached the correct temperature for serving, simply add a few ice cubes to the ice bucket to maintain its cool, bearing in mind that it is important not to over-chill. The same principles apply when using a wine cooler or an insulated thermal bag. Sparkling wines are treated in the same way.

WARMING A WINE. Ideally, the bottle should be left for 2–3 hours in a room where the temperature is at around 64°F (18°C). Never place wine near a source of heat such as a fireplace, radiator, or oven; this risks giving it "heat stroke" and will adversely affect the flavors. Red wines should be treated with particular care—especially old, rare vintages, since these are most susceptible to extremes of temperature. Once taken from the cellar, give them time to warm up gradually in a still, temperate room.

The temperature at which wine should be served depends not only on its color, but also on its character, the season, and the temperature of the room where it is to be enjoyed.

Every wine style has its own temperature

How does temperature affect the taste of wine? Warmth causes aromatic components to evaporate, which simply means that it allows the wine's pleasant bouquet to come to the fore. As aromas vary from one wine to another, different wines are at their best at different temperatures.

WHITE WINES COOLER THAN REDS. This is the general principle, but the range of temperatures is wide in both cases. The rule of "white wine at refrigerator temperature and red wine at room temperature" is rather perfunctory. It tends to encourage serving white wines too cold and red ones too warm. In reality, each style of white wine requires a different temperature, and many reds—if not all—should be served a few degrees below room temperature.

NOT TOO COLD, NOT TOO WARM. Wine suffers far more from heat (which may bring out any possible flaws)

> To warm an over-chilled bottle of wine, just leave it for a while in a temperate room.

than from cold. A great red wine may become completely unbalanced if served at 72°F (22°C). As heat accentuates the presence of alcohol, white wines should, in general, be served well chilled to modify the alcohol. When the bottle is chilled, the wine's acidity blends with its fruitiness, making it pleasantly refreshing, as should be expected from all white wines. However, it's a mistake to serve great white wine too cold, as their particular qualities—on the nose as well as in the mouth—may be enhanced if they are just cool. In warm weather, wines should be served slightly cooler than normal, in order to prevent the bottle from warming up too quickly. Conversely, in cold weather (even if the room is well heated), wines (whites or young reds) should not be over-cooled, even if they are supposed to be tasted chilled.

IT ALL DEPENDS ON THE CHARACTER OF THE WINE. A straightforward, supple wine should be served cooler to accentuate its slight acidity. Likewise, an alcohol-rich wine should also be served cooler. On the other hand, a very crisp or tannic wine should not be over-chilled as cold accentuates any bitter, acidic characters.

TRUE OR FALSE?

It's better to serve a wine too cold than too warm.

TRUE. The wine's aromas will be revealed as the temperature rises. If the wine is served too warm, the aromas will be masked by the alcohol.

WINES AND SERVING TEMPERATURES		
WINE TYPE	**EXAMPLES**	**TEMPERATURE**
SPARKLING WINES		
Dry sparkling wines	Cava, *crémant*, Saumur, Champagne	43–46°F (6–8°C)
Sweet sparkling wines	Medium-dry Champagne, Moscato d'Asti	43–46°F (6–8°C)
Special selections	Vintage Champagne	46–50°F (8–10°C)
WHITE WINES		
Ordinary off-dry whites	White Anjou, Loupiac, Muscat	43–46°F (6–8°C)
Medium-dry whites	Medium-dry Vouvray, Riesling Spätlese, Soave	43–46°F (6–8°C)
Sweet whites	Sauternes, Tokaj, Vin Santo, Muscat du Cap-Corse	43–46°F (6–8°C)
Ordinary dry whites	Muscadet, Sancerre, Pinot Gris, dry Riesling, Sauvignon Blanc	50–54°F (10–12°C)
Full-bodied dry whites	Burgundy, Graves, Orvieto, Sémillon, Viognier, Chardonnay, Chenin	50–54°F (10–12°C)
Classy dry whites	Burgundy, Pessac-Léognan, Savennières	54°F (12°C)
ROSÉ WINES		
	Ordinary rosés are served as for dry white wines	50–54°F (10–12°C)
RED WINES		
Young, fresh reds	Loire wines, Beaujolais, Côtes-du-Rhône, Valpolicella, Cabernet Franc, Grenache	57°F (14°C)
Ordinary reds	Bordeaux, Burgundy, Cabernet Sauvignon, Chianti Classico, Merlot, Pinot Noir, Sangiovese, Syrah, Tempranillo	61°F (16°C)
Great reds	Bordeaux, Côte-Rôtie, Gevrey-Chambertin, Corton, Vino Nobile de Montepulciano, Brunello, Barolo, top Rioja	63–64°F (17–18°C)
FORTIFIED WINES		
	French *vins doux naturels* (whites)	46–50°F (8–10°C)
	Fino and manzanilla sherry	50–54°F (10–12°C)
	Amontillado sherry, sercial madeira, French *vins doux naturels* (red)	54°F (12°C)
	Oloroso or cream sherry, bual madeira	57°F (14°C)
	Ruby port	57°F (14°C)
	Tawny port	61°F (16°C)
	Vintage port	61–64°F (16–18°C)

OPENING THE BOTTLE

Serving a wine is not something that should be improvised; each part of the process contributes to the pleasure of tasting. The host should therefore be versed in all aspects of serving wine, including the essential stage of opening a bottle of wine with ease.

The corkscrew

There are two criteria for choosing a good-quality corkscrew. First, the part that penetrates the closure (cork) should be of the right shape. Only a helix (sometimes called "the worm") that is sufficiently long and wide, and with a good point, will provide a solid grip without the danger of the closure crumbling or breaking. The traction mechanism is also important. The most basic corkscrews with a T-shaped handle require too much effort from the arm and shoulder muscles: a tight closure will resist you. It's better to choose a corkscrew with a lever system that wedges itself against the neck of the bottle. There is a wide range of models available, from the "waiter's friend" to the corkscrew with

Opening a bottle is a great moment, and it should not be done abruptly. Having been enclosed in the bottle after many production processes, the wine now comes into contact with the air and is ready to reveal all its qualities.

a counter-screw mechanism or the "Screwpull," which works on the boring/digging principle (*see* pp.190–1). Finally, it is definitely not a good idea to use devices powered by gas or air; not only could the pressure of the gas spoil the wine, but if the bottle has a manufacturing defect, there's a danger that it may shatter or explode when being opened.

Opening a still wine

The closure should be extracted without having to resort to force and without tearing it, since the wine is susceptible to abrupt changes in pressure.

ACTIONS. Any difficulties experienced in opening a bottle of wine depend on the type of corkscrew used, but the process is always

OPENING A STILL WINE

Troublesome closures

Sometimes cork or plastic closures stubbornly resist extraction. Here are some solutions.

The closure is sticking. Warm the neck of the bottle by running hot water over it—but keep the closure dry. This will moisten and expand the glass. Alternatively, hold the corkscrew at a slight angle while turning it.

The closure is broken. Hold the corkscrew at a slight angle and turn it carefully into the remaining closure. If this doesn't work, push the closure into the bottle. When pouring the first glass, use the corkscrew's worm to keep the closure away from the neck; it will then float on the surface of the wine.

A few pieces of closure in the wine will not affect its taste. If there are more, the wine can be decanted (see p.193) into a clean bottle, carafe, or pitcher.

the same. First, the foil wrapper on the neck should be cut and (at least the upper part) removed; this ensures that the wine will not come into contact with the foil. If the wine is to be decanted (*see* p.193), the whole of the wrapper should be removed to give a better view of the wine. Next, wipe the neck and top with a clean cloth, then drive the worm of the corkscrew through the centre of the closure, taking care not to split it. Finally, extract the closure in a single smooth movement. Of course, this procedure assumes the bottle is not sealed with a screwcap.

SHOULD A BOTTLE BE OPENED IN ADVANCE? In general, simple red, white, or rosé wines such as Beaujolais or Côtes-de-Provence rosé are opened at the last moment, unless they are required to be decanted. Fuller-bodied, but still young, white wines may be opened 1–2 hours in advance; they also can be poured into a carafe or decanter half an hour before serving. Still-young but distinguished red wines will benefit from being opened 2–4 hours before being served, or decanted 1–2 hours in advance. As for old wines, they should not be opened too early; if they are first left standing upright, any sediment will drop to the bottom.

EXCEPTIONS. Some cork closures, especially those of mature Bordeaux wines, are very long and often fragile. In such cases, it is necessary to proceed in two movements. When the worm of the corkscrew has penetrated the closure fully, draw it up by a fraction of an inch, give it an extra twist inward (taking care that the worm does not go right through the closure), and then extract the whole closure.

"Waiter's friend" corkscrews are often effective in dealing with very old closures. Particular care is also necessary with a delicate bottle, such as an old Burgundy. When it is being carried from storage to where it is to be served, it should be kept lying on its side. (Carrying it in a basket may be a good idea.) The slightest abrupt movement should be avoided throughout the whole process, including when the bottle is being opened.

Opening sparkling wines

A bottle of sparkling wine is always opened in front of the guests. But never do this directly in front of anyone or toward a window: turn the bottle toward a wall.

PRECAUTIONS. Since the wine is under pressure, opening the bottle clumsily or quickly may force the closure out violently. You will lose a lot of mousse (and wine), not to mention whatever damage the closure might do as it shoots out of the bottle. Therefore start by chilling the wine, and avoid shaking the bottle so as not to increase the pressure of the gas. The wine should be cooled to between 43–48°F (6–9°C). So avoid leaving it in the refrigerator too long. Once it has left the cellar, it is preferable to chill it for a while in a bucket containing a mixture of water and ice; accelerated chilling can only damage to the wine.

ACTIONS. First take off the foil wrapper, in order to access the wire cage and the closure. Gently untwist the wire, keeping your thumb on top of the cork, then take off the wire cage and its cap. The secret of successful opening consists of holding the bottle at a slight angle, and keeping the cork closure well supported with one hand while with the other gently turning the bottle (not the closure). You will feel the closure rising, pushed up by the pressure of the gas. Use your thumb to lever the closure out gently as soon as it begins to move up the neck.

OPENING A SPARKLING WINE

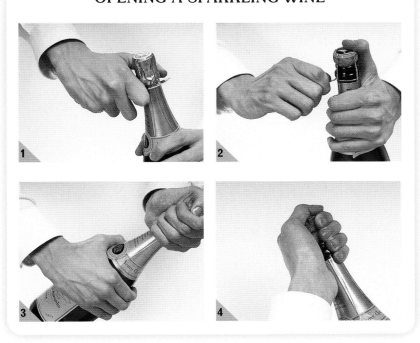

CORKSCREWS

Although they are tools for a very specific task, some corkscrews are a pleasure to look at, hold, and even collect.

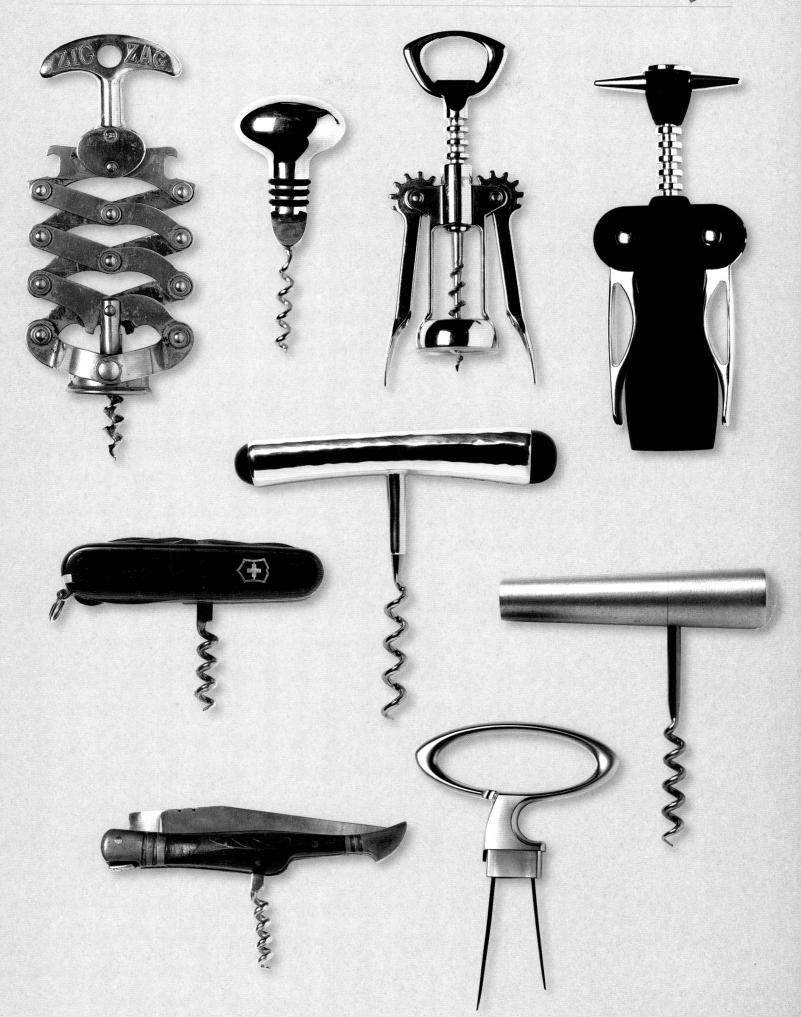

DECANTING THE WINE

Decanting is a delicate operation, requiring a degree of dexterity to achieve three objectives: to separate any sediment from the wine, to aerate the wine, and to modify its temperature.

Advantages and disadvantages

Most wines can be served directly from the bottle, but some benefit from being decanted into a carafe or a pitcher. In almost every case where the wine shows traces of sediment, it should be decanted. For other wines, it depends on their age and the time they will remain in a decanter (*see* box below).

Advocates of decanting assert that a young wine that has been decanted for one or even several hours will become softer, rounder, and generally more pleasurable to taste. However, if left too long in a decanter, it may lose its freshness and vitality. Decanting can invigorate vintage wines, but it can also harden them and dissipate their precious aromas.

Do not forget that wine continues to aerate when passing from the decanter to the glass, and also if gently swirled in the glass. Before decanting, therefore, take the precaution of tasting the wine.

> *Decanting can improve the wine in two ways: it removes any sediment (or even pieces of cork closure), and it aerates the wine, which may offer greater pleasure.*

Sediment: quality or defect?

CRYSTALS. Some young, light, white wines occasionally show deposits of crystals. These are caused by the crystallization of potassium bitartrate following a sudden drop in temperature. Despite their appearance, these crystals present no danger to health and will not affect the taste of the wine. Stand the bottle upright and the deposit will collect under the closure in a few seconds. They can be avoided by careful pouring.

COLORED SEDIMENT. Older red wines produce natural sediment from precipitation of color and tannin molecules. This is a fairly light sediment and requires careful handling of the bottle to avoid.

Decanting is necessary unless the wine has become too fragile (*e.g.* old wines from Burgundy). The decision should be made immediately after the bottle is opened and the wine initially tasted: an immature, slightly hard wine will benefit from decanting, but a delicious wine in full bloom does not require it.

What wines should be decanted?

RED WINES WITH SEDIMENT

Bordeaux: *premiers crus, grands crus,* classified growths, St-Émilion *grands crus,* great Pomerols.

Rhône Valley: Hermitage and other wines from the northern valley, as well as Châteauneuf-du-Pape in the south.

Other French wines: the best wines from Provence, Madiran.

Italy: Barolo, Brunello di Montalcino, Sassicaia, Ornellaia.

Spain: Vega-Sicilia, Pingus, and the better wines of Penedès. Also, some Riojas tend towards sedimentation.

Portugal: vintage and crusted ports. Late bottled and tawny ports do not need to be decanted.

New World: Cabernet Sauvignons and Syrah/Shiraz from California, Washington State, Australia, and Chile.

YOUNG RED WINES

Bordeaux: good vintage wines from the smaller châteaux of Bordeaux. Also, many good Cabernet Sauvignon wines from elsewhere in the world.

Burgundy: the Beaujolais crus and the communal appellations of the Côte d'Or. Also, many good Pinot Noir wines from elsewhere in the world.

Rhône Valley: all the reds. Also, many Syrah and Rhône-style blends from elsewhere in the world.

Other French wines: Cahors, red Bandol, Chinon, Faugères, and those wines with good acidity and tannin content when young; or all traditionally vinified, highly concentrated wines. In Italy, Barolo, Barbaresco, and Brunello.

WHITE WINES

Some white wines improve from being decanted just before serving: young Loire wines, white Graves, Alsace *vendanges tardives*, great Rhine and Mosel wines from Germany, white oak-aged Riojas from Spain. Others do not benefit: very mature white Bordeaux and Burgundies, mature white wines except for the ones cited above, most young white wines, Champagne, and other sparkling wines.

> Young wine is aerated in a carafe or decanter with a broad base.

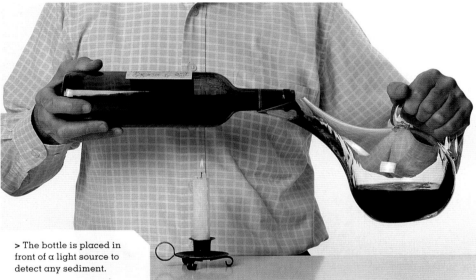

> The bottle is placed in front of a light source to detect any sediment.

it into a clean carafe. The wine may be poured fairly quickly: if it splashes near the top of the carafe, it will simply aerate better. Then it's best to allow the wine to rest for at least an hour before drinking, with the open decanter in the room where it will be served. This will allow it to reach room temperature gradually.

DECANTING A MATURE WINE. Due to the fragility of the wine, this is a delicate operation requiring patience and dexterity. It is done just before serving the wine, and the decanter should be stoppered. If the bottle has been left standing upright in the cellar about two days early, the sediment will collect at the bottom. If the bottle is left lying down, the sediment will collect on the side; in the latter case, take it from the cellar in a wine cradle. When the closure has been pulled, the wine should be poured very slowly (but steadily, to avoid any swirling) into a decanter. A light source such as a candle or flashlight positioned under the neck of the bottle will show when the first sediment comes to the top. As soon as sediment reaches the neck, stop pouring and set the bottle upright.

How to decant

WHAT CONTAINER? Wine can be decanted into a carafe, a jug, or a pitcher. However, the shape and size of the vessel play an important role in decanting, specifically in how large a surface area of wine is put in contact with air. In fact, following the initial "shock" of aeration to a wine that has always been in a closed environment, the aromas will expand more or less rapidly in the decanter depending on its shape. So, for young, good quality wines, a flat decanter with a very broad base best facilitates the interaction of the wine with air; for older wines, it's better to choose a decanter that exposes only a small surface of the wine to the air. Also, fill it up and replace the stopper afterward. Always, rinse and drain the decanter before use; and if using a funnel or a fabric filter, also wash them beforehand. When pouring the wine into the decanter, make sure you are well balanced and do not hold the bottle at arm's length.

DECANTING A YOUNG WINE. The aim of this operation is to aerate the wine and allow it to soften and reveal its bouquet. All that is necessary is to open the bottle and pour

Caring for decanters

Decanters should be clean and washed with the same care as glasses, using plenty of hot water to rinse them as much as possible. To dry a decanter, first wipe the outside with a clean cloth, then turn the decanter upside down to let any remaining water flow out. The best way to drain a decanter is to place it on a well-anchored rack, to ensure stability, and leave it in a well-aired place. It should not be kept enclosed and empty for too long and should always be rinsed well with hot water before every use.

If your decanter shows traces of previously decanted wines, use unrefined sea salt and wine vinegar to clean it, shaking until all traces have disappeared. Rinse well in clean, hot water.

GLASSES

Faced with an enormous range of choices, the important thing is to select glasses that will enhance the appreciation of wine and that also reflect your own taste. The aesthetic factor should not be neglected, as it often enhances the pleasure of tasting.

Choosing glasses

To permit good tastings, the glass should satisfy the demands of the eye, the nose, and the mouth. Wine tastes different, and better, when consumed from the appropriate glass. Points to bear in mind when choosing glasses are, in order of importance: shape, size, and what they are made from.

SHAPE. The bowl of a wine glass should be in the shape of a semi-closed tulip. The rim of the bowl should curve slightly inward to capture the wine's aromas and channel them toward the nose. A glass with a shallow bowl creates more wine surface area to expose to air and will not retain the aromas. The stem of the glass should be sufficiently long to hold without the fingers touching the bowl. A glass of chilled white wine will warm up rapidly when in contact with the hand.

SIZE. The glass should be big enough to hold an adequate amount of wine without being more than a quarter or one-third full. If the glass is too small or too full, the wine cannot be swirled to release its aromas, nor can the glass be tilted to examine the wine. A normal serving of wine is around 3 oz (90 ml); ideally, the capacity of a glass should be at least 9.5 oz (280 ml). Some restaurants use much bigger glasses; avoid this at home to spare yourself the disagreeable impression of having just a drop of wine in the bottom of your glass. In any case, these glasses have a special purpose as the large surface area helps to volatilize the aromas of a young wine; but they should not be used

The same wine consumed from different shaped glasses will not taste the same. A classic wine glass should have the same qualities as a tasting glass, as well as being both attractive and hardwearing.

for old, delicate wines. On the other hand, a large glass, with a capacity of 12 oz (350 ml), is necessary for the best red wines when served at their peak.

MATERIAL. The glass should be transparent, smooth, and without facets. Heavy glasses in cut crystal or gilded are certainly beautiful, but they detract from the appreciation of wine and the pleasure of tasting. Colored glasses make it impossible to admire the wine's color and intensity. The ideal material is fine crystal, which provides optimal clarity and quality for an unimpeded view of what is in the glass. Experts who have carried our comparative tastings are convinced that the quality of the glass contributes to tasting pleasure. All the same, the material is of less importance than the shape or size of the glass.

A glass for every wine?

In addition to standard wine glasses, there are others—traditional (*see* box) and those specially designed to enhance a particular type of wine. After years of research, great crystal manufacturers such as Riedel and Spiegelau have created lines of glasses designed to optimize tasting of the world's great wines. However, it is by no means essential to have a different wine glass for every appellation or style; though it is accepted that white wine glasses are smaller than those for red wine. The tulip shape of the glass is the chief consideration. For sparkling wines, a flute is the preferred shape. To these classic glasses,

> Water glass

> Burgundy glass

> Bordeaux glass

> White wine glass

Traditional glasses

Most wine-producing regions have developed a glass thought to be ideal for tasting local wine. Such glasses have great charm, and when they are used, traditions should be respected. In general, their chief purpose is to celebrate easy-drinking wines with no pretensions. The most famous example is the Alsace wine glass: a small balloon set on a long, green-tinted stem. The purpose is to reflect a light color into the white wine, while also highlighting the freshness of the wine served. Obviously, the high quality wines of Alsace don't need such a prop.

> The bowls of wine glasses should be tulip-shaped to retain aromas.

a Burgundy glass may possibly be added and another for port, sherry, and liqueurs. Only the water glass is free from any constraints in shape and material.

There also are specialized or technical wine-tasting glasses, such as those approved by INAO (*Institut National des Appellations d'Origine*) or the "Les Impitoyables" line. Used by professional tasters, these high-specification glasses are designed to reveal any defects in a wine (*see also* p.204.).

Caring for wine glasses

Many wine tastings are ruined by dirty glasses. But the "dirt" isn't always visible: detergents or rinsing products can leave a film that may be undetectable by sight or smell when the glass is empty, but they can react when in contact with wine (or water), giving it a bad taste.

Glasses attract and retain odors; these may come from the washing or drying processes, or from how they are stored. However, they are all easy to avoid. It's best not to put wine glasses in the dishwasher, but to wash them by hand in plenty of hot water. If necessary, use just a little gentle detergent or soap. While still warm and damp, they should be wiped and polished with a clean cotton or linen cloth, which itself has been rinsed after washing to remove any smell of detergent or fabric conditioner. Avoid using new cloths, which might leave fluff or threads on the glasses.

Store the glasses in a closed cupboard, preferably not in the kitchen. Stand them upright or slip the bases (foot) into glass-holders. If stored upside-down, they will absorb the smell of the cupboard. Finally, take them out well beforehand so that you can check they are clean and air them before arranging on the table.

> Port glass   > Flute

What glass for bubbles?

The Champagne *coupe* has long been associated with this wine. Though, from a formal tasting point of view, it's useless. The wide bowl immediately dissipates the wine's bouquet and instantly disperses the mousse, not to mention the stream of bubbles. For Champagne and, in general, for all sparkling wines, the flute is the best choice. The wine should be poured to fill the tall glass three-quarters full. The height of the bowl means that bubbles will form easily and last longer; the narrow rim will ensure that none of the bouquet is lost. The tulip glass is an acceptable alternative to the flute.

DINING WITH WINE

Ever since the first harvest in some ancient vineyard, wine was destined to end its journey in a glass at a table, as part of a meal. And yet, sometimes even a tiny mistake in serving the wine is enough to spoil the pleasure of tasting it: every detail matters and brings tangible reality an aspect of pleasure.

Choosing and preparing the wines

First, it is acknowledged that wines to be served should be chosen according to the occasion and the foods that constitute the meal (*see* pp.168–83). Figure on at least one 750ml bottle for three or four guests. The selected wines should be carefully checked since, from the minute they are taken from storage to the moment they are consumed, details are important. Although wines for immediate drinking, including rosé wines, can be opened and consumed with no delay, other—certainly mature red—wines require more care due to their style and their age.

INSPECT THE BOTTLES. If possible, choose any mature wines to serve at a meal about two days beforehand. Check the bottles in storage, which ideally are kept lying down, with the label up. This way, you can be sure that the sediment is localized, opposite from the label. Handle the bottles gently, with no sudden movements. Keep them oriented as they were laid, and use a good flashlight to check the clarity of the wine and the amount of the sediment.

BRING TO THE CORRECT TEMPERATURE AND NEUTRALIZE THE SEDIMENT. Young, dry white wines can be chilled a few hours before serving. Mature white wines showing some sediment should be stood upright the previous evening before being chilled. Young red wines generally have very little sediment; it's sufficient to place them upright the morning before your dinner party. Mature red wines with sediment should be gently set upright two days in advance before being decanted, if necessary.

The order in which wines are served follows a few simple rules: dry white wine should be served before red wine; young red wine before mature red; lighter wines before fuller-bodied ones; simplest wines before the most complex.

How many wines should be served?

A single wine can be consumed throughout a meal, or a different wine can be served for every course. (Or no wine at all needs be served.) The number of wines served also varies depending on whether it is a question of lunch or dinner, a family meal, or a meal for real foodies (*see also* p.168).

FAMILY OR FRIENDS. A meal for family or friends implies simplicity. A single, well-made, unpretentious wine is fine; and the color is a matter of choice. A Sunday meal or one with friends is an occasion where a choice of wines adapted to the menu is welcome. In addition to the aperitif — which may be the wine planned for the first course—three or four wines may reasonably be expected to follow: a white wine for the first course, a red wine for the main course, another wine for the cheeses, and finally a dessert wine.

AMONG CONNOISSEURS. If the meal has been specially planned as "fine dining," the wine selection may be doubled; although it should be remembered that all of these wines will be swallowed and not spat out, as in a professional tasting. The danger lies not in the variety of wines served, but rather in an excessive amount of wine being consumed.

Setting

About two hours before the guests arrive, it's a good idea to attend to final preparations. Anticipating some details in this way will help the service go smoothly at the table.

OPENING THE BOTTLES. Except for sparkling wines, which should be opened in front of guests, all bottles can be opened and the wines tasted quietly in advance in order to check their condition (*see also* the box on p.197). White wines should then be resealed and returned to the refrigerator. Any red wines requiring decanting should be decanted into carafes (*see* p.193). These should be stoppered afterward, and kept at optimum temperature. It is pointless to reseal red wines that have not been decanted. Finally, in case more wine is required, it's good to have an unopened bottle of each wine in reserve.

POINTS TO REMEMBER. Don't forget to have a napkin handy in order to wipe the neck of the bottle (or a damp bottle) while you are serving. Chill several bottles of mineral water, both still and sparkling.

PLACING THE GLASSES. At each place setting, the glasses are arranged in order of serving, from left to right facing the plate. To avoid laborious manipulations during the meal, it's best to set out all the necessary glassware right away. The water glass

should be placed behind the wine glasses. If it happens that several bottles of the same memorable great wine are served during the meal, the possibility of having to change glasses with each bottle opened should be catered for, as there can be great differences from one bottle to another.

Always taste before serving

As soon as the selected bottles have been opened, it's time to check the wine. First, check each closure (if natural cork) by sniffing it in order to detect possible defects. Then proceed to a "control" tasting. Some musty smells disappear quickly; but "corky" smells are more serious. If a musty smell is very light, the first glass may be the only one affected, and simple aeration is often enough to clear it. If it persists, it's best to open another bottle. If in doubt, do not hesitate to change. Once verified, each bottle can be decanted (just in case), and then served.

Table service: be as attentive as a wine waiter

THE HOST'S ROLE. Throughout the meal, the host generally plays the role of wine waiter and shoulders the responsibility of serving the wine. As a courtesy, the host will taste each bottle before pouring, and make sure that wines remain (as much as possible) at the right serving temperature. They also see that each glass is filled to one-third of capacity throughout the meal.

THE CORRECT TEMPERATURE. Sparkling and white wines should be kept sufficiently chilled by standing them in a bucket containing water and some ice cubes. It is a good idea to serve red wines one or two degrees colder than prescribed: as soon as they are poured into a glass they warm up by a degree or so.

TRUE OR FALSE?

Dry Champagne goes well with desserts.

FALSE. Contact with sugar hardens the taste of dry Champagne. For desserts, you should make a point of choosing the wines that are made for them, collectively called "dessert wines." Examples are late-harvest Muscat or Sémillon. Dry Champagne is ideal as an aperitif or served throughout a meal. For dessert, it's best to serve a medium-dry Champagne.

WINE IN A RESTAURANT

A restaurant is chosen for the quality of its food, its decor, its wine selection, and its price bracket. It's not always easy to navigate your way through a long, impressive wine list; but a quick glance can establish a fairly good idea of the choices and their prices. Additionally, you can ask the sommelier (or wine waiter) for advice.

Choosing wine

Wine selection rests on several criteria, but a quick glance helps the customer get an idea of the attention the restaurant gives to wine. A short and well-chosen selection is better than a big accumulation of famous appellations, the service of which is not always to be trusted. The wine list should reflect the style of the restaurant's cuisine; so it's interesting to note the influence of certain wine-producing regions. The presence of a sommelier confirms that real attention is paid to selection and service.

FOOD/WINE HARMONY. Good servers will never be offended if asked both for the menu and the wine list. This shows the customer cares about both aspects of the meal. In a first-time visit to a restaurant, it is hard to know whether the food should be ordered first, followed by the wines, or vice versa. Creative cuisine should be explained, and a simple listing of the ingredients may guide the choice of wines. If it's impossible to resist a dish whose composition might alter the wine, it's best to ask the sommelier's advice. Conversely, if a particular wine attracts your attention, the server or sommelier will be able to recommend the best dish to complement it.

The sommelier is simultaneously wine waiter, oenophile, psychologist, jurist, and foodie. He or she presides over the wine "ceremony" and is a skilled guide to the subtle relationships between the wines and the foods on the menu.

Wine lists

PRESENTATION. Restaurant efficiency is reflected in the simplicity of the wine list. It should be clear so that the client can immediately understand how to read it. The wines should be classified by color, then by some combination of varietals,

countries, regions, or appellations. Additionally, a good list will show wines by vintage, and maybe even by sub-appellation. And, obviously, they should always clearly show price—by the glass (for some wines) and by the bottle (for all wines). Whatever format of presentation, it should be consistent throughout the list. The best restaurants should show (as appropriate) each wine's village, site, *clos*, proprietor's name, and the vintage. When a "house wine" is listed, it generally means an honest wine selected to complement the restaurant's style of cuisine, but it will never be a truly great wine.

USEFUL SPECIFICS. A sommelier will always be able to impart useful additional information such as the quality of a vintage, the grape varieties, production techniques, the exact location of the estate, etc. Learn from your sommelier, but do not monopolize them indefinitely. His or her work involves seeing to other tables, preparing glasses and bottles, and serving wine.

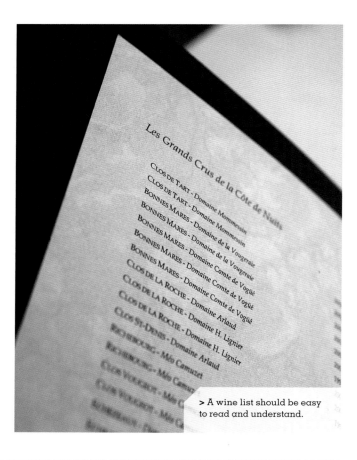

> A wine list should be easy to read and understand.

DID YOU KNOW...?

The profession of sommelier is more than 4,000 years old. In fact, it goes back to the time of the Pharaohs, when the sommelier was responsible for preparing drinks for the country's kings and nobles, making and serving both beer and wine. Until the middle of the 20th century, the sommelier also bottled the wine in the cellar of the restaurant where he worked. When it became customary to bottle wine at estates, sommeliers began working on the restaurant floor (see also pp.200–1).

What if there's something wrong with the wine?

The wine served is defective: it may be musty, maderized, oxidized, flat, "corked," etc. Defects should be noted by the customer, the server, or the sommelier when they first taste the wine, in which case the bottle should be changed. If there is even the slightest doubt, it is the customer's prerogative to ask for another bottle. However, some restaurants may warn you that rare bottles or those from an old vintage are ordered at your own risk and will be charged whatever happens.

You don't like the wine. There's nothing wrong with the wine, which has been warmly recommended by the waiter or the sommelier, but for whatever reason you do not like it. You should mention this, and the staff should make another suggestion to suit your taste. Having taken the risk, it's incumbent on the restaurant to behave both nobly and with modesty.

> When the person who has ordered the wine approves it, the sommelier will fill the glasses.

Sommeliers

Lost and bewildered among pages of *crus* from different regions and varying prices, the customer should turn for advice to a helpful professional. Although it can be a delicate matter to bring up prices, a talented sommelier will pick up small hints from guests on just how far to go. There is no reason for embarrassment if a suggestion is unsuitable; just ask for another, being as precise as possible about what you like. And while the sommelier's suggestion is almost always a good one, the customer remains the final decision maker and should not feel any constraints. The sommelier will know the wines he or she suggests, but that counts less than the customer's preference and the etiquette of service.

Serving the wine

Once the order has been taken, the sommelier prepares the appropriate glasses and gets the selected bottles. The service, as it is properly called, then begins. Each bottle is presented to the client so that she or he can check and agree that the appellation, vintage, and producer are just as ordered. The sommelier then opens bottles, sniffing closures and often tasting each wine. If necessary, they will decant the wine and keep it at the correct temperature.

In top restaurants, the signal to serve a wine is given by the person who has ordered it. The sommelier will serve him or her first, so that he or she can taste the wine. This enables the host to check the wine's intrinsic quality and its temperature. If the customer approves it, the service continues in order of precedence, not forgetting to refill the glass of whoever has tasted first. Drinks should be served from the right, giving each guest the opportunity, if he or she wants, to glance at the label while the sommelier may discreetly murmur the wine's name and vintage. The sommelier will fill the glasses to one-third and will be vigilant to ensure no guest is without wine. He or she will also serve any bottled water. At all times, a sommelier will respond to the customer's demands. If the customer cannot find a wine he or she likes—or notes a defect in quality, such as the wine being "corked" or having a temperature problem—he or she is within his rights to point it out and to ask for another bottle.

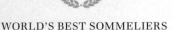

WORLD'S BEST SOMMELIERS

2008   Andreas Larsson (Sweden)

2004   Enrico Bernardo (Italy)

2000   Olivier Poussier (France)

1998   Markus Del Monego (Germany)

1995   Shinya Tasaki (Japan)

1992   Philippe Faure-Brac (France)

1989   Serge Dubs (France)

1986   Jean-Claude Jambon (France)

FRANCE'S BEST SOMMELIERS

2008   Manuel Peyrondet (Hotel Bristol, Paris)

2006   Pascal Leonetti (Auberge de l'Ill, Illhaeusern)

2004   Dominique Laporte (Le Phare, Palavas-les-Flots)

2002   David Biraud (Hotel Crillon, Paris)

2000   Franck Thomas (consultant)

Sommelier as wine ambassador

Light and shade. What better image could define the sommelier's craft? "Shade" because it is his or her role to perform in the proverbial shadow of the wines. "Light" because a sommelier is both an actor and a producer of a perfectly choreographed scene on the "stage" of the restaurant, and in the spotlight of direct contact with customers.

CONNOISSEUR AND MANAGER

In the so-called shade, the sommelier must keep training throughout his or her career. This means visits to vineyard regions to become familiar with wines and wineries, and to learn about every new vintage. Education never stops, and its goal is to find wines best suited to the cuisine and clientele of the restaurant. There are two key criteria: the style of the wine and, obviously, its price. Since the sommelier is first and foremost a manager: he or she is responsible for the proper maintenance of the cellar, controlling inventory, development of the wine list, establishing prices in agreement with supervisors, and taking responsibility for it. In well-known establishments that can afford to acquire and store very expensive bottles, she or he must also be able to forecast the wines' potential and decide whether to save or serve them. Finally, he or she routinely sets up the inventory for the day, where the bottles are stored at service temperature to meet the restaurant's immediate requirements.

IT'S LIKE BEING ON STAGE

This is where the sommelier steps into the light. The uniform is unchanging: black apron, matching jacket, and gold lapel pin in the shape of a cluster of grapes. The tools are at the ready: corkscrew, white napkin, decanter, and small dish in which to lay the closure, if necessary. The role is always the same: advise the customer, bearing in mind the food selected; present the wines and spirits; and serve them. "It's a complex scenario," emphasizes Philippe Faure-Brac, World's Best Sommelier in 1992. "The script and the partners change a

1. Recording wines taken from the cellar.
2. Opening: sure, precise actions.
3. Checking the wine before serving.
4. Insignia of a master sommelier.

every meal. You need to have a sense of who you are dealing with: wine lover, novice, business executive wanting to impress guests, lovers, the affluent or not…"

SOMMELIER COMPETITIONS …

To prepare for this often twice-daily performance, increasing numbers of sommeliers enter various competitions organized by their trade associations. They compete for the title of best regional sommelier, best sommelier in France, or in Europe, or in the world. For beginners, there's one for best student sommelier; and later there's one for the best young (under 24) working sommelier. The elements are often the same from one competition to another, but there's a clear difference in the difficulty of the questions and the level of the contestant skills.

The theory section will involve tests on regional history and geography of vineyards and wineries; as well as oenology; technology; legislation; the organization of a wine list; the spelling of wines and appellations; cellar management; knowledge of spirits, coffees, teas, mineral waters, cigars — nothing is left out.

Next, the top candidates undergo a series of practical tests: serving wine, wine and food pairings, taking an order in a foreign language, correcting an inaccurate wine list (a white wine slipped in among the reds, a non-existent vintage, faulty spellings, an incorrect price, for example).

Jean-Luc Jamrozik, sommelier of the Hotel Baltimore in Paris, is a member of the Union of French Sommellerie (UDSF) and regularly prepares candidates for various competitions. "I get to play

difficult clients," he explains with a gently sadistic smile. "The kind who want red wine with fish or white with game, or who say they are allergic to sulfur, or who play at being blasé and demand to be surprised…"

Apart from the prestige of being singled out from among peers, the winner generally does not receive money but far more appropriate prizes: distinguished bottles of wine, trips to vineyard regions around the world, a chance to meet the great names in the profession, meals in the best Michelin-starred restaurants, the opportunity to develop new wines, etc. Every year more and more candidates are drawn to the challenge of these contests, including more women. The number of women in this profession is still deplorably low, as is sadly shown in the list of winners of the most prestigious contests. But change is on the menu.

HOW TO TASTE WINE

THE BASICS OF SUCCESSFUL TASTING

Tasting a wine brings experiences that can be described concretely—the color, the aromas, the flavors, and the texture all speak to our senses. Most often, though, the enthusiastic amateur lacks an adequate vocabulary to describe these sensations. He or she is unable to "decode" the different elements making up the wine; in other words, how to taste.

The art of tasting

Tasting is above all a technical exercise, taking place in three stages during which three of our senses in turn are brought into play: sight, smell, and taste. Although there are several tasting groups open to the general public, wine lovers often organize private events with friends, a practice open to all and requiring only a little attention to detail and a few material conditions.

Choosing a venue

Choosing the right room is important. It should be bright, with sufficient daylight or neutral lighting (and certainly no strip lighting or colored lamps). The air should not be "polluted" with cooking smells, flowers, tobacco, or perfume. The ideal room temperature is somewhere between 64°F and 68°F (18°C–20°C), as this will enable your wine to show its best. (The idea of allowing the wine to stand in a room for a few hours so that it warms up from cellar temperature and tastes better dates back to a time before central heating.) The table should be covered with a white cloth, or, in the absence of one, the glasses should be placed on a piece of white paper, which will allow people to judge the color of the wine objectively.

Tasting will help you learn about wine. Practiced regularly, tasting sharpens the senses and gradually improves the specific vocabulary required to communicate wine-related opinions clearly.

Selecting your equipment

GLASSES. Choosing these correctly is important because they influence the appearance and aroma of the wine. Do not use colored glasses. A tulip-shaped glass with a transparent stem, sometimes known in France as an *Angoulême*, is a great choice. Many ideal glasses used by wine professionals are available from companies including Riedel, Schott Zwiesel, and Spiegelau. Their semi-elliptic form has a narrower mouth than its curved bowl, allowing it to concentrate aromas and to avoid spills when swirling the wine. These glasses are available from department stores and any good wine merchant. A taster should smell their glass before using it to make sure there are no residual odors (from the box or dish detergent). The glass may be rinsed with water or, better still, moistened with the first wine to be tasted. The ideal approach is to provide a fresh glass with every wine. If this is not possible, provide a minimum of two glasses per taster so that wines may be compared.
SPITTOONS. These are indispensable accessories, allowing tasters to empty their glasses and to spit (*see* box p.205). If you have no spittoons, you can use other vessels, such as deep bowls, vases, and Champagne buckets.

lip

bowl

stem

base

Getting wine ready

The wines, which will have been stored horizontally in a cellar, should be placed upright one day early so that any natural deposit will settle at the bottom of the bottle. They should be opened an hour before the tasting and, if necessary, decanted into a carafe. The whites should be placed on ice or refrigerated for a few hours and then taken out half an hour before tasting to reach the right temperature; they should be opened just before being tasted.

What is blind tasting?

This is a completely objective method of tasting wines without knowing their identity. The bottle is covered with paper or some kind of sleeve—whatever the taster's level of expertise, there is always the danger of being influenced by the label. A wine with a great reputation will always raise expectations and the reverse can also be true. In blind tasting, the intrinsic quality of the wine is left to speak for itself, and this experience may lead to some surprises.

Appropriate physical conditions

A taster should be fresh and rested, and in good health. Discomfort from fatigue will affect judgment, and colds in particular are a considerable handicap to taking in the aromas and flavors of the wine. The technically best time for wine tasting is in the morning, when the senses are sharpest and concentration is at a maximum. But wine lovers generally prefer to get together at the beginning of an evening before dinner, when the agenda is about friends and fun. Tasting after a meal should be avoided; the senses are "saturated" and the body's systems are committed to digestion.

Before tasting, wine lovers should refrain from drinking coffee or smoking cigarettes, since this will "spoil" the palate. By the same token, bread—a neutral foodstuff—is preferable to cheese or salty crackers to "cleanse" the palate between the wines that are particularly tannic or acidic.

A few simple rules for successful tasting

When tasting, it is best to observe at least a little silence, as this encourages concentration. As fascinating as it is to share your thoughts, there will be time for this later. The person leading the tasting may therefore suggest a summary of the wines tasted, after sampling a set number of bottles. Each guest will keep notes of their observations on a tasting sheet provided for this purpose (for a few examples, see pp.222–5). There is no substitute for this exercise in reinforcing a taster's judgment. The notes will provide a starting point as your tasting ability develops, and you trace the evolution of wines. Tasting is an exercise in memory as well—the more you taste, noting colors, aromas, and flavors in your "reference library" of experience,

> Bottles disguised with paper sleeves at a blind tasting.

the more you will be in a position to identify a wine's sensory characteristics and, by comparing many, to assess its qualities. Equally important rules include honesty, modesty, and respect for others: virtues to be practiced throughout life! There actually is no such thing as "good" or "bad" in tasting—everyone has their own ideas and may defend these in discussion, always preserving respect for others.

DID YOU KNOW...?

Spitting out a wine is normal at tastings.
For a beginner, spitting might seem odd and a bit disgusting, not to mention the frustration one might feel at not being able to enjoy the wine fully. The practice is explicable, though, as a question of physical necessity. Formal tastings do not take place at mealtimes, and so drinking wine means imbibing alcohol on its own. While not actually bringing about a state of drunkenness, it likely will dull the senses or cause the individual to lose concentration. Furthermore, actually swallowing the wine does not bring into play any additional criteria for assessment, as everything takes place between the nose and the mouth. So people spit in order to appreciate the aroma and the body of several wines more keenly.

APPEARANCE

The first contact with a wine is visual—the eye perceives the color and depth of color that the wine offers as soon as it is served. To the attentive taster, wine begins to tell its story while it is still in the glass. Looking at what is known in French as the wine's robe *("dress")—its hue, brilliance, surface, and its "legs"—allows a taster to uncover many valuable clues as the wine reveals its origins, its age, its personality, and indeed its quality.*

Noting the appearance

At first, a taster will try to define a wine's color: its hue, its intensity, and its clarity. To see these clearly, the wine should be held—in good lighting—in front of a neutral background (a white tablecloth, for example) or placed on any white surface.

HUE. The color of a wine is evaluated according to two parameters, its hue and its intensity. The vocabulary used to describe the first quality draws its terms from the world of precious stones (ruby, topaz), metals (gold, copper), flowers (rose, violet), and fruits (lemon, cherry). *See also* box below.

INTENSITY. Since there are so many different shades of color, it is important to define the hue by its intensity. This varies between "pale" and "very dark," moving through "light," "dark," "deep," "intense," and "profound." Some of the vocabulary used, such as "poor," "soft," and "weak," are already indications of quality.

Visually inspecting a wine is the first step in waking the senses. It prepares and conditions the mind and the other senses for tasting the wine.

CLARITY. This should be perfect and not compromised by any foreign particles in suspension, such as dust, flakes, or any residue from finings or dead yeast that may float around in the liquid. If it is not, it may be described as "cloudy," "hazy," or "opalescent." These are all signs of poor winemaking or contamination of the wine, and generally render it unfit for enjoyment. As wine production advances, though, these occurrences are fortunately less and less likely.

What does the appearance of a wine tell us?

A wine's color not only tells us its type—white, red, or rosé—but it can reveal details about the age of the vines, the yield, the year, the age of the wine, and even the manner of its maturation.

VARIETIES AND VINTAGES. The substances that lend a wine its color originate with pigments contained in grape skins. There are few of these to be found in white grapes, but they are very prevalent in red grapes, with different intensities according to variety. A wine made with Gamay grapes has a pretty ruby color; and it's distinct from one made with Cabernet Sauvignon, which is a deep garnet. The gradual development of the vines partially determines the maturity of the grape pigments, although the color intensity of a wine is more predicated on actual vintage quality. Thus a 1994 Médoc will have a less intense hue than the more concentrated 1996, which was a hotter year. In the same way, white wines will have a deeper color when

> To inspect a wine's appearance, it should be placed above a white surface.

The palette of colors

Red wines: peony, light ruby, dark ruby, vermilion, garnet, deep garnet, carmine, deep purple. When aged: brick red, russet, chestnut, mahogany, coffee.

Rosés: pale gray, very light rose, pink, raspberry, carnation, strawberry, cherry, salmon pink. When older, they become: salmon, orange, brick, copper, onion skin.

White wines: pale yellow with a hint of green, pale yellow, lemon, pale gold, golden yellow, straw gold. After several years of maturing: old gold, bronze, copper, amber, mahogany, coffee.

the grapes were harvested in hotter years, which encourage slight over-maturity.

VINE YIELD. The color intensity is also a function of the yield that the winemaker has obtained from the vines. The higher the yield, the less concentrated the grapes and the lighter the resulting liquid. By contrast, the lower the yield, the more the wine will gain in intensity. This is often the case with old vines, which bear fewer grapes and which almost always produce a wine with a pronounced coloration.

CONDITION OF THE GRAPES. The health of grape clusters is also a factor that influences a wine's appearance. If made with a spoiled lot of grapes, the wine will have less color intensity, whatever the variety or yield.

WINE AGE. The color of a white wine intensifies with age, while that of a red wine fades. As a result, inspecting a wine can allow you to assess its age. When very young, reds (and some rosés) have a slight blue tinge that often lends a purple hue to their overall appearance. In time, they will acquire shades of deep orange as the pigments and tannins start to yellow. As whites

DID YOU KNOW...?

A wine "throwing a deposit" or looking cloudy is not necessarily a bad sign. If unfiltered or only partially filtered, some young wines will display a slight haze, arising from fine lees in suspension that will go on to form an entirely normal deposit. By the same token, it is entirely normal to find deposits in old wines or, in certain bottles, small crystals resulting from a precipitation of tartaric acid, one of the ingredients of wine. The latter come from a sudden change in temperature.

Inspecting sparkling wines

Much like still wines, sparkling wines are judged on their color, clarity, and brilliance.

In addition to these criteria, the froth of the bubbles should be examined. For this, a tall "flute" glass is preferable to a standard "cup" glass, which can spoil the wine's effervescence. In the first instance, a taster will study the foam that forms spontaneously in the glass when the wine is poured, noting the size, duration, and the size of the bubbles. A good foam is of a reasonable size, long-lasting, and made up of small bubbles. Once this has subsided, the *cordon*, a ring of bubbles adhering to the side of the glass, will remain. These bubbles, which should be small, will rise regularly from the bottom of the glass to the ring at the top in columns known in French as the *cheminée*. Large bubbles that burst immediately at the surface, the absence of a ring of bubbles, or minimal effervescence do not suggest high quality wine. But note that the serving temperature and the choice of glass both play a role in the formation of bubbles and froth—cold inhibits effervescence and heat encourages it.

> The stream of bubbles rising to form a *cheminée* replenishes the ring of froth that forms at the edge of the glass.

contain few tannins, their color develops much more slowly, from shades of green and yellow to gold.

VINIFICATION. This too plays a role in wine color. For reds, a long maceration allows more of the pigmented substances to be extracted (*see* p.68). Because of their methods of production, either by crushing or by *saignée* ("bleeding") of the vats (*see* p.66), rosés will have different shades: rather pale in the case of the former method, and darker in the latter. A new barrel will intensify wine hue as it boosts the combination of the substances causing coloration. Whether white or red, a wine will have a darker shade when matured in barrels than the same wine that has been stored in steel tanks.

The surface and the meniscus

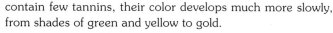

THE SURFACE (the topmost view of a wine). To observe the surface accurately, tasters first place themselves directly above the glass—the top view—and then hold the wine up to light—the side view. The surface is judged according to the brilliance of its appearance and by the way it catches the light. Observing the surface should confirm the clarity of the color. A wine with clarity issues will also present a surface with the same problems; and a suspect will be described as "matte," "dull," "flat," and "lusterless." More positively, the wine's surface might be described as "brilliant," "lustrous," "luminous," or "intense." For white wines and rosés, luster is an important and fundamental index of quality. For reds wines, such a quality should be considered in light of the recent winery trend to avoid filtration, an operation otherwise carried out just before bottling and intended to increase the clarity and brilliance of a wine (*see*

p.76). Without filtration, a wine will lose in brilliance but gain in color intensity.

THE MENISCUS (OR RIM). When inspecting the surface of red wines, and to a lesser extent rosés, tasters will pay special attention to its outside edge, known as the "meniscus." Because the wine is at its thinnest here, the wine's true color will be most apparent. If there is a touch of blue, it suggests that the wine is still very young; if it reveals more shades of terracotta and brick red, it will be an older wine. This development of color, a result of pigments taking on an orange or brick tint with time due to the ageing of tannins, is of varying significance and meaning for different wines. Thus, hints of purple or a bold red are appropriate for wines that are enjoyed young; by the time these have taken on an orange meniscus, they are no longer fresh. Orange and ochre go in tandem with a more developed wine, which has some age. Shades of brown and garnet, how-

Common visual faults

The most common faults encountered today are a lack of color intensity and, in the case of red wines, a color that has prematurely turned to one reminiscent of brown bricks; this is most often the result of a spoiled harvest or insufficiently matured grapes. It could also show too high of a yield, or winemaking that was rushed or badly carried out.

ever, are acceptable only in wines capable of very long ageing. For wines that do not have sufficient physical or aromatic capabilities for long ageing, these are signs of decrepitude. Much like the wine's color, the meniscus should be in proportion to the year printed on the label. Thus, if the label suggests that the wine is still young but the meniscus already shows signs of age, it is not likely to be a wine of good quality. The color then will be described as "old," "tired," or "impaired." In the reverse case (an old wine with a less well developed meniscus), the taster will note the youth of its color.

The "legs"

WHAT EXACTLY ARE LEGS? By placing the glass up to light and swirling the wine, or rotating it to slide up the sides of the glass, tasters will be able to see traces of a transparent liquid that slips down more slowly than the rest of the wine. These are the "legs," and inspecting them is the last stage of a visual examination of wine. They are the result of twin phenomena arising from physical tension between water and alcohol and from the mixture of alcohol, sugars, and glycerols in the wine. The legs display the body of a wine—its viscosity or tactile thickness. Well-defined, viscous legs that flow gently down the glass are a sign of wine rich in residual sugars and/or alcohol. By contrast, a less rich wine will have fewer, finer, and more fluid legs that move more quickly. The phenomenon is described in terms of the wine's fluidity or viscosity, using words like "watery," "liquid," and "fluid" for a wine with a low alcohol or sugar content and "thick," "syrupy," and "unctuous" in the opposite case.

HOW SHOULD LEGS BE INTERPRETED? "Legs" are rarely considered a sign of good or bad quality in a wine. Instead, they provide more information about its personality or categorization in the great wine families (see pp.154–61). For

> Inspecting a wine's "legs" will give you an idea of the its alcohol and/or sugar content.

white wines, abundant "legs" with a certain viscosity suggest a sweet or medium-sweet style of wine, rich in sugars (a Sauternes or Jurançon, for example) rather than a dry wine. In blind tastings, where the wine's identity is unknown, inspecting such details will yield helpful clues for tasters.

IF WINE IS LUSTROUS, IT IS ALIVE

Jean-Michel Deluc, Master Sommelier.

"The brilliance of a wine is a visual expression of its acidity. A young wine, whether it is red, white, rosé, sparkling, sweet, or dry, will have a brilliance from undiminished acidity. This acidity beds down and softens with age, and the wine loses its luster. Acidity is the life of a wine, and as long as it remains, the wine will have a shine. A wine that has lost this has reached the end of its time.

The oldest wine I have ever tasted was an 1834 Pedro Ximenez sherry. It was a coffee color, with a sweet texture. Its density had made it opaque, and yet it still had a shine, a surprise that bowled me over!"

Tastevin

An accessory popular with Old World cellar masters, the tastevin is a shallow, round metal receptacle resembling a little cup. It is not really possible to "nose" a wine with a tastevin because of its low profile; it is primarily used to judge the fine detail and intensity of a wine's appearance and clarity, thus helping to estimate the general state of the wine more objectively.

Professional winemakers are thus able to follow the development of the different wines held in their cellars.

WINE AROMA OR "NOSE"

Sniffing a glass of wine, identifying the different aromas, and investigating its complexity and subtlety is one of the great pleasures of tasting. Nonetheless, this exercise is one that often frustrates novice tasters, who have trouble telling aromas apart. A short refresher course will be useful in reawakening your olfactory memory.

Analyzing the "nose" of a wine

A wine's aroma delivers about 70 percent of all information about that wine. For the best results in analyzing the aroma of a wine, tasters should choose a tulip-shaped glass and fill it to only about a third of its capacity. They will also monitor the serving temperature of the wine—somewhere between 46 and 64°F (8–18°C) depending on wine color and origin (*see* p.186–7)—which influences the volatility of the aromatic ingredients of the wine. If it is too cold, the aromas will not be able to vaporize easily; if it is too hot, they will evaporate too quickly and be overpowered by alcohol fumes.

The best advice is to sniff the glass several times without inhaling too hard, in order to avoid saturating your senses. Also, wait a little between each inhalation. Analyzing the aroma of a wine splits into three stages.

FIRST NOSING. For the initial olfactory contact with a wine, tasters will angle their glasses and lightly breathe in the wine aromas. They make sure, on the one hand, that the wine is not tainted with undesirable smells and, on the other, that they capture the delicate, volatile scents of the wine (those present in the upper part of the glass). The latter soon disappear after serving.

SECOND NOSING. This stage is intended to identify the wine's aromatic personality. Tasters will grasp the glass by its base and rotate it to swirl the wine and oxygenate it. This will accelerate the vaporization of the various aromatic compounds. (To make this easier, feel free to keep the glass on the table while swirling it.) They will then inhale a few times, dipping their noses into the glass for several seconds, in order to assess the strength, the intensity, and the richness of the nose, while trying to identify the different aromas of which it is composed.

THIRD NOSING. This shows the wine's character after a long period of oxygenation in the glass. Once the wine is in contact with the air, its various aromatic compounds develop at different rates according to their volatility. So it's an interesting exercise to dip your nose back into the glass (without swirling its contents) after leaving the wine to stand for a while. Tasters often note the development of new aromas and changes in intensity.

> *The term "nose" describes the collection of scents that characterize a wine. One might use the term "aroma" to designate the fresh and fruity scents of young wines, and "bouquet" to express the aromatic richness of a wine at the height of its powers or in its old age.*

> Giving the wine a gentle swirl in its glass will oxygenate it.

DID YOU KNOW...?

Smell is the most active of our senses and yet, paradoxically, the least educated. Although smell is the most developed sense among newborns, as adults we just react to odors in an instinctive and primary manner, accepting or rejecting them but rarely analyzing them. This often causes problems for tasters called upon to identify the characteristic aromas of a wine. To help, good tasters attempt to smell everything around them that produces a scent (flowers, fruits, spices, as well as the scents of the countryside, the kitchen, the bakery, etc.), hoping to capture and catalog them in each of the family groups of smells. It's not a difficult exercise and certainly not an unpleasant one—tasting is a little like "dusting off" our memory, diving into our life history to bring up memories associated with particular smells.

Nasal and retronasal passages

The sense of smell is called upon not only during the sniffing stage, but also during the actual tasting itself. Aromatic molecules in a vaporized state will rise toward the back of the nasal cavity along two routes: the nasal passage, which passes directly through the nostrils when we breathe in, and the less direct retronasal passage, which links the mouth to the nose via the throat when we breathe out.

It's therefore only at the moment of drinking that tasters complete their olfactory analysis of the wine, by uncovering the aromas that are not directly accessible to the nose. Indeed, because of their low volatility, some scents need to be warmed in the mouth in order to pass from a liquid state to a gaseous one. Only at that moment do flavors and aromas mix and juxtapose themselves. What we recognize, for example, as the taste of strawberries is in fact the smell of strawberries; the "taste" is thus the sum total of sensations that are as much olfactory (aromas) as they are gustatory (flavors).

> Analyzing the nose of a wine requires concentration and an effort of memory from a taster.

Describing the bouquet of a wine

The best way to describe the aromas or bouquet of a wine is in stages, starting with an overall impression before pointing out the different scents and aromas you find in the wine.

AROMATIC CHARACTERISTICS. At first, tasters will try to describe the wine's aromatic features in a general way, assessing intensity in terms of "strong" or "weak" or the various gradations between them. The vocabulary used might include terms such as "expressive," "intense," "powerful," "generous," and "exuberant." By contrast, there is "inexpressive," "weak," "poor," and "limp." In certain circumstances, the wine does not develop any clear aroma in the glass, such as when it has just been poured or when served too cold; the bouquet is then said to be "closed." This objective and descriptive vocabulary is often augmented with more subjective thoughts such as "pleasing," "agreeable," "elegant," or "classy." As well, there is "banal," "ordinary," "simplistic," or "vulgar."

IDENTIFYING DIFFERENT AROMAS. The next level of analysis may be a more difficult exercise. Rather than trying to identify a specific aroma, it is often easier to identify the "family" of scents to which it belongs, referring to such groups as floral, fruity, vegetal, mineral, spicy, balsamic, toasted, and chemical aromas (see table on p.214).

Aromas may also be distinguished according to the origins, age, and production methods of the wine, as some of these groups of scents overlap with others.

PRIMARY AROMAS. These show the fruit characteristics of the grape variety (or varieties) that comprise the wine. They may be floral, fruity, vegetal, mineral, or spicy, according to the grape varieties. They are at their strongest when the wine is young, especially if it has been matured exclusively in vats.

SECONDARY AROMAS. These are the result of fermentation, the process that transforms grapes into wine. Consequently, they often are called "fermentation aromas." They are determined by the nature of the yeast and the style of winemaking, and are part of the "chemical" family of aromas: amylic (bananas or nail varnish), fermentative (yeast, soft bread), or lactic (butter, milk, cream). These aromas are associated with young wines and disappear after a couple of years of bottle age. Secondary aromas are also introduced by maturing the wine in barrels, and these are spicy scents (pepper, vanilla, cinnamon) or toasted (grilled, roasted, smoked).

TERTIARY AROMAS. These appear when wines develop or age in the bottle (i.e. a reductive medium) or in oak barrels (under the influence of slight oxygenation). Tertiary aromas are the result of a long period of ageing and contribute to the complexity of a wine, adding musky and vegetal notes to the aromatic framework.

What can the nose of a wine tell you?

Just like its appearance, the nose of a wine reveals important information about its personality and its quality. Pleasant intensity and a large palette of aromas are signs of high

quality and will excite a taster who encounters them. The primary or tertiary aromas are usually the dominant scents—the secondary ones are rarely the most prominent, unless they overpower everything else—and they will provide valuable information about the grape or grapes used, the age of the wine, the production methods, indeed even the year and the yield.

FRUIT RIPENESS. To a large extent, the quality of the aromas contained in the glass depends on the ripeness of the grapes. A less ripe, dilute Sauvignon Blanc will give off an unsophisticated grassy scent with just a hint of citrus fruits. When more mature and made from a low yield, it will reveal complex aromas of pineapple and pink grapefruit zest.

WINE ORIGIN. A Chardonnay produced in Chablis will have a fresh bouquet with mineral and white flower notes, very different from one made in Meursault, which will be more opulent with hints of almond and hazelnut. Furthermore, a wine created beneath the Languedoc sun is even heavier, with potent notes of ripe fruit.

WINE AGE. A wine best expresses its complexity with time; the different perfumes of a wine—the primary, secondary, and tertiary aromas—evolve while the wine is being matured in a tank or a barrel, and then later as it ages in the bottle. In the best examples, a wine captures the scents from its whole history, expressing the quintessence of the land where it was made and yet always retaining the memory of the original fruit.

CONFIRMATION OF VISUAL INSPECTION. A wine's bouquet should back up its visual appearance. A wine with a young appearance should thus have young, fruity notes; a great

red wine that has been laid down and reached its peak will have more complex aromas. If this is not the case, the wine will suffer from an imbalance and disharmony that tasting will only confirm (*see* pp.216–8). To sum up, tasters will note the complexity or simplicity of the bouquet offered by the wine, its rusticity or sophistication, its coherence or dissonance, its youth or its maturity. They use terms such as "elegant," "vigorous," or "distinguished," or, in the opposite case, "banal," "ordinary," "simple," "lacking harmony," "undistinguished."

Olfactory flaws

The most common faults in wine are those resulting from its production methods. Poor hygiene in the winery can leave a taint of mold or mildew. A wine that has not been oxygenated will have a reduced, "closed" nose; on the other hand, too much oxygen is harmful to wine and results in an oxidized odor. Inappropriate addition of sulfur can also have a detrimental effect. In too great a quantity, sulfur has an acrid and penetrating smell. When poorly integrated, it has a rotten egg odor known as "mercaptan." A fault in the wine's aroma may also be caused by an external factor such as a bad cork or certain wood treatment products used in the framework of the barrels or the storage pallets, which can leave a "corky" smell.

Aroma families

This table outlines the various aroma families (floral, herbaceous, fruit, mineral, etc.) by color and by category (primary aromas: *i.e.* stemming from each grape variety; secondary, resulting from fermentation; tertiary, from maturation and ageing).

AROMA FAMILY	RED WINES AND ROSÉS
FLORAL GROUP	
Primary aromas	Iris, peony, rose, violet.
Tertiary aromas	Dried flowers, pressed roses.
FRUIT GROUP	
Primary aromas	Small red and black fruits (blackcurrant, cherry, strawberry, raspberry, Morello cherry, redcurrant, blackberries), fruit jams, black olives, prunes.
Secondary aromas	Bananas, licorice.
Tertiary aromas	Cooked fruits, fruit liqueurs.
HERBACEOUS GROUP	
Primary aromas	Blackcurrant stems, humus, black pepper, green tomato.
Tertiary aromas	Mushroom, humus, forest floor, truffle.
MINERAL GROUP	
Primary aromas	Chalk, clay, flint.
SPICE GROUP	
Primary aromas	*Garrigue*, bay leaf, pepper, thyme.
Secondary aromas	Cloves, licorice.
CHEMICAL GROUP	
Secondary aromas	Acetone, banana, yeast, sulfur, nail varnish.
MUSK GROUP	
Tertiary aromas	Leather, fur, game, meat juices, venison.
BALSAMIC GROUP	
Secondary aromas	New wood, oak, pine, resin, turpentine, vanilla.
TOASTED GROUP	
Secondary aromas	Cocoa, cigars, smoke, tar, grilling, roasting, tobacco, soot, tea, warm bread.

AROMA FAMILY	WHITE WINES
FLORAL GROUP	
Primary aromas	Acacia, hawthorn, orange flower, geranium, rose, lime blossom.
Tertiary aromas	Camomile, dried flowers.
FRUIT GROUP	
Primary aromas	Apricot, citrus fruits (lemon, orange, grapefruit), pineapple, banana, quince, fig, fruit candies, exotic fruits (lychee, mango, papaya), nuts (almond, hazelnut), melon, peach, pear, green apple, cooked apple.
Secondary aromas	Pineapple.
Tertiary aromas	Dried fruits, honey.
HERBACEOUS GROUP	
Primary aromas	Blackcurrant stems, boxwood, mushroom, fennel, fern, hay, fresh-cut grass, fresh mint, straw, "cat's pee."
Tertiary aromas	Rare or non-existent.
MINERAL GROUP	
Primary aromas	Chalk, iodine, gasoline, flint, silica.
SPICE GROUP	
Primary aromas	White pepper.
Secondary aromas	Cinnamon, cloves, vanilla.
CHEMICAL GROUP	
Secondary aromas	Fresh butter, *brioche*, cream, milk, yeast, bread, sulfur.
MUSK GROUP	
Tertiary aromas	Rare or non-existent.
BALSAMIC GROUP	
Tertiary aromas	New wood, oak, pine, resin, turpentine, vanilla.
TOASTED GROUP	
Secondary aromas	Grilling, *brioche*, mocha, tea, warm bread, roasting.

TASTE

The third and final stage is the tasting itself! The wine will now reveal its complete personality, including flavors, texture, structure, and balance. But thanks to the clues they have gathered, tasters are not going into this with absolutely no idea of what they are about to taste. Tasting must confirm and complete all the previous observations, and, in the best cases, deliver total satisfaction.

Tasting: no easy task

It's a sight to see tasters at work: grimacing and gurgling the wine around their mouths before spitting it out again, all with a thoughtful look on their faces.

Far from being done for show, the whole procedure is indispensable to proper appreciation of wine, and it's explained by the many factors that are part of the process of tasting. There is the tongue, which detects the four principal flavors; but there also is the whole mouth—the gums, cheeks, and palate—which registers sensations such as temperature, texture, and chemical qualities such as astringency or effervescence, where present. A wine taster's facial expressions are no more than an attempt to get the most from the sense organs.

Although the technique is simple, the art of tasting turns out to be more difficult. In effect, in a short space of time (less than a minute), a taster will assess various sensations that

Anyone can attempt a tasting exercise, though it requires attention and concentration. And even a little practice and curiosity can bring some amateurs to a level of competence that would not shame a true professional.

combine and conjoin among themselves, thereby making their analysis relatively difficult. The best approach is to ask oneself appropriate questions about the structure, balance, harmony, and complexity of the wine's flavors.

The three stages of tasting

While the practical aspect of tasting is conducted in one action, the associated analysis is carried out in three successive stages.

ATTACK PHASE. The attack phase corresponds to the first impression that the liquid gives to the tongue when the taster takes a small sip of wine. From the very start, the taster will note the temperature and the presence of any gas, and will also form an idea of the wine's overall personality. The attack phase of a quality wine will be open, clean, and precise, but may also turn out to be generous, aromatic, and fruity. If this first contact does not make much of an impression on the taster, the attack is said to be "weak," fleeting," or "watery;" in other circumstances, it is "aggressive" if it elicits a strong or unpleasant taste sensation.

MID-PALATE STAGE. This "evolution" stage corresponds to the development of the wine in the mouth. Tasters roll a sip of wine around their mouths for a few seconds, giving the impression of "chewing," and then breathe in a column of air through the mouth in order to accelerate the flow of aromatic particles to the olfactory bulb—an organ at the back of the nasal cavity designed to capture these—via the retronasal passage (*see* box on p.211). These olfactory sensations, both tactile and thermal, will combine and increase to deliver an overall impression. The taster's task is thus to try to differentiate these in turn before analyzing and assessing the balance of the wine.

FINISH. This last stage deals with the length of flavor of the wine "in the mouth" once it has been swallowed (or spat out). This gives an idea of the "size" of a wine. The longer the impression, the higher the quality and the greater the wine's potential for laying down. The finish is measured in seconds (a unit of time known to French tasters as a *caudalie*, from the Latin *cauda*, "tail"). The finish is described as "long" or "lingering"—in the very finest cases, the French compare it to a "peacock's tail"—although a less substantial finish is referred to as "short," "brief," "fleeting," or "non-existent." The difficulty lies in not confusing the flavor length with the sensations elicited by the acidity, alcohol, or tannins—burning, warmth, or

---

Flaws in flavor

Some olfactory faults (see p.213) will become more apparent during tasting. Dirty or musty smells reveal themselves as a "bad taste" comparable to the smell of rotting vegetation or of an animal pen. A wine with too much sulfur will have an unbalanced flavor reminiscent of garlic, rubber, or rotten eggs (mercaptan). An oxidized wine will have an acidulated flavor in the case of whites, and a sweet-and-sour taint sometimes called *rancio* in the case of reds. A wine with a "corky" aroma will taste like the smell of cardboard. Other faults are inherent in a poorly balanced wine and are not always perceptible in the wine's aroma.

A burning sensation indicates an excess of alcohol or acidity. A large dose of sugar, unbalanced by alcohol and appropriate acidity, will deliver a feeling that is cloying, heavy, and lacking in finesse. Poorly ripened tannins will present a strong acrid sensation from a young wine, and a dryness in an older wine.

> Once the wine has been analyzed in the mouth, it can be swallowed or spat out.

astringency—which tend to obscure it. The simplest approach is to concentrate on the most dominant flavor and then, having swallowed (or spat out) the wine, stay on its trail until it has disappeared.

Every assessment needs a conclusion! A rapid summing up is called for, not only in respect of the wine's quality at that precise moment, but also of its future. (Is it ready to be enjoyed, for example, or does it require more ageing, or has it passed its best?) Here, of course, is where tasters can give free rein to their own tastes!

Analyzing flavors and aromas

Flavors come from different wine components. Acidity comes from various acidulating elements; sweetness comes from possible residual sugar but also from alcohol; bitterness is linked with the presence of tannins; saltiness is rare, existing only in very weak quantities and deriving from various saline elements. These flavors combine during tasting as juxtapositions, sometimes cancelling each another out (see box, p.218), but almost always complementing the aromas. The latter, which will have been identified in part during a taster's olfactory analysis, will be confirmed at the tasting stage.

So a red wine whose bouquet has notes of very ripe red fruits should also "taste" of red fruits. Backed up by a sweet flavor, that

Tannins

Only found in red grape varieties, tannins are extracted from the skins during maceration or they may arise during storage in barrels (as "noble" tannins). Their quality and quantity is defined by various factors: the maturity of the fruit, the duration of maceration, and even the grape variety (Gamay is less tannic than Cabernet Sauvignon). Tannins are responsible for the structure of the wine and play an essential role in ageing.

In the mouth, they are perceptible as a sensation of astringency (or dryness), which gives a "chewiness" to the wine. This is more or less pronounced according to its quality and age. Tannins are described (from most to least) in terms of "rough," "bitter," "firm," "round," and "fine." In time, tannins evolve from harsh to soft, from heavy to fine, and never the other way around.

Wine texture

Texture reflects a combination of tactile sensations in the mouth. It can be appreciated from the very start by an amateur, even before any analysis of the different elements of balance. It is a function of the relationship between the principal constituents of a wine: alcohol, acidity, tannins, and sugars. The vocabulary used to describe it often borrows from the world of fabrics: a texture is said to be "supple," "caressing," "satiny," "velvety," "silky," or by contrast, "grainy," "coarse," "rough," or "rustic." Comparisons to the human frame are frequently drawn, and the "body" of a wine may be "fleshy," "full-bodied," "robust," or conversely "thin," "lean," or "sinewy." Other terms, such as "suave," "unctuous," "viscous," "creamy," and "syrupy," are commonly used to describe the texture of white wines that are rich in residual sugars.

The quality of the texture may also be understood within the context of the appellation—a Médoc wine, made predominantly from Cabernet Sauvignon grapes and rich in tannins, will not have the same velvety feel as a Pomerol, where Merlot, rich in alcohol and often lower in tannins, reigns supreme.

> In red wines, astringency reinforces the sensation of acidity.

character will be all the more apparent. By contrast, a dominant acidic flavor will point toward an imbalance between flavour and aroma, and this does not say much for the wine's quality. However, in a dry white wine with prominent citrus aromas (lemon, grapefruit), a fresh bite of acidity is the very character that should predominate in the mouth. The perception of the harmonious interaction of flavors in the mouth and the aromas detected in the nose of a wine are thus essential elements that allow the wine's quality and balance to be assessed.

Analyzing tactile sensations

In addition to the aromatic and olfactory sensations it generates, a wine generates different different tactile sensations in the entire mouth, and especially in its mucous membranes:

SOFTNESS. The sensation of softness is evoked by alcohol, which has a soft and slightly sweet character; this is reinforced by the possible presence of actual residual sugars. Alcohol is what gives dry white wines their softness and, in the case of reds, provides an idea of the wine's richness.

ACIDITY. The sensation of acidity is provided by various acidic elements in the wine. Although these can be less apparent in red wines, they come more to the fore in white wines and in rosés made using the pressing process. Acidity encourages salivation and thus a sensation of freshness.

ASTRINGENCY. A sensation of dryness in the mouth, induced by tannins (*see* box, previous page), is most often encountered in red wines; but it's also a feature of rosés made using the bleeding process. Along with acidity and alcohol, tannins are one of the elements that make up the framework or "skeleton" of a wine.

Each of these sensations can be analyzed separately, although in most cases they combine to form a composite experience. In a sweet or dry white wine, and in some rosés, the wine's tactile personality is defined by the pairing of acidity and softness; for reds and other rosés, the defining factors are the trio of acidity, softness, and astringency. There are as many combinations possible as there are wines, but the result must be balanced. It should not elicit any unpleasant sensations from an excess of one of the components. Examples include a "burn" from excess of alcohol or acidity, or a dryness and harshness caused by insufficiently ripened tannins, or by a lack of softness in the wine (*see* pp. 220–1). An appreciation of the texture of the wine results from the sum total of these tactile sensations, and this is known as the "body" or "fullness" of the wine.

DID YOU KNOW...?

We recognize four basic tastes: sweetness, saltiness, sourness, and bitterness. Despite a widespread misconception, our taste buds as they are set out on the tongue are not specialized and each can recognise the entire range of flavors. During tasting, the flavors inter-react, forming partnerships or cancelling out their opposites: saltiness reinforces bitterness, sweetness dominates saltiness but diminishes the perception of acidity and slows the perception of bitterness. When tasting, it is thus important to assess the balance of flavors in general. There is the balance of sugars on one hand and acidic and bitter elements in particular on the other. These are a direct index of the balance of the wine (see pp. 220–1). In the final analysis, each individual has a personal sensitivity or threshold of perception for each taste component.

THE SYNTHESIS OF TASTING

It is now time to assess the quality of the wine, and this may be summed up in three words: balance, harmony, and pleasure. Balance many be appreciated directly during tasting, and harmony is a synthesis of all the data gathered—tastes, aromas, and visual impression. Pleasure is a matter for the taster alone.

Balance and harmony

When judging the overall quality of a wine, two criteria are usually applied: balance and harmony.

BALANCE. A wine is said to be balanced when the various tasting components—acidity and sweetness for white wines; tannins, acidity, softness for reds—combine in a satisfactory manner, creating a subjective impression of balance. This idea, both structural and quantitative, should be distinguished from that of harmony, which is aesthetic and qualitative.

HARMONY. A wine is considered harmonious when its constituents combine but do not all tell the same story. Each group of components, taken individually, should have no disagreeable element (bitter tannins, piercing acidity, a softness that is too alcoholic); and when taken as a whole, each of them should have a great relationship with the others, making an overall aesthetic impression.

Such a situation is most often brought about by a graduated hierarchy of the three groups of tasting components

Knowing how to taste means being able to distinguish every aspect of a wine. Becoming a good taster involves nothing more than having an open and inquiring mind, cultivating a little sensory discernment, and, above all, applying your memory.

rather than their absolute equality; and as it is a function of wine education and cultural norms, the concept of harmony varies from country to country.

Balance in dry whites

The balance of dry white wines is a function of the relationship between acidity and alcohol. The former brings freshness and vivacity, and the latter brings the wine sweetness and softness—in other words, its body. In the mouth, the two sensations should be in equilibrium. To understand how they are related, the simplest approach is to imagine two perpendicular axes (*see* diagram). The nearer the wine is to the crossing point, the more balanced it will be considered. A wine with strong acidity and little alcohol will reveal itself as aggressive, thin, and insubstantial, while one with weak acidity and a normal alcohol level is described as *nerveux* or "nervous."

In the same fashion, higher alcohol levels with the same acidity will lead to suppleness, roundness, and body, or even to a heaviness that reveals itself as an unpleasant sensation of warmth in the mouth.

Nuances in this balance exist and define the different styles of wine. An Alsace Riesling can be distinguished by its "nervousness," while a Meursault should yield certain opulence. Despite these differences, neither wine would be considered imbalanced. The combination of flavors and aromas also plays a role in the balance of the wine by reinforcing or dulling tactile sensations.

The balance of sweet whites

The two axes present in all white wines—acidity and alcohol—are joined by that of the residual sugars specific to sweet and very sweet wines (*see* diagram). This component reinforces the tactile sensation of softness engendered in the mouth by alcohol. Balance is achieved when no single one of the characteristics is allowed to dominate the other two.

The secret of harmonious wines is found in two important rules: the richer a wine is in sugars, the higher its alcohol level must be raised; the higher these two ingredients are raised, the more the acidity level should pull the balance back toward the center. Insufficiency of any one of the constituents will immediately cause imbalance. When dominated by sugars, for example, a wine will be syrupy.

BALANCE IN DRY WHITES

ACIDITY +

"green" wine: thin or little body

rich and hard wine

aggressive
cutting
"nervous"
lively
fresh

ALCOHOL −

thin · insubstantial · gentle · supple

good body
supple · heavy · warm · burning

ALCOHOL +

fresh
smooth
flat
gentle

flat and insipid wine

rich and heavy wine

zone of balance

ACIDITY −

THE BALANCE OF SWEET WHITES

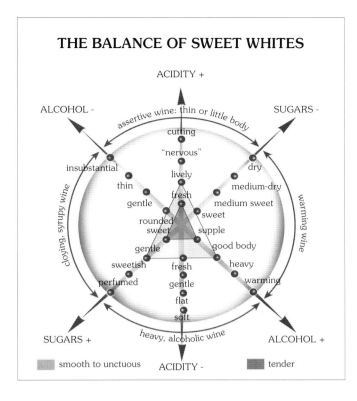

smooth to unctuous

tender

Even at the heart of this balance there are nuances in texture—it may be tender, supple, unctuous—that will define the wine's richness as well as its style. By the same token, some sweet wines have a considerable acidity that, far from being aggressive, brings a pleasant "nervousness" to the wine. This is the case for sweet wines from the Loire Valley such as Coteaux-du-Layon and Vouvray. During tasting, the amateur taster will also bear in mind the power of the aromas and flavors, which should back up and confirm the richness of the wine.

The balance of reds

Assessing the balance of red wines is made more difficult by the presence of tannins. Such a balance is a value expressed on three axes, representing alcohol, acidity, and tannin respectively (see diagram). Their meeting point is an ideal of equilibrium, with possible nuances dictated by the style of wine: solidly made if the tannins somewhat dominate the alcohol/acidity coupling, or rounded and integrated in the opposite case. The further one travels from the center of the diagram, the more robust a specimen of its style a wine will be, until reaching a point where the harmony is upset as one or two of the dominant characteristics are sidelined. The more tannin a wine possesses, the greater a sensation of astringency will be felt—and perceived as unpleasant if it is not compensated by acidity and alcohol at a proportional level. From tannic, a wine then becomes harsh, rough, bitter, and astringent. When dominated by tannins and acidity, a wine gains in firmness to the point where, as the sensation of softness is obscured, it feels austere, rigid, and cutting. This state of affairs can be seen in wines made with Cabernet Sauvignon grapes that are rich in tannins. When ripe, they display a certain austerity that dulls with age. When less ripe, they can be more "angular," eliciting an unpleasant sensation that is a mixture of astringency and bitterness.

The balance of sparkling wines

The family of sparkling wines is a large one because of the diversity of grape varieties that can be used to make them (both reds and whites) and the different production methods (see pp.70-1). Nonetheless, they bear a structural resemblance to white wines, bubbles apart.

Sparkling wines are balanced across two axes: acidity and sweetness. To them, we must add effervescence, whose role it is to reinforce or attenuate the sensation of acidity. The bubbles are assessed during the attack phase according to their abundance and fineness. This gives the "tone" of the wine, showing it to be more or less aggressive, more or less subtle. A wine that foams excessively in the mouth is a bad sign. Sparkling wines often display a higher level of acidity than dry white wines; this guarantees vivacity, but in excess will impart a disagreeable cutting sensation. The bubbles should mellow this component, and do the same for the sweetness, without making the wine insipid. The finish should be fresh and aromatic, without retaining the burning sensation caused by acidity or the sweetish flavor of a poorly balanced *dosage* (sugars added during production).

THE BALANCE OF REDS

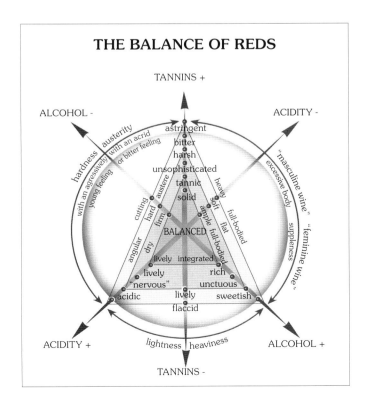

Some sample tasting notes

Judging the quality of a wine is not just a matter of taste—it is an exercise based on considerable learning and a diversity of tasting experiences. The greater an amateur's mastery of these, the better she or he will be able to understand wine and to evaluate its qualities and faults.

What's the point of tasting notes?

When tasting wine, the perception of aromas and flavors is always accompanied by a judgment reflecting the pleasure (or lack thereof) experienced by the taster. In contrast to a tasting of this kind, which is purely for pleasure, there is also tasting in the technical sense, the aim of which is to judge the quality of the wine. This includes detailed analysis of the sensations experienced according to a very precise set of criteria; but it is also reliant on a good knowledge of wine and winemaking. While tasting notes come as pre-printed documents of some precision for professionals, they are nothing so formal for amateurs, who might jot down impressions in their cellar books (*see* p.143) or in just a notebook.

FOR THE PROFESSIONAL. Professional tasters are looking, above all, for any flaws in the wine: imbalance, weakness, lack of local character, lack of fruit, bitterness, etc. Professionals will examine the appearance, nose, and mouth-feel of a wine to gain an overall impression. They will assess the wine's qualities, its potential for laying down, and the period when it will be at its peak (when the wine will taste its best). They will note the purchase price and potential price changes with age and suggest serving conditions (temperature, decanting.). They may suggest potential foods to accompany it. The wine is scored out of 100, 20, 10, or even 5 points, a ranking sometimes expressed as stars.

FOR THE AMATEUR. Amateur tasters follow the same visual, olfactory, and gustatory steps, and will attempt to assess the harmony of the wine. They may suggest thoughts on the wine's evolution, and perhaps note potential food-pairing suggestions. They may also include notes from various guides or articles. Tasting notes will allow collectors to follow the development of the wines in their cellars; and where wine has been passed on, tasting notes will allow the recipients to get to know the wines.

TASTING NOTES
Wine no. 1

Date:	January 2009
PROVENANCE	
Region:	Bordeaux
Appellation and/or wine name:	Pauillac
Producer:	La Rose Pauillac
Year:	2005
VISUAL APPEARANCE	
Color:	Intense ruby color with hints of purple.
Intensity:	Sparkling and glistening.
Concentration:	Full and rich.
BOUQUET	
Intensity:	Good intensity.
Quality:	Elegant, subtle, powerful, and complex.
Aromas:	Floral notes (rose, peony) mingling with ripe red fruit (strawberry, raspberry) and black fruits (blackcurrants, blackberries), followed by woody notes and hints of spices, toast, and licorice.
TASTING	
Attack:	Open, creamy, and velvety.
Mid-palate:	Rich and ample mouth-feel with plenty of suppleness that combines freshness with vinosity. Dominant fruit flavors with toasted and roasted notes from its maturation toward the back.
Finish:	Good flavorful length.
Balance:	Very well balanced.
CONCLUSION	
Quality:	An excellent Pauillac at an age to drink.
Drinking notes:	May be enjoyed now, after being left to breathe for an hour in a carafe. Also worth leaving to mature until 2014. Can be kept until 2020 in a good cellar. Serve with red meat or duck.

TASTING NOTES
Wine no. 2

Date:	January 2009
PROVENANCE	
Region:	Burgundy
Appellation and/or wine name:	Savigny-lès-Beaune, Cuvée de Réserve
Producer:	Maison Aegerter
Year:	2004
VISUAL APPEARANCE	
Color:	Charming ruby coloration with tinges of purple and a mauve edge.
Intensity:	Sparkling and velvety.
Concentration:	Average.
BOUQUET	
Intensity:	Good intensity.
Quality:	Elegant, aromatic, and fruity.
Aromas:	Floral notes (roses) mingling with ripe red and black fruit (blackcurrants, Morello cherries, raspberries) and a slight hint of spices, smoke, and licorice. Extremely harmonious nose.
TASTING	
Attack:	Open and perfumed.
Mid-palate:	Ample, smooth mouth-feel with plenty of suppleness, marrying freshness with fruit. Dominant flavors of Morello cherries, with a background of minerals and spices.
Finish:	Long and flavorful finish.
Balance:	Very well balanced.
CONCLUSION	
Quality:	A very nice nose from a well-rounded wine.
Drinking notes:	May be enjoyed now with roasted white meats or game terrines. Open the bottle an hour before serving. Will carry on maturing until 2015 in a good cellar.

TASTING NOTES
Wine no. 3

Date:	January 2009
PROVENANCE	
Region:	Alsace
Appellation and/or wine name:	Gewürztraminer Fronholtz late harvest
Producer:	Domaine Ostertag
Year:	2006
VISUAL APPEARANCE	
Color:	Intense golden color, good clarity.
Intensity:	Scintillating.
Concentration:	Plenty of nice substantial legs.
BOUQUET	
Intensity:	Nose initially closed, opening a little after aeration.
Quality:	Elegant but still a little understated.
Aromas:	Charming rose notes with a hint of spices, exotic fruits, and very ripe grapes.
TASTING	
Attack:	Supple and sweet.
Mid-palate:	Smooth body, coats the mouth well. A sugary character is apparent but not overpowering, with plenty of freshness, nice weight, aroma of roses clearly there.
Finish:	Long and flavorful finish.
Balance:	Good balance with no heaviness; sugars well integrated.
CONCLUSION	
Quality:	A very attractive wine with perfect balance, showing delicacy and concentration in equal measure.
Drinking notes:	Too young for the moment, will reach its peak somewhere between 2012 and 2020. Decant into a carafe if it is to be enjoyed in its first three years.

TASTING NOTES
Wine no. 4

Date:	January 2009
PROVENANCE	
Region:	Champagne
Appellation and/or wine name:	Champagne, Cuvée "La Grande Dame"
Producer:	Veuve Clicquot Ponsardin
Year:	1999
VISUAL APPEARANCE	
Color:	Golden appearance with a glint of pale green.
Intensity:	First foam fine and aerated. Ring of bubbles present.
Concentration:	Very fine bubbles rising in streams to the ring. Effervescence continues in the glass.
BOUQUET	
Intensity:	Good intensity.
Quality:	Elegant, fresh, and sophisticated.
Aromas:	Floral notes of white flowers mingling with ripe white fruit (peaches) and hints of citrus (grapefruit zest), followed by fleeting notes of toasted almonds and mocha.
TASTING	
Attack:	Good intensity.
Mid-palate:	Rich, ample mouth-feel with plenty of suppleness, marrying freshness and vinosity. Dominant fruit flavors with toasted and roasted notes in the background.
Finish:	Very long and flavorful finish.
Balance:	Very well balanced.
CONCLUSION	
Quality:	A very fine wine from a rich and mature year.
Drinking notes:	To be enjoyed now, with fine fish and slightly creamy sauces. Also worth laying down until 2014. Will keep until 2020, in a good cellar.

TASTING NOTES
Wine no. 5

Date:	January 2009
PROVENANCE	
Region:	Languedoc
Appellation and/or wine name:	Corbières rosé, Cuvée Pompadour
Producer:	Cave de Castelmaure
Year:	2008
VISUAL APPEARANCE	
Color:	Reasonably soft rosé, with a raspberry color with glints of salmon pink and copper; good clarity.
Intensity:	Refulgent.
Concentration:	Nice flowing legs, but few in number.
BOUQUET	
Intensity:	Expressive.
Quality:	Appealing fruit notes (red fruits).
Aromas:	Pronounced red fruits-strawberries, raspberries, and morello cherry jam- with intense peppery aromas and a delicate floral hint.
TASTING	
Attack:	Good attack, with plenty of suppleness.
Mid-palate:	Ample and generous; a rounded mouth-feel with bold fruit flavors.
Finish:	Average length; aromatic, with a hint of agreeable bitterness.
Balance:	Alcohol and acidity in perfect balance.
CONCLUSION	
Quality:	A vinous rosé with a generous body, but not out of balance.
Drinking notes:	Drink chilled by 2012. Should be served with grilled pork or fresh-water fish.

TASTING NOTES
Wine no. 6

Date:	January 2009

PROVENANCE

Region:	Spain
Appellation and/or wine name:	Rioja Gran Reserva
Producer:	Marqués de Riscal
Year:	2001

VISUAL APPEARANCE

Color:	Ruby-red appearance with good intensity; still fresh and clear.
Intensity:	Just beginning to mature with a slight orange rim.
Concentration:	Fine, flowing legs.

BOUQUET

Intensity:	Good intensity.
Quality:	Elegant, sophisticated with some charming hints of maturity.
Aromas:	Slightly fleshy notes linked with more integrated woody, toasted notes. When aerated, cooked fruit notes and spices become apparent.

TASTING

Attack:	Supple, quite soft.
Mid-palate:	Average mouth-feel, underlined by fine, well-integrated tannins. Bold fruit character.
Finish:	Good aromatic length.
Balance:	Balance correct.

CONCLUSION

Quality:	A wine that has developed very well; a great example of Spanish winemaking. Elegant and vinous.
Drinking notes:	Having reached its peak, the wine will be drinkable until 2013. Decanting recommended just before service to best bring out its fruit aromas.

TASTING NOTES
Wine no. 7

Date:	January 2009

PROVENANCE

Region:	Argentina
Appellation and/or wine name:	Mendoza, Finca El Portillo, Malbec
Producer:	Bodegas Salentein
Year:	2007

VISUAL APPEARANCE

Color:	Intense ruby appearance, going over into a bluish-black with purple at the rim.
Intensity:	Scintillating and profound.
Concentration:	Rich and bold intensity.

BOUQUET

Intensity:	Intense and deep.
Quality:	Elegant, powerful, and spicy.
Aromas:	Interplay of power and character. Shades of fruit couli sauce (blackcurrants, blackberries, myrtle), spice notes (pepper, cinnamon, vanilla), and licorice. Toast and cocoa notes.

TASTING

Attack:	Full-bodied and flavorful.
Mid-palate:	Structured wine with rather masculine acidity and tannins integrating with the fruit flavors.
Finish:	Average length with hints of licorice and pepper.
Balance:	Again rests on the strength of its structure.

CONCLUSION

Quality:	Excellent Malbec, comparable with a well-made Cahors.
Drinking notes:	Ready for drinking now after breathing in a carafe for 2 hours, or for laying down in a cellar until 2015.

DESCRIBING WINE

Mastering the techniques of tasting is equally a matter of being able to describe the sensations and building experience. The best way to understand the vocabulary used by professional tasters is to bear in mind that it is based on two basic principles.

Tasting vocabulary

There is no official body of tasting terminology, but a certain number of basic terms are widely used, and these are set out on the following pages in alphabetical order with their definition. They have become established through their use in describing the aromas, character, and structure of wines. Many of them work by analogy: the aromas of a wine are described in terms of familiar scents (fruits, spices, etc.); its texture (the tactile sensation it engenders in the mouth) is described by referring to the quality of a fabric, for example; and its structure is compared to that of the human body. The personality of a wine is described in much the same way: it may be "simple," "complex," "unsophisticated," or "elegant." Given all of these terms, the taster may create an almost infinite vocabulary to describe and analyze sensations.

The terms associated with formal tasting of wine are complementary to the technical vocabulary connected with winemaking contained in the glossary (pp.494–503) and the chapter "from the vine to the bottle."

A

ACACIA The charming scent of acacia flowers often features in the aroma of young Chardonnay and Chasselas wines, when their acidity is tempered.

ACERBIC Of a rather sharp nature; used where perceptible acidity is accentuated by the presence of unripe tannins.

ACIDITY Sensed by the tongue, but also through the secretion of saliva, which it promotes through the sharp sensation it leaves on the mucous membranes. Acidity plays a fundamental role in the mouth-feel of a wine and the general balance of its flavors. *See also,* CRISP.

ACRID Said of a wine with unpleasant bitterness, often due to tannins that are very pungent.

AGGRESSIVE Characteristic of a wine producing an attack of excess acidity or astringency on the mucous membranes.

ALCOHOL Alcohol is the principal constituent of wine after water. It eventually loses its burning and dehydrating character (as encountered in brandies), and instead takes on a distinctly sweet taste, which is a major contributor to softness in dry wines.

ALMOND, ALMOND BLOSSOM A flavor of almond blossom is sometimes detected in Sauvignon Blanc and Sylvaner white wines. The aroma of dried almonds, which is similar to vanillin, is often encountered in Chardonnays as they age. Notes of bitter almonds are a feature of many very young white wines, and are also an element of the muted, nutty taste found in some old red wines. The aroma of toasted almonds is part of the attraction and the distinction of white wines of a certain age.

AMBER Of great distinction, the subtle scent of amber is sometimes found in the finest Chardonnay wines (Champagne, Chablis, Côte d'Or) and certain sweet wines from southwestern France.

AMBERING Ambering is a feature of sweet wines of a certain age, but is also found in dry or low-sugar white wines from good vintages that are apt to age without oxidation or becoming excessively dry.

AMIABLE Characteristic attributed to a pleasing wine without pretension.

AMPLE The term applied to wines that "fill the mouth" without a sense of heaviness.

ANISEED Aroma found as a trace element in the bouquet of certain white wines that have reached a good age.

APPEARANCE The color, brilliance, and overall visual impression of a wine.

APPLE The various varieties of apples each have their own flavors, and each are found in different concentrations in a number of white wines (Muscadet, Sauvignon Blanc, Riesling, etc.).

APRICOT Aroma characteristic of certain white wines, particularly in the Rhône Valley; associated with the Viognier grape variety when very ripe.

ASTRINGENCY Sense of dehydration resulting from tannins, notably those present in red wines. As wine ages, astringency mellows as the tannins are "used up" and lose intensity, sharpness, and general presence.

ATTACK The first impression felt when wine enters the mouth.

AUSTERE The term applied to red wines whose tannins and acidity are most prominent and where a bouquet that might make this more agreeable is absent.

B

BALANCE Quality found in wine where the various flavor groups (alcohol, acidity, and sweetness in white wines; alcohol, tannins, acidity, and softness in red wines) play off one another in a satisfactory manner, without any single one dominating or underperforming.

BALSAMIC More or less resinous odors (pine, cedar, juniper, wood, etc.) found in young wines matured in new barrels. Also a feature of ripeness in great red wines.

BANANA Aroma frequently occurring in wines meant for early drinking, especially in batches made using carbonic maceration. It should be tempered with other floral and fruit aromas, as in Beaujolais or white Mâcon wines; otherwise the nose will be reminiscent of nail polish.

BAY LEAF Spicy aroma characteristic of certain grape varieties originally found in the South of France, such as Syrah and Grenache.

BEER An aroma similar to that of beer is sometimes found in the white Chasselas wines of Switzerland as they begin to lose their freshness.

BERGAMOT The extremely pleasant odor of this essential oil is found in aromatic wines at a certain stage of their bottle ageing.

BILBERRIES Aroma very often associated with WILD BLACKBERRIES (*see* under BLACKBERRIES below) and found under the same conditions.

BITTER Bitterness is not a feature of good wine, except perhaps in a few reds as a mild and transitory state. It is an anomaly when found elsewhere.

BLACKBERRIES, WILD Aroma often referred to in red wines of some maturity with rich and varied fruit notes.

BLACKCURRANTS The aroma of blackcurrant fruit or juice is invariably an element of the bouquet of Cabernet Sauvignon, irrespective of the country where it was harvested. It is sometimes found in the fruit scents of a large number of red varieties (Merlot, Syrah, Mourvèdre, etc.) when they reach their tasting peak.

BODY Terms such as "body," "full-bodied," and the like are used of wines where the joint dominance of tannins and sweetness is perceptible and imply a certain alcoholic fullness.

BOUQUET The entirety of the aromatic impressions conveyed by a mature wine in the sense that they combine to form a coherent and homogeneous whole. Various subtle notes alternate and intertwine in a subtle and agreeable ensemble.

BOUQUET GARNI Term used to describe the scents of aromatic dried herbs often found in Mediterranean red wines.

BRETTANOMYCES Spoilage yeast imparting bad aromas or flavors (mustiness, acetic spoilage, or mold) to a wine; a fault arising during the storage of empty barrels.

BRICK RED Color found in mature red wines, where the brownish hue is reminiscent of old tiles or bricks.

BRILLIANCE Term qualifying the luminosity of a wine, *i.e.* its ability to reflect light. A lack of brilliance—dullness—is considered a flaw.

BROOM The yellow flowers of Spanish broom have a pleasant and penetrating odor, reminiscent of wallflowers, which forms part of the aroma of some Chardonnay and sweet wines.

BURNED *see* EMPYREUMATIC

BUTTER An aromatic nuance sometimes found in very ripe batches of white wine, when low in acid and high in richness. Also attributed to maturation in new oak barrels.

C

CARAMEL An aroma common in white wines that are past their best, oxidized, or maderized.

CARNATION Aroma often referenced for some red wines with a slightly austere bouquet.

CAUDALIE French term for a unit of "length" (*see* LENGTH) after swallowing. One *caudalie* = one second.

CHERRY Various aromas of different varieties of cherries are often found as constituents of the bouquet in many red wines.

CHERRY PLUM Aroma found in white wines from very ripe years, with an overall richness that imparts an extremely enticing appeal to the bouquet.

CINNAMON Aroma sometimes found in fine examples of sweet (Jurançon, Sauternes) or dry (Pouilly-Fuissé, Corton-Charlemagne) white wines.

CIVET Fairly pronounced musky scent, not always unpleasant, and reminiscent of game meats. A feature of older red wines such as Burgundy's Pinot Noirs.

CLARITY The transparency of a wine's appearance, which may be: crystalline, brilliant, limpid, veiled, hazy, troubled, or opaque.

CLEAN Said of a wine whose aromas and flavors are upfront and precise, without ambiguity.

CLOSED A term referring to a wine with a "mute" or undeveloped bouquet.

CLOSURE Generic term for a wine bottle stopper, whether natural cork, synthetic or screwcap.

CLOVES Scent found in Rhône Valley reds after a few years of ageing.

CLOYING Said of slightly thick wines whose heaviness is exacerbated by lack of acidity.

COCOA Aroma sometimes found in wines with a fruity and spicy nose when they reach great maturity. Also attributed to maturation in new oak barrels.

COFFEE Aroma that develops in the bouquet of good quality old wines. Also attributed to maturation in new oak barrels.

CORKED Unpleasant smell of damp and rotten cork or cardboard, arising either from a fault in the closure itself or a lack of hygiene in the cellar.

CRISPNESS Sensation of freshness attributed to the action of acidity on the tongue. *See also* ACIDITY.

CUT HAY Scent typical of wines most often encountered as they pass from a phase of fermentation aromas to those of maturity.

D

DELICATE Said of wines with a subtle structure, but not lacking in charm or character.

DRY Term applied to white wines that are not sweet. White wines are called dry where any sweetness is subtle or masked, without this harming the balance of the whole.

E

EASY-GOING Said of a wine that offers immediate pleasure, with few tannins and a good balance of sweetness and acidity.

EGLANTINE Rose-like aroma sometimes found in light and very subtle wines.

ELEGANT Description implying a certain class and an absence of heaviness.

EMACIATED Said of a wine that has lost its "body" or its softness, due to too much or faulty ageing.

EMPYREUMATIC Referring to a category of aromas including tar, soot, burned wood, caramel, singed bread, and also, in a more attenuated manner, tea, coffee, cocoa, tobacco, biscuits, etc. Such aromas are often spoken of as "smoky," "toasted," "roasted," or "burned."

F

FADED A faded wine has lost its brilliance, its best aromas, and its freshness.

FENNEL An aroma sometimes found in very ripe dry white wines.

FERMENTATION Fermentation as a type of scent is not well known, and comes from the decomposition of yeasts when the wine is on the lees.

FERN-LIKE Aromatic characteristic found in white wines of great quality, and which gives them an airy bouquet.

FIG The aroma of dried figs, often combined with that of stewed or preserved strawberries, is a typical feature of soft red port or Banyuls wines, and also of dry red wines from very ripe vintages after some age.

FILLED OUT Said of a red wine with sufficient—but not excess—tannin and flavor, giving a good impression of body.

FIRM Typical of a young red wine; equates to a slight dominance of tannins and acidity.

FLINTY Aroma found in some lively, light white wines (Sauvignon Blanc, Muscadet, Burgundy made with Aligoté grapes).

FLORAL Wine bouquet where the aroma of flowers is dominant.

FRESH Term used to refer to aromas such as mint and citronella, which evoke sensations associated with coolness or refreshment.

FRUIT First stage of a wine's bouquet, after alcoholic fermentation, where the dominant aromas are of fresh fruit. The term is more often applied to reds and rosés, although white wines may possess pronounced fruit aromas such as apple, lemon, banana, and others.

FULL Said of a wine that seems to fill the mouth with a substantial and balanced richness, or an impression of abundance.

FULL-BODIED Term describing the tactile sensation of softness in a wine, when it is rich in alcohol and/or sugar.

FUR Nuance in the musky group of aromas, found in some red wines with some age.

G

GAMEY Animal aromas that may feature to a greater or lesser degree in the bouquet of old red wines. At its slightest, it is the scent of prepared fur; when more obtrusive, it is the smell of wildfowl—or of "fox" in old Pinot Noirs. Some develop into more varied venison aromas, while others take on a repellent nature known in French as *ventre de lièvre* or "hare belly."

GENEROUS Term most often applied to wines rich in alcohol.

GLUGGABLE Said of a wine that is easy to drink, due to a lack of astringency and to having the correct proportion of fresh acidity and sweetness (without heaviness).

GRAPEFRUIT Aroma often perceived in very crisp sparkling white wines, which are yet to be stripped of their fermenting agents; disappears after secondary fermentation and clarification of the wine. Also recognized in some naturally high-acid white varietals.

GRASSY Aromas or flavors reminiscent of freshly mown lawns or vegetal shoots. Generally considered disagreeable.

GREEN Used in reference to under-ripe fruit characters in a white, red, or rosé wine that is very crisp, where excess of acidity comes through.

GRENADINE An aroma typical of Côtes du Rhône and Provence rosés.

H

HARD Describes red wines with a synergy of tannins and acidity that provide astringency and also aggressiveness. Lack of any soft fruit characters in the wine reinforces this characteristic still further.

HARMONIOUS Quality ascribed to well-made wines, where each group of flavors (alcohol, acidity, and sweetness in white wines; alcohol, tannins, acidity, and softness in red wines) melds pleasantly with the others to create a charming whole.

HARSH Excessive astringency, where tannins "grate" on the mucous membranes of the mouth with real intensity and insistence.

HAVANA Scent of green tobacco leaves features as a trace element in very fine red wines.

HAWTHORN Aromatic characteristic found in young, dry, and slightly green white wines.

HAZELNUT Aroma often found in high quality white wines after several years of ageing (Chardonnay).

HEADY Characteristic of wines where rich body is accompanied by an elevated alcohol content.

HEAVY Characteristic of a wine lacking any lightness, suppleness, or freshness.

HONEY Aroma typical of lightly sweet to very sweet wines.

HONEYSUCKLE Aroma found in some Chardonnay and Sauvignon Blanc white wines, as well as other gently aromatic grape varieties.

HUMUS Aroma reminiscent of the forest floor or dead leaves, encountered in fairly good quality red wines that have aged.

HYACINTH Floral aroma often encountered with aromatic white grape varieties after a few years of bottle age (Sauvignon Blanc, Rhine varieties, fine Muscats).

IN BLOOM Said of a wine that has reached its peak and where its full personality comes to the fore, both in taste and aroma.

INTEGRATED Said of a wine where all flavor sensations express themselves in unity.

IODINE Term applied to wines whose aromas evoke the seaside.

IVY Ivy leaf aromas are often referenced in many Cabernet wines, when their bouquet is first forming.

JAMMY Used in tasting to express an aroma or taste that is reminiscent of jam or cooked fruit.

JUNIPER Aroma often encountered in some highly perfumed wines.

LACTIC Aroma arising from faulty malolactic fermentation or from an indeterminate combination of circumstances, more or less resulting in the odor of *fromage frais* or fermented cheese.

LEATHER Leather aromas of various kinds are often encountered in certain red wines after a few years of ageing (Bandol, Châteauneuf-du-Pape, Madiran, Corton, Hermitage, Chambertin, etc.).

LEGS Transparent streams of liquid that run down the inside walls of the glass when the wine has been agitated. Indicates a wine's richness in alcohol or residual sugar.

LEMON (CITRONELLA) Quite a common aroma in young, crisp, and light white wines.

LEMON BALM An aroma found in young white wines. Close to that of lemon zest, but more rarefied and less acidic.

LENGTH Duration of a wine's flavor in the mouth after swallowing. *See also* CAUDALIE.

LICHEN Herbal aroma present in certain red wines.

LICORICE Aroma and flavor often found at the finish of certain red wines.

LIGHT-BODIED Said of wines with a distinct lack of richness or structure.

LIME (BLOSSOM) Aroma found in certain white wines with very subtle bouquets.

LONG Said of a wine with considerable length of aroma or flavor after swallowing.

MADERIZATION Oxidation in a white wine to the point of browning its color and giving it the taste of Madeira; a serious flaw.

MEDIUM SWEET Descriptor for wines lightly dosed with residual sugar, where sweetness provides more suppleness than an overtly sugary sensation.

MERCAPTAN Very strong, unpleasant sulfurous odor. Reminiscent of rotten eggs. A chemically faulty wine.

MINT Two separate aromas should be distinguished here: those of peppermint and fresh mint. Both are found as trace notes in certain white wines, and create the freshness and vivacity of the bouquet.

MOUTH-FEEL Term designating the entirety of the sensations felt in the mouth.

MUSHROOM Pleasant aroma, similar to Portobello mushrooms, often found in mature wines. It can be unpleasant and resemble mildew if the wine has been made with botrytized grapes.

MUSK Aroma reminiscent of animals. It is slightly fetid in a state of reduction, but extremely pleasant when aerated. Often referred to in various high quality wines of a certain age.

MUSKY Generic term designating a family of animal-related smells (fur, game, leather, etc.) that feature in older red wines. When encountered in young wines, such odors are often unpleasant but will disappear with aeration.

NERVOUS Physical character attributed particularly to white wines, and sometimes to reds, where the interplay of high acidity and sweetness create an impression of opposition or tension.

NOSE The overall olfactory characteristics of a wine.

NUTMEG Aromatic spice often referred to in very sweet white wines of a certain age, and in some red wines.

ONION Aroma caused by chemical reduction and occasionally found in very old red wines.

ORANGE (FLOWER) Aroma found in the bouquet of some Sauvignon Blancs and other aromatic white grape varieties.

ORANGE (ZEST) References are often made to orange zest characters in respect to young white wines made from extremely ripe harvests. Also present in some fortified wines.

P

PEACH Flavors and aromas of white or yellow peaches are often found in aromatic white wines (Viognier and Pinot Gris) as well as in some Côtes du Rhône reds and Beaujolais wines.

PEACH (BLOSSOM) Very delicate aroma, similar to pistachio or bitter almonds, sometimes found in young and fresh aromatic white wines.

PEAR Aroma very often encountered in young unoaked white wines, and in some high quality red wines—in the most evanescent and subtle phase of the nose and in the final phase of the palate.

PEONY The slightly peppery aroma of this flower is also found in wines that share its color.

PEPPERS (GREEN) Aroma and flavor perceptible in red wines that are rich in tannins and whose fruit flavors are less than ideally ripe.

PINE Resinous or medicinal aroma referred to in some red wines.

PINEAPPLE Aromatic quality found in a large number of white wines made from very ripe grapes.

PISTACHIO Very subtle aroma, similar to bitter almonds but more delicate. Sometimes found in red wines with sophisticated bouquets.

PRUNES Aroma also known as *rancio*, defined by hints of stewed fruits such as prunes. Typical of port and old red wines, but considered a flaw in young red wines.

PUNGENCY Describes a juxtaposition of astringency and tartness, combined with a certain roughness that is more or less repellent.

Q

QUINCE Aroma found in rich and sweet white wines, linked with other aromas of very ripe or candied fruit.

R

RANCIO Aromas (prunes, tobacco, leather, Madeira) that develop with age, typical of naturally soft old wines, port, mature red wines, and old brandies.

RASPBERRIES Common constituent scent of Pinot Noir, Grenache, and numerous other red wines (including Beaujolais).

REDCURRANT Aromatic feature found in light red wines and reds intended for early drinking.

RESIN Balsamic-like aroma that features in the bouquets of certain red wines.

ROSE Primary aroma in Gewürztraminer and various varieties of Muscat. A delicate note of faded roses is found in some high quality, old red wines.

ROUGH High levels of astringency.

ROUNDED Term applied to wines with no angularity, in other words where softness and suppleness dominate without heaviness.

S

SAPPY Professional term used to express an expansiveness of aromas and abundance of flavors as the wine passes through the mouth.

SEVERE A wine under the joint dominance of tannin and acidity, accompanied by austere aromas. Not appealing.

SHARP Said of a wine with marginally dominant acidity and tannin, giving a slightly aggressive edge. Not appealing.

SILKY Term expressing the sheer feel of a wine in the mouth. Very appealing.

SMOKY Aroma evoking a wood fire. Almost a given in Pessac-Léognan reds and some Côte de Nuits wines. Also attributed to maturation in new oak barrels. *See also* EMPYREUMATIC.

SMOOTH Physical characteristic of a wine with high viscosity, a result of a judicious balance of tannin and acidity and no shortage of softness.

SOFT Name given to the overall effect of various sweet constituents in a wine (alcohol, glycerol, sugar), especially in red wines, and in particular when this group of substances dominates and is enhanced by a lack of hard sensations.

SOFTNESS Characteristic of wines lacking acidity relative to their tannin content, which is normal.

SOLID Said of wines possessing a good, sound framework of tannins on a balanced base of fruit and acidity.

SOURNESS Characteristic most often associated with a wine that is beginning to spoil.

SPICES Considerable number of aromas. Includes the full range of spices used in cooking and baking. Sometimes found in various white and red wines that have reached some maturity.

STALE Characteristic odor of wines that have been left open without a stopper, and generally accompanied by the loss of any expected aromas in the wine.

STALKY A disagreeable, acerbic character with a more or less herbaceous character. Caused by prolonged maceration with shredded grape stems during vinification.

STAR ANISE Similar aroma to aniseed, but more intense.

STRAWBERRY Aroma of wild strawberries is common in young red wines intended for early drinking. Stewed or preserved strawberry aromas are often found in tandem with those of dried figs in soft red wines and old, dry red wines.

SUCROSITY Neologism used in tasting to express the level of a wine's apparent sugar content, which may be, in ascending order: fruity, medium-sweet, sweet, or syrupy.

SUPPLE Texture displayed by restrained tannin and acidity, allowing the natural softness of the wine to shine through.

SWEET White wines and rosés are called sweet when a perceptible amount of sugar remains in the wine, imparting a soft feel and sweet taste.

TANNIN Substance extracted from grape skins giving red wines their structure and some character.

THICK Said of red wines with such soft tannins that subtlety or harmony is lost.

THIN Term applied to wine of a weak consistency, where all of its constituent elements are generally lacking.

THOROUGHBRED Said of a wine of incomparable elegance and distinction.

THYME Aroma found fairly frequently in certain white wines from the south of France and Haute-Provence.

TIRED Said of a wine that has lost its coherence and its tone.

TOASTED A note of toasted or "grilled bread" is found in some red wines, and "toasted almonds" is an aroma encountered in fine white wines as they begin a phase of reduction in the bottle. Also attributed to maturation in new oak barrels.

TOBACCO Notes of green tobacco leaves, associated with the hints of Havana beloved of *parfumiers*, are sometimes found in very fine red wines.

TRUFFLE Very distinguished aroma found in high quality, old red wines. White truffle is sometimes encountered in certain vintages of aged white or sweet wines.

VANILLA Aromatic element of numerous white and red wines. It develops naturally in the woody part of the grape stem or (more frequently) in the oak of the wooden vats or barrels for wine production.

VEGETAL Aromas reminiscent of the world of plants. Also said of tannins that supply a certain astringency due to a lack of maturation or robust extraction.

VELVETY Said of a wine whose mouth-feel evokes velvet.

VENISON *see* GAMEY

VINOUS Said of a wine whose richness in alcohol is clearly apparent. Also known as alcoholic.

WALLFLOWER Small ornamental plant whose aroma is often compared with the finest Chardonnays and Chenin Blancs.

WARMING Term expressing the sensation of warmth in the mouth, under the influence of a certain richness in alcohol.

WAX The aroma of wax is common in some great expressions of Chardonnay and Sémillon, especially some sweet wines from the Loire Valley.

WEAK Implies, on the one hand, a certain lack of alcohol and, on the other, a shortfall in constitution—indicating potential fragility and difficulties in storage.

WOODY One of the balsamic group of aromas, found in wines aged in new barrels.

YOUNG A wine is considered young if it has retained a good portion of its initial fruit aromas and flavors.

GREAT WINE REGIONS OF THE WORLD

KEY WINE REGIONS

50° N

40° N

30° N

0° Equator

30° S

40° S

CANADA

UNITED STATES

MEXICO

Pacific

Ocean

PERU

CHILE   URUGUAY

ARGENTINA

BRAZIL

Atlantic

Ocean

Wine-producing regions

WORLD OF WINE

Vines are found on every continent of the world, although their distribution is anything but equal. While Europe still largely leads the field in terms of total land area devoted to vineyards, the two Americas, Asia, and especially Australia and New Zealand are witnessing expansion in their respective grape-growing regions. Even so, real changes are occurring in the areas of consumption and production.

Global vineyards

LARGEST VINEYARDS. According to figures supplied for 2009 by the International Organization of the Vine and Wine (OIV), the vineyards of the world cover 18.8 million acres (7.6 million hectares). In descending order, the largest vine-growing nations by surface area are: Spain, France, Italy, the USA, Portugal, and Argentina. These figures are often adjusted (with the exception of those relating to the vineyards of Turkey, China, Iran, and Romania) since the data gathered by the OIV includes the total surface area of planted vines, without distinguishing between grapes for eating, winemaking, and distilling.

SOUTHERN MIGRATION. Vineyard plantings worldwide are witnessing a gradual reduction in surface area from year to year. European growing areas remain the largest, with more than 55 percent of total world production, followed by Asia, America, Africa, and Oceania (Australia, New Zealand). Setting aside the difficulty of measuring the portion of vineyards just for wine production in some countries (China, for example), certain basic changes are apparent: the most significant have been a 20-year slide in production in Europe and growth in the southern hemisphere.

DROPPING CONSUMPTION. America became the world's largest consumer of wine in 2009, but global consumption has tended to fall—in line with a sustained decrease in demand from European countries that have traditionally been the largest producers and consumers (France, Italy, Spain, and Germany). Equally noteworthy is the meteoric rise of China, which in a very short time has become one of the world's top 10 wine consumers, and should reach seventh place in 2012.

Europe in decline

The Old World has witnessed a year-on-year reduction in its wine-producing area, most notably from official policy to tear out vines in European countries; more grubbing up plans, as seen in France; or a restructuring of vineyards in the countries that have recently joined the EU. The wine-producing regions of the EU (of which there are 27) amounted to 9.1 million acres (3.7 million hectares) in 2009. Depending on the particular harvest, France and Italy take turns in holding the title of largest global producer; but Spain devotes the most actual land to wine production.

> *Italy is now the number one wine producer by volume, outpacing France, Spain, the USA, Argentina, and Australia. Global wine production in 2006 amounted to about 3 billion cases (282 million hectoliters).*

Booming New World

South America and Oceania have seen their grape plantings grow dramatically during the past 20 years; and Argentinian, Brazilian, and, to a lesser extent, Chilean vineyards are still expanding. As far as production is concerned, a slight drop witnessed in Argentina over the past few years has been balanced out by Chile's performance; so wine production in South America thus maintained its high levels throughout 2008 and 2009. Production in South Africa, New Zealand, and Australia was also up in 2008.

New wine-producing countries

Asia continues to be a focal point for growth among the world's wine producers. Chinese growers have experienced a rapid rise since 1998, and this expansion seems to have continued, albeit at a less frantic rate, over the past five years. China is, without doubt, the principal force behind growth in the wine market in Asia. South Africa (which occupies 10th place in world rankings) has reduced the area devoted to vineyards and is concentrating on improving the quality of its wines.

India—a promising but reticent region

The Indian market is an exceptional case, since the country's population is very young (three-quarters of its citizens are under 35 years of age). Wine consumption—estimated at an annual 1.2 million cases (11 million liters), of which 20 percent is imported—could well grow in the next few years. India also can now claim more than 50 wine producers distributed between three areas of wine production: Nasik and Sangli, both in Maharashtra, and Bangalore in Karnataka. Even if India remains a large

consumer of beer and spirits (especially whisky), the national market is promising for wine and its economic weight should not be underestimated. The actual buying market is approaching 30 million inhabitants—meaning consumers who for the most part live in three states: Maharashtra, Karnataka, and Delhi, and who belong to the most leisured classes. These three states alone account for 75 percent of India's entire wine consumption.

China, the top wine consumer in Asia

It's estimated that Asia accounts for five percent of the world's wine consumption; but among these nations China will see the largest expansion over the next few years. Consumption of still wine across that country (including Hong Kong) amounted to 62.7 percent of total Asian wine consumption in 2006, and this number is still increasing. By late 2012, China will go from being the 10th to the 7th-largest consumer of the world's still wine, surpassing Russia and Romania. France still remains the principal supplier to the Asian countries, followed by the USA, Italy, Australia, and Chile. Finally, it's worth noting that Hong Kong is now the key market through which quality wines are funnelled into all of East Asia.

International changes

The global wine market suffered an abrupt slowdown during 2008 and 2009, and several big players, such as Australia, France, and Italy, saw exports fall. The economic crisis put the brakes on growth in almost all wine-exporting countries and reduced consumption everywhere. France, once the market leader, is now seeing the drop in its exports accelerate. Italy has retained its position as world leader in terms of volume of wine exported, and now accounts for 19 percent of global wine circulation; Spain is close behind, with 183 million cases (16.5 million hectoliters), and France is third. A group of six countries is emerging from the New World (southern hemisphere and USA) to account for 30 percent of the world market in 2008. It should be noted that international exports represent nearly 37 percent of world consumption (as opposed to 18 percent at the beginning of the 1980s)—in other words, more than a third of the world's wine is consumed in a country other than where it was produced.

WINE-PRODUCING COUNTRIES		
COUNTRY	SURFACE AREA (thousands of acres/hectares)	PRODUCTION (millions of gallons/thousands of hectoliters)
WESTERN AND CENTRAL EUROPEAN ZONE		
Austria	119/48	61.9/2,346
Bulgaria	200/81	52.8/2,000
Czech Republic	47/19	15.5/585
France	2,075/840	1,203/45,558
Germany	252/102	242.5/9,180
Greece	284/115	95.1/3,600
Hungary	172/70	89.8/3,400
Italy	2,021/818	1,207.2/45,699
Portugal	600/243	158.5/6,000
Romania	506/205	147.9/5,600
Slovakia	49/20	10.5/400
Slovenia	44/18	15.6/593
Spain	2,750/1,113	858.7/32,506
Switzerland	37/15	29.3/1,110

There are wine-producing countries in this zone other than the ones mentioned above, but their yield is either very low or the most recent figures are unreliable or unavailable. These include (in probable order of size): Republic of Macedonia, Croatia, Cyprus, Bosnia, Luxembourg, the UK, and Malta.

EASTERN EUROPEAN ZONE – EAST ASIA – MIDDLE EAST		
Georgia	(87/35)	(25/950)
Israel	25/10	11.9/450
Lebanon	30/12	37.9/500
Moldova	(363/147)	(60.7/2,300)
Russia	185/75	(52.8/2,000)
Turkey	129/52	46.2/1,750
Ukraine	(215/87)	(60.7/2,300)

– For countries with figures in parentheses, information dates from 2006 at the most recent, and is not entirely reliable.
– Several countries in this zone not mentioned above have grape-growing areas, but these are wholly or partly devoted to table grapes or grapes destined to become raisins. In some cases, wine production can be estimated as almost zero.
– In Turkey and Lebanon, whose total production is known, the proportion of grape cultivation devoted to winemaking is estimated at 10 percent in the case of Turkey and 25 percent for Lebanon.
– Grape-producing countries that do not feature in this table include: Afghanistan, Armenia, Azerbaijan, Iran, Iraq, Jordan, Kazakhstan, Kyrgyzstan, Syria, Tajikistan, Turkmenistan, Uzbekistan, Yemen.

AMERICAN ZONE		
Argentina	563/228	320.4/12,135
Brazil	227/92	77.9/2,950
Chile	494/200	260.5/9,869
United States	983/398	544.5/20,620

Several other countries in this zone produce wine. These are, in order of output: Mexico, Uruguay, Canada, Peru, Bolivia, Venezuela.

AFRICAN ZONE		
Morocco	(25/10)	(7.9/300)
South Africa	326/132	90.3/3,419
Tunisia	(30/12)	(9.2/350)

The portion of grape cultivation devoted to winemaking is estimated in the case of Tunisia and Morocco.

OCEANIC ZONE		
Australia[1]	400/162	306.3/11,600
New Zealand[2]	72/29	54.1/2,050
ASIAN ZONE		
China[3]	371/150	316.9/12,000
India	(171/69)	Note 4 (below)
Japan	49/20	24.3/920

1 Australian Bureau of Statistics, 2009.
2 New Zealand Winegrowers, 2008.
3 Estimated for China, based on the OIV's statistics for 2006 and a deduction made from blended production with imported wines. It should be noted that grape cultivation is widespread in this country (more than 1.1 million acres/450,000 ha) but the majority of the yield is destined for other uses (table grapes, raisins, distillation).
4 No reliable information is available for India.

Sources: OIV, definitive figures for 2006, economic overview for 2010, unless otherwise mentioned.

FRANCE

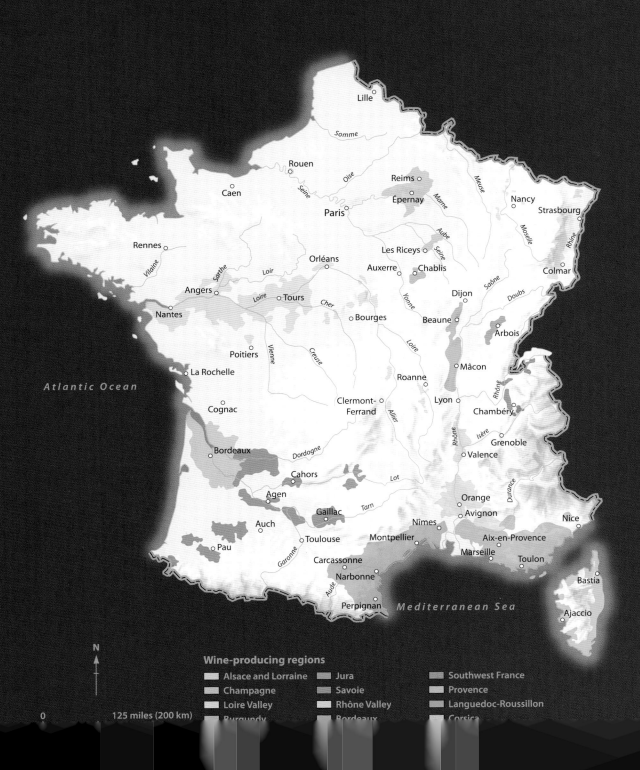

Lille

Somme

Rouen
Caen
Oise
Reims
Seine
Nancy
Épernay
Strasbourg
Marne
Paris
Meuse
Moselle
Rhine
Rennes
Aube
Les Riceys
Seine
Auxerre
Chablis
Colmar
Vilaine
Orléans
Sarthe
Loir
Dijon
Saône
Doubs
Angers
Loire
Tours
Cher
Bourges
Beaune
Arbois
Nantes
Yonne
Loire
Poitiers
Vienne
Creuse
Mâcon
Roanne
Rhône
La Rochelle
Atlantic Ocean
Clermont-
Ferrand
Lyon
Chambéry
Cognac
Allier
Rhône
Isère
Grenoble
Bordeaux
Dordogne
Valence
Cahors
Lot
Durance
Agen
Tarn
Orange
Gaillac
Avignon
Nice
Auch
Nîmes
Pau
Toulouse
Montpellier
Aix-en-Provence
Garonne
Carcassonne
Marseille
Toulon
Narbonne
Bastia
Aude
Mediterranean Sea
Perpignan
Ajaccio

N

Wine-producing regions

- Alsace and Lorraine
- Jura
- Southwest France
- Champagne
- Savoie
- Provence
- Loire Valley
- Rhône Valley
- Languedoc-Roussillon
- Burgundy
- Bordeaux
- Corsica

0   125 miles (200 km)

BORDEAUX

All over the world, Bordeaux is synonymous with wine. It has come to symbolize exceptional vineyards and legendary châteaux: Bordeaux is home to some of the greatest wines on earth. Their excellence has inspired wineries in other countries, from Italy to Australia to California in the USA.

Long-standing reputation

ORIGINS. Wine production began in the Bordeaux region early in the 1st century with the arrival of the Roman legions. Its wines soon became famous—by the 4th century the poet Ausonius was already singing their praises. However, Bordeaux's wines did not really flourish until the 12th century, with the marriage in 1152 of Eleanor of Aquitaine to the future Plantagenet King Henry II of England. This marked the beginning of significant wine trade between Bordeaux and England.

FROM THE 17TH TO 19TH CENTURIES. A new era of trade began in the 17th century with the arrival of the Dutch, who bought wine for distillation. This was also the period when the great châteaux, such as Haut-Brion, were built. In the 18th century, wine began to sell in bottles, and exports increased. London society developed a taste for the wines of Bordeaux, particularly red wines of the Médoc, which the English called the new French clarets. Meanwhile, new vine-growing practices developed in the Médoc. The "Place de Bordeaux" (a marketing system) started to play, and still plays, a key role. It was supported by the emergence of new winemaking and storage techniques, and the influence of new wine merchants, who were largely responsible for the distribution of the wines (as they are today: merchants sells around 75 percent of the Gironde's production and 95 percent of the

> **BORDEAUX STATISTICS (AOC)**
>
> **Vineyard area:** 293,855 acres (118,919 ha)
>
> **Production:** 53 million cases (4,778,000 hl)
>
> **Red:** 87%
>
> **White:** 9%
>
> **Rosé:** 4%
>
> (CIVB, 2008)

grands crus). The 19th century was a golden age for Bordeaux vineyards. They saw, among other things, the establishment of a hierarchy among the wineries of the left bank of the Garonne, with the 1855 classification of the Médoc *grand crus*. Then, at the end of the 19th century, the vineyards suffered devastating attacks of phylloxera and mildew. Then came the First World War, global economic crisis, and then war again.

FROM THE 20TH CENTURY TO TODAY. It was not until the 1950s that the vineyards recovered. New classifications—of Graves, St Émilion, and the *crus bourgeois*—were created. With the exception of the *crus bourgeois* classification, which was annulled in 2007, these continue to reflect the excellence of Bordeaux's wines. There have been a few scandals (involving fraud) and increasingly serious challenges to its supremacy from foreign competition. But Bordeaux appears to have armed itself with the means of continuing its success. Bordeaux's *en primeur* sales continue to constitute the major event of the year in the wine world. Vinexpo, the biennial international trade fair, and "open days" throughout the vineyards, attract many thousands of visitors. Anxious to improve their image, become more competitive, and provide greater transparency, producers have created unions and other groups. One is Sweet Bordeaux (an association of producers of sweet wines, *see also* p.271). On a larger scale is the new Côtes-de-Bordeaux appellation,

> Château de Monbadon in the Libourne region.

introduced in 2008—a real force representing one-sixth of Bordeaux's output, with a total area of 35,000 acres (14,000 ha) and producing 7.8 million cases (700,000 hl).

Climate

Bordeaux's vineyards enjoy a temperate, maritime climate. The large Landes forest forms a shield to protect the vines from westerly winds and regulates area temperatures. But the proximity of the ocean is an important factor. Mild, wet winters are followed by early springs (which are prone to hail storms and cold rain) and then hot, dry summers. Finally, sunny weather blesses the fall, with mists that are ideal for the development of the noble rot (*botrytis cinerea*) that is necessary for the production of great sweet wines.

Vineyard landscape

Bordeaux's vineyards occupy the entire *département* of the Gironde. Three generic appellations—Bordeaux, Bordeaux Supérieur, and Crémant de Bordeaux—are produced throughout the region. The other appellations are grouped into three broad geographical areas.

THE LEFT BANK AND THE CITY OF BORDEAUX. This area covers the Médoc (northwestern Bordeaux), Graves, and Sauternes (southeastern Bordeaux). The soil is composed mainly of various types of gravel. Pebbles of uneven sizes are mixed with clay, alluvial deposits, or sand, with some areas of clay-limestone. This base produces red wines and both dry and sweet white wines. The Médoc is itself divided into two regional appellations: the Médoc and the Haut-Médoc. The latter contains well-known appellations at the level of the communes (in alphabetical order: Listrac, Margaux, Moulis, Pauillac, St-Estèphe, and St-Julien). The Left Bank is home to some very fine wines and some of the most famous châteaux in the world, such as Château Lafite-Rothschild, Château Margaux, Château Léoville-Las-Cases, and Château Cos d'Estournel in the Médoc; Château Haut-Brion in Graves; Château d'Yquem, Château Climens, and Château Rieussec in Sauternes.

THE RIGHT BANK AND THE PORT OF LIBOURNE. This area encompasses the vineyards of Blaye and Bourg to the north; Libourne at the center, with St-Émilion, Pomerol, and Fronsac; and Castillon to the east. The soils are mostly clay and limestone (Fronsac, St-Émilion) or made up of gravel (Pomerol). The Right Bank also has several world-famous

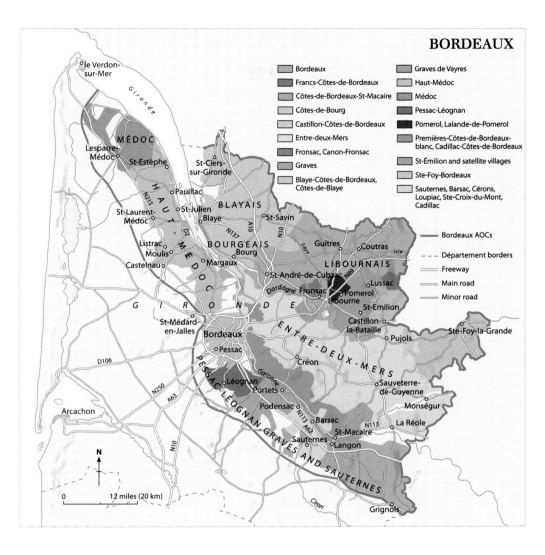

BORDEAUX

Legend:
- Bordeaux
- Francs-Côtes-de-Bordeaux
- Côtes-de-Bordeaux-St-Macaire
- Côtes-de-Bourg
- Castillon-Côtes-de-Bordeaux
- Entre-deux-Mers
- Fronsac, Canon-Fronsac
- Graves
- Blaye-Côtes-de-Bordeaux, Côtes-de-Blaye
- Graves de Vayres
- Haut-Médoc
- Médoc
- Pessac-Léognan
- Pomerol, Lalande-de-Pomerol
- Premières-Côtes-de-Bordeaux-blanc, Cadillac-Côtes-de-Bordeaux
- St-Émilion and satellite villages
- Ste-Foy-Bordeaux
- Sauternes, Barsac, Cérons, Loupiac, Ste-Croix-du-Mont, Cadillac
- —— Bordeaux AOCs
- - - - Département borders
- ═══ Freeway
- ═══ Main road
- ─── Minor road

Bordeaux stars

There is an elite group of about ten prestigious *grands crus* that are the stuff of dreams. They are never far from the minds of serious wine lovers, collectors, and investors. Each of these properties has a unique personality, a soul. Their names? Château Margaux (Margaux), the jewel of the Médoc; Château d'Yquem (Sauternes), the only wine in Bordeaux to be awarded the special rank of *premier cru supérieur*, the "best of the best" of sweet white wines; Château Haut-Brion (Pessac-Léognan), which did so much for the reputation of Bordeaux wines in Britain; Pétrus (Pomerol), a cult wine; Château Latour (Pauillac), the ultimate expression of Cabernet Sauvignon; Château Cheval-Blanc and Château Ausone (St-Émilion Premier Grand Cru), among the rarest wines in the world; Château Lafite-Rothschild, the first of the first growths (*premier des premiers crus*) in 1855; and Château Mouton-Rothschild (Pauillac), which was made a *premier cru* in 1973, and is famous not only for the quality of its wines but also for its labels by well-known artists.

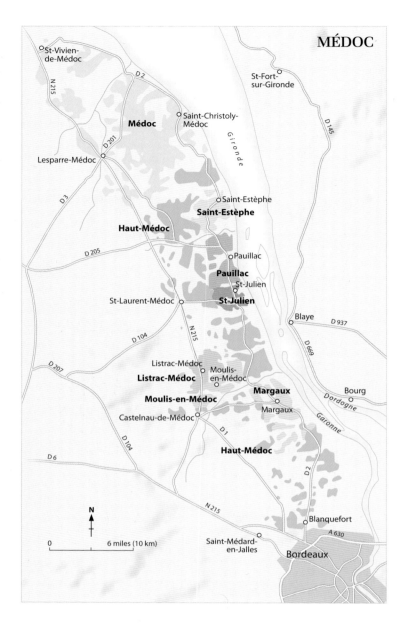

MÉDOC

CABERNET SAUVIGNON. This is Bordeaux's star red wine grape, and the main variety grown in the Médoc and Graves. Harvested when fully ripe, it produces fine, dark, distinguished, extremely complex wines known for their exceptional length on the palate, tannic structure, and capacity for ageing. It is also an important element in blends, appearing in the wines of the Bordeaux Supérieur, Haut-Médoc, and Côtes-de-Bordeaux appellations.

CABERNET FRANC. A popular red wine grape in the Libourne area, where it competes with Merlot, it can produce wines that, even after 50 years in the cellar, still show incredible youth. It is grown almost everywhere in the Gironde.

PETIT VERDOT. This red variety has a long history and is used in several wines of the Médoc, bringing color, tannin, and spicy notes.

MALBEC (ALSO KNOWN AS AUXERROIS AND CÔT). This great red variety of the Cahors region is used in many blends in Bordeaux, bringing fruity flavors and structure.

SÉMILLON. This white grape is the king of Sauternes, and of all the sweet wines produced in the Gironde (and in neighboring Monbazillac). Offering high yields, it is also widespread in Graves and the Entre-Deux-Mers region. Sémillon's fruit and finesse enable the production of truly great white wines, both dry and sweet. It partners particularly well with Sauvignon Blanc.

SAUVIGNON BLANC. The other great white grape of the Bordeaux region. Its yields are low, but it is prized for structure, freshness, and length on the palate. It produces very flavorful dry white wines with pronounced herbaceous notes (Bordeaux, Pessac-Léognan, Blaye, Entre-Deux-Mers) that develop great complexity with age. It is also used in sweet wine blends.

MUSCADELLE. A traditional Bordeaux white grape variety, Muscadelle gives wines a pleasant floral aroma. But it is now in danger of disappearing due to its extreme sensitivity to disease.

> **TRUE OR FALSE?**
>
> *Bordeaux's grands crus can age for more than 50 years.*
>
> **TRUE.** Although they are now enjoyable in their relative youth, as fruity, fresh wines, the wines of Bordeaux have the potential to improve with age and should be kept for five to 15, or even 20 years. However, only wines from great vintages—the most recent being 2000, 2003, and 2005—from Médoc, St-Émilion, Pomerol, and Graves, and the best appellations (Pauillac, Margaux, St-Julien) can be kept for 50 years without a few wrinkles developing.

châteaux, with Petrus and Château L'Église-Clinet in Pomerol, and Château Ausone and Château Cheval-Blanc in St-Émilion.

BETWEEN THE GARONNE AND THE DORDOGNE. This region consists mainly of vineyards in the Entre-Deux-Mers appellation. It produces dry and sweet white wines, as well as full-bodied reds (primarily with Merlot). The soil is made up of clay and gravel. The AOCs of Ste-Croix-du-Mont, Loupiac, and Cadillac, which produce sweet wines, are located along the right bank of the Garonne River.

Bordeaux grape varieties

Eight grape varieties are used to create the blends that make up Bordeaux's wines.

MERLOT. References to Merlot in St-Émilion date back to the 18th century. It is the most widely grown red wine grape in Bordeaux, dominating the appellations of St-Émilion, Pomerol, Côtes-de-Bordeaux, Bordeaux Rouge, and Bordeaux Supérieur. Ripening early, it produces full-bodied, fruity wines that are simultaneously supple and elegant.

Bordeaux and branded wines

In 1930, Baron Philippe de Rothschild had the idea of selling his second wine under the brand name "Mouton Cadet" with a different label from that of his prestigious property, Château Mouton-Rothschild (Pauillac). Success quickly followed. Today, Mouton Cadet, a blend of different wines from the Bordeaux region, is the leading brand of Bordeaux wine in the world. Other brand names followed. Among the largest, there are: Baron de Lestac, Malesan, Blaissac, Cellier d'Yvecourt, Croix d'Austéran, Julien & Martin Batiste.

"Châteaux"

Bordeaux has more than 6,000 wine-producing châteaux. One would think that any label mentioning a château is referring to a "real" château. This is not the case. Often, the only château is the one in the name—and these are no more than ordinary houses, farms buildings, or winemaking facilities. There are, of course, some authentic châteaux; but they are rare. Indeed, in Bordeaux, the term "château" is simply applied to wine-producing properties and has nothing to do with architecture. For example, there is no château associated with the legendary estates of Pétrus, Latour, or Mouton. However, not everyone can claim the term: a château implies a vineyard owned by a sole proprietor cultivating their own vines and making their own wine.

> The *terroirs* of the vineyards in Bordeaux offer the best expressions of Cabernet Sauvignon.

Bordeaux blends

The wines of Bordeaux are made by blending different components. This solid tradition has developed over many years, and it has become a real art. Bordeaux's wines, whether they are a generic appellation or a *grand cru classé*, are generally a combination of several grape varieties from various parcels or *terroirs*. The proportions of each will vary depending on the vintage, the winemaker, and the main grape varieties specified for that appellation. The goal is to obtain the best balance and the best expression of the *terroir*. As a rule, there are at least two grape varieties involved in each wine, often three, and sometimes four.

Style of wines

The wines of Bordeaux are defined by their immense diversity. The region produces red, rosé, dry white, sweet white, and sparkling wines. Plus, their styles can be very different, even within an appellation. While there is comparative unity in terms of grape varieties and winemaking techniques, there are huge variations in the soil, microclimates, and the composition of the blends.

RED. These wines may be light, for drinking when they are young and fruity (Bordeaux); full-bodied with a fine tannic structure, for consumption within five years (Bordeaux Supérieur); full-bodied and supple with good ageing potential (St-Émilion, Pomerol, Fronsac); or finally, complex and tannic when young, but with a huge capacity to age (Pauillac, St-Julien, etc.).

ROSÉ. Produced all over the Gironde department under two appellations, Bordeaux rosé and Bordeaux clairet, these are fresh wines that should be consumed young.

DRY WHITE. Produced all across the department of the Gironde, these are lively and pleasant to drink (Entre-Deux-Mers, Côtes-de-Bordeaux-Blaye, and the vast Bordeaux appellation); but they also can be supple and powerful with good ageing potential (Pessac-Léognan, Graves).

SWEET WHITE. Lead by Sauternes and Château d'Yquem, these wines are made primarily in the appellations of Sauternes, Cérons, Cadillac, Ste-Croix-du-Mont, Barsac, and Loupiac, totaling around 7,400 acres (3,000 ha). They are also produced in a few other areas such as Graves Supérieur and

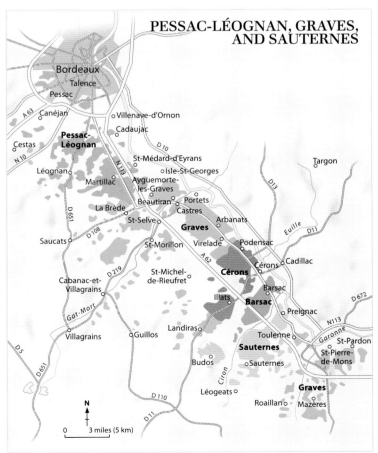

PESSAC-LÉOGNAN, GRAVES, AND SAUTERNES

> Barrels in the cellar of Château Lascombes in the Margaux appellation.

CLASSIFICATION OF THE WINES OF SAUTERNES AND BARSAC. This also dates from 1855. Château d'Yquem stands alone as the only superior first growth (*premier cru supérieur*) and is followed by 11 first growths and 14 second growths.

CLASSIFICATION OF GRAVES. The first classification of Graves was in 1956, with a revision in 1959. It contains 16 estates representing 13 red wines and nine white wines.

CLASSIFICATION OF ST-ÉMILION. None of the *grands crus* of St-Émilion were included in the 1855 classification. The wine union (*syndicat viticole*) therefore established its own classification, which is reviewed every ten years. The first classification took place in 1954.

CRUS ARTISANS. This group existed for over a century and a half, disappeared in the 1930s, and was restored in the 1990s. In 1994, the word "artisan" was recognized by the European Union and a classification took place in 2002. "Cru Artisan" implies a family-scale operation that is responsible for the growing of the grapes and the making and selling of the wines. The classification recognizes 44 *crus artisans* covering 840 acres (340 ha), mainly in the Médoc and Haut-Médoc.

CRU BOURGEOIS. The term *cru bourgeois* appeared in the 19th century in the Médoc, as an intermediate ranking between the *crus classés* and the *crus artisans*. The first official list, which dates from 1932, records 490. The classification was gradually forgotten, but then regained popularity in the 1980s. In 2003, a new, very official list was drawn up; but it was immediately challenged in court. Annulled in 2007, *cru bourgeois* returned in

TRUE OR FALSE?

The legendary wine of Pétrus is a grand cru classé.

FALSE. There is no classification in Pomerol. Despite its rarity, prestige, and quality, Pétrus does not appear in any of the official classifications (*see also p.267*).

Côtes-de-Bordeaux-St-Macaire. Some of these wines may be kept for a remarkably long time.

SPARKLING. White and rosé sparkling wines are produced throughout the Bordeaux region, and are currently very popular.

Classifying Bordeaux wines

The first classifications of the region's wines appeared at the end of the 17th century; but the most famous is the 1855 classification, which established rankings for the red wines of the Médoc. Over time, it was followed by several others. Bordeaux now has a total of 171 classified growths (*crus classés*), corresponding to approximately 13,000 acres (5,300 ha) of vines.

THE 1855 CLASSIFICATION (OF THE WINES OF THE MÉDOC). This hierarchy consists of 61 wines divided into five categories, from first to fifth growth. It has been revised just once, in 1973, when Château Mouton-Rothschild was promoted from second to first growth.

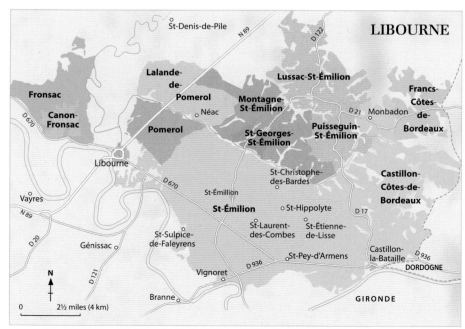

2009 in a new form. The term was authorized for use on bottles from 2008 onward. Rather than a classification, it is now a type of certification, awarded every year by an independent body on the basis of certain criteria. The certification applies to a specific vintage and is granted two years after the harvest.

"Second" wines

To make their *grand vins*, the châteaux of Bordeaux use the best possible blending components. Anything that does not qualify for the "*premier*" (or "*grand*") wine is used to produce a "*second*" wine (and sometimes even a "*third*" and a "*fourth*"). These are sold under a different label, and generally offer excellent quality at lower prices. Sometimes the second wine is as good as the first wine. This should not come as a surprise: both are the product of an excellent *terroir*.

> Less concentrated than the *grand vin*, a "second" wine is ready for drinking when it is younger.

Selected "second" wines

Château Ausone: Chapelle d'Ausone

Château Beychevelle: Amiral de Beychevelle

Château Cheval-Blanc: Le Petit Cheval

Château Cos d'Estournel: Pagodes de Cos

Château Haut-Brion: Château Bahans Haut-Brion

Château Lafite-Rothschild: Les Carruades

Château Lafleur: Les Pensées de Lafleur

Château Lascombes: Chevalier de Lascombes

Château Latour: Les Forts de Latour

Château Léoville-Las-Cases: Clos du Marquis

Château Léoville-Poyferré: Château Moulin Riche

Château Margaux: Pavillon Rouge du Château Margaux

Château Montrose: La Dame de Montrose

Château Mouton-Rothschild: Le Petit Mouton

Château Palmer: L'Alter Ego

Château Pavie-Macquin: Les Chênes de Macquin

Château Pichon-Longueville Comtesse de Lalande: La Réserve de la Comtesse

Château Pontet-Canet: Les Hauts de Pontet-Canet

Château Sociando-Mallet: La Demoiselle de Sociando-Mallet

Bordeaux AOCs

REGIONAL AND GENERIC APPELLATIONS
- Bordeaux
- Bordeaux clairet
- Bordeaux rosé
- Bordeaux sec
- Bordeaux supérieur
- Côtes-de-Bordeaux
- Crémant de Bordeaux

LEFT BANK
- Barsac
- Cérons
- Graves
- Graves supérieur
- Haut-Médoc
- Listrac-Médoc
- Médoc
- Moulis-en-Médoc
- Margaux
- Pauillac
- Pessac-Léognan
- St-Estèphe
- St-Julien
- Sauternes

RIGHT BANK
- Côtes-de-Bourg
- Côtes-de-Blaye
- Blaye
- Blaye-Côtes-de-Bordeaux
- Cadillac
- Cadillac-Côtes-de-Bordeaux
- Canon-Fronsac
- Castillon-Côtes-de-Bordeaux
- Francs-Côtes-de-Bordeaux
- Fronsac
- Lalande-de-Pomerol
- Lussac-St-Émilion
- Montagne-St-Émilion
- Pomerol
- Puisseguin-St-Émilion
- St-Émilion
- St-Émilion Grand Cru
- St-Georges-St-Émilion

ENTRE DEUX MERS
- Côtes-de-Bordeaux-St-Macaire
- Entre-deux-Mers
- Entre-deux-Mers-Haut-Benauge
- Loupiac
- Ste-Croix-du-Mont
- Ste-Foy-Bordeaux

Bordeaux's classified growths (*crus classés*)

CLASSIFICATION OF THE WINES OF THE MÉDOC (1855)

First Growths (*Premiers Crus*)
- Château Haut-Brion, Pessac
- Château Lafite-Rothschild, Pauillac
- Château Latour, Pauillac
- Château Margaux, Margaux
- Château Mouton-Rothschild, Pauillac (added in 1973)

Second Growths (*Seconds Crus*)
- Château Brane-Cantenac, Cantenac
- Château Cos d'Estournel, St-Estèphe
- Château Ducru-Beaucaillou, St-Julien-Beychevelle
- Château Durfort-Vivens, Margaux
- Château Gruaud-Larose, St-Julien-Beychevelle
- Château Lascombes, Margaux
- Château Léoville-Barton, St-Julien-Beychevelle
- Château Léoville-Las-Cases, St-Julien-Beychevelle
- Château Léoville-Poyferré, St-Julien-Beychevelle
- Château Montrose, St-Estèphe
- Château Pichon-Longueville, Baron de Pichon, Pauillac
- Château Pichon-Longueville, Comtesse de Lalande, Pauillac
- Château Rauzan-Ségla, Margaux
- Château Rauzan-Gassies, Margaux

Third Growths (*Troisièmes Crus*)
- Château Boyd-Cantenac, Cantenac
- Château Calon-Ségur, St-Estèphe
- Château Cantenac-Brown, Cantenac
- Château Desmirail, Margaux
- Château Ferrière, Margaux
- Château Giscours, Labarde
- Château d'Issan, Cantenac
- Château Kirwan, Cantenac
- Château Lagrange, St-Julien-Beychevelle
- Château La Lagune, Ludon
- Château Langoa-Barton, St-Julien-Beychevelle
- Château Malescot-St-Exupéry, Margaux
- Château Marquis d'Alesme-Becker, Margaux
- Château Palmer, Cantenac

Fourth Growths (*Quatrièmes Crus*)
- Château Beychevelle, St-Julien-Beychevelle
- Château Branaire-Ducru, St-Julien-Beychevelle
- Château Duhart-Milon, Pauillac
- Château Lafon-Rochet, St-Estèphe
- Château Marquis de Terme, Margaux
- Château Pouget, Cantenac
- Château Prieuré-Lichine, Cantenac

- Château St-Pierre, St-Julien-Beychevelle
- Château Talbot, St-Julien-Beychevelle
- Château La Tour-Carnet, St-Laurent-en-Médoc

Fifth Growths (*Cinquièmes Crus*)
- Château d'Armailhac, Pauillac
- Château Batailley, Pauillac
- Château Belgrave, St-Laurent-Médoc
- Château Camensac, St-Laurent-Médoc
- Château Cantemerle, Macau-en-Médoc
- Château Clerc-Milon, Pauillac
- Château Cos Labory, St-Estèphe
- Château Croizet-Bages, Pauillac
- Château Dauzac, Labarde
- Château Grand-Puy-Ducasse, Pauillac
- Château Grand-Puy-Lacoste, Pauillac
- Château Haut-Bages-Libéral, Pauillac
- Château Haut-Batailley, Pauillac
- Château Lynch-Bages, Pauillac
- Château Lynch-Moussas, Pauillac
- Château Pédesclaux, Pauillac
- Château Pontet-Canet, Pauillac
- Château du Tertre, Arsac

CLASSIFICATION OF THE SWEET WHITE WINES OF SAUTERNES AND BARSAC (1855)

Superior First Growth (*Premier Cru Supérieur*)
- Château d'Yquem, Sauternes

First Growths (*Premiers Crus*)
- Château Climens, Barsac
- Château Clos Haut-Peyraguey, Bommes
- Château Coutet, Barsac
- Château Guiraud, Sauternes
- Château Lafaurie-Peyraguey, Bommes
- Château Rabaud-Promis, Bommes

- Château de Rayne-Vigneau, Bommes
- Château Rieussec, Fargues-de-Langon
- Château Sigalas-Rabaud, Bommes
- Château Suduiraut, Preignac
- Château La Tour Blanche, Bommes

Second Growths (*Seconds Crus*)
- Château d'Arche, Sauternes
- Château Broustet, Barsac
- Château Caillou, Barsac
- Château Doisy-Daëne, Barsac
- Château Doisy-Dubroca, Barsac

- Château Doisy-Védrines, Barsac
- Château Filhot, Sauternes
- Château Lamothe, Sauternes
- Château Lamothe-Guignard, Sauternes
- Château de Malle, Preignac
- Château de Myrat, Barsac
- Château Nairac, Barsac
- Château Romer du Hayot, Fargues-de-Langon
- Château Suau, Barsac

CLASSIFICATION OF THE WINES OF GRAVES (1959)

Premier Grand Cru

- Château Haut-Brion (red), Pessac

Crus classés

- Château Bouscaut (red and white), Cadaujac
- Château Carbonnieux (red and white), Léognan
- Domaine de Chevalier (red and white), Léognan
- Château Couhins (white), Villenave-d'Ornon
- Château Couhins-Lurton (white), Villenave-d'Ornon
- Château Fieuzal (red), Léognan
- Château Haut-Bailly (red), Léognan
- Château Laville-Haut-Brion (white), Talence
- Château Malartic-Lagravière (red and white), Léognan
- Château La Mission-Haut-Brion (red), Talence
- Château Olivier (red and white), Léognan
- Château Pape Clément (red), Pessac
- Château Smith-Haut-Lafitte (red), Martillac
- Château La Tour-Haut-Brion (red and white), Talence
- Château La Tour-Martillac (red and white), Martillac

CLASSIFICATION OF THE RED WINES OF ST-ÉMILION (1996)

PREMIERS GRANDS CRUS

Premiers Grands Crus classés A

- Château Ausone, St-Émilion
- Château Cheval-Blanc, St-Émilion

Premiers Grands Crus classés B

- Château Angélus, St-Émilion
- Château Beau-Séjour-Bécot, St-Émilion
- Château Beauséjour (Duffau-Lagarrosse), St-Émilion
- Château Belair, St-Émilion
- Château Canon, St-Émilion
- Château Figeac, St-Émilion
- Château La Gaffelière, St-Émilion
- Château Magdelaine, St-Émilion
- Château Pavie, St-Émilion
- Château Trottevieille, St-Émilion
- Clos Fourtet, St-Émilion

Grands Crus classés

- Château Balestard La Tonnelle, St-Émilion
- Château Bellevue, St-Émilion
- Château Bergat, St-Émilion
- Château Berliquet, St-Émilion
- Château Cadet-Bon, St-Émilion
- Château Cadet-Piola, St-Émilion
- Château Canon-la-Gaffelière, St-Émilion
- Château Cap de Mourlin, St-Émilion
- Château Chauvin, St-Émilion
- Château Corbin, St-Émilion
- Château Corbin-Michotte, St-Émilion
- Château Curé-Bon, St-Émilion
- Château Dassault, St-Émilion
- Château Faurie de Souchard, St-Émilion
- Château Fonplégade, St-Émilion
- Château Fonroque, St-Émilion
- Château Franc-Mayne, St-Émilion
- Château Grand Mayne, St-Émilion
- Château Grand Pontet, St-Émilion
- Château Guadet-St-Julien, St-Émilion
- Château Haut-Corbin, St-Émilion
- Château Haut-Sarpe, St-Christophe-des-Bardes
- Château L'Arrosée, St-Émilion
- Château La Clotte, St-Émilion
- Château La Clusière, St-Émilion
- Château La Couspaude, St-Émilion
- Château La Dominique, St-Émilion
- Château La Serre, St-Émilion
- Château La Tour du Pin Figeac (Giraud-Bélivier), St-Émilion
- Château La Tour du Pin Figeac (J.-M. Moueix), St-Émilion
- Château La Tour-Figeac, St-Émilion
- Château Lamarzelle, St-Émilion
- Château Laniote, St-Émilion
- Château Larcis-Ducasse, St-Laurent-des-Combes
- Château Larmande, St-Émilion
- Château Laroque, St-Christophe-des-Bardes
- Château Laroze, St-Émilion
- Château Le Prieuré, St-Émilion
- Château Les Grandes Murailles, St-Émilion
- Château Matras, St-Émilion
- Château Moulin du Cadet, St-Émilion
- Château Pavie-Decesse, St-Émilion
- Château Pavie-Macquin, St-Émilion
- Château Petit-Faurie-de-Soutard, St-Émilion
- Château Ripeau, St-Émilion
- Château St-Georges Côte Pavie, St-Émilion
- Château Soutard, St-Émilion
- Château Tertre Daugay, St-Émilion
- Château Troplong-Mondot, St-Émilion
- Château Villemaurine, St-Émilion
- Château Yon-Figeac, St-Émilion
- Clos de l'Oratoire, St-Émilion
- Clos des Jacobins, St-Émilion
- Clos Saint-Martin, St-Émilion
- Couvent des Jacobins, St-Émilion

Bordeaux's most famous wines

Bordeaux abounds with great wines and prestigious appellations. We have chosen the following order in which to present these appellations: first, the generics, meaning those produced throughout the département of the Gironde; then the appellations on the Left Bank of the Gironde estuary and the Garonne River; followed by those on the Right Bank; and finally, those that lie between the Dordogne and Garonne rivers (or Entre-Deux-Mers).

BORDEAUX AOC

This is the largest appellation in the Gironde: it covers the entire department (109,000 acres or 44,000 ha). It sits alongside the Atlantic Ocean, divided into two sub-regions separated by the Gironde estuary and the Garonne River. The AOC produces about 27.8 million cases (2.5 million hectoliters) of wine, mostly red, but also some dry whites. It is hard to find any common characteristics that unify these wines. They vary so much due to the different *terroirs* and the dominant grapes (Merlot or Cabernet Sauvignon). In general, they are harmonious, pleasant, and for drinking relatively young.

> **GRAPE VARIETIES** Merlot, Cabernet Franc, Cabernet Sauvignon, Malbec, and Petit Verdot for the red wines; Sémillon, Sauvignon Blanc, and Muscadelle for the white wines.

> **SOIL** Alluvial deposits, gravel, clay-and-limestone, silica-clay-sand.

> **STYLE** Along with their classic color, the red wines present, depending on the blend, a bouquet dominated by red and dark fruit (raspberries, strawberries, black-currants), flowers (violets), and pepper embellished with hints of spice. The palate is well-structured, fruity, round, supple, and not very full-bodied. The whites typically have a pale golden color with hints of green. The nose develops aromas of fruit (citrus, peach) and white flowers, underscored with occasional notes of sweet spices. In the mouth, they are dry, lively, and fruity, with good balance.

Color:
Red and white.

Serving temperature:
About 50°F (10°C) for the white wines;
59 to 61°F (15 to 16°C) for the reds.

Ageing potential:
2 to 3 years for the whites;
2 to 5 years for the reds.

BORDEAUX SUPÉRIEUR AOC

Produced across the same area as Bordeaux AOC, Bordeaux Supérieur wines are subject to more stringent production conditions—with more limited yields and a maturation period of at least 12 months (increasingly in oak barrels). They also generally have a higher alcohol content. The vast majority of the appellation's production is red wine, but there some sweet white wines are also produced, unlike in the standard Bordeaux appellation.

> **GRAPE VARIETIES** Merlot, Cabernet Franc, Cabernet Sauvignon, Malbec, and Petit Verdot for the red wines; Sémillon, Sauvignon Blanc, Muscadelle for the white wines, with Ugni Blanc, Ondenc, Chenin Blanc, Merlot Blanc, and Mauzac as possible secondary varieties.

> **SOIL** Identical to those for Bordeaux AOC: alluvial deposits, gravel, clay-and-limestone, silica-clay-sand.

> **STYLE** The red wines are deeply colored. The nose is more concentrated and more complex than for Bordeaux AOC, with aromas of red and dark fruit, notes of vegetation, and hints of spice and vanilla. The palate is generous, smooth, fruity, and well-structured, and supported by powerful, firm tannins that need a little time to soften. The finish is fruity and refreshing. The sweet white wines have a golden color; a rich, complex nose; and a fruity palate, with a good balance of fruit, alcohol, and acidity.

Color:
Red and white.

Serving temperature:
46 to 50°F (8 to 10°C) for the white wines;
59 to 61°F (15 to 16°C) for the reds.

Ageing potential:
3 to 5 years for the whites;
5 to 10 years for the reds.

CRÉMANT DE BORDEAUX AOC

This recent appellation upholds a long-standing Bordeaux tradition and provides a regulatory framework for sparkling wines. They may be produced anywhere in the Gironde department, through the method of secondary fermentation in bottle. *Crémant* is mostly white (about 100,000 cases or 9,000 hl), but there is also some rosé.

> **GRAPE VARIETIES** Sémillon, Sauvignon Blanc, Muscadelle, Ugni Blanc, Colombard for white crémant; Cabernet Sauvignon, Cabernet Franc, Merlot, Malbec, and Petit Verdot for the rosé.

> **SOIL** Gravel, clay-and-limestone, silica-clay-sand, alluvial deposits.

> **STYLE** Pleasantly flavorful, Crémant de Bordeaux has a pale golden color and fine bubbles. The nose is fresh and fruity with floral notes (white flowers) and hints of citrus and hazelnut. The palate is well-constructed, with a good balance between well-integrated acidity and flavor complexity. A generally elegant wine. Rosé crémant has a delightful bouquet of small red berries.

Color:	Serving temperature:	Ageing potential:
White and rosé.	*42 to 46°F (6 to 8°C).*	*Drink within a year.*

BORDEAUX ROSÉ AOC

This is the only regional appellation that produces exclusively rosé wines. Charming and easy to drink, there are about 2 million cases (180,000 hl) produced every year; and, like all rosés in France, it is very popular.

> **SOIL** Sand, gravel, clay-and-limestone, silica-clay-sand.

> **STYLE** Bordeaux rosé has a pure, clear color—in all shades of pink. It develops delicate flavors of small red berries (strawberries) and flowers, accompanied by hints of spice. The palate is supple, well balanced between freshness and fruit, with a fine tannin structure and a long, fruity finish.

Color:	Serving temperature:	Ageing potential:
Rosé.	*About 46°F (8°C).*	*Drink within a year.*

Two superior Bordeaux Supérieur

In 2001, Dominique Méneret, a former fine wine merchant working in the "place de Bordeaux," bought a 156-acre (63-ha) property near Castillon, 67 acres (27 ha) of which were planted with Merlot. Since then, he has gone to great lengths to obtain expert advice, including that of Stéphane Derenoncourt. His desire is to make great wine, like the ones that he used to sell. It seems he has achieved his ambition. At the 2007 *en primeur* tastings, his Château de Courteillac delighted the American critic Robert Parker, who awarded it a score of 89–91 out of 100. Some *grands crus classés* would be very happy with such a result! Meanwhile, Château de Brondeau, a 25-acre (10-ha) property near Libourne, run by Dominique Méneret's wife, Marie-Claude, produces another Bordeaux Supérieur that is the equal of many a *cru classé*.

GRAND VIN DE BORDEAUX

CHATEAU DE BRONDEAU

— 2006 —

MARIE-CLAUDE MENERET

BORDEAUX CLAIRET AOC

Historically the first style of wine produced in Bordeaux, *clairet* is the same light red that the French were exporting to England in the Middle Ages. Due to its delicate color the English called it "French claret." The name remained to describe wines with a color somewhere between rosé and red—which is obtained by a light maceration of red grapes. This rather small appellation consists of 2,300 acres (925 ha) spread throughout the Gironde, and it produces about 578,000 cases (52,000 hl) per year.

> **GRAPE VARIETIES** Merlot (dominant), Cabernet Sauvignon, Cabernet Franc, Malbec.

> **SOIL** Sand, gravel, clay-and-limestone, silica-clay-sand.

> **STYLE** Light, fresh, and delicate, Bordeaux Clairet has a bright, pale red color. The bouquet expresses aromas of strawberries, redcurrants, and flowers. The fresh, light palate is highlighted by a fine tannin structure.

Color:
Red.

Serving temperature:
42 to 46°F (6 to 8°C).

Ageing potential:
2 years.

MÉDOC AOC

In Latin, "Médoc" means "in the middle of the water." And this sub-region is shaped like a peninsula, bordered to the west by the ocean and to the east by the Gironde estuary. The appellation covers 14,100 acres (5,700 ha) and benefits from an exceptional geographical location. A distinction is made between the "Haut-Médoc" (at the south), which contains the grands *crus classés*, and the "Bas-Médoc" (at the north end of the peninsula), which corresponds to the actual Médoc appellation. Production is substantial: 3.3 million cases (300,000 hl) of entirely red wine.

There are no *cru classé*.

> **GRAPE VARIETIES** Cabernet Sauvignon, Merlot, Cabernet Franc, Malbec, Petit Verdot.

> **SOIL** Gravel.

> **STYLE** Appealing and balanced, Médoc wines have a deep color and a bouquet with a fine range of aromas: dark and red fruit, notes of pepper, licorice and even, when the wine is young, a suggestion of mushrooms and undergrowth. The palate is well-structured and generous, with well-defined, delicious tannins. With age, the flavors soften with roasted, gamey notes.

Color:
Red.

Serving temperature:
59 to 63°F (15 to 17°C).

Ageing potential:
Drink from the second year onward; it will keep 5–10 years.

Selected Médoc and Haut-Médoc producers

MÉDOC

- **Château Bournac (Civrac-en-Médoc).** Lots of class, with good capacity to age. Reliable wines for this appellation.

- **Château Fontis (Ordonnac).** Elegant, balanced, refined wines.

- **Château La Tour de By (Bégadan).** Very fine, delightfully supple wines capable of ageing for a very long time.

- **Château Les Ormes-Sorbet (Couquèques).** A deep, balanced, elegant, refined Médoc with excellent potential for ageing.

HAUT-MÉDOC

- **Château Camensac (St-Laurent-du-Médoc).** Top quality wine.

- **Château Carone Ste-Gemme (St-Laurent-du-Medoc).** Distinguished, deep, tannic wine, with great potential to improve with age.

- **Château Clément-Pichon (Parempuyre).** Very elegant, refined wine. Also, the second wine: Château de Conques.

- **Château Preuillac (Lesparre).** Excellent wine, well-structured and fruity: typical of the appellation.

GRAND VIN DE BORDEAUX

CHÂTEAU
CLÉMENT-PICHON
HAUT-MÉDOC

Mis en Bouteille au Château
2007
VIGNOBLES CLÉMENT FAYAT

HAUT-MÉDOC AOC

This appellation consists of the vineyards located at the south end of the Médoc peninsula *(see* Médoc AOC), upstream of the Garonne. It covers 11,780 acres (4,765 ha), and produces exclusively red wines (2.7 million cases or 242,315 hl). The Haut-Médoc is where many of Bordeaux's best wines are found, including five of the 1855 classified growths. The same region contains the prestigious single-commune appellations of Pauillac, St-Julien, St-Estèphe, Margaux, Listrac, and Moulis.

> **GRAPE VARIETIES** Cabernet Sauvignon, Merlot, Cabernet Franc, Malbec, Petit Verdot.
> **SOIL** Gravel, clay, and limestone.
> **STYLE** The wines are more full-bodied than those of Médoc AOC. Deep red garnet in color, the wines of the Haut-Médoc develop a delightful bouquet expressing ripe red fruit, dark fruit (black-currants), hints of sweet spices, vanilla, and roasted notes. The palate is full-bodied and generous with all the same characters as the nose, supported by a fine tannin structure, and a long finish.

Color:
Red.

Serving temperature:
62 to 64°F (17 to 18°C).

Ageing potential:
7 to 16 years.

ST-ESTÈPHE AOC

St-Estèphe is the northernmost of the six Médoc appellations. The vineyards were planted during the Roman conquest and are located around the commune of the same name, forming an enclave with Pauillac to the south and the Haut-Médoc wrapping around. The appellation covers about 3,000 acres (1,200 ha) and produces 778,000 cases (70,000 hl) of earthy, austere, robust wines (exclusively red). The St-Estèphe appellation contains five of the 1855 classified growths.

> **GRAPE VARIETIES** Cabernet Sauvignon, Merlot, Cabernet Franc.

> **SOIL** Clay-gravel.
> **STYLE** Virile, powerful, and well-structured, the wines of St-Estèphe have a concentrated color and a bouquet, when young, that expresses aromas of lilies, red and dark fruit, sweet spices, and violets. With age, there are tertiary notes of game and undergrowth. The palate is harmonious, powerful, and well-structured with fine, closely textured, distinguished tannins that need time to soften; the finish is very fresh and distinctive. This is an excellent wine for laying down.

Color:
Red.

Serving temperature:
62 to 64°F (16 to 18°C).

Ageing potential:
15 to 25 years, or more for certain grands crus.

ST-JULIEN AOC

Located between Pauillac and Margaux, St-Julien is the smallest appellation in the Médoc (2,200 acres or 900 ha), but it is one of the most prestigious in terms of its châteaux. The vineyards, which cover the communes of St-Julien and Beychevelle, produce about 511,000 cases (46,000 hl) of exclusively red wine. The appellation contains 11 classified growths, which include five second growths. The style of the wines varies considerably depending on the château, but with one common characteristic: the wines are all powerful and concentrated.

> **GRAPE VARIETIES** Cabernet Sauvignon, Merlot, Cabernet Franc.
> **SOIL** Gravel, marl, pebbles.
> **STYLE** The wines are potent, harmonious, and refined, with a typically dense, dark purple color. The delicate bouquet offers distinctive aromas of dark fruit (blueberry, blackcurrant, blackberry) with notes of plum, licorice, tobacco, a slight smokiness, and a hint of game. The palate is full-bodied, rich, beautifully structured, balanced, and sappy, supported by fine tannins that are close-knit, yet velvety and elegant. The finish is long, spicy, and fruity.

Color:
Red.

Serving temperature:
62 to 64°F (16 to 18°C).

Ageing potential:
15 to 25 years, or more for certain grands crus.

PAUILLAC AOC

Pauillac is the wine capital of the Médoc; it has excellent soil, a superb climate, and centuries-old expertise in winemaking, uniting truly exceptional conditions for the production of extremely fine wines. Furthermore, it is home to three of the five 1855 first growths (*premiers grands crus classés*)—Lafite, Latour, and Mouton—along with a plethora of other wines. Perched on superb gravel hilltops, the vineyards stretch over 2,940 acres (1,190 ha) and produce 717,000 cases (64,500 hl) of exclusively red wine, with very few exceptions (such as Mouton-Rothschild, which also makes a white wine). The red wines vary enormously, ranging from the austerity of Château Latour to the suppleness of Château Lafite-Rothschild.

> **GRAPE VARIETIES** Cabernet Sauvignon (dominant), Merlot, Petit Verdot, Malbec.
> **SOIL** Gravelly hilltops.
> **STYLE** Rich, dense, and profound, the wines of Pauillac have a deep ruby color. The bouquet is delicate, elegant, and complex, evoking dark fruit (Morello cherries, blackcurrants) and flowers (roses, irises), mixed with roasted notes and hints of cedar, smoke, leather, and incense. The rich, full-bodied, smooth palate is highlighted by a fine framework of powerful, tight tannins that need time to soften. The finish is long, with lots of fruit. These wines have an exceptional capacity to improve with age; you somehow just have to manage to wait for them.

Color:
Red.

Serving temperature:
61 to 64°F (16 to 18°C).

Ageing potential:
15 to 25 years, or more for some grands crus.

Château Cordeillan-Bages

The name of this Pauillac estate may not ring any bells. However, the château's restaurant was developed by Michelin-starred chef Thierry Marx, now at the Mandarin Oriental in Paris. The wine is a match for such great cuisine: an opulent Cabernet Sauvignon (80 percent) grown and produced by Château Lynch-Bages, a fifth growth. This magnificent wine has a beautiful, dark red color and a delicate, complex bouquet that offers a delightful combination of ripe fruit and hints of spice (vanilla, cinnamon) with toasted notes. The full-bodied, smooth palate is supported by delicious, refined tannins. Complex, powerful, and distinguished, this is a wine that ages very well.

LISTRAC-MÉDOC AOC

Initially famous during the 18th century, the commune of Listrac became popular again in the early 20th century. In 1913, it was one of the largest wine-producing communes of the Médoc peninsula, with 3,410 acres (1,380 ha) of vines. However, all of this changed during the economic crisis of the 1930s. In 1957, Listrac was granted AOC status and became one of the six single commune appellations of the Médoc. Spread across three terraces on the edge of the Haut-Médoc, the vineyards (1,640 acres or 665 ha) are protected from the prevailing winds by a vast pine forest, enabling slow and steady ripening of the grapes. It produces about 420,000 cases (37,580 hl) of exclusively red wine.

> **GRAPE VARIETIES** Merlot (dominant), Cabernet Sauvignon, Cabernet Franc, Petit Verdot.
> **SOIL** Gravel, clay-and-limestone.
> **STYLE** Listrac-Médoc has a dark color with hints of deep purple. The nose is intense, with aromas of red fruit, balsamic notes, and hints of spice with vanilla and toast. The palate is powerful and harmonious—with good volume and fine, powerful tannins that, over time, soften to yield a generous, elegant wine.

Color:
Red.

Serving temperature:
62 to 64°F (16 to 18°C).

Ageing potential:
8 to 12 years.

The Lords of Listrac

This small Médoc appellation is worthy of attention. It is home to the excellent Château Clarke and four châteaux that are grouped together under the name *Quatuor de Listrac* (The Listrac Quartet).

- **Château Clarke (Rothschild family).** The star of the appellation. This château's fortunes were confirmed in 1973 when it was purchased by Baron Edmond de Rothschild, who thoroughly modernized the vineyard and the winery facilities, with the help of the oenologist Michel Rolland. The wines gradually joined the ranks of the Gironde's finest. After the death of Baron Edmond, who was so attached to Château Clarke that he asked to be buried there, his son

Benjamin took over. The wines are all he could hope for: powerful, elegant, and with a great potential to improve with age.

- **Quatuor de Listrac.** For 30 years, these four châteaux have worked together for recognition of the quality and originality of Listrac's wines. However, each has its own personality. Their wines are to be explored and enjoyed.
  – Château Fonréaud (Chanfreau family)
  – Château Fourcas Dupré (Patrice Pagès)
  – Château Fourcas Hosten (Renaud and Laurent Mommeja)
  – Château Lestage (Chanfreau family)

MOULIS-EN-MÉDOC AOC

LEFT BANK (MÉDOC)

This is the smallest of the Médoc appellations. Planted with vines since the 13th century, Moulis covers 1,480 acres (600 ha) and produces 386,000 cases (34,750 hl) of wine. It owes its name to the numerous windmills (*moulins*) that used to exist in the commune. The appellation stretches away from the Gironde, to the west of Margaux, along a narrow strip 7.5 miles (12 km) long. Now sheltered from winds by a pine forest, the microclimate is well suited to ripening grapes. It produces exclusively red wines and contains no classified growths.

> **GRAPE VARIETIES** Cabernet Sauvignon, Merlot.

> **SOIL** Gravel, alluvial deposits, limestone.

> **STYLE** Refined, powerful, and complex, the wines of Moulis have a deep ruby color with dark glints. The fine, rich bouquet presents aromas of stewed and ripe red fruit mixed with notes of toast, licorice, and hints of violet, humus, and undergrowth. The palate is harmonious and elegant, with plump, silky tannins.

Color:
Red.

Serving temperature:
61 to 63°F (16 to 17°C).

Ageing potential:
5 to 15 years.

MARGAUX AOC

LEFT BANK (MÉDOC)

Château Margaux, the legendary first growth, is famous all over the world. However, the Margaux appellation has many other very fine châteaux, with a total of 21 in the 1855 classification. Set among prairies and woods, the vineyards enjoy very favorable conditions for the ripening of grapes: good soil, excellent natural drainage, and proximity to the Gironde estuary. The appellation lies at the south end of the Médoc, encompassing 3,480 acres (1,410 ha) and five communes: Margaux, Cantenac, Labarde, Soussans, and Arsac. The appellation produces about 867,000 cases (78,000 hl) of exclusively red wine, with the exception of Château Margaux's white wine, Pavillon Blanc.

> **GRAPE VARIETIES** Cabernet Sauvignon, Merlot, Cabernet Franc, Malbec, Petit Verdot.

> **SOIL** Gravel hilltops.

> **STYLE** Refined and elegant, the wines of Margaux have a dense ruby color that becomes tinged with garnet as they mature. The very delicate, complex nose is full of finesse—with aromas of red and dark fruit, flowers mixed with roasted notes, wood, truffle, and vanilla, underscored with hints of tobacco, violets, cinnamon, and prunes. With age, they evolve into aromas of undergrowth and mushrooms. The palate is harmonious and full-bodied, supported by finely textured, delicate, delicious tannins. The finish continues with total harmony and elegance.

Color:
Red.

Serving temperature:
61 to 63°F (16 to 17°C); decanting is essential.

Ageing potential:
Drink from the third year onward, up to 20 years.

1. The dovecote in the vineyards.
2. Cabernet Sauvignon grapes.
3. Barrel bungs covered with gauze.
4. Bottles wrapped in tissue paper.
5. The winery.
6. The cellar.

Château Latour

It's a plain, understated label with a simple name ("The Tower"). It's a strong, reassuring image, and it has immense prestige: this is Château Latour. For centuries, its mention has evoked magnificence and the perpetuity of tradition. Its long, complex history presents a fascinating story that continues today.

HISTORIC PRESTIGE

Château Latour's site was highly desirable from a strategic perspective during the Hundred Years War; but its wine history did not really begin until 1718, when the Marquis Nicolas-Alexandre de Ségur planted the first vineyard. The reputation of its wines quickly spread beyond France's borders. In 1787, Thomas Jefferson, then the ambassador of the newly formed United States of America, noted the château's name in his travel journal and bought a few bottles of its wine. At that time, Latour's wines were already 20 times the price of a standard Bordeaux. Château Latour received official recognition in 1855, with the classification ordered by Napoleon III, when it was awarded the title of *premier cru classé* along with just three other châteaux in the whole of the Médoc and Graves region.

BRITISH CONTROL

In 1963, Château Latour was sold to a British group. The château's consistently high quality remained unaltered, and the wine's prestige was preserved. In 1993, the French businessman and wine connoisseur François Pinault acquired the property; and after 30 years of loyal service from the British, the château was returned to French hands.

PERFECT TERROIR

Latour's terroir meets all the criteria for excellence. The vineyard covers just under 200 acres (80 ha). The 116 acres (47 ha) that surround the château, known as the Enclos, are special. Château Latour's Grand Vin is made exclusively from grapes from the Enclos. Though the pebbly soil would be too poor for any other crop, it is ideal for vines. The gravel hilltop here enables perfect drainage of rainwater into the river. Its three gentle slopes are in constant sunshine. Whatever the vagaries of the weather, the vines are

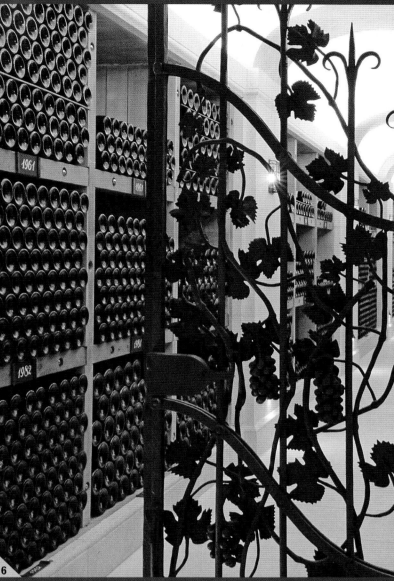

easily able to find the right amount of nourishment and water. Furthermore, the proximity of the Gironde protects the vineyards from extreme temperatures.

GRAPE VARIETIES

Cabernet Sauvignon is king here, occupying 75 percent of the planted area. It gives the wine tannic structure, color, and concentration. It also ensures slow, harmonious ageing, and consequently wines that can be kept for a very long time. A delicate balance is provided by a smaller quantity of Merlot (23 percent), which is softer, more supple, and packed with flavor. The remaining two percent consists of Cabernet Franc and Petit Verdot, which may or may not be used in the final blend.

METICULOUS CARE

To keep the average age of the vineyards as high as possible, each vine serves until its natural death before being replaced by young stock. At the time of the harvest, the vines selected are those whose grapes are worthy of being included in Latour's grand vin. In order not to have more than eight bunches of grapes per vine, some bunches are removed during a "green harvest" in July, thereby producing more concentrated berries. After meticulous hand harvesting, intensively monitored vinification, 18 months' maturation in barrels, and painstaking attention to detail at the bottling stage, it is hardly surprising that the wine of Château Latour is of exceptional quality, has a remarkable capacity to age beautifully, and is always consistent, whatever the vintage.

TASTE OF LATOUR

Château Latour's grand vin is exceptional in almost every way. While austere in its early years, after about 12 years in the cellar this *premier cru classé* reveals the accomplishment of a masterpiece. Over time, the wine's great power and density combines with its very distinguished tannins to achieve perfect harmony. Structured, succulent, powerful, and very long on the palate, this wine has a natural ability to age magnificently for 30, 40, or 50 years, and even longer in great vintages. It needs to be decanted so that the bouquet can fully open. Served at 64°F (18°C), it is an excellent accompaniment for the local lamb of Pauillac, red meat, or game.

LES FORTS DE LATOUR

There is also Les Forts de Latour, the château's "second wine," whose high quality has been justly recognized for many years. Its style is impeccable; and while it may not reach the heights of its elder brother, it is the equal of many of the Médoc's second growths. It ages very well (15 years) and also needs to be decanted.

> Vines growing at Château Larrivet Haut-Brion, in the appellation of Pessac-Léognan.

PESSAC-LÉOGNAN AOC

LEFT BANK (GRAVES)

This appellation was created when the AOC of Graves was divided in 1987. The *graves de Bordeaux* region has always been known for its superb vineyards, concentrated in two main areas: Pessac and Léognan. Located on the southern and southwestern outskirts of Bordeaux, the appellation covers 10 communes (Cadaujac, Canéjan, Gradignan, Léognan, Martillac, Mérignac, Pessac, Saint-Médard-d'Eyrans, Talence, and Villenave d'Ornon), and contains all of the Graves *grands crus classés*, including the legendary Château Haut-

Brion. It mainly produces red wines (3,200 acres or 1,300 ha, yielding 744,000 cases or 67,000 hl), with some dry white wines (655 acres or 265 ha, yielding 167,000 cases or 15,000 hl).

> **GRAPE VARIETIES** Merlot, Cabernet Sauvignon, Cabernet Franc, Malbec, and Petit Verdot for the red wines; Sauvignon Blanc (at least 25 percent), Sémillon, and Muscadelle for the white wines.

> **SOIL** Gravel, rounded pebbles.

> **STYLE** Rich and elegant, the reds have a cherry color tinged with black. The nose develops intense aromas of very ripe red

fruit and flowers (violets), underscored by mingling notes of toasted almonds, resin, and smoke. The palate is full-bodied and well-structured, with closely knit tannins and a long, fruity finish with hints of licorice. The dry whites are a light golden color that deepens with age. The intense, complex nose exudes aromas of stone fruit (peaches, nectarines), citrus, and flowers, with hints of hazelnut and beeswax. The palate balances acidity and fruit with smoothness and strength. The lingering finish returns to all the flavors of the bouquet.

Color:
Red and white.

Serving temperature:
46 to 50°F (8 to 10°C) for the white wines; 61 to 63°F (16 to 17°C) for the reds (which may require decanting).

Ageing potential:
3 to 8 years for the white wines; 10 to 15 years for the red wines.

Château de France

This château's buildings date from the 17th century and are part of the history of Bordeaux. Château de France—developed in turn by Taffard, a member of the Guyenne parliament, and then Jean-Henri Lacoste, a fabric merchant—was acquired by Bernard Thomassin in 1971, who raised it to new heights. Advised by Michel Rolland and currently managed by Arnaud Thomassin, Château de France is a member of the Union des Grands Crus de Bordeaux and produces red wines made primarily from Cabernet Sauvignon (60 percent) and Merlot (40 percent)—called Château de France, Château Coquillas, and Le Bec en Sabot—as well as whites made from Sauvignon Blanc, namely Château de France and Château Coquillas. Its wines are among the best in the Pessac-Léognan appellation.

GRAND VIN DE GRAVES

MIS EN BOUTEILLE AU CHÂTEAU

CHÂTEAU DE FRANCE
PESSAC-LÉOGNAN
2007

GRAVES AOC

Graves is the only appellation in France to be named after a type of soil: *graves de Bordeaux* (Bordeaux gravel). The vineyards, located along the left bank of the Garonne, to the south of Bordeaux, cover 6,700 acres (2,700 ha) in a 30-mile long (50-km) strip. As a result, they are very diverse. Production is largely red wines (about 1.3 million cases or 120,000 hectoliters), with less than a third devoted to fine white wines, both sweet and dry. The sweet white wines are sold under the Graves Supérieur appellation.

> **GRAPE VARIETIES** Merlot (dominant), Cabernet Sauvignon, Cabernet Franc for the reds; Sauvignon Blanc, Sémillon, and Muscadelle for the whites.

> **SOIL** Gravel.

> **STYLE** Elegant and sensual, the red wines have a deep garnet color. The nose is fragrant and complex, combining aromas of red and dark fruit, floral notes, hints of spice and vanilla, and roasted, smoked notes. The palate is well-structured, with a long, generous finish. With age, these wines develop richness and complex flavors. The dry white wines are fresh with an attractive, bright, gold-green color. The nose is refreshing with aromas of white fruit, citrus, floral notes, and hints of spice and beeswax. The palate balances acidity with smoothness and richness. The finish lingers with fruit, freshness, and warmth. Deep yellow in color, the sweet white wines have a very aromatic nose (white fruit, citrus, notes of acacia); the palate is generous and structured, with a long fruity finish.

Color:	*Serving temperature:*	*Ageing potential:*
Red and white.	46 to 50°F (8 to 10°C) for the dry and the sweet white wines; 61 to 63°F (16 to 17°C) for the reds.	2 to 3 years for the dry white wines; 5 to 10 years for the sweet white wines; up to 8 years for the reds.

The Women of Graves

In 1991, the *Syndicat des Graves* was the first union of wine producers in France to elect a woman, Françoise Lévêque, as its president. She remained president until 1997. Today, quite a number of wines in the Graves region are made by women. After following very different paths—some were raised in the vineyard, others come from diverse backgrounds—they are all passionate about producing their wines with a feminine touch. Though they refuse to say that these are "wines made by women." We cannot list them all, so here is a small selection.

- **Catherine Gachet, Château La Tour des Remparts (Preignac).** Superb Graves.

- **Isabelle Labarthe, Château d'Arricaud (Landiras).** Lively, fruity wines.

- **Florence Lafragette, Château de l'Hospital (Portets).** Balanced, elegant wines.

- **Catherine Martin-Larrue, Château Haut-Pommarède (Portets).** Very personal red Graves of excellent quality.

CÉRONS AOC

Northwest of Barsac, Cérons is named after the Ciron River, which runs through it and which is responsible for the nocturnal mists that are conducive to the development of *botrytis cinerea*. With only 100 acres (41 ha) producing 14,400 cases (1,300 hl), this sweet white wine is not widely available. It has the distinction of being either *moelleux* or *liquoreux* (the latter has a higher level of residual sugar) depending on the year and weather conditions.

> **GRAPE VARIETIES** Sémillon (dominant), Sauvignon Blanc, Muscadelle.

> **SOIL** Gravel, sand, limestone.

> **STYLE** Golden in color, the wines present an intense bouquet with aromas of fruit (citrus, exotic, and crystallized) as well as hints of honey, caramel, vanilla, and acacia flowers. The palate is very fragrant, full-bodied, smooth, and voluptuous, with a remarkably long, aromatic finish.

Color:	*Serving temperature:*	*Ageing potential:*
White.	About 46°F (8°C).	10 years or more.

BARSAC AOC

This appellation is located on the left bank of the Garonne, northwest of Sauternes, from which it is separated by just a small river (the Ciron). The climate in Barsac is rather special: in the fall, misty mornings are often followed by direct afternoon sunshine, creating favorable conditions for the growth of *botrytis cinerea* or "noble rot," the fungus that produces the greatest sweet white wines. The wines, renowned for their complexity (the AOC contains 10 1855 classified growths), may be sold under the Barsac or the Sauternes appellation—but the same does not apply to the wines of Sauternes.

> **GRAPE VARIETIES** Sémillon (dominant), Sauvignon Blanc, Muscadelle.

> **SOIL** Clay, limestone, or gravel.

> **STYLE** Refined, sleek, and elegant, the wines have a golden color that evolves with age to shades of amber. The nose is intense with a mixture of stone fruit (peaches), exotic fruit, notes of honey, hazelnuts, and dried apricots with hints of crystallized orange peel, vanilla, and brioche. This intensity reappears on the palate, which is full-bodied and perfectly balanced with smoothness and freshness. The finish is long and lingering.

Color:
White.

Serving temperature:
About 46°F (8°C).

Ageing potential:
20 years or more.

SAUTERNES AOC

This is the most famous of Bordeaux's sweet wine appellations, and it includes the iconic Château d'Yquem (*see* pp.264–5), one of the greatest sweet wines in the world. The vineyards of Sauternes cover 4,290 acres (1,735 ha), about 25 miles (40 km) south of Bordeaux. They are spread over five communes, including Barsac (which has its own AOC), and enjoy excellent conditions: protection from bad weather by the pine forests to the west, night mists owing to the proximity of the Garonne, and plenty of sunshine in the fall, encouraging the development of the famous noble rot—vital for the production of great sweet wines. The appellation produces exclusively sweet white wines (380,000 cases or 34,260 hl). The method of producing these nectars, appreciated all over the world, are rigorous—with manual harvesting of overripe grapes, berry by berry, in a series of selective pickings. The best *terroirs* are on the high ground furthest from the river. This is where most of the classified growths are located.

> **GRAPE VARIETIES** Sémillon (dominant), Sauvignon Blanc, Muscadelle.

> **SOIL** Gravel, clay-and-limestone, limestone.

> **STYLE** The wines have a sumptuous "old gold" color that evolves with age to a warm amber. The Sauternes bouquet is typically very complex and intense, exploding with an exuberant symphony of fruit, floral notes, hints of honey, spices, almond paste, and beeswax, all delicately combined. The palate is full-bodied, powerful, smooth, refined, and elegant, with a perfect balance between fullness and acidity, and a very long finish.

Color:
White.

Serving temperature:
42 to 46°F (6 to 8°C).

Ageing potential:
Enjoyable when young, but will keep for up to 100 years.

Selected Sauternes

Other than Chateau d'Yquem, there are some extremely fine sweet wines.

- **Cru Barréjats (Pujols-sur-Ciron).** A tiny vineyard, but huge in terms of finesse, purity of flavor, and depth.

- **Château Climens (Barsac).** Perhaps the finest and most *liquoreux* (having high residual sugar) of Sauternes wines.

- **Château de Fargues (Fargues).** Superb; worthy of a *premier cru*.

- **Château La Tour Blanche (Bommes).** Harmonious Sauternes with a superb bouquet.

- **Château Rieussec (Fargues-de-Langon).** A powerful *premier cru* with enormous personality.

- **Château Sigalas-Rabaud (Bommes).** Unparalleled finesse.

- **Château Suduiraut (Preignac).** A rich, deep, elegant *grand cru* with exceptional longevity.

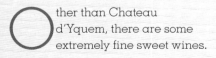

BLAYE-CÔTES-DE-BORDEAUX AOC

RIGHT BANK (BLAYE REGION)

Vines were planted in the Blaye region well before they were in neighboring Médoc. Wine estates here developed along the estuary, taking advantage of the dynamic, flourishing shipping industry. The vineyards, located to the north of Bordeaux, across from the Médoc, cover about 16,000 acres (6,500 ha) and produce mostly red wines (3.6 million cases or 325,000 hl), along with a few white wines (167,000 cases or 15,000 hl).

> **GRAPE VARIETIES** Merlot (70 percent), Cabernet Sauvignon, Cabernet Franc, Malbec for the reds; Sauvignon Blanc, Sémillon, and Muscadelle for the whites.

> **SOIL** Clay-and-limestone.

> **STYLE** These wines have an intense ruby color; the bouquet is powerful and fruity (red and dark fruit), embellished with hints of spice. The palate is supple and harmonious, with well-integrated tannins and a long finish returning to the flavors of the bouquet. The white wines are pale yellow in color, tinged with green, and present aromas of yellow fruit, citrus notes, and hints of juniper. The palate is well-balanced between acidity and fruit, which linger on the finish.

Color:
Red and white.

Serving temperature:
61 to 64°F (16 to 18°C). (Grands crus *should be decanted two hours before serving.*)

Ageing potential:
7 to 20 years (and up to 25 years for the grands crus).

CÔTES-DE-BLAYE AOC

RIGHT BANK (BLAYE REGION)

On the right bank of the Gironde—north of Bordeaux and near the town of Blaye, with its citadel built by Vauban—the vineyards are planted on hills and in small valleys, and receive lots of sunshine. This small appellation (620 acres or 250 ha) produces 178,000 cases (16,000 hl) of red wines and dry white wines. The white grapes are scheduled to be phased out by 2020, with the Ugni Blanc and Colombard gradually being replaced by red grape varieties.

> **GRAPE VARIETIES** Merlot, Cabernet Franc, Cabernet Sauvignon for the red wines; Sémillon, Sauvignon Blanc, Muscadelle, Colombard, Ugni Blanc for the whites.

> **SOIL** Clay-and-limestone, gravel.

> **STYLE** The red wines have a deep, but bright, color. The nose offers notes of red and dark fruit (raspberries, strawberries, cherries, blackberries, blackcurrants), underscored with hints of flowers (peppery rose, violet), vegetal aromas (mint, pepper), spices, chocolate, and wood. The palate is supple, rounded, and well-balanced, with beautifully textured, fine, silky tannins and a long, fruity finish. Very full-flavored, the white wines are deep yellow in color; the nose offers a delightful range of citrus notes (lemon, grapefruit, tangerine) and stone fruit, with hints of toasted almonds; the palate is very elegantly balanced between fruit and freshness.

Color:
Red and white.

Serving temperature:
50 to 54°F (10 to 12°C) for the white wines; 61 to 63°F (16 to 17°C) for the reds.

Ageing potential:
Drink within a year; white wines keep for 2 to 3 years; reds for 3 to 7 years.

> The underground cellars at Château Bertinerie (Blaye-Cotes-de-Bordeaux AOC).

Château d'Yquem

Visible from afar, the imposing **Château d'Yquem** dominates the several hundred acres of vineyards that surround it. The Lur-Saluces family reigned here for more than four centuries, with unwavering passion and rigor. Now controlled by a large company, the property produces one of the most prestigious—and most expensive—sweet wines in the world.

A LONG-STANDING REPUTATION

The history of this exceptional vineyard dates back to the 16th century. By the time it came into the possession of the Lur-Saluces family, 200 years later, its wines were already highly prized. In 1790, the future president of the United States, Thomas Jefferson, ordered "thirty dozen" bottles for the incumbent president, George Washington, and a few for himself. The work carried out by early generations of the Lur-Saluces family on this exceptional terroir was rewarded in the 1855 classification of Bordeaux's wines, when **Château d'Yquem** was raised to the unique rank of *premier cru supérieur* (superior first classified growth) of Sauternes. All the royal courts of Europe and all the palaces and prestigious restaurants placed their orders. This infatuation continues today. In its category, **Château d'Yquem** is often considered to be the best wine in the world.

YQUEM'S GRANDEUR REMAINS UNCHANGED

After years of prosperity, Château d'Yquem had to face the phylloxera crisis; and then many of the Lur-Saluces family went away to fight in the first and second world wars; and Europe also became engulfed in economic crisis. Alexandre de Lur-Saluces took the reins in 1968, and upheld the wine's reputation for more than 35 years. All of the vintages that he produced are monumental. In 1999, the **LVMH** group became the majority shareholder and kept Alexandre de Lur-Saluces in charge of the property. Pierre Lurton took over in 2004. Descended from a long line of respected Bordeaux winemakers, he also contributes to the excellence of the famous Château Cheval-Blanc, a *premier grand cru classé* in St-Émilion. His experience, humility, and talent have been important factors in the extraordinary success of recent vintages of Yquem.

1. Château d'Yquem.
2. Once fermentation has stopped, the wine is matured in oak barrels.
3. Old vintages demonstrate the longevity of this "golden nectar."
4. A bunch of Sémillon with "roasted" berries.
5. Château d'Yquem's emblem.
6. The 2005 vintage.

REMARKABLE TERROIR REQUIRING GREAT CARE

The explanation for the continuing excellence of this wine is not obvious. The terroir that produces it certainly plays a vital role. Pebbles sit on a layer of clay soil that covers a mosaic of subsoils, which seem to have been created for vines and give the wine its exceptional complexity.

The fall climate—with mist in the morning and sunshine in the afternoon—and the proximity of the little Ciron River that joins the Garonne, together favor the development of "noble rot." This is the famous *botrytis* that grows on the grape skins, feeding on water from the pulp inside and concentrating the sugar in the grapes without increasing their acidity. Since this fungus grows in an irregular fashion, the pickers have to pass through the rows of vines up to 10 times in order to pick only the berries that are at just the right stage (described as *rôti* or "roasted").

This is a risky operation because the selective picking process requires time, during which any rain could wipe out the crop. Nine vintages of Château d'Yquem were lost during the 20th century due to poor weather conditions. To this must be added an incredibly low yield: in the Médoc, as a rule of thumb, each vine produces an average of one bottle of wine; at Yquem, each vine produces a single glass. During a slow fermentation in new barrels, yeasts convert the sugar in the must into alcohol. The richness of sugar slows the process and ultimately stops the fermentation: not all of the sugar is converted into alcohol; some remains. The wine then spends three long years in oak barrels.

A SUBLIME NECTAR

In its early years, wine from Château d'Yquem is already remarkable, offering immediate sensual pleasure. The golden color and generous bouquet of crystallized citrus fruit, flowers, spices, and honey are totally captivating. On the palate, it is the smoothness that is the most striking; this is balanced by an exquisite freshness and length, full of fruit and exotic flavors. Some would say that it is a crime to drink the wine when it is young. They know what it will offer when it reaches maturity, after at least another 15 or 20 years. And it is true that the wine is truly sublime when, with age, the color becomes tinged with topaz, and the aromas of crystallized fruit mingle with sweet spices, beeswax, and toasted brioche. In the mouth, smoothness competes with richness, mellowness with vigor, silk with velvet, and there is that infinitely long finish—with bursts of apricot, white pepper, and ginger. To enjoy the full symphony of flavors, serve the wine at 54°F (12°C), in the finest crystal glasses, and only to people who will appreciate it!

CÔTES-DE-BOURG AOC

The Côtes de Bourg has some of the oldest vineyards in Bordeaux; their wines have competed with those of the Médoc since the 19th century. Located south of the town of Blaye, across from Margaux, this appellation covers 15 communes on hillsides overlooking the Gironde estuary. The 9,600 acres (3,900 ha) of vineyards, known as the "Little Switzerland of the Gironde," produce about 1.4 million cases (130,000 hl) of mostly red wines that are very pleasant and fruity, and age well.

> **GRAPE VARIETIES** Merlot (dominant), Cabernet Sauvignon, Cabernet Franc, Malbec for the reds; Sémillon, Sauvignon Blanc, Muscadelle, and Colombard for the whites.

> **SOIL** Alluvial deposits, sandy-clay, and limestone.

> **STYLE** Rustic and charming, the reds have a deep color and an intense nose of fresh and stewed dark fruit and spices. With age, they develop notes of mushroom, humus, and venison. The palate is generous, powerful, and well-structured with fine, silky tannins, and a long, flavorful finish. Dry and fruity, the white wines have a pale color, and a very aromatic nose of flowers and white fruit; the palate is harmonious, smooth, and well balanced between fruit and freshness.

Color:	**Serving temperature:**	**Ageing potential:**
Red and white.	About 50°F (10°C) for the white wines; 61 to 63°F (16 to 17°C) for the reds.	2 to 3 years for the whites; 3 to 8 years for the reds.

FRONSAC AOC

Bordered by the Dordogne and Isle rivers, these very old vineyards enjoyed a golden period in the 17th century under Richelieu, the Duke of Fronsac, who built a villa in the area to host sumptuous parties. The appellation extends to the gates of Libourne, covering about 2,100 acres (830 ha) and producing around 489,000 cases (44,000 hl) of exclusively red wine. The wines produced in the communes of Fronsac and St-Michel-de-Fronsac may also be sold under the Canon-Fronsac appellation. There is no official classification in Fronsac.

> **GRAPE VARIETIES** Merlot, Cabernet Sauvignon, Cabernet Franc, Malbec.

> **SOIL** Alluvial deposits (Fronsac molasse), clay-and-limestone.

> **STYLE** Charming and full-bodied, the wines of Fronsac have a concentrated ruby color. The nose develops intense aromas of mainly red fruit mixed with spicy notes (pepper) with touches of undergrowth. The balanced, robust, rich, full palate is supported by solid, flavorful tannins that require several years to settle down.

Color:	**Serving temperature:**	**Ageing potential:**
Red.	61 to 63°F (16 to 17°C). (Decant, if possible.)	5 to 10 years.

Châteaux Vrai Canon Bouché and Le Tertre de Canon

In 2005, Philip Haseth-Möller bought 30 acres (12 ha) of land on the high plateau near the village of Fronsac. Self-taught, he engaged the services of Stéphane Derenoncourt, a consultant who advises many of the vineyards in St-Émilion (Pavie-Macquin and Canon-la-Lagaffelière among others), and of the renowned agrobiologist Claude Bourguignon, who specializes in matching grape varieties with soil types. The result was two very fine wines (with Merlot as the dominant grape): Vrai Canon Bouché and Le Tertre de Canon, both excellent expressions of the *terroir*.

POMEROL AND LALANDE-DE-POMEROL AOCS

One of the jewels of Bordeaux, the Pomerol appellation contains the equally famous Pétrus, one of the rarest and most expensive wines in the world. Paradoxically, it is one of the few appellations that does not have a classification system for its wines. The vineyards of Pomerol, a commune that does not have a village, date back to Roman times. It is located about 30 miles (50 km) east of Bordeaux, near the town of Libourne. The vineyards are spread over 1,940 acres (785 ha) of terraces above the Isle River and produce 453,000 cases (40,800 hl) of exclusively red wine. In the same region as Pomerol, separated from the prestigious appellation by a stream called the Barbanne, the Lalande-de-Pomerol appellation covers two communes, Lalande-de-Pomerol and Néac. It produces, from the same grape varieties, wines that are similar to those of its prestigious neighbor—even, in some cases, managing to rival them.

> **GRAPE VARIETIES** Merlot (80 percent to 100 percent), Cabernet Franc, Cabernet Sauvignon, Malbec.

> **SOIL** Clay-gravel.

> **STYLE** Powerful, rounded, and supple with a very deep, dense color, the wines of Pomerol develop full, complex aromas of red and dark fruit, spices, and hints of violet. They are underscored with hints of tobacco, licorice, truffle, and game, which become more complex with age. The palate is full, smooth, and fleshy, steeped in fruit flavors with a powerful structure of silky, dense tannins. The lingering finish is long and fragrant. The wines of Lalande-de-Pomerol are deep red and powerful, with a fine bouquet and elegant, well-integrated tannins.

Color:
Red.

Serving temperature:
61 to 64°F (16 to 18°C). (Decant several hours before drinking.)

Ageing potential:
3 to 15 or 20 years.

Selected Pomerol producers

After Pétrus, the "king" of the appellation, and other famous châteaux such as L'Évangile, La Conseillante, and Vieux Château Certan, there are some very good wines to be found in Pomerol:

- **Château Belle-Brise (Libourne).** Pomerol elegance and class.

- **Château Bellegrave (Pomerol).** A very typical Pomerol with great finesse and concentration.

- **Château Gombaude-Guillot (Pomerol).** Both of the property's wines (Clos Prince and Château Gombaude-Guillot) are organic; well-balanced and harmonious, they combine power and great elegance.

- **Château La Ganne (Libourne).** Very good value.

AOC ST-ÉMILION

RIGHT BANK (LIBOURNE REGION)

St-Émilion is the first wine-producing area to be included in Unesco's World Heritage List as a "cultural landscape." It is also one of the most famous in the world. The vineyards enjoy a temperate climate thanks to the nearby Dordogne River. They cover 13,300 acres (5,400 ha) and eight communes, producing 567,000 cases (51,000 hl) of exclusively red wine. Depending on the soil, exposure, and age of the vines, as well as the concentration of the grapes, wine producers may sell their wines under two appellations: St-Émilion and St-Émilion Grand Cru *(see* below). In 1955, a classification was drawn up for the *grands*

crus, with the proviso that it be updated every 10 years.

> **GRAPE VARIETIES** Merlot (dominant), Cabernet Franc, Cabernet Sauvignon.
> **SOIL** Limestone, clay-alluvial deposits (Fronsac molasse), gravel alluvium, sand.
> **STYLE** With the passing of time, the dark color of the wines of St-Émilion quickly becomes a beautiful garnet, tinged with brown and orange. The complex nose offers ripe, stewed red and dark fruit, with notes of leather, sweet spices, and woody-smokiness. With age, aromas of undergrowth and humus develop, with notes of game. The palate is full, fleshy, well-structured, and

supported by delicate, silky tannins. A beautiful finish offers fruit, spice, and smoky notes.

Color:	Serving temperature:	Ageing potential:
Red.	61 to 63°F (16 to 17°C). *(Decant if possible.)*	3 to 8 or 10 years, or more.

ST-ÉMILION GRAND CRU AOC

RIGHT BANK (LIBOURNE REGION)

This appellation covers the same area as that of St-Émilion *(see above)*. To be described as *grand cru*, wines must meet certain quality criteria (yields limited to 2.4 tons/acre (40 hl/ha), maturation in barrels for 12 months). The appellation has two *grands crus classés A*, namely Château Ausone and Château Cheval-Blanc, and 11 *grands crus classés B* (see p. 251).

> **GRAPE VARIETIES** Merlot (dominant), Cabernet Franc, Cabernet Sauvignon.
> **SOIL** Limestone, clay-alluvial deposits

(Fronsac molasse), gravel alluvium, sand.
> **STYLE** The wines of St-Émilion Grand Cru have a purple color and present a very fragrant, concentrated, complex nose— mingling ripe, dark fruit and flowers, with notes of prunes, hints of spice, vanilla, and toasted almonds. The palate is full-bodied, fleshy, and well structured, with good quality, fine, closely knit tannins that need time to soften. The finish is long, fresh, and full-flavored.

Color:	Serving temperature:	Ageing potential:
Red.	61 to 64°F (16 to 18°C). *(Decant if possible.)*	7 to 20 years, or more for the crus classés.

Grand crus and organic farming

The number is still few, but the list of St-Émilion Grand Cru properties that have adopted organic or biodynamic methods does become longer every year. Among the main names are: Château Barrail des Graves (Gérard Descrambe, St-Sulpice-de-Faleyrens), one of the very first; Châteaux Fonroque and Moulin du Cadet (Moueix, St-Émilion and Libourne); Château Franc-Pourret, Domaine du Haut-Patarabet, Clos Chante l'Alouette (Vignobles Ouzoulias, St-Émilion); and Château Laroze (Georges Meslin, St-Émilion). In addition to their diversity, these wines offer superb quality with an extra something that makes a difference.

THE ST-ÉMILION "SATELLITES"

Four communes neighboring St-Émilion are permitted to add that name to their own. To the far north is Lussac-St-Émilion (3,560 acres or 1,440 ha, producing 944,000 cases or 85,000 hl). Following on from the vineyards of Pomerol and St-Émilion to the north is Montagne-St-Émilion (4,000 acres or 1,600 ha, producing 1 million cases or 91,600 hl) and St-Georges-St-Émilion (494 acres or 200 ha, producing 128,000 cases or 11,500 hl). Facing the St-Émilion plateau lies Puisseguin-St-Émilion (1,840 acres or 745 ha, producing 478,000 cases or 43,000 hl). Using the same grapes as St-Émilion AOC, these appellations offer wines with personality and represent excellent value.

> **GRAPE VARIETIES** Merlot (dominant, sometimes up to 90 percent), Cabernet Franc, Cabernet Sauvignon, Malbec.

> **SOIL** Clay and limestone. Lussac's soil is varied: clay-gravel in the valleys, sandy clay on the plateaus, and clay-limestone on the hillsides.

> **STYLE** The wines of Lussac are elegant and well-structured; Montagne's are classy, generous, and distinguished; St-Georges' are full-bodied and powerful; Puisseguin's are full-bodied and fleshy.

Color:
Red.

Serving temperature:
59 to 63°F (15 to 17°C).

Ageing potential:
5 to 9 years

FRANCS-CÔTES-DE-BORDEAUX AOC

The name "Côtes de Francs" dates back to the 6th century. After the battle of Vouillé in 507, Clovis, the king of the Franks, defeated the Visigoths and seized Aquitaine. The place where a detachment of the Frankish army established itself was called *Ad Francos*, which later became "Francs." Located about 30 miles (50 km) northeast of Bordeaux, this appellation is one of the smallest and the most easterly. The vineyards cover 1,300 acres (525 ha) spread over the three communes of Francs, Saint-Cibard, and Tayac. It produces about 289,000 cases (26,000 hl) of red wine and a small quantity of white wine, both dry and sweet.

> **GRAPE VARIETIES** For the red wines: Merlot (dominant), Cabernet Sauvignon, and Cabernet Franc; for the white wines: Sémillon (dominant), Muscadelle, and Sauvignon Blanc.

> **SOIL** Limestone covered with Agen molasse (to the south), and limestone with Fronsac molasse.

> **STYLE** The red wines have a very dark color. The nose offers aromas of very ripe red and dark fruit with spicy notes. The palate combines smoothness and volume with a tannin structure that needs time to soften. The whites develop a citrus and exotic fruit bouquet, with hints of honey. The palate is full and well-balanced.

Color:
Red and white.

Serving temperature:
46 to 50°F (8 to 10°C) for the whites;
57 to 61°F (14 to 16°C) for the reds.

Ageing potential:
1 to 3 years for the whites;
3 to 5 years for the reds.

CASTILLON-CÔTES-DE-BORDEAUX AOC

This is a land steeped in history—the battle of Castillon in 1453 ended the Hundred Years War. The appellation covers 7,400 acres (3,000 ha) on the right bank of the Gironde, to the east of St-Émilion. It produces 1.8 million cases (160,000 hl) of full-bodied, generous, exclusively red wines. It joined the new Côtes-de-Bordeaux appellation in 2007.

> **GRAPE VARIETIES** Merlot, Cabernet Franc, Cabernet Sauvignon.

> **SOIL** Clay-and-limestone, gravel.

> **STYLE** The wines have a dark ruby color. The nose is expressive and complex, with aromas of ripe red fruit and prunes. It is underscored with notes of vegetation (ivy), spices, licorice, leather, undergrowth, and game. The palate is fruity and well-structured, with powerful, generous tannins.

Color:
Red.

Serving temperature:
61 to 64°F (16 to 18°C).

Ageing potential:
5 to 10 years.

ENTRE-DEUX-MERS AOC

This region consists of a plateau crisscrossed with valleys, and it takes its name from a location between two rivers, the Dordogne and the Garonne—forming its borders to the north and south. This vast appellation stretches over 6,700 acres (2,700 ha) and produces an average of 1.56 million cases (140,000 hl) per year. They are mostly dry white wines, and some sweet wines. Nine communes (Arbis, Cantois, Escoussans, Gornac, Ladaux, Mourens, Soulignac, St-Pierre-de-Bat, and Targon), located in the same area, are entitled to the appellation Entre-Deux-Mers-Haut-Benauge.

> **GRAPE VARIETIES** Sauvignon Blanc (dominant), Sémillon, Muscadelle.

> **SOIL** Limestone, silica, gravel, alluvial deposits.

> **STYLE** Entre-Deux-Mers wines have a brilliant golden color with hints of green; they are lively, fruity, supple, and very fresh tasting. The nose presents notes of lemon, blackcurrant buds, and just a hint of iodine. The finish is relatively long and full-flavored with citrus notes.

Color:
White.

Serving temperature:
About 46°F (8°C).

Ageing potential:
2 to 3 years.

STE-FOY-BORDEAUX AOC

Located between Bordeaux, Perigord, and Agen, this ancient medieval zone lies on the eastern boundary of the Bordeaux wine-producing region. Containing 19 villages, it follows a series of hills and plateaus that overlook the Dordogne River. With only about 790 acres (320 ha), Ste-Foy-Bordeaux's production is limited; but it is highly appreciated by connoisseurs. It mainly produces red wines, plus a few rare dry and sweet white wines.

> **GRAPE VARIETIES** Cabernet Sauvignon, Cabernet Franc, Merlot for the red wines; Sauvignon Blanc, Sémillon, Muscadelle, Sauvignon Gris for the whites.

> **SOIL** Gravel, sand.

> **STYLE** Opulent and powerful, the red wines have a magnificent bouquet of red fruit, dominated by cherries, mixed with delicate notes of leather and undergrowth. The palate is fleshy, full-bodied, and powerful, with a solid tannin structure that needs time to soften. The finish is long and flavorful. The sweet white wines have a beautiful warm golden color. Their delicate nose expresses aromas of white flowers and honey with a subtle hint of musk. The palate is rounded, full, and smooth, and is highlighted by a superb freshness. The finish is very long and fragrant. The dry white wines have a pale yellow color, and a lively, fruity bouquet (citrus); the palate is well-balanced between fruit, acidity, and smoothness.

Color:
Red and white.

Serving temperature:
46 to 50°F (8 to 10°C) for the dry and the sweet white wines; 61 to 63°F (16 to 17°C) for the reds.

Ageing potential:
2 to 3 years for the dry whites;
3 to 6 years for the reds;
4 to 7 years for the sweet whites.

CADILLAC AOC

Overlooked by Cadillac's château in that beautiful 17th-century walled town, the appellation extends along the right bank of the Garonne River, 19 miles (30 km) southeast of Bordeaux. The microclimate in the vineyards is suitable for the development of noble rot. Some 22 communes have the right to the appellation. Representing excellent value, the wines of Cadillac are well worth exploring. This appellation should not be confused with Cadillac-Côtes-de-Bordeaux AOC, which produces only red wines.

> **GRAPE VARIETIES** Sémillon, Sauvignon Blanc, Muscadelle.

> **SOIL** Clay-and-limestone, gravel.

> **STYLE** The wines of Cadillac have a golden color with hints of topaz; the bouquet typically offers aromas of honey, acacia, honeysuckle, and crystallized fruit. The smooth, flavorful palate has plenty of substance, with some roasted notes that linger on the finish.

Color:
White.

Serving temperature:
About 46°F (8°C).

Ageing potential:
10 to 15 years, or more.

"Sweet Bordeaux"

In the Gironde, 11 sweet wine appellations—Sauternes, Barsac, Loupiac, Ste-Croix-du-Mont, Premières-Côtes-de-Bordeaux, Graves supérieur, Cadillac, Cérons, Bordeaux supérieur, Côtes-de-Bordeaux-St-Macaire, and Ste-Foy-Bordeaux—have joined together to form "Sweet Bordeaux," a group that shares tastings and celebrates a "sweet attitude" with a view to conquering new markets: "sweet hours," "sweet music," and "sweet parties" are organized in an attempt to attract a younger clientele and show that these wines can be enjoyed with a wide range of foods, and not only the traditional *foie gras*. Here are some of the Sweet Bordeaux wines.

- **Château Haura**, Barsac (Cérons AOC). High in residual sugar, this is a delicious, full-bodied, complex wine with excellent balance.
- **Château La Grave**, Ste-Croix-du-Mont (Ste-Croix-du-Mont). This offers a "Sentiers d'Automne," a powerful, full-bodied, smooth wine.
- **Château Petit Clos Jean**, Cérons (Loupiac AOC). The Cuvée Prestige is full of charm, elegance, and power.
- **Château Peyruchet**, Loupiac (Loupiac AOC). The *liquoreux* (high residual sugar) wines represent the appellation magnificently.

LOUPIAC AOC

ENTRE-DEUX-MERS

Located on small hills 25 miles (40 km) south of Bordeaux, the vineyards of Loupiac (860 acres or 350 ha, producing 139,000 cases or 12,550 hl) enjoy excellent sunshine, very good natural drainage, and mists in the fall that—with the presence of the Garonne—create ideal conditions for the growth of *botrytis cinerea*, the noble rot necessary for the production of sweet wines.

> **GRAPE VARIETIES** Sémillon (dominant), Sauvignon Blanc, Muscadelle.
> **SOIL** Clay, gravel.
> **STYLE** A beautiful yellow color with hints of gold, the wines of Loupiac are generous and very refined. Elegant and complex, the nose presents aromas of crystallized fruit, exotic fruit, and figs, with notes of spiced bread, yellow flowers, honey, acacia, currants, and prunes. The palate is full and creamy, with an elegant structure supported by good acidity. The finish is long and flavorful.

Color:
White.

Serving temperature:
About 46°F (8°C).

Ageing potential:
As much as 100 years, or more.

STE-CROIX-DU-MONT AOC

ENTRE-DEUX-MERS

This slightly unusual appellation is located to the southeast of Bordeaux, across from Sauternes, and covers 1,100 acres (450 ha) of steep hills in the commune of the same name. The vineyards of this appellation enjoy a microclimate that favors the development of *botrytis cinerea*, with mild weather in the fall and humidity at night. Ste-Croix-du-Mont produces about 167,000 cases (15,000 hl) of exclusively sweet white wine.

> **GRAPE VARIETIES** Sémillon, Sauvignon Blanc, Muscadelle.
> **SOIL** Clay-and-limestone, limestone.
> **STYLE** The wines of Ste-Croix-du-Mont have a charming, intense golden color; the nose offers aromas of jam (peach, apricot), citrus, and exotic fruit, mixed with notes of raisins and figs, and underscored with hints of honeysuckle, acacia, and honey. The palate is full-bodied, creamy, and very flavorful with a long, smooth finish that lingers with the same fruit flavors as the nose.

Color:
White.

Serving temperature:
46 to 50°F (8 to 10°C).

Ageing potential:
Up to 10 years, or more.

BURGUNDY

A highly symbolic wine region, Burgundy today covers the same area as the medieval province of the same name. Its land produces some of the greatest wines of France (and the world), both white and red. While the complex layout of its estates and its diverse hierarchical structure is part of its charm, it can render the region inaccessible to the layman.

Monks, *clos*, and complicated classifications

Burgundy is a land that bridges the north and south, not only of France but also of Europe. This is something that has long encouraged awareness and dissemination of its wines.

FROM THE FOUNDATION OF THE ABBEYS TO THE FRENCH REVOLUTION. It is believed that the vine developed in the Beaunois region as early as 200 AD. Yet the real boom in Burgundy wine production is linked to Christianity, not only due to the demand for sacramental wine (communion was given in bread and wine until the 13th century, and the faithful often received it daily), but also due to the location of monasteries in the Middle Ages,

where the vineyards were often handed down by important local leaders, and served as a means of raising money. The monks, who enjoyed a good standard of living, patiently selected the plots (or "*climats*") that would produce the best wines, which could be sold at the highest prices (*see also* p.17). They were even supposed to have tasted the earth in order to evaluate a particular location! It is more likely that they marked out plots by tasting wines for the payment of tithes in kind. To protect their most precious spots (and avoid disputes with their neighbors), they built stone walls and created the famous Burgundy *clos*, or enclosed vineyard.

FROM THE REVOLUTION TO THE FIRST CLASSIFICATIONS. The French Revolution was an opportunity for winemakers in Burgundy to take revenge on the

BURGUNDY STATISTICS (AOC)

Vineyard area: 123,854 acres (50,122 ha)
Production: 29.3 million cases (2,640,724 hl)
Reds and rosés: 59.8%
Whites: 35.6%
Sparkling: 4.6%

(BIVB, 2007; Inter-Beaujolais, 2005)

> Hôtel-Dieu de Beaune has a roof of brightly colored, painted tiles arranged in geometric patterns.

Hospices de Beaune Auction

Founded in 1452 by Nicolas Rolin and Guigone Salins to rescue and care for the poor, the Hospices de Beaune owns a vast inherited estate of more than 148 acres (60 ha), which produces plenty of *premiers crus* and *grands crus*. Each year, the estate's wines are sold in *pièces* (the name for 60-gallon (228 l) Burgundian barrels) on the third Sunday of November at the largest sale of wine in the world. Organized since 2005 by the great British auction house Christie's, the sale is held by candlelight. The proceeds from this sale (€2.8 million in 2008) are still used to finance the Hôtel-Dieu, which has become a regional health center. The prices received during the auction serve as an indicator to determine the average price for Burgundy wines of that vintage.

> Harvest in a village in Burgundy.

aristocratic and monastic estates. The fragmentation of estates there began in 1791 with a selling off of national assets, such as those of Clos de Vougeot (*see also* p.283) and Romanée-Conti (*see also* pp.288-9). By 1861, a classification of the "Agricultural Committee of the District of Beaune" prefigured the modern system of *appellation contrôlée*. They could already distinguish very fine wines or *têtes de cuvée*, which included Romanée-Conti, Clos de Vougeot, and Chambertin *grands crus* and *premiers crus*. This classification has been simplified (somewhat) by the National Institute of Appellations of Origin (INAO), which removed the highest classification, retaining only the *grands crus* and *premiers crus*. The appellation regulations started to appear in 1936, and the first were for the *grands crus*, followed quickly by local appellations.

Chablis and Yonne vineyards

Chablis is the hallmark of fine, dry, white wine, where the balance between freshness, provided by acidity, and fruit character results in wines that are very similar to the great whites of the Côte d'Or, but more sleek and taut. However, making wine in the Chablis region is not easy, since it is located at the northernmost limit of commercial viticulture. The great enemy here is frost, so much so that growers must sometimes, in winter, install vineyard heaters (a kind of oil-fired brazier) or sprinkle water on the vines to form a protective coating around the plant.

Chardonnay, here called "Beaune," grows especially well on the marl and limestone soils of the Yonne district. The *premiers crus* sites of Chablis (*see* p.281), and even more so the *grands crus*, rival the great whites of the Côte d'Or, with greater minerality and lesser richness. The *grands crus* are all concentrated around the town of Chablis itself, between the villages of Fyé and Poinchy.

In other vineyards around Yonne, Auxerre, and Tonnerre, there are good-quality red wines such as Bourgogne Côte-Saint-Jacques (formerly Coteaux de Joigny) or Bourgogne Vézelay, but

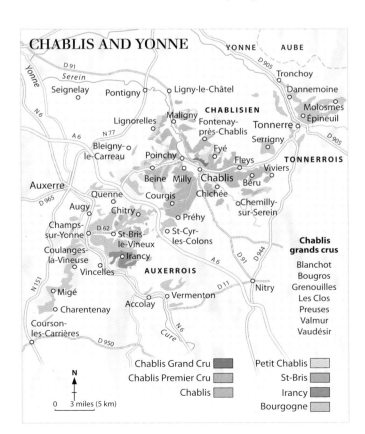

CHABLIS AND YONNE

Chablis grands crus

Blanchot
Bougros
Grenouilles
Les Clos
Preuses
Valmur
Vaudésir

Chablis Grand Cru
Chablis Premier Cru
Chablis
Petit Chablis
St-Bris
Irancy
Bourgogne

0   3 miles (5 km)

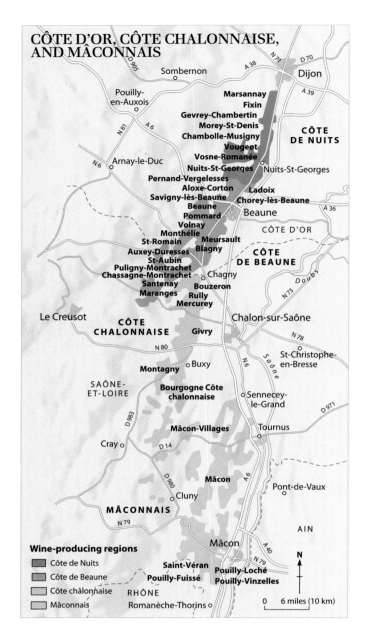

CÔTE D'OR, CÔTE CHALONNAISE, AND MÂCONNAIS

Wine-producing regions
- Côte de Nuits
- Côte de Beaune
- Côte châlonnaise
- Mâconnais

severe winters and hot, dry summers, which is the reason why not all the wines are of comparable quality. The vineyards are located on steep slopes, which are composed of marl and limestone. The altitude varies between 500 and 1,300 ft (150 and 400 m), and the best wines are almost always mid-slope. The local village itself is generally located lower down.

Côte Chalonnaise

This region is the continuation of the last villages of the Côte d'Or to the south. Its geology is similar to the Côte d'Or, with outcrops of limestone and marl, and some steep sites are very exposed; but the clear line of the Côte d'Or here breaks down into a succession of hills and valleys. The wines have generic or regional appellations such as the AOC Bourgogne Côte Chalonnaise. In addition, five villages can use their own names: Bouzeron, Rully, Mercurey, Givry, and Montagny. Red, white, and sparkling wines are produced.

Mâconnais

This vast vineyard area, comprising 17,100 acres (6,920 ha) south of the Côte Chalonnaise, produces AOC Mâcon red and white wines. Several villages are allowed to use their own name; and some, like Pouilly, have acquired an excellent reputation. There are also many limestone hills, perfect for Chardonnay, as well as areas of granite rock with sandy soil, more suitable for Gamay. Near Viré, Clessé, and Lugny, the soil is favorable for light white wines. The highest hills and best slopes are located toward the south of the region. This is where well-known villages develop good white Chardonnays, such as Pouilly-Fuissé and Saint-Véran.

Beaujolais

At 37,065 acres (15,000 ha), this is the largest and southernmost vine-growing area in Burgundy. Beaujolais extends from south of Mâcon to the suburbs of Lyon. Yet it has little in common with the rest of Burgundy, apart from the business network and geographic proximity. Limestone, while dominant elsewhere, gives way here to the granite and igneous rocks of a mountain range separating the Loire River, to the west, from the Saône.

in a style that is much lighter than their prestigious neighbors further south in the rest of Burgundy.

Côte d'Or

Côte d'Or stretches from Dijon in the north to Santenay in the south, via Beaune. The wines produced here are more complex, more expensive, and more lasting than elsewhere in Burgundy. They come from famous villages such as Vosne-Romanée, Pommard, Volnay, Meursault, and Puligny-Montrachet. They often have these appellations of origin, as well as *"climats,"* of which the most notable are classified as *premier cru* and *grand cru*. The region is divided into two parts, Côte de Nuits to the north and Côte de Beaune to the south. The first produces almost exclusively red wine, the second both reds and whites. Côte d'Or takes its name from the Orient: the vines face east to make the most of often limited sunlight. As with Chablis, this area marks the northern limit of viticulture, with long,

DID YOU KNOW...?

Gamay, the main grape of Beaujolais, was at one time banned in Burgundy. In 1395, Philip the Bold banned across Burgundy (and ordered uprooting of) the "very bad and foul Gamay vine, a plant that produces a great abundance of wine [...] which is of the sort that is very harmful to human beings... because it is full of great and terrible bitterness." This edict was hardly enforced, especially since Gamay can make great wines when its yields are controlled, as in Beaujolais!

Here, the Gamay grape dominates. The region is often considered an appellation producing just "thirst-quenching wines" designed to accompany snacks in the bars of Lyon. But it also develops high quality wines, particularly the 10 Beaujolais *crus*, capable of being aged for several years. Even so, the adjective most often used by producers is "drinkable," which usually refers to refreshing, unpretentious wine with fresh grape flavors. Production of white is small-scale, but often of good quality.

Burgundy grape varieties

The three main varieties of Burgundy are well known: two are red, Pinot Noir and Gamay, and one is white, Chardonnay. While Pinot Noir and Chardonnay exist worldwide, Gamay is rarely cultivated elsewhere, except in the Loire Valley. Other grape varieties, such as Sauvignon

> Vines around the hill of Vieille Morte, near the village of Rivolet in Beaujolais.

Gris and Aligoté, are even less common: Aligoté does not exist outside of Burgundy; Sauvignon Gris is found virtually nowhere except St-Bris.

PINOT NOIR. This delicate variety is difficult to cultivate. And Burgundy represents the northern limit of its cultivation, as in Champagne and Jura. Yet here it produces the best results, particularly in Côte d'Or, where the red *grands crus* are among the greatest wines in the world.

GAMAY. This grape has a bad reputation because of overproduction. It is true that, if badly cultivated, it provides diluted and bland wines, where only carbonic maceration (*see next page*) reveals a few flavors. But this does not take into account the fact that if the harvest is restricted, Gamay is able to produce wines that are delicious, fresh and light. Plus, the best Beaujolais wines can come, with ageing, to closely resemble their neighbors from Côte d'Or. The issue is how, if not to replace, at least to supplement it with other varieties, especially in Beaujolais, to tackle global warming. Syrah from neighboring Côtes du Rhône to the south has been suggested.

CHARDONNAY. Which variety seems most closely linked to Burgundy? And yet, if there is a truly international grape, it is Chardonnay. It is particularly fond of limestone, found extensively in Burgundy. It can vary enormously in its flavor profile, depending on the winemaking and soil. For example, Chardonnays from Burgundy aged in wood contain particular notes of butter and toast.

ALIGOTÉ. A simple and rustic grape variety, this is intended to produce thirst-quenching, refreshing, but not too complex, wines. They do, however, have a little more depth and character around the village of Bouzeron, where the wines are described as "Aligoté-Bouzeron."

SAUVIGNON GRIS. This grape variety, originally from the Loire, is present on a small scale, in the Yonne in particular, producing the superb, aromatic whites of St-Bris.

BEAUJOLAIS

Mâcon
SAÔNE-ET-LOIRE
Chasselas
Leynes
Pruzilly
Saint-Vérand
Chânes
St-Mamert
Julliè
St-Amour
Juliénas
Émeringes
Chénas
RHÔNE
Moulin-
à-Vent
La Chapelle-
de-Guinchay
Vauxrenard
Fleurie
Romanèche-Thorins
Les Ardillats
Chiroubles
Villié-Morgon
Lancié
Beaujeu
Morgon
Lantignié
Corcelles
Régnié
BEAUJOLAIS-
VILLAGES
Quincié
Ardières
Cercié
St-Jean-d'Ardières
Marchampt
St-Lager
Belleville
Brouilly
Côte-de-
Brouilly
Charentay
St-Étienne-la-Varenne
Le Perréon
St-Étienne-
des-Oullières
AIN
Vaux
Salles-
Arbuissonnas
Saint-Julien
Montmelas
Arnas
Morgon
Rivolet
Villefranche-
sur-Saône
Denicé
Chamelet
Cogny
Gleizé
Liergues
Létra
BEAUJOLAIS
Saint-Laurent-
d'Oingt
Pommiers
Theizé
Anse
St-Vérand
Lachassagne
Le Bois-d'Oingt
St-Jean-
des-Vignes
Sarcey
Châtillon
Chazay-
d'Azergues
Bully
Turdine

N

0   3 miles (5 km)

Burgundy wine production

RED BURGUNDY. Pinot Noir requires a delicate balance in its maturity, and this needs to be correctly extracted by the wine producer: harvested too early or during cool years, it will result in vegetal flavors and a light wine with excessive acidity; harvested too late or subjected to excessive extraction, it will yield a heavy, alcoholic wine that lacks finesse. Traditionally, portions of the stems (the "skeletons" of the grape clusters) were retained, as these were supposed to give the wine tannic structure; but this practice is no longer common. Oak ageing is now more popular than ever, especially for *grands crus*; but new oak is used less frequently than in Bordeaux. As little wine as possible is extracted from the barrels to avoid any contact with air during maturation. Filtration is also less prevalent than in other regions, such as Bordeaux, for example.

WHITE BURGUNDY. The whites may be less demanding in their development. If it is a *premier* or *grand cru* from the Côte d'Or or Chablis, the wine is produced in small oak barrels. If it is a generic Chablis or Mâcon wine, stainless steel or cement tanks are used to preserve freshness, lightness, and a simple and pleasant fruitiness. This fermentation is sometimes followed by ageing in oak barrels, until the end of malolactic, in order to add some complexity. The wine then remains on its lees, with fining and filtering kept to a minimum. The *grands crus* generally benefit from stirring (mixing of lees with a stick placed in the barrel), which adds complexity, richness, and depth.

> Clos des Barraults (red) and Vignes de Maillonge (white), two Mercureys from the Juillot estate.

Beaujolais Nouveau

Following the development of *vins de primeur* since 1951, Beaujolais Nouveau arrives on tables after the third Thursday of November each year (since 1985). This is a fruity and refreshing young wine, which has no pretensions and brightens up the late fall. It has a bright, purplish, sometimes fluorescent color, and its flavors of exotic fruits and fresh grapes (when it is successful and has little or no chaptalization) go very well with the cooked meats and various other nibbles served up at bars in Lyon or Paris.

THE CASE OF BEAUJOLAIS. To preserve the fresh and delicate flavors of Gamay, winemakers employ a novel technique called "carbonic maceration" (*see also* p.68). This involves fermenting grapes (that have been destemmed but not crushed) in a closed vessel. The weight of the grapes causes the berries to break up gently and gradually, activating their natural yeasts. Carbon dioxide emitted by the fermentation keeps the must under pressure and prevents oxidation of the upper layer. The must is then pressed and extracted, and the two types of juice are blended (with a generally lower proportion of pressed juice) to continue fermentation in stainless steel vats. The wine is then matured in tanks or barrels until bottling in September the following year.

Appellations and *crus*: a complex system

At the bottom of the scale are regional appellations, followed by village or local appellations, then *premiers crus*, and finally *grands crus*.

REGIONAL APPELLATIONS. These cover wines from many vineyards in Burgundy (*e.g.* Bourgogne Passetoutgrain) or wines from a large sub-region (*e.g.* Bourgogne Hautes-Côtes-de-Nuits).

VILLAGE WINE. These are local appellations attached to the *terroir* around a specific village. Thus, the label of a wine produced in the Gevrey-Chambertin commune has the words "*Appellation Gevrey-Chambertin Contrôlée*" written on it. However, some "village" AOCs overlap with nearby villages, and others do not include all the land of the commune. Thus, an AOC Nuits-Saint-Georges wine can come from Premeaux, a nearby village.

PREMIERS CRUS. This name distinguishes certain plots among the villages of the Côte d'Or and Chablis. The label offers the name of the village and the specific plot, for example Gevrey-Chambertin Clos St. Jacques. A *premier cru* wine can

TRUE OR FALSE?

All Burgundy wines are made from a single grape variety.

FALSE. Bourgogne Passetoutgrain is one-third Pinot Noir with the rest Gamay, and generic white Burgundy and Crémant de Bourgogne can include Chardonnay, Pinot Blanc, Aligoté, and Melon de Bourgogne (as well as Sacy in Yonne).

Brotherhood of the Knights of Tastevin

While the name of this famous brotherhood evokes the Middle Ages, it is actually a relatively recent creation. Founded in 1934 by Georges Faiveley and Camille Rodier, its goal was to restore the reputation of Burgundy wines, which had been battered by the crisis of 1929. The Brotherhood owns the famous Château du Clos de Vougeot (but not the vineyards), in which it holds its "chapters," during which new members are inducted. (They now have almost 10,000 worldwide.) It brings together statesmen and men of letters, famous people and enthusiasts—all with the aim of making them ambassadors for Burgundy wines. Since 1950, it has organized selections of Burgundy wines under the name "Tastevinage." This labeling process is rigorous and very modern in its outlook despite the somewhat old-fashioned logo on the bottles!

come from a single site, for example Beaune-Grèves, or be a blend of *premiers crus* from different great sites (such as Beaune Premier Cru without any further indication).

GRANDS CRUS. These are small, but famous appellations; and on labels their name is always followed by the words "Appellation Grand Cru Contrôlée." For example, the *grand cru* Romanée-Saint-Vivant is labeled "Romanée-Saint-Vivant, Appellation Grand Cru Contrôlée." A *grand cru* can straddle several villages; for example, Grand Cru Corton is produced from certain plots in the Aloxe-Corton, Ladoix-Serrigny, and Pernand-Vergelesses districts.

Here is a trick to figure out Burgundy: the shorter the name, the better the wine. Thus, Musigny (*grand cru*) is better than Chambolle-Musigny (a village appellation); Chambertin (*grand cru*) is better than Gevrey-Chambertin (a village appellation), and so on. But alas, there are many exceptions to this rule.

Main market players

As in many other regions, wine production is divided among independent producers, *négociants*, and cooperatives, but with specific features and important differences.

INDEPENDENT WINE PRODUCERS. The great wines of Burgundy have traditionally been expensive, and the prices achieved in recent years have done nothing to change that tradition. Côte d'Or is the home of small independent producers. This is reflected in small lots of handcrafted wines, the fragmentation of the *climats*, and the complexity of

appellations. Bottling in-house has grown significantly since the 1970s. But the small size of plots means that the producers, apart from a few major estates (Leroy, Prieur, and De Vogüé, for example), rarely have older wines for sale. In fact, they may have nothing to offer apart from the most recent harvest. It is the size of the plots that explains the extreme diversity of wines within the same appellation: a small producer is not generally free to blend several plots to counteract a bad or less favorable vintage. Good and bad sit side by side. So the consumer sometimes finds it difficult to figure out, even if helped by labeling systems such as Tastevinage (*see* box left). Prices also act as a reliable guide, and a wine priced significantly lower than its neighbors must be treated carefully and with circumspection. Accordingly, wines from elite wine producers (Chandon de Briailles, Coche-Dury, Comtes Lafon, or Méo-Camuzet, for example) are often expensive and sold mainly abroad and for major events.

BURGUNDY *NÉGOCIANTS*. In Burgundy, wine merchants are not content, as elsewhere, to simply sell wines made by others. We can distinguish ordinary *négociants* from *négociants* who buy grapes, make wine, blend, age, and put it on the market. They have often been criticized for the uniformity of their wines and some poor vintages. But the quantity of wine they produce enables them to precisely control the blending, and erase the imperfections of a wine-producing area as fragmented and capricious as Burgundy. They often have an estate themselves, producing *premiers crus* and *grands crus*, including wines to rival those of elite independent wine producers. But such high standards have a price! Above all, like the estates in Champagne, Burgundy *négociants* provide the bulk of exports.

COOPERATIVES. It would be wrong to think that the independent or individual nature of the wine producers in Burgundy would make them reject cooperatives as a means of production. But they are definitely more important on the periphery, in Chablis, Hautes Côtes, Mâconnais, and Beaujolais, than in Côte d'Or or the heart of Burgundy. Some are excellent, such as La Chablisienne or the Buxy cooperative, producing wines of very high quality. They now have advanced facilities (which are often lacking in independent wine producers) and encourage their members to produce the best possible grapes.

DID YOU KNOW...?

During the late 19th century, several villages in the Côte d'Or were awarded the right to add to their name the name(s) of the grands crus *produced in their locality. Thus, in 1882, Chambolle took the name Chambolle-Musigny, Gevrey became Gevrey-Chambertin, both Puligny and Chassagne villages share the name of their* grand cru, *the famous Montrachet. Aloxe added the name Corton, although this wine is also produced in the villages of Pernand-Vergelesses and Ladoix, while Vosne has naturally benefited from the reputation of Romanée.*

Burgundy AOCS

** *grand cru*   ***** general appellation including *premiers crus*

REGIONAL AND GENERIC APPELLATIONS (produced throughout Burgundy)
- Bourgogne Aligoté
- Bourgogne Rosé or Bourgogne Clairet
- Bourgogne Grand Ordinaire or Bourgogne Ordinaire
- Bourgogne Passetoutgrain
- Crémant de Bourgogne

CHABLIS
- Petit Chablis
- Chablis *
- Chablis Grand Cru **
- Bourgogne Côte-de-St-Jacques

AUXERRE, TONNERROIS, AND VÉZELIEN
- Bourgogne Chitry
- Bourgogne Côtes d'Auxerre
- Bourgogne Coulanges-La-Vineuse
- Bourgogne Épineuil
- Bourgogne Vézelay
- Irancy
- St-Bris

CÔTE DE NUITS
- Bonnes-Mares **
- Bourgogne Hautes-Côtes-de-Nuits
- Bourgogne La Chapelle-Notre-Dame
- Bourgogne Le Chapitre
- Bourgogne Montrecul
- Chambertin **
- Chambertin-Clos de Bèze **
- Chambolle-Musigny *
- Chapelle-Chambertin **
- Charmes-Chambertin **
- Clos de la Roche **
- Clos de Tart **
- Clos de Vougeot **
- Clos des Lambrays **
- Clos St-Denis **
- Côte-de-Nuits-Villages
- Échezeaux **
- Fixin *
- Gevrey-Chambertin *
- Grands Échezeaux **
- Griotte-Chambertin **
- La Grande Rue **
- La Romanée **
- La Tâche **
- Latricières-Chambertin **
- Marsannay
- Mazis-Chambertin **
- Mazoyères-Chambertin **
- Morey-Saint-Denis *
- Musigny **
- Nuits-Saint-Georges or Nuits *
- Richebourg **
- Romanée-Conti **
- Romanée-Saint-Vivant **
- Ruchottes-Chambertin **
- Vosne-Romanée *
- Vougeot *

CÔTE DE BEAUNE
- Aloxe-Corton *
- Auxey-Duresses *
- Bâtard-Montrachet **
- Beaune *
- Bienvenues-Bâtard-Montrachet **
- Blagny *
- Bourgogne Hautes-Côtes de Beaune
- Chassagne-Montrachet *
- Chevalier-Montrachet **
- Chorey-lès-Beaune or Chorey
- Corton **
- Corton-Charlemagne and Charlemagne **
- Côte-de-Beaune
- Côte-de-Beaune-Villages
- Criots-Bâtard-Montrachet **
- Ladoix-Serrigny or Ladoix *
- Maranges *
- Meursault *
- Monthélie *
- Montrachet **
- Pernand-Vergelesses *
- Pommard *
- Puligny-Montrachet *
- St-Aubin *
- St-Romain
- Santenay *
- Savigny-lès-Beaune or Savigny *
- Volnay *

CÔTE CHALONNAISE
- Bourgogne Côte Chalonnaise
- Bourgogne Côtes-du-Couchois
- Bouzeron
- Givry *
- Mercurey *
- Montagny *
- Rully *

MÂCONNAIS
- Mâcon
- Mâcon followed by a village name
- Mâcon Supérieur
- Mâcon-Villages
- Pouilly-Fuissé
- Pouilly-Loché
- Pouilly-Vinzelles
- Saint-Véran
- Viré-Clessé

BEAUJOLAIS
- Beaujolais
- Beaujolais-Villages
- Beaujolais Supérieur
- Brouilly
- Chénas
- Chiroubles
- Côte-de-Brouilly
- Fleurie
- Juliénas
- Morgon
- Moulin-à-Vent
- Régnié
- St-Amour

Best-known wines of Burgundy

Burgundy is fairly homogeneous in terms of wine style, with the exception of red Beaujolais wines. Whites are drier and with greater minerality in the north, richer and more aromatic in Côte d'Or. They are mostly Chardonnay, which gives them, if not an exact likeness, at least a family resemblance. The reds have a greater diversity: there is little in common between a Passetoutgrain and a fine Côte de Nuits.

CRÉMANT DE BOURGOGNE AOC

THE WHOLE REGION

In Burgundy, sparkling wines have been produced since the 19th century; but since 1975 they have been entitled to the appellation Crémant de Bourgogne (if they are produced from wines that undergo a second fermentation in bottle). Without the reputation of their neighbors in Champagne, they generally offer good value for money.

> **GRAPE VARIETIES** Pinot Noir and Gamay (20 per cent maximum) for rosés; Chardonnay (30 percent minimum) with the addition of Aligoté, Melon, or Sacy for whites.

> **SOIL** All Burgundy *terroirs* are suitable, with a preference for calcareous marl, chalky soil as in Champagne, or granite to the south.

> **STYLE** The *blanc de blancs* shows white flowers, citrus, and green apple flavors that evolve with time towards note of white orchard fruit and toast. The *blanc de noirs* presents aromas of berry fruit (cherry, blackcurrant, or raspberry). It is a powerful wine on the palate, long and persistent. Keeping it results in a little more roundness and warmth, with dried fruit flavors that are sometimes honeyed or spicy. The rosé (Pinot Noir, with or without Gamay) is a delicate wine with subtle red fruit flavors.

Color:	Serving temperature:	Ageing potential:
White and rosé.	*39 to 48°F (4 to 9°C) depending on the occasion (as an aperitif or with a meal).*	*3 to 5 years maximum.*

BOURGOGNE PASSETOUTGRAIN AOC

THE WHOLE REGION

This appellation (which is also written "Passe-tout-grain"), established in 1937, applies to red or rosé wines from all over Burgundy. It is produced from up to two-thirds Gamay and one-third Pinot Noir. The grapes are blended in the tank, not as finished wines. In a region that history has led to focus on single-variety wines, it is a sufficiently original trait to be worth noting. Rosé wines, which are less common, must be produced by fermenting grapes, whether crushed or not, without pressing them before fermentation.

> **GRAPE VARIETIES** Pinot Noir and Gamay.

> **SOIL** Pinot Noir is found almost everywhere in Burgundy, Gamay particularly in Mâconnais on siliceous, clay, sandy, or granite soil.

> **STYLE** For red wines, the style varies according to the proportion of Gamay and Pinot, but these are usually fruity, light, "thirst-quenching wines." They can assume a purplish, almost fuchsia hue, and they are full of light in their youth. The rosés are a little more intense in color, with a slight hint of orange; their fruity, delicious flavors evoke gooseberries.

Color:	Serving temperature:	Ageing potential:
Red and rosé.	*54°F (12 °C) for both reds and rosés.*	*3 to 5 years maximum.*

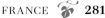

CHABLIS AND PETIT CHABLIS AOC

Before the onset of phylloxera, the Chablis region produced one-third of all Burgundy wines. It is centered round the small town of Chablis, whose dry whites have been well known since the 9th century. This vineyard, the most northerly in Burgundy, is particularly vulnerable to spring frosts. Worldwide, Chablis is synonymous with dry, mineral-laced white wine. Its name has been stolen again and again for anything similar. Petit Chablis AOC, less well known, produces wines that are lighter, with fewer flavors than Chablis… but it's cheaper!

> **GRAPE VARIETY** Chardonnay.
> **SOIL** Kimmeridgian limestone and clay.
> **STYLE** Chablis used to be produced and aged in oak barrels, but these were seldom new. The use of stainless steel tanks for vinification has opened up new horizons. Now oak ageing results in wines that are richer, and sometimes more complex; but Chablis' hazelnut flavor may be found in wine aged in steel tanks, after a few years. If we let the wine age three or four years, it acquires complexity and richness.

Color:
White.

Serving temperature:
50 to 52°F (10 to 11°C).

Ageing potential:
3 to 6 years for Chablis;
4 years at most for Petit Chablis.

CHABLIS GRAND CRU AND CHABLIS PREMIER CRU AOC

The *grands* and *premiers crus* from Chablis are among the finest white wines of Burgundy. The grands crus come from seven "*climats*," and their names come after the words Chablis Grand Cru: Blanchot, Bougros, Les Clos, Grenouilles, Preuses, Valmur, and Vaudésir. More affordable than their counterparts from the Côte de Beaune, they can age longer than regular Chablis irrespective of *cru*, and they gain complexity and richness as they mature. The *premiers crus* are more numerous. Among the best known are Fourchaume, Montée de Tonnerre, Mont de Milieu, Montmains, and Vaucoupin.

> **GRAPE VARIETY** Chardonnay.
> **SOIL** Limestone in which there are still deposits of tiny oysters from the time when a shallow, warm sea covered Burgundy.

STYLE The various *crus* are not always easy to recognize, since their differences are as much based on style of cultivation and wine production as from different *terroirs*. After at least five years in the cellar, a *premier* or *grand cru* from Chablis is a complex yet open wine, where flavors of flint and stone give way to hints of lime, dried fruit, and sometimes of mushrooms.

Color:
White.

Serving temperature:
54 to 57°F (12 to 14°C).

Ageing potential:
10 years for premiers crus;
10 to 15 years (and sometimes more) for grands crus.

Selected Chablis producers

- **La Chablisienne.** This excellent cooperative is responsible for about a third of the production of Chablis. Its wines are always impeccable, and include a selection of the oldest vineyards classed as *premier cru*. Its finest wine is the Château Grenouilles (*grand cru*), which is very rare and much sought after.

- **Château de Béru.** A dynamic, 400-year-old estate. The vineyard, devastated by phylloxera in the early 20th century, was not replanted until 1987. The estate now produces Chablis Clos Béru, a Chablis Premier Cru Vaucoupin, and a top quality "village" Chablis.

- **Domaine Laroche.** One of the biggest estates in Chablis, comprising some 247 acres (100 ha). Its best "village" wine is the Chablis St-Martin. Smart (and wealthy!) wine lovers seek the rare and famous Réserve de 'Obédience, a Grand Cru Chablis from a tiny plot of old vines in Blanchot.

- **William Fèvre.** This *négociant*, a subsidiary of the Beaune estate Bouchard Père & Fils, has the largest area of *grands crus* from this appellation. It is one of the major proponents of new oak for ageing, though this approach has eased in recent years.

FIXIN AOC

This little village, the most northerly of the Côte de Nuits, produces mainly high quality red wines. Though little known to wine lovers, some of them are reminiscent of Gevrey-Chambertin in terms of their character. The appellation includes several *premiers crus*, including Les Hervelets, La Perrière, Le Clos du Chapitre, and Le Clos Napoléon.

> **GRAPE VARIETY** Pinot Noir.

> **SOIL** Brown calcareous soil, fairly homogeneous for the *premiers crus*, with marl in some places (*e.g.* Les Hervelets), as well as a combination of limestone and marl elsewhere.

> **STYLE** The wines are powerful yet delicate, with good tannic structure, but without being too aggressive. They are rather deep in color and suggest aromas that are typical of Pinot Noir (violet, blackcurrant, cherry), developing after a few years to more gamey and spicy notes.

Color:
Red.

Serving temperature:
55 to 59°F (13 to 15°C).

Ageing potential:
10 to 15 years.

GEVREY-CHAMBERTIN AOC

This extensive appellation is one of the most famous in Côte de Nuits, and also one of the most understandable! Here, no *grand cru* has a name that is completely different from the main village. The nine *grands crus*–Chambertin, Charmes-Chambertin, Chambertin-Clos de Bèze, Chapelle-Chambertin, Griotte-Chambertin, Latricières-Chambertin, Mazis-Chambertin, Mazoyères-Chambertin, and Ruchottes-Chambertin total 215 acres (87 ha), more than from any other village. Napoleon was reputed to drink only Clos de Bèze wines—diluted, they say, with water. There also are no fewer than 26 *premiers crus*.

> **GRAPE VARIETY** Pinot Noir.

> **SOIL** Hard rock, covered with a thin layer of brown silt on top. Marl and limestone are on the slopes.

> **STYLE** The best Gevrey-Chambertins are powerful, fruity, and tannic, with a structure that will last. The wines have a bright color when young, ranging from dark red to black cherry. On the nose, notes of cassis, cherry, and raspberry evolve over time into cocoa, coffee, and hints of damp woodlands. In the mouth, full and fleshy textures dominate. The *grands crus* here rarely disappoint, but fragmentation sometimes leads to variable quality. Some *premiers crus*, including the famous Clos-St-Jacques, can compete with *grands crus*.

Color:
Red.

Serving temperature:
57 to 61°F (14 to 16°C).

Ageing potential:
10 to 30 years.

MOREY-ST-DENIS AOC

This small village rests between two famous neighbors (Gevrey-Chambertin and Chambolle-Musigny). The vineyards lie on a limestone hill that runs from Gevrey to Vougeot. Two of the *grands crus* around the village are from old walled monastery cloisters that are typical of Burgundy: Clos de Tart (which is a monopole) and Clos St-Denis, as well as the Clos de la Bussiere Premier Cru. The other *grands crus* are the Clos de la Roche and Clos des Lambrays, and part of Bonnes-Mares (the other part being on Chambolle-Musigny). Morey-St-Denis Burgundy develops red wines that are to be laid down in the classic, solid, and well-structured style of Côte de Nuits. Because it is not well known by the general public, this appellation represents good value for money, at least in comparison to its prestigious neighbors.

> **GRAPE VARIETY** Pinot Noir.

> **SOIL** Clay-and-limestone.

> **STYLE** Depending on their origin, the red wines of Morey derive their full-bodied nature from Gevrey-Chambertin in some cases, while others gain their delicacy from Chambolle. Overall, these are wines with class and power, including a rich bouquet of violets and strawberry, which sometimes also is reminiscent of truffles.

Color:
Red.

Serving temperature:
57 to 61°F (14 to 16°C).

Ageing potential:
10 to 30 years.

CHAMBOLLE-MUSIGNY AOC

In 1878, only the commune of Chambolle was allowed to append its name to that of its most famous *climat*, Musigny, which overlooks the Clos de Vougeot. A former stronghold of Cîteaux Abbey, Chambolle-Musigny has two *grands crus*: Bonnes-Mares (shared with Morey-St-Denis) and Musigny. Lighter than the Chambertins, the red wines of Chambolle-Musigny have an admirable bouquet and sweetness; and they are usually considered the finest, most delicate, and most elegant of the Côte de Nuits. The very timbre of the name of the village conjures up a sense of elegance and lightness when you say it. The *premier crus* are also top quality, the best being Les Amoureuses, located below the plots of Musigny. White Musigny is found only occasionally.

> **GRAPE VARIETY** Pinot Noir.

> **SOIL** Limestone, often mixed with clay marl.

> **STYLE** Restrained power, combined with elegance: this is the hallmark of the best wines of the village, which are some of the greatest reds from Burgundy. They are less tannic and less structured than the wines of Morey-St-Denis and Gevrey-Chambertin. They have a potent violet and red berry nose in their early years, giving way with age to riper, spicier, more gamey aromas (such as prunes, truffles, and damp woodland).

Color:
Red.

Serving temperature:
57 to 61°F (14 to 16°C).

Ageing potential:
10 to 20 years.

VOUGEOT AOC

Clos de Vougeot is probably the most famous or the flagship Burgundy wine, although its dispersal among multiple owners with small plots (80 owners across 124 acres/50 ha) can result in quite different wines depending on their location and the work of the producer. But the appellation, which owes its name to the Vouge, a small local river, is more than just that famous Clos, owned by Cîteaux Abbey from the 12th century, whose medieval castle is the headquarters of the Brotherhood of Knights Tastevin of Burgundy (*see box* p.278). It develops a small amount of white wine, too—in particular the Clos Blanc Premier Cru (sometimes called Vigne Blanche), which is quite rare in Côte de Nuits.

> **GRAPE VARIETIES** Pinot Noir for red; Chardonnay for white.

> **SOIL** Brown, calcareous, rather thin soils at the top of the hills; marl clay and limestone lower down on the hills.

> **STYLE** Vougeot reds have a dark color, almost purple when young, as well as a powerful, rich, almost sweet flavor at that age, enhanced by a bouquet of violets and berries (blackcurrant). This distinct combination, elements of which are present in other wines, albeit less systematically, enables them to be recognized. While not the most subtle Burgundy wines, they are full-bodied and generous in the mouth and have a velvety texture. The white wines are rather dry, with a floral bouquet (of hawthorn and acacia) enhanced with notes of toast. The mouth can be quite mineral, similar to Aloxe-Corton wines, in a lighter style than the great whites of the Côte de Beaune. It develops a more spicy and full-bodied flavor after a few years.

Color:
Red and white.

Serving temperature:
54 to 55°F (12 to 13°C) for the whites;
57 to 61°F (14 to 16°C) for the reds.

Ageing potential:
5 to 10 years for the whites;
10 to 20 years for the reds.

VOSNE-ROMANÉE AOC

This appellation is bordered by Nuits-St-Georges to the south, and Chambolle-Musigny and Vougeot to the north, around and above the charming villages of Vosne-Romanée and Flagey-Échezeaux. It includes no fewer than eight *grand crus*, including La Romanée-Conti (*see* pp.288–9), held as a monopole with La Tâche by the estate that bears its name. Some *grands crus* are tiny in size (La Romanée and La Grande Rue, promoted from *premier cru* status in 1992), but the others are not much larger in area (Richebourg, Romanée-St-Vivant, Échezeaux, Grands Échezeaux).

However, this does not prevent them from being divided between multiple owners. The *grands crus* and *premiers crus* are grouped above the village plots. These *grands crus* achieve the highest prices for Burgundy wines, in particular those sold by Domaine de la Romanée-Conti. Fortunately, some *premiers crus*, like Les Malconsorts, Les Suchots, Les Chaumes, Aux Brûlées, and Les Beaux Monts, are excellent and produce outstanding wines that, in good years, can rival the *grands crus*.

> **GRAPE VARIETY** Pinot Noir.

> **SOIL** Calcareous soils often mixed with clay loam, with the depth varying from an inch or two to three or four feet at most.

> **STYLE** The *grands crus* are always rich, heady, and opulent, especially those of the Domaine de la Romanée-Conti. Tannic structure is a common characteristic of wines from Vosne-Romanée, as well as their richness and character, both smooth and powerful. After a few years, their tertiary bouquet develops, revealing aromas of spice, leather, damp woodlands, and violets.

Color:
Red.

Serving temperature:
57 to 61°F (14 to 16°C).

Ageing potential:
10 to 30 years, and beyond for grands crus in the best vintages.

Selected Côte de Nuits producers

Should we prefer wines from independent producers to those from a *négociant*? Such is the dilemma facing those who are fans of the great Burgundies. The former may be exceptional, but cannot be found. The latter are not always the most successful of the appellation, nor the most affordable, but they generally have constant quality. One solution may be to focus on wines from the private estates of the *négociant*, which are generally very high quality, because they constitute a kind of "calling card."

• **Domaine Faiveley:** Les Damodes. A Nuits-St-Georges Premier Cru AOC produced in a manner that is both modern (cold maceration) and traditional, without too much new oak, is a wine with deep color that comes from one of the best Nuits *premiers crus* (there are no *grands crus*).

• **Domaine Liger-Belair:** Richebourg Grand Cru AOC. In 2001, Thibault Liger-Belair decided to re-establish the vineyards of this estate, founded in 1720, which had previously been in a sharecropping system. He converted the estate to biodynamics after a few years, with the sole objective of elevating of its soil. Just try his wonderful Richebourg to be convinced that he has succeeded.

• **Domaine Méo-Camuzet:** Clos de Vougeot Grand Cru AOC. This beautiful family estate in Vosne-Romanée produces one of the best Vougeots, a rich, complex, and concentrated wine. The excellent location of its plot, at the top of the Clos, near the castle, makes this not at all surprising.

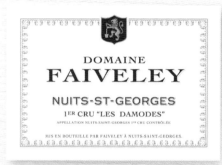

NUITS-ST-GEORGES AOC

The small town that gave its name to the Côte de Nuits was for a long time the rival of Beaune in the wine trade. While it still has a few large *négociants* (Faiveley, Labouré-Roi), the field today is dominated by Beaune. The vineyards are distributed from Nuits-St-Georges to Premeaux-Prissey along a 4.5-mile (7-km) strip on the hillsides, which explains their diversity. They are almost all red, predominantly from Pinot Noir (98 percent). Some Chardonnays still exist (less than two percent), and they provide remarkable white wines, albeit in very small numbers. There is no *grand cru* but 40 *premiers crus*. Nuits-St-Georges has its own hospice, just like Beaune. Much more modest in size, it has a beautiful vineyard of 21.7 acres (8.8 ha). Hospice wines are very good quality.

> **GRAPE VARIETIES** Pinot Noir for reds; Chardonnay for whites.

> **SOIL** This consists of alluvial scree on the north slope, with marl clay and limestone to the south, all on a limestone bedrock.

> **STYLE** Depending on whether they are from the north, near Vosne, or the south, around Premeaux, the reds have a distinct character: they are more opulent and perfumed in the north (the Premier Cru Les Damodes is from near Vosne-Romanée), and more aromatic and robust to the south, partly due to the heavier soil. Generally full-bodied, these wines are intense in color, sometimes almost mauve. They offer red fruit, blackcurrant, and licorice flavors when young, progressing to leather and truffle as they age. Whites, which are quite rare, have a nice golden color after a year or two, and brioche aromas that turn to white flowers.

Color:
Red and white.

Serving temperature:
54 to 55°F (12 to 13°C) for the whites;
57 to 61°F (14 to 16°C) for the reds.

Ageing potential:
4 to 8 years for the whites;
5 to 10 years for the reds.

ALOXE-CORTON AOC

The village of Aloxe-Corton is dominated by the hill of Corton and its two *grands crus*: Corton (the only red *grand cru* in the Côte de Beaune, and the largest in Burgundy) and Corton-Charlemagne (whites only). It is said that the vineyard of Corton-Charlemagne was the personal property of the emperor Charlemagne, who donated it to the collegiate church at Saulieu in 775 AD. Other, more or less apocryphal, stories are reported regarding this legendary wine, the first of which claims Charlemagne must have preferred it because it would not stain his beard…

> **GRAPE VARIETIES** Pinot Noir for the reds; Chardonnay for the whites.

> **SOILS** Corton occupies the eastern slope of the hill, Corton-Charlemagne the south and southwest slopes. There is lighter soil at higher levels, with a high percentage of chalk. The bottom of the hill produces wines that are less powerful and more flexible.

> **STYLE** The reds are very tannic when young, and powerfully aromatic. They have a strong regional flavor, from which fruity and spicy notes emerge after several years in bottle. One should not drink these before they are five years old. The whites are among the best in the world, with a spicy bouquet. They are very mineral when young, but really start to open up and reveal the subtle aromas of hazelnut and spice after five years. They should be kept for 15 or 20 years.

Color:
Red and white.

Serving temperature:
54 to 57°F (12 to 14°C) for the whites;
57 to 61°F (14 to 16°C) for the reds.

Ageing potential:
10 to 20 years for the whites;
10 to 30 years for the reds.

LADOIX-SERRIGNY AOC

The most important village of the Côte de Beaune, Ladoix includes Aloxe-Corton and Pernand Vergelesses along with Corton and Corton-Charlemagne *grands crus* on its beautiful hills. Recently, the INAO elevated some *climats* to *premier cru* status, including Hautes-Mourottes, which produces red wine in a style reminiscent of the *premiers crus* of Aloxe. White wines are less common (20 percent of production), but of good quality.

> **GRAPE VARIETIES** Pinot Noir for the reds; Chardonnay for the whites.
> **SOIL** Consists of gravel, limestone, and some marl.
> **STYLE** The best reds are reminiscent of Corton, without acquiring the fullness and body of that *grand cru*. They have a fleshy body and more delicate flavors—raspberry and cherry, but also spices and cocoa as the reds age. Whites can be confusing, with buttery notes and more vegetal flavors. They do not, however, have the richness and power of the great whites from closer to Beaune.

Color:
Red and white.

Serving temperature:
52 to 54°F (11 to 12°C) for the whites;
57 to 61°F (14 to 16°C) for the reds.

Ageing potential:
5 to 10 years for the whites;
10 to 15 years for the reds.

BEAUNE AOC

The charming medieval town of Beaune has become wealthy as a result of the Côte d'Or wine trade over the centuries, and it shows! A tourist, as well as a cultural, attraction, it becomes the center of the region in connection with the auction at the Hospices de Beaune on the third Sunday in November (*see p.272*). It is a large appellation of some 790 acres (320 ha), with many *premier crus*—some of which can almost rival *grands crus* (Clos des Mouches, Clos du Roi, and the Vigne de l'Enfant-Jésus from the *négociant* Bouchard Père & Fils on the *climat* of Grèves). It mainly produces reds (98 percent). Among the rare whites, some are outstanding, such as the Joseph Drouhin Clos des Mouches, if you have the chance to taste it.

> **GRAPE VARIETIES** Pinot Noir for the reds; Chardonnay for the whites.
> **SOIL** Between 680 and 980 ft (200 and 300 m) in altitude, the AOC has a limestone base with thin brown soils, marls interspersed with iron oxide, and clay-limestone soil at the foot of the hill.
> **STYLE** The reds are powerful and feature a rich, aromatic spectrum (black and red fruits), supported by rather elegant tannins. They evolve into typically Burgundian flavors of damp woodland and truffle accented with a touch of spice. The whites are more straightforward and easier to drink, with the exception of *premiers crus* that can sometimes, at their best, compete with their neighbors from Puligny and Chassagne.

Color:
Red and white.

Serving temperature:
54 to 57°F (12 to 14°C) for the whites;
57 to 61°F (14 to 16°C) for the reds.

Ageing potential:
5 to 10 years for the whites;
6 to 10 years for the reds.

POMMARD AOC

A name that is almost synonymous with the great wines of Burgundy, this village produces exclusively red wines, but does not have a *grand cru*. The vineyards, bordered to the south by Volnay and to the north by Beaune, consist of a wide strip. The *premiers crus* (27 *climats*) are almost all around the village of Pommard, and Les Épenots and Les Rugiens are generally regarded as the best. The appellation, which was granted in 1936, was among the first in the region.

> **GRAPE VARIETY** Pinot Noir.
> **SOIL** Clay-and-limestone. Alluvial rock and stony debris with brown limestone soil, sometimes containing iron oxide.
> **STYLE** The wines are deep colored, with intense flavors and concentration that allows them to improve. The bouquet has notes of fruit (blackcurrant, currant, cherry) and evolves with time into more gamey aromas (such as damp woodland, leather, and chocolate).

Color:
Red.

Serving temperature:
57 to 61°F (14 to 16°C).

Ageing potential:
5 to 15 years.

VOLNAY AOC

The village is located high on the hillside, with the vineyards stretching from one side to the other and below. Volnay is bordered to the southwest by Meursault and Monthélie, and to the northeast by Pommard. The appellation produces only red wines (whites are entitled to the appellation Meursault). The *premiers crus*—Caillerets, Champans, Clos des Chênes, and Clos des Ducs— are renowned for a quality of wine that highlights finesse and sensitivity.

Santenots, another *premier cru*, is found nearby in the commune of Meursault, although it falls within the Volnay AOC.

> **GRAPE VARIETY** Pinot Noir.

> **SOIL** Mostly limestone at the top of the hill, the soils are stonier on the mid and lower slopes.

> **STYLE** A delicate perfume of violet and strawberry emerges from Volnay when it is young; and while age brings greater complexity (with plum and spice notes)

and greater softness, it does not detract from its natural elegance, even if it fades a little.

Color: Red.	**Serving temperature:** 57 to 61°F (14 to 16°C).	**Ageing potential:** 5 to 15 years.

MONTHÉLIE AOC

This old village with a castle is perched on the hill at Meursault. It was long operated by the Abbey of Cluny. The Burgundians typically pronounce the name "montli," as if they were quickly finishing a drink. It is true that until the mid-1980s, the village wines (mostly red) were regarded as rustic and unpretentious. Since then, talented winemakers have taken advantage of the potential of their plots, and the best wines have developed character, structure, and flavor, and are

now sought after on account of their good value. The best known of the nine *premiers crus* from Monthélie are Sur la Velle and Les Champs Fulliot.

> **GRAPE VARIETIES** Pinot Noir for the reds; Chardonnay for the whites.

> **SOIL** A limestone base covered with marl and red clay.

> **STYLE** The reds are quite light, rather like their light relatives or neighbors from Volnay. The nose is delicate, often with notes of black and red fruits, and

is sometimes accented with flowers (peony, violet). It evolves with age to damp woodland and spice notes. The tannins are mild and often supple, even when the wines are young. The whites are reminiscent of Meursault to an extent, but are lighter and less concentrated, with a more floral and less complex nose, at least when young.

Color: Red and white.	**Serving temperature:** 50 to 54°F (10 to 12°C) for the whites; 57 to 61°F (14 to 16°C) for the reds.	**Ageing potential:** 5 to 10 years for the reds and the whites.

AUXEY-DURESSES AOC

Auxey-Duresses (pronounced "ossai") is a former possession of the Abbey of Cluny, situated in a narrow valley that rises in the Hautes Côtes between Meursault (to the south), Monthélie (to the north), and St-Romain (to the west). Before the AOC establishment, wines from this small village were sometimes sold as Volnay or Pommard. The pleasant wines produced here, especially the

reds (but with a significant proportion of whites), are generally sold at quite modest prices for wines from the Côte de Beaune.

> **GRAPE VARIETIES** Pinot Noir (70 percent) for the reds; Chardonnay for the whites.

> **SOIL** On the Monthélie side, marl limestone on a stony base for the red *terroirs*; finer limestone is the soil for

the whites, on the *climats* of Val and Mount Mélian.

> **STYLE** The *premiers crus*, like Les Duresses and Clos du Val, can produce fine reds with raspberry flavors, leading to a comparison with some Volnays. The best whites, with a delicious toast and hazelnut note, have no reason to envy Meursault, since they have enough body, but should be consumed younger.

Color: Red and white.	**Serving temperature:** 54 to 57°F (12 to 14°C) for the whites; 57 to 61°F (14 to 16°C) for the reds.	**Ageing potential:** 5 to 10 years for the whites and the reds.

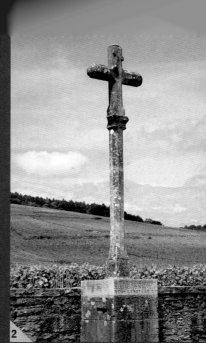

1. Vineyards and village of
   Vosne-Romanée.
2. The cross in the middle of
   the vines is the symbol of the
   estate.
3. In the cellar.
4. The term "monopole"
   indicates that a single estate is
   responsible for the production
   of this *grand cru*.
5. Oak barrels at the winery.

Romanée-Conti

At the heart of the **Côte de Nuits**, this modest plot of land, covering around 4.5 acres (1.8 ha), enjoys worldwide prestige. The red wine produced in Romanée-Conti has long held legendary status, so that it is talked about more than it is actually consumed.

ANCIENT HISTORY
The Romans had noticed the extraordinary potential of the soil in this region. Later, **Cistercian monks** made the same observation; and from 1512, the limits of the *cru* were established. In 1760, the **Prince de Conti**, a Burgundian and adviser to **King Louis XV**, bought the plot at an exorbitant price. During the French Revolution, the prince was dispossessed of his domain, and it was sold in 1792 as a national asset. It is after this event that the vineyard acquired its final name: **Romanée-Conti**.

TERROIR MAKES ALL THE DIFFERENCE
Wine from Romanée-Conti demonstrates the importance of *terroir*. On this tiny area of land, with the same grape variety used throughout Burgundy—**Pinot Noir**—unique scents and flavors are revealed. Its immediate neighbors, just a few yards away, are treated with the same care and the same methods, and certainly produce remarkable wines, yet they are nonetheless very different. It is a longstanding situation and a complete mystery. Facing the east, on a slightly sloping plot, the vineyard benefits from perfect exposure and drainage. Pinot Noir feels at home here and finds its fullest expression. For many years, everything had been done to retain the original vines; but after the harvest of 1945, long ravages of phylloxera forced the owners to completely uproot and replant—as elsewhere, with rootstocks resistant to the parasite. Thus, between 1946 and 1951 inclusive, there was no Romanée-Conti.

FROM VINE TO CELLAR: A FAULTLESS PROCESS
Today, Aubert de Villaine and Henry-Frédéric Roch, joint owners of the estate,

operate the vineyard based on the principles of biodynamics. For it is in the vineyard that it all begins: with healthy and ripe grapes. Nothing is forced with the use of chemicals that could facilitate the work, but would deplete the soil and vines. The essential treatments carried out are sparing, punctual, and natural; and yields are kept under strict control.

At harvest time, each cluster is tested: any suspect or insufficiently mature berries are removed. Depending on circumstances, the grapes are only slightly or not de-stemmed and fermentation continues easily until it is complete. The wine is then aged for at least 18 months in new oak barrels from the forest of Tronçais.

Once bottled—in addition to 750 ml bottles, some magnums and jeroboams are used—the wine stays one more year in the cool cellars at the estate, before being offered to handpicked enthusiasts and hundreds of wine merchants. They then take responsibility for the slow and indispensable ageing process. An impeccable wine cellar is necessary because this wine is demanding and admits no compromise. From a good year, it will keep at least 20 years; from a great year, it will keep for 30 years, 40 years, or more.

DIAMOND WITH A THOUSAND FACETS

To fully appreciate this legendary wine, it should be served at 61°F (16°C). There is no need to decant it. For older vintages, which will contain sediment, simply turn the bottle slowly upright two days before serving and pour the wine into glasses, avoiding abrupt movement. The glass should be made of very thin crystal and tulip-shaped to enjoy its wonderful bouquet. At its peak, the wine of Romanée-Conti is a unique combination of density and delicacy. The nose has extraordinary complexity, with hints of dark fruit, macerated cherry, blueberry, damp woodland, light tobacco; then there are hints of wood, sweet spice, old rose, Russian leather, and truffle. In the mouth, the richness is tender, delicate, soft, and smooth; and the wine lasts a long time without fading at all, but with a light touch of flowers and licorice. After Mozart, the silence that follows is still Mozart.

MEURSAULT AOC

This village is synonymous with rich and fleshy white wines, where Chardonnay is at its best and produces an iconic Burgundy. Meursault has no *grands crus*, but an impressive number of *premiers crus* (Les Charmes, Les Perrières, Les Gouttes d'Or, etc.), a total of 21. Production is sometimes of variable quality; so we must rely primarily on named producer (apart from the *premiers crus*). The idea of producing red wine (less than four percent of the vines) would seem ridiculous were it not for the wonderful Clos de Mazeray, from Domaine Jacques Prieur. The reds are also entitled to use the appellation Blagny, after the nearby hamlet of that name. The latter may also sell its whites under the appellation Meursault or Puligny-Montrachet, depending on where they originate.

> **GRAPE VARIETIES** Pinot Noir for the reds; Chardonnay for the whites.

> **SOIL** Calcareous marls.

> **STYLE** About 96 percent of the wines are white. The *premiers crus* produce the finest and most concentrated wines, while the *vins de village* have less character. These wines have strong and persistent flavors, and can age and improve remarkably. The bouquet is delicate when young, with floral and plant tones (ferns, lime, white flowers), but develops toward more pronounced notes of hazelnut and dried fruit, honey, and characteristic buttery notes. In the mouth, richness often dominates; but a proper Meursault can keep the balance necessary for freshness—a restrained, yet clearly crisp context. The red wines are similar to wines from Blagny and a few Volnays (in terms of smoothness), but rather unusual due to the very small quantities produced. You really have to want to make red Meursault.

Color:	Serving temperature:	Ageing potential:
White and red.	54 to 57°F (12 to 14°C) for the whites; 57 to 61°F (14 to 16°C) for the reds.	5 to 10 years for the reds; 10 to 15 years for the whites.

PULIGNY AND CHASSAGNE AOCs

These two picture-postcard communes are home to the most famous white wines in Burgundy (and the world). These are the *grand crus* from Montrachet (pronounced "mown-rah-shay"): Le Montrachet, Chevalier-Montrachet, Bienvenues-Bâtard-Montrachet, Bâtard-Montrachet, and Criots-Bâtard-Montrachet. Le Montrachet covers just under 20 acres (7.99 ha), and few owners possess more than a couple of acres of it. This shows the rarity of this wine, which has a smooth, penetrating, and haunting bouquet that very few enthusiasts can boast of ever having tasted. Only the top experts can distinguish the Chevalier-Montrachet from its fuller-bodied neighbor, and if Le Montrachet outstrips its neighbors, it is by a short head. Besides the *grands crus*, the two municipalities produce red and white *vins de village* for the Chassagne-Montrachet and Puligny-Montrachet AOCs. Curiously, Chassagne-Montrachet is better known for its reds, which are certainly worthy of note, than for its whites, which nonetheless represent 60 percent of its production.

> **GRAPE VARIETIES** Pinot Noir for the reds; Chardonnay for the whites.

> **SOIL** A limestone base is sometimes covered with reddish marls or thin and stony soils.

> **STYLE** The white *grands crus* are powerful and need to be left to develop: it is unwise to open them before five years, and they can be enjoyed at their best after 10 years. Their bouquet is rich and heady with notes of butter, gingerbread, hazelnut, and dried fruit. A richness and creaminess are evident in the mouth, always with a nice balance from crisp acidity, which give these wines a significant freshness that you would not necessarily expect. The *premiers crus* are generally excellent; for Puligny, Les Pucelles and Les Caillerets are noteworthy; for Chassagne, En Remilly. The reds are powerful and tannic, with flavors of red or black fruit (cherry and blackcurrant). Clos Pitois, Morgeot, and La Maltroye are among the best *premiers crus* from Chassagne. They are often good value for money.

Color:	Serving temperature:	Ageing potential:
White and red.	54 to 57°F (12 to 14°C) for the whites; 57 to 61°F (14 to 16°C) for the reds.	5 to 15 years for the reds; 10 to 30 years for the whites.

SANTENAY AND MARANGES AOCs

At the southern end of the Côte de Beaune, red wine dominates the landscape. There are several *premiers crus* that produce wines that are somewhat rustic, and have a pronounced regional character. They should not be kept for too long, but should be consumed between five and 10 years. The Santenay AOC has several towns and hamlets, and shares the appellation of Santenay with Remigny. The Maranges AOC is shared by three villages: Dezize-lès-Maranges, Sampigny-lès-Maranges, and Cheilly-lès-Maranges, and it has six *premiers crus*.

> **GRAPE VARIETIES** Pinot Noir for the reds; Chardonnay (13 percent) for the whites.

> **SOIL** The top of the hills consist of limestone soil, while further down, this is mixed with marl.

> **STYLE** The reds combine floral characters (peony, violet) and red fruit with hints of licorice. The tannins are firm, sometimes a bit rustic, with a real fullness in the mouth. The whites are vigorous and refreshing, with mineral and floral tones developing into dried fruits and herbaceous notes.

Color:
White and red.

Serving temperature:
50 to 54°F (10 to 12°C) for the whites;
57 to 61°F (14 to 16°C) for the reds.

Ageing potential:
5 to 10 years for the reds and whites.

Selected Côte de Beaune producers

- **Domaine Chandon de Briailles:** white Corton, Corton Grand Cru AOC. A lovely estate in Savigny, it's owned by the Nicolay family, which has very nice plots in Corton, especially in Bressandes. It produces very fine wines—very traditional. They need to be set aside to mature in order to enjoy them fully.

- **Domaine Drouhin:** Clos des Mouches, Beaune Premier Cru AOC. Purchased plot by plot in the 1920s, this Beaune producer tends one of best *premiers crus* of the appellation, for both white and red.

- **Domaine Jacques Prieur:** Clos Santenots, Volnay Premier Cru AOC. This 52-acre (21 ha) estate, taken over in recent years by the Labruyère family, has plots in the greatest *terroirs* of Burgundy, including a plot of Le Montrachet. Its Volnay Clos des Santenots has both balance and finesse.

- **Maison Louis Jadot:** Clos Malta, Santenay Premier Cru AOC. This wine, which comes from the Jadot estate, is fresh and powerful without the hardiness occasionally found in Santenays. It comes in white and red. Louis Jadot also distributes the Domaine du Duc de Magenta, with a good selection of *premiers crus* in Chassagne and Puligny.

- **Domaine Leflaive:** Les Pucelles, Puligny-Montrachet Premier Cru AOC. The most beautiful estate for whites in the Côte de Beaune, it is operated entirely by biodynamics under the management of Anne-Claude Leflaive, assisted by Pierre Morey. Its *premiers crus* are almost as good as a *grand cru*, and Les Pucelles is certainly the best. Unfortunately the prices are far from affordable.

- **Domaine Louis Latour:** Corton Grancey, Corton Grand Cru AOC. Purchased in 1749 from Count Grancey, this is the seat of the estate. Corton from the Latour family has been allowed to add "Grancey" after the name Corton. Corton-Charlemagne Grand Cru from the estate is also top quality.

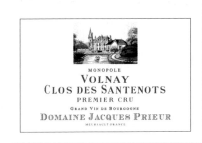

MERCUREY AOC

Mercurey is one of five appellations in the Côte Chalonnaise (along with Bouzeron, Rully, Givry, and Montagny) and certainly the most prestigious. It spans two communes, Mercurey and St-Martin-sous-Montaigu. Here, reds dominate (though there are some whites) in 1,581-acre (640-ha) vineyard area: three times larger than the one in Rully, to the north. This appellation has large, well-managed estates and a number of *négociants* (Antonin Rodet is the most well-known). A Mercurey from a good producer can represent excellent value for money (for a Burgundy, that is) and can be aged for several years. Some *terroirs* have been classified as *premiers crus* by the INAO (32 *climats* have been so classified); but others, including unclassified *climats*, have an excellent reputation. The best vineyards include Clos du Roy, Clos Voyen, Les Champs Martin, Clos des Barrault, and Clos l'Evêque.

> **GRAPE VARIETIES** Pinot Noir for red wines; Chardonnay and Aligoté for white wines.

> **SOIL** Outcrops of limestone and marl.

> **STYLE** The white wines are refreshing, with a hint of minerality as well as floral and spicy flavors. Although much more affordable than their neighbors in Côte d'Or, they are less complex and less powerful. The reds are firm but delicate when young, with flavors reminiscent of raspberry, strawberry, or cherry. With age, they develop spicy and gamey characters.

Color:
Red and white.

Serving temperature:
50 to 54°F (10 to 12°C) for the whites;
57 to 61°F (14 to 16°C) for the reds.

Ageing potential:
3 to 6 years for the whites;
4 to 8 years for the reds.

Selected Côte Chalonnaise producers

- **Comte de Ternay: Château de Rully, Rully AOC.** The former medieval castle dominates this appellation, not only because of its location but also in terms of the quality of its wines. Distributed by the key Côte Chalonnaise *négociant* Antonin Rodet, there are whites and reds, but it is the whites that are of most interest in the way they balance finesse and richness.

- **Domaine Faiveley: La Framboisière, Mercurey AOC.** This beautiful Côte de Nuits estate also owns vineyards in Mercurey, notably among the finest *premiers crus* (Clos du Roy and Clos des Myglands). La Framboisière is aptly named, as it is a delicious wine that brings to mind raspberries and red fruit. It is typically velvety.

- **Domaine De Villaine: Aligoté-Bouzeron, Bouzeron AOC.** The manager of the Domaine de la Romanée-Conti operates this beautiful estate of approximately 50 acres (20 ha) with his wife. Two-thirds of its production is white. The Aligoté produced here has an unexpected vigor and depth, something that owes as much to the rigor of Aubert de Villaine as to the *terroir*.

- **Marquis de Jouennes d'Herville: Château de Chamirey, Mercurey AOC.** This old estate of 100 acres (40 ha) (including 10 *premiers crus*) is a one of the finest distributed by *négociant* Antonin Rodet. Its red Mercurey is delicate and delicious, and represents a good introduction to regional production.

- **Michel Juillot: Clos des Barraults, Mercurey Premier Cru AOC.** A beautiful family estate of nearly 79 acres (32 ha), located mainly in Mercurey. Harvesting here is carried out by hand, and the wine production process is very traditional. Its white Mercurey Premier Cru, a superb combination of richness and freshness, is remarkable.

Selected Mâconnais producers

- **Domaine Cordier: Vieilles Vignes, Pouilly-Fuissé AOC.** This wine displays a beautiful complexity of flavors—revealing hints of vanilla and white flowers leading on to honey, with just enough richness and liveliness to support it.

- **Domaine Guffens-Heynen: Mâcon-Pierreclos AOC.** A tiny but hugely successful estate, established in 1976 by a Belgian couple that apparently had not forgotten that Flanders and Burgundy were once united. The Mâcon (white) is exceptionally similar to its northern neighbors, and renowned worldwide.

- **Domaine Jacques et Nathalie Saumaize:** Produced from a 50-year-old vineyard and aged in wood, these elegant wines have no shortage of depth, with a nice balance between richness and freshness.

- **Domaine de la Bongran: Tradition, Viré-Clessé AOC.** Jean Thévenet has demonstrated that you can harvest late in Mâconnais, which has often landed him in trouble with the AOC authorities. However, he continues to produce particularly original wines.

MÂCON AND MÂCON-VILLAGES AOCs

MÂCONNAIS

The Mâconnais is the heart of southern Burgundy. It spans some 40 miles between the end of the Côte Chalonnaise and the famous Solutré Rock. The region is further south than the Côte d'Or, and the climate is gentler. The red wines are entitled to the Mâcon AOC (or the Mâcon-Supérieur, if they have an additional degree of alcohol). They are often produced from Gamay, although Pinot Noir may be used. White should be produced from 100 percent Chardonnay. Twenty villages have the right to include their name alongside the AOC. This is the case for Chardonnay, Lugny Prissé, Igé, Loché, La Roche-Vineuse, and Pierreclos

in particular. The Mâcon-Villages AOC is for white wines only. The new Viré-Clessé appellation (689 acres/279 ha) replaced the Mâcon-Viré and Mâcon-Clessé AOC in 2002.

> **GRAPE VARIETIES** Gamay and Pinot Noir for reds; Chardonnay for whites.
> **SOIL** Pinot likes brown calcareous soils, while Gamay prefers granite soils similar to those of Beaujolais. Sandy, clay, or silica soils will be better suited to Chardonnay.
> **STYLE** The whites are quite variable, depending on whether they are aged in wood or stainless steel vats. In the first case, they gain in complexity and

richness for they can lose in terms of freshness and liveliness. In the second instance, the emphasis is on fruit character and simplicity. This style is more representative of white Mâcon: pale, fresh, light, and clean. It whets the appetite without tiring it. Reds made from Pinot Noir are entitled to the appellation Bourgogne (or that of Passetoutgrain, if they contain the required proportion of Gamay). As for rosés, they are rich and lively, with subtle, slightly tart, red berry flavors.

Color:	*Serving temperature:*	*Ageing potential:*
Red, rosé, and white.	*50 to 54°F (10 to 12°C) for the whites; 57 to 59°F (14 to 15°C) for the reds.*	*3 to 6 years.*

POUILLY-FUISSÉ AOC

MÂCONNAIS

Three appellations here begin with the name of Pouilly; but Pouilly-Fuissé produced in Fuissé, Solutré, Vergisson, and Chaintré is better known than Pouilly-Loché and Pouilly-Vinzelles, because of its larger level of production (approximately 467,000 cases/42,000 hl). This is where

the best white wines in the Mâconnais are produced—something that has long been known by the monks of Cluny, who had many of their vineyards here.

> **GRAPE VARIETY** Chardonnay.
> **SOIL** Clay-and-limestone slopes.
> **STYLE** In the classic style of Burgundian

whites, Pouilly wines are marked by a minerality and crispness well balanced by their fullness. Without reaching the power of some of their neighbors to the north, they have clear character and a good range of flavors. As they get older, they develop dried fruit and honey notes.

Color:	*Serving temperature:*	*Ageing potential:*
White.	*50 to 54°F (10 to 12°C).*	*3 to 6 years.*

BEAUJOLAIS AND BEAUJOLAIS-VILLAGES AOCs

These vineyards are located in the Rhône department, except for the canton of La Chapelle-de-Guinchay, which is located in the Saône-et-Loire. The picturesque hills, where vineyards ascend to 1,600 or even 2,000 ft (500 or 600 m), dominate the Saône Valley. Profiting from a regulatory decision in the 1950s that allowed the initial harvest to be put on sale early, the Beaujolais AOC was popularized worldwide by the Beaujolais Nouveau. This opportunity is focused on the third Thursday of November, just weeks after the harvest. But its sudden popularity, which created an image of an unambitious easy-to-drink red wine, was a double-edged sword. Its top producers would now like to be taken more seriously. It should be remembered that the best of Beaujolais are these 10 *crus*: Brouilly, Chénas, Chiroubles,

Côte-de-Brouilly, Fleurie, Juliénas, Morgon, Moulin-à-Vent, Régnié, and St-Amour.

> **GRAPE VARIETIES** Gamay for reds and rosés; Chardonnay for whites.

> **SOIL** The soil in this area consists of granite alluvium from the Tertiary and Quaternary periods, which allows expression of all the fruitiness and charm in Gamay.

> **STYLE** Beaujolais Nouveau is naturally designed for fun, as it provides a refreshing and instantly pleasing accompaniment to snacks and conversation. A standard Beaujolais or a "Villages" wine is fresh with red fruit (currants), grape, and spice flavors that enable it to be consumed over an entire meal, where it usually goes very well with meats from the deli and simple dishes. White Beaujolais (and even rosés) are produced in limited numbers, but are often very

good quality. If made from Chardonnay, they can bear comparison with the wines of Mâconnais or Côte Chalonnaise, when they are well produced.

Color:
Red, rosé, and white.

Serving temperature:
61 to 63°F (16 to 17°C) for the reds;
50 to 54°F (10 to 12°C) for the whites and rosés.

Ageing potential:
3 to 5 years.

JULIÉNAS AOC

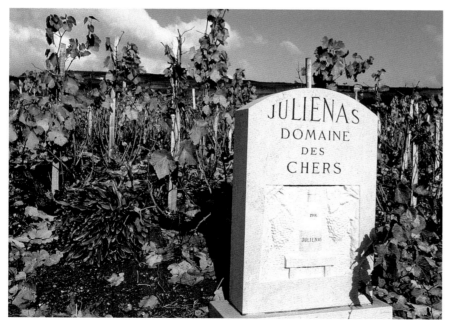

Juliénas includes some of the oldest wine-producing sites in Beaujolais. Its high and steep slopes provide excellent locations for ripening grapes. The appellation straddles the departments of Saône-et-Loire and the Rhône, facing south to the valley of the Mauvaise River, a tributary of the Saône. It has a planted area of 1,509 acres (610 ha), twice the size of St-Amour, through the annexation of two neighboring hamlets: Jullié and Emeringues. The La Bottière, Les Capitans, Les Chers, and Les Paquelets *climats* are particularly renowned.

> **GRAPE VARIETY** Gamay.

> **SOIL** Granite.

> **STYLE** Juliénas wines are more potent and less refined than those of St-Amour. They are at their best two to four years after harvest.

Color:
Red.

Serving temperature:
57 to 61°F (14 to 16°C).

Ageing potential:
3 to 5 years.

MOULIN-À-VENT AOC

Named after a windmill located on a hilltop, this wine is generally considered the best in Beaujolais. Beaune *négociants*, such as Louis Jadot, who owns vineyards here, are not mistaken. This is certainly the most suitable Beaujolais for ageing, and the most expensive. Some producers carry out maturation in oak barrels, which is not typical for this appellation, to make the most of the structure of the wines.

> **GRAPE VARIETY** Gamay.

> **SOIL** The granite subsoil, covered with a sandy layer rich in manganese, gives the wine a distinctive character.

> **STYLE** The best wines, which are a dark ruby color, may retain an impressive structure and density for more than 10 years. Their body and their class are reminiscent of several wines from the Côte d'Or.

Color:
Red.

Serving temperature:
57 to 61°F (14 to 16°C).

Ageing potential:
10 to 15 years.

ST-AMOUR AOC

Located a few miles south of Mâcon, St-Amour is the northernmost of the Beaujolais *crus*, and one of the smallest. Most vineyards are planted on slopes facing east-southeast at an altitude of 820 ft (250 m). With a name like this, it would be surprising if the wine did not sell well. Added to the small size of the vineyard 793 acres (321 ha), prices are quite high in terms of the average quality. Some producers of Chardonnay here sell their products under the St-Véran appellation.

> **GRAPE VARIETY** Gamay.

> **SOIL** The appellation is located on a granite plateau at the south end of the Saône-et-Loire department.

> **STYLE** Lightweight and subtly fruity, the wines are produced to be consumed while young. They do improve after two or three years in bottle, though.

Color:
Red.

Serving temperature:
57 to 61°F (14 to 16°C).

Ageing potential:
3 to 5 years.

Selected Beaujolais producers

• **Domaine des Jacques: Moulin-à-Vent AOC.** So what is a *négociant* from the Côte de Beaune doing at Moulin-à-Vent? Quite simply, Louis Jadot is making a top quality Burgundy wine, since buying this excellent estate in 1996. Part of the harvest is aged in oak barrels for 10 months, which adds complexity and durability to the wine.

• **Domaine du Vissoux: Fleurie Poncié, Fleurie AOC.** Pierre-Marie Chermette has become known for his unchaptalized Beaujolais wines, which demonstrate that one can limit yields and harvest at optimal ripeness here for a naturally full-bodied wine. His Fleurie and Moulin-à-Vent wines have

character, yet they are not much more expensive than others that are much less impressive.

• **Domaine Jean Foillard: Morgon Côte du Py, Morgon AOC.** Jean Foillard combines respect for the land and modern techniques to produce a genuine and balanced Morgon, which is both uncompromising and noted for its *terroir*.

• **Henry Fessy: Beaujolais AOC.** This quality producer was acquired in 2008 by Louis Latour, a Beaune *négociant*. It produces, with this simple Beaujolais, a typically fruity, supple, and rounded wine.

CHAMPAGNE

Champagne is the wine par excellence *for celebrations. French in origin, it has now conquered the world and inspired its own lifestyle. Everything about Champagne adds to its magic, from its mysterious beginnings to its production, a blending technique jealously guarded by each major house or brand. It is the most famous wine in the world, and also the most copied; but it is made in the Champagne region alone and nowhere else.*

A brief history of Champagne

As is often the case in France, the origins of the Champagne region's vineyards can be traced back to the Roman legions. During the 5th and 6th centuries, it was the Benedictines in particular who took over their development. These wines were served in the courts of French kings; Louis XIV was very fond of them. The wines of that era have nothing in common with the tiny bubbles that we know and enjoy today. They were lively wines, both light reds or still whites.

THE FIRST CHAMPAGNES. The Champagne legend only really took off once effervescence was mastered in the 1670s, thanks to a second fermentation in bottle. This discovery is attributed to Dom Pérignon (*see* box on facing page, also p.71). Whether or not this story is true, it is the case that the era marks a turning point in the history of Champagne. The large wine production houses opened for business and, from the 18th century onward, established

Champagne's renown worldwide. In this period, the use of blends was already a preferred technique in order to achieve more homogenous wines. Then vineyards were destroyed by phylloxera at the end of the 19th century, which caused several economic crises, with that of 1911 being particularly memorable. Various advanced production programs were introduced to re-establish the vineyard region, and these remain in use today.

INFORMED CHOICES. Mindful of its vineyards and their impact on the environment, the Champagne region introduced sustainable viticulture in 2001. It could do so because the world of sparkling wine is no longer in crisis; indeed it's enjoying great success. Champagne can barely produce enough to meet the demand. In 2003, a process designed to extend the appellation's boundaries was launched. The new area, which is planned to include 40 villages, should be in use by 2013; and the first vines in new plots of land there will be planted around 2015, for initial harvesting a few years later.

CHAMPAGNE STATISTICS

Vineyard area:
86,500 acres (35,000 ha)

Average production:
338 million bottles /
28 million (9-l) cases

(CIVC, 2007)

Climate and soil

The Champagne region is centered some 90 miles (150 km) northeast of Paris. These are France's most northerly vineyards, and the northernmost limit of commercial wine cultivation. The hillside vine rows are cut into terraces, at elevations of between 295 and 1150 ft (90 and 350 m), around 319 villages across five *départements*: Aube, Haute-Marne, Marne, and some villages in Aisne and Seine-et-Marne.

CLIMATE. Characterized partly by continental extremes, with its cold winters—and sometimes destructive frosts—as well as sun-drenched summers,

> Winter pruning at the Champagne Roederer estate in France.

Champagne AOCs

- Champagne
- Coteaux Champenois
- Rosé des Riceys

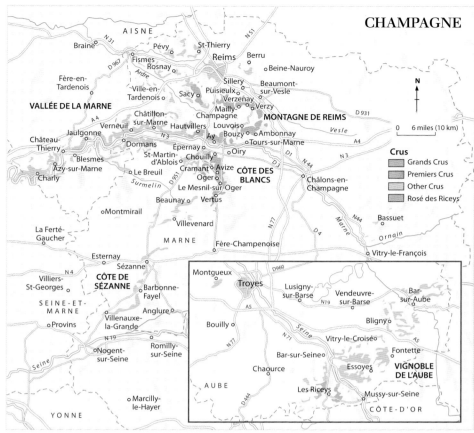

CHAMPAGNE

and partly by a relatively temperate Atlantic influence with high humidity.

SOIL. Limestone soils are an essential contributor to the quality of Champagne wines. They consist mostly of sand and clay over a chalky subsoil, which regulates moisture and temperature very efficiently and plays a vital role in maturing the grapes. Furthermore, the chalk allows deep caves to be excavated, in which wine can be stored for ageing.

Vineyard landscape

MONTAGNE DE REIMS. This vast plateau, covered with forests, is situated between Épernay and Reims. It is the realm of the Pinot Noir grape (around 70 percent in some areas), but Chardonnay and Pinot Meunier are also grown. The region boasts the largest number of villages classed as *grand cru*.

CÔTE DES BLANCS. Situated to the south of Épernay, this is a stronghold for Chardonnay, which reigns supreme here— predominantly between Cramant and Le Mesnil-sur-Oger. Some villages, such as Vertus, produce good red wines (AOC Coteaux Champenois).

VALLÉE DE LA MARNE. This area extends from just west of Château-Thierry to east of Épernay. It is dominated by red grape varieties, particularly the Pinot Meunier. Various *grands crus* can be found.

VIGNOBLE DE L'AUBE. This area stretches more than 60 miles (100 km) to the southeast of Troyes. The region's subsoils tend to be marl and are mostly planted with Pinot Noir. The appellation Rosé de Riceys lies to the south.

CÔTE DE SÉZANNE. Planted during the 1960s, this region is an extension of the Côte des Blancs southward. This Chardonnay stronghold produces full, rich wines.

Grape varieties and wine styles

Three grape varieties are permitted in the Champagne region: Chardonnay for the whites and two Pinot varieties for the reds.

CHARDONNAY. Planted across 28 percent of regional vineyards, it produces elegant wines that are lively and full of spirit, offering delicate aromas with floral and sometimes mineral notes. It is well suited to ageing.

PINOT NOIR. This red represents 39 percent of plantings, and brings body, richness, and longevity to the blend.

Two legendary names, two famous brands

A literal contemporary of Louis XIV (they both lived from 1639–1715), Dom Pérignon was responsible for the vines and cellars at the Hautvillers abbey near Épernay, where he wrote *l'Art de bien traiter la vigne et du Champagne* (How to care for the vine and Champagne). It is uncertain whether he was the creator of Champagne as we know it, but he was a wine expert ahead of his time. He developed the process of blending *crus* and grape varieties, the basis for the preparation of Champagne. Today, Dom Pérignon is also the name of a *prestige cuvée* made by Moët & Chandon, produced since 1936 and always a vintage wine. The other "Dom," Dom Ruinart (1657–1709), specialized in the study of "antiquities," specifically the study of monuments and cemetary inscriptions. He met Dom Pérignon in 1696 at Hautvillers abbey. Dom Pérignon is credited with being the inspiration for his nephew Nicolas Ruinart, founder of the house that carries his name. Ruinart, the oldest Champagne house, dedicated their *prestige cuvée* to Dom Ruinart in homage.

PINOT MEUNIER. This grape accounts for the remaining third. It provides flavor and fruitiness. The wines produced from it are supple and fruity, and have an intense bouquet.

A blended wine

Champagne is produced according to a winemaking technique known as the "Champagne" or traditional method (*see* pp.70–1). Only Champagne may use the title "Méthode Champenoise." Champagne is a blended wine *par excellence*. Few *cuvées* come from just one vineyard or one village. The wine producer may choose to blend two or three grape varieties, or simply to use one. Similarly, he or she combines various *crus* and various vintages. The red grape varieties are almost always vinified in the style of white wine. Every year, the cellar master puts together a *cuvée* or blend corresponding to the house or brand quality and image.

TRUE OR FALSE?

Champagne ages better in 750 ml bottles.

FALSE. Experience shows that Champagne is best preserved in a magnum (which holds 1.5 liters). It seems to mature better, and age for longer, in these bigger bottles.

Types of Champagne

There are several different types of Champagne, according to grape varieties, blends, *dosage* (addition of sugar), and ageing.

BLANC DE BLANCS **CHAMPAGNE.** An exception to the blending rule, this wine is made from the Chardonnay grape variety on its own, and it offers great finesse.

BLANC DE NOIRS **CHAMPAGNE.** This wine is made from Pinot Noir or Pinot Meunier. It is a relatively rare Champagne, as

Vineyard hierarchy

The name of a *cru* rarely features on Champagne labels, but *crus* represent a rigorous classification system. Called the "*échelle des crus*" or "ladder of growth" by residents of the Champagne region, it sets percentages that determine the price of grapes. Of the total 319 villages producing Champagne, 17 have the privilege of receiving a 100 percent *cru* rating. They may claim the appellation *grand cru*. Some 44 villages are classified between 90 and 99 percent and may call themselves *premier cru*. The others, classed between 80 and 89 percent, may use the designation *second cru*. Far from being just theoretical, this classification determines the wine's quality, with the best *cuvées* and *prestige cuvées* being made from top or "100 percent" *crus*.

Pinots are primarily used in the preparation of *cuvées* or blends. Powerful and vinous, it is always extremely elegant.

ROSÉ CHAMPAGNE. Champagne is the only European wine region where it is permitted to mix red and white wines to produce rosés. Of course, that red wine (Pinot Noir), which makes up 10 to 20 percent of the wine, must come from the Champagne region. Other rosé Champagnes may be produced using the *saignée* technique following a short maceration. This refined variety of Champagne has become so popular that nearly all of the Grand Marques (big brands) offer "their" rosé.

> The *remueurs* or "riddlers" turn up to 50,000 bottles per day to ensure that the yeast deposits accumulate in the neck.

CHAMPAGNE SANS ANNÉE. Non-vintage Champagne it is a blend of various grape varieties and various years.

VINTAGE CHAMPAGNE. This wine is produced only in great years, generally one out of three, and must be aged on the lees for at least three years. It is a *Grand Champagne*, distinctive and with an ability to generate extraordinary sensations.

PRESTIGE CUVÉE. A rare bottling, this high-end Champagne is generally presented in an original and distinctive bottle. It brings together the best *cuvées* of a given brand. It is *the* Champagne for important occasions. Some of the most famous examples are: Roederer's Cristal, Pol Roger's Sir Winston Churchill, Laurent-Perrier's Cuvée Grand Siècle, chez Ruinart's Dom Ruinart.

***GRAND CRU* OR *PREMIER CRU* CHAMPAGNE.** Just 17 villages can claim this first title (grand) for their wine; and 44 may do so for the second (*see* box on the facing page).

RD (*RÉCEMMENT DÉGORGÉ*) CHAMPAGNE. This Champagne spends a very long time resting on its lees, and thus reaches a maximum level of maturity. The most famous is Bollinger's RD.

BRUT NATURE, DOSAGE ZÉRO OR "NON-DOSAGE" CHAMPAGNE. This Champagne does not contain added sugar—or at least less than 3 g/l. A dry Champagne, it is honest and fresh.

EXTRA-BRUT CHAMPAGNE. This is similar to Brut Nature, but a little more rounded than that style, with no more than 6 g/l of sugar.

BRUT CHAMPAGNE. This is the most widely produced type of Champagne. It contains less than 15 g/l of residual sugar.

> Champagne bottles tilted in "A-line" racks, in the Roederer house cellars in Reims.

Selected Grande Marque Champagnes

- **Bollinger (Aÿ).** A Champagne institution. Its inimitable style, instantly recognizable, has long established this house's reputation through three legendary *cuvées*: the Spécial Cuvée (the non-vintage Brut Maison), the Grand Cuvée, and the RD (*récemment dégorgé*).

- **Billecart-Salmon (Mareuil-sur-Aÿ).** A style of finesse, harmony, and balance.

- **Duval-Leroy (Vertus).** Known for their extremely rare Rosé de Saignée Champagne.

- **Champagne Gosset (Aÿ).** Their Cuvée Celebris is dense and powerful, and their Grand Rosé is superbly vinous.

- **Jacquesson (Dizy).** Known for their reliable quality.

- **Krug (Reims).** Some people consider this to be the Champagne *par excellence*; others say one of the most sophisticated available. Known for their Grande Cuvée, their Clos du Mesnil, and their Brut rosé.

- **Laurent-Perrier (Tours-sur-Marne).** Acclaimed for their elegant non-vintage Brut, their non-*dosage* Ultra Brut, and their mythical and dazzling Cuvée Grand Siècle.

- **Louis Roederer (Reims).** A superb range of Champagnes—distinguished, straightforward, and well balanced, including the world-famous prestigious *cuvée* "Cristal."

- **Moët & Chandon (Épernay).** The ubiquitous Champagne label. Their Brut Impérial (non-vintage), with its inimitable style, light and fruity, is the most widely sold *cuvée* in the world. Their classification Cuvée Dom Pérignon is one of the most famous and most expensive.

- **Philipponnat (Mareuil-sur-Aÿ).** Known for the jewel in their crown, the Clos de Goisses.

- **Pol Roger (Épernay).** Wines of great finesse. This was Winston Churchill's favorite Champagne.

- **Ruinart (Reims).** A very small production, but very elegant wines, notably the *blanc de blancs* Cuvée Dom Ruianart.

- **Salon (Le Mesnil-sur-Oger).** Their Cuvée S is unique: one grape variety, one *cru*, always a vintage wine.

- **Veuve Clicquot Ponsardin (Reims).** Their non-vintage Brut, with the famous sunset yellow label, is one of the best examples of the genre. So is the Grande Dame, named in homage to the widow who gave it its renown.

EXTRA-DRY CHAMPAGNE. This Champagne is deliberately rounded, rich, and supple, with 12 to 20 g/l of residual sugar; but it also has a certain freshness.

DRY AND MEDIUM-DRY CHAMPAGNE. Despite its name, this variety contains from 17 to 40 g/l of residual sugar, making it an excellent accompaniment for desserts.

SWEET CHAMPAGNE. Very rare, this is particularly high in residual sugar: more than 55 g/l.

Major houses and grower Champagnes

Prestige requires distinction. There are no châteaux or estates here, but rather "houses" or marques.

MAJOR HOUSES. These companies shaped the history of Champagne and perpetuate a truly French art and tradition. The most powerful are listed on the stock exchange. In first place is the LVMH group (Moët & Chandon, Veuve Clicquot Ponsardin, Mercier, Krug, Ruinart), an empire of 55 million bottles. Next are the Rémy Cointreau group (Charles Heidsieck, Piper-Heidsieck), the Vranken group (Vranken, Pommery, Charles Lafitte, Heidsieck & Co Monopole), and BCC (Boizel, Chanoine, de Venoge, Philipponnat, Lanson, and Alfred Rothschild). Others, equally prestigious, have remained within the family: Louis Roederer, Bollinger, Henriot, etc. There are more than a hundred producers of this kind, making up a large percentage of the market. A few rare examples (such as Bollinger) have their own vineyards; generally, houses buy their grapes from growers.

GROWER CHAMPAGNES. These wines are often contrasted with the so-called Grand Marques. They are the expression of a particular person, a *cru*, or a *terroir*. The emergence of these *terroir* Champagnes is a recent phenomenon, led by a new generation of wine producers (Selosse, Égly, Vesselle, Fleury, etc.).

Selected Grower Champagnes

- **Pierre Gimonnet (Cuis).** Original wines that are remarkably evolved.

- **Marie-Noëlle Ledru (Ambonnay).** Their Champagnes, matured on the lees for three to five years, are dense.

- **Jacques Selosse (Avize).** The owner is one of the Champagne region's most remarkable characters. Their superb and delicious Champagnes, biodynamically cultivated, announce their *terroir* loud and clear.

- **Paul Bara (Bouzy).** Valued *cuvées* full of character.

- **Égly-Ouriet (Ambonnay).** Their *Grand Champagnes*, with little added sugar, and their red Bouzy are wines with character that balance vinosity and elegance.

- **Pierre Moncuit (Le Mesnil-sur-Oger).** Champagnes marked by minerality, purity, and the character of their *terroir*.

- **Roses de Jeanne (Celles-sur-Ources).** Their Champagnes play the cards of finesse and elegance.

- **Jean-Pierre Fleury (Courteron).** A pioneer of biodynamics in Champagne, this producer creates wines full of finesse, aromatics, and elegance. Magnificent expressions of the *terroir*.

- **Champagne Drappier (Urville).** *Terroir* Champagnes with character, especially non-dosage *cuvées*. They also use extraordinary containers, the Solomon (18 l), the Primat (27 l), and the Melchizedek (30 l).

- **Larmandier-Bernier (Vertus).** Beautiful, well-balanced Champagnes boasting the best *crus* and excellent value for money.

- **De Sousa (Avize).** Distinguished wines, deep and long-lasting to an extent scarcely matched in the Champagne region.

- **Agrapart & Fils (Avize).** Light, fresh, distinguished *blancs de blancs*, full of charm.

- **Jacques Beaufort (Ambonnay).** Their *cuvées*, blending fruit and *terroir*, produced from grapes given homeopathic and aromatherapy treatments, have no equal.

- **Françoise Bedel (Crouttes-sur-Marne).** A remarkable range of Champagnes produced organically.

> Vines in the area
around Ay, in the
Vallée de la Marne.

A few label idiosyncrasies

Champagne promotes its difference, even on its labels. It is not mandatory to state *"appellation contrôlée"* on the label; but, alongside standard information (see p.108), the occupational category of whoever bottled the wine must be stated. This is generally printed at the bottom of the label in very small letters (see also p.111).

NM: *négociant-manipulant.* The producer or house either harvests or buys its grapes, and then vinifies them in its own cellars.

RM: *récoltant-manipulant.* The grower-winemaker produces, vinifies, and markets his or her own wine.

RC: *récoltant-coopérateur.* The grower sends grapes to the cooperative to be made into wine, and then reclaims all or some of the completed bottles for sale.

R: *récoltant.* Neither a producer nor the member of a cooperative, the grower has the wines from his or her harvest produced by a Champagne house.

CM: *cooperative de manipulation.* The wines are produced and sold by a cooperative.

SR: *société de récoltants.* Quite rare, this is an association of independent wine producers who produce and market their wines jointly.

ND: *négociant-distributeur.* A wine merchant who buys bottles produced by other producers and redistributes them under his or her own label.

MA: *marque d'acheteur.* A label custom-produced for a purchaser, who then markets it under their own name. This is often used for wines sold in supermarkets.

They have refused to sell their grapes to big Champagne groups, and focus on the characteristics of their *terroir*. There are more than 6,000 of these innovative, dynamic producers competing in the market with their truly luxurious flagship products. They represent about 25 percent of total Champagne production. The properties are small (often less than 40 acres, or 15 hectares), many passed down from generation to generation. Their wines are mostly marketed at the property itself or through direct sales.
COOPERATIVES. These collectives have become more widespread in recent years. Among the most famous are Champagne Jacquart, which brings together 600 growers (one of the most active cooperatives on the market); also Veuve A. Devaux; Beaumont des Crayères; Union Auboise; and CV-CNF (Centre Vinicole-Champagne Nicolas Feuillatte). Their Champagnes are generally blended to a uniform style: light, fruity, well-balanced wines that appeal to all. This does not stop them developing particularly elegant, special *cuvées*: Champagne Jacquart's Cuvée Allegra and Nicolas Feuillatte's prestigious Palmes d'Or, with its special bottle and cloth bag (paying homage to a diva); its vintage *grand crus*; and its *cuvées* aged in oak barrels.

Champagne without bubbles

Alongside its famous sparkling wines, the vineyards of the Champagne region also produce still wines under two appellations.
COTEAUX CHAMPENOIS. This appellation covers the entire Champagne region. It produces still, dry wines in white, rosé, and red styles. The whites are cool and light, supported by a beautiful freshness. The rosés are full of elegance and finesse. The reds are also elegant, with a beautiful structure and wonderful raspberry or cherry aromas. The most famous bears the name of the *village* of Bouzy (Pinot Noir *grand cru*). Like various others (such as Vertus, Ambonnay, Aÿ, Cumières), it is permitted to add its name after that of the appellation.
ROSÉ DES RICEYS. One of France's greatest rosés, this wine is produced in limited quantities in the Aube, at the south end of the Champagne region, grown in limestone soil and Kimmeridgian marls. Produced from Pinot Noir through a short maceration—which must be halted at the precise moment when the *"goût de Riceys"* flavors appear—it is a full wine, dense with a pretty nose that is delicately fruity and yet complex.

The art of Champagne according to Krug

The house of Krug made its debut in the world of Champagne in 1843. Over time, it has been able to gain and retain a reputation at the pinnacle of prestige and excellence. This is the result of striving consistently for authenticity and perfection, already a guiding principle under the house's founder, Johann-Joseph Krug. The sixth generation of the family still retains the same enthusiasm and passion. First fermentation is in oak barrels to enrich the wine's complexity, while ensuring that it develops over time, and the blending process is followed by a long ageing period in the cellars (at least six years): these factors all contribute to the Champagne's overall excellence.

GRANDE CUVÉE, A HOUSE EMBLEM

One of the house of Krug's great strengths is an enormous reserve of old wines from top vineyard blocks. These still wines, allowed to age in cool cellars, are regularly used in the final blend of Grand Cuvée, a true emblem of the house of Krug. Being non-vintage, it is able to combine various *crus* from different areas of the Champagne region, to use wines from previous years, and to integrate the three grape varieties Chardonnay, Pinot Meunier, and Pinot Noir in suitable proportions. It achieves, year after year, Krug's emblematic style. Fifty years, some-times even more, go into making the end product. Grande Cuvée has a lightly golden, brilliant appearance, and it is fringed in the glass with a lasting ring of delicate bubbles. The rich bouquet reveals ripe yellow and citrus fruits with hints of toasted hazelnut, brioche, and white flowers. On the palate, the wine slowly develops a rich, vinous density, aromatic and full of flavor; the deli-cate sparkle literally blends into the fruity softness. All of this is steadily prolonged through continuous freshness and rare mineral notes. The richness and complexity of this Champagne demand an experienced palate. A wine for contemplation and for celebration,

1. Main building in Reims.
2. Chardonnay vines planted at Clos du Mesnil.
3. Olivier Krug selects *vins clairs*.
4. Grande Cuvée.
5. Bottles stored in the cellars at an inclined position, before disgorgement.
6. Oak barrel with wine from the Clos du Mesnil.

at the table it is an excellent accompaniment for sophisticated shellfish, meat, and poultry in creamy sauces (with chanterelles), and even roasted small game.

VINTAGE KRUG

Krug's vintage Champagne, or Krug Vintage, meets a different set of criteria. There is no option to draw upon reserve wines. Although the vintage wine is determined by the climate that year, the Krug style can still be recaptured by exploiting vine maturity, a range of *terroirs*, and judicious proportions of the three grape varieties. During fermentation in oak barrels, the wine's development can be seen up close: the *nouveau* wine is tasted every day. Then, at a crucial moment in the blend, the entire Krug family can choose from a wide variety of still wines from the same year to create a wine that is loyal both to the vintage and to its own character. These Champagnes, with excellent ageing properties, remain surprisingly fresh after 20 or 30 years in the cellar.

KRUG ROSÉ

Rosé is now part of the Krug line, demonstrating the family's willingness to move into new *cuvées*. The first Krug rosé was produced with the magnificent 1976 vintage. At initial tastings, in 1983, it enjoyed immediate success. The blend (as meticulous as ever) includes a small amount of skin-fermented Pinot Noir, giving the wine its own particular, significantly more robust, nuance and flavor. Made to accompany great cuisine, this vinous Champagne continues to reflect the Krug spirit.

CLOS DU MESNIL AND CLOS D'AMBONNAY

Two extraordinary rarities add the finishing touches to this portrait gallery: the *blanc de blancs* Clos du Mesnil and the *blanc de noirs* Clos d'Ambonnay. In 1971, the Krug family acquired the Clos du Mesnil, 4.57 acres (1.85 hectares) planted with Chardonnay in a layout unchanged since 1698. This wine exists only in exceptional vintages and does not undergo any blending (highly unusual for Krug). Yet, it is one of the cleanest and most accomplished Champagnes. Even rarer, almost extravagantly so, the Clos d'Ambonnay is the exceptional fruit of a 1.692-acre (0.685-hectare) *clos* planted exclusively with Pinot Noir. The wine has a coppery golden appearance, and provides a magnificent richness of aroma and flavor. What better testimony to the house of Krug?

ALSACE, JURA, AND SAVOIE

Alsace, Lorraine, Jura, Savoie, Bugey—the vineyards of eastern France are some of the country's smallest. Little in size, they are nevertheless great and unique in terms of the wide range and originality of their grape varieties, and the typicity of their wines, some of which (such as Château-Chalon) are among the most famous in the world.

ALSACE

A narrow ribbon of valleys and hillsides, the Alsace vineyards extend along some 106 miles (170 km) of a line between Thann in the south and Marlenheim in the north. The region is notable in France for its grape varieties and the style of its wines—and of course for its appellation system, where bottles have always been allowed to display grape varieties: Gewurztraminer, Riesling, Muscat, Pinot Noir, etc. There are only three appellations: one for *vins de cépage*, another for *grands crus*, and the third for *crémants*.

Yesterday and today

Established by Roman legions, who introduced their own grape varieties, the vineyards of Alsace reached a peak in the Middle Ages. This period of prosperity—which also saw the arrival of large wine merchants—actually continued until the 17th century, when its dynamism was undermined by war, German annexation, and phylloxera. At the end of the First World War in 1918, though, the vineyards recovered by focusing specifically on quality.

Since the 1970s, Alsace has been committed to organic production, led by wine producers such as Jean-Pierre Frick, a pioneer in the field. The region contains 110 organically or biodynamically cultivated estates, covering an area of some 2,470 acres (1,000 hectares). This may seem like a modest amount, but the pace of conversion has gathered real momentum.

ALSACE STATISTICS (AOC)

Vineyard area: 38,300 acres (15,500 ha)

Production: 12.8 million cases (1.15 million hl)

Whites: 91%

Reds and rosés: 9%

(CIVC, 2007)

Vineyard landscape

CLIMATE. Protected by the Vosges mountain range, Alsace benefits from a dry continental climate with warm springs, dry and sunny summers, long and mild autumns, and cold winters, all of which are particularly conducive to growing vines.

SOILS. The vineyards contain no fewer than 13 types of soil—including volcanic, sandstone, granite, gneiss, schist, marly limestone, clay marl, and loess—most of which are closely intermixed. This great diversity allows a single grape variety to produce a huge range of flavors in wines.

Grape varieties and wine styles

Alsace can proudly claim a formidable collection of grape varieties, some of which can be found nowhere else in France.
RIESLING. This is the most prestigious of local grape varieties. Lively and distinguished, it produces wines with a characteristic bouquet of lemon, honeysuckle, citronella, and grapefruit, supported by a pleasant minerality that takes on fascinating notes of petroleum with age.
GEWURZTRAMINER. The name means "spiced Traminer" in German and Alsatian. Gewurztraminer creates a full-bodied, highly expressive wine offering exceptional aromatic complexity

> Vines near the village of Riquewihr.

DID YOU KNOW...?

Alsace and Lorraine are traditionally considered together. Lorraine is noted for producing Côtes-de-Toul, famous for its vin gris (in fact a rosé made from direct pressing) with its unusual gray color. It is a fairly lively wine offering aromas marked by flowers and soft fruits.

End of the single variety?

In Alsace, the rule for *grands crus* is: one *terroir*, one grape variety. If a wine producer does not respect this rule, the wine loses its appellation. However, some wineries are daring to take the plunge. Take the example of Marcel Deiss. He was not content to define his wines as simply varietal expressions of the *terroir* that he manages with great care biodynamically. He instead chose to pursue "complantation"—the practice of planting different grape varieties in one *terroir* without identifying them—and to produce blends of more than one variety. His Burg and his Grasberg, among others, have met with major success.

dominated by rose and lychee, mingling with white and exotic fruit flavors, as well as spicy notes.

PINOT GRIS. This variety provides rounded, well-structured, rich, complex whites, offering fruity aromas tinged with spice.

MUSCAT. Two varieties are used, often in blends: Muscat d'Alsace (also called Muscat à Petits Grains or Muscat de Frontignan) and Muscat Ottonel. They produce dry wines with an intense nose and palate of fresh grapes.

SYLVANER. This variety yields a pleasant, fresh, light, discreetly fruity wine, with an acacia scent accented by mineral notes. It's often delightfully lively.

PINOT BLANC. This rising star of a grape variety forms a rounded, tender wine. It is fresh and supple, with an aromatic range offering notes of fruit and flowers.

PINOT NOIR. This is Alsace's only red grape variety. It is used to make rosé or red wine. For the latter, it is aged in barrel, and creates reds with a little less depth than their counterparts from Burgundy, but with a typical fruitiness and hints of cherry. These wines can become extraordinary in great years.

KLEVENER DE HEILIGENSTEIN. This is simply Savagnin Rose. Grown in just five villages of Bas-Rhin, it produces original, well-structured wines, with exotic fruits emphasizing spicy notes.

Alsace specialties

GENTIL AND EDELZWICKER. These blended wines are made from various grape varieties, and are pleasant and thirst-quenching. One or other of these terms will therefore follow the appellation AOC Alsace on the label.

***VENDANGE TARDIVE* AND *SÉLECTION DE GRAINS NOBLES*.** These descriptions (not appellations) may be added to AOCs Alsace or Alsace Grand Cru. They are given only to sweet wines made from Riesling, Gewurztraminer, Muscat, and Pinot Gris, which are particularly rich in sugar when harvested. These exceptional wines, capable of competing with the world's greatest sweet wines, are well suited to being aged for long periods, sometimes for more than half a century.

ICE WINE. Some producers are trying their hand at these rare wines, produced from grapes harvested in December and January, at temperatures of between 14 and 19°F (−7 and −10°C). Ignored by French legislation, these sweet wines sell for astronomical prices.

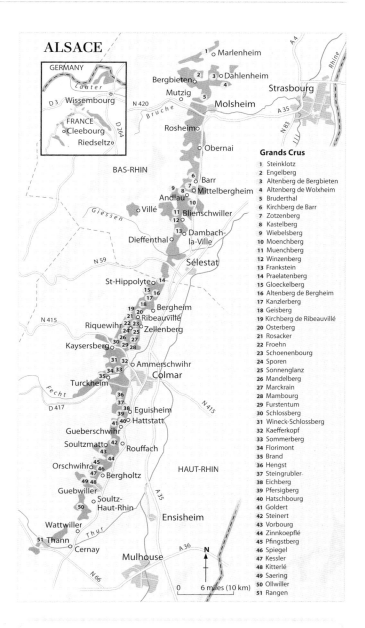

ALSACE

Grands Crus
1. Steinklotz
2. Engelberg
3. Altenberg de Bergbieten
4. Altenberg de Wolxheim
5. Bruderthal
6. Kirchberg de Barr
7. Zotzenberg
8. Kastelberg
9. Wiebelsberg
10. Moenchberg
11. Muenchberg
12. Winzenberg
13. Frankstein
14. Praelatenberg
15. Gloeckelberg
16. Altenberg de Bergheim
17. Kanzlerberg
18. Geisberg
19. Kirchberg de Ribeauvillé
20. Osterberg
21. Rosacker
22. Froehn
23. Schoenenbourg
24. Sporen
25. Sonnenglanz
26. Mandelberg
27. Marckrain
28. Mambourg
29. Furstentum
30. Schlossberg
31. Wineck-Schlossberg
32. Kaefferkopf
33. Sommerberg
34. Florimont
35. Brand
36. Hengst
37. Steingrubler
38. Eichberg
39. Pfersigberg
40. Hatschbourg
41. Goldert
42. Steinert
43. Vorbourg
44. Zinnkoepflé
45. Pfingstberg
46. Spiegel
47. Kessler
48. Kitterlé
49. Saering
50. Ollwiller
51. Rangen

Alsace AOCs

- Alsace
- Crémant d'Alsace
- Alsace Grand Cru, followed by the name of one of 51 lieux-dits (named vineyards):
  - *Altenberg de Bergbieten*
  - *Altenberg de Bergheim*
  - *Altenberg de Wolxheim*
  - *Brand*
  - *Bruderthal*
  - *Eichberg*
  - *Engelberg*
  - *Florimont*
  - *Frankstein*
  - *Froehn*
  - *Furstentum*
  - *Geisberg*
  - *Gloeckelberg*
  - *Goldert*
  - *Hatschbourg*
  - *Hengst*
  - *Kaefferkopf*
  - *Kanzlerberg*
  - *Kastelberg*
  - *Kessler*
  - *Kirchberg de Barr*
  - *Kirchberg de Ribeauvillé*
  - *Kitterlé*
  - *Mambourg*
  - *Mandelberg*
  - *Marckrain*
  - *Moenchberg*
  - *Muenchberg*
  - *Ollwiller*
  - *Osterberg*
  - *Pfersigberg*
  - *Pfingstberg*
  - *Praelatenberg*
  - *Rangen*
  - *Rosacker*
  - *Saering*
  - *Schlossberg*
  - *Schoenenbourg*
  - *Sommerberg*
  - *Sonnenglanz*
  - *Spiegel*
  - *Sporen*
  - *Steinert*
  - *Steingrubler*
  - *Steinklotz*
  - *Vorbourg*
  - *Wiebelsberg*
  - *Wineck-Schlossberg*
  - *Winzenberg*
  - *Zinnkoepflé*
  - *Zotzenberg*

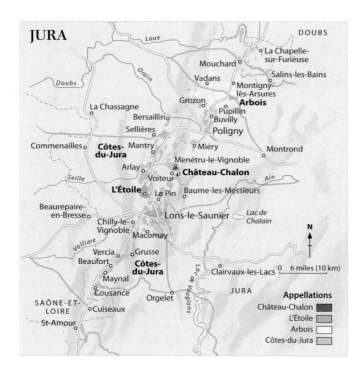

JURA

. . . .

Facing Burgundy across the Saône River, the Jura wine region occupies a stretch of terrain between plains and mountains. Although particularly famous for its *vins jaunes*, this region still produces an unbeatable range of red, rosé, and white wines (both dry and sweet), and even sparkling styles.

Vineyard landscape

Established during the 1st century BC, Jura's vineyards were really developed by religious communities during the 5th and 6th centuries. At the end of the 19th century, they covered some 49,420 acres (20,000 hectares). Phylloxera ravaged the region, but wine producers decided to pursue quality, and in 1936 received the first French AOC with Arbois.

CLIMATE AND SOIL. Jura enjoys a semi-continental climate, which is favorable to the vine's development and maturation. It is characterized by severe winters, cold and wet springs, hot summers, and sunny autumns. The vines are set in generally west-facing tiers on the hillsides of the Revermont region, at altitudes of between 650 and 1300 ft (200 and 500 m). They benefit from a wide variety of *terroirs* based on various clays and marls, marly limestone soils, limestone scree, and alluvium.

Jura AOCs

. . . .

- Arbois
- Arbois-Pupillin
- Côtes-du-Jura
- Château-Chalon
- Crémant du Jura
- L'Étoile
- Macvin du Jura

JURA STATISTICS (AOC)

Vineyard area: 38,300 acres
(15,500 ha)

Production: 1 million cases
(93,000 hl)

Whites: 40%

Reds and rosés: 40%

Crémants: 16%

Others: 4%

(CIVJ, 2007)

Grape varieties and wine styles

Jura grows five major grape varieties, each highly suited to the *terroir* and each producing original, very distinctive wines.

POULSARD (OR PLOUSSARD). Grown particularly in AOC Arbois, this variety produces a clear, ruby red wine. It's not very tannic, with aromas of small soft fruits that develop into spicy and damp woodland notes.

TROUSSEAU. This wine is characterized by an intense ruby color and a nose of soft fruits with slightly peppery spices. They are supported by firm tannins, which ensure that the wine has great potential for ageing. Quite often, it is vinified with Pinot Noir or Poulsard.

PINOT NOIR. This grape produces characterful wines profoundly marked by their *terroir* here, with raspberry and cassis aromas enhanced by spicy notes.

SAVAGNIN. This is *the* major white grape variety in Jura, the base for the famous *vin jaune*. Its rich aromatics range from apple to toasted almond, from fresh walnuts to wheat, and from curry to coffee. It is vinified with or without topping up (*see* p.78), alone or as a blend with Chardonnay; and it produces very distinctive wines, endowed with remarkable freshness and suited to a long ageing period.

CHARDONNAY. This is the most widespread grape variety (42 percent of the vineyard area). In this region, it creates wines with their own distinct qualities—including floral, fresh, and well-structured aromas.

Jura specialties

Alongside *vin jaune*, Jura offers two other specialties: Macvin du Jura and *vin de paille*.

MACVIN. This is a *vin de liqueur* produced from two-thirds unfermented grape must and one-third fermented, fortified with Jura brandy. Aged in barrel for 18 months, it provides a superb balance between the sweetness of the fruit and the power of the alcohol.

VIN DE PAILLE. A sweet wine that is produced using a very distinctive production technique (*see* p.66).

> As *vin jaune* is aged, a film of yeast forms on its surface.

VIN JAUNE. This unique wine is made with just one grape variety: Savignin. Harvested late, it is vinified as dry white wine and then stored in 60-gallon (228-liter) barrels, where its mysterious transformation begins. Aged without topping up, the wine's surface becomes covered with a film of yeast, protecting it from acetification (which would turn it to vinegar) and giving it the inimitable *jaune* taste. After six years and three months, the wine can finally be decanted into its special bottle, the famous 620 ml *clavelin*. Its capacity corresponds to the amount of wine remaining from a liter once the ageing process is complete.

SAVOIE

· ·

Savoie is better known for its snow and its glaciers than for its wines, which is a great pity. In this region of lakes and mountains, grain fields and rolling pastures, the Savoie vineyards are set in terraces on hillsides at altitudes of between 980 and 1,970 feet (300 and 600 m), between Lake Geneva and Chambéry. They produce a wide and appealing variety of wines that are mainly consumed locally.

Vineyard landscape

Savoie is blessed with a continental climate, meaning cold winters, hot summers, and sunny late autumns—all tempered by the presence of lakes. The soils are varied, with limestone scree, stony moraines, and sandstone being the most common. Vines have been grown here since the Roman era. The vineyards reached their peak in the 19th century, when they exceeded 19,770 acres (8,000 hectares). But the phylloxera crisis reduced this to less than 4,940 acres (2,000 hectares). They were slow to re-establish themselves, but began to pick up after the 1950s and have continued to increase ever since.

Grape varieties and wine styles

Savoie has a wide variety of mostly native, very original, grape varieties. They are largely white and produce very stylish wines.
JACQUÈRE. The most widely planted variety, it creates fresh and light wines. This is the principal grape variety in Abymes and Apremont *crus*.
ROUSSETTE (OR ALTESSE). This grape variety, growing in popularity, produces rich and fruity wines with some spicy notes. It forms the base for wines under the AOC Roussette de Savoie.
ROUSSANNE (OR BERGERON). Produced in very small quantities, it creates high quality wines, sometimes even exceptional wines to lay down—notably in Chignin with the Chignon-Bergeron.

SAVOIE STATISTICS (AOC)

Vineyard area: 4,940 acres (2,000 ha)

Production: 1.6 million cases (145,000 hl)

Whites: 65%

Reds: 35%

(Syndicat des vins de Savoie, 2007)

The Savoie AOCs

· ·

- Vin de Savoie with or without *cru* name
- Roussette de Savoie with or without *cru* name
- Roussette de Seyssel

A small neighboring region

Between Jura and Savoie, Bugey covers some 1,235 acres (500 hectares) and three production areas—Cerdon, Montagnieu, Belley—on sandy-limestone and sandy-clay soils. It primarily produces still and sparkling white wines from Savoie and Burgundy grape varieties. Worthy of note are Bugey-Cerdon, sparkling wines and lightly sparkling wines, white or rosé, created using the local ancestral method (*see p.70*).

CHASSELAS. This variety covers 70 percent of the vineyards, and is the sole base for Marin, Marignan, Ripaille, and Crépy *crus*.
MOLETTE. This grape produces a clear, light white wine, fairly alcoholic and very fruity, with some herbaceous notes. With high acidity, it is used in Seyssel sparkling wine.
GRINGET. Equivalent to Jura's Savagnin, this produces the famous Ayze sparkling wine.
CHARDONNAY. Introduced in the 1960s, this variety is grown across practically the entire Savoie area. Whether alone or in a blend, it produces lively and fruity wines.
GAMAY. This is the dominant red grape variety, making fresh and light wines. The best examples are to be found in the Chautagne region.
MONDEUSE. This old grape variety traditionally produces well-structured and tannic red wines, notably in Arbin, where it is the only variety used.
PERSAN. This old, red grape variety had practically disappeared. Today, it is being grown again by some producers in Combe de Savoie and Maurienne. It makes tannic, rather colorful wines that are well suited to ageing.

Famous wines from Alsace, Jura, and Savoie

Small vineyards, but great wines. Alsace, Jura, and Savoie can claim to produce several grand vins, some of which are counted among the best in the world.

ALSACE AOC

This is the most important of the Alsace AOCs. It covers the entire area, and primarily produces white wines (92 percent). Where the label mentions the grape variety, this is the only variety used and the wine name follows that of the appellation—such as Alsace Muscat, Alsace Riesling, Alsace Gewurztraminer, Alsace Pinot Noir, Alsace Sylvaner. If the grape variety is not indicated, then the wine is a blend of more than one variety and is sold under the appellations Alsace Edelzwicker or Gentil.

> **GRAPE VARIETIES** Riesling, Sylvaner, Gewurztraminer, Pinot Blanc, Pinot Gris, Muscat, Pinot Noir.

> **SOIL** Schist, granitic, volcanic, marly limestone.

> **STYLE** The whites are generally dry, fruity, and aromatic, with each grape variety having its own specific characters. Gewurztraminer offers powerful, full, structured wines, with notes of rose and lychee. Riesling produces fullbodied and well-structured wines with notes of petroleum (more tactfully known as "mineral"), and a tang of citrus fruit. Muscat yields winning wines with a nose of fresh grapes, heightened by hints of exotic fruits: you can almost feel the crunch of the fruit. Pinot Blanc produces powerful wine with an intense floral, white fruit nose. Alsace reds, made from Pinot Noir, are slightly tart with aromas of currant and cherry; with age, a crisp palate develops with flavors of ripe soft fruits, from which emerge some gamey notes. Sweet wines in the categories *vendange tardive* (VT) or *sélection de grains nobles* (SGN; *see* p.305) are high-quality wines that produce an exceptional concentration of aromas.

Color:	Serving temperature:	Ageing potential:
White and red.	*46 to 50°F (8 to 10°C) for whites; 54 to 57°F (12 to 14°C) for reds.*	*Within a year for Muscat; 1 to 3 years for Gewurztraminer, Riesling, Pinot Blanc; 1 to 3 years for reds; 2 to 10 years for VT and SGN whites.*

CRÉMANT D'ALSACE AOC

The number one sparkling wine consumed in France (as an AOC), Crémant d'Alsace is very popular. Its method of production includes a second fermentation in bottle (*see* p.71).

> **GRAPE VARIETIES** White: Pinot Blanc, Pinot Gris, Riesling, Chardonnay, either blended or alone (in which case the variety name appears on the label). Rosé: Pinot Noir.

> **SOIL** Granitic, chalky, sandstone, marl.

> **STYLE** Alsace sparkling wines are light and airy with wonderful aromatic range and delicate bubbles. These are wines for pleasure.

Color:	Serving temperature:	Ageing potential:
White and rosé.	*43 to 46°F (6 to 8°C), put on ice.*	*Consume within a year.*

ALSACE GRAND CRU AOC

Grape variety is less important than the *terroir* here, as this appellation is designed to show off the character of the best sites. For this reason, there are 51 such *terroirs* (*see* p.305) defined according to strict climatic and geologic criteria. They follow stringent rules regarding viticulture, choice of grape varieties, yield, alcohol content, vinification, *etc*. These wines represent just four percent of production. As well as the vintage and the name of the *cru*, the label must specify the grape variety, unless it is a blend (permitted for the *lieux-dits* Altenberg de Berghem and Kaefferkopf).

> **GRAPE VARIETIES** Gewurztraminer, Riesling, Pinot Gris, Muscat. The Sylvaner variety is granted as an exception for the Alsace Grand Cru Zotzenberg.

> **SOIL** Schist, granitic, volcanic, marly limestone, sandstone.

> **STYLE** It would be impossible to describe the styles of all 51 *grand crus* here; great Alsace whites are so different from each other thanks to each *terroir*. These wines, which reflect and refine their *terroir*, are generally distinguished, powerful, and very well suited to ageing.

Color: White.

Serving temperature: Around 46°F (8°C), fresh but not icy.

Ageing potential: 10 to 15 years for all grands crus. 15 to 20 years for the VT and SGNs, or even more for the greatest vintages.

CHÂTEAU-CHALON AOC

Château-Chalon is the cradle of *vin jaune* and the only appellation entirely dedicated to it. The AOC covers four villages and 120 acres (50 hectares), with a production of around 16,700 cases (1,500 hl) depending on the vintage, since wine is only produced in great years. In other years, Château-Chalon is not produced at all.

> **GRAPE VARIETY** Savignin.

> **SOIL** Blue or gray marl.

> **STYLE** A wine with a unique character, which may sometimes be a little disconcerting, and a complex and rich nose combining the aromas of walnut, apple, curry, and mushrooms. Its palate is both rich and dry, with an extremely long finish (known as the "peacock tail").

Color: White.

Serving temperature: 57 to 61°F (14 to 16°C).

Ageing potential: 50 to 100 years.

Selected Alsace producers

- **Cave des Vignerons de Pfaffenheim.** The most dynamic and award-winning cellar in Alsace, offering a wide range of excellent quality and good value.

- **Domaine Dopff & Irion (Riquewihr).** A wide range of regionally representative wines, notably the Kaefferkopf made with Gewurztraminer, the Rouge d'Ottrott, and the Crément d'Alsace rosé.

- **Domaine Hugel (Riquewihr).** One of the most famous of the Alsace estates, founded in 1639. The *vendanges tardives* and *sélections de grains nobles* are quite simply remarkable.

- **Domaine Pierre Frick (Pfaffenheim).** This estate producing biodynamically cultivated, extremely pure wines should not be overlooked.

- **Domaine Ostertag (Epfig).** The *Vins de Fruit*, *Vins de Pierre*, and *Vins de Temps* are real success stories.

- **Domaine Seppi Landmann (Riquewihr).** The Gewurztraminers and Rieslings produced as *vendanges tardives* and *sélection de grains nobles* deserve special attention.

- **Maison Trimbach (Ribeauvillé).** Exceptional Gewurztraminers and Rieslings, notably the Clos Sainte-Hune.

- **Domaine Weinbach (Kaysersberg).** Impressive wines, among the greatest sweet wines in the world.

- **Domaine Zind-Humbrecht (Turckheim).** Biodynamically cultivated *grands crus* that clearly emphasize the idea of *terroir*.

- **Marcel Deiss (Bergheim).** One of the biggest estates in Alsace. Biodynamically cultivated *grand crus* that are always exceptional.

Selected Jura producers

- **Château d'Arlay (Arlay).** One of Jura's most famous producers. The white wines and *vins jaunes* are quite simply magnificent.

- **Domaine André et Mireille Tissot (Montigny-lès-Arsures).** For the organic wines, and notably for the Cuvée La Mailloche (Arbois Blanc) and the Spirale, a remarkable *vin de paille*.

- **Domaine Berthet-Bondet (Château-Chalon).** Remarkable *vins jaunes* and Côtes-du-Jura whites.

- **Jacques Tissot (Arbois).** Superb Jura *crémants* and *vins jaunes*.

- **Domaine Henri Maire (Arbois).** Symbolic of Jura, Henri Maire has restored his reputation in the region. A beautiful and wide range of wines, and good value.

- **Domaine Pierre Overnoy-Emmanuel Houillon (Pupillin).** Excellent, very pure wines: intense whites, sulfur-free reds, biodynamically cultivated.

- **Frutières Vinicoles (Arbois, Voiteur, Pupillin, Caveau des Byards).** Offering a wide range of wines and excellent value.

- **Michel Gahier (Montigny-lès-Arsures).** Notable for natural wines and the purity of their cuvées.

ARBOIS AOC

JURA

The most important of the Jura AOCs (40 percent of total production), it covers 13 villages around the town of Arbois; but only the village of Pupillin may couple its name with that of the appellation. A favorite *terroir* for Trousseau and Poulsard, the AOC is most famous for its red wines; but it also produces white wines, *vins jaunes*, *vins de paille*, and *crémants*.

> **GRAPE VARIETIES** White: Chardonnay and Savignin; red and rosé: Poulsard, Trousseau, Pinot Noir.

> **SOIL** Clay and limestone scree.

> **STYLE** The reds are generous and tannic, with a rich bouquet of soft fruit aromas supported by gamey notes. Great length on the palate. The Chardonnay whites are elegant—their fruity and floral aromas seasoned with spicy, walnut, and honey notes. The Savagnin examples are more opulent with notes of walnut and spices, and a beautiful length on the palate.

Color:
White and red.

Serving temperature:
46 to 50°F (8 to 10°C) for whites and rosés;
57 to 61°F (14 to 16°C) for reds;
57 to 61°F (14 to 16°C) for vin jaune;
45 to 50°F (7 to 10°C) for vin de paille;
43 to 46°F (6 to 8°C) for sparkling wines.

Ageing potential:
Within a year for crémants;
1 to 3 years for whites;
3 to 5 years for reds;
more than 10 years for vin de paille;
50 to 100 years for vin jaune.

CÔTES-DU-JURA AOC

JURA

The largest AOC in Jura, this appellation stretches from Salins in the north to St-Amour in the south, across a wide variety of terroirs. It covers 105 villages, the most famous being Voiteur, Poligny, Gevingey, and Arbois. Whites are clearly dominant here, whether dry or sweet, still or sparkling.

There is also a wide range of Jura red wines, rosés, *vins jaunes*, and *vins de paille*.

> **GRAPE VARIETIES** White: Chardonnay and Savignin; red: Poulsard, Trousseau, and Pinot Noir.

> **SOIL** Clay and limestone scree.

> **STYLE** The whites offer a wide variety of styles depending on the terroir, the vinification method, and the blends. Two categories emerge: fresh floral whites, made from Chardonnay; and distinctive whites made from Savignin. The reds are tannic, rounded, and rich, with soft fruit aromas. *Vins de paille* produce a perfume of exotic and dried fruits.

Color:
White and red.

Serving temperature:
46 to 50°F (8 to 10°C) for whites and rosés;
57 to 61°F (14 to 16°C) for reds;
57 to 61°F (14 to 16°C) for vin jaune;
45 to 50°F (7 to 10°C) for vin de paille;
43 to 46°F (6 to 8°C) for sparkling wines.

Ageing potential:
Within a year for crémants;
1 to 3 years for whites;
3 to 5 years for reds;
more than 10 years for vin de paille;
50 to 100 years for vin jaune.

VIN DE SAVOIE AOC

This is the main Savoie appellation. The name may be used alone or coupled with the names of 16 *villages*, or zones, known as *crus*: Abymes, Apremont, Arbin, Ayze, Chautagne, Chignin, Chignin-Bergeron, Crépy, Cruet, Jongieux, Marignan, Marin, Montmélian, Ripaille, St-Jean-de-la-Porte, St-Jeoire-Prieuré. The wines of this appellation, which covers four *départements*, may be made from more than one grape variety. The AOC Vin de Savoie primarily produces dry whites (70 percent of production), the rest being shared among reds, rosés, and sparkling wines. With demand being greater than supply, these mountain wines are often consumed locally, and while still young. However, some deserve to be laid down for a few years.

> **GRAPE VARIETIES** White: Jacquère, Altesse or Roussette, Chasselas, Molette, Gringet, Roussanne. Red: Mondeuse, Pinot Noir, Gamay Noir.

> **SOIL** Limestone scree and glacial moraines.

> **STYLE** Generally, the red wines made from Mondeuse have a beautiful purple appearance, with wild aromas of mountain fruits and violet, and highly pronounced spicy notes. Their astringent and persistent tannins become pleasantly rounded with age. The whites are light, very dry, and fruity, especially those made with Jacquère. Roussanne whites, with their floral and exotic fruit scents, are more well-structured and can be aged for longer. Those from Roussette have great finesse.

Color:
Red, white, and rosé.

Serving temperature:
46 to 50°F (8 to 10°C) for whites and rosés; 54 to 55°F (12 to 13°C) for reds, or 59 to 63°F (15 to 17°C) for Mondeuse reds; 43 to 46°F (6 to 8°C) for sparkling wines.

Ageing potential:
Within a year for sparkling wines; within 2 years for whites and rosés; 2 to 6 years for reds.

ROUSSETTE DE SAVOIE AOC

The vines of this appellation are grown along the Rhône between Frangy and Jongieux. The wine takes its name from the Roussette grape variety, the sole variety used for the four *crus* Frangy, Marestel, Monthoux, and Monterminod. Other white wines may be made from either Chardonnay or Roussette.

> **GRAPE VARIETIES** Roussette (also known as Altesse), Chardonnay.

> **SOIL** Limestone scree and glacial moraines.

> **STYLE** These wines have great finesse, and are extremely fresh and lively. Flavors include dried fruit and walnut, and they linger on the palate for some time.

Color:
White.

Serving temperature:
43 to 46°F (6 to 8°C).

Ageing potential:
Within a year, but can be kept for a few years.

Selected Savoie and Bugey producers

- **Château de Ripaille (Ripaille).** Lively Chasselas wines with fruity and mineral notes, pleasantly long.

- **Château de la Violette (Les Marches).** Very elegant Jacquère whites.

- **Domaine Raphaël Bartucci (Mérignat).** A worthy representative of Bugey wines, the Cerdon rosé produced through organic agriculture contains beautiful small bubbles, merry and lively.

- **Domaine Belluard (Ayze).** Delicate and enchanting sparkling wines, and still Gringet wines, too.

- **Domaine Dupasquier et Fils (Jongieux).** Very well-balanced Roussettes.

- **Domaine Louis Magnin (Arbin).** Wonderful Mondeuses and superb Bergerons, well suited to ageing.

- **Domaine André et Michel Quénard (Chignin).** Remarkable Gamay and Mondeuse reds, and whites from Abymes and Chignin-Bergeron.

- **Domaine Raymond Quénard (Chignin).** The Mondeuses and Bergeron cuvées are magnificently fruity and full of quality.

THE LOIRE VALLEY

The Loire Valley is one of the most versatile wine regions in France. It produces a range of wines with flavors and textures so different that it is difficult to find common characteristics.

Long journey

The vineyards of the Loire have been established in the furrow plowed by the longest river in France. The Loire rises from the south of the Massif Central, at more than 4,265 ft (1,300 m) in altitude, where vines are rare. Halfway along its passage to the sea, where it begins turning to the west, it reaches the region of Sancerre and Pouilly, where its altitude is no more than 656 ft (200 m). It then runs alongside the forest of Orleans before continuing its course westward through the vast expanses of Touraine, Anjou, and Saumur, at an altitude of only 164 ft (50 m). Finally, it reaches Nantes, which is next to the ocean.

The 629-mile (1,013-km) journey passes through a wide variety of geologic terrains that, together with fluctuations in climate and grape varieties, greatly influence the character of the wines.

LOIRE VALLEY STATISTICS (AOC AND AOVDQS)
Vineyard area: 180, 500 acres (52,000 ha)
Production: 33 million cases (c. 3,000,000 hl)
Whites: 52%
Reds: 26%
Rosés: 16%
Sparkling: 6%
(www.vinsvaldeloire.fr)

From the 10th century, winemaking monks in abbeys and monasteries contributed to the further development of vineyards. In the 12th century, Henry Plantagenet, Count of Anjou, became King of England and served the wines of Anjou to his court. Later, during the 15th and 16th centuries, the castles of the Loire and their royal owners encouraged the work of wine producers, who sought to improve their wines by carefully selecting grape varieties and improving their cultivation.

Until the middle of the 19th century, Loire wines really flourished, thanks in particular to trade with the Netherlands via the port of Nantes. But the phylloxera epidemic devastated its vineyards, just as it did everywhere else. A fresh start was made in the 20th century, and quality became the watchword. Sancerre, Vouvray, and Quincy were among the first AOC wines here

Historic inheritance

Regional vineyards date back to Roman times. During the 4th century, St. Martin, the bishop of Tours, encouraged the development of viticulture by reserving the use of wine for the demands of religious worship and the needs of the sick.

Quality revolution

The Loire Valley now has some 60 wine appellations. They collectively represent the largest producer of white AOC wines in France, and the leading region in the production of sparkling wines (excluding Champagne). For several recent years, there has been a real reawakening about local *terroir*. Lower yields, better segmentation of appellations, more care in winemaking and wine ageing: all substantive endeavors intended to improve wine quality. It has already led to new appellations being created, the latest being those of Orléans and Orléans-Cléry in 2005. This revolution in quality would never have happened without the efforts of many new, young, talented wine producers, who come from diverse backgrounds—ranging from children or grandchildren of established winemakers to wine enthusiasts ready to participate in the adventure.

Sub-regions

The Loire Valley is divided into several sub-regions, each with its own identity and style of wines. The vineyards actually alongside the Loire River, as

ANJOU AND PAYS NANTAIS

well as its tributaries—the Cher, Indre, Allier, and Vienne—are among the most important.

THE CENTRE. This sub-region begins north of the Auvergne Mountains, stretches around the city of Bourges, and then continues to the outskirts of Gien. The white wines of Sauvignon Blanc dominate here, and the leading appellations are Sancerre and Pouilly-Fumé.

TOURAINE. This district starts west of Orléans and reaches Chinon at the outskirts of Saumur. The vineyards here cover a large number of appellations. In typical soils, locally known as "*tufs*" or tuffeau, white wines are produced with mineral aromas—particularly rocks or abraded stones—with a quite salty texture in Chinon and Vouvray. The red wines, produced from Cabernet Franc, are included in the appellations Bourgueil and Chinon. Along with neighboring Anjou, Touraine is the largest producer of red wines from the Loire. It is also from within this sub-region that many of the sparkling wines produced in the Loire Valley originate, including Crémant de Loire and the sparkling and lightly sparkling Vouvray and Montlouis-sur-Loire wines.

ANJOU AND SAUMUR. This vast region extends some 20 miles east of Nantes and along the Loire to Saumur and Angers. The notable appellations here are for white wines—dry ones such as Savennières, and sweet ones like Coteaux du Layon and other Coteaux de l'Aubance. In the area around Saumur, there also are several red and sparkling wines.

PAYS NANTAIS AND VENDÉE. Located close to Nantes and partly in Vendée, these vineyards near the ocean produce mostly white wines, quite refreshing and full of flavors perfect to accompany seafood. The grape variety Melon de Bourgogne finds its finest expression in the Muscadet appellation, producing bright and crisp wines; some of them, which are made on their lees, have a lightness and obvious freshness. The wines from the hills of Ancenis are made from the Malvasia grape, whereas Folle Blanche, also grown in southwest France, displays freshness and panache in the Gros Plant du Pays Nantais, a slightly sharp wine that goes well with the local cuisine. Somewhat isolated southwest of the Loire, the appellation Fiefs Vendéens, with its Mareuil, Vix, Brem, and Pissotte *crus*, produces red wines and a few whites.

Climate change in the Loire Valley

The year 2003 made its mark in the world of wine because scorching sunshine and high temperatures made life difficult for both grapes and producers. Since then, winemakers have wondered about changes in their *climats*, with a certainty that they will suffer global warming and its consequences in the future. Many of them are trying to counter the effects of rising annual temperatures by turning to varieties that have not been previously grown in Loire vineyards, but might be suited to the new conditions. Syrah, normally used for wines from the Rhône Valley, is making an appearance for the first time. Also, Chasselas or Petit Meslier are grape varieties already present in the vineyards of the Loire, and are interesting for their freshness and liveliness. In the future, without actually completely changing the identity of appellations, the rules regarding permitted grape varieties can no longer be the same.

> A number of microclimates, soils, and grape varieties are responsible for the variety of wines from the Loire.

Loire Valley soils

The geographic extent of the Loire Valley gives it a wide variety of soils and subsoils. Here is a selection of the most significant.

Caillottes (chalky stone) On the hard limestone ground in Sancerre, the Sauvignon Blanc grape finds its *terroir* of choice. When the limestone is slightly more friable, the stones are called "grillottes." They give the wine pretty intense flavors and plenty of liveliness.

Chailloux (quartz) Among the vineyards of the Centre, this soil of silica and colluvium is mainly seen in the Pouilly Fumé appellation. It gives the wine a deep minerality and exotic fruit flavors.

Schist In the Pays Nantais, this soil gives wines freshness and minerality.

Tuffeau This hard limestone is found mainly in Vouvray and Montlouis. It is an ideal medium for producing minerality. It's also home to many cellars, literally carved into tuffeau cliffs.

Varennes A mixture of sand and gravel, this soil type is found in Chinon. It produces wines of finesse. In St-Nicolas-de-Bourgueil, varennes also designates sandy loam soil.

Grape varieties

The variety of grapes cultivated in the Loire Valley enables producers to diversify the style of their wines. It is not uncommon for a winery to offer red wine and white wine, still and sparkling. Some grape varieties here produce wines of exquisite quality, such as Chenin Blanc in Vouvray. Also, Sauvignon Blanc in Sancerre displays the outstanding purity of its fruit.

DOMINANT VARIETIES. In the vineyards of the Centre, you will find Sauvignon Blanc and some Chardonnay for white wines, Pinot Noir and Gamay for the reds. From Touraine to Pays Nantais, Chenin Blanc and Melon de Bourgogne (the latter only in the Muscadet AOC) dominate for whites, while the Cabernet Franc stands out as the major red variety.

RARE VARIETIES. Apart from these well-known varieties, there are in places some rare varieties to please the palate. Thus, Pinot Gris produces a rosé Reuilly wine with a fresh, sappy texture. In the St. Pourçain appellation, the Tressalier and Saint Pierre Doré yield white wines with invigorating texture. The Gris Meunier, a synonym for Pinot Meunier, plays a significant part in the rosé wines of Orleans; while in the Touraine appellation Gamay Noir is supplemented with Gamay de Bouze and Gamay de Chaudenay. Finally, in the hills of Ancenis, the full-bodied

TRUE OR FALSE?

White Sancerre is best in its early years, very young.

FALSE. The white wines produced from Sauvignon Blanc (as well as Chenin Blanc) are very enjoyable in their youth. But they may also be aged in a cellar for more than 15 years.

> Vines at Sauzay, for the Saumur-Champigny appellation.

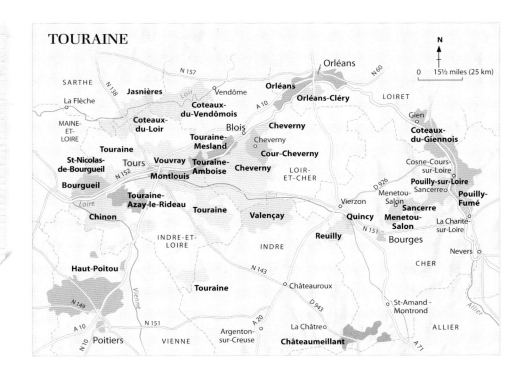

and generous Malvasia grape, a relative of Pinot Grigio, makes its distinctive mark on wines.

Négociants and estates

The Loire Valley is a region of small estates, and therefore closer to Burgundy than to Bordeaux. However, while the Burgundians have been enriched by the reputation of their wines, it has not been the same for producers in the Loire, whose talent has not always received its due reward. Muscadet, Sancerre, Pouilly Fumé (white), Bourgueil, and Saumur-Champigny (red) represent the only relatively successful wines produced.

Few wine cooperatives guarantee an income for their producers, which means total freedom in terms of available stocks and the demands of *négociants*. Most often located in the region of Muscadet, between Saumur and Nantes, *négociants* buy wine from different estates to blend them. Purchases are generally based on price, and winemakers only release their less successful wines, which explains why bottled Sancerre in the Nantes region is often disappointing.

Loire Valley AOCs and AOVDQSs

REGIONAL APPELLATIONS
• Rosé de Loire
• Crémant de Loire

CENTRE
• Châteaumeillant
• Coteaux-du-Giennois
• Menetou-Salon
• Orléans
• Orléans-Cléry
• Pouilly-sur-Loire
• Pouilly Fumé (or Blanc Fumé de Pouilly)
• Quincy
• Reuilly
• Sancerre

TOURAINE
• Bourgueil
• Chinon
• Cour-Cheverny
• Cheverny
• Coteaux-du-Vendômois
• Coteaux-du-Loir
• Jasnières

• Montlouis-sur-Loire
• St-Nicolas-de-Bourgueil
• Touraine
• Touraine-Amboise
• Touraine-Azay-le-Rideau
• Touraine-Mesland
• Touraine-Noble-Joué
• Valençay
• Vouvray

ANJOU AND SAUMUR
• Anjou
• Anjou blanc
• Anjou Coteaux-de-la-Loire
• Anjou Gamay
• Anjou mousseux
• Anjou-Villages
• Anjou-Villages-Brissac
• Bonnezeaux
• Cabernet d'Anjou
• Cabernet de Saumur
• Coteaux-de-l'Aubance
• Coteaux-du-Layon
• Coteaux-du-Layon-Chaume
• Coteaux-de-Saumur

• Quarts-de-Chaume
• Rosé d'Anjou
• Saumur
• Saumur-Champigny
• Saumur mousseux
• Savennières, whether or not followed by the name of the particular site
• Thouarsais

PAYS NANTAIS, VENDÉE, AND POITEVIN
• Coteaux-d'Ancenis
• Fiefs Vendéens
• Gros-Plant Nantais
• Haut-Poitou
• Muscadet
• Muscadet-Sèvre-et-Maine
• Muscadet-Coteaux-de-la-Loire
• Muscadet-Côtes-de-Grandlieu

AUVERGNE
• Côtes-d'Auvergne
• Côte-Roannaise
• Côtes-du-Forez
• Saint-Pourçain

Famous wines of the Loire Valley

From Centre to Pays Nantais, following the course of river, these are the remarkable wine appellations of the Loire Valley.

REUILLY AOC

This vineyard district was established in the 7th century by the monks of the Abbey of St-Denis. The wines, originally intended only for the city of Bourges, have gradually gained attention throughout France and neighboring countries. The appellation spans two *départements*, Cher and Indre, southeast of Bourges, with an area of 460 acres (186 ha). Reuilly and Sancerre are the only AOC vineyards of Centre, which produces wines in three styles.

> **GRAPE VARIETIES** Sauvignon Blanc for white wines; Pinot Gris and Pinot Noir for rosés. Pinot Noir is the only variety used for reds.

> **SOIL** Limestone marl and sand on the hills, which provide the wine of this appellation with perfect depth and some slightly sharp notes.

> **STYLE** First, rosé. The significant presence of Pinot Gris always ensures a full and generous palate. The white wines are harmonious and burst with flavor. In the red wines, Pinot Noir impresses with its rich character and its delicacy—flavors are punctuated with strawberry, raspberry, and various wild berries.

Color:
White, rosé, and red.

Serving temperature:
46 to 50°F (8 to 10°C) for the whites and rosés; 61°F (16°C) for the reds.

Ageing potential:
3 to 7 years.

QUINCY AOC

Located a few miles east of Bourges, Quincy is the oldest vineyard district in the region. It was also the first vineyard in the Loire Valley to acquire AOC status in 1936. The appellation covers 554 acres (224 ha) and is spread over two areas, Quincy and Brinay. The Sauvignon Blanc grape was first brought to the Notre Dame de Beauvoir Abbey here by monks of the Cistercian order.

> **GRAPE VARIETY** Sauvignon Blanc.

> **SOIL** There are three types of soil, namely sandy-gravelly soils, soils based on formations of red sand, and sandy-silt formations containing various amounts of clay.

> **STYLE** Quincy is a dry, fine, and lively wine. In tasting, it shows a very light color that is always bright and clear. The nose has an array of fresh citrus, like kaffir lime or grapefruit, and exotic fruits. Those continue on the palate, which is very fresh and pure. It is always best to leave this wine for at least three years before tasting.

Color:
White.

Serving temperature:
46 to 50°F (8 to 10°C).

Ageing potential:
3 to 10 years.

Easy-to-drink, good value Loire wines

DRY WHITES

- Coteaux-du-Giennois AOC: Émile Balland (Cosne-sur-Loire).
- Montlouis-sur-Loire AOC: Clos de la Bretonnière, Domaine de la Taille aux Loups (Montlouis-sur-Loire).
- Orléans AOC: L'Excellence, Clos Saint-Fiacre (Mareau-aux-Prés).
- Pouilly Fumé AOC: Domaine Michel Redde (Saint-Andelain).
- Sancerre AOC: Florès et Nuance, Domaine Vincent Pinard (Bué).

SPARKLING WHITES

- Montlouis-sur-Loire AOC: *Brut traditionnel*, Domaine François Chidaine (Montlouis-sur-Loire).
- Vouvray AOC: *Brut* (Traditional method), Domaine du Clos Naudin (Vouvray). Quality sparkling wine: Cuvée Ludwig Hahn, Domaine de l'Écu (Le Landreau).

ROSÉS

- Sancerre AOC: Domaine François Cotat (Chavignol).

REDS

- Chinon AOC: Les Varennes du Grand Clos, Domaine Charles Joguet (Chinon).
- Orléans-Cléry AOC: Clos Saint-Fiacre (Mareau-aux-Prés).
- Sancerre AOC: À Nicolas, Domaine Pascal et Nicolas Reverdy (Maimbray); Domaine Francois Cotat (Chavignol) ; Domaine François Crochet (Bué).

Les Varennes du Grand Clos
CHINON
2007
CHARLES JOGUET

SANCERRE AOC

CENTRE

This is the flagship wine appellation from Centre. It covers the slopes and hills around the village of Sancerre, over an area of 6,845 acres (2,770 ha). It also covers the best *terroirs*, traditionally known for the quality of their wines, in Chavignol and Bué.

> **GRAPE VARIETIES** Sauvignon Blanc is the only grape used for white wines; Pinot Noir is the only grape variety for reds and rosés.

> **SOIL** The appellation is spread across a vast array of soils: *caillottes* and *grillottes*, but also white or flinty soils. They combine to produce wines full of flavor with many different characteristics.

> **STYLE** Long considered as a fruity, slightly sharp, and refreshing wine, the style of the appellation has changed greatly. While in the past Sancerre was matured in bottle, there are now wines aged in barrel that have intense mineral notes.

Color:
White, rosé, and red.

Serving temperature:
46 to 50°F (8 to 10°C) for the whites and rosés; 61°F (16°C) for the reds.

Ageing potential:
5 to 10 years.

POUILLY FUMÉ AOC (OR BLANC FUMÉ DE POUILLY AOC)

CENTRE

The Pouilly Fumé appellation has long shown Sauvignon Blanc in the best possible light. There is flinty soil on top of the hill at St-Andelain, which is ideal for raising the minerality and crystalline purity of this grape variety.

> **GRAPE VARIETY** Sauvignon Blanc.

> **SOIL** Just like Sancerre, this appellation covers a variety of soils; and they provide evidence of the impact of both time and nature. Chailloux (quartz), marl limestone, and flint are the best soils for this wine, as far as wine producers are concerned.

> **STYLE** These wines always match the sites from which they come. The wines from marl limestone are often valued for their fairly straightforward flavors: herbal infusions and fruit; the Chailloux sites convey the expected minerality and some exotic hints; while the flint sites produce a sublime mineral burst, highlighted by stony notes.

Color:
White.

Serving temperature:
46 to 50°F (8 to 10°C).

Ageing potential:
5 to 15 years.

ORLÉANS AND ORLÉANS-CLÉRY AOCs

Orléans has always occupied a special place in terms of wine production in the Loire Valley. In the past, coopers lived there and produced the best barrels for the finest estates in the region; but it's an activity that has gradually been abandoned. The award of its AOC in 2005 restored the wines of Orléans (previously classified as VDQS) to their former honor. The Orléans-Cléry appellation applies only to red wines.

> **GRAPE VARIETIES** Chardonnay for white wines, Pinot Noir and Pinot Meunier for Orléans AOC reds; Cabernet Franc for Orléans-Cléry reds.
> **SOIL** The vineyards, located mainly south of Orléans, are based in soils composed of alluvial deposits left by a river millions of years ago. It should also be noted that silica and limestone are present, giving the wines mineral tones.
> **STYLE** Recent vintages have produced white Chardonnay wines with slightly exotic, very pleasant hints of citrus—and a refreshing palate. The rosés have a very expressive fruitiness shifting toward a slightly sharp finish. The Orléans reds are flexible and have a silky texture. The Orléans-Cléry has more depth and structure as well as notes of Sichuan pepper and leather.

Color:
White, rosé, and red for Orléans; red only for Orléans-Cléry.

Serving temperature:
46 to 50°F (8 to 10°C) for the whites and rosés; 61°F (16°C) for the reds.

Ageing potential:
5 to 7 years.

JASNIÈRES AOC

This tiny district of 160 acres (65 ha) is one of the oldest Loire appellations. Set slightly back from the river, it has produced wines solely from Chenin Blanc for many ages. They are designed for their minerality and offer an incredible potential for ageing.
> **GRAPE VARIETY** Chenin Blanc.
> **SOIL** The vines face south, and are on a soil that is dotted with flint and tuffeau stones. Consequently, when the warm weather comes, perfect grape ripeness is ensured.
> **STYLE** The appellation creates dry, taut, crystalline white wines that show notes of quince on the palate with a sublime directness. Also, its sweet wines are synonymous with balance and harmony. It is a sweetness that rewards the palate with touches of wax, quince, and acacia honey.

Color:
White.

Serving temperature:
46 to 50°F (8 to 10°C) for the moelleux; 50 to 54°F (10 to 12°C for the secs.

Ageing potential:
3 to 15 years for the white secs; 10 to 30 years for the moelleux and liquoreux.

VOUVRAY AND MONTLOUIS-SUR-LOIRE AOCs

Vouvray, at 4,945 acres (2,000 ha), and Montlouis-sur-Loire, at 915 acres (370 ha), are twin appellations separated by the Loire River, near Tours. They are the source of great Loire whites. Chenin Blanc, their sole grape variety, offers multiple styles of wine: from the driest and most vigorous, to sparkling wine, all the way through to sweet wines.

> **GRAPE VARIETY** Chenin Blanc.
> **SOIL** Vouvray and Montlouis-sur-Loire are based in a tuffeau *terroir*, a fairly soft limestone and chalk rock. It passes on the most crystalline and mineral elements to the wine. It is the *terroir* of choice for Chenin Blanc.
> **STYLE** The hallmark of these two appellations is variety: dry (*sec*) white wines and lightly sweetened *demi-secs*, as well as delightful sweet wines and bubbly sparkling wines. Regarding flavors, there are hints of quince, lime, and bergamot against a background of acacia honey. All are typical features of these two appellations.

Color:
White.

Serving temperature:
46 to 50°F (8 to 10°C) for the moelleux *and sparkling whites;* 50°F (10°C) for the secs.

Ageing potential:
3 to 10 years for the secs; 7 to 30 years (or more for the best vintages) for the moelleux.

CHINON AOC

This vast appellation covers 5,683 acres (2,300 ha) on the south bank of the Loire River, across from Bourgueil, around the town of Chinon. This appellation mainly produces red wines in which the Cabernet Franc shows its full potential, offering both significant depth and tannic subtlety.

> **GRAPE VARIETIES** Cabernet Franc and Cabernet Sauvignon for the reds and rosés; Chenin Blanc for white wines.

> **SOIL** Limestone. There are also hillocks of flinty clay and sand in the area.

> **STYLE** The reds require several years of development in the cellar for the Cabernet Franc to reveal its entire character and subtlety. They then release blackberry, blackcurrant, and elderflower fragrances. Their longer development will make them turn smoky, fiery, and peppery. The whites offer the right balance between a broad texture and chalky or flinty characters. As for the rosés, they show all the richness to be expected from this appellation.

Color:
White, rosé, and red.

Serving temperature:
46 to 50°F (8 to 10°C) for the whites and rosés;
61°F (16°C) for the reds.

Ageing potential:
3 to 5 years for the whites and rosés;
7 to 20 years for the reds.

BOURGUEIL AND ST-NICOLAS-DE-BOURGUEIL AOCs

Located on the right bank of the Loire, a few rows of vines upstream from Saumur, these AOCs are appreciated for the structure and depth of their red wines. It is worth pointing out the expansion in quality there in recent years, especially in terms of maturation, and the rise of enthusiastic and committed new wine producers.

> **GRAPE VARIETIES** Cabernet Franc and Cabernet Sauvignon.

> **SOIL** Many of the vineyards in these AOCs are located on hillsides. Soil composition is much more sandy than in other parts of the region, interspersed with patches of clay that have an effect on the power of the wine.

> **STYLE** These reds are a glowing color, accompanied by scents of blackberry and plum, as well as a firm palate with fine, subtle tannins. In order to fully enjoy these wines, it is best to leave them in the wine cellar for a few years.

Color:
Red.

Serving temperature:
61°F (16°C).

Ageing potential:
5 to 25 years.

COTEAUX-DU-LAYON AOC

This represents a major benchmark for sweet wines in the Loire Valley. The vineyard area of 3,460 acres (1,400 ha), located near Angers, extends on each side of the Layon River, a small tributary of the Loire. In the fall, under the cover of mists from the river, botrytis appears on the golden Chenin Blanc berries. The best villages of this appellation, which have *cru* status, are allowed to include their name on the label: Beaulieu-sur-Layon, Faye-d'Anjou, Rablay-sur-Layon,

Rochefort-sur-Loire, St-Aubin-de-Luigné, and St-Lambert-du-Lattay. The Coteaux du Layon-Chaume AOC, established in 2007, precisely defines the Chaume *terroir*, situated on a hillside facing south, on schist and sandstone soils. Wines from 2005 and 2006 are eligible for this appellation.

> **GRAPE VARIETY** Chenin Blanc.

> **SOIL** This is a real melting pot in which the limestone mingles with the schist and sandstone to provide the Chenin

Blanc grape with many different features and flavors.

> **STYLE** Only sweet (*moelleux*) wines are produced, and only the sugar content varies. Each vineyard has its own interpretation of the way to produce Chenin Blanc, and they all show great balance. Alongside the sweetness are perfumes and flavors of crystallized fruit (plum, greengage, and quince) as well as scents of brioche and truffle, showing during the later development of wine.

Color:
White.

Serving temperature:
46 to 50°F (8 to 10°C).

Ageing potential:
5 to 50 years.

Refined *terroirs* and patience at Clos Rougeard

For more than a century, Clos Rougeard at Chacé, south of Saumur, has been developing great red wines in the Loire Valley. The Foucault brothers are following the tradition of previous generations, by working on a small scale and crafting the most exquisite wines of the Saumur-Champigny and Coteaux de Saumur appellations. In the vineyard, everything is done to enhance the development of Cabernet Franc, the red grape, and Chenin Blanc, the only white grape variety. Artificial products and chemical treatments are banned, and the land is instead treated much more sensitively. Each individual plot is weeded and plowed, and yields are deliberately kept low to preserve quality. The grapes are harvested by hand when ready. For the winemakers, it is simple: "We take our time," as Nady Foucault says. After lengthy maturation (24 to 36 months), which is rare in French wineries, the wines are ready to last for decades, as is shown by some bottles from 1953, 1937, and 1921.

SAUMUR AND SAUMUR-CHAMPIGNY AOCs

Both of these appellations are spread around the town of Saumur. Saumur AOC, covering 6,425 acres (2,600 ha), produces dry reds and whites, as well as sparkling wines. Saumur-Champigny AOC, which covers 3,700 acres (1,500 ha), produces only reds and has two styles of wines. The *négociants* make soft wines that should be consumed within the first few years, while the independent wine producers, like Clos Rougeard (see above), aim to make wines that will keep for a much longer period of time.

> **GRAPE VARIETIES** Chenin Blanc, Sauvignon Blanc, and Chardonnay for whites; Cabernet Franc, Cabernet Sauvignon, and Pineau d'Aunis for reds.
> **SOIL** The vineyards of Saumur cover land enriched with chalk. The Saumur-Champigny appellation is based on much richer and deeper soil, as well as tuffeau, limestone clay, and sand-clay.
> **STYLE** The sparkling wines of Saumur impress with the delicacy of their bubbles, subtle flavors, and light texture. It is slightly strange, but this appellation has developed to include a sparkling red made from Cabernet de Gamay, which is utterly delightful. Whites, when carefully produced and matured, have juicy fruit flavors and hints of verbena. On the palate, there is a dominant minerality from the limestone. Saumur-Champigny reds are very able to demonstrate depth. They offer an elegant sensation, supplemented by slightly sharp scents of black fruit, wood smoke, and soft spices. Those from Saumur are somewhat more flexible and concentrated.

Color:
White and red.

Serving temperature:
46 to 50°F (8 to 10°C) for whites (still or sparkling) and rosés; 61°F (16°C) for reds.

Ageing potential:
3 to 10 years for whites; 5 to 20 years for reds.

SAVENNIÈRES AOC

Curnonsky, the Prince of Gastronomy, rated Savennières at the same level as the legendary Montrachet, Château d'Yquem, and even Château-Chalon. Suffice it to say that Savennières is exceptional in the Anjou wine-production landscape. Ideally located, looking over the course of the Loire River, the 306 acres (124 ha) of vineyards are spread across three communes (Savennières, Bouchemaine, and La Possonnière). The wines are always produced from grapes with high levels of maturity, and tasting each bottle really is a special moment. The name of the appellation may be followed by the name of one of these sites: La Roche-aux-Moines and Coulée-de-Serrant.

> **GRAPE VARIETY** Chenin Blanc.
> **SOIL** The appellation is rooted on slopes perpendicular to the Loire, traversed by schist veins with a sandy base. This soil, which is quite unique, imbues Chenin Blanc with a noble austerity.
> **STYLE** Savennières need time. Subtle and restrained at first, it must sit for at least 10 years in the cellar before delivering an array of juicy yellow fruit flavors such as plum, quince, and apricot. In the mouth, there is an almost tannic texture that strikes the palate: a Savennières relies on a firm texture and an elegant bitterness with a saline tone.

Color:
White.

Serving temperature:
50 to 54°F (10 to 12°C).

Ageing potential:
10 to 50 years.

QUARTS-DE-CHAUME AOC, BONNEZEAUX AOC

If the great wines of the Loire Valley were ranked, these two names would occupy the top positions. Bonnezeaux, comprising 222 acres (90 ha), is located at the heart of the vineyards of the Coteaux du Layon; Quarts de Chaume, made up of 123 acres (50 ha), is on the banks of the Loire. Taking advantage of the mesoclimates in the meandering twists and turns of Layon, these appellations, whose origins date back to the Middle Ages, work magic with the Chenin Blanc grape variety from which they are made. As far as wine lovers are concerned, they are the quintessential sweet wines and fully capable of surviving the test of time.

> **GRAPE VARIETY** Chenin Blanc.
> **SOIL** Composed of sandstone and schist, the soil combines with the morning mist of Layon to produce botrytis.

> **STYLE** These wines make a distinct impression with a richness of residual sugar that is refined and developed with evolution in the cellar. If you enjoy them when they are young, notes of bergamot, citrus fruits, pine honey, and quince are apparent. When they are older, after 10 or 20 years, the palate is enriched with aromatic notes of white ground pepper, pear jam, confectionery, and white truffle.

Color: White.

Serving temperature: 50 to 54°F (10 to 12°C).

Ageing potential: 10 to 50 years.

MUSCADET AOC

Close to the city of Nantes and near the mouth of the Loire River, the vast vineyards of Muscadet occupy some 8,900 acres (3,600 ha). They are bounded on the north by Brittany, to the south by the Vendée woodland, and on the west by the Atlantic coast. As early as the 16th century, Rabelais extolled the virtues of Melon de Bourgogne, the Muscadet grape. Recently, many growers have made real qualitative improvements. Note the progress in winemaking and ageing techniques that have produced wines with a lot more finesse.

> **GRAPE VARIETY** Melon de Bourgogne (also known as Muscadet).
> **SOIL** The soil is very diverse. You can find schists, mica schists, gabbros, and, to a lesser extent, granite.
> **STYLE** The best wines are often produced after a very long period of maturation in tank, which gives the wines more palate texture and depth. New work being done in barrels makes it certain that they will be kept for some time in cellars—which is unusual for a wine largely sold and consumed in youth. At tasting, the nose has a floral scent of freshly cut grass and

lime, then moves to notes of citrus and white fruit. In the mouth, its freshness invigorates the palate with liveliness and panache.

Color: White.

Serving temperature: 46 to 50°F (8 to 10°C).

Ageing potential: 3 to 20 years.

Fine wines

DRY WHITES
- AOC Anjou: Les Rouliers, Richard Leroy (Rablay-sur-Layon).
- AOC Blanc Fumé de Pouilly: Silex, Didier Dagueneau (Saint-Andelain).
- AOC Montlouis-sur-Loire: Stéphane Cossais, Maison Marchandelle (Montlouis-sur-Loire).
- AOC Sancerre: Clos La Néore, Edmond Vatan (Chavignol).

SWEET WHITES
- AOC Coteaux-de-Saumur: Clos Rougeard (Chacé).
- AOC Montlouis-sur-Loire: Domaine François Chidaine (Montlouis-sur-Loire).
- OC Vouvray moelleux: Romulus, Domaine de la Taille aux Loups (Montlouis-sur-Loire) ; Domaine du Clos Naudin (Vouvray).
- AOC Quarts-de-Chaume: Château de Suronde (Rochefort-sur-Loire).

REDS
- AOC Chinon: L'Huisserie, Domaine Philippe Alliet (Cravant-les-Coteaux).
- AOC Sancerre: Charlouise, Domaine Vincent Pinard (Bué) ; Belle Dame, Domaine Vacheron (Sancerre).
- AOC Saumur: Les Arboises, Romain Guiberteau (Mollay).
- AOC Saumur-Champigny: Les Poyeux, Clos Rougeard (Chacé).

THE RHÔNE VALLEY

*Situated between Lyon and Marseille, bordered to the west by the Massif Central, to the
east by the Alps, and to the south by the Mediterranean, the Rhône Valley has a dual
personality. Vineyards grow in granite and are restricted to pretty much one grape variety
in the north, while limestone soils and the use of multiple grape varieties frames the south.
Commonalities are the sunshine, or arid climate, and the wind—as well as a profound belief
in regional cohesion. Its current and well-deserved success is due to a combination of the
worldwide popularity of its grape varieties and a succession of good vintages.*

Geographic location

The appellations of the valley are spread over six
départements. These are, from north to south,
Côte-Rôtie in the Rhône *département*; Château-
Grillet, Condrieu, and St-Joseph in the Loire;
another part of Saint-Joseph, Cornas, and
then further south, Côtes-du-Vivarais
in Ardèche; plus Hermitage, Crozes-
Hermitage, and the appellations of Diois
in the Drôme.

The southern part begins in Drôme
Provençal, with Vinsobres and Coteaux-du-
Tricastin. Châteauneuf-du-Pape, Gigondas,
Vacqueyras, Beaumes-de-Venise, Ventoux, and
Luberon are in Vaucluse. The eastern Gard contains Lirac,
Tavel, and Costières-de-Nîmes.

**RHÔNE STATISTICS
(AOC)**

Vineyard area: 190,701 acres
(77,174 ha)
Production: 31.3 million cases
(2,815,434 hl)
Reds: 83%
Rosés: 12%
Whites: 5%

(Inter-Rhône, 2008)

Tumultuous geologic history

The Rhône Valley is the result of the clash of the Massif
Central and the Alps, as well as a depression that
was filled by the Mediterranean. The granite rock
found in the north was produced by volcanic
activity in the Massif Central about 300
million years ago. The south was a gulf
of a great ocean, where a succession of
fluvial and marine deposits assembled—in
particular the limestone that would later form
peaks such as the Dentelles de Montmirail
and Mont Ventoux. So the grape-growing
character of the north, with granite, and the
south, with limestone, were already being laid down.

The actual emergence of the Alps, 40 million years ago,
created this valley between two massifs. It was then flooded
by the Mediterranean several times: each flood brought new
deposits, and with each drainage the river cut its bed several
hundred yards deeper—yielding terraces on the sides of its valley,
and mixing different elements along the slopes between terraces.

Soil and wine style

The soil of the Rhône Valley is built from three types of rock, which
allows us to speak of wine style according to these categories.
GRANITE. Dominant in the northern Rhône Valley as bedrock
and deposits (in Côte-Rôtie, Condrieu, Cornas, Château-Grillet,

> The tiny appellation de
Château-Grillet is renowned
for producing excellent
Viognier whites.

Recurring drought

Despite some differences in climate—a bit more sun
and wind in the south, a little cooler and wetter in the
north—the issue of drought affects all the vineyards
of the Rhône Valley. Across 2003–2008, for example,
rainfall numbers dropped (likely evidence of climate
change, further supported by earlier and earlier
harvest dates). This has resulted in lower yields, the
death of some plants, and some imbalances in the
wines. While the lack of water requires the grower
to pay more attention to the plant, it also can reduce
the need for chemical treatments (against mold or
rot problems).

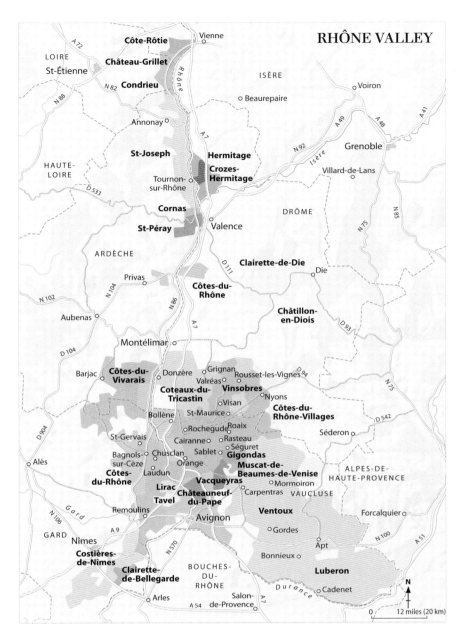

RHÔNE VALLEY

du-Pape). The white, rosés, and reds wines are full but structured.

LIMESTONE. Found only in traces in the northern valley, as glacial alluvium (in Hermitage, St-Péray), limestone yields white and red wines that are rather fine and fresh. But it is most prevalent in the south, as sedimentary deposits that have become bedrock (in Châteauneuf-du-Pape, Coteaux-de-Die, Tavel). The whites and rosés are full of flavor, but again are fresh. Also in the south, there are limestone boulders forming the slopes of the Dentelles de Montmirail and Mont Ventoux. The wines here are warm (alcoholic) and red (as Côtes-du-Rhône, Beaumes-de-Venise, Gigondas, Vacqueyras, Côtes-du-Ventoux).

Vineyard history

GRECO-ROMAN ORIGIN. In the south, toward Marseilles, it seems that the vine was flourishing in Ancient Greek times, around the 4th century BC. In the north, the culture of the vine did not develop until well after the Roman conquest, toward the second half of the 1st century AD. Pliny the Elder, in his *Natural History*, said that a new variety of grape had made the vineyards of the Allobroges famous, and he called it Allobrogica. Its unique feature was its adaptation to colder conditions than the Mediterranean. The fall of the Roman Empire then marked a setback to vineyard development in Rhône because it was deprived of its markets, except for the vineyards near the Mediterranean ports and the vineyards of the far north, which primarily supplied Lyon.

FROM THE POPES TO THE PHYLLOXERA CRISIS. The presence of the papal court in Avignon for the majority of the

St-Joseph, Hermitage), granite supplies red and white wines with minerality and means that they need to be laid down for a long time.

SILICA (SAND). In the north, silica is the decomposition of the granite (in St-Joseph, Crozes-Hermitage); and in the south, it is marine and river deposits on the terraces and the valley floor (Châteauneuf-du-Pape, Lirac). This type of soil produces light wines with finesse. Sometimes, especially in the south, the silica has reformed into large pebbles (in Châteauneuf-du-Pape, Lirac, Costières-de-Nîmes, Tavel). These help ripen the grapes by a process of retaining and re-radiating the sun's heat. These pebbles produce structured red wines with high alcohol and tannins, which need time to mature.

CLAY SOILS. In the north of the valley, the clay is the result of the decomposition of the granite (Hermitage, Crozes-Hermitage, Saint-Joseph); in the south it is marine or even glacial marl (south of the appellation Côtes-du-Rhône, Beaumes-de-Venise, Vinsobres, Gigondas, Vacqueyras). The clay in the soil in particular balances the grapes warmed by the pebbles (red Châteauneuf-

> Côte Brune is one of the two slopes forming the famous vineyards of Côte-Rôtie in the northern Rhône Valley.

14th century encouraged planting in the countryside around Châteauneuf, Tarascon, Avignon, and Arles. The grape varieties were still the ancient ones, originating from Italy or Spain. For centuries, almost all Rhône wines were consumed only locally. Then, in the late 19th century, a profound change took place: phylloxera decimated the vineyards in much of the valley, especially in Provence. At the same time, the sandy areas of the Gard, Vaucluse, and nearby Languedoc were quickly planted (or overplanted) with vines, since this louse would not thrive on this type of soil. The ensuing crisis of overproduction led to the creation of wine cooperatives.

Collective competition

The Rhône Valley has played an active role in creating the modern structure of French wine production, and it continues to demonstrate faith in the AOC system.

BARON WINEMAKER. Baron Pierre Le Roy Boiseaumarié (1890–1967), a First World War hero and then (by marriage) a winemaker in Châteauneuf-du-Pape, fought for official recognition of that appellation—first through the courts, then by decree in 1933. The model collectively developed there subsequently became the standard for all French AOC decrees: delineation of the area of the appellation, the grape varieties, cultivation methods, harvest dates, production techniques and more. The Baron's work continued to the surrounding Côtes-du-Rhône, turning an old regional name into an official appellation by decree in 1937; he also was president of that association. Finally, he helped found the National Institute of Appellations

of Origin (INAO), of which he was president (1947–1967), and the International Office of Vine and Wine (OIV) *(see also p.22)*.

FAITH IN AOC. Ever since, getting an *appellation d'origine contrôlée* has been a source of motivation to an entire vineyard district, whose villages seek to demonstrate their uniqueness and quality. Consequently, the likes of Gigondas, which had mere mention appended to Côtes-du-Rhône-Villages, secured its own full AOC in 1970. Vacqueyras did the same in 1990, and finally Vinsobres and Beaumes-de-Venise did so in 2005. Rasteau (which has an AOC for its *vins doux naturels*) and Cairanne, which already has a reputation to some extent, are waiting for this recognition, too.

"Natural" wine

As in all French regions, a minority of Rhône wine producers are becoming known for "natural" wines, that is to say wines made with as little chemical input as possible, and even with minimal use of modern technology. These wines often offer a more original and diverse expression of flavor. In the north, these are the Domaines Dard et Ribo, Titi et Moustique, Christophe Curtat, La Tache, Texier, Stéphan, and Allemand; in the south, Gramenon, Le Mazel, La Soutéronne, Marcel Richaud, Élodie Balme, La Ferme St-Martin, Chaume-Arnaud, L'Anglore, or even La Cave d'Estézargues.

Reviving the past in Côte-Rôtie

Brigitte Roch and Gilbert Clusel, wine producers in Côte-Rôtie, have always felt limited by the five clones of Syrah available at nurseries. So, in 1990, they began to propagate the 30 indigenous strains present in their oldest vines, belonging to their grandfather. The experiment was extended to the entire appellation; a vine nursery has been created; and a groundswell to replant these old strains is on the move. The wines are more complex and more tannic, but last longer than those from modern clones, and the reintroduction of biodiversity can limit the spread of disease.

> Châteauneuf-du-Pape: the small stones absorb the sun's heat and release it back to the vines at night.

Popular grape varieties

Rhône Valley wines have attracted great interest in the English-speaking world because they reflect a global trend. Coming from a warm climate, they possess the popular, concentrated fruit flavors of many New World wines. Three Rhône varieties are particularly noteworthy. Syrah, an indigenous grape variety, is now widely planted in Australia, Argentina, South Africa, and California. Recent genetic discoveries have shown it to be derived from Mondeuse Blanche, a variety of grape from Savoie, and Dureza, a black Ardèche grape, reportedly a distant relative of Pinot Noir. Also a descendant of the Mondeuse Blanche, the white variety Viognier is now grown in the United States, Argentina, and South Africa. Finally, Grenache, the great grape of the south, is also widely cultivated in Spain, especially in Priorat, but also in Australia.

This does not detract from appreciation for the subtlety of other varieties. For red, there is Mourvèdre, with a dark and bitter but appealing character; the delicate Cinsaut, perfect for easy-to-drink wines; and sometimes Carignan, which is delicious when ripe. For white, there is the rich Grenache Blanc, the floral Clairette, the plump Bourboulenc and Marsanne, the aromatic Roussanne and Muscat, and the unctuous Rolle.

TRUE OR FALSE?

Sweet wines are produced only in the southern Rhône Valley.

FALSE. Besides the Muscats Beaumes-de-Venise and the Rasteau *vins doux naturels*, there is a real collector's item in the *vin de paille* of Hermitage. It is produced in the same way as the wine of that name from Jura, leaving grapes to dry for three months after picking to concentrate the sugars. Produced in very small quantities, and very expensive to manufacture, this wine is unique. Its flavors move between fungi and exotic fruits.

Recent vintages

Since 1998, the Rhône Valley has enjoyed an impressive series of good vintages. The exceptions are 2002, which was badly damaged by rain at harvest time, and, to a lesser extent, the 2008 vintage. As for the great years, 2005 and 2007 are particularly worthy of note, since these two vintages are both powerful and balanced. Better than average, the 2003 vintage is very full-bodied, but a potential greenness on the palate finish and a lack of sharpness could lead these wines to go downhill quickly. In general, wines from the 2000 vintage for the great appellations—like Hermitage, Côte-Rôtie, Cornas, and Châteauneuf-du-Pape—are now mature and ready; but those of the 2005 vintage still need time.

Rhône Valley AOCs

- Côtes-du-Rhône
- Côtes-du-Rhône-Villages
- Beaumes-de-Venise
- Château-Grillet
- Châteauneuf-du-Pape
- Châtillon-en-Diois
- Clairette de Die
- Condrieu
- Cornas
- Costières-de-Nîmes
- Coteaux-de-Die
- Côte-Rôtie
- Côtes-du-Vivarais
- Crémant de Die
- Crozes-Hermitage
- Gigondas
- Hermitage (with some *vin de paille*)
- Lirac
- Luberon (formerly Côtes-du-Luberon)
- Muscat de Beaumes-de-Venise (VDN)
- Rasteau (VDN), rancio
- St-Joseph
- St-Péray
- Tavel
- Tricastin
- Vacqueyras
- Ventoux (formerly Côtes-du-Ventoux)
- Vinsobres

Leading Rhône Valley wines

The Rhône Valley produces an amazing variety of wines. Its northern zone begins south of the Rhône département (toward Vienne), reaches the Loire and Isère, then goes as far as the north of Ardèche and Drôme (toward Valence); the southern zone includes Vaucluse and Drôme (toward Montélimar), and reaches east to Gard Vaucluse (around Avignon).

CÔTES-DU-RHÔNE AND CÔTES-DU-RHÔNE-VILLAGES AOCs

Côtes-du-Rhône is a regional appellation: any wine produced in the Rhône Valley can claim it, except for wines produced as AOCs for Luberon, Ventoux, Côtes-du-Vivarais, Coteaux-du-Tricastin, and Costières-de-Nîmes, as well as in the Diois. The Côtes-du-Rhône-Villages AOC can be appended with the name of one of the following 18 villages: Cairanne, Chusclan, Laudun, Massif d'Uchaux, Plan de Dieu, Puyméras, Rasteau, Roaix, Rochegude, Rousset-les-Vignes, Sablet, St-Gervais, St-Maurice, St-Pantaléon-les-Vignes, Séguret, Signargues, Valréas, and Visan. The vast majority of Côtes-du-Rhône AOC wines are produced in the southern part of the valley (77 percent of red and rosé, and 84 percent of whites are from Gard and Vaucluse).

> **GRAPE VARIETIES** Grenache Noir, Syrah, Mourvèdre, Carignan, Cinsaut, Counoise, Muscardin, Camarèse, Vaccarèse, Picpoul Noir, Terret Noir, Grenache Gris, and Clairette Rosé for the reds and rosés; Grenache Blanc, Clairette, Marsanne, Roussanne, Bourboulenc, Viognier, Ugni Blanc, and Picpoul Blanc for the whites.

> **SOIL** The Rhône Valley is mainly granite to the north and limestone to the south, in both cases with a significant presence of clays and sands. The vineyards are divided between base rock and terraces of varying heights.

> **STYLE** The reds, concentrated and full-bodied, have ripe red fruit and herb flavors. The whites are often rich in flavor, and for a long time were heavy; but they are increasingly enjoyable with improved temperature control techniques. The rosés are full-bodied and more colorful than in Provence. Côtes-du-Rhône-Villages is more structured wine, sometimes aged in barrel, something that tends to be done with the more prestigious *crus*. Character varies, though. Any two places produce different wines: in Cairanne, the wine shows red fruit (raspberry) and is easy to drink, but distinctive. In Rasteau, it is black fruit (blackberry, blackcurrant) that dominates the wine.

Color:
Red, rosé, and white.

Serving temperature:
46 to 54°F (8 to 12°C) for the whites and rosés;
54 to 61°F (12 to 16°C) for the reds.

Ageing potential:
3 years for rosés and whites;
3 to 5 years for the reds.

CÔTE-RÔTIE AOC

This small appellation—598 acres (242 ha), on steep slopes—is the northern-most in the valley. It produces red wines for ageing, most of them with time in barrel. After an initial period of bright expression, the wines often close down for three years, before reopening when they are about seven or eight years old.

> **GRAPE VARIETIES** Syrah (here called "Serine") and Viognier.

> **SOIL** Granite to the south, schist to the north.

> **STYLE** The style is inclined toward concentrated black fruit, mocha, licorice, and chocolate, but also includes specific characteristics from the *terroirs* across this appellation. The wines furthest south in the AOC, where there is more granite, especially along a slope called "Côte-Blonde," sometimes have more floral notes and are more marked by pencil lead aromas than the wines of the north, especially along the slope called "Côte-Brune."

Color:
Red.

Serving temperature:
61°F (16°C).

Ageing potential:
At least 15 years.

CONDRIEU AOC

With completely granite soils, the 329 acres (133 ha) of this AOC produce white wines exclusively from Viognier. The qualities displayed by this grape variety vary greatly according to the *terroir*; here it can produce wine that demonstrates the minerality of the soil, when the winemaker so chooses. Depending on the year, part of the production can be dedicated to making sweet (*moelleux* or *liquoreux*) wines. These should soon be designated as *sélection de grains nobles*, allowing the buyer to make an informed decision. Condrieu wines can be consumed young, if you like fresh fruit flavors; but they also benefit from ageing to gain more minerality.

> **GRAPE VARIETY** Viognier.

> **SOIL** Biotite granite (white mica), producing wines noted for their minerality; Muscovite granite (black mica), producing more generous wines.

> **STYLE** Minerality aside, the flavors produced by the wines of Condrieu are often both diverse and subtle, marked by white flowers, white pepper, peach, apricot, and even orange peel, mixed with aromatic herbs.

Color:
White.

Serving temperature:
50 to 54°F (10 to 12°C)

Ageing potential:
4 or 5 years, if you like a fruitier style,
10 years, if you prefer minerality

ST-JOSEPH AOC

This appellation produces red and white wines. Occupying 2,718 acres (1,100 ha), it starts in the north, around the Condrieu district, and ends in the south, across from Hermitage, just above Cornas. The St-Joseph hill, which gives its name to the AOC, is located between the towns of Mauve and Tournon, hence its former name of "vin de Mauve." The appellation has a great diversity of soils, which can result in a wide variety of production. Note, however, that larger estates in the northern Rhône region, renowned for production of Cornas, Côte-Rôtie, or Hermitage, are buying more and more vineyards in St-Joseph. The value represented by these wines is often significant. While the center of the appellation is less prestigious, it still contains many nice surprises.

> **GRAPE VARIETIES** Syrah for the reds; Marsanne and Roussanne for the whites.

> **SOIL** Similar to those of other appellations of the region: partially granite, sometimes broken clay.

> **STYLE** Red wines generally have a nose of red and black fruit with floral elements (violets), becoming a little smoky. They have a striking fruit palate with excellent freshness, and a licorice or peppermint finish. The whites (nine percent of production) convey some smoothness from the clay soils; but they are rarely heavy, especially when the grape variety blend is mainly Roussanne.

Color:
Red and white.

Serving temperature:
50 to 54°F (10 to 12°C) for the whites;
54 to 61°F (12 to 16°C) for the reds.

Ageing potential:
3 to 10 years.

Big names in the Rhône

Hermitage, Côte-Rôtie, and Châteauneuf-du-Pape wines have long been recognized by enthusiasts. They represent three of the most prestigious terroirs in this region, with bottles priced between €25 and €70 (around $34 to $90+/£20 To £50+), depending on the district and vintage. To the north, the négociant Guigal established the reputation of Côte-Rôtie, before expanding with a line of fairly good quality into the other terroirs of the valley. This producer was later joined by many top estates, such as Mathilde et Yves Gangloff, renowned for magnificent Condrieu wines. In Hermitage, alongside the Jaboulet operation, Michel Chapoutier has produced extraordinary wines over the years, often from plots farmed organically or using biodynamics. To the south, the Château Rayas, on sandy terroirs, and Château de Beaucastel, on stony soils, are the two estates most sought-after for Châteauneuf-du-Pape.

HERMITAGE AOC

Hermitage—338 acres (137 ha) located on a hill around the town of Tain—is a large, single swathe of land; yet it has amazingly complex geologic composition. This allows each producer to adopt his own style, whether distinctive wines from single micro-plots or interesting blends. About 25 percent of the wines from Hermitage are white; they are among the finest in France, and made mostly from Marsanne. Enthusiasts of fruit flavors enjoy Hermitage wines when they are young; those who are more patient wait from 7 to 15 years to enjoy their complexity.

> **GRAPE VARIETIES** Syrah for red; Marsanne and Roussanne for white.

> **SOIL** Hermitage was originally a block of granite that separated the Rhône from the Massif Central. The hill, topped by a small chapel, rises to the east of the AOC and produces great, austere reds. The central and western parts (75 percent of the land) are covered with multiple alluvial deposits. Areas of limestone and clay, or even sandy deposits, are often planted with white grapes.

> **STYLE** The great complexity of the soil, the south-facing exposure, and the maturation in barrel produces notes of juniper and acacia, butter, white fruit, licorice, nuts, gentian, or even truffle in the whites. The reds are often smooth, with chocolaty black fruit flavors. They have hints of licorice, pepper, spices, or even violet, and a very long finish.

Color:
Red and white.

Serving temperature:
54°F (12°C) for the whites;
61 to 63°F (16 to 17°C) for the reds.
(Wines younger than 6 years should be decanted for 1 or 2 hours.)

Ageing potential:
More than 20 years, for both reds and whites.

CROZES-HERMITAGE AOC

Crozes is a large—3,625-acre (1,467-ha)—AOC in the northern Rhône Valley. While it can be said that the Hermitage is its *grand cru*, it represents an interesting variety of styles. Limited to 1,235 acres (500 ha) in 1937, the AOC was expanded in the 1950s to incorporate similar land in the region. Despite the extension, the wines are mostly of uniform quality and are a very good value. Note the local cultivation of white wines, often largely from Marsanne, a rich grape variety that requires barrel ageing.

> **GRAPE VARIETIES** Syrah for the reds; Marsanne and Roussanne for the whites.

> **SOIL** The Châssis *terroir* consists, for the most part, of sandy clay alluvial deposits; while in the northern part of the appellation, it is granite-like in Hermitage. There are also some limestone areas, and some rare kaolin (white clay) in the Larnage area.

> **STYLE.** The classic style of wine (in the Châssis area) is fresh and fruity, offering a nice balance between full-bodied character and a supple body. But there also are wines that have been matured (from the areas of granite and kaolin) with more marked tannins, even some gamey hints.

Color:
Red and white.

Serving temperature:
50 to 54°F (10 to 12°C) for the whites;
54 to 61°F (12 to 16°C) for the reds.

Ageing potential:
3 to 10 years.

Selected Crozes-Hermitage estates

- **Domaine Combier (Pont-de-l'Isère).** Organic farming that develops distinctive whites and reds for ageing.

- **Domaine Les Bruyères (Beaumont-Monteux).** This biodynamic estate produces reds that are full-bodied yet very at ease.

- **Domaine Mucyn (Gervans).** Oak-aged wine in a Burgundy style. Very successful.

- **Domaine Pradelle (Chanos-Curson).** Supple and velvety reds and whites in a classic style.

- **Domaine Yann Chave (Mercurol).** Wines that strike a perfect balance between conveying elements of the terroir and being easy to drink.

- **Cave de Tain (Tain-l'Hermitage).** This cooperative produces very well-crafted wines, especially whites.

CORNAS AOC

This is a small vineyard district of just 287 acres (116 ha), but one with great character! Unlike Hermitage and Côte-Rôtie, which face directly south, some Cornas vineyards face east—which may explain why some wines are more rustic in style, and always take a little longer to reveal themselves. But style varies by producer, with the most traditional ones not de-stemming the grape clusters and crafting firmer wines, which need to be aged for between 8 and 10 years. For those who do remove the stems, the bottle-ageing period is considerably shorter or even nonexistent—except for certain vintages like 2005.

> **GRAPE VARIETY** Syrah.

> **SOIL** The soil in this district is mainly granite, with a few limestone areas (from Vercors) on the hill at Chaillots in St-Joseph.

> **STYLE** Cornas is marked by powerful notes of smoke and black fruits. Plots with more limestone produce wines with a more fruity nose, but they are

sometimes firm on the palate. As Cornas ages, very clear notes of menthol, game, and pepper emerge.

Color:
Red.

Serving temperature:
61°F (16°C).

Ageing potential:
More than 20 years.

CÔTES-DU-VIVARAIS AOC

Although located in Ardèche, this is the first southern Rhône appellation, and it uses a majority of Grenache varieties for both red and white wines. Côtes-du-Vivarais is a small appellation, occupying 1,225 acres (496 ha), but one boasting two major advantages: an unusual character and very reasonable prices.

> **GRAPE VARIETIES** Grenache Noir, Syrah, Carignan, and Cinsaut for the reds and rosés; Grenache Blanc, Marsanne, and Clairette for the whites.

> **SOIL** Limestone pebbles on clays located around the gorges of Ardèche. This soil is warm on the surface and cool as you penetrate to any depth. The area suffers less from drought than much of the valley, while still taking advantage of the sun.

> **STYLE** The wines here are very different from those found throughout the Rhône Valley. They are concentrated like all wines from the south, but also supported by a lovely freshness.

Color:
Red, rosé and white.

Serving temperature:
46 to 50°F (8 to 10°C) for the rosés and the whites;
57°F (14°C) for the reds.

Ageing potential:
3 years for the rosés and the whites; 3 to 8 years for the reds

Good value wines from the southern Rhône

• **Cave de Rasteau (Rasteau).** This cooperative produces Côtes-du-Rhône in all three colors, notably in the Les Viguiers line.

• **Cave Terra Ventoux (Villes-sur-Auzon-Mormoiron).** Wine crafted very well at a wide range of prices in Ventoux.

• **Domaine de la Boisserelle (St-Remèze).** Excellent value white, red, and rosé Côtes-du-Vivarais wines.

• **Domaine de Beaumalric (Beaumes-de-Venise).** A superb, low-priced Beaumes-de-Venise.

• **Domaine Coulange (Bourg-St-Andéol).** Distinctive Côtes-du-Rhône produced by an excellent winemaker.

• **Domaine Brusset (Cairanne).** A very good Cairanne wine producer that also makes very affordable Côtes-du-Rhône and Ventoux.

• **Domaine de Durban (Beaumes-de-Venise).** Amazing value for a characteristic Beaumes-de-Venise AOC wine.

• **Domaine de Grange Blanche (Blovac).** A very nice Côtes-du-Rhône-Villages Rasteau.

• **Domaine Terre des Chardons (Bellegarde).** Superb Costières-de-Nîmes for as little as €8 ($10/£7).

• **Nicolas Croze (St-Martin-d'Ardèche).** Very good, full-bodied Côtes-du-Rhône.

VINSOBRES AOC

SOUTHERN RHÔNE

Vinsobres, which is one of the two most recent appellations in the Rhône (2005), has been a great success. A limited area of 1,220 acres (494 ha) consists of well-drained soils, often located at high altitudes (up to 1,640 ft or 500 m), combined with an environment protected from the Mistral winds to ensure that the wine has good structure. As with all recent appellations, this represents good value. Note that the rules establishing the AOC specifies that young vines can produce Vinsobres only after seven years, which is particularly demanding.

> **GRAPE VARIETIES** Grenache Noir (at least 50 percent), Mourvèdre, and Syrah, with five percent white grape varieties.

> **SOIL** Clay mixed with pebbles or sand.

> **STYLE** Wine with a nose of red and black fruit, supported by a great mineral depth and a well-structured palate—without heaviness.

Color:
Red.

Serving temperature:
57 to 61°F (14 to 16°C).

Ageing potential:
8 to 10 years.

GIGONDAS AOC

SOUTHERN RHÔNE

This appellation is located northwest of the Dentelles de Montmirail, and its vineyards are situated between 330 and 1,640 ft (100 and 500 m) in altitude on the side of the massif. The red wines may be enjoyed within three years of the harvest, sometimes five years for firm vintages. It also produces rosés.

> **GRAPE VARIETIES** Grenache Noir (mostly), Syrah, and Mourvèdre, as well as other varieties from the Rhône Valley (except Carignan).

> **SOIL** Red clay dotted with limestone, sand, and pebbles.

> **STYLE** These wines are rather heady, often with nice red fruit notes and good tannic structure.

Color:
Red and rosé.

Serving temperature:
46 to 50°F (8 to 10°C) for the rosés;
57 to 61°F (14 to 16°C) for the reds.

Ageing potential:
8 to 10 years.

CHÂTEAUNEUF-DU-PAPE AOC

SOUTHERN RHÔNE

This appellation is defined more by the method used to classify AOCs than by the actual extent to which commonalities are found here; but it does follow a certain geologic logic. It is certainly more relevant than any claimed differences attributed to the 13 grape varieties that make Châteauneuf—especially the reds, most of which are dominated by Grenache. Red Châteauneuf wines should be kept from 5 to 10 years depending on the vintage. The white wines are good, mostly aged in barrel, like the reds, but they can be consumed as soon as they go on sale.

> **GRAPE VARIETIES** Grenache Noir, Syrah, Mourvèdre, Terret Noir, Counoise, Muscardin, Vaccarèse, and Cinsaut for the reds; Picpoul Blanc, Clairette, Roussanne, Bourboulenc, and Picardan for the whites.

> **SOIL** On a base of Urgonian limestone (shells), various sands and clays were deposited as sediment. Also pebbles of quartzite and silica from the Alps.

> **STYLE** The limestone terroir is well suited for producing white wines that are full of flavor, yet possess a good level of freshness. Clay, which is very common in the southern part of the appellation, produces a structured red wine that is both warm and deep. This represents the classic wines of Châteauneuf-du-Pape. But a current trend is to redevelop the sandy terroirs, situated to the northwest of the AOC, which will produce finer, lighter, and spicier wines.

Color:
Red and white.

Serving temperature:
50 to 54°F (10 to 12°C) for the whites;
57 to 61°F (14 to 16°C) for the reds.
(For young wines, decant for 1 or 2 hours.)

Ageing potential:
More than 10 years for the whites;
More than 20 years for the reds.

BEAUMES-DE-VENISE AOC

This appellation is one of the most recently established (2005). As with the vineyards of Gigondas and Vacqueyras, it lies at the foot of the Dentelles de Montmirail. We also should point out the extremely reliable uniformity of the wines here—a result of the very farsighted set-up of the AOC, both in terms of production regulations and official review of the wines. Note that bottles from this Triassic *terroir* are still very affordable, and will certainly be worth a lot more in a few years.

> **GRAPE VARIETIES** Grenache Noir (at least 50 percent), Syrah (at most 25 percent), and all the other Côtes du Rhône grape varieties among reds; white grape varieties are, at most, five percent of production.

> **SOIL** Clays mixed with sand or limestone pebbles that have come down from the Dentelles de Montmirail into this Triassic (200 million years old) *terroir*. It is generally a mixture of gypsum, clay, and limestone.

> **STYLE** Wines have the flavor of very ripe red fruits, with notes of kirsch and often an interesting mineral structure. Depending on the *terroirs*, the wines are either light (clay), concentrated (limestone rocks), or for laying down with a great structure and finesse (Triassic).

Color:
Red.

Serving temperature:
57 to 61°F (14 to 16°C).

Ageing potential:
8 to 15 years.

VACQUEYRAS AOC

To the west of the Dentelles de Montmirail, this appellation occupies 3,487 acres (1,411 ha), and is close to its neighbor to the north, Gigondas AOC. But it's distinguished by a slightly warmer *climat*, and hence the style of its wines. The whites are enjoyed immediately; the reds need three to six years to be ready.

> **GRAPE VARIETIES** Grenache Noir (at least 50 percent), Syrah, and Mourvèdre for the reds and rosés; Grenache Blanc, Clairette, Bourboulenc, Marsanne, Roussanne, and Viognier for the whites.

> **SOIL** Red clay dotted with limestone pebbles and sand.

> **STYLE** These wines have black fruit flavors, with mineral, smoky, and even gamey notes. The palate finishes marked by licorice and pepper.

Color:
Red, rosé, and white.

Serving temperature:
46 to 50°F (8 to 10°C) for the whites and rosés;
57 to 61°F (14 to 16°C) for the reds.

Ageing potential:
3 years for the rosés;
7 to 8 years for the whites;
8 to 10 years for the reds.

Château de la Gardine

The style of this Châteauneuf-du-Pape estate is a successful union of finesse and power. Located in the town of Châteauneuf, the property's vineyards combine the three types of soil (limestone, sand, and clay with pebbles) found for the AOC. This enables the development of wines (both white and red) that are very balanced and highly representative of the appellation. The search for balance is also found in the methods of vinification: Patrick, Philippe, and Maxime Brunel are followers of current best practice, such as cold soaking or total de-stalking of some vintages.

They cultivate the art of "Castelneuvois" blending of grapes for winemaking, a practice dating from a time when vines were planted "en masse," regardless of variety. Pursuit of balance does not prevent use of the imagination; in recent years the estate produced a wine made without any addition of sulfur, called "Peur bleue" (blue fear) in reference to the terror inspired by this risky winemaking procedure! Their Châteauneuf-du-Pape wines are sold at very high prices; but their line includes productions of white, rosé, and red Château St-Roch Lirac and a delicious, low-priced Côtes-du-Rhône.

TAVEL AOC

The only Côtes-du-Rhône appellation to produce just rosé wines, the Tavel AOC consists of three types of *terroir*. This allows for a blending of styles: full of flavor or well-structured, deep-colored or lighter. The resulting wine is quite different from many regional rosés, pale and light, in the Provençal style. In recent years, the appellation has suffered some irregularity in production—sometimes involving wine that was heavy or not very clear, or containing too much sulfur. But it seems that a new generation of wine-makers is ready to take over.

> **GRAPE VARIETIES** Grenache, Cinsaut, Clairette, Picpoul, Calitor, Bourboulenc, Mourvèdre, Syrah, and Carignan.

> **SOIL** Limestone rocks or slabs, clay pebbles, sandy soil.

> **STYLE** These are powerful rosés that are boldly colored, have a long finish, and are ideally suited as table wines.

Color:
Rosé.

Serving temperature:
46 to 50°F (8 to 10°C).

Ageing potential:
5 years.

LIRAC AOC

Lirac has had AOC status since 1947. This appellation sums up the different *terroirs* in the southern Rhône Valley. But whereas Châteauneuf, though five times larger, has found a lucrative market with consistent quality, Lirac is divided between a somewhat diluted, entry-level production and more demanding estates, often from neighboring Castelneuvois, who want to showcase great *terroirs*. This results in moderate price levels, which are the delight of enthusiasts familiar with the "big wines from little estates" concept.

> **GRAPE VARIETIES** Grenache Noir (at least 40 percent), Syrah, Mourvèdre, Cinsaut, and Carignan for the reds and rosés; Clairette, Grenache Blanc, Bourboulenc, Ugni Blanc, Picpoul, Marsanne, Roussanne, and Viognier for the whites.

> **SOIL** Limestone boulders, sand, and clay scree.

> **STYLE** Lirac wines are warm and full of flavor, and structured to a varying extent.

Color:
Red, rosé, and white.

Serving temperature:
46 to 50°F (8 to 10°C) for the rosés and whites;
57 to 61°F (14 to 16°C) for the reds.

Ageing potential:
3 years for the rosés;
3 to 6 years for the whites;
3 to 10 years for the reds.

VENTOUX OR CÔTES-DU-VENTOUX AOC

Since 2008, Ventoux has been the new name of the former Côtes-du-Ventoux AOC. Mount Ventoux has a traditional Mediterranean foothill landscape. The local climate has contrasting summer temperatures 41 to 50°F (5 to 10°C) in the morning up to 86 to 104°F (30 or 40°C) in the afternoon, which allows for optimal ripening of the grape tannins. The result is an original style, also present in the local AOC *vin de table*, the Muscat du Ventoux. But the appellation suffers from its vast scale (15,792 acres or 6,391 ha), more than all of the Côtes-du-Rhône-Villages with their local names put together. This condemns even good producers to an economically precarious situation because of fluctuations in the supply and price of the wine. We hope these difficulties will not deter the top cooperatives or estates, which are growing in number, from continuing to improve their production. In fact, the AOC currently represents an amazingly good value red wine. This is also true for whites.

> **GRAPE VARIETIES** Grenache Noir, Syrah, Cinsaut, Mourvèdre, Carignan, Picpoul Noir, Counoise for the reds and rosés; Clairette, Bourboulenc, Grenache Blanc, Roussanne for the whites.

> **SOIL** Mainly limestone.

> **STYLE** Both whites and reds have very ripe fruit flavors and a freshness on the palate.

Color:
Red, rosé, and white.

Serving temperature:
46 to 50°F (8 to 10°C) for the rosés and whites;
57 to 61°F (14 to 16°C) for the reds.

Ageing potential:
3 years for the rosés;
3 to 5 years for the whites;
3 to 8 years for the reds.

LUBERON OR CÔTES-DU-LUBERON AOC

Since 2008, Luberon has been the new name of the former Côtes-du-Luberon AOC. With a soil similar to the nearby Ventoux AOC, Luberon does not have as large a temperature variation, and the wines are more in line with those from the southern Côtes-du-Rhône, except for one small detail: the prestige of the name has enabled some producers to move to maturation in new oak barrels and an international style, with resulting higher prices. However, there are interesting estates that offer value from their *terroirs*.

> **GRAPE VARIETIES** For red and rosé: Syrah and Grenache Noir (at least 60 percent), Mourvèdre, Carignan, Cinsaut. For white: Grenache Blanc, Ugni Blanc, Clairette, Rolle, Bourboulenc, Roussanne, Marsanne.
> **SOIL** Mainly limestone.
> **STYLE** The red wines are warm, with a significant proportion of them getting barrel ageing. The rosés resemble Rhône wines rather than those from Provence. The whites are a specialty of the AOC, with sometimes obvious age, but also some more interesting successes. In blending,

an increasing share of the Rolle grape, which is full of flavor and refined, indicates a resemblance to Provençal wine.

CHÂTEAU LA CANORGUE

2008 LUBERON
APPELLATION LUBERON CONTRÔLÉE

Color:
Red, rosé, and white.

Serving temperature:
46 to 50°F (8 to 10°C) for the rosés and whites;
57 to 61°F (14 to 16°C) for the reds.

Ageing potential:
3 years for the rosés;
3 to 8 years for the whites;
3 to 10 years for the reds.

COSTIÈRES-DE-NÎMES AOC

Administratively located in Languedoc-Roussillon, this vast AOC of 10,653 acres (4,311 ha) finds its geologic home in the Rhône Valley. It has a number of wines that represent good value, and some estates are increasing production.
> **GRAPE VARIETIES** Syrah, Grenache, Mourvèdre, Carignan, and Cinsaut for the

reds and rosés; Grenache Blanc, Marsanne, Roussanne, Clairette, Bourboulenc, Maccabeu, and Rolle for the whites.
> **SOIL** While the surface consists of Castelneuvois silica and quartzite pebbles interspersed with gravel, the clay layer is quite thin and it is sand, which is very porous, that dominates.

> **STYLE** They have the flavor of very ripe concentrated fruit, as can be found throughout the Rhône Valley, but on rather light structures with little tannin, which means the wines need to be consumed fairly quickly. The smoothness of the whites can be significant if the maturation is well handled.

Color:
Red, rosé, and white.

Serving temperature:
46 to 50°F (8 to 10°C) for the rosés and whites;
57 to 61°F (14 to 16°C) for the reds.

Ageing potential:
3 years for the rosés;
3 to 5 years for the whites;
3 to 8 years for the reds.

MUSCAT DE BEAUMES-DE-VENISE AOC

Small in scale (133,000 cases or 12,000 hl) compared to its cousins in the Languedoc-Roussillon, this Muscat is fermented mainly using indigenous yeasts (that is to say, naturally present on the skin of grapes and not artificially inoculated), and transferred with 5% alcohol. Some plots still produce red Muscatel, allowing the development of

red and rosé Muscat de Beaumes de Venise. Producing sweet wines is really popular here, and there are sometimes other interesting versions, such as a late harvest of Mourvèdre and *vin de paille*.
> **GRAPE VARIETIES** Muscat with small berries, called "de Frontignan."
> **SOIL** Clays mixed with sand or limestone pebbles.

> **STYLE** The white wines create a magical world of flowers (acacia, gladiolus, lime, rose, violet) and fruit (apricots, quince, candied orange peel, lemon, pear, mango), with notes of menthol, juniper, licorice and spicy nuances, even sharpness, as well as a crystallized fruit finish. The red wines and rosé wines have beautiful currant flavors.

Color:
Red, rosé, and white.

Serving temperature:
50°F (10°C).

Ageing potential:
5 to 10 years.

SOUTHWEST FRANCE

Set between the vast expanses of Languedoc-Roussillon to the east and the famous reaches of Bordeaux to the west, the vineyards of the southwest—the most diverse in France—boast a wide variety of soils, grape varieties, and appellations. Scattered over 10 départements, southwestern French wines maintain a character of their own, concealing a few pearls at value prices—one of the major benefits of the era of wine globalization.

History

As with many other French wine areas, viticulture was brought here during the Roman occupation. Certain wines, such as Cahors, Madiran, and Gaillac, found great favor with the kings of France during the Middle Ages, and their fame spread throughout Europe (to England and the Netherlands, for example). But this region could not evade the domination and the envy of its prestigious neighbors in Bordeaux, who prevented access to their port until all their own wine had been sold.

The phylloxera crisis at the end of the 19th century brought about the destruction of almost every vineyard here, and winemaking would not be revitalized until the 1970s, under the aegis of dynamic cooperatives and enthusiastic winemakers who emphasized the area's quality and unique character.

SOUTHWEST FRANCE STATISTICS (AOC)

Vineyard area: 183,000 acres (74,000 ha)

Production: 48 million cases (4.3 million hl)

Reds: 68%

Whites: 22%

Rosés: 10%

(CIVSO, CIVRB, 2007)

Vineyard districts

Although the hallmark of southwestern France is its variety, there are four key wine-producing areas.

BERGERACOIS. Following both banks of the Dordogne, the area is famed for Bergerac, of course, but can also lay claim to Monbazillac, Pécharmant, Montravel, and many others.

GARONNE. Set along both banks of the Garonne from Langon to Agen, the vineyards here are upstream from Bordeaux and include the territory of Côtes-de-Duras, Côtes-du-Marmandais, and Buzet wines.

HAUT-PAYS. This zone to the north and northwest of Toulouse includes Gaillac, Côtes-du-Frontonnais, Cahors, and others.

PYRENEES. Found to the south between the Adour and the Pyrenees, this area includes a number of leading appellations: Madiran, Irouléguy, Pacherenc-du-Vic-Bilh, Jurançon, and others.

Climate and soils

The climate naturally varies among the banks of the Garonne, the Basque country, and the Pyrenees, but a maritime climate with continental and

> Vines at Château de Haute-Serre, in the Cahors region.

Nine new AOCs?

The southwest boasts more AOVDQS appellations than any other region of France. This designation is being reclassified (see p.96), and no fewer than nine districts are awaiting official recognition (Coteaux-du-Quercy, Côtes-de-Millau, Côtes-du-Brulhois, St-Mont, St-Sardos, Tursan, Vin d'Entraygues et du Fel, Vin d'Estaing, Vin de Lavilledieu). Their quality and originality make this distinction well deserved.

SOUTHWEST FRANCE

Alpine influences dominates. There are humid springs and wet winters, as well as hot summers and long, glorious, and sun-drenched autumns. The diversity of the soils supports the plurality of these wines, with a general preponderance of molasse, limestone, and alluvial soils on the terraces formed by the many rivers and watercourses.

Grape varieties

Bordeaux varieties grow side by side with local grapes here; and this gives the wines their unique character.

FRENCH COLOMBARD lends dry white wines aromas of grapefruit and exotic fruits.

DURAS is a key to Gaillac, producing light reds with fine tannins and spicy aromas (pepper).

FER SERVADOU Also known as Pinenc and Mansois, this variety originally hails from the Basque country and produces fruity red wines with deep colors and tannins.

GROS MANSENG Another native of the Pyrenees, this grape is used to make dry white wines; but it has also been pressed into service with Courbu and Petit Manseng to make sweet whites.

LEN DE L'EL (also known as Len de l'Eh or Loin de l'Oeil) The grape at the heart of Gaillacs and Gaillac-Premières-Côtes.

MALBEC Also known as Auxerrois and Côt Noir, this grape is the staple variety for Cahors wines—to which it lends characteristic aromas and color.

MAUZAC A Gaillac grape sought for its power and its aromatic character of apples and pears; it is used to make dry whites and sparkling wines.

NÉGRETTE A Côtes-du-Frontonnais variety that produces very spicy and aromatic reds (violet, licorice).

PETIT MANSENG This Pyrenean grape is the foundation of white wines from Jurançon; when affected by noble rot (botrytized), it produces sweet wines of great subtlety with characteristic aromas of crystallized and exotic fruit, cinnamon, honey, and citrus zest.

TANNAT A native of Béarn, this variety is used for blends in a number of different appellations (including Béarn, Madiran, and Irouléguy). It produces a tannic wine with deep coloration and raspberry aromas (*see also* box above).

Wine styles

Southwestern France produces a great variety of wines—with 21 reds, 15 rosés, 15 dry whites, 10 sweet whites, and two sparkling wines. Made with Tannat, Malbec, and Cabernet Sauvignon, the reds are powerful, structured, and tannic. They have an aromatic and spicy nose, and are ideal for laying down. There are also lighter wines that can be enjoyed younger, and these are sometimes reminiscent of certain Bordeaux.

The white wines generally boast an agreeably floral and fruity nose, with delightful freshness and charming lightness. The sweet wines are fine and elegant, and some among them are a match for their neighbors from Sauternes.

Southwestern France's AOCs

- Béarn
- Béarn-Bellocq
- Bergerac
- Buzet
- Cahors
- Côtes-de-Bergerac
- Côtes-de-Duras
- Côtes-du-Frontonnais or Fronton
- Côtes-du-Frontonnais-Villaudric
- Côtes-du-Marmandais
- Côtes-de-Montravel
- Gaillac
- Gaillac doux (sweet Gaillac)
- Gaillac mousseux (sparkling Gaillac)
- Gaillac-Premières-Côtes
- Haut-Montravel
- Irouléguy
- Jurançon
- Jurançon sec (dry Jurançon)
- Madiran
- Marcillac
- Monbazillac
- Montravel
- Pacherenc-du-Vic-Bilh
- Pécharmant
- Rosette
- Saussignac

Famous wines of southwestern France

Beyond the leading appellations of Madiran, Jurançon, and Gaillac, this region boasts a multitude of wines worth discovering for their originality, unique character, and easy-drinking quality.

BERGERAC AND CÔTES-DE-BERGERAC AOCs

BERGERACOIS

At the heart of Périgord, along the border with Bordeaux—from which it has adopted a version of every grape variety—Bergerac's vineyards extend over some 17,300 acres (7,000 ha). The landscape is one of sunny hills and plateaus on both sides of the Dordogne Valley, forming a strip about 6 to 9 miles (10 to 15 km) long around the town of Bergerac. It is made up of a mosaic of microclimates, and produces both red and white wines. The most sophisticated are grouped under the Côtes-de-Bergerac AOC label, which represents the top flight of the appellation.

> **GRAPE VARIETIES** Cabernet Sauvignon, Cabernet Franc, Merlot, Malbec, Fer, and Merille for reds and rosés; Sémillon, Sauvignon Blanc, Muscadelle, Ondenc, Chenin Blanc, and Trebbiano for whites.
> **SOIL** Clay, limestone, and sand in the northern Dordogne; molasse, marl, and limestone in the south.
> **STYLE** The reds are supple, easy to drink, and rather fruity, with notes of strawberries, blackcurrants, and other berry fruits. Often matured in barrel, Côtes-de-Bergerac wines are more tannic with complex aromas (ripe fruits, toasted notes, spices), and further ageing can be beneficial. Made by the *saignée* (draining the vats) technique, the rosés have a salmon-pink color with crisp fruit flavor (raspberries, wild strawberries) supported by fresh aromas. The dry whites are lively with a charming nose and good length in the mouth. The medium-sweet and sweet Côtes-de-Bergerac whites combine freshness, finesse, and full body with a fairly pronounced bouquet.

Color:
Red, rosé, and white.

Serving temperature:
46°F (8°C) for sweet whites;
50 to 54°F (10 to 12°C) for dry whites and rosés;
59 to 63°F (15 to 17°C) for reds.

Ageing potential:
Rosés within a year;
reds and whites within 2 to 3 years;
Côtes-de-Bergerac within 5 to 6 years.

MONBAZILLAC AOC

BERGERACOIS

This appellation is one of the oldest in the region. After falling out of favor for a while, Monbazillac has regained its reputation and is now one of the best-known of all the Dordogne wines. The vineyards are dispersed around five villages located in the steep hills of the Dordogne Valley, south of Bergerac: Pomport, Rouffignac, Colombier, St-Laurent-des-Vignes, and Monbazillac. The temperate climate is conducive to developing the noble rot necessary to make the finest sweet wines. In good years, Monbazillac is a match for some Sauternes.

> **GRAPE VARIETIES** Sémillon, Sauvignon Blanc, Muscadelle.
> **SOIL** Clay-limestone with high clay content.

> **STYLE** These golden, sweet wines exude a complex bouquet of white flowers, almonds, hazelnuts, honey, and gentle spices. They boast a nice balance of liveliness and power, with a long and aromatic finish.

Color:
White.

Serving temperature:
43 to 46°F (6 to 8°C)

Ageing potential:
5 to 30 years.

BUZET AOC

Buzet is the oldest and the most famous of the appellations to emerge from the Garonne. It only just avoided falling to the phylloxera crisis, but recovered thanks to the dedication of members of the powerful Vignerons de Buzet growers' association. They never ceased in their efforts to restore it to its former vigor. The AOC now covers 5,000 acres (2,000 ha) situated between the left bank of the Garonne and the edge of the Landes *département*. Buzet produces wine in all three colors, with reds being dominant.

> **GRAPE VARIETIES** Merlot, Cabernet Franc, Cabernet Sauvignon for reds and rosés; Sémillon and Sauvignon Blanc for whites.

> **SOIL** Gravelly, clay-limestone, boulbène.

> **STYLE** Reds are powerful and full-bodied, featuring red and black fruit tones with spicy and smoky notes resting on a good framework of tannins. As they age, the tannins grow more supple and the wine gains in aromatic complexity, tending toward forest floor, humus, and game scents. Wines of this caliber are a match for their Bordeaux cousins. The whites are fresh with aromas of fruit and white flowers, and the rosés have a powerfully aromatic nose.

Color:
Red, rosé,
and white.

Serving temperature:
46 to 50°F (8 to 10°C) for whites
and rosés;
59 to 63°F (15 to 17°C) for reds.

Ageing potential:
1 to 2 years for the whites and rosés;
3 to 6 years for the reds.

CAHORS AOC

Nicknamed "black tie" by the British because of its almost ebony appearance, Cahors wines were a favorite of King Francis I of France and also the Russian court. This is one of the oldest wines in France. The appellation cultivates 10,400 acres (4,200 ha) of land on each side of the Lot Valley south of Quercy. It produces 2.1 million cases (192,700 hl) of exclusively red wine. A number of producers under the aegis of Pascal Verhaeghe (Château du Cèdre) have banded together to set up the "Cahors Excellence" seal of quality, establishing extremely strict specifications for the production of top wines.

> **GRAPE VARIETIES** Malbec (known here as Auxerrois or Côt Noir), Merlot, Tannat.

> **SOIL** Limestone, alluvial, and gallet soils in Lot; clay and limestone elsewhere.

> **STYLE** Cahors is traditionally a powerful and generous wine, with a deep red-garnet hue that can be almost black. The nose shows aromas of macerated red and stone fruits, typical characteristics of the Malbec from which it is made. The tannins soften and the nose becomes more complex with age—with notes of prunes, chocolate, humus, and licorice, and all acquiring good length in the mouth. Today, you also will find Cahors that are predominantly made with Merlot grapes, and these are more supple and easy to drink.

Color:
Red.

Serving temperature:
59 to 63°F (15 to 17°C).
Best decanted.

Ageing potential:
3 to 10 years, or more for great vintages.

CÔTES-DU-FRONTONNAIS OR FRONTON AOC

This is the signature wine of Toulouse. Located between the Tarn and the Garonne, the vineyards of Fronton cover 5,900 acres (2,400 ha) of terraces—with soils particularly favorable for Négrette, the local grape that lends the wine its distinct characteristics. Annual production totals 1.1 million cases (100,000 hl) of almost exclusively red wines.

> **GRAPE VARIETIES** Négrette, Cabernet Franc, Cabernet Sauvignon, Syrah, Gamay, Fer, Malbec, Cinsaut.

> **SOIL** Gravel, iron-rich soils, boulbène.

> **STYLE** Reds are supple, elegant, and typical of their variety, the Négrette, with a deep, ruby red color. The nose mixes aromas of red fruit, flowers (violets and peonies), and spices (licorice and pepper). The rosés are lively, with a charming bouquet that combines white flowers with red and exotic fruits.

Color:
Red and rosé.

Serving temperature:
46 to 50°F (8 to 10°C) for rosés;
59 to 63°F (15 to 17°C) for reds.
Best decanted.

Ageing potential:
Rosés should be enjoyed within a year;
reds can be kept for 4 to 5 years.

Cooperatives in the spotlight

Cooperative wineries have played a central role in saving appellations that were on the point of being lost forever; and these endeavors continue to this day. Some have set the bar extremely high, such as the Producteurs Plaimont, the largest cooperative in Gascony. It unites the wineries of St-Mont and Crouseilles, and has also awarded its seal of approval to wines from Madiran and Pacherenc-du-Vic-Bilh. Other honorable mentions are due to the Vignerons de Buzet, Cave d'Irouléguy, Cave des Vignerons de Rabastens (Gaillac), Cave de Fronton, Berticot (Côtes-de-Duras), and Cave de Cocumont (Côtes-du-Marmandais), all of whom guarantee excellent value.

GAILLAC AOC

HAUT-PAYS

Once famed for its sparkling white wine, this district is one of the oldest in the region and, at 6,200 acres (2,500 ha), also one of the largest in southwest France. Gaillac produces a palette of wines with breadth and depth: reds and rosés, as well as dry, sparkling, and sweet whites—not to mention both red and white *nouveaux* wines. The Gaillac-Premières-Côtes appellation produces a dry white wine.

> **GRAPE VARIETIES** Duras, Braucol (Fer Servadou), Gamay, Syrah, Négrette, and Cabernet Franc for reds; Mauzac, Len de l'El, Muscadelle, Sauvignon Blanc, Ondenc, and Sémillon for whites.

> **SOIL** Gravelly on the left bank of the Tarn, which favors red wines; granite and limestone on the right bank, which is better for whites.

> **STYLE** The dry whites are elegant, lively, and fresh, with a nose of green apples and pears that is characteristic of Mauzac grapes. The palate is light with a slight fizz. A creamier dry white is a Gaillac speciality. It has a very gentle effervescence that reinforces freshness and vivacity, and brings out the natural aromas of the Mauzac and Len de l'El grapes. The sweet white wine reveals notes of stewed apples, honey, figs, and white flowers. The sparkling wine,

whether made by the traditional method or the Gaillac method (*see* p.70), is a seductive ensemble of apple aromas and fine bubbles. The rosés are also lively and fresh, with a delightfully aromatic bouquet. The *nouveau* red—which is not supposed to be consumed until the third Thursday in November—has a nose typical of Gamay, the single grape from which it is made. There are aromas of red berries underpinned by a charming freshness. The traditional red is tannic, structured, and agreeable, with a nose of red fruits and spices, and admirable balance.

Color:	Serving temperature:	Ageing potential:
Red, white, and rosé.	43 to 46°F (6 to 8°C) for the sweet whites and the sparkling wines; 46 to 50°F (8 to 10°C) for the dry whites and rosés; 54 to 63°F (12 to 17°C) for the reds.	Nouveaux reds should be consumed during the winter after bottling; sparkling and dry whites and the rosés should be enjoyed within a year; sweet whites can be kept for 2 to 3 years; traditional reds can age for 2 to 5 years.

PACHERENC-DU-VIC-BILH AOC

PYRENEES

In Gascon dialect, "pacherenc du vic bihl" means "marked out with stakes from the old country." Located in the same wine-producing area as Madiran, a region of hills and dales, this small appellation produces 95,400 cases (8,500 hl) of exclusively white wine. Most are sweet

or very sweet, although a few are dry.

> **GRAPE VARIETIES** Arrufiac, Petit Manseng, Petit Courbu, Gros Manseng, Sauvignon Blanc, Sémillon.

> **SOIL** Argilo-siliceous, alluvial soils.

> **STYLE** Made with over-ripe grapes that are hand-harvested in multiple passes,

Pacherenc is a refreshing, aromatic, and crisp wine of great freshness. It has a charming nose that combines notes of preserved lemons and grapefruit with exotic and dried fruits.

Color:	Serving temperature:	Ageing potential:
White.	43 to 46°F (6 to 8°C) for sweet wines; 50 to 54°F (10 to 12°C) for dry.	Dry wines should be enjoyed within a year; sweet wines can be kept for 5 to 10 years.

MADIRAN AOC

Madiran was long the wine of choice for pilgrims to Santiago de Compostela, before becoming a fashionable wine in 1970s Paris. Set northeast of Pau in the middle of Béarn, the appellation covers 3,200 acres (1,300 ha) along terraces at the foot of the Pyrenees. It produces about 778,000 cases (70,000 hl) of exclusively red wine with the distinct character of the Tannat grape, which lends the wine its typical tannic strength.

> **GRAPE VARIETIES** Tannat, Cabernet Franc, Cabernet Sauvignon, Fer Servadou.

> **SOIL** Clay-and-limestone, siliceous, gravel.

> **STYLE** Madiran is concentrated, showing notes of raspberry and black fruits with hints of spices and truffles. It has a framework of robust tannins and a generous helping of alcohol. The tannins soften with age, and the wine's aromas become spicier with hints of black fruits (prunes) and roasted notes, mingling with licorice and mint. Thanks to their rich structure, the wines are prime candidates for laying down.

Color:
Red.

Serving temperature:
61 to 63°F (16 to 17°C).
Definitely to be decanted.

Ageing potential:
1 to 5 years for basic wines;
10 to 15 years for fine vintages from larger producers.

JURANÇON AND JURANÇON SEC (DRY) AOCs

History has it that Henry IV of France was baptized with a drop of Jurançon and a clove of garlic. Its 2,500 acres (1,000 ha) of terraced vineyards are arranged at an elevation of 980+ feet (300 m) among fields and meadows at the gates of Pau. From these vines, the appellation produces some 422,000 cases (38,000 hl) of exclusively white wine. The sweetest of these are some of the finest in France. The AOC Jurançon produces nothing but sweet wines, and making these with late-harvest grapes has been official since 1996. There is a separate appellation—Jurançon sec—for dry wines.

> **GRAPE VARIETIES** Gros Manseng, Petit Manseng, Courbu.

> **SOIL** Marl and clay-limestone. Also siliceous limestone and conglomerate soil.

> **STYLE** Jurançon wines have a striking bouquet, with notes of slightly crystallized lemon and grapefruit. There is a palate of tropical fruit, and a hint of honey; the finish is long and flavorful. Dry Jurançon is replete with floral scents and exotic fruit notes underpinned with plenty of ebullience and a slight effervescence.

Color:
White.

Serving temperature:
46 to 50°F (8 to 10°C) for Jurançon;
50 to 54°F (10 to 12°C) for dry Jurançon.

Ageing potential:
2 and 5 years, or up to 15 years for
great vintages, for Jurançon;
3 to 4 years for dry Jurançon.

IROULÉGUY AOC

Vines once ruled this area nestled in the heart of the Atlantic Pyrenees (Pyrénées-Atlantiques *département*) or Basque country, with vineyards covering more than 2,500 acres (1,000 ha). Today, there remains only a single private estate. Crouching timidly around five villages clustered not far from the Spanish border at the base of the St-Étienne-de-Baïgorry hills, the appellation produces a wide variety of red wines as well as several sought-after whites and rosés.

> **GRAPE VARIETIES** Tannat, Cabernet Franc, and Cabernet Sauvignon for reds and rosés; Gros Manseng, Petit Manseng, and Petit Courbu for whites.

> **SOIL** Clay-and-limestone, siliceous clay, red pebbles.

> **STYLE** The reds have a deep purple color, with slightly rustic aromas of red fruits and violets. They are heightened by spicy notes against a background of gentle tannins. The finish is long and aromatic. The rosés are lively and fruity, with hints of red fruits lifted by a delightful freshness.

Color:
Red, rosé,
and white.

Serving temperature:
46 to 50°F (8 to 10°C) for rosés
and whites;
59 to 63°F (15 to 17°C) for reds.

Ageing potential:
Within 2 years for rosés and whites;
5 to 8 years for reds.

LANGUEDOC-ROUSSILLON

This wine region is one the oldest in France. It has long suffered because of its image as a producer of very ordinary wines. But it accounts for more than a third of national production today, and many of the wines are well worth discovering.

LANGUEDOC

The Languedoc sub-region is almost unique in the French countryside with its patchwork of vineyards and its wide range of wines. After making great strides in the past 30 years, it is now aiming to become one of the world's leading wine regions. Three appellations—Corbières, Coteaux du Languedoc, and Minervois—represent three-quarters of sales.

Yesterday and today

While the Greeks introduced vines to the region during the 6th century BC, it was the Romans who really developed them, under the Emperor Domitian, after the latter had created the vast province of Narbonne. Despite later occupation by the Visigoths, the vine continued to flourish, benefiting from the expansion of monasteries (Lagrasse, Caunes, etc.) during the 9th century. The opening of the Canal du Midi in 1681 and development of railroads during the 19th century further promoted the growth of viticulture. However, by the late 19th century phylloxera had destroyed these vineyards. They reappeared, but quality was sacrificed to productivity. Today, the vineyards here have regained their identity and sense of authenticity, and they are asserting a pivotal role.

> **LANGUEDOC STATISTICS (AOC)**
>
> Vineyard area: 93,542 acres (37,855 ha)
>
> Production: 147 million cases (13,270,000 hl)
>
> Reds: 80%
>
> Whites: 13%
>
> Rosés: 7%
>
> (CIVL, 2008)

Vineyard landscape

Languedoc vineyards cover three *départements*: Gard, Herault, and Aude. It is a region spanning, east to west, from Nîmes to Carcassonne. It is bordered to the north by the foothills of the Massif Central, and to the south by the Mediterranean and the mountains of Corbières. A variety of soils—schist, pebbled terraces, sandstone, marl, limestone, and alluvium—give the wines their distinctive character. The Mediterranean climate, with its high summer temperatures, sporadic rainfall, and strong winds, gives the region a certain unity and allows perfect ripening of its grapes.

Varieties and styles

Key grape varieties are from Bordeaux and the Mediterranean.

RED GRAPES. Carignan, which finds its ideal *terroir* here, gives the wines their structure, appearance, and color. Grenache provides warmth and full flavors, while Syrah provides tannins. As for Mourvèdre, it produces elegant wines that are suitable for ageing. Cinsault is mainly used for making rosés.

WHITE GRAPES. Grenache Blanc produces full-bodied, round, crisp wines with a good finish. Maccabeu produces a dry wine with some color, a balance of richness and delicacy, and relatively subtle but ripe fruit on the nose. Picpoul provides a very crisp and fresh wine, and Bourboulenc is used to create floral expressions. Chardonnay (in Limoux) and Marsanne are also grown, along with Roussanne and Rolle.

DRY STYLES AND *VINS DOUX NATURELS*. The red wines of Languedoc are generally a beautiful garnet color. They are

> Vineyards near Carcassonne.

Languedoc AOCs

- Blanquette de Limoux
- Cabardès
- Clairette du Languedoc
- Corbières
- Corbières-Boutenac
- Crémant de Limoux
- Faugères
- Fitou
- Languedoc or Coteaux-du-Languedoc
- Limoux
- Malepère
- Minervois
- Minervois-La Livinière
- Muscat de Frontignan
- Muscat de Lunel
- Muscat de Mireval
- Muscat de St-Jean-de-Minervois
- St-Chinian

powerful, generous, and increasingly elegant. Besides *appellation contrôlée* wines, there are simple table wines from many different parts of the region, and they are mostly red. Some, like those of Mas de Daumas Gassac, are recognized as truly great wines. The region's white wines are often full and rich, with some sparkling wines (Blanquette de Limoux, Crémant de Limoux), and some *vins doux naturels* (Muscat de Lunel, Muscat de Frontignan) of outstanding quality, but of relatively restricted quantity.

LANGUEDOC-ROUSSILLON

The map shows place names including: GARD, Languedoc, Pic-St-Loup, Terrasses du Larzac*, HÉRAULT, Lodève, Clairette du Languedoc, Grès de Montpellier*, Muscat de Lunel, TARN, Lacaune, Bédarieux, Montpellier, Castres, St-Pons-de-Thomières, Faugères, Pézenas et Cabrières*, Muscat de Mireval, Mazamet, St-Chinian, Muscat de Frontignan, Muscat de-St-Jean-de-Minervois, Languedoc, Picpoul-de-Pinet*, Minerve, Béziers, Étang de Thau, Cabardès, Terrasses de Béziers*, Minervois, Valras-Plage, Cap d'Agde, Carcassonne, Aude, La Clape*, Malepère, Narbonne, Gruissan, Lagrasse, Corbières, Mediterranean Sea, Limoux, AUDE, Mouthoumet, Fitou, Fitou, Blanquette de Limoux, Tuchan, Étang de Leucate, AUDE, Axat, Maury, Côtes-du-Roussillon-Villages, ARIÈGE, Caramany, Latour-de-France, Tét, PYRÉNÉES-ORIENTALES, Prades, Perpignan, Côtes-du-Roussillon, Rivesaltes, Collioure, Céret, Banyuls, Tech, SPAIN*

0 — 12 miles (20 km)

N

* The asterisk indicates the sub-appellations and the Languedoc AOC.
NB. Since 2007, the Languedoc AOC has been extended to include the combined Languedoc and Roussillon territory.

Roussillon AOCs

- **Banyuls**
- **Banyuls Grand Cru**
- **Collioure**
- **Côtes-du-Roussillon**
- **Côtes-du-Roussillon-Les Aspres**
- **Côtes-du-Roussillon-Villages**
- **Maury**
- **Muscat de Rivesaltes**
- **Rivesaltes**

ROUSSILLON

This sub-region is home to exceptional *vins doux naturels*: Banyuls, Maury, and Rivesaltes. The area produces 80 percent of these wines in France, but also offers a nice range of traditional wines—reds, rosés, and whites.

History

Wine production here dates back to Ancient Greek times. And though the wines of Roussillon have been well known since the Middle Ages, the real development of the vineyards took place from the middle of the 17th century. Then phylloxera devastated plantings, leading to an economic crisis. The industry recovered by focusing on quality, and that work led to AOC status for Rivesaltes, Banyuls, and Maury in 1936.

Vineyard landscape

Vineyards occupy a large amphitheater facing the Mediterranean between the Massif des Corbières in the north, Canigou in the west, and the Albères to the south. They enjoy a Mediterranean climate with mild winters and hot summers. Soils are very diverse: black and brown schist, sandy granite, and clay-and-limestone.

ROUSSILLON STATISTICS (AOC)

Vineyard area: 60,284 acres (24,396 ha)

Production: 7.6 million cases (680,000 hl)

Vins Doux Naturels: 80%

Red and rosé: 15%

White: 5%

(CIVR, 2007)

Varieties and styles

GRAPE VARIETIES. Roussillon cultivates all the Mediterranean varieties—Carignan, Grenache Noir, Mourvèdre, Syrah, and Cinsault for red and rosé wines; Grenache Blanc, Maccabeu, Roussanne, and Marsanne for whites. There are also some native varieties: Malvasia du Roussillon Blanc produces wines with a golden color, richness, delicacy, aromatics, and crispness; Lladoner Pelut (also known as Grenache Poilu) produces dry wines with some color. Muscat of Alexandria and Muscat Blanc à Petits Grains, grapes with very rich flavors, are used in blends for *vins doux naturels*.

VINS DOUX NATURELS. Produced from Grenache (Banyuls, Maury) or Muscat (Muscat de Rivesaltes and Rivesaltes), the wines are at once powerful, elegant, and floral. Very unfairly ignored, they suffer from a negative image as *vins cuits* (overdone, "cooked") or *vins d'apéritif bon marché* (cheap glugging wine). This is a shame because they deserve to be enjoyed for what they are: great food wines with a remarkable capacity for ageing.

TRADITIONAL STYLES. Reds are fine and light, and should be consumed when young; or they are powerful, concentrated, and suitable for ageing (including Côtes du Roussillon-Villages). The rosés combine finesse and power. The more rare white wines (Côtes du Roussillon) are full of fruit flavor and well balanced.

Top Languedoc-Roussillon wines

This region, one of the world's largest in terms of area, produces many high-quality wines. Some of them, including the vins doux naturels, *are highly sought after for their distinct character.*

LANGUEDOC AOC

LANGUEDOC-ROUSSILLON

In 2007, the Languedoc AOC replaced Coteaux du Languedoc, which may still appear on labels until 2012. It covers all other appellation areas in Languedoc and Roussillon, approximately 23,475 acres (9,500 ha). It comprises red, rosé, and several whites. The appellation is divided into districts that correspond to particular terroirs: La Clape, Picpoul-de-Pinet, Pézenas, Grès de Montpellier, Terrasses du Larzac, Pic-St-Loup, Terrasses de Béziers, and Terres de Sommières. Producers also are able to append one of the following geographic names: Cabrières, La Méjanelle, Montpeyroux, Quatourze, St-Christol, St-Drézéry, St-Georges-d'Orques, St-Saturnin, and Vérargues.

> **GRAPE VARIETIES** Grenache Noir, Syrah, Mourvèdre, Cinsault, Carignan, and Lladoner for red and rosé wines; Grenache Blanc, Clairette Blanche, Bourboulenc, Picpoul Blanc, Roussanne, Marsanne, Rolle, and Viognier for the white wines.

> **SOIL** Limestone, schist, gravel.

> **STYLE** Whether they are produced in the traditional way or by carbonic maceration, reds can range from soft and light with red fruit flavors embellished with spices, to more elaborate, more concentrated, and with more tannins and notes of leather, dried fruit, and mineral flavors. The rosés are round and soft with a nice floral and fruity nose. As for the whites, they are fresh and have an aromatic bouquet of white and yellow flowers with notes of honey, spice, and garrigue.

Color:
Red, rosé, and white.

Serving temperature:
46 to 50°F (8 to 10°C) for whites and rosés;
54 to 57°F (12 to 14°C) for light reds;
59 to 63°F (15 to 17°C) for concentrated reds.

Ageing potential:
Within a year for whites;
1 to 2 years for rosés;
2 to 4 years for reds (sometimes up to 8 years).

CORBIÈRES AOC

LANGUEDOC

The vineyards of Corbières are at the heart of the Aude, in a rectangle of 31,750 acres (12,850 ha) between Carcassonne, Narbonne, Perpignan, and Quillan. They mainly produce red wines. The variety of soils is such that there are 11 *terroirs*: Montagne d'Alaric, St-Victor, Fontfroide, Quéribus, Boutenac, Termenès, Lézignan, Lagrasse, Sigean, Durban, and Serviès. Since 2005, Boutenac has had its own AOC.

> **GRAPE VARIETIES** Grenache, Syrah, Mourvèdre, Carignan, and Cinsaut for the reds and rosés; Grenache Blanc, Bourboulenc, Maccabeu, Marsanne, Roussanne, and Vermentino for the white wines.

> **SOIL** Schist, limestone, sandstone, marl.

> **STYLE** It is difficult to describe the Corbières since the *terroirs*, and hence the wines, are varied. The reds, whether produced traditionally or by carbonic maceration, are powerful, concentrated, and well-structured. They display a complex nose that combines black fruits, spices, and garrigue notes. The palate is long and persistent, with rounded tannins. With age, the flavors develop notes of coffee, cocoa, damp woodland, humus, and game. The rosés are powerful, full of flavor, and fruity. Whites offer a fine, delicate nose of white flowers and exotic fruits, with nice palate roundness.

Color:
Red, rosé, and white.

Serving temperature:
50 to 54°F (10 to 12°C) for the whites and rosés;
61 to 64°F (16 to 18°C) for the reds (which should be decanted).

Ageing potential:
1 to 2 years for the whites and rosés;
3 to 10 years, or even 15 years, for the reds.

BLANQUETTE DE LIMOUX AOC

This is the oldest sparkling wine in France. Its history dates to the 16th century, when the wine was developed (in 1531) by monks at the Abbey of St-Hilaire, near Limoux. Located in the hills bordering the valley of the Aude, and overlooking the Pyrenees to the south of Carcassonne, the vineyards cover 2,965 acres (1,200 ha) and yield 556,000 cases (50,000 hl) of sparkling white wine (*blanquette*). Production is by the traditional method or the ancestral method (*see* p.70), which has its own appellation. These sparkling wines, which are all white, can be *brut*, *demi-sec*, or *sec*.

> **GRAPE VARIETIES** Traditional method: Mauzac, also known as Blanquette (90 percent at least), Chenin, and Chardonnay. Ancestral method: Mauzac.

> **SOIL** Clay-and-limestone, stones, marl, sandstone.

> **STYLE** With small, fine bubbles and a fruity nose dominated by the scent of ripe apples and a few floral notes (white flowers), the wine fills the palate with a lingering finish.

Color:
White.

Serving temperature:
43 to 46°F (6 to 8°C).

Ageing potential:
1 to 3 years.

MINERVOIS AOC

This appellation derives its name from the goddess of wisdom, Minerva. The territory of Minervois is an amphitheater of 10,324 acres (4,178 ha) bounded by the Canal du Midi in the south and the Montagne Noire to the north. It produces very different wines, soft and fruity or structured and meant for ageing. The AOC produces mostly reds, but also white and rosé wines. At the heart of its territory, across six different districts, is the first "village" appellation of Languedoc to be created: Minervois-La Livinière.

> **GRAPE VARIETIES** For red and rosé: Syrah, Mourvèdre, Grenache, Carignan, Cinsaut, Terret Noir, and Picpoul Noir; for white: Maccabeu, Bourboulenc, Clairette, Grenache, Vermentino, and Muscat.

> **SOIL** Terraces of pebbles, sandstone, schist, and limestone soils.

> **STYLE** The red wines typically display complexity and concentration, with a deep ruby red color. The nose shows aromas of red and black fruit, hints of garrigue and spice or licorice, as well as delicate violets. The palate has a frame of tannins and a long finish. The rosés are powerful, but fresh. The white wines combine white and exotic fruits in a fine balance.

Color:
*Red, rosé,
and white.*

Serving temperature:
*50 to 54°F (10 to 12°C) for whites
and rosés;
61 to 63°F (16 to 17°C) for reds.*

Ageing potential:
*Within a year for whites and rosés;
5 to 8 years for the reds.*

Selected Languedoc producers

BLANQUETTE DE LIMOUX

- **Blanquette Beirieu (Roquetaillade).** Superb *blanquettes* using the ancestral method and respecting tradition absolutely, with no added sulfur.

- **Sieur d'Arques (Limoux).** Full range of sparkling wine from this major wine cooperative.

CORBIERES

- **Domaine Montmija (Lagrasse).** Organically grown wines with exquisite flavors.

- **Château Pech-Latt (Lagrasse).** One of the major estates of the appellation.

LANGUEDOC

- **Château Puech-Haut (St-Drézéry).** Superb red wines.

- **Domaine Peyre-Rose (St-Pargoire).** One of the most impressive wines from Languedoc.

- **Prieuré St-Jean-de-Bébian (Pézenas).** An exceptional estate producing legendary reds and whites.

MINERVOIS

- **Château La Grave (Badens).** Fine wines that balance finesse and power. A benchmark.

- **Domaine Pierre Cros (Badens).** Powerful and generous wines.

CÔTES-DU-ROUSSILLON AND CÔTES-DU-ROUSSILLON-VILLAGES AOCs

These regional appellations cover 12,350 acres (5,000 ha) right across Roussillon. They mainly produce red wines, but also rosés and occasional white wines from the region. Northern Roussillon, between the Massif des Corbières and Têt, is the stronghold of the Côtes-du-Roussillon-Villages, an appellation consisting entirely of red wines. Four villages, Caramany, Latour-de-France, Lesquerde, and Tautavel, can add their name to the appellation.

> **GRAPE VARIETIES** For red and rosé: Carignan, Grenache, Mourvèdre, Syrah, and Lladoner; for white: Maccabeu, Grenache Blanc, Malvoisie, Marsanne, and Roussanne.

> **SOIL** Granite, schist, limestone.

> **STYLE** Powerful and generous, the reds are distinguished by a nose of wild fruits and mineral notes. Those of the Côtes-du-Roussillon-Villages AOC display a complex nose of crystallized fruit with vanilla notes on a frame of rounded, long-lasting tannins. The palate is firm and lively. Produced by *saignée*, the roses are full-bodied and fruity. The whites are light with aromas of flowers and wood.

Color:
Red, rosé, and white.

Serving temperature:
50°F (10°C) for the whites and rosés; 59 to 61°F (15 to 16°C) for the reds.

Ageing potential:
Within a year for whites and rosés; 2 to 5 years for reds.

RIVESALTES AOC

This appellation derives its name from the town of Rivesaltes (meaning "high banks" in Catalan). Located mostly in Roussillon, but also in Corbières, it is the largest appellation for *vins naturels doux*. It covers about 13,345 acres (5,400 ha) and produces an average of 3.3 million cases (300,000 hl) of red and white wines. Its name may be supplemented by the terms "tuilé," "ambré," and "hors d'âge."

It is important to note that you should not confuse Rivesaltes AOC with Muscat de Rivesaltes AOC, a white *vin doux naturel*, which covers the same territory. Muscat de Rivesaltes is made from the Muscat of Alexandria and Muscat à Petits Grains grapes.

> **GRAPE VARIETIES** Grenache (Noir, Gris, or Blanc), Maccabeu, and Malvoisie du Roussillon.

> **SOIL** Schist, limestone, and silt.

> **STYLE** Young Rivesaltes has aromas of slightly crystallized red fruit, supported by round tannins. "Tuilé" Rivesaltes has a nose dominated by caramel, mixed with aromas of sweet spices, orange peel, cocoa, quince, coffee, and nuts. "Hors d'âge" Rivesaltes is aged for a minimum of five years after production. Most are aged for much longer.

Color:
White and red.

Serving temperature:
54 to 61°F (12 to 16°C).

Ageing potential:
10 to 20 years or more.

Selected *vins doux naturels*

MAURY

- **Domaine de la Coume du Roy (Maury).** Wines of great substance, impressive in their density, concentration, and depth of flavor.

- **Mas Amiel (Maury).** Great Maury wines, beautiful Muscat de Rivesaltes, and a remarkable range of Côtes-du-Roussillon wines that are very elegant.

BANYULS

- **Domaine du Mas Blanc (Banyuls-sur-Mer).** An estate famous for its Banyuls and Collioure wines, which are among the best of the appellation.

- **Domaine de la Rectorie (Banyuls-sur-Mer).** Superb and beautiful Banyuls that are stylistic benchmarks, as well as lovely rosé and red Collioure appellation wines.

- **Domaine du Traginer (Banyuls-sur-Mer).** Full-bodied and powerful wines produced from organic grapes.

RIVESALTES

- **Domaine Cazes (Rivesaltes).** A safe bet. Muscats that are harmonious, rich, and beautifully produced, using biodynamics.

MAURY AOC

At the heart of the Agly Valley, in northwestern Roussillon, these vineyards cover some 4,200 acres (1,700 ha) and produce 533,000 cases (48,000 hl) of fortified wines. The zone covers the town of Maury and three of the neighboring villages, forming an enclave within the much larger Rivesaltes and Côtes-du-Roussillon-Villages appellations. There are two kinds of Maury: the vintage (or *rimage*), which is bottled soon after vinification, and *rancio*, which is intentionally oxidized, either in wooden casks or in glass demijohns exposed to the elements.

> **GRAPE VARIETIES** Grenache Noir (at least 75 percent), Grenache Gris, Grenache Blanc, and Maccabeu.

> **SOIL** Schist.

> **STYLE** Vintage Maury boasts heady scents of black and red fruits that explode against a chocolate background. The palate is smooth, packed with pulpy tannins, and the finish is long and full of flavor. With its ruby red color, Maury Rancio has a nose of caramel, smoke, toast, dried and crystallized fruit, tea, nuts, coffee, and cocoa. The palate is rich and fragrant, just like the nose, with very good persistence.

Color:
Red and white.

Serving temperature:
54 to 57°F (12 to 14°C) for young wines;
57 to 61°F (14 to 16°C) for old wines.
(Vintage wine should be decanted.)

Ageing potential:
5 to 10 years, or even 20 to 30
years for the very best.

BANYULS AND BANYULS GRAND CRU AOCs

This historic wine region dates to the Carthaginian era, five centuries before Christ. Located on the Mediterranean, along the Spanish border, this *vins doux naturels* appellation spans the towns of Banyuls, Collioure, Port Vendres, and Cerbère. It covers 2,965 acres (1,200 ha) of vines grown in steep terraces, with a yield of around 322,000 cases (29,000 hl). As with Maury wines, there are two kinds of Banyuls: *rimages*, which have been quickly bottled to retain their freshness and fruit; and *rancios*, which have been aged in either tank or demijohn to develop a complex flavor—blending notes of chocolate, coffee, and prunes. Banyuls Grand Cru, which is prepared in the same appellation area, is aged for 30 months (as against 12 months for Banyuls).

> **GRAPE VARIETIES** Grenache Noir (50 percent for Banyuls, 75 percent for Banyuls Grand Cru), Grenache Gris, Grenache Blanc, Carignan, and Maccabeu.

> **SOIL** Schist.

> **STYLE** Young *rimage* Banyuls have flavors of stone fruit, blueberry, and blackberry. They are naturally sweet and mellow, even smooth, and have a very long palate. Old *rimages* develop a very balanced mix of leather and roasted notes (coffee, chocolate). The nose is intense and aromatic with a bouquet mingling notes of licorice, coffee, tea, dried fruits, and sweet spices. The palate is soft and gentle. With age, the color has tinges of bronze and the nose becomes even more complex, revealing lingering hints of toast, nuts, and caramel. *Rancio* Banyuls are much more "oxidated" with very persistent notes of spices and toast.

Color:
Red and white.

Serving temperature:
54 to 57°F (12 to 14°C) for young wines;
57°to 61°F (14 to 16°C) for old wines.

Ageing potential:
10 to 20 years, or more.

PROVENCE AND CORSICA

Provence and Corsica may be the oldest vineyard regions in France. Their modern production is full of surprises, and a far cry from the reputation that their wines are only easy-to-drink and for the summer.

PROVENCE

Sunshine, vacations, and rosé: this is the image of Provence. And yes, the region's production is 75 percent rosé. But the vineyards of Provence are not limited solely to pink; they also produce great red wines and quality whites that are well worth a look.

Ancient vines

Vine cultivation was introduced to Provence during the 6th century BC by the Phoenicians or the Phocaeans (Anatolian Greeks)—historians are still uncertain who planted the first vines in Provence and France. Vineyards then prospered under the influence of the great monastic orders. From the 15th century, the industry suffered many disasters, plague, and wars. And they had scarcely recovered when attacked by phylloxera during the 19th century, which destroyed all their work. In the 20th century everything was restored, with just a single watchword for all the appellations: quality.

Climate and soils

Given the broad expanse occupied by the vineyards of Provence, between Nice, Marseille, and St-Rémy-de-Provence, they are subject to significant variations in climate. They can be maritime or continental, depending on latitude and topography. However, there is one common: sunshine. Soils are very varied in nature: granite and schist in the Maures, limestone soil in Cassis, and so on.

Varieties

The spectrum of terrain and climate is matched by a wide range of grapes, with traditional varieties coexisting alongside indigenous ones.

RED GRAPE VARIETIES. Grenache, which is very common in Coteaux-d'Aix-en-Provence, brings power, richness, and elegant red fruit flavors. Cinsault imbues rosé wines with freshness, finesse, and fruit. Tibouren offers a rich bouquet. Mourvèdre, the star grape of Bandol, provides smoothness, complexity, and spicy notes. Carignan produces wines that are well-structured, generous, and colorful.

WHITE GRAPE VARIETIES. Rolle, especially in the Bellet AOC, produces wines with flavors of citrus and pear; they are rich, balanced, and fine. Clairette lends the wines flavor and bouquet, while Bourboulenc generates finesse and roundness.

Styles

Three appellations, Côtes-de-Provence, Coteaux-d'Aix-en-Provence, and Coteaux-Varois, account for 95 percent of production. Rosé wines are usually very aromatic, fruity, dry, and lively. But there are more complex rosés, which are structured and full-bodied, with powerful fruit flavors and the ability to accompany a gourmet meal. Red wines fall into two broad categories. There are lively and fruity wines with aromas of red fruits and flowers, which are consumed while young; and there are more

> **PROVENCE STATISTICS (AOC)**
>
> Vineyard area: 70,425 acres (28,500 ha)
>
> Production: 13.3 million cases (1,200,000 hl)
>
> Rosés: 75%
>
> Reds: 20%
>
> Whites: 5%
>
> (CIVP, 2007)

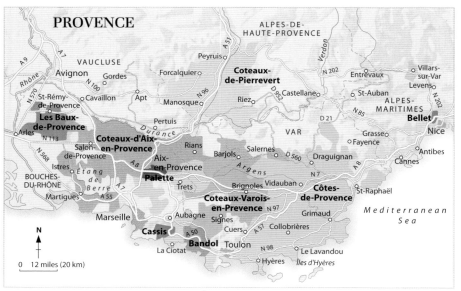

> ### Provence AOCs
>
> - Bandol
> - Bellet
> - Cassis
> - Coteaux-d'Aix-en-Provence
> - Coteaux-de-Pierrevert
> - Coteaux-Varois-en-Provence
>
> - Côtes-de-Provence (with or without a geographic designation: Fréjus, La Londe, Ste-Victoire)
> - Les Baux-de-Provence
> - Palette

elaborate and concentrated wines, with more tannins and a potential for ageing. As for the whites, they generally offer a wonderful aromatic complexity with a pleasant creaminess.

Provence also produces a *vin cuit*: the grapes are extensively heated so as to concentrate flavors and substance. This wine does not come under any appellation.

CORSICA

History

Viticulture in Corsica is more than 2,500 years old. It was developed under Greek and Roman influence. During the 17th century, vineyards occupied much of the territory, and viticulture was the lifeblood of virtually the entire population. But, as elsewhere, phylloxera ravaged the entire region. It was not until the 1960s and the arrival of expatriates from North Africa that the vineyards were reborn. After a period of productivity at all costs, it is now definitely geared toward quality and authenticity.

Climate and soils

Corsica is more than just an island; it is a mountain massif. It enjoys a Mediterranean climate tempered by the combined influences of the sea and mountains, which is particularly favorable for the maturation of grapes. Across this rugged terrain, there are a wide variety of soils, ranging from schist in the east to granite soil on the west coast and in the south.

CORSICA STATISTICS (AOC)

Vineyard area: 6,920 acres (2,800 ha)

Production: 1.1 million cases (98,000 hl)

Reds: 44%

Rosés: 42%

Whites: 14%

(CIVP, 2007)

Corsica AOCs

- Ajaccio
- Muscat du Cap-Corse
- Patrimonio
- Vin de Corse

Varieties and styles

GRAPE VARIETIES. As well as standard southern French grapes (Grenache and Syrah), Corsica takes pride in its own varieties. Related to Sangiovese (from Tuscany), the Nielluccio grape is the basis of red wines from Patrimonio. It presents flavors of red berries, violets, spices, and apricot. Another red grape variety, the Sciacarello, is grown mainly in the granite soils of southern Corsica; it displays great finesse, combined with an unforgettable peppered bouquet. Among the white grape varieties, the most characteristic is Vermentino, which is also called Malvasia here. It produces a very distinctive wine, which is very rich and has strong floral aromas. It is also used for the development of rosés.

WINES. Corsican rosé and white wines are rich and full of flavor, with a nice balance. They should be consumed young. Red wines are generally light, but those of Patrimonio and Ajaccio have dense tannins with good length on the palate, and may be aged for a few years.

> In northern Corsica, Patrimonio vineyards occupy a privileged position, sheltered from the winds.

Leading wines of Provence and Corsica

Whether large or small, Provençal appellations are widely known for their rosés; but their reds and whites are also worth investigating. We also should explore the sunny wines and Muscats from Corsica.

CÔTES-DE-PROVENCE AOC

PROVENCE

Occupying a vast area, this AOC extends from Gardanne to St-Raphaël over some 46,950 acres (19,000 ha) across three *départements* (Var, Bouches-du-Rhône, and Alpes-Maritimes) and a mosaic of *terroirs*—each with its own distinctive geography, climate, and character. The appellation is made up of five major districts: Mont Ste-Victoire, the Beausset basin, the limestone highlands, the interior valley, and the coastal region. It is especially renowned for its rosé (87 percent of production, nearly half of the rosés sold in France). It also produces quality reds and several whites. The Côtes-de-Provence

AOC includes 18 classified growths: Château Minuty, Château Ste-Roseline, Château Ste-Marguerite, Château de la Clapière, Domaine de l'Aumérade, Clos Cibonne, Domaine de Rimauresq, Château Roubine, Château du Galoupet, Château de St-Martin, Château St-Maur, Clos Mireille, Château de Selle, Château de Brégançon, Château de Mauvanne, Domaine de la Croix, Domaine du Noyer, and Domaine du Jas d'Esclans.

> **GRAPE VARIETIES** Grenache, Syrah, Carignan, Mourvèdre, Tibouren, Cinsaut, and Cabernet for reds and rosés; Clairette, Sémillon, Ugni Blanc, and Rolle for whites.

> **SOIL** Stony.

> **STYLE** The rosés are rather pale and display pleasant, subtle scents of red fruit mixed with hints of spice and licorice. The reds may be supple and light with a nose of red berries and flowers, or they may be generous, powerful, and elegant with complex flavors of black fruit with touches of damp woodland and spicy notes that linger on the palate. The whites are smooth with a delicate balance between freshness and richness.

Color:	Serving temperature:	Ageing potential:
Red, rosé, and white.	*43 to 46°F (6 to 8°C) for whites; 46 to 54°F (8 to 12°C) for rosés; 61 to 63°F (16 to 17°C) for reds (ideally decanted).*	*Consume rosés the summer after vintage; consume whites within a year; 3 years for reds; 10 to 12 years for classified growths.*

COTEAUX-VAROIS-EN-PROVENCE AOC

PROVENCE

This appellation covers 28 villages in the heart of Provence—around Brignoles, between the massifs of Ste-Baume to the south and Bessillons to the north. It climbs over 1,150 ft (350m) along slopes that are subject to a continental climate. It mainly produces rosé wines, but also reds and whites.

> **GRAPE VARIETIES** Syrah, Grenache, Mourvèdre, Cinsault, and Cabernet

Sauvignon for reds and rosés; Clairette, Grenache, Rolle, Sémillon, and Ugni Blanc for whites.

> **SOIL** Clay-and-limestone.

> **STYLE** With pretty, nuanced colors, the rosés have red fruit flavors (strawberry and raspberry) enhanced by notes of spice and garrigue; and they are highlighted by an attractive freshness and good balance. The well-structured, fleshy, tan-

nic red wines blend floral and red fruit flavors, with herbaceous hints. They need time to soften. The whites have a nose delicately scented with flowers, fruits, and citrus, with good balance between freshness and roundness.

Color:	Serving temperature:	Ageing potential:
Red, rosé, and white.	*43 to 46°F (6 to 8°C) for whites; 46 to 54°F (8 to 12°C) for rosés; 61 to 64°F (16 to 18°C) for reds.*	*Consume rosés within a year; 1 to 2 years for whites; 3 to 8 years for reds.*

BANDOL AOC

This vineyard region on the edge of Toulon is one of the oldest in France. Limited to eight districts in Var, its terraces cover about 4,200 acres (1,700 ha). It produces primarily red wines of great character, but also rosés and whites.

> **GRAPE VARIETIES** Mourvèdre (at least 50 percent), Grenache, Cinsaut, Syrah, and Carignan for reds and rosés; Bourboulenc (at least 60 percent), Clairette, and Ugni Blanc for whites.

> **SOIL** Sand-and-limestone.

> **STYLE** Stamped with the letter "B," the reds, which spend at least 18 months in barrel, are powerful. These wines offer complex black fruit, pine, and garrigue flavors. With age, they develop peony, spice, and licorice characters, with a finish that remains full of flavor. The rosés have a range of red fruit flavors highlighted by herbaceous notes. Fewer in number, the whites display hints of white and yellow flowers and fruits, and a pleasing finesse.

Color:
Red, rosé, and white.

Serving temperature:
46 to 50°F (8 to 10°C) for rosés;
48 to 52°F (9 to 11°C) for whites;
61 to 64°F (16 to 18°C) for reds.

Ageing potential:
1 to 3 years for whites and rosés;
10 years or more for reds.

CASSIS AOC

Located near the charming little port of Cassis, and blown by the Mistral wine, this vineyard area extends over 420 acres (170 ha) between the Calanques and Cap Canaille, the highest cliff in France at 1,312 ft (400 m). It produces highly regarded white wines, as well as some rosés and reds.

> **GRAPE VARIETIES** For red and rosé: Grenache, Carignan, Mourvèdre, and Cinsaut; for white: Clairette, Ugni Blanc, Sauvignon, Marsanne, and Bourboulenc.

> **SOIL** Limestone.

> **STYLE** Young whites offer a refreshing palate with a beguiling nose of white fruits, citrus, and an iodized hint that is reminiscent of the nearby sea. All these flavors have a long finish. With age, the nose becomes complex and releases aromas of honey, and the wine becomes more rounded and softer. The rosés, which are light and supple, present pleasing fruity and floral notes. Fewer in number, the reds offer herbaceous hints of bay leaf and thyme. There also are touches of red fruit (blackcurrant) mixed with some spice and licorice notes.

Color:
Red, rosé, and white.

Serving temperature:
46 to 50°F (8 to 10°C) for whites
and rosés;
59 to 63°F (16 to 17°C) for reds.

Ageing potential:
Consume rosés within a year;
3 to 5 years for reds;
up to 8 years for whites.

Selected Provence producers

- **Château de Pibarnon (La Cadière-d'Azur).** A classic of its appellation. Deep and balanced wines from the Bandol AOC.

- **Château du Gros Noré (La Cadière-d'Azur).** Authentic, exquisitely expressive wines that are among the best in the Bandol AOC.

- **Château La Calisse (Pontevès).** Seductive rosés and lovely reds from Coteaux-Varois-en-Provence

- **Clos Ste-Magdeleine (Cassis).** A key estate for the Cassis appellation, producing wines of character that are tempting and delicious.

- **Domaine de La Courtade (île de Porquerolles).** Exceptional red Côtes-de-Provence produced from Mourvèdre.

- **Domaine de Garbelle (Garéoult).** Some fantastic Coteaux-Varois-en-Provence reds that are powerful and generous.

- **Domaine Hauvette (St-Rémy-de-Provence).** A great estate of the Coteaux-d'Aix-en-Provence AOC, which produces top quality organic wines.

- **Domaine Rabiega (Draguignan).** One of the best in the Côtes-de-Provence AOC. Its wines are an authentic expression of the *terroir*; its Clos Dière is excellent.

- **Les Maîtres Vignerons de la Presqu'île de Saint-Tropez (Gassin).** A range of superb quality Côtes-de-Provence wines; their red Château de Pampelonne is colorful, rich, dense, and generous.

Domaine de Trévallon: majestic *vin de pays*

Eloi Dürrbach came from his native Alsace in 1973 and took over the estate established by his father on the northern slopes of the Alpilles near St-Etienne-du-Grès. To develop its reds, he chose a blend of the two varieties he considers particularly well suited to his *terroir*: Syrah and Cabernet Sauvignon. The latter is not recognized by the authorities of the INAO here and simply has the status of *vin de pays* in Bouches-du-Rhône. Nevertheless, it is a major estate of Provence, renowned worldwide.

COTEAUX-D'AIX-EN-PROVENCE AOC

Aix-en-Provence was the city of 15th-century King René, who was both a king and a winemaker. He developed the vineyards; and today, these vast plantings cover the Bouches-du-Rhône *département*. Across sheltered hillsides, woods, and scrubland, they extend over 7,400 acres (3,000 ha). The appellation produces rosé wines, but also some reds and whites.

> **GRAPE VARIETIES** Grenache, Cabernet Sauvignon, Carignan, Mourvèdre, Cinsaut, Syrah, and Counoise for reds and rosés; Clairette, Rolle, Bourboulenc, Ugni Blanc, Grenache, Sémillon, and Sauvignon for whites.
> **SOIL** Sand-and-limestone.
> **STYLE** The rosés are light and soft, with delicate colors. They display a nice variety of fruits (strawberry, peach), flowers (lime), and mineral notes on a fresh palate. The red wines, which are rich and full, combine flowers (violet), herbaceous notes, and hints of spices with persistent palate length. While the white wines are fresh, elegant, and full of flavor, yielding a bouquet of flowers, fruits, and citrus.

Color:
Red, rosé, and white.

Serving temperature:
43 to 46°F (6 to 8°C) for whites;
46 to 54°F (8 to 12°C) for rosés;
61 to 64°F (16 to 18°C) for reds.

Ageing potential:
1 to 2 years for whites;
2 to 5 years for rosés;
2 to 6 years for reds.

PATRIMONIO AOC

Rising in terraced rows that curve above of the Gulf of St-Florent in northwest Corsica, and influenced by both mountains and sea, the vineyards of Patrimonio grow over an area of about 4,695 acres (1,900 ha). They are best known for their red wines, but also produce rosés and whites in small numbers but of high quality.
> **GRAPE VARIETIES** For reds and rosés: Niellucio, Sciacarello, and Grenache; for whites: Vermentino and Ugni Blanc.
> **SOIL** Schist covered with limestone.
> **STYLE** The reds, based mainly on Niellucio, have a powerful nose of macerated red fruits and spices. They are rich and generous with spicy notes. The roses have a savory nose of spices and fresh fruit (strawberry, cherry), supported by a very full body. The whites are typical of their grape variety, Vermentino. They are dry and crisp, and have a very aromatic bouquet combining notes of white flowers and exotic fruits with a hint of dried grass, all highlighted by a fine freshness.

Color:
Red, rosé, and white.

Serving temperature:
45 to 46°F (7 to 8°C) for whites;
46 to 50°F (8 to 10°C) for rosés;
59 to 61°F (15 to 16°C) for reds.

Ageing potential:
Consume rosés within a year;
up to 2 years for whites;
3 to 8 years for reds.

VIN DE CORSE AOC

Backing into rocky ridges, these vineyards cover some 5,312 acres (2,150 ha) and produce 844,000 cases (76,000 hl) of mainly reds, but also some very distinctive whites and rosés. The wines, which can be produced throughout Corsica, come mainly from the east coast, and may add the name of one of these *terroirs*: Sartène, Figari, Porto-Vecchio, Calvi, and Coteaux-du-Cap-Corse.

> **GRAPE VARIETIES** Nielluccio, Sciacarello, and Grenache for reds and rosés; Vermentino and Ugni Blanc for whites.
> **SOIL** Granite, schist.
> **STYLE** The red wines have very nice aromas of red fruit, with mineral tones that linger on the palate. The whites, produced mostly from Vermentino grapes, have a generous, floral, and fruity nose. They also have hints of citrus and tropical fruit enhanced by a lovely freshness. As for rosés, they are bright and lively, with floral notes punctuated by subdued herbaceous touches.

Color:
Red, rosé, and white.

Serving temperature:
46 to 50°F (8 to 10°C) for whites and rosés; 59 to 63°F (15 to 17°C) for reds.

Ageing potential:
1 to 2 years for whites and rosés; 4 to 9 years for reds.

MUSCAT DU CAP-CORSE AOC

Muscat is a very old Corsican specialty. The *vin doux naturel* is rare—with only some 22,000 cases (2,000 hl) produced—and delicate. It comes from terraced vineyards covering 220 acres (90 ha) at the north end of the island. Production encompasses 17 villages, the area of Patrimonio, and the Vin de Corse-Coteaux-du-Cap-Corse AOC. There is also a local variation called *passito*, a non-fortified wine produced by *passerillage*, the raisining of grapes on the vine.

> **GRAPE VARIETY** Muscat Blanc à Petits Grains.
> **SOIL** Schist at Cap Corse, limestone boulders in Patrimonio.

> **STYLE** Produced by fortification, Muscat du Cap-Corse is a wine of great finesse. It offers a rich and complex bouquet combining notes of dried fruit (figs, currants), tropical fruit, and hints of spices (cinnamon). It all lingers on the palate with a nice balance between freshness and generosity.

Color:
White.

Serving temperature:
46 to 50°F (8 to 10°C).

Ageing potential:
10 years.

Selected Corsica producers

- **Clos d'Alzeto (Sari-d'Orcino).** Red, rosé, and white wines of great character in the Ajaccio AOC.

- **Domaine Arena (Patrimonio).** Very pure white, red, and rosé wines of the Patrimonio appellation, and a Muscat du Cap-Corse Grotte di Sole.

- **Domaine Comte Peraldi (Mezzavia).** A safe bet from the Ajaccio AOC.

- **Domaine Leccia (Poggio-d'Oletta).** Major estate of the Patrimonio appellation; its dry whites and reds highlight the qualities of their *terroir*.

- **Domaine de Torraccia (Porto-Vecchio).** Powerful, organically produced red Vins de Corse.

ITALY

Wine-producing regions
- Northern
- Central
- Southern and islands
- --- Border
- --- Regional border

N

0   125 miles (200 km)

VAL
D'AOSTA

PIEDMONT

Turino

Asti

Como

LOMBARDY

Milan

Genova

LIGURIA

Bolzano

TRENTINO-
ALTO-ADIGE

Trento

Adda

Adige

Lake
Garda

VENETO

Vicenza

Verona

Venice

Plave

FRIULI-
VENEZIA-
GIULIA

Trieste

Po

Modène

EMILIA-ROMAGNA

Reno

Bologna

Ravenna

SAN MARINO

Pisa

Florence

Arno

TUSCANY

Montepulciano

Perugia

UMBRIA

Tiber

Ancona

MARCHE

Ligurian
Sea

Pescara

LAZIO

ABRUZZO

Rome

MOLISE

Fòggia

CAMPANIA

Naples

Bari

PUGLIA

BASILICATA

Tarento

SARDINIA

Tyrrhenian
Sea

Cagliari

Adriatic
Sea

CALABRIA

Ionian
Sea

Reggio
di Calábria

Mediterranean
Sea

Palermo

Messina

SICILY

Catania

PANTELLERIA

ITALY

Italy produces about 20 percent of the world's wine. In other words, one bottle out of every five on earth is Italian. A land of art and culture, with a vibrant instinct for food and flavor, the Italian peninsula is full of great classics and local surprises, thanks to the its many different regions and their rich history.

Wonderful (and confusing) diversity

In an Italian wine cellar, an expert in French wine feels somewhat lost. Each winery follows its own aesthetic inspiration, and the shape of the bottle does not indicate in any way—as it does in France, via the specific bottle shapes for Bordeaux, Burgundy, etc.—the region of production. The only distinctive bottle is the straw-covered flask used for basic Chianti, which Tuscany discards for its other wines, preferring instead to adopt the Bordeaux-shaped bottle.

Reading the labels fails to solve the mystery. Except for the most famous names (Chianti Classico, Barolo, and Brunello), the 41 DOCG (*Denominazione di origine controllata e garantita*), the 316 DOC (*Denominazione di origine controllata*), the 120 IGT (*Indicazione geografica tipica*), and the countless references and trademarks of *vino da tavola* (table wine) can completely baffle the novice. In terms of the number of appellations for wines and spirits, Italy leads the world. The price ranges are also extensive. So what should we expect

ITALY STATISTICS

Vineyard area: 1,690,200 acres (684,000 ha)

Production: 519 million cases (46,700,000 hl) (average 2005–2009)

Whites: 55%

Reds and rosés: 45%

(Assoenologi and Istat, 2010)

when we open the bottle? Is the wine light, full-bodied, dry, sweet, or sparkling? Is it best for simple drinks or for dinner? Which foods will it complement?

To understand and appreciate Italian wines, some key explanatory notes will prove as useful as a corkscrew: the names of key grape varieties, the rich tapestry of soils and climates, and the history of the people and viticulture in the various regions.

A long history of wine

FROM ANCIENT ORIGINS... The vine is an experienced traveler. After beginning its journey in Asia Minor, it moved to Ancient Greece; and they then taught the Etruscans how to ferment grapes. Many Roman texts detail winemaking methods, classifications of wines (including by the Academy of Medicine in Rome), and the export of its highly priced and very popular nectar to wealthy Gauls: "a slave or an amphora [of wine]," said Diodorus Siculus. The renowned *terroir* of Campania, between Rome and Naples, suffered from the eruption of Vesuvius at Pompeii in 79 AD. The city was buried under volcanic ash, but even today there are traces of poles that supported vines. So Italian winemakers have refined their know-how for millennia. The Antinori family, as one example, has been making wine since 1385, for 26 generations. But there are countless dynasties of Italian wine entrepreneurs whose names we don't know.

...TO MODERN THREATS... There have been three key threats to the modern Italian wine industry: phylloxera, excessively high yields, and the globalization of style. The first was handled during the late 19th century by planting American vine rootstocks that were resistant to phylloxera—to which any European grape varieties could be grafted as required. But what grape varieties were chosen? Traditional ones with local names unfamiliar to anyone outside the province? Or famous international varieties (Merlot, Chardonnay, etc.), which would often produce higher yields and could be readily exported? Entire regions, such as Veneto, Sicily, and Tuscany, planted international grapes on a large scale. During the 20th century, the second threat was the era of "bulk wine," with Italy exporting boatloads of cheap wine for blending. These

> Barrels being made in Florio, Sicily.

> Terraced vineyards in Trentino-Alto Adige, northeast Italy.

came from vineyards with very high yields and generous alcohol content and color; and these still equate to one-third of the volume produced in Italy. Calling them "pizzeria plonk" would be unfair. They are not very subtle, but they nevertheless can represent a decent house wine. Note that "bulk" is not necessarily synonymous with poor quality. Many producers sell appealing wine in 3-liter or 5-liter boxes.

...TO THE ERA OF ESTATE BOTTLING. Today, the Italian wine market has matured. Consumption is "less but better." So the area occupied by vineyards has decreased from 3,039,396 acres (1,230,000 million ha) in 1980 to 1,690,200 acres (684,000 ha) in 2009. Sources of bulk wine (in order of size: Puglia, Sicily, Emilia-Romagna, and Abruzzo) have reduced their cheap exports to improve quality and sell higher-value bottles. To attract orders, some winemakers are adapting their production to the desires of the international market and accentuating sweeter or oakier flavors. At times, this standardization of such unique varieties is a matter of regret; but other winemakers are reviving local grapes, which provide a fitting response to the more uniform flavors produced by the New World.

Northern regions

In its journey around the world, the vine would have become less attached to Italy if the terrain there been a dreary plain with a uniform climate. But this is one of the few nations in the world where every corner of the country cultivates its own varieties—meaning there is a broad spectrum of climates and styles.

Val d'Aosta, Trentino-Alto Adige, and Friuli have a mountain climate. Vines planted in the snow of Val d'Aosta, at an altitude of more than 3,940 ft (1,200 m), are among the highest in Europe. That climate is reflected in the wines, which have a bracing freshness. But the mosaic of climates and the many varieties found across Italy's northern regions yield some nice discoveries. In Piedmont (literally "the foot of the mountains"), vines grow on remarkably steep hills, with the rice fields of the Po plain below them. Rich alluvial land, with water from the Alps and warm sunshine, permits the high yields seen in Lombardy and Veneto: up to 8.8 tons/acre (150 hl/ha). By contrast, to create more concentrated wine, appellations like Barolo limit their production to less than 3 tons/acre (52 hl/ha). From a total of 20 Italian regions, the six northern ones (Piedmont, Lombardy, Trentino, Veneto, Friuli, and Emilia-Romagna) provide half the total volume of Italian wine and account for more than half of DOCGs.

TRUE OR FALSE?

Italy is the largest wine producer in the world.

TRUE. The current volume of wine produced and exported puts Italy in first place. However, the numbers vary according to the year, markets, and crops. (Sometimes France is number one.) In terms of total planted area, Spain has the largest vineyard area in the world.

Central regions

In the so-called "green heart" of Italy, the hills of Tuscany produce the world-famous Chianti. This region takes its name from the ancient Etruscans (or Tusci), who learned winemaking from the Greeks before passing this skill on to the Romans. In fact, the Greek word *oinos* became *vinum* in Etruscan and Latin, before becoming "vin" in French and ultimately "wine" in English. During the 20th century, Tuscany started crafting premium wines created with grape varieties such as Cabernet Sauvignon and Cabernet Franc—and they became known as Super Tuscans. The Marquis Incisa della Rocchetta, a great fan of Bordeaux wines, produced the first bottles of Sassicaia during the 1940s (*see also* pp.368–9). Then other creative winemakers followed, such as the Antinori family with their Solaia. A local appellation,

Bolgheri, was even created to formalize this new style of wine. The other aim of this work was to reveal the qualities of Tuscan *terroir* in terms people understood. From the Apennines to the Adriatic, the areas of Lazio, Abruzzo, and Molise benefit from climates and soils of great diversity—from sunny beaches to year-round snow. These zones of ancient viticulture also have the advantages of proximity to Rome, which has been a major wine market for several millennia.

Southern regions

Southern Italy is a land of sunshine. The volcanic soils of Campania and the dry hills of Puglia, Basilicata, and Calabria were appreciated by the Ancient Greeks, who called this part of the Italian peninsula "Oenotria" (the land of vines). These age-old

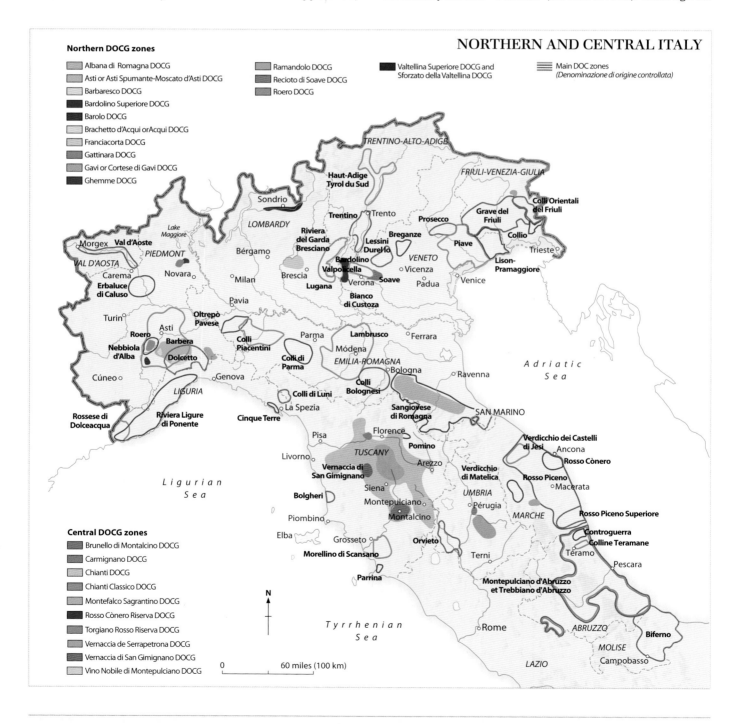

NORTHERN AND CENTRAL ITALY

Northern DOCG zones
- Albana di Romagna DOCG
- Asti or Asti Spumante-Moscato d'Asti DOCG
- Barbaresco DOCG
- Bardolino Superiore DOCG
- Barolo DOCG
- Brachetto d'Acqui or Acqui DOCG
- Franciacorta DOCG
- Gattinara DOCG
- Gavi or Cortese di Gavi DOCG
- Ghemme DOCG
- Ramandolo DOCG
- Recioto di Soave DOCG
- Roero DOCG
- Valtellina Superiore DOCG and Sforzato della Valtellina DOCG
- Main DOC zones *(Denominazione di origine controllata)*

Central DOCG zones
- Brunello di Montalcino DOCG
- Carmignano DOCG
- Chianti DOCG
- Chianti Classico DOCG
- Montefalco Sagrantino DOCG
- Rosso Cònero Riserva DOCG
- Torgiano Rosso Riserva DOCG
- Vernaccia de Serrapetrona DOCG
- Vernaccia di San Gimignano DOCG
- Vino Nobile di Montepulciano DOCG

0   60 miles (100 km)

> Tuscan hills around the abbey of Sant'Antimo, near Montalcino.

regions—long dominated by large suppliers of bulk wine—are also changing. Cooperatives and large private cellars still supply the mass market at low prices, but small producers are making niche wines from local varieties.

The islands

With a Mediterranean climate, the islands are a different world from mainland Italy. The mountains of Sardinia have retained grape varieties from the period of Spanish rule. Sicily has a volcano that is still active, and the soils at the foot of snow-capped Mount Etna are unique. At the south end of the island, on the dark sands of Pachino, vineyards are located at a more southerly latitude than Tunis (North Africa). The dry and windy climate limits fungal diseases (such as mildew or powdery mildew) caused by dampness, so chemical plant treatments are less necessary than in northern vineyards—making Sicily the largest region in Europe for organic production. The southernmost Italian vineyard is on Pantelleria, an island between Sicily and Africa, where the grapes are left to dry naturally on the vine.

Key Italian varieties

The broad spectrum of climates and soils, across a distance of 750 miles (1,200 km) from north to south, is the main reason for the diversity of Italian vineyards. The other reason is cultural: until the 19th century, the peninsula was a patchwork of small independent states that were constantly at war. Each one proudly cultivated its local varieties of grape, which had been selected and differentiated by generations of winemakers.

To understand Italian wine, knowing the grape varieties is essential. The front or back label on the bottle often specifies the variety. One-third of the appellations mentioned on pages

Giant vines of Campania

The vine is a creeper that the Greeks left to grow along the ground. Later winemakers invented the "small tree'" method that is still practiced in Italy (alberello) and France (gobelet). To limit any damage to fragile young vines from the wind and their own weight, growers had to find a means of support or something for them to cling to. The best-known solution was the wooden post. The famous Falerno wine of antiquity, described by Pliny (23–79 AD), even takes its name from the word for "post." Another idea for support was the poplar tree. In Campania, near Aversa, Asprinio grapevines have been "married to poplars" for over a century. They intertwine with the branches of the tree about 50 feet (15 meters) up. They are harvested using a ladder.

> Sangiovese grapes, the main variety of Chianti.

360–73 are names of grape varieties associated with a particular geographic zone, such as Cannonau di Sardegna DOC (Sardinia) or Montepulciano d'Abruzzo DOC (Abruzzo). But even originally French varieties (Merlot, Chardonnay, etc.) have been adopted by the Italians, and many DOC and DOCG appellations now include them.

TRUE OR FALSE?

Sicily produces mostly red wine.

FALSE. White wine represents 61 percent of Sicilian production. So white grapes are not the exclusive preserve of northern vineyards, just as reds are not exclusive to southern *terroirs*.

AGLIANICO. Red, mainly grown in Campania, Basilicata, Molise, and Puglia. Probably brought by Ancient Greek colonists, it derives its name from the word "Hellenic." Sometimes vinified as a white (without the skins), as a sparkling or sweet wine, or as a *riserva*.

ARNEIS. White Piedmont produced both as a dry and sometimes a sweet wine. In the Piedmont dialect, its name means "little rascal."

BARBERA. Red from Piedmont, now grown throughout Italy.

BONARDA. Red used in appellations of Piedmont, Lombardy, and Emilia-Romagna, it's transformed into sparkling or still wine and is sometimes cultivated as dessert grapes.

BRACHETTO. Light red from Piedmont that produces a slightly sparkling wine, low in tannins.

CANNONAU. Red grown in Sardinia, also known as Grenache in French, that yields a high level of alcohol. Also vinified as a rosé and *vin doux naturel*.

DOLCETTO. Fresh and light red from Piedmont.

FALANGHINA. White from Campania. The Romans would have used this in their famous Falerno.

FIANO D'AVELLINO. White used for a yellow *vin de paille*. Little is actually produced, and it was recently saved from extinction.

GRECO DI TUFO. White grown in Campania. In Italy, several varieties are called "Greco," probably due to their Greek origins.

In danger of extinction, it has been revived for production line with modern tastes.

INZOLIA. White used to create Marsala, and also used as a blended wine. Wineries now offer a single grape variety version, or blended versions with other whites (Chardonnay, Sauvignon Blanc, Grecanico). It is also known as "Ansonica" on the island of Elba, in Lazio, and in Tuscany.

LAMBRUSCO. Red grown in Lombardy and Emilia-Romagna. The Romans called the vines that grew wild on the edge (*labrum*) of cultivated fields (*bruscum*) *vitis labrusca*.

MONTEPULCIANO. Intense red from the south (Abruzzo, Puglia, Marche, Lazio).

MOSCATO. White grown throughout all of Italy. It is transformed into still, lightly sparkling, or fully sparkling wines, as well as sweet wines or late-harvest wines. There is also a red variation.

NEBBIOLO. Red from Piedmont and Lombardy. Slow to mature at altitude, it is harvested in mid-October or even November, when there is an autumnal fog (*nebbia*), hence its name. It does best in limestone soils.

NERO D'AVOLA. Red from Sicily, with wild flavors. It is blended with more restrained grape varieties (Cabernet Sauvignon, Merlot, Syrah) or produced on its own for those who like a powerful style. Also available as a sweet red. There are some 20 Sicilian appellations.

PRIMITIVO. Red that is genetically similar to California's Zinfandel. "These are twin brothers that have been separated for a long time," claim wine producers from Puglia. It is the first grape to fully ripen each year, hence its name ("early").

PROSECCO. White from Veneto, made in a closed tank as a sparkling "extra dry," "brut," or "dry" wine. This method was developed by Charmat (according to the French) or by Martinotti (according to the Italians). Available in a sweet, *passerillé* version with 16% ABV.

SANGIOVESE. Its name comes from the Latin *sanguis Iovis* (Jupiter's blood). An emblematic red from Tuscany, but it's also cultivated in central and southern Italy. There are several clones with very different styles and yields.

TOCAI FRIULANO. White grown in Friuli and Veneto. After some legal wrangling with neighboring Hungary, this grape is now called Friulano. It has nothing in common with the Hungarian Tokaj (sweet) and Friuli Tocai (dry).

Pervasive promotion

In Italy, wine is more than a product: it is a symbol of cultural identity. Tourist brochures mentions it alongside the frescoes in

---

DID YOU KNOW...?

Italian grape varieties often have colorful names.
Coda di Volpe, an ancient variety from Campania, takes its name from the resemblance of its clusters to a fox tail. In Emilia-Romagna, the Bombino variety, often exported to blend with German wines, is nicknamed pagadebit *("repaying the debt") as a reference to its efficiency and profitability.*

monasteries, an opera by Rossini, a contemporary sculpture, or traditional cheeses, meats, and vegetables. Local agencies (cities, regions, wine-producing guilds) and national groups (chambers of commerce, the Italian Institute for Foreign Trade [ICE]) publish many brochures, pamphlets, books, guides, educational maps, and websites such as www.terroirsditalie.com (in English) and www.enoteca-italiana.it (in Italian and English). The *Strade del Vino* (Wine Routes) indicates tours through vineyards and wineries open to the public.

Deciphering labels

AESTHETIC MESSAGE. Wine is a very mobile agricultural product. When it is a long way from its home region, it needs a means of identifying itself, a kind of passport. Even the Romans attached labels to their amphora, engraving the name of the manufacturer, the place of origin, and the type of wine. Today, packaging is more diverse. On one hand, electric blue bottles of low-priced whites are aimed at a young audience, with minimal refinement and synthetic corks the same color as the label. On the other, prestigious wines such as Barolo communicate their message with a restrained or traditional label, or with a chic, contemporary design. On store shelves, the objective remains the same for all wines: stand out or lose out.

QUALITY PYRAMID. There are three levels to note (*see also* p.96): DOCG (*Denominazione di origine controllata e garantita*), identified by a purple numbered collar on the neck of the bottle, and DOC (*Denominazione di origine controllata*); IGT (*Indicazione geografica tipica*); and table wine or *vino da tavola*. Each of these three levels (DOC / DOCG, IGT, and *vino da tavola*) represents approximately one-third of the total volume produced in Italy every year.

GUARANTEE OF QUALITY? DOC and (especially) DOCG wines, with lower yields than IGT and *vino da tavola*, in principle have richer and more concentrated flavors. Generally, a given

> A grocery store in Siena, Tuscany.

winemaker will use the most successful expressions of his or her best plots for these wines. The point of the appellation is to define a method of production so that consumers will be able to find, across various producers, a distinct style reflective of that region. Yet many winemakers are creating original, exciting wines that are not part of the appellation system—which is why some IGTs secure higher prices than a DOCG. As always, the market is the ultimate judge. For other wine lovers, the key to quality is respect for the environment through wines produced using organically farmed grapes. Italy also produces kosher certified wines.

GLOSSARY OF ITALIAN WINE TERMS

Some terms found on Italian wine labels:

amabile: medium sweet
amaro: bitter (or very dry)
asciutto: demi-sec
bianco: white
cantina: cellar, winery
cantina sociale: cooperative winery
chiaretto: clairet (light rosé wine)
classico: from the historic center of an appellation area
cerasuolo: dark rosé wine (cherry-colored)
consorzio: regional wine producer association

dolce: sweet
frizzante: lightly sparkling
gradi: degrees of alcohol
invecchiato: aged
in purezza: pure, from a single grape variety, not blended
metodo classico: sparkling wine using traditional method (Champagne style)
nero: dark red
novello: new
passito: dessert wine produced from *passerillage* (clusters are dried in crates or hung to dry)
recioto: some dry sweet wines from Veneto

riserva: wine aged for a period defined by the appellation
rosato: rosé
rosso: red
secco: dry
spumante: sparkling
tenuta: estate
vendemmia: harvest, vintage
vendemmia tardiva: late harvest

Leading Italian wines

Tasting Italian wines is a voyage through the history and terrain of the peninsula. A real mosaic, the map of Italian appellations reflects a certain alchemy of the terroirs, the biodiversity of the grape varieties, and the natural and human landscape.

AOSTA

VALLE D'AOSTA DOC

The smallest of all Italian wine regions is located between Switzerland and France, where they officially speak both Italian and French. Mountain wine producers here cultivate vineyards reputed to be the highest in Europe. The output of this *terroir* represents only a tiny fraction of total Italian wine production, but it nevertheless is divided into 30 categories such as "Enfer d'Arvier" or "Petite Arvine." Wine produced from grapes dried on the vine is both of high quality and small scale.
> **GRAPE VARIETIES** The appellation recognizes 22 varieties: Piemontese (Nebbiolo, Dolcetto, Moscato, etc.),

French (Chardonnay, Pinot, Gamay), German (Müller-Thurgau), and local (Petite Rouge, Petite Arvine, Vien, Malvasia).
> **SOIL** Alpine terraces, some over 3,900 ft (1,200 m) in altitude.
> **STYLE** Valle d'Aosta is the only DOC in the region, and it includes a range of distinctive wines from the mountains. The altitude gives them freshness, a pleasant sharpness, and a reduced alcohol content (at least 9% ABV for white, 9.5% ABV for the basic red).

Color:	*Serving temperature:*	*Ageing potential:*
Red (lightly colored), white, and rosé.	*46 to 50°F (8 to 10°C) for whites and rosés; 57 to 59°F (14 to 15°C) for reds.*	*1 to 2 years.*

PIEDMONT

ASTI DOCG

With 80 million bottles of wine shipped every year, this appellation is second only to Chianti in volume. The vines cover the limestone hills and plains of the provinces of Asti, Cuneo, and Alessandria. In winemaking, the tank is cooled to stop fermentation while there is still sugar in the grape must. The alcohol level is stabilized at between 7 and 9.5% ABV; though it would reach 12% ABV if the yeasts transformed all of the sugar.

Next, secondary fermentation occurs in a closed tank using the Charmat or Martinotti technique (*see box* p.71), though some wines are made in bottle (the traditional method). Poorly produced or stored bottles have damaged the modern reputation of Asti. However, this very affordable sparkling wine is truly modern in terms of its low alcohol content, its sweetness, and its freshness.
> **GRAPE VARIETY** Muscat Blanc, which

the Romans called *uva apiana* (a grape popular with bees).
> **SOIL** Limestone hills and plains.
> **STYLE** Its mousse is thin, and the wine is a pale yellow color. The nose and palate have intense fruit flavors. Asti goes with desserts that are not too sweet, pastries, and Piedmont cookies containing hazelnuts.

Color:	*Serving temperature:*	*Ageing potential:*
White.	*43 to 46°F (6 to 8°C).*	*Less than 2 years.*

BAROLO DOCG

Barolo is a rare wine and one of the most prestigious in Italy. It is often compared to Burgundy: both are single-variety wines, produced toward the northern edge of a region, on *terroirs* that have been worked for several centuries. Similarly, the wines, whether in a fresh style for early consumption or with potential for ageing, command a premium price. In addition, the Barolo bottle sometimes has the same shape as the Burgundy version. The wine is produced to a 13% ABV minimum and aged in wood for three years (five years if the word *riserva* appears on the label). Finally, something called Barolo Chinato is flavored with quinine. The six million-bottle production of the "king of wines and wine of kings" remains a limited amount, just one-thousandth of total Italian output. Barolo has near relatives produced from the same Nebbiolo grape: Barbaresco commands an equally expensive range of prices, but more affordable are Albugnano, Boca, Bramaterra, Carema, Lessona, Gattinara, Ghemme, Nebbiolo d'Alba, and Roero.

> **GRAPE VARIETY** Nebbiolo.

> **SOIL** Clay-and-limestone hills of Langhe.

> **STYLE** Barolo has a moderately intense ruby color, with orange highlights. Even in a young wine, it has an expressive nose of violets, dried roses, crystallized fruit, and prunes with *eau de vie*. On the palate, there are velvety flavors of cooked fruit, licorice, and spices. It has a slight sharpness, firm tannins, and a long finish. Depending on the winemaking style and length of maturation in barrel, freshness or full-bodied flavors dominate.

Color:	Serving temperature:	Ageing potential:
Red.	*61 to 63°F (16 to 17°C).*	*10 to 30 years.*

FRANCIACORTA DOCG

Around 1960, Lombardy producers who were enthusiastic about Champagne decided to produce sparkling wine. However, at that point their region was more famous for its factories than for its wines. They invested in vineyards in Franciacorta, built modern cellars, and financed winemakers and training for technical personnel. Thus Franciacorta wine came into being. Its secondary fermentation takes place in the traditional manner, in bottle, and not in closed tanks like simple sparkling wines. The minimum alcohol is 11.5%. The *blanc de blancs* or *satèn* (sparkling) is made only from white grapes, and the rosé is with a minimum of 15 percent Pinot Noir. Vintage Franciacorta contains at least 85 percent of the wine from that particular year. Today, 4,200 acres (1,700 ha) of vineyards will produce 10 million bottles each year of the most prestigious sparkling wine in Italy. More demanding than Champagne, this appellation limits its yield to 4 tons/acre and needs to be aged on lees for at least 18 months. It should not be confused with the DOC Terre di Franciacorta, which produces still white or red wines.

> **GRAPE VARIETIES** Chardonnay (70 percent of the area compared to only 26 percent in Champagne), Pinot Blanc, and Pinot Noir.

> **SOIL** Sub-alpine moraine hills, gravel.

> **STYLE** The wines, which are a straw yellow color with green or golden glints, have a fresh, floral, or fruity bouquet. On the palate, they show roundness and less acidity than many northern sparkling wines. "In Franciacorta, lack of ripeness in the grapes is never a problem, quite the contrary!" So say local producers, always quick to make fun of Champagne.

Color:	Serving temperature:	Ageing potential:
White and rosé.	*50°F (10°C).*	*2 to 5 years.*

OLTREPÒ PAVESE DOC

LOMBARDY

Located, as its name suggests, "on the other side of the Po" near Pavia, this appellation includes some 20 districts. It comprises white wines, rosés, sparkling whites, reds such as Bonarda (16 million bottles per year), sweet wines, and two amazing specialties: Sangue di Giuda and Buttafuoco. The Sangue di Giuda ("Blood of Judas" is a red that is both sweet and sparkling, hence the humorous name of the wine "traitor." It is all too easy to drink, and is just 12% ABV minimum. The Buttafuoco, literally "fire-breathing," is a deep red, full-bodied, often sparkling wine, though again just 12% ABV.

> **GRAPE VARIETIES** Barbera, Croatina, Pinot Noir, Uva Rara, Vespolina, and Cabernet Sauvignon for the red wines; Chardonnay, Cortese, Malvasia, Moscato, Pinot Gris, Riesling Italico, Riesling Renano, and Sauvignon Blanc for the white wines.

> **SOIL** Sedimentary hills and clay soils.

> **STYLE** The wines come in all kinds of styles. They may be consumed with a meal, or as an appetizer (for the lightly sparkling wines), or as a dessert (for the sweet sparkling wines).

Color:
White, rosé, and red.

Serving temperature:
46 to 50°F (8 to 10°C) for whites and rosés;
57 to 61°F (14 to 16°C) for reds.

Ageing potential:
2 to 3 years.

VALPOLICELLA DOC

VENETO

Valpolicella is fourth among Italian appellations in terms of production volume, selling more than 40 million bottles per year. Most are exported from Veneto. This is a red wine for dinner, at least 11% ABV. The *superiore*, 12% ABV, is aged for one year. The term "classico" indicates that the wine is produced in the historic zone. There is also a territorial *denominazione* called Valpantena. Valpolicella should not be confused with the Recioto della Valpolicella dessert wine derived from desiccated grapes, which also exists in a sparkling (*spumante*) style.

> **GRAPE VARIETIES** Corvina Veronese (from 40 to 70 percent), Rondinella (from 20 to 40 percent), and Molinara. Other permitted varieties in the blend include Negrara Trentina and/or Rossignola and/or Sangiovese and/or Barbera. Bardolino (*see below*) comes from the same grapes and the same region.

> **SOIL** Fertile alluvial plains.

> **STYLE** The wines have an intense ruby color and a characteristic bouquet of red fruit (cherry) and bitter almonds. On the palate, they have a dry or velvety texture, as well as a fruity, slightly bitter and spicy sensation.

Color:
Red.

Serving temperature:
61 to 63°F (16 to 17°C).

Ageing potential:
3 to 5 years.

BARDOLINO DOC

VENETO

With a production of almost 26 million bottles per year, this red wine from the shores of Lake Garda is one of the best known in Italy, particularly through its *novello* (very young) version. Its *Chiaretto*, which is somewhere between red and rosé, is produced after a very short maceration of the must with the grape skins. Bardolino Superiore DOCG is aged for at least one year, with 12% ABV minimum. The *classico* comes from the historic area of the appellation. Until the early 19th century, the must was fermented in cavities in impermeable rock, covered with stone slabs.

> **GRAPE VARIETIES** Corvina Veronese (from 35 to 65 percent), for body and color; Rondinella (from 10 to 40 percent) and Molinara for flavor; also Rossignola, Barbera, Sangiovese, Garganega, Merlot, and Cabernet Sauvignon. These are the same grape varieties as for Valpolicella (*see above*).

> **SOIL** Fertile alluvial plains and moraine hills.

> **STYLE** These wines have a clear ruby color and cherry flavors. They are easy to drink and light and fruity on the palate.

Color:
Red and chiaretto.

Serving temperature:
57 to 59°F (14 to 15°C).

Ageing potential:
1 to 3 years.

SOAVE DOC, RECIOTO DI SOAVE DOCG

The most famous dry white Italian wine, Soave ranks third in volume after Chianti and Asti. Each year, more than 70 million bottles of Soave leave the region, and 65 percent are for export. "If there are Italian wines in a store anywhere on earth, there will be a wine from Veneto!" jokes Luciano Piona, the president of UVIVE (the syndicate of consortia producing DOC wines in Veneto). Soave is the name of a town, but the word also means "sweet, delicate." Almost *novello* in color, this wine hits the market on December 1st of the year it is harvested. The *classico* is matured for longer, and comes from the historical area of the Colli Scaligeri *terroir*. Soave Superiore DOCG is sometimes aged in barrels, giving it hints of vanilla. It remains at least three months in bottle before being put on the market. Matured for two years from November 1st following the harvest, the DOCG Riserva must reach at least 12.5% ABV. There is also a DOCG "Riserva Classico." Within the same appellation, winemakers also produce the Recioto di Soave DOCG, a very sweet wine made from *passerillés* (partially dried) grapes. Before being vinified, they are hung out or deposited in crates for months to desiccate. Pressed in March, they yield only about 20 liters per 100 kg of source grapes, hence the high price for 50 cl bottles.

> **GRAPE VARIETIES** Garganega (70 percent minimum), Trebbiano di Soave and/or Pinot Blanc and/or Chardonnay (25 to 30 percent), and other local white grape varieties.

> **SOIL** Fertile alluvial plains.

> **STYLE** Soave is a straw yellow color with green and gold glints. Floral notes on the palate are succeeded by flavors of apple, peach, lemon, and grapefruit. It is a fresh, dry, slightly sharp wine. Recioto di Soave suggests dried apricot, crystallized fruit, and lychées, but has an intense sweetness.

Color of wine:
White.

Serving temperature:
46 to 50°F (8 to 10°C).

Ageing potential:
1 to 4 years, depending on quality
(superiore, riserva).

Which is the best Italian wine?

Assoenologi* lists about 700,000 producers in all regions of Italy—from the large wineries to the small part-time farmers, and even individuals who bring a few baskets from their private garden to a cooperative. Of course, not all actually make wine with their grapes, even if home production is common and deserves further study in terms of both society and wine. But if we limit the choice to bottles sold commercially, which is the best Italian wine? Several rankings (available online) try to answer this question. Every year, Wine Spectator's team tests thousands of products and identifies between 10 and 20 Italian wines in their global Top 100. A Brunello di Montalcino was actually named Best Wine in the World in 2006. Such a designation often comes with prices between $70 and $100, though the Wine Spectator has Proseccos and Barberas at $12 and $13. Other ratings are provided by the Festival Grand Tasting, Duemilavini dell'AIS, L'Espresso, Gambero Rosso, and guides by Maroni and Veronelli. The magazine Civiltà del bere publishes a wine guide that summarizes all the ratings.

Among top Italian wines, here are some listed according to region.

- **Val d'Aoste:** Crêtes.
- **Piedmont:** Fratelli Cavallotto, Giacomo Contero, Gaja, Bruno Giacosa, Massolino.
- **Lombardy:** Bellavista.
- **Trentino-Alto Adige:** Cantina Bolzano, Kellerei Kaltern, Tenuta San Leonardo.
- **Tuscany:** Antinori, Castello del Terriccio, Colle Massari-Podere Grattamacco, Montervertine, Ornellaia, Petrolo, Podere Il Carnasciale, Poliziano, San Guido, Tenimenti Luigi D'Alessandro.
- **Umbria:** Arnaldo Caprai, Còlpetrone.
- **Marche:** Ercole Velenosi.
- **Campania:** Galardi, Mastroberardino, Montevetrano.
- **Basilicata:** Basilisco.
- **Sicily:** Abbazia Santa Anastasia, Donnafugata, Palari.

*Associazione Enologi Enotecnici Italiani, www.assoenologi.it

PROSECCO DI CONEGLIANO VALDOBBIADENE DOC

Italians like bubbles in their mineral water, and in their white, rosé, and red wines. Across northern regions in particular, it is common to find wine bars named *proseccheria*, specializing in sparkling wines. Almost all Italian regions produce their own sparkling wines, but the area most famous for its Prosecco is the province of Treviso, specifically around the towns of Conegliano and Valdobbiadene. *Spumante* style generates more bubbles than *frizzante*. Prosecco is produced in "brut," "extra dry," and "dry" versions, with at least 10.5% ABV.

> **GRAPE VARIETIES** Prosecco, Verdiso, Bianchetta, Perera, Chardonnay, Pinot Blanc, and Pinot Noir.

> **SOIL** Fertile alluvial plains allowing high yields.

> **STYLE** Straw yellow in color and bubbly. Despite its fruity flavors, Prosecco remains fresh and dry on the palate. An aperitif wine, also used for celebrations, Prosecco may accompany fish, pasta, or risotto.

Color:	Serving temperature:	Ageing potential:
White.	*46 to 50°F (8 to 10°C).*	*1 to 2 years.*

AMARONE DELLA VALPOLICELLA DOC

Wine producers in the Veneto have retained an instinct for international trade from ancient Venice. Their region, the largest producer of wines in Italy, accounts for 30 percent of Italian exports by value alone. But the Veneto also produces limited quantities of niche wines, renowned for their individual style, such as Amarone della Valpolicella. Red grapes are handpicked and dried on a lattice for one to three months, which increases sugar concentration. After pressing and fermentation, a classic sweet wine is produced. The unique vinification of Amarone is allowed to continue until the yeasts convert all of the grape sugars into alcohol. This produces a dry wine at 15 or 16% ABV. It is aged for at least two years.

> **GRAPE VARIETIES** Corvina Veronese (from 40 to 70 percent), Rondinella (from 20 to 40 percent), Molinara, Barbera, Negrara Trentina and/or Rossignola and/or Sangiovese.

> **SOIL** Fertile alluvial plains.

> **STYLE** The wine has a garnet color, and a nose with aromas of ripe red fruits, plums, raisins, cherry jam, and spices (clove, cinnamon, etc.). On the palate it is intense with flavors of *eau-de-vie* fruit.

Color:	Serving temperature:	Ageing potential:
Red.	*61 to 63°F (16 to 17°C).*	*Up to 15 years.*

How to match Italian food and wine

The Sardinian restaurant Fontanarosa is one of the most famous Italian eateries in Paris. It has more than 200 wines on its menu. How does Flavio Mascia guide his customers? Does he advise, as is often done in Italy, choosing wine from the same region as the selected dish? No, because he sells more than just Sardinian wines. How does he match food and wine? Which are his favorite producers? Here is his response.

"Giving you a list of names would be a big mistake. And we must stop the standard clichés that such-and-such a wine goes with polenta, etc. I suggest a light wine for lunch, and a full-bodied one for dinner. I am not talking about alcohol content, but rather its impact on the palate. I observe customers, I ask them a few questions, I try to understand whether they want to focus on and explore the food or the wine, which are two different approaches. Similarly, I ask what they want in terms of price. My advice is this: if you like a wine, write its name down, find the estate on the Internet, try to learn more about it. Even better: find the name of the winemaker and the other wines he produces. In three simple words: read the label!"

ALTO ADIGE DOC - SÜDTIROL DOC

This *terroir* has a unique history. Until 1919, the region was Austrian—after a brief period of French rule under Napoleon. Today, the autonomous province of Bolzano is home to only 25 percent native Italian speakers, but the complexity of a DOC label has reached its peak. A bilingual label is required featuring the name of the appellation and grape variety in both German and Italian, hence Alto Adige DOC Pinot Bianco and Südtirol DOC Weissburgunder are the same wine. Then the name of one out of six sub-denominations is added: Colli di Bolzano, Meranese, Santa Maddalena, Terlano, Valle Isarco, or Valle Venosta, along with their German equivalent, given the importance of the German market. An even more precise translation of the label, with references to *vigna*, *gewächs*, or *wachstum*, is possible. But the complications continue: the appellation authorizes some 20 varieties for dual- and single-variety wines (Cabernet-Lagrein, Cabernet-Merlot, and Merlot-Lagrein), and everything is listed bilingually. There are also terms such as "late-harvest" for sparkling wines and some rosés. The word *riserva* describes wines that are aged for at least two years.

> **GRAPE VARIETIES** There are about 20 German, Italian, and French grape varieties in this area, a living relic of the Napoleonic period.
> **SOIL** Alpine hills and mountain vineyards planted on terraces.
> **STYLE** White wines (55 percent of production) are fresh and fragrant; reds (45 percent) are fresh and bright.

Color:
White, rosé, and red.

Serving temperature:
46 to 50°F (8 to 10°C) for whites, sparkling wines and rosés;
57 to 59°F (14 to 15°C) for reds.

Ageing potential:
1 to 2 years.

COLLI ORIENTALI DEL FRIULI DOC

This appellation includes 30 different sparkling or sweet wines, all produced in the province of Udine. White wines account for 60 percent of production, reds 40 percent. The DOC indicates the wine's geographic origin (with two sub-regions, Cialla and Rosazzo) as well as the grape variety, if it amounts to more than 85 percent. Thus the Colli Orientali del Friuli Rosazzo Ribolla Gialla comes from the Rosazzo area and contains at least 85 percent of the white grape Ribolla Gialla. Wine producers looking for greater freedom in blends produces a generic Colli Orientali del Friuli Bianco. The reds follow the same principle in terms of appellation. Colli Orientali del Friuli Dolce is a sweet white wine produced from desiccated grapes. The word *riserva* on wines indicates those aged for at least two years; in the Cialla area, a minimum of four years is required.

> **GRAPE VARIETIES** For white: Sauvignon Blanc, Traminer Aromatico, Verduzzo Friulano, Chardonnay, Malvasia, Pinot Blanc, Pinot Gris, and Tocai Friulano (now called Friulano); for red: Cabernet Franc, Cabernet Sauvignon, Merlot, Pinot Noir, Pignolo, Schioppettino, Refosco Nostrano, Refosco dal Peduncolo Rosso, and Tazzelenghe. Wine producers love collecting grape varieties!
> **SOIL** Steep cliffs between the Alps and the Adriatic.
> **STYLE** The Friuli region is characterized by fresh, mineral-laced white wines that are light in alcohol, and produced as a result of excellent technical winemaking. Oysters and oily fish go very well with the dry whites and their hints of white flowers and citrus (lemon and grapefruit). The fresh, light, and mineral-edged red wines are not as well known, despite the undoubted expertise in their production. Some wine producers, however, adopt a more intense and full-bodied style after ageing in barrel.

Color:
White and red.

Serving temperature:
46 to 50°F (8 to 10°C) for whites;
57 to 59°F (14 to 15°C) for reds.

Ageing potential:
1 to 3 years.

CINQUE TERRE DOC

Set in a crescent around the Gulf of Genoa, the tiny province of Liguria is penultimate in production volume among

wine-producing regions. Cinque Terre is a white wine (two-thirds of Ligurian output) developed by versatile wineries. As in Val d'Aosta, vines grow on the sides of cliffs and on terraces, but at a lower altitude and under a more intense sun. Some vineyards are right on the waterfront, others cling high up in the mountains. Five areas produce the wine, hence its name. There is also a Cinque Terre Sciacchetrà, a sweet *passerillé* version.

> **GRAPE VARIETIES** Bosco (at least 40 percent), Albarola and/or Vermentino

(at least 40 percent), and other local white grapes.

> **SOIL** Steep terraces between the mountains and the Mediterranean.

> **STYLE** The wine is pale yellow in color, with dry but fruity and floral flavors. Cinque Terre Sciacchetrà wines are sweet and have a golden yellow color with glints of amber and scents of honey and apricot. This sweet wine goes with strong cheeses and desserts that are not too sweet, as well as slightly sharp fruit.

Color:
White.

Serving temperature:
46 to 50°F (8 to 10°C) for dry and sweet wines served as an aperitif;
54°F (12°C) for sweet wines served with dessert.

Ageing potential:
1 to 3 years.

LAMBRUSCO DI SORBARA DOC

Vast fertile plains in Emilia-Romagna are home to high-yield vineyards that produce an original yet cheap red wine: Lambrusco. Its production is similar to that of Asti (*see* p.360): fermentation is stopped by refrigeration and filtration before the yeast has converted all the grape sugar into alcohol. Instead of reaching 11.5% ABV, the final content is only 8 or 9% ABV and the residual sugars provide its characteristic sweetness. A second fermentation car-

ried out in closed tanks causes *prise de mousse*. This wine, which is widely exported, was mischievously called the "Italian Coca-Cola™." It provided young people with an introduction to sweet and sparkling wine. There are other Lambrusco appellations, such as Lambrusco di Grasparossa Castelvetro, produced from 85 percent of the Grasparossa grape variety, as well as high-end wines crafted with great care by smaller producers.

> **GRAPE VARIETIES** Lambrusco di Sorbara, Lambrusco Grasparossa, and Lambrusco Salamino.

> **SOIL** Alluvial and clay plains.

> **STYLE** Lightly sparkling wine with light, fruity, and sweet characters. Suitable as an aperitif, with cold cuts and antipasti, as well as with desserts.

Color:
Red and rosé.

Serving temperature:
54 to 55°F (12 to 13°C).

Ageing potential:
1 year.

BRUNELLO DI MONTALCINO DOCG

Unlike the many appellations derived from ancient traditions, this red wine is a recent invention of the Tuscan industry. Around 1870, during the phylloxera crisis, Ferruccio Biondi-Santi replanted his vineyard and gambled on the production of a wine stored for a long time in barrel, and then bottled. At the time, local wines were consumed young, and may have been lightly sparkling. The first

vintage of Brunello di Montalcino dates back to 1888. The creation of this wine prefigures the "Super Tuscans" Sassicaia (*see* pp.368–9) and Solaia—produced a century later by other winemakers in the region. Brunello di Montalcino is released for drinking six years after it is harvested, and its *riserva* only after seven years. Both must be aged for at least two of those years in oak casks, then in bottle.

> **GRAPE VARIETIES** Sangiovese (locally known as Brunello).

> **SOIL** Clay-and-limestone hills.

> **STYLE** The wine is a ruby red color. On the nose, it has aromas of red fruits and jam, as well as vanilla and spices. It is intense, fleshy, fruity, and tannic on the palate, with a long finish.

Color:
Red.

Serving temperature:
61 to 63°F (16 to 17°C).

Ageing potential:
10 to 20 years.

CHIANTI DOCG

The most famous Italian red wine is popularly pictured in the straw flask that used to protect it during shipping.

Today, wine producers more often sell it in Bordeaux-shaped bottles. Chianti comes from a large area of Tuscany, but the label restricts the geographic designation to grapes grown in the following areas: Colli Aretini, Colli Fiorentini (Florence), Colli Senesi (Siena), Colline Pisana (Pisa), Montalbano, Montespertoli, and Rùfina. If aged for at least two years, including three months in bottle, and if it is at least 12% ABV, it is labeled *riserva*. This should not be confused with *classico*, describing wine from the historic heart of the area, and indicated on the bottle by a black rooster surrounded by a red circle. The *classico riserva* is aged for the same length of time, but is a minimum of 12.5% ABV. Using a traditional method called *governo*,

performed just after racking, the wine has slightly desiccated grapes added to trigger a slow second fermentation, increasing alcohol, roundness, and possibly a slight beading to the wine.
> **GRAPE VARIETIES** Sangiovese (at least 75 percent), Canaiolo Nero, Trebbiano Toscano, and Malvasia del Chianti.
> **SOIL** Clay-and-limestone hills.
> **STYLE** Chianti is a bright ruby color. It displays aromas of violets, and has a dry palate. There are often notes of cherry, vanilla, cinnamon, or even leather. It is slightly tannic and velvety.

Color:	Serving temperature:	Ageing potential:
Red.	59 to 63°F (15 to 17°C), depending on age and complexity.	5 to 7 years.

VERDICCHIO DEI CASTELLI DI JESI DOC

Verdicchio Bianco is an Italian variety used in nine appellations, including Verdicchio dei Castelli di Jesi DOC. In the area of Jesi, it produces 11.5% ABV wines in both *spumante* and *passito* (made from dried grapes) styles. If aged for at least 24 months, including six in bottle, and at least 12.5% ABV, the term *riserva* is added. The *spumante* can also have

this term appended. The wine from the traditional area is called *classico*, and its *superiore* version is at least 12% ABV, with the *classico riserva* containing at least 12.5% ABV. Verdicchio di Matelica, also produced in the Marche, is a close relative.
> **GRAPE VARIETIES** Verdicchio Bianco, along with other white grape varieties, the latter limited to a maximum of 15 percent.

> **SOIL** Hills between the mountains and sea.
> **STYLE** Shades of green are reflected in the straw-yellow color. It displays fruity and floral notes; and on the palate, Verdicchio is fresh, dry, and slightly bitter.

Color:	Serving temperature:	Ageing potential:
White.	46 to 50°F (8 to 10°C).	1 to 2 years.

ORVIETO DOC

Produced near Rome, this white wine was popular with popes, princes, and the city's vast middle-class market. The term *classico* describes wine from the historic center of the appellation; *superiore* is a wine of at least 12% ABV, sold after March 1st following the year of harvest. If harvested

after October 1st, the Orvieto DOC qualifies for the addition of the term *vendemmia tardiva* (late harvest).
> **GRAPE VARIETIES** Grechetto, Trebbiano Toscano, Canaiolo Nostrano, and other local grape varieties.
> **SOIL** Clay-and-limestone hills.

> **STYLE** On the nose, it has a floral bouquet; but on the palate, the wine is dry, with a slight sharpness. It goes with fish, risotto, or pasta.

Color:	Serving temperature:	Ageing potential:
White.	46 to 50°F (8 to 10°C).	1 to 2 years.

Sassicaia, the "Super Tuscan"

"On these rocks, I will build my vineyard." Those could have been the words of Marchese Mario Incisa della Rocchetta back in 1944. He was a keen enthusiast of Bordeaux wines, so he decided to plant Cabernet, the top Bordeaux grape variety, because he had noticed that the soils in Graves resembled those in part of his Tuscan property, Tenuta San Guido on the Mediterranean coast near Siena. In Tuscan dialect, Sassicaia means "stony ground," and that would be the name of the wine.

BEGINNINGS

The three or four acres he first planted were increased by two or three extra acres after the Baron Philippe de Rothschild offered the Marchese additional Cabernet Sauvignon plants directly from the Château Mouton-Rothschild. How encouraging! But for 20 years, from 1948 to 1968, the wine was consumed exclusively by the family of the Marchese, at the estate. Initially, it had little appeal; but the vines grew older, as did the bottles in the cellar—so over time it became both interesting and viable. The idea of a Tuscan wine produced from 100 percent Bordeaux grape varieties at first unsettled many people. In addition, the wine was entitled to only a modest place in the hierarchy of Italian appellations, as a *vino da tavola* (table wine).

REVELATION

In 1977, *Decanter* magazine organized a blind tasting in London of the great Cabernets Sauvignons of the world. The best wine critics participated. Sassicaia 1974 won first place ahead of many world-class wines, including top Médocs and Graves. In an instant, this new wine, which was so original as to be almost incongruous, had made its mark in the panoply of legendary wines. Upon the death of the Marchese in 1983, his son Nicolò pursued his father's vision with the same vigor. Finally, in 1994, a new DOC (*Denominazione di origine controllata*) was established in Italy under the name Sassicaia Bolgheri, granting formal and unquestionable recognition to the wine.

MODEL VINEYARD

The vineyard now covers just less than 150 acres (60 ha) and consists of 85 percent Cabernet Sauvignon and 15 percent Cabernet Franc. Very fragmented

1. Vines at the San Guido estate, which produces Sassicaia.
2. Marchese Nicolò Incisa della Rocchetta, son of the creator of Sassicaia.
3. Palazzo San Guido, near the village of Bolgheri, in Tuscany.
4. Sassicaia's 2004 label, with the Incisa della Rocchetta family crest.

the various plots extend over stony hills that are well protected from sea winds. The only treatments carried out on the vines use Bordeaux mixture. Numerous nearby groves contain natural predators of any local insects harmful to the vine. Added to these natural advantages is a constant effort to avoid, by virtue of rigorous pruning and green harvesting techniques, excessive production that is harmful to the concentration and quality of the grapes.

CAREFUL PRODUCTION, EXTENDED AGEING

After harvest and vinification are carefully completed, the new wine is stored in 225-liter (60 gal) oak barrels. Each year, 40 percent of the barrels are replaced with new stock. The oak used is from the forests of Allier in France, and it is universally recognized as one of the best materials for ageing fine wines. The wine spends 24 months in barrel. After bottling, the bottles are kept resting for six months before they are shipped around the world.

A GREAT NECTAR

Sassicaia is treated like great Bordeaux. Despite its humble profile, it has the virtue of Latin elegance and charm. Strictly speaking, it is a wine from two Cabernet varieties—Sauvignon and Franc—and so it could be an austere or rigid wine. Yet the Mediterranean climate makes it undeniably smooth. Time and patience provide the rest, giving the wine a supreme and necessary harmony. Like its distant relatives from Bordeaux, Sassicaia needs to be developed for 8 to 12 years before reaching its peak, and therefore must be stored in optimal cellar conditions. Its capacity for ageing means that it can be held for many years, even decades, without any deterioration.

EMOTIONAL ENGAGEMENT

It is easy to see how, at that famous blind tasting, Sassicaia was able to make the grade as one of the best wines. But is it really so easy to recognize it among its illustrious rivals? The greatest tasters willingly admit their embarrassment. All truly great wines provide enjoyment and, often, engage the emotions. Now, this great Tuscan wine—showing the cultural richness of the homeland—has entered the pantheon of the best wines in the world.

ABRUZZO

MONTEPULCIANO D'ABRUZZO DOC

ABRUZZO

The Montepulciano grape (bearing the same name as a town in Tuscany) is grown in many parts of Italy and is included in some 100 appellations. But it has a special place among Abruzzo wines. Montepulciano d'Abruzzo DOC is at least 11.5% ABV and must be aged for at least five months. The *riserva* is at least 12.5% ABV and is aged in tank for at least two years. The finest in the lineup, Montepulciano Colline Teramane DOCG, is produced in the area of Teramo, at 12.5% ABV. It is matured for at least two years, or three years for the *riserva*, including at least one year in oak or chestnut barrels, then six months in bottle.

> **GRAPE VARIETY** Montepulciano. Regulations allow the addition of another variety blended to a 15 percent maximum, often Sangiovese.

> **SOIL** Ranging from the Apennines (rising 9,560 ft/2914 m) to the Adriatic, there are clay-and-limestone, alluvial, sandy, and stony soils.

> **STYLE** Montepulciano d'Abruzzo has a ruby color and intense red fruit, licorice, and spice characters. In the mouth, it is robust, fruity, and tannic.

 | **Color:**
Red and cerasuolo (cherry colored). | **Serving temperature:**
61 to 63°F (16 to 17°C). | **Ageing potential:**
10 years or more.

TREBBIANO D'ABRUZZO DOC

ABRUZZO

As is often the case, the name of this appellation combines both the name of the grape and the name of the region. Trebbiano is a white grape known by many synonyms here, including Bombino Bianco and Pagadebit. The appellation covers the four provinces of Abruzzo: L'Aquila, Chieti, Pescara, and Teramo. The area is renowned for its great geographic diversity, since it extends from the Adriatic coast to the Apennine mountains.

> **GRAPE VARIETIES** Trebbiano d'Abruzzo and/or Trebbiano Toscano (85 percent minimum), along with other local grape varieties.

> **SOIL** Between the coastal plains and the mountains, there are several types of soil: clay-and-limestone, alluvial, sandy, and stony.

> **STYLE** Trebbiano d'Abruzzo is an easy-to-drink wine. It has a straw-yellow color with green highlights. The nose is intense, fruity, and floral; but the palate is dry.

 | **Color:**
White. | **Serving temperature:**
50 to 54°F (10 to 12°C). | **Ageing potential:**
1 to 2 years.

GRECO DI TUFO DOCG

CAMPANIA

Along with Fiano, Aglianico, and Falanghina, Greco is one of the recently endangered local grape varieties that wine producers in Campania, such as Mastroberardino or Francesco Paolo Avallone (Villa Matilde), have worked to revive. Greco di Tufo is a white wine produced near Tufo, northeast of Naples. The name of the grape variety recalls the Greek origins of Italian viticulture. There are also sparkling wines, *brut* or *extra-brut*, employing traditional secondary fermentation in bottle.

> **GRAPE VARIETIES** Greco and Coda di Volpe Bianca at 85 percent minimum, along with other local white grapes.

> **SOIL** Volcanic and alluvial.

> **STYLE** Greco di Tufo has a golden straw-yellow color. The nose has fruity aromas of peach and pineapple. Pleasant lemony acidity surprises the palate. It can be enjoyed during a meal, but also as an aperitif due to the freshness and richness of its flavors.

 | **Color:**
White. | **Serving temperature:**
46 to 50°F (8 to 10°C). | **Ageing potential:**
2 to 3 years.

TAURASI DOCG

This robust red comes from a single grape variety, Aglianico—though it's possibly combined in the vineyard with other regional varieties. The growing zone is in the province of Avellino, east of Naples. DOCG conditions require the winemaker to age the wine for at least three years (including at least one year in barrel), or four years if the term *riserva* is applied. The minimum alcohol content is 12 and 12.5% ABV, respectively.

> **GRAPE VARIETY** Aglianico.

> **SOIL** Volcanic and alluvial.

> **STYLE** The wine is ruby red in color, with orange glints typical of old wine, even when the wine is young. The bouquet is intense, with notes of black cherry, cinnamon, vanilla, and nutmeg, supported by a good tannic structure.

Color:
Red.

Serving temperature:
61 to 63°F (16 to 17°C).

Ageing potential:
10 years or more.

CASTEL DEL MONTE DOC

An emblematic monument in the province of Bari has given its name to the generic Puglian appellation. Among wines here, the Castel del Monte Aglianico requires 90 percent of the blend to be the Aglianico grape variety; the *riserva* is aged for two years, including one year in oak. Using the same production methods, the appellation includes the following other reds and rosés: Castel del Monte Bombino Nero, Castel del Monte Cabernet, Castel del Monte Pinot Nero, and Castel del Monte Uva di Troia. The generic Castel del Monte Rosso (red) is produced from a minimum of 65 percent Aglianico, Montepulciano, or Uva di Troia, blended with a maximum of 35 percent of other red grapes. For whites, the methodology is identical. When the appellation lists a Castel del Monte grape variety, it must be greater than 90 percent of the wine. The generic Castel del Monte Bianco (white) is produced with a minimum of 65 percent Bombino Bianco or Chardonnay Pampanuto, blended with other local white varieties.

> **GRAPE VARIETIES** For whites: Bombino Bianco, Chardonnay, Pinot Bianco, and Sauvignon Blanc; for reds: Aglianico, Aglianico Rosato, Bombino Nero, Cabernet Sauvignon, Pinot Nero, and Uva di Troia.

> **SOIL** Limestone, gravel, silt deposits.

> **STYLE** This panorama of inexpensive wines offers the chance to discover a spectrum of local grapes and their individual characters—especially since they are generally quite simple (except for the *riservas*).

Color:
White, rosé, and red.

Serving temperature:
46 to 50°F (8 to 10°C) for whites and rosés;
57 to 59°F (14 to 15°C) for reds;
61 to 63°F (16 to 17°C) for riservas.

Ageing potential:
1 year for whites and rosés;
3 years for reds and riservas.

CIRÒ DOC

Calabria has a rich history of viticulture. Archaeologists have even found traces of clay pipes for wine, presumably evidence of some kind of "vinoduct." It is a rugged region with microclimates ranging from the mountains to the Ionian coast and the shores of the Tyrrhenian Sea. The Cirò DOC spreads over low maritime hills. In recent years, Calabria has moved forward from its past of only over-ripe oxidized, and very alcoholic wines. Thanks to modern methods of vinification and temperature control, the Cirò DOC now displays fruit and freshness. The term *classico* indicates a provenance of the historic areas of Cirò and Cirò Marina. *Superiore* indicates greater than 13.5% ABV, and *riserva* an ageing period of two years.

> **GRAPE VARIETIES** At least 95 percent Gaglioppo, sometimes with the addition of whites such as Trebbiano Toscano and Greco Bianco. Nine-tenths of regional production consists of red and rosé wines.

> **SOIL** Apennine limestone, granite, and alluvial deposits.

> **STYLE** The wine is a deep ruby color. The nose shows aromas of red fruits and berries, and jam. The palate is dry, full bodied, warm, and velvety.

Color:
Red.

Serving temperature:
59 to 61°F (15 to 16°C).

Ageing potential:
3 to 5 years (up to 10 years for riservas).

CANNONAU DI SARDEGNA DOC

Sardinia was occupied by the Spanish for a long time, and its iconic red wine comes from the Cannonau grape variety, also known as Garnacha in Spain (or Grenache in France). The Cannonau DOC has three sub-regions: Oliena, Capo Ferrato, and Jerzu. The wines are aged for a minimum of seven months and have a minimum of 12.5% ABV. The *riserva* is aged for two years and is at least 13% ABV. The appellation also produces a rosé.

> **GRAPE VARIETIES** Cannonau and other local varieties.

> **SOIL** The soil is complex. There are clay and limestone sediments, granite, Tertiary volcanic rocks, and Quaternary alluvial deposits in the plains.

> **STYLE** The wines have a ruby color, and ripe fruit and spice characters. On the palate they are dry and tannic, and they confirm jam-like aromas on the nose. They have a long finish.

Color:	Serving temperature:	Ageing potential:
Red and rosé.	*46 to 50°F (8 to 10°C) for rosé;* *61 to 63°F (16 to 17°C) for red.*	*1 to 2 years for rosé;* *3 to 5 years for red.*

ALCAMO DOC

Located in the provinces of Trapani and Palermo, the Alcamo appellation includes several styles of wine: white, red, rosé, sparkling (white and rosé), as well as late-harvest. The term *classico* refers to wines from the historic heart of the area, and *riserva* applies to wines that are aged for longer than average. When the grape variety is mentioned alongside the DOC, it must constitute at least 85 percent of the blend. So the Alcamo Grecanico contains at least 85 percent of the Grecanico grape. Alcamo Bianco DOC is a blend of Catarratto (at least 60 percent), Inzolia, and other white grapes of the region.

> **GRAPE VARIETIES** Inzolia (also called Ansonica), Catarratto, Chardonnay, Grecanico, Grillo, Müller-Thurgau, and Sauvignon Blanc for the whites; Cabernet Sauvignon, Calabrese or Nero d'Avola, Merlot, and Syrah for the reds.

> **SOIL** Volcanic, limestone, clay, and sand.

> **STYLE** The Alcamo Bianco has a pale straw yellow-color with green glints, and a fruity nose. On the palate, there is a hint of sharpness and real freshness. The reds are more diverse.

Color:	Serving temperature:	Ageing potential:
White, rosé, and red.	*46 to 50°F (8 to 10°C) for whites and rosés;* *57 to 63°F (14 to 17°C) for reds, depending on complexity.*	*1 to 2 years for whites and rosés;* *3 years for reds.*

MARSALA DOC

How did early modern merchants transport wine to distant destinations without it spoiling and turning into vinegar? They "fortified" the wine with additional alcohol, which acted as a preservative. Based on this principle, the British merchant John Woodhouse established the export of Marsala to England and the world at large during the 18th century. This wine, fortified with sweet must, has lost some of its prestige because current fashion runs against overtly sweet wines—and long-term use in cooking never enhances a wine's status. Marsala is classified as "fine" (1 year old), "superiore" (2 years old), "superiore riserva" (4 years old), "vergine" and/or "soleras" (5 years old), or "soleras stravecchio" (10 years old).

> **GRAPE VARIETIES** Grillo, Catarratto, Inzolia, and Damaschino for the whites; Pignatello, Calabrese, Nerello Mascalese, and Nero d'Avola for the reds.

> **SOIL** Volcanic, limestone, clay, and sand.

> **STYLE** The whites are gold and amber, the reds are ruby colored. The typical flavors of Marsala are crystallized fruits and *eau-de-vie* fruits. Its level of sweetness varies from "dry" containing the least sugar (less than 40 g/l), "semi-dry" (41 to 99 g/l), and "sweet" (more than 100 g/l).

Color:	Serving temperature:	Ageing potential:
White (amber) and red.	*43 to 46°F (6 to 8°C) served as an aperitif;* *57 to 59°F (14 to 15°C) served as a dessert wine.*	*5 to 20 years, depending on the type.*

"Natural" wine at the foot of Mount Etna

Frank Cornelissen is a leading winemaker promoting "natural" wines. They are most often produced from organic grapes, with minimal intervention from vine to bottle. The wines do not contain added yeast, they are unfiltered, and no sulfur is used in the production process. They can be recognized by their deep color and a pleasant hint of vinegar scents, known as "volatile acidity." In his winery near Etna, Frank fills a glass to the brim, and then dips his finger into it. Wine flows over the sides. "If we add something, we need to remove something else." Without fertilizers or treatments, he obtains

a very low yield: only 10,000 bottles from the 25 acres (10 ha) of his estate. "I do not treat the vine, because I want it to stand up for itself. The same goes for my wines. For the wine to be preserved without sulfur, it needs a good concentration, and a certain minerality." At harvest, fermentation of the grapes (in terracotta jars) does not start with standard, commercially available yeast. "My yeasts are the air in the cellar." Frank produces vigorous wines with complex, floral, fruity, and mineral flavors. Cornelissen exports 95 percent of production at prices between €10 and €150 ($15 to $210/£10 to £130) per bottle.

SICILY

ETNA DOC

In his study *De Naturali Vinorum Historia*, published in 1596, Andrea Bacci, the physician of Pope Sixtus V, indicated the conditions required for agriculture in the volcanic ash of Catania. This mountainous area, still dominated by black sand, is particularly rich in those ashen minerals. Etna, the largest volcano in Europe, and one of the most active in the world, is 10,974 ft (3,345 m) high. It creates a humid climate and provides the fertile soil for viticulture. The Etna appellation produces wines in three styles around the town of Milo (whose name is not derived from the Venus of that same name).

> **GRAPE VARIETIES** Carricante, Catarratto Bianco Comune, and possibly Trebbiano and Minella Bianca for the whites (Etna Bianco Superiore is produced from Carricante.); Nerello Mascalese and Nerello Mantellato or Cappuccio for the reds and rosés. (The latter include a small proportion of white grapes.)

> **SOIL** Volcanic.

> **STYLE** The white has a straw-yellow color, with hints of green or gold. Its palate is dry, fresh, and fruity; and it contains a minimum of 11.5% ABV. The white *superiore* is at least 12% ABV. The red presents ruby colors, and has spice and red fruit (plum, blackberry) flavors. On the palate, it is dry and full-bodied. As for the rosé, it is fruity, light, and refreshing.

Color:	Serving temperature:	Ageing potential:
White, red, and rosé.	*46 to 50°F (8 to 10°C) for whites and rosés; 57 to 61°F (14 to 16 °C) for reds.*	*2 to 3 years for whites and rosés; 3 to 5 years for reds.*

ÎLE DE PANTELLERIA

MOSCATO DI PANTELLERIA DOC

This naturally sweet wine, meaning there is no addition of fortifying alcohol, made the island famous when it was exported to Europe. Located between Sicily and Africa, Pantelleria cultivates vines where the grapes ripen quickly and dry easily on the vine or after harvest. This white Muscat is at least 15% ABV. It should not be confused with the *passito liquoroso* Pantelleria, made from dried grape clusters and fortified with grape spirit during its fermentation.

> **GRAPE VARIETY** Muscat of Alexandria, also called Zibibbo.

> **SOIL** Volcanic.

> **STYLE** This soft white wine has a golden color and intense aromas, which are typical of Muscat. On the palate, the flavors of dried fruit, apricot, and honey dominate. Moscato may be enjoyed as an aperitif. Those who like foie gras with *vin liquoreux* will enjoy it, too. Still others advise it should be sipped with desserts that are not too sweet or acidic, such as a plum tart. It also goes well with blue cheese.

Color:	Serving temperature:	Ageing potential:
White.	*46°F (8°C).*	*1 to 2 years.*

SPAIN

Wine-producing regions

- Denominación de origen (DO)
- Denominación de origen calificada (DOC)
- Border of autonomous community
- Border

0   125 miles (200 km)

N

Map labels (mainland)

La Coruña
GALICIA
Oviedo
ASTURIAS
Santander
Txakoli de Bizkaia
Txakoli de Getaria
San Sebastián
Santiago de Compostella
CANTABRIQUE
Bilbao
BASQUE COUNTRY
Ribeira Sacra
Biérzo
León
Vitoria
Pamplona
Ampurdán-Costa Brava
Rías Baixas
NAVARRA
Logroño
Navarra
Pyrenees
Vigo
Ribeiro
Miño
Burgos
Rioja
LA RIOJA
Somontano
CATALONIA
Valdeorras
CASTILLE AND LEÓN
Huesca
Ebro
Pla de Bages
Monterrei
Cigales
Campo de Borja
Zaragoza
Costers del Segre
Alella
Atlantic Ocean
Douro
Ribera del Duero
Lleida
Barcelona
Valladolid
Cariñena
Priorat
Tarragona
Toro
Rueda
Calatayud
Terra Alta
Penedès
Salamanca
Mondéjar
ARAGON
Conca de Barberà
MADRID
Tajo
Tarragona
PORTUGAL
Madrid
Los Vinos de Madrid
Méntrida
Toledo
Mediterranean Sea
Tajo
Utiel Requena
VALENCIA
EXTREMADURA
La Mancha
Valencia
Mérida
Guadiana
CASTILLA-LA MANCHA
Xúqueri
Ribera del Guadiana
Almansa
Valencia
Valdepeñas
Jumilla
Alicante
Valdepeñas
Yecla
Alicante
Cordoba
Bullas
MURCIA
Murcia
Condada de Huelva
Guadalquivir
Genil
Montilla-Moriles
Binissalem
Palma
Huelva
Seville
ANDALUSIA
MAJORCA
Jerez/Xérès
Málaga
Grenada
Jerez de la Frontera
Málaga
Pla í Llevant
Cádiz
Balearic Islands

Inset (Canary Islands)

Atlantic Ocean
Lanzarote
Valle de la Orotava
Tacoronte-Acentejo
La Palma
Valle de Güímar
Ycoden Daute-Isora
Abona
El Hierro
CANARY ISLANDS

0   60 miles (100 km)

N

SPAIN

After a long period in the doldrums, Spain is now a source of excitement, and it possesses some of the world's best vineyards and wines. Why such success? Meticulous identification of terroirs and use of native grape varieties appropriate to their appellation, as well as technical progress in the fields of vine growing and winemaking.

Then and now

RICH HISTORY. Today's Spanish wine industry is on a history encompassing conquest, the crusades, and the successive contributions of individuals who have, little by little, created and enriched the wine-producing landscape.

The Phoenicians were the first to bring vines to Spain, in the 7th century BC, particularly to the Malaga and Cadiz regions. Romans arrived in Spain during the 3rd century BC, and they gave the Spanish a better understanding of vine pruning, the process of fermentation, and the maturation of wine which, at that time, took place not in barrels but in amphorae. The grape variety Muscat of Alexandria, with its sumptuously exuberant bouquet, was then brought to Spain by the Arabs from the Maghreb during the 8th century.

SPAIN STATISTICS
Vineyard area: 2,935,000 acres (1,174,000 ha)
Production: 424 million cases (38,173,000 hl)
Reds: 52%
Whites: 24%
Rosés: 17%
Sparkling wines: 4.5%
Fortified wines: 2.5%
(OIV [International Office of Vines and Wine], 2006)

PHYLLOXERA ATTACKS. By the time this devastating aphid descended on Spanish vineyards in the late 1800s, a way of dealing with its ravages had already been determined: grafting European varieties onto resistant American rootstocks. Consequently, growers got to work replanting. Many of the most reputable wineries today date from this era.

RECENT DEVELOPMENT. During the second half of the 20th century, Spain started to move from producing just anonymous wines for bulk sale to the creation of real quality. In the 1970s, Rioja wines began significant exports, quickly followed by such estates as Vega Sicilia (*see* pp.384–5), and then by those of Valdepeñas and Catalonia. During the 1980s, Spanish wine underwent a complete quality revolution, and the wine-producing areas were remapped into 17 autonomous regions (*autonomías*), each producing their own distinctive wines.

> Vines planted on terraces in Catalonia.

Climate and geography

Spain is dominated by a vast central plain (*meseta*), with an elevation of 2,150 ft (650 m) above sea level, surrounded on all sides by mountains. So its best wines are made from grape varieties that grow well at altitude—up to 1,640 ft (500 m) in Rioja, for example. Vineyards here benefit from good exposure to the sun without suffering from scorching heat or temperatures that fall too low at night.

Most great Spanish wines are produced north of Madrid, which is to say, going from west to east, Galicia, the valleys of the Duero and the Ebro, and Catalonia. The best sites are most often found in these mountainous valleys with relatively poor soils based on clay subsoil. On the other hand, much of the valleys of the Ebro and the Douro are rich in alluvial soil.

The climate is similarly diverse: the Atlantic Ocean brings freshness and humidity to the west; the climate in the central and northern zones is of the continental type, with hot summers and cold winters; the Catalan coast enjoys a Mediterranean climate.

> Vines at Bodega Gonzáles Byass, the largest producer of sherry in Andalusia.

Vineyard landscape

Spain has the world's largest area under vine cultivation. There are vineyards in almost every region of the peninsula.

GALICIA AND THE BASQUE COUNTRY. These are Spain's most northerly vineyards. The Atlantic Ocean influences the climate, the economy (based mainly on fishing), and the wines, which are generally light, dry whites that are an excellent accompaniment to seafood.

NAVARRA, RIOJA, AND ARAGON. Also situated in the north, across the high valley of the Ebro, these regions produce mainly powerful red wines with the potential for long cellaring, as well as robust whites.

CATALONIA. Located around the mouth of the Ebro, Catalonia has a very distinctive culture. The importance of its fishing industry and its Mediterranean climate quite naturally lead to the production of white wines. It is also the birthplace of Cavas, Spanish sparkling wines.

CASTILE AND LEON. Here are the traditional vineyards of the Duero Valley. A continental climate is tempered by proximity to the river. Red wines are fleshy and powerful, and dry whites here are full-bodied. This is home to the legendary Ribera del Duero (*see* p.382) appellation.

ANDALUSIA. In the extreme south, Andalusia forms a single, vast, autonomous region. Its legendary Jerez or sherry wines undergo a lengthy maturation under a veil of *flor*—the beneficial yeast that develops on the surface of the wine there (*see* p.74). Constantly progressing, the Montilla–Moriles and Condado appellations of Huelva make sweet wines, fortified or otherwise, as well as a few dry wines. Finally, after almost disappearing (*see box* p.378), Malaga continues to produce a vast range of sweet wines.

OTHER REGIONS. Most top Spanish wines are produced in northern regions, as mentioned above; but vines are very much a force in the center and the south of the country, too. Cultivation extends across Castile–La Mancha and Vinos de Madrid, on the plateau of the *meseta*, as well as in the Levante, which includes the autonomous regions of Valencia and Murcia—all producing wine for everyday drinking. A small amount of wine is produced also in the Spanish islands—the Balearics and the Canaries.

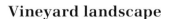

DID YOU KNOW...?

Vineyard yields in Spain are among the lowest in the world. The average yield is just 1.4 tons per acre (25 hl/ha). This figure is remarkably low, especially when compared with that of neighboring countries (4.2 tons per acre/70 hl/ha on average in France). It can be attributed to the presence of very old vines in the various growing areas, as well as the rigorous climatic conditions that make life quite tough for the vine—but to the benefit of the wine.

Grape varieties: protected heritage

Spain has preserved its native grape varieties, which form a kind of "memory" of the country's wine heritage. They drive the expression of many appellations to great heights, producing wines with enormous personality.

AIRÈN. This white grape (the most commonly grown white variety in the world) can be found in southern Spain, in Castile–La Mancha, across more than one million acres (420,000 ha). It produces very refreshing, aromatic wines.

ALBARIÑO. This white grape variety has a strong personality and is often compared to Sauvignon Blanc and even Viognier. It is fascinating for the great complexity of its bouquet, sometimes evoking exotic fruit and very elegant, floral notes. Albariño flourishes in Galicia, in northwestern Spain, largely in the Rías Baixas appellation.

CARIÑENA. Known in France as Carignan, this red grape variety is grown on a massive scale in Catalonia, where it produces inviting aromas of chocolaty, dark fruits and a dense and focused impact on the palate. It has pride of place in the blends of the great Priorats.

GODELLO. Abandoned for many years, this white grape variety has since made a most convincing comeback. It is valued both for its supple, mineral texture and touches of rubbed stone and pebbles. It forms part of the blend in the Valdeorras and Bierzo appellations, among others.

MENCIA. Even from its youth, this red grape variety offers up notes of crisp red fruits, and promises an extremely satisfying sweetness on the palate. The appellations where Mencia produces the best results are Monterrei, Valdeorras, Ribeiro, and Ribeira Sacra.

PALOMINO AND PEDRO XIMÉNEZ. This duo of white varieties is cultivated in the Jerez DO (*Denominacion de Origen*—the Spanish equivalent of the French AOC): Palomino brings a natural vivacity and "PX," as it is known locally, expresses a range of varied aromas and, most notably, a rich sweetness.

TEMPRANILLO. If only one Spanish variety could be cultivated, it would have to be Tempranillo. The standard bearer of national wine production, it produces dark red wines with a sustained tannic structure. At the same time, it shows freshness and achieves a sumptuous balance. It is expressed to the fullest in the Ribera del Duero appellation, where it works miracles. Tempranillo is also known as: Tinto Fino, Cencibel, Tinto del Pais, Tinto de Toro, Tinto de Madrid, and so on.

Wine styles

Well known for its fortified wines, such as the famous sherries of Jerez, Spain also produces red wines, rosés, white wines,

> Advertising for Malaga painted on ceramic.

Malaga rescued

Historic Andalusian wine fortified with brandy, Malaga almost disappeared from local wine production—threatened by land development for the vacation property market, and a strong demand for raisin grapes. But since the 1980s, a new generation of wine producers has been flying the flag for this appellation once more. Malaga is a sweet white wine that owes its complex character to the addition of sweet grape syrups or concentrated musts. The wine is aged in *conos* (casks made from chestnut) according to a *solera* system (fractional blending), which can be compared with the technique for making sherry in Jerez (see p.74). Its quality depends on a long maturation in those casks. The best wines can be kept in bottle for decades, even centuries. Several categories are recognized, according to the ageing period: Malaga (from 6–24 months), Malaga Noble (2–3 years), Malaga Añejo (3–5 years), and Málaga Trasañejo (more than 5 years). Malaga is also classed according to its color, from *dorado* (golden) to *negro* (black). Since 1995, it has been officially possible to make dry white wines in this region (*Malaga Blanco Seco*) as well as naturally sweet whites—those made without raising the alcohol content by the addition of spirits—as well as all three colors of dry wines under the Sierras de Malaga DO.

> *Chai* (barrel cellar) for ageing at Señorío de Arinzano, near Estella, in Navarra.

and sparkling wines that range from very modest to highly sophisticated. Almost crunchy reds with sharp tannins are found in the Ribeira Sacra appellation, as well as in Monterrei from Galicia. The best and fleshiest red wines are made principally in Priorat (*see* p.386), Toro (*see* p.381), or even in Ribera del Duero (*see* p.382). Spanish white wines have a distinct vivacity, such as Rías Baixas (*see* p.380), Txakoli (*see* p.380), or other wines from Navarra and Rioja (*see* p.383). Several of the best sweet wines—both white and red—are also produced in Penedès, Navarra, and Murcia.

Cava, a sparkling wine with vivacious bubbles, is produced mainly in Catalonia (*see* p.389). The production techniques are the same as those in Champagne (*see* pp.70–1) , but using different grape varieties.

Widely known, Jerez or sherry, a family of fortified white wines, offers a whole range of styles, from the driest to the sweetest. Long popular among the British (who originally called them "sack"), they owe their delightful flavor to the way they are vinified beneath a film of yeast known as *flor* (*see* pp.74 and 388). The only other place in the world where this develops naturally is the Jura (France), where it plays an essential role in the making of *vin jaune* (*see* p.307).

Pagos wines

The Spanish system of appellations (*see* p.96) is similar to the system that exists in France. *Pagos* wines are at the very top of the quality scale. They each reflect a tiny *terroir*, a specific microclimate, and they are demarcated after long years of observation and tasting. As such, they often are signature wines from a single producer. In France, these wines would correspond to *monopoles* (vineyards that have only one owner) revered by all who have tasted them, such as Romanée-Conti in Burgundy, Château-Grillet in the Rhône Valley, or Coulée-de-Serrant in the Loire Valley. *Pagos* wines are produced mainly in Castile and Leon. Marqués de Griñón, Manuel Manzaneque, Dominio de Valdepusa, and Finca Elez are some of the most famous.

Spain's best-known wines

Spain's dynamic vineyards produce a wide range of wines that are winning spectacular popularity on the international market. From north to south, here are the main appellations and their characteristics.

TXAKOLI DO

At the center of Basque Country, nicknamed "Green Spain," in the provinces of Bilbao and San Sebastián, this appellation includes three geographic denominations: Bizkaia, Getaria, and Alava. Situated close to the Atlantic Ocean, the vines are grown on the slopes of steep hills where typical climatic conditions consist of copious amounts of rain and moderate sunshine.

> **GRAPE VARIETIES** Hondarribi Zuri for white wines and Hondarribi Beltza for reds.
> **SOIL** Vineyards are on soil that is, for the most part, granitic. But there is limestone in some cases.
> **STYLE** Almost the entire appellation produces white wine; though some red wine is made for early consumption, when they are young and fruity. In terms of white wine, a pale, silvery color is paired with aromas of Granny Smith apples and the zest of citrus fruit. The same is expressed on the palate with a crisp vivacity.

Color:
White and red.

Serving temperature:
46 to 50°F (8 to 10°C) for whites;
61 to 64°F (16 to 18°C) for reds.

Ageing potential:
3 to 5 years for whites;
3 to 7 years for reds.

RÍAS BAIXAS DO

This DO is located in southern Galicia, very close to the border with Portugal. It contains several production zones, such Valle del Salnes, Condado del Tea, and O Rosal. The region owes its living to the sea and its rich wine-making history.
> **GRAPE VARIETIES** Albariño, Loureiro, Treixadura, Caiño Blanco, Torrontés, and Godello for white wines; Caiño Tinto, Sousón, Espadeiro, Brancellaon, Mencia, and Loureiro for reds.
> **SOIL** The area is strongly influenced by the sea. The soil—limestone, chalk, or even rocky scree—is therefore ideal for making white wines with mineral notes.
> **STYLE** Virtually the entire appellation is given over to making white wines.

They are pale yellow or very light in color, and very aromatic with notes of orchard fruit, such as peach or apricot. As they evolve over time, hints of greengage and Mirabelle plum jam begin to emerge. There is a saline base to the structure of the mouth-feel, enhanced with mineral qualities and a convincing finish.

Color:
White and red (less than 1 percent of the latter).

Serving temperature:
50°F (10 °C) for whites;
61°F (16 °C) for reds.

Ageing potential:
3 to 5 years for reds;
5 to 7 years for whites.

VALDEORRAS DO

Valdeorras lies south of the Orense province, between the border with Portugal and the Atlantic Ocean. Home to a number of talented winemakers, this DO has been producing white wines that arouse a great deal of interest due to their mineral character and the mouth-feel they offer. Reds make up only a very small part of total production. The climate, often damp because of its proximity to the sea, is ideal for wine maturation. The vine-yards cling tenaciously to the sides of the mountains, but they also extend into the heart of local valleys.

> **GRAPE VARIETIES** Godello, Palomino, Doña Blanca, for white wines; Mencia for the reds.

> **SOIL** Granite and slate soils bring a great deal of tautness to the wines, and honesty to the often fleshy palate.

> **STYLE** The white wines exude aromas of white fruit in *eau-de-vie*, such as pears and Mirabelle plums. On the palate, they have a dense, fleshy feel with an interesting mineral quality. For the red wines, the Mencia variety shows a purplish-crimson color. It goes on to present notes of crisp red fruit and silky tannins offering a welcome richness.

Color:
White and red.

Serving temperature:
50°F (10 °C) for whites;
61°F (16 °C) for reds.

Ageing potential:
3 to 5 years for reds;
5 to 7 years for whites.

TORO DO

Established in 1987, this DO became—in just a decade—one of the prime locations in which to make great wines. The average yield is scarcely a ton per acre (15 hl/ha) and the atmospheric temperature range—one of the widest in the country—is ideal for the process of grape development.

> **GRAPE VARIETIES** Malvasia and Verdejo for whites; Tinto de Toro and Garnacha for the reds and rosés.

> **SOIL** The vineyards grow at altitude (between 2,000 and 2,800 ft/600 and 800 m), where the nights are often very cold. The soil—mainly siliceous-clay—provides the vines just the right amount of heat retention, along with the trace elements that they also need.

> **STYLE** It is mainly the red wines that grab attention here. They are generally made from pure Tinto de Toro. The dark red, almost black, color of the wines is striking. To the nose, they offer warm tones of leather, damp earth, and old varnish around a core of ripe, juicy fruit. On the palate, the concentrated aromas join in a soft and velvety texture. Then comes a series of slightly toasted, spicy flavors, all coupled with great breeding. The white and rosé wines are more classic in character.

Color:
White, rosé, and red.

Serving temperature:
46 to 50°F (8 to 10°C) for whites and rosés;
61°F (16 °C) for reds.

Ageing potential:
5 to 20 years.

Numanthia, the jewel in Toro's crown

Vineyards are planted at an altitude of more than 2,100 ft (650 m). The Tinto de Toro grape variety, better known as Tempranillo, produces vigorous wines of great depth—with aromas of juicy black fruit and spices. But one winery in particular stands out in the heart of this region: Numanthia–Termes. Established in 1998, this estate is first and foremost the story of a family, the Egurens, whose talent brings out the best in an exceptional vineyard. The estate (about 100 acres/40 ha) has a remarkable heritage, with old vines that lend great distinction to the wines. Every wine receives special care: very low yields, careful monitoring of fruit ripening, and, above all, meticulous attention to the production process. It all gives these wines a rare persistence and velvetiness. The Cuvée Termanthia, made solely from pre-phylloxera—*i.e.* ungrafted—vines, has become established in recent vintages as one of the greatest Spanish wines.

BIERZO DO

Situated below the Cantabrian Cordillera, Bierzo vines are grown at more than 1,600 ft (500 m), and so benefit from ideal temperature variation. This is the perfect *terroir* for the Mencia grape variety, which produces some striking red wines here.

> **GRAPE VARIETIES** Godello, Doña Blanca, Malvasia, Palomino, and Chardonnay for whites; Mencia, Garnacha (Grenache), Tempranillo, Cabernet Sauvignon, and Merlot for reds and rosés.

> **SOIL** High elevation together with the proximity of the mountains results in a soil that is made up mostly of alluvial deposits with some lim stone. This combination produces slow-maturing wines, with strong mineral notes.

> **STYLE** The white and rosé wines here have been eclipsed in recent years by the progress made with red wines from the Mencia variety. A dark, almost opaque, color from the very beginning, they offer a concentrated, deep nose with notes of cherry or blackcurrant that become smoky and mineral. There are also rich, intense tannins that require a few years' ageing in order to keep their promise.

Color:	*Serving temperature:*	*Ageing potential:*
White, rosé, and red.	46 to 50°F (8 to 10 °C) for whites and rosés; 61°F (16 °C) for reds.	3 to 5 years for whites and rosés; 5 to 15 years for reds.

RIBERA DEL DUERO DO

This red wine appellation is to Spain what Margaux and Côte-Rôtie are to France. A real standard bearer for Spanish expertise, today more than ever, Ribera del Duero proves—vintage after vintage—that it is truly the queen of the Iberian peninsula and the cradle of the greatest wines. For example, the legendary estate Vega Sicilia (*see* pp.384–5) was established here in 1864. This appellation is one of the best examples of the Spanish system for classifying wines according to age (*see also* p.96), with a clear vision of the wines it produces. Consequently, *crianza* wines, bottled after two years, are for early drinking; the *reservas* are at least three years old, including one year spent in cask; the *gran reservas*, produced in particularly good vintages, are at least five years old, including two years in cask and three in bottle.

> **GRAPE VARIETIES** Tinto Fino, Cabernet Sauvignon, Merlot, Malbec, and Garnacha (Grenache) for reds; Albillo for whites (though the production of white wine is close to non-existent here).

> **SOIL** In this high-altitude *terroir*, the soil is mainly formed from alluvial deposits, chalk, and ancient limestone. This combination produces a wine with unrivalled tactile definition.

> **STYLE** The aromas of the red wines tend toward crisp red fruit, mild spices, and exotic wood passing through hints of smoked meat to finish with essence of dried roses: Ribero del Duero can be intriguing and passionate. The *crianza* wines offer a fair compromise between flavorsome texture and attractive expression of Tinto Fino. The *reservas* and *gran reservas* are wines that are much more profound, seductive, and velvety.

Color:	*Serving temperatures:*	*Ageing potential:*
Red and white.	50°F (10°C) for whites; 64°F (16°C) for reds.	10 to 50 years or longer, depending on vintage and the particular winery.

RIOJA DOC

The Rioja region, following the Ebro River in northern Spain, actually derives its name from Rio Oja, a small river that crosses the appellation from west to east. During the 19th century, the producers of Rioja were greatly inspired by the wines of Bordeaux. Enough so that, in the midst of the phylloxera crisis, some of them moved to Bordeaux and returned later with new techniques and expertise. As in the Ribera del Duero appellation, the ageing process is very strictly controlled, resulting in a wine of excellent quality. Rioja spends several months in oak barrels: *crianza* is aged for at least two years, including one year in oak; *reserva* is aged for at least three years, including one year in oak; gran *reserva* is aged for at least two years in oak and at least three in bottle.

> **GRAPE VARIETIES** Grenache Blanc, Viura, and Malvasia for whites; Tempranillo, Garnacha, Graciano, and Mazuelo for reds and rosés.

> **SOIL** Most of the soil is a mix of clay and limestone, but specific variations have an impact on wine style. In Rioja Baja, one of the three Rioja *terroirs*, ferruginous clay yields powerful wines; while in Rioja Alavesa, limestone yields more acidity.

> **STYLE** The white wines depend mainly on Grenache Blanc. They are pale in color and have soothing aromas of white fruit (Japanese pears, peaches) and nuances of damp pebbles. The palate is full and fleshy. During recent years, the reds—dark red with deep purple glints—have gradually been losing their former warmth and generosity. But the aromatics still perfectly express the personality of this great appellation. Imbued with sanguineous notes (venison, game, musk), blackberry jam, and touches of cocoa

powder, the palate is characterized by structure and vigor. The rosés offer a range from fresh to fruity.

Color:
White, rosé, and red.

Serving temperature:
46 to 50°F (8 to 10°C) for whites and rosés;
61°F (16°C) for reds.

Ageing potential:
3 to 15 years for whites and rosés;
5 to 20 years for reds.

NAVARRA DO

One of the best-known Spanish appellations, Navarra dates back to the origin of the DO system. Located just 37 miles (60 km) south of the French Pyrenees, the appellation stretches from Pamplona in the north and Logroño in the west to the Sierra de Moncayo in the south. There are several production zones within the DO: Baja Montaña, Tierra Estella, Valdizarbe, Ribera Alta, and Ribera Baja. The immense Navarra terroir covers more than 37,500 acres (15,000 ha) and is immediately adjacent to the Rioja region.

> **GRAPE VARIETIES** Viura, Chardonnay, Moscatel de Grano Menudo, and Malvasia, for white wines; Garnacha (Grenache), Tempranillo, Cabernet Sauvignon, Merlot, Mazuelo, and Graciano for reds and rosés.

> **SOIL** The vineyards are extensive and impressive. Some border the Ebro River, extending north toward the hills and mountains beyond. The soils are as diverse as the vineyard exposures are numerous. There is clay and sand, and a substantial amount of limestone, all providing a noticeable mineral support to the wines.

> **STYLE** The whites are mostly crisp and refreshing, with fruity notes that are extremely well expressed. Worthy of note are the Chardonnays matured "a la Bourgignonne"—*i.e.* with a period in barrel to give them fleshiness and fullness. Wine lovers on the hunt for rare vintages and new discoveries should try the appellation's sweet wines. For several years now, Muscats have been produced

with great success. Made from grapes dried on the vine, these wines offer rich sweetness. The style of red wine here is dominated by the Bordeaux school of blending. There is significant use of Merlot and Cabernet Sauvignon, which may rob the wines of a part of their authenticity and local color. On the other hand, Navarra wines made from Tempranillo are dense and well formed, delivering the scents of blackberry or juniper berries on a spicy base.

Color:
White, rosé, and red.

Serving temperature:
46 to 50°F (8 to 10°C) for whites and rosés;
61°F (16°C) for reds.

Ageing potential:
3 to 10 years for whites and rosés;
5 to 15 years for reds.

1. View over the Vega Sicilia estate.
2. Tempranillo grapes.
3. In the winery.
4. Emblem of Vega Sicilia.
5. Unico label.

Vega Sicilia's Unico

The name of this famous Spanish estate is unusual with its Italian overtones. Equally unusual, the name of the local river changes, some 62 miles (100 km) south of Burgos, from the Spanish Duero to the Portuguese Douro. Unusual again, this amazing wine (Unico) is made from several French grape varieties. And finally, and still more unusual, is the way it is matured. All these oddities aside, Vega Sicilia's Unico has achieved legendary status.

FROM TABLE WINE TO OFFICIAL ACCLAIM

After an instructive visit to Bordeaux in 1864, Don Eloy Lecanda y Chaves established his vineyard in Castile with vines he had brought back from France: Cabernet Sauvignon, Malbec, Merlot,

and Carmenère—to which he added the famous local grape variety Tempranillo (also known as Tinto Fino). His initial efforts were mediocre, and it was not until 1903, in the hands of a new proprietor, Antonio Herrero, that the estate acquired a reputation for greatness. In 1982, the estate was bought by the Alvarez family, and Vega Sicilia achieved worldwide acclaim. That same year, the wine (until then classed as a simple *vino de mesa* [table wine]), was awarded the prestigious status of Denominacion de Origen for Ribera del Duero.

CLIMATE, SOIL, AND GENTLE HANDLING

Perched at an altitude of 2,300 ft (700 m), the vineyard benefits from a semi-continental climate with hot, dry summers and

cold, rainy winters. The spring frosts represent a considerable danger, as they can occur right up to the start of May. But Vega Sicilia's Unico is produced only during great vintages. In mediocre years—1992, 1997, 2000, 2001—this wine simply does not exist. The *terroir* of the 575 acres (230 ha) at the estate contains no fewer than 19 soil types. The relative nutritional poverty of the soils combined with their great variety produces complexity in the final wine. Five different tiers of wine are produced across the estate, but for the one bearing the name Vega Sicilia Unico, only fruit from the oldest vines is used. Gentle, natural production methods are the norm here. Pruning is carried out after seasonal vine growth has already started, which limits the yields and improves the quality of the fruit. Harvest is left as late

4

3

5

as possible to obtain maximum ripeness, and the grapes are stripped gently from their clusters so fermentation begins immediately and naturally.

MATURATION PROCESS

Each grape variety brings its own distinctive touch to the blend, and contributes to a wide aromatic range. Once the final wine has been crafted, the long and exceptional maturing process of Vega Sicilia Unico begins. The cellar master, Xavier Aussas, follows the development of the wine in barrel for at least seven years! His work requires great patience, and consists of maturing the wine—for various periods— first in new barrels of French oak, then in older American oak barrels, then in new American oak barrels, and then again in French barrels. Xavier is the unchallenged master of this meticulous process. After such a treatment, any other wine would

become dull and lifeless; but it is quite the opposite for Unico.

FINISHED A DECADE AFTER HARVEST

After the long process of barrel maturation, the wine is bottled. But to refine it further and achieve complete balance, it will remain at the winery for another four years. Only then is it put on the market, and the few privileged customers who receive it are on a long waiting list. A wine delivered 10 years— at least—after the harvest likely breaks all records. It is said that even the king of Spain has to wait patiently for it. At the most prestigious wine merchants in the world, Vega Sicilia Unico secures stratospheric prices. And to reach its peak of perfection, the wine must remain in the cellar for several more years. Keeping it for even another 50 years wouldn't be a problem—quite the contrary.

TASTING AND ENJOYING

This is a wine for a great occasion, and it requires tremendous care in its presentation. To appreciate its wide aromatic palate to the full, it should be decanted an hour before it is served at 64°F (18°C). Poured into tulip-shaped glasses, its deep purple color seduces people right away. Turned slowly in the glass, it offers the entire array of its bouquet, holding nothing back: first black fruit, preserved or macerated, then woody-smoky spices and gamey and floral notes, then touches of undergrowth, and finally, subtly, the scent of amber. When finally savoring the wine in your mouth, there is the flavor of ripe fruit, textured tannins that are in a class of their own, and a constant freshness, welcome and particularly sensuous. It's an opulent wine, beautifully supple, with a soft and infinite finish. It's undoubtedly an aristocrat among wines— a Spanish prince.

CAMPO DE BORJA DO

The region of Aragon is a vast expanse crossed by the almost never-ending Ebro River. The appellation Campo de Borja, situated at the southern edge of the Navarra DO, derives its name from *campo*, which means the area surrounding the old city of Borja. It accurately reflects the quality and nobility of the wines produced from its *terroirs*. The average altitude of most vineyards here is 1,600 ft (500 m). The landscape is made up of long strips of land punctuated by hills with gentle slopes.

> **GRAPE VARIETIES** Garnacha (Grenache), Tempranillo, Mazuelo, Cabernet Sauvignon, Merlot, and Syrah for reds and rosés; Maccabeu, Moscatel, and Chardonnay for whites.

> **SOIL** Limestone, fairly brownish in color, with touches of ferrous oxide.

> **STYLE** The appellation's reputation is based largely on its red wines, mainly from Grenache. Their color is suffused with purplish, even opaque, tints. On the nose, the aromas develop notes of macerated black fruit (blackberry, bilberry, fig) over a firm structure that is pleasing to the palate. The tannins progress to a supple, velvety texture. The (far fewer) white wines and the rosés are characterized by fresh aromas and invigorating, crisp textures.

Color:
White, rosé, and red.

Serving temperature:
46 to 50°F (8 to 10°C) for whites and rosés;
61°F (16°C) for reds.

Ageing potential:
3 to 5 years for dry whites;
7 to 10 years for sweet and "mellow" whites;
7 to 20 years for reds.

PRIORAT DOC

This is the queen of Catalan appellations. Twenty years ago, Priorat wines sold in wine-boxes for barely a dollar (equivalent) per liter; the best wines now exceed $500 a bottle. The DOC has undergone a complete transformation and now offers wines of great character. They have "rewritten" their *terroir*. White and red wines with *crianza* on the label are matured for at least six months in oak barrels; the *gran reservas* spend a minimum of 24 months in barrel and three years in bottle before going on the market.

> **GRAPE VARIETIES** Grenache Blanc, Maccabeu, Parellada, Chenin Blanc, Viognier, and Pedro Ximénez for whites; Cariñena, Garnacha (Grenache), Cabernet Sauvignon, Merlot, Pinot Noir, Syrah, and Tempranillo for reds.

> **SOIL** The landscape is a succession of terraces and plateaus at altitudes of up to almost 3,000 ft (900 m), on soils comprised of shale and granite.

> **STYLE** Dry whites, still produced in limited quantities, are a typical expression of the Grenache Blanc and a true marker of *terroir*. The sweet whites—those in the *rancio* style—are truly irresistible but of lesser importance in terms of production. The reds are purple in color, with aromas of redcurrant jam, blackberries, and spices. They rest on firm tannins nuanced by flavors of black fruit and pencil lead.

Color:
White and red.

Serving temperatures:
50 to 54°F (10 to 12°C) for both dry and sweet whites;
61°F (16°C) for reds.

Ageing potential:
3 to 5 years for dry whites;
7 to 10 years for sweet and rancio whites;
7 to 20 years for reds.

Ten top Spanish wineries

- **Agustí Torelló** – Cava DO
- **Bodegas Chivite** – Navarra DO
- **Bodegas Aalto** – Ribera del Duero DO
- **Bodega Álvaro Palacios** – Priorat DOC
- **Bodegas Arzuaga** – Ribera del Duero DO
- **Bodegas Numanthia-Termes** – Toro DO
- **Bodegas San Roman** – Toro DO
- **Bodegas Vega Sicilia** – Ribera del Duero DO
- **Clos Mogador** – Priorat DOC
- **Vall Llach** – Priorat DOC

PENEDÈS DO

Spread across more than 75,000 acres (30,000 ha), this symbolic appellation covers a large part of Catalonia and includes several subzones: Alt Penedès, Baix Penedès, and Garraf. The vast extent of the area means that several different styles of wine can be produced here.

> **GRAPE VARIETIES** Maccabeu, Parellada, Xarel-lo, Moscatel, Chardonnay, Sauvignon Blanc, Gewurztraminer, Riesling, and Chenin Blanc for white wines; Tempranillo, Grenache, Cariñena, Monastrell, Cabernet Sauvignon, Merlot, Pinot Noir, and Syrah for reds and rosés.

> **SOIL** This large wine-producing area and its different types of landscape include a number of soils: at altitude, the predominant limestone guarantees wines with a remarkable freshness; there are also chalk soils and granite; the plain is dominated by a mixture of sand and clay.

> **STYLE** White wines are based on several grape varieties—the presence of international varieties such as Chardonnay or Sauvignon Blanc means that all styles of wine can be produced here, even the most oaky. On the palate, the aromatic range and the textures will, therefore, all be different. As for the reds, they often go through expertly controlled maturation that gives the wines a deep color and a bouquet of black fruit (plum, blackcurrant) and spice powder. The tannic composition varies according to the blending of the varieties, but is always relatively supple and velvety.

Color:
White, rosé, and red.

Serving temperature:
46 to 50°F (8 to 10°C) for whites and rosés;
61°F (16°C) for reds.

Ageing potential:
1 to 3 years for rosés;
3 to 10 years for dry whites;
7 to 10 years for reds.

VALDEPEÑAS DO

Sheltered by the Toledo Mountains and the Sierra de Segura, this DO covers more than 75,000 acres (30,000 ha). The wines are made in all three colors, generally using classic techniques that are true to the appellation.

> **GRAPE VARIETIES** Airén and Maccabeu for whites; Cencibel, Grenache, and Cabernet Sauvignon for reds and rosés.

> **SOIL** Val de peñas means "valley of the stones," so it is easy to imagine the arid, barren landscape on which the vines are planted. The most promising plots in this appellation are made up of chalk-and-limestone soils.

> **STYLE** The white wines are based on the duo Airén and Maccabeu. The former brings freshness and vivacity, while the latter is appreciated for its abundant and fleshy mouth-feel, revealing a sumptuous minerality. The red wines are made mostly from the purely Spanish variety Cencibel, which serves up some fine surprises for lovers of deep, concentrated, and velvety wines.

Color:
White, rosé, and red.

Serving temperature:
46 to 50°F (8 to 10°C) for whites and rosés;
61°F (16°C) for reds.

Ageing potential:
3 to 5 years for dry whites and rosés;
8 to 10 years for reds.

JUMILLA DO

Located in southeastern Spain, in the Levant, Jumilla extends over more than 100,000 acres (40,000 ha). The landscape in certain zones looks almost lunar—arid and even baked by long hours of intense sun.

> **GRAPE VARIETIES** Airén, Maccabeu, Moscatel, Malvasia, and Pedro Ximénez for white wines; Monastrell, Garnacha (Grenache), Tempranillo, Cabernet Sauvignon, Merlot, and Syrah for the red wines.

> **SOIL** A mix of stones and chalk, it ensures a good supply of trace elements and mineral salts: ideal conditions for the growth of vines.

> **STYLE** The whites and rosés are produced to show off the aromatic qualities of their different grape varieties; they are generous and invigorating on the palate. But the most interesting wines are the reds made from Monastrell (Mourvèdre) grapes left to desiccate on the vine. Wineries first began making them, with great success, at the beginning of the 20th century. These purple-red, dark wines are bursting with aromas of cooked fruit (raspberry, plum, figs) allied with a subtle palate, all within an ideally balanced whole. The sweetness remains harmonious, never heavy.

Color:
White, red, and rosé.

Serving temperature:
46 to 50°F (8 to 10°C) for whites and rosés;
59°F (15°C) for reds.

Ageing potential:
3 to 5 years for dry whites and rosés;
7 to 30 years for reds.

YECLA DO

This southern appellation has achieved a real turnaround in quality with its latest vintages. With a much more limited yield—relative to the area cultivated—than neighboring Jumilla DO, Yecla comprises two zones: Campo Arriba and Campo Abajo. Both produce wines that are greatly appreciated for their maturity.

> **GRAPE VARIETIES** Airén, Maccabeu, Merseguera, and Sauvignon Blanc for the whites; Monastrell (synonymous with Mourvèdre, and with a presence of at least 75 percent in the blends), Tempranillo, Garnacha (Grenache,) Cabernet Sauvignon, Merlot, and Syrah for the reds and rosés.

> **SOIL** Like several other appellations in southern Spain, Yecla rests on chalk-and-limestone soil, which gives the wines great freshness and balance.

> **STYLE** The whites and rosés are always very expressive, bringing out textures that are crisp, invigorating, and redolent of sunshine. The reds always have an intense color, underlined by tinges of dark red and crimson. The wines are heavy, powerful, well supported by generous tannins; and the aromas range through spicy, chocolaty, and slightly balsamic.

Color:
White, rosé, and red.

Serving temperature:
46 to 50°F (8 to 10°C) for whites and rosés;
61°F (16°C) for reds.

Ageing potential:
3 to 5 years for dry whites and rosés;
3 to 10 years for reds.

JEREZ DOC

The southern tip of Spain, and the region of Andalusia, is anchored by the Jerez (or Xérès or Sherry) appellation. A DOC since 1933, it has been famous for centuries—courtesy of the English, who have long enjoyed its character. The Palomino grape variety, which on other *terroirs* produces wine with a narrow aromatic range and little interest, seems to have found ideal conditions here.

> **GRAPE VARIETIES** Two varieties stand out. The first, Palomino Fino, also called Palomino Blanco or Listan, represents 90 percent of the growing area. The second, Pedro Ximénez, called "PX" for short, is involved mostly in the production of sweet wines.

> **SOIL** Mainly chalky soils and subsoils (a *terroir* known as *albariza*) dominate in this region. This base material is one of the qualifying criteria for the great wines of Jerez. It is expressed in the wine as a distinct mineral quality, and it presents an aromatic palate with real tactile sensation.

> **STYLE** The complexity and diversity of this appellation flows from a unique style of production. It creates both the driest and most lively wines, such as *fino* and *manzanilla*, as well as almost syrupy wines that are rich in tertiary aromas, such as *oloroso* and cream. There are two main families of sherry wines: the dry and light *finos* and the deeper colored and stronger *olorosos*. The *finos* are dependent on the *flor* process (*see* p.74), but the *olorosos* are not. The rare *palo cortados* are a hybrid of the two.

- Finos. These are very dry and aromatic wines (with notes of walnut, almonds, leather); and their alcohol content is lower than that of *olorosos*. They are consumed very young. There are several categories according to the location and length of ageing, and final character: *manzanilla*, *manzanilla pasada*, *fino*, and *amontillado*.

- Olorosos. These differ from *finos* in their higher alcohol content (between 16 and 18% ABV), and especially in the length of time they are matured in barrel. Their aromatic range includes dried fruit (fig), malt, roasted coffee, and chocolate, but also leather and more balsamic nuances. The categories are: *dry*, *cream*, and *pale cream*. Separate sweet styles include *moscatel* and *Pedro Ximénez*.

Color:
White.

Serving temperature:
46 to 54°F (8 to 12°C) for finos;
57°F (14°C) for olorosos.

Ageing potential:
1 to 3 years for finos;
7 to 100 years for olorosos.

PLA Í LLEVANT DO

This appellation, recent in terms of classification, is located on the island of Majorca. Within its 625 acres (250 ha), a very small area for Spain, there are nine producers who grow their vines in a fine climate of abundant sunshine and sea air. The result is harvests of great quality. Note that a choice of grapes based on native varieties captures all the richness of the island.

> **GRAPE VARIETIES** Prensal, Moscatel, Maccabeu, Parellada, and Chardonnay for the white wines; Callet, Fogoneu, Tempranillo, Manto Negro, Monastrell, Cabernet Sauvignon, and Merlot for the reds and rosés.

> **SOIL** The vines are planted on limestone terrain strewn with lumps of chalk, ensuring ideal water retention.

> **STYLE** Muscat of Alexandria, with its small grapes, seems to have found the perfect *terroir* in which to grow here. Generally dried before use, this grape variety yields wines with floral scents of lavender and mimosa, going on to deliver a vigorous and aromatic palate. The rosé wines are worth a close look. They catch the eye with pronounced color, then develop aromatic touches of crystalized orange, new leather, and a hint of smokiness. On the palate, fleshiness and opulence are very evident. All the generosity of

wines from the Mediterranean basin can be found in the reds here. Made mostly from Callet and Tempranillo, they attract attention with their dark red color and offer aromas of blackberry jam on an entrancing chocolate base. The textures on the palate are very apparent thanks to solid and well-ripened tannins.

Color:
White, rosé, and red.

Serving temperature:
46 to 50°F (8 to 10°C) for whites and rosés;
59°F (15°C) for reds.

Ageing potential:
3 to 5 years for whites, rosés, and reds.

CAVA DO

Nicknamed "Champaña" by the Spaniards, the best-known sparkling wines from the Iberian peninsula take their name from the word *cava*, which means 'cave' or 'cellar' in Catalan. Cava's origins are much later than those of Champagne. The first written records date to 1872, when José Raventos—of the famous Cordoníu winery—returned from a journey to Champagne. He decided to produce a local equivalent of the famous sparkling wine using native grape varieties. After much research and many attempts, he finally managed to create a satisfactory version at his San Sadurni d'Anoia winery. Cava is made principally in Catalonia, but it also can be produced in Aragon, Estremadura, Rioja, Navarra, the Basque country, and in Valencia. It therefore covers an immense area (more than 87,500 acres/35,000 ha).

> **GRAPE VARIETIES** Chardonnay, Maccabeu, Malvasia, Parellada, and Xarel-lo for white wines; Garnacha (Grenache), Monastrell, Trepat, and Pinot Noir for rosés.

> **SOIL** The extensive winemaking area means there are many different types of soil. Even so, producers are almost unanimous in the belief that the best wines are produced from limestone or chalky soils that are capable of contributing the necessary minerality and maturity.

> **STYLE** Cavas all show the same scintillating colors, enlivened by strings of bubbles that rise to the surface. On the nose, aromas of lime tree, acacia, and verbena are clearly recognizable in the floral bouquet. These lead to touches of finely ripened yellow fruit, such as Mirabelle plums and greengages, and the whole is lightened by chalky hints. On the palate, the effect is of dynamic and lively effervescence. As they develop, these wines gain in fullness and subtlety. The final olfactory experience is one of rubbed pebbles, acacia honey, and juicy pears, which persist for as long as you like. Note that in 1986, Chardonnay became an authorized grape variety. It has an ever-greater presence in new blends, and

helps develop very delicate buttery aromas, as well as the *moelleux* of bubbles that is sought in good sparkling wines.

Color:
White and rosé.

Serving temperature:
46 to 54°F (8 to 12°C) according to the cuvée and the state of the wine's development.

Ageing potential:
3 to 15 years.

PORTUGAL

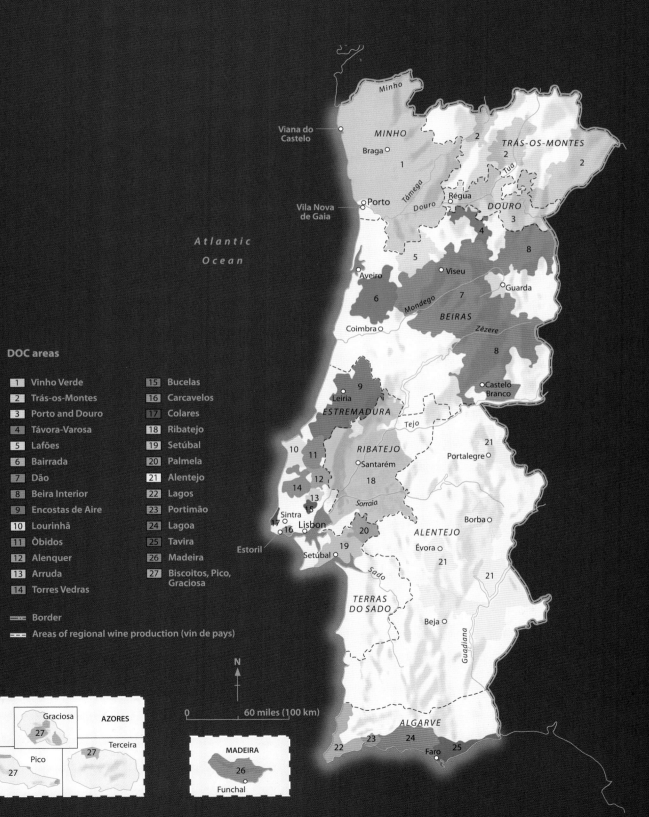

DOC areas

1	Vinho Verde
2	Trás-os-Montes
3	Porto and Douro
4	Távora-Varosa
5	Lafões
6	Bairrada
7	Dão
8	Beira Interior
9	Encostas de Aire
10	Lourinhã
11	Óbidos
12	Alenquer
13	Arruda
14	Torres Vedras
15	Bucelas
16	Carcavelos
17	Colares
18	Ribatejo
19	Setúbal
20	Palmela
21	Alentejo
22	Lagos
23	Portimão
24	Lagoa
25	Tavira
26	Madeira
27	Biscoitos, Pico, Graciosa

▭▭ Border

▬▬ Areas of regional wine production (vin de pays)

AZORES

Graciosa — **27**

Terceira — **27**

Pico — **27**

MADEIRA

26

Funchal

0   60 miles (100 km)

N

Minho

Viana do Castelo

MINHO

Braga

1

2

TRÁS-OS-MONTES

2

Tua

2

Porto

Vila Nova de Gaia

Tâmega

Douro

Régua

DOURO

2

3

4

8

Aveiro

5

Viseu

Guarda

6

Mondego

7

BEIRAS

Coimbra

Zêzere

8

Castelo Branco

9

Leiria

ESTREMADURA

Tejo

21

Portalegre

10

11

RIBATEJO

Santarém

18

12

14

13

Sorraia

15

Sintra

17

Lisbon

16

Estoril

19

Setúbal

20

ALENTEJO

Évora

21

Borba

Sado

TERRAS DO SADO

Beja

Guadiana

21

ALGARVE

22

23

24

Faro

25

Atlantic Ocean

PORTUGAL

Set on the western edge of Europe, Portugal offers a wide variety of wine styles from its relatively narrow territory. Renowned for centuries for the fortified wines port and Madeira, it now also produces some fine dry reds and increasingly attractive white wines.

Long history

PORT INDUSTRY. Portuguese vineyards date back to antiquity, but it is rather more recently that its wines have acquired a degree of fame. Trade links with England began in the 12th century, and they were the main engine of development for Portugal's wine industry. This long collaboration most famously gave birth to port during the 18th century— a dark red wine from the Douro Valley, fortified to withstand long sea voyages. The Douro region adopted extensive legislation as early as 1756, making it the world's first appellation of origin, 179 years before the introduction of the AOC system in France. But Portugal's slow economic growth and political isolation, until the 1974 revolution, meant that its viticultural practices were virtually frozen in time. This allowed Portugal to retain almost intact its tremendous wealth of local varieties.

RECENT PROGRESS. Since Portugal's admission to the European Union in 1986, an extraordinary energy has been driving many of its producers—from large historic houses, which have always played a leading role, to cooperatives, often fully modernized, to private domains (*quintas*), which have multiplied since the 1990s. Some vineyards have been replanted, and others have been newly established. Some regions previously without a great wine tradition, such as Alentejo, have become places of experimentation. However, there is still a contrast between the old family estates operating according to past practices and domains at the forefront of progress; though the rapid spread of new technology goes a long way to reducing the gap.

PORTUGAL STATISTICS

Vineyard area: 600,000 acres (237,000 ha)
Production: 83.3 million cases (7.5 million hl)
Reds and rosés: 69%
Whites: 31%

(Instituto do Vinho e da Vinha, OIV, 2007

Topography and climate: a country of contrasts

Portugal is a land of contrasts—some very marked—and they are reflected in the wines. Relative to its total land area, the total Portuguese vineyard area is vast: 600,000 acres (237,000 ha) spread throughout the country, except for the high mountain areas in the center and northeast.

Relatively narrow from east to west, Portugal has 380 miles (600 km) of coastline. The Atlantic Ocean exerts a strong

> An estate in the Douro Valley.

influence over the coastal regions, with fairly abundant rainfall, temperatures cooled by sea breezes, and lush vegetation, especially in the north. This influence fades rapidly toward the east. In the north, mountain ranges halt the advance of moist sea air and shelter an arid landscape with extreme temperatures in both summer and winter.

South of the Tagus River, which cuts the country in half, the terrain flattens, giving way to vast plains. They are occasionally punctuated by low hills, but all are battered in summer by relentless sun and drought.

> Every year, hundreds of pickers harvest grapes on the sunny slopes overlooking the Douro River.

Northern regions

Portugal's northern vineyards extend from the Douro Valley up to the north and northeast border with Spain. This is where the two largest and most renowned appellations are located: Vinho Verde and Porto, producing wines in entirely different styles.

VINHO VERDE. The vineyards of Vinho Verde form a vast amphitheater looking out toward the Atlantic. This densely populated region is wet, with lush vegetation, and is known mainly for its slightly sparkling, dry, light white wines made from a wide variety of local grapes.

PORT AND DOURO. Toward the east, the green countryside slowly gives way to an austere, arid landscape in the central mountains. This is where the Douro and port vineyards are located. Both DOCs share the same area, which follows the Douro River and its tributaries from the Spanish border to the outskirts of the city of Resende, about 60 miles (100 km) inland. The rivers have cut deep canyons into the mountain schist. Vines are planted in hillside plots and are supported either by traditional stone walls or arranged in sloping terraces of more recent construction (*patamares*). Port, fortified by the addition of grape spirit, is a powerful, warm, and spicy wine. It is born out of these spectacular stony vineyards, which are subjected to a harsh, dry climate that is particularly hot in summer. Since the 1990s, this region has also been successfully producing dry red wines bearing the Douro DOC, and made with the same grapes as port.

TRAS-OS-MONTES. The vineyards of this recent DOC (2006), at the northeastern end of the country, are part of the vast Transmontano Vinho Regional (VR) area. Production is dominated by cooperatives.

Central regions

The wine regions between the Douro and the Tagus rivers account for more than 40 percent of the country's production, half of which is table wine. Including some famous DOCs, this area is divided into three Vinho Regional zones—Beiras in the north, Ribatejano and Estremadura in the southwest—all permitting the planting of international varieties alongside local ones.

BAIRRADA. This humid, rural area is sandwiched between the coast and the granite hills that border the Dão DOC to the east. Famous during the 18th century, the region has rediscovered its potential through the work of some visionary producers including Luis Pato (whose wines sell under the Beiras Vinho Regional appellation). The soils are mostly clay-and-limestone, and the main grape variety, Baga, gives local red wines a powerful and structured character. They often need time to shed the austerity they display in their youth.

DÃO. Set adjacent to Bairrada, this DOC is undergoing a revolution since local cooperatives lost (in 1989) their monopoly on wine production for the entire appellation. Today, it offers some of the country's most successful red wines, along with some generous and compelling whites. The vineyards grow on a granitic plateau, sheltered from the influence of the Atlantic by the Serra do Caramulo mountains. The style of wine ranges from soft to powerful and structured.

RIBATEJO. The Ribatejo (or Tejo) region, crossed by the Tagus River, continues to produce mainly table wines and Vinho Regional (under the appellation Ribatejano), including some good Cabernet Sauvignon and Syrah. The Ribatejo DOC amounts to less than 10 percent of regional production, but showcases the interesting local varieties.

Four categories

In Portugal, brand loyalty is very strong. The Portuguese consumer will choose a brand name or a trusted producer over that of an appellation of origin. Even so, wine legislation has had to comply with European requirements, and it's now based around four categories: DOC (Denominação de Origem Controlada), IPR (Indicação de Proveniência Regulamentada), although their numbers are dwindling, Vinho Regional ("vin de pays"), and Vinho de Mesa (table wine). This classification structure is intended to be a scale of quality, but many of the best producers prefer to use the Vinho Regional tier, since it allows them greater freedoms, especially in their choice of grape varieties.

ESTREMADURA. These vineyards extend for about 20 miles (30 km) along the coast north of Lisbon. Most of the area (62,500 acres/25,000 ha) is devoted to ordinary wine production, and the nine DOCs of the region amount to scarcely five percent of total production. Most are struggling to emerge, and some historic DOCs on the outskirts of Lisbon, like Carcavelos and Colares, are threatened by the capital city's extension. Bucelas, north of Lisbon, could suffer the same fate, but the current fashion for its fresh and fragrant whites from local variety Arinto is protecting it for now.

Southern regions and islands

SETÚBAL PENINSULA. Along with vineyards on the actual Setúbal Peninsula, this region also includes those situated south of the Sado Estuary. The peninsula enjoys a relatively mild oceanic climate, while the vineyards east of Setúbal, in the fertile plain of the Sado River, are subject to a much more harsh climate. There are only two DOCs: Palmela, planted mainly with Castelão, a red grape known locally as Periquita, yielding soft and fruity wines; and Setúbal, renowned for its sweet white wines from Moscatel de Setúbal. Half of the wines are now labeled Terras do Sado Vinho Regional, as this appellation allows greater freedom of grape variety choice. The white wines, from local or international varieties, have improved dramatically in the past 10 years. For the red wines, Castelão is still the main variety, but it is becoming increasingly challenged by Cabernet Sauvignon, Syrah, Aragonês, and Touriga Nacional.

ALENTEJO AND THE ALGARVE. The Alentejo is a vast, sparsely populated area covering nearly a third of Portugal. This is a land of vast agricultural estates, and it is subject to a very hot and dry climate with scorching summers. It used to

> Red ports are classified into two groups, ruby and tawny. The production of white ports remains marginal.

Port vinification

Grapes are first crushed underfoot in traditional stone vats called lagares, or by conventional mechanical means. During fermentation, the must is fortified by the addition of about 10 percent grape spirit to halt the yeast fermentation and to preserve some of the natural grape sugars. Independent producers who make wine only from their own quinta (domain) mature the wine at their estate. But the great houses of Porto have a very different tradition. In the spring following the harvest, the wines are transported to Vila Nova de Gaia, at the mouth of the Douro, across from Porto, where they will age in wooden containers of different sizes: tuns, the traditional pipes (pipas, about 140 gal/630 l), or barrels. Here, away from the summer heat of the Douro Valley, the damp cellars of the great port producers age the wine slowly. The length of maturation is quite variable, and depends on the style of wine desired (see p. 396).

be best known for its cork production, but it is now recognized for its powerful and fleshy red and white wines, made with the modern consumer in mind. The production is divided between Alentejano Vinho Regional and Alentejo DOC—with eight sub-regions, all with their own DOCs. Although local cooperatives still play an important role, the vitality of the Alentejo is due mostly to private investors, large and small, who have contributed to the current success of its wines. The small vineyards of the Algarve (10,000 acres/2,500 ha), on the southern tip of Portugal, are being encroached by the development of new tourism infrastructure, but the domains have been modernized and produce above all soft and fruity red wines from Castelão, Negra Mole, or Syrah.

ISLAND VINEYARDS. The vineyards of the Azores and Madeira are small in size, but Madeira has given its name to an historic and famous fortified wine, unique in its vinification process and for its extraordinarily long ageing capability (*see box on following page*).

Portuguese grapes: great riches

Long isolated and therefore oblivious to international taste, Portugal has preserved its great range of grape varieties.

DID YOU KNOW...?

Portugal has more than a third of the world's cork-oak forests. Seventy percent are in the Alentejo, the largest cork-producing region on earth.

> A vineyard in Alentejo, southern Portugal, where the vines grow in arid conditions.

Portugal's entry into the European Union, along with new international interest in Portuguese wine, was the trigger for a much-needed classification of its varieties. As many as 341 have been documented, including many varieties not found outside the country. While some international varieties do yield excellent results here (Shiraz, Cabernet Sauvignon, and Chardonnay), it is the native varieties that make Portuguese wines so special.

RED GRAPES. Touriga Nacional is the great red Portuguese grape variety, and it's currently very much in vogue. Originally from Dão, it frequently forms the backbone of port wines and the dry reds of the Douro; but it has proved its worth in other regions, such as the Alentejo and Ribatejo. It presents concentrated, tannic, and intense wines. The widely planted Spanish Tempranillo (known here as Tinta Roriz or Aragonês) makes very powerful wines, though often more supple than those from Touriga Nacional. Baga is the great grape of Bairrada. Hardy and late maturing, it produces very dark, structured, tannic wines with acidity for long ageing. Trincadeira thrives in the hot, dry soils of the Alentejo in the south, and on the hillsides of the Douro (where it is known as Tinta Amarela). When fully ripe, it produces dark and spicy wines for long ageing. Castelão (or Periquita) is one of the most widely planted red varieties, especially in the south, and it's appreciated for its fruity and relatively fresh wines.

WHITE GRAPES. Alvarinho and to a lesser degree Loureiro are highly prized in the region of Vinho Verde, where they make fresh and aromatic wines. Bical offers fresh, intense aromas, and is one of the star varieties in the still and sparkling wines of Bairrada. It is also found in the Dão appellation, alongside the powerful and remarkable Encruzado, one of the most promising white grapes. Arinto grows in most wine regions, but is at its best in the Bucelas DOC, where it is renowned for fresh and lemony wines. Fernão Pires, the most widely planted white variety (especially in the central and southern parts of the country), produces well-rounded, charming, and rather warming wines.

Madeira, unchanged

The wine industry on this Portuguese island, 400 miles (640 km) off the coast of Morocco, had its heyday during the 18th century, when its fortified wines graced the tables of royalty. Powdery mildew and phylloxera in the 19th century, the loss of its traditional markets, and the use of mediocre grape varieties have all gradually tarnished its reputation, and Madeira eventually found its main outlet reduced to the kitchen! Today, just 1,000 acres (400 ha) of vineyards are spread over a patchwork of small plots. But some historic houses still carry on the tradition of the great Madeiras—wines fortified to varying degrees of sweetness, whose unique character reflects their unusual ageing. The wines are heated to 115°F (45°C) in stainless steel tanks for three months (or for two years in sun-baked lofts). The best (vintage or frasqueira) wines are from a single harvest and spend a minimum of 20 years ageing in cask. These are powerful wines, both warm and fresh. They have a bouquet of rare complexity—with notes of caramel, leather, candied fruit, dried fruit, iodine, plus balsamic notes—and extraordinary longevity.

The best-known Portuguese wines

Portugal's wine revolution is now in full swing, and great producers are emerging in all regions, whether DOC or Vinho Regional.

PORTO DOC

This DOC is reserved for the fortified red and white wines produced within a defined area along the Douro Valley in northern Portugal. It extends over 625,000 acres (250,000 ha), but only 115,000 acres (45,000 ha) are actually planted. There are three sub-regions: Baixa Corgo in the west; Cima Corgo, the historic heart; which was first regulated in 1756; and Douro Superior in the east. The Porto appellation is the world's most strictly controlled—at every stage of production, from a meticulous classification of individual vineyards to particularly demanding certification tastings. The wines take their character both from local geographic conditions—schist soils, a particularly hot and dry climate during the ripening season, well-adapted grape varieties—and the vinification and maturation techniques that ultimately shape the diversity of styles of port.

> **GRAPE VARIETIES** Touriga Nacional, Tinto Cão, Tinta Roriz, Tinta Barroca, and Touriga Franca for reds. Sercial (Esgana Cão), Folgasão, Verdelho, Malvasia, Rabigato, Viosinho, and Gouveio for whites.

> **SOIL** Port can only be produced from the schist soils of the Douro Valley and its tributaries.

> **STYLE** Red ports are sweet, powerful, and intense. They fill the palate with a gentle warmth and provide a rare sensation of fullness. There are two main types of red port.

- Tawny ports. These are aged in barrel for a long period. Under the influence of a controlled oxidation, the color evolves (tawny means "reddish" or "amber") and powerful tertiary aromas (coffee, nuts, dried fruit, fig, cedar) become sharper and increasingly complex over time. Most tawny ports are produced by blending wines of different vintages, whose average age should be the minimum required by law. This category includes, in order of quality: tawny (minimum three years in oak); tawny reserve (seven years); and tawny with an indication of age (10, 20, 30, or 40 years). The colheitas (seven years minimum) are vintage tawny ports, meaning from a single year, as shown on the label.

- Ruby ports. These wines are oak-aged for a much shorter period than the tawny ports, and they keep their youthful "ruby" color. Young ruby ports are bright, and intense with aromas of ripe red and black fruit, as well as spicy notes. On the palate, the most ambitious retain a tannic structure that can be very powerful in the best wines. Ruby and ruby reserve are young and exuberant wines, intensely fruity with relatively little tannin. Late bottled vintage (LBV) are from a single vintage, bottled four to six years after harvest. They are more supple than the final category, vintage. Vintage port is a wine from an exceptional year and is bottled two to three years after harvest. Thanks to their intensity and tannic structure, LBVs and,

even more so, vintage ports can be kept for several decades. Vintage ports are traded on international markets in the same way as great Bordeaux and Burgundies.

- There is also a very limited production of white port, made solely from white varieties and aged in wood. They may be semi-dry or sweet, and are generally soft and round, but often lacking the complexity of red ports.

> **LEADING PRODUCERS** Barros, Burmester, Churchill, Croft, Dow, Fonseca, Gould Campbell, Ferreira, Graham, Niepoort, Quinta do Crasto, Quinta do Noval, Quinta do Vale, D. Maria Ramos Pinto, Andresen, Taylor Fladgate, Warre's.

Color:
White and red.

Serving temperature:
52 to 57°F (11 to 14°C) for whites;
59 to 63°F (15 to 17°C) for reds.

Ageing potential:
Whites are best consumed young;
up to 50 years for the reds.

DOURO DOC

This appellation covers the same area of production as Porto DOC (see opposite). Red and white table wines have always been produced in the Douro for local consumption, but they were made either from excess crop for port, or from lower-quality grapes. A few port houses, such as Ferreira (from the 1950s with their *cuvée* Barca Velha) or, later, Quinta do Crasto, saw the potential of the area for high quality dry red wines. So the region has rapidly devloped to become a benchmark for this type of wine, which increasingly comes from dedicated vineyards. The wines of Douro DOC can be made with all the grape varieties permitted for port, though certain varieties dominate.

> **GRAPE VARIETIES** Touriga Nacional, Tinto Cão, Tinta Roriz, Tinta Barroca, Touriga Franca, Trincadeira, and Souzão for reds; Malvasia, Rabigato, Viosinho, and Gouveio for whites.

> **SOIL** Schist.

> **STYLE** Red wines (about 80 percent of production) come in a variety of styles. They are usually deep in color, with intense aromas of very ripe red and black fruit, plum, and flint or slate-like mineral notes. They are powerful and tannic on the palate, sometimes with a lovely mineral freshness. They are well able to support lengthy ageing in wooden barrels. The white wines are supple and aromatic, the best displaying a remarkable balance with surprising freshness and a very reasonable alcohol level.

> **LEADING PRODUCERS** Alves de Sousa, Barca Velha, Quinta do Côtto, Quinta do Crasto, Quinta do Fojo, Quinta do Passadouro, Quinta de la Rosa, Quinta de Roriz, Quinta do Vale D. Maria, Quinta do Vallado, Niepoort, Sogrape, Ramos Pinto, Wine and Soul, Prats, and Symington.

Color:
White and red.

Serving temperature:
48 to 54°F (9 to 12°C) for whites;
57 to 61°F (14 to 16°C) for reds.

Ageing potential:
3 to 5 years for whites;
10 years or more for reds.

VINHO VERDE DOC

This old DOC (1908) in northwest Portugal is one of the largest and best known. Its name immediately evokes fresh and aromatic light white wines, best consumed young (hence the name Verde, meaning "green" in the sense of young or undeveloped). But the region also produces a similarly fresh red and some sparkling white and rosé. The DOC covers 95,000 acres (38,000 ha), bounded by the Minho River to the north, the Douro River to the south, and mountains in the east. Facing the Atlantic, the region receives about 47 inches (1,200 mm) of rainfall per year. The lush vines are traditionally trained high, on trellises or pergolas, although the most recent plantings are trained low. The appellation has been divided into nine sub-regions according to their geographic and cultural aspects. The region of Moncao in the north is particularly renowned for its whites from the Alvarinho variety (Albariño in Spain).

> **GRAPE VARIETIES** Alvarinho, Arinto, Avesso, Azal, Batocera, Loureiro, and Trajadura for whites; Alvarelhão, Amaral, Borraçal, Espadeiro, Padeiro, Pedral, Rabo de Anho, and Vinhão for reds.

> **SOIL** Shallow, mainly granite, low in nutrients, and fairly acidic.

> **STYLE** The white wines are low in alcohol, vigorous, and aromatic with notes of green apple, citrus fruits, and white flowers. The sensation of freshness they provide is sometimes enhanced by a slight sparkle. The red wines are colorful, lively, and fruity, with mostly soft tannins.

> **LEADING PRODUCERS** Palácio da Brejoeira, Ponte de Lima, Quinta do Ameal, Quintas Melgaço, Reguengo of Melgaço, Sogrape, Casa de Vila Verde, Aveleda, Paço de Teixeiro.

Color:
White and red.

Serving temperature:
46 to 54°F (8 to12°C) for whites
57 to 59°F (14 to 15°C) for reds.

Ageing potential:
2 years for whites;
3 years for reds.

BAIRRADA DOC

Created in 1979, this DOC is situated in the Beiras region, between the Atlantic coast and the eastern hills that mark the border with Dão. The climate is mild and particularly wet (up to 63 inches/1,600 mm of rainfall per year), which unfortunately promotes the development of vine diseases. The vineyard area covers 30,000 acres (12,000 ha) intermingled with other crops. Red wines account for most of the production (70 percent); the main variety, Baga, must comprise at least 50 percent of the blend. The quality of the DOC's dry whites has risen sharply recently, and the region has retained a tradition of sparkling winemaking notably using Arinto. Such star producers as Luis Pato choose to produce wines under the Beiras Vinho Regional appellation.

> **GRAPE VARIETIES** Baga, Alfrocheiro, Camarate, Castelao, Jaen, Touriga Nacional, Aragones, Cabernet Sauvignon, and Merlot for reds; Fernão Pires, Arinto, Cercial, and Chardonnay for whites.

> **SOIL** Clay-limestone and sandy; fairly fertile and heavy.

> **STYLE** The red wines are austere in their youth—particularly tannic and crisp; so they need long ageing. When fully mature, the best display great complexity. A more modern style has recently emerged (better grape ripeness, destemming, etc.), and the wines have become more supple and rounded, ready to drink sooner. The white wines are fresh, aromatic (citrus fruit, white flowers, freshly mown grass), and well balanced, especially those from Arinto. Fernão Pires yields more rounded wines.

> **LEADING PRODUCERS** Caves Aliança, Casa de Saima, Caves São João, Luis Pato, Quinta de Baixo, Quinta do Poço do Lobo, Quinta da Rigodeira, Sidónio de Sousa, and Sogrape.

Color:
White and red.

Serving temperature:
48 to 54°F (9 to12°C) for whites;
59 to 63°F (15 to 17°C) for reds.

Ageing potential:
3 years for the whites;
10 years or more for reds.

DÃO DOC

This old DOC (1908), set in Beira Alta to the east of Bairrada, is named after the river that runs through it. The region is a granite plateau, with vineyards extending over 50,000 acres (20,000 ha) and planted at altitudes of 1,300 to 2,300 feet (400 to 700 m). The surrounding mountains, especially in the west, protect the area from oceanic influences. The climate is more continental with cold, wet winters and particularly hot, dry summers. Red wines (about 80 percent of total production) are dominated by Touriga Nacional and Tinta Roriz (Tempranillo). They are sometimes vinified as single varietals, but are often blended with other varieties such as Jaen (Mencia in Spain) or Alfrocheiro. The dry white wines and a few sparkling wines are mainly Encruzado, often blended with Bical, Cercial, or Malvasia fina.

> **GRAPE VARIETIES** Alfrocheiro, Alvarelhão, Tinta Roriz, Bastardo, Jaen, Rufete, Tinto Cão, Touriga Nacional, and Trincadeira for reds and rosés; Barcelo, Bical, Bercial, Encruzado, Malvasia Fina, Rabo de Ovelha, Terrantez, Uva Cão, and Verdelho for whites.

> **SOIL** Schist, sand, and granite.

> **STYLE** Today's clean, modern Dão wines have replaced the mediocre wines produced in the days dominated by cooperatives, whose monopoly was abolished in 1989. Among reds, the styles are diverse, but good Dãos display very ripe red and black fruit aromas with spice and vanilla (if aged in barrel), as well as floral notes. On the palate, they are clean, rich, well-structured, tannic, and ready for a few years' cellaring. Encruzado-based whites are aromatic (yellow fruit), substantial, fairly rich, and well-balanced. There also are light and aromatic rosés.

>**LEADING PRODUCERS:** Caves Aliança, Dão Sul, Quinta dos Carvalhais, Quinta das Maias, Quinta da Pellada, Quinta do Perdigão, Quinta dos Roques, and Quinta Saes.

Color:
White, red,
and rosé.

Serving temperature:
48 to 54°F (9 to12°C) for whites;
50 to 54°F (10 to 12°C) for rosés;
57 to 61°F (14 to 16°C) for reds.

Ageing potential:
1 year for rosés;
4 years for whites;
10 years for reds.

ALENTEJO DOC AND ALENTEJANO VINHO REGIONAL

Alentejo is a vast region in central and southern Portugal. Its vineyards cover only 55,000 acres (22,000 ha), but the wines have made remarkable progress in the past decade, thanks to the dynamism of its cooperatives and newly established producers. The region is divided into eight sub-regions: Reguengos, Borba, Redondo, Vidigueira, Évora, Granja-Amareleja, Portalegre, and Moura—soon to be followed by a ninth. Each of them can claim a specific DOC, but more than half the wines are labeled Alentejano Vinho Regional. Note that the DOC is Alentejo, but the Vinho Regional is Alentejano (*see* Quinta do Carmo label, right). The climate is particularly hot and dry. Lots of sunlight helps the grapes to ripen fully, but it also means irrigation is necessary and harvesting has to take place earlier than elsewhere, particularly for the whites.

> **GRAPE VARIETIES** Alicante Bouschet, Aragones, Cabernet Sauvignon, Moreto, Periquita, Syrah, Tinta Caiada, Touriga Nacional, and Trincadeira for reds; Antão Vaz, Arinto, Rabo de Ovelha, Roupeiro, and Fernão Pires for whites.

> **SOIL** Clay, sand, granite, and schist.

> **STYLE** In a region where more than 50 grape varieties are authorized (for Vinho Regional), styles necessarily vary. But the reds are characterized by their fullness, the ripeness of their fruit, and their warmth. Very pleasant in their youth, the more tannic reds can be kept for a few years. The whites also have volume, roundness, and power.

> **LEADING PRODUCERS** Adega Cooperativa de Borba, Adega Cooperativa de Portalegre, Adega Cooperativa de Redondo, Cortes de Cima, Quinta do Mouro, Herdade da Malhadinha Nova, Herdade do Mouchão, Sogrape, Quinta do Carmo, and Quinta do Monte d'Oiro.

Color:
Red and white.

Serving temperature:
48 to 54°F (9 to 12°C) for whites;
59 to 61°F (15 to 16°C) for reds.

Ageing potential:
4 years for whites;
10 years for reds.

Five favorite wines
from George Dos Santos

IMPORTER AND WINE MERCHANT (ANTIC WINE, PORTO PORTO PORTO).

- **Maria Gomes, Beiras Vinho Regional (Luis Pato).** A "quaffer" par excellence. A fresh, fruity, pure, and mineral white wine, at a very affordable price. Ideal with Mediterranean cuisine (seafood, shellfish, saffron, olive oil).

- **Loureiro Girosol, Vinho Verde (Niepoort).** All the purity of the Loureiro variety, bursting with soft and fresh citrus fruit, with a well-rounded finish. By one of the best producers in Portugal. A summer wine to share with friends.

- **Cuvée Ex æquo, Estremadura Vinho Regional (Bento).** Dense and concentrated wine with aromas of black fruit, smoked bacon, black olives, and elderberry. Grown in the sunshine of Estremadura, it is perfect with grilled meats like the local porco preto.

- **Vintage Port 2004 (Quinta do Noval).** A prestigious house at the top of its game with this vintage port that rewrites the rulebook—intense and imposing. Full and rich herb aromas, with a freshness that complements its power.

- **Vintage Port 2006 (Quinta do Vesuvio).** The taste of a legend. A huge wine, from century-old vines grown in an enclosed vineyard, which gives a unique feeling of both fullness and fresh unctuousness.

GERMANY

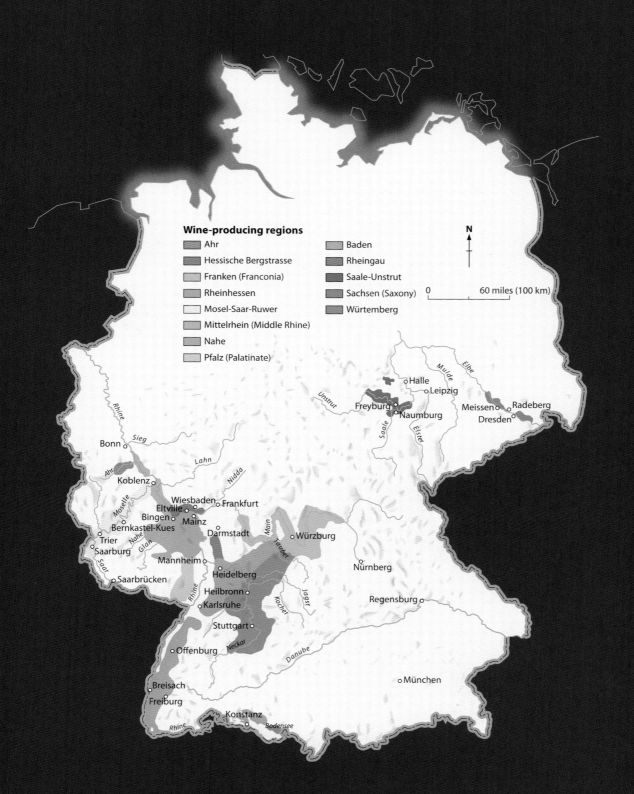

Wine-producing regions

- Ahr
- Hessische Bergstrasse
- Franken (Franconia)
- Rheinhessen
- Mosel-Saar-Ruwer
- Mittelrhein (Middle Rhine)
- Nahe
- Pfalz (Palatinate)
- Baden
- Rheingau
- Saale-Unstrut
- Sachsen (Saxony)
- Würtemberg

N

0   60 miles (100 km)

Bonn
Koblenz
Wiesbaden   Frankfurt
Eltville
Bingen   Mainz
Bernkastel-Kues
Trier   Darmstadt
Saarburg
Mannheim
Saarbrücken   Heidelberg
Heilbronn
Karlsruhe
Stuttgart
Offenburg
Breisach
Freiburg   Konstanz

Halle   Leipzig
Freyburg   Meissen   Radeberg
Naumburg   Dresden
Würzburg
Nürnberg
Regensburg
München

Rhine
Sieg
Lahn
Nidda
Moselle
Nahe
Glan
Saar
Rhine
Neckar
Kocher   Jagst
Tauber
Main
Danube
Bodensee
Rhine
Unstrut
Saale
Elster
Mulde   Elbe

GERMANY

The best German wines are among the finest in the world; and even though some very large volume wines may be disappointing, recent efforts by young winemakers are full of promise.

Vine cultivation

The earliest vines here were planted in the 3rd century BC, in the Ahr region; and viticulture had spread along the Rhine and Mosel by the 1st century BC. After the fall of the Roman Empire, no new vines were planted until the emperor Charlemagne came to power; but the foundation of numerous convents and abbeys during the Middle Ages did much to improve the quality of the wines. German wine production expanded between the 11th and the late 16th centuries, peaking at a cultivated area of 740,000 acres (300,000 ha); but war during the 17th century laid waste to a large proportion of the vines. The advent of phylloxera (1874), mildew, and oidium further reduced the area under cultivation to 247,000 acres (100,000 ha), and it is of a similar size today.

GERMANY STATISTICS

Vineyard area: 252,000 acres (102,000 ha)

Production: 115 million cases (10,365,000 hl)

Whites: 63%

Reds and rosés: 37%

(Statistisches Bundesamt, Deutscher Weinbauverband e.V., 2007)

Difficult conditions

German wines are produced in a climate of limited suitability for viticulture, and this may explain their often low alcohol content and acidity levels that at times can be high. Cold weather makes it difficult to achieve good levels of maturity in grapes, and the vagaries of the northern climate can negate the efforts of an entire year. Growers compensate for this handicap by planting vines on the least exposed sites.

With this said, climate change over the past few decades has been good news for German wine growers—a rise in average annual temperatures of nearly 3°F (2°C) has allowed them to achieve riper grapes and to plant red grape varieties, which were previously extremely rare in Germany.

> Hard at work among the vines in Meissen, Sachsen.

GLOSSARY OF GERMAN WINE TERMS

Words you may find on the label:

Grauburgunder: Pinot Gris

Halbtrocken: medium-dry

Eiswein: "ice wine"

Erzeugerabfüllung: estate-bottled

Grosses/Erstes Gewächs: grand/premier cru (first growth)

Schwarzriesling: Pinot Meunier

Spätburgunder: Pinot Noir

Spätlese: late harvest (although a wine with this label may be sweet or dry)

Süss: sweet (generally reserved for very sweet wines)

Trocken: dry

Weingut: estate

Weinkellerei: wine merchant/cellar

Weissburgunder: Pinot Blanc

Winzergenossenschaft: wine-producing cooperative

(See also Glossary, pp.494–503, for more German terms)

> Vineyards overlooking
the Rhine near the town of
Bacharach (Mittelrhein).

Along the rivers

Germany has 13 traditional wine-producing areas (*Anbaugebiete*, as described on pp.406–11), each of which are divided into districts (*Bereiche*). Most of these are located to the west and the south of the country and follow the curves of river valleys— even a glance at the distribution of the main growing areas is enough to demonstrate the importance of a location near a watercourse.

Baden's vineyards are never far from the Rhine. The Neckar and its tributaries wind through the hills of Württemberg before rejoining the Rhine at Mannheim; the Main, another Rhine tributary, shapes the vineyards of Franconia or Franken as it passes through them. The little region of Hessische-Bergstrasse meets the Rhine Valley north of Heidelberg, and the Rhine Palatinate or Pfalz stretches out along the other side of the river. Rheinhessen,

lying immediately to the north, is bordered to the east and north by the river, and the vineyards of the Rheingau are found on the east bank here.

The vineyards covering the northwest Rhine Valley combine to form a region known as the Mittelrhein or Middle Rhine. The Nahe, yet another tributary, has also given its name to a growing area. The Mosel, the area that has most gained a name for itself beyond Germany's borders, includes the vineyards along the banks of the Saar and the Ruwer. The beautiful little region of Ahr is not far from the furthest northern reaches of wine production in the west of the country. Then the region of Saale-Unstrut, in the east, takes its name from the two rivers that cross it. Finally, also in the east, Sachsen or Saxony's vineyards lie along the banks of the Elbe.

TRUE OR FALSE?

Most German white wines are sweet.

FALSE. This may have been true at one time, but today Germany produces a multitude of excellent medium-dry and dry wines. Improved selection of varieties and soils, combined with the climate change of the past few years, has allowed the production of riper grapes than in the past. Wine producers are no longer obliged to chaptalize, and fermentation now results in balanced dry and medium-dry wines.

Wide range of varieties

German researchers have been cross-breeding classic grape varieties since the end of the 19th century, with the aim of creating new strains more resistant to disease and capable of producing wines of character with better yields and higher sugar levels. These hybrids are today often planted alongside traditional varieties. A striking development here over the

DID YOU KNOW…?

Germany produces some of the best ice wines in the world? *Well-ripened grapes are harvested when vineyard temperatures dip to –10 °C, so the fruit will be at most –7 °C in the press. Cryoextraction (see p.62) is forbidden. The wines have an alcohol content of about 8% by volume, and their fine mineral content lends them great freshness and subtle aromas (dried apricots, citrus fruits, caramelized apples, horseradish, aniseed, candied ginger, honey). They can be laid down for decades.*

> Riesling grapes.

> Trollinger grapes.

past 15 years is the growth in red grapes (Pinot Noir, Cabernet Sauvignon), which now occupy 40 percent of the planted land.

CLASSIC WHITE VARIETIES. Riesling is the benchmark for all German wines. Capable of achieving great ripeness during Germany's sunny autumns, it produces wines in a number of different styles. It has been long planted across all the best sites, notably in the central Mosel (Mittelmosel) and the Rheingau. The grape once lost ground as various hybrid varieties were introduced, but its plantings have now stabilized. The decline of Sylvaner, another classic grape variety, has been much more significant. This variety is associated mainly with Franken, although the largest vineyards are in Rheinhessen. It produces dry wines that are concentrated and yet lively, with great ageing potential if the vineyards are well situated and the yields reasonable. Other key grapes include Weissburgunder (Pinot Blanc), Grauburgunder (Pinot Gris, sometimes known as Ruländer), and Chardonnay.

HYBRID WHITE GRAPES. Müller-Thurgau, the first hybrid to be created by researchers (*see* p.35), produces quality white wines as long as the yield is low. Scheurebe—the best of the hybrids, judged by wine quality—has been very successful in the Pfalz. This wine is establishing itself thanks to fine bouquet, judicious acidity, and real potential for laying down. Kerner is a variety prized for the consistency of its yields, producing wines of character with fruity and vegetal aromas (elderberry blossom and mown grass), as well as hints of honey and spices that are reminiscent of Riesling. Due to their sugar content, they are often considered "late harvest" wines, such as *spätlesen* or *auslesen*.

CLASSIC RED VARIETIES. The main varieties are Spätburgunder (Pinot Noir), which has tripled in acreage over 20 years, and Blauerportugieser, which produces light wines. Other reds under

cultivation include Trollinger, Schwarzriesling (Pinot Meunier), and Samrot (a mutation of Pinot Meunier).

HYBRID RED GRAPES. Dornfelder is a recent hybrid that has enjoyed remarkable success. The wines have a garnet red appearance and aromas of red fruits (blackberries, cherries, prunes) with notes of bitter chocolate on the palate and supple tannins. Cabernet Cubin, which is reminiscent of Cabernet Sauvignon, is generally used in conjunction with other red varieties; it produces good results when aged in barrels. Domina and Regent produce reds with hints of garnet and fruity aromas.

Private producers and cooperatives

Leaving aside the Baden-Württemberg state, the greatest share of the best wines are made by private domains, state holdings (Rheinland-Pfalz, Hesse, Bavaria), or indeed municipal vineyards. The cooperatives receive grapes from their members and their output accounts for more than a third of national production—though cooperatives produce Baden-Württemberg's entire range of wines. This said, the quality and style of wines vary according to each producer's strategy. Generally, a new desire to produce better wines at higher prices seems to be emerging, and these are often estate-bottled (*Erzeugerabfüllung*).

Seeking quality

Climate change, clonally selected vines returning better yields, and training initiatives for young growers have all combined to improve wine quality in Germany. If geographic origin is the principal criterion for classifying German wines, the second is their official tier of quality. This is simply a measure of their sugar or grape juice content. An official hierarchy has been established according to the idea that the riper the grapes, the better the wine. A distinction is thus made between *tafelwein* (table wine), *landwein* (country wine, equivalent to *vin de pays*), QbA (*qualitätswein bestimmter anbaugebiete*, quality wine from a specified area), and *prädikatswein* (quality wine, a recent direct replacement for the old QmP, *qualitätswein mit prädikat*, classification). The *prädikatswein* label may be applied to one of six categories, reflecting their natural sugar content level (*see* p.98).

Labels marked "Classic" and "Selection"

In 2000, the Deutsches Weininstitut (German Wine Institute) approved two new categories intended to make the available range of wines more transparent. The terms "Classic" and "Selection" that now appear on some labels are found only on quality dry white wines made with a single grape variety. The "Classic" category must feature the name of the grape variety, the producer, the production region, and the year. "Selection" wine must also name the estate of origin and is subject to certain production regulations (harvest yields, minimum potential alcohol content, etc.).

DID YOU KNOW...?

Sparkling wine is called Sekt in Germany (and in Austria). Some 800 producers generate an annual total of nearly 500 million bottles of Sekt. If the label features the term "Deutscher Sekt," the wine was made exclusively with German grapes. This category includes a few wines of considerable quality, but in general almost all Sekt is made with industrial production methods and sold at reasonable prices under a brand name. Only estate Sekt (Winzersekt) conveys a sense of provenance, but sells at higher prices. A vintage Sekt must contain at least 85 percent of its grapes from the same year declared on the label.

CULTURAL PRACTICES. This said, some producers are reconsidering their traditions and abandoning sweeter styles in favor of drier wines that satisfy international consumer demand. This trend also encourages growers to limit their yields, with the resulting concentration ensuring an element of balance usually provided by residual sugars. Several estates also have converted to organic and biodynamic production, and that number is growing every year, whether the growers are affiliated to a certifying body (Ecovin, Bioland, Naturland, Demeter, Gäa) or not.

Quality and awards labels

These are found on the label or directly on the bottle.

An eagle with outstretched wings. This is the emblem of the Verband Deutscher Prädikatsweingüter (VDP), an association for top producers of Prädikatswein (the old QmP classification). The eagle represents wines of great quality, although there are many producers of fine wines who are not members. In 2002, the VDP decided to apply its own classification system to the best vineyard areas: the designation Grosses Gewächs or Erstes Gewächs corresponds to the notion of grand or premier cru (first growth) wine. Strict production regulations are observed for the grape variety planted, yield, levels of ageing, and vinification techniques.

A roundel or neck label. This represents a medal (gold, silver, or bronze) awarded to the wine by a local jury of the Deutsche Landwirtschafts-Gesellschaft (DLG), the Germany agricultural authority.

A colored *Weinsiegel* (seal). This, too, is awarded by the DLG. A yellow seal denotes trocken (dry) wine, green halbtrocken (medium-dry), and red all other wines.

> Vats at a Franken estate; on the right, a *Bocksbeutel*, the characteristic bottle of the region, can just be seen.

Leading German wines

Improvements in wine quality have increased demand across Germany's domestic and export markets. Exports rose to 24.4 million cases (2.2 million hl) in 2008, principally destined for the UK, the Netherlands, the USA, Russia, Sweden, France, and Norway. From north to south, these are the main wine-producing regions and their wines.

SAALE-UNSTRUT AND SACHSEN (SAXONY)

These two wine-producing areas were part of communist East Germany until 20 years ago. Saale-Unstrut (1,630 acres/660 ha) is located in the valleys of the two rivers after which it is named, and Sachsen's wine district (1,160 acres/470 ha) extends along the banks of the Elbe River north and south of Dresden. These regions mainly produce dry and medium-dry white wines, with red grape varieties representing less than 20 percent of planted land. The quality of the wine here has improved considerably since reunification.

> **GRAPE VARIETIES** Whites: Müller-Thurgau, Weissburgunder (Pinot Blanc), Riesling, and Sylvaner; reds: Portugieser, Dornfelder, and Spätburgunder (Pinot Noir).

> **SOIL** Shelly limestone, red sandstone, clay-loess, and copper slate in Saale-Unstrut; schist, granite, sandstone, and strata of loess covered with clay and alluvial sand in Sachsen.

> **STYLE** Saale-Unstrut whites feature fruit aromas (apples, lemon zest, and nuts) with extremely refreshing mineral notes. Red wines made with Portugieser grapes have black fruit aromas (blackberries, cherries) and hints of violets, juniper, and star anise. Sachsen whites made with Müller-Thurgau feature aromas of apples, peaches, and nuts, while those made with Riesling have scents of apples, apricots, citrus fruits, and little white flowers, all underpinned with agreeable mineral notes. Reds made with Dornfelder reveal aromas of red fruits, violets, and cocoa, whereas Spätburgunders have aromas of red fruits, forest floor, and peppery notes.

> **TOP VINEYARDS** Saale-Unstrut: Freyburg Edelacker, Karsdorf Hohe Gräte, Bad Kösen Saalhäuser, Bad Sulza Sonnenberg, Gosecker Dechantenberg, Höhnstedt Kreisberg, Kaatschen Dachsberg, Naumburg (Sonneneck, Steinmeister), Schulpforte Köppelberg, and Weischütz Nüssenberg. Sachsen: Dresdner Elbhänge, Meissen (Kapitelberg, Rosengründchen), Pesterwitz Jochhöhschlösschen, Pillnitz Königlicher Weinberg, Radebeul (Johannisberg, Steinrücken), Schloss Proschwitz, Seusslitz Heinrichsburg, and Weinböhla Gellertberg.

> **NOTABLE PRODUCERS.** Saale-Unstrut: Günter Born, Gussek, Klaus Böhme, Lützkendorf, Bernard Pawis, Kloster Pforta, Thüringer, and Weingut Bad Sulza. Sacshen: Klaus Zimmerling, Schloss Proschwitz (Prinz zur Lippe), and Vincenz Richter.

AHR

Ahr is a region of just 1,300 acres (530 ha) located very close to the confluence of the Rhine and the river that gives the area its name. Set across steep slopes, the vines grow in soils principally composed of clay and schist, and they can produce excellent Pinot Noir. Only 12 percent of the area is planted with white grape varieties.

> **GRAPE VARIETIES** Spätburgunder (Pinot Noir), Portugieser, and Domina for reds; Riesling for whites.

> **SOIL** Clay and schist

> **STYLE** Red wines made with Pinot Noir have pronounced aromas of black fruits and spices. Good vintages can be kept for up to 20 years. Portugieser grapes give wines hints of red and black fruits (cherries, raspberries, blackcurrants, and prunes), as well as spices, leather, and even smoke at the finish. Rieslings, which are usually made medium-dry and sweet, display aromas of bright fruit (apples, apricots, citrus fruits, and wild strawberries), as well as acacia flowers, aniseed, and mineral notes.

> **TOP VINEYARDS** Ahrweiler Rosenthal, Altenahr Eck, Dernau Hardtberg, Heimersheim Burggarten, Neuenahr Schieferlay, and Walporzheim (Gärkammer, Kräuterberg).

> **NOTABLE PRODUCERS** J. J. Adeneuer, Deutzerhof-Cossmann-Hehle, Meyer-Näkel, and Jean Stodden.

MITTELRHEIN (MIDDLE RHINE)

This region of just 1,090 acres (440 ha) begins south of Bonn at the Königswinter estates on the right bank of the Rhine. It takes in Bad Hönningen and Vallendar near Koblenz before arriving at the area around the town of Nassau, which is also the most romantic part of the Rhine. Here we find wine villages of great pedigree, such as Boppard, St Goar, and Bacharach. Vineyards are set on extremely steep slopes, making for hard physical labor. The region is renowned worldwide for its late-harvest wines. Red varieties represent no more than nine percent of plantings, although this figure is growing.

> **GRAPE VARIETIES** Riesling (70 percent) and Müller-Thurgau for whites; Spätburgunder (Pinot Noir) for reds.

> **SOIL** Schist and *Grauwacke* (sedimentary sandstone).

> **STYLE** Riesling produces dry, medium-dry, and sweet wines of very high quality. They feature aromas of citrus fruits, lime, and elderberry blossom, along with very spicy notes, hints of mineral and great potential for ageing. The reds are best consumed young.

> **TOP VINEYARDS** Bacharach Hahn, Boppard Hamm Feuerlay, Engelhöll Bernstein, Oberwesel Ölsberg, and Steeg St. Jost.

> **NOTABLE PRODUCERS** Didinger, Friedrich Bastian, Toni Jost-Hahnenhof, Dr. Randolf Kauer, Lanius-Knab, Helmut Mades, Matthias Müller, August and Thomas Perll, and Ratzenberger.

MOSEL-SAAR-RUWER

The region around the Mosel and its tributaries, the Ruwer and the Saar, is one of the most beautiful vineyard areas in Germany. There are 21,750 acres (8,800 ha) of vines, with more than a quarter of them growing on very steep slopes overlooking the river. Wine producers are categorized by the sub-regions of Mosel, Saar, and Ruwer, although only the name Mosel has featured on wine labels since 2009. The cool climate has led growers here to plant exclusively white grape varieties for centuries. And despite many extensively chaptalized wines of mediocre quality, there have always been great Mosel wines: at the turn of the 20th century, prices for late-harvest Rieslings and ice wines here often surpassed those of the great Sauternes. Today, the best Rieslings—which are dry or off-dry—are appreciated when young for their lightness and freshness, but also for their ability to transform themselves with age into fascinating and complex wines. Sweeter Rieslings—*spätlese, auslese, beerenauslese, trockenbeerenauslese*, and *eiswein*—are wines to lay down (some for 30 years and more). Finally, some attempts have been made in a few locations to grow red varieties such as Pinot Noir and Dornfelder.

> **GRAPE VARIETIES** Riesling and Müller-Thurgau for whites; Dornfelder and Spätburgunder for reds.

> **SOIL** Limestone in the upper Mosel, schist in the central Mosel (Mittelmosel), limestone and sandstone around the Terassenmosel, and schist in the Saar.

> **STYLE** Great Rieslings, whether sweet or dry, have an astonishing range of aromas and flavors. They offer fruits characters (apples, peaches, apricots, and citrus fruits), floral notes (elderberry blossom), and spices (aniseed, cumin). They are fresh, with excellent mineral notes and good length in the mouth.

> **TOP VINEYARDS** Mosel: Bernkastel Doctor, Brauneberg (Juffer and Sonnenuhr), Erden (Prälat and Treppchen), Graacher Himmelreich, Piesporter Goldtröpfchen, Trittenheimer Apotheke, Ürziger Würzgarten, Wehlener Sonnenuhr, and Winningen Uhlen. Saar: Kanzem Altenberg and Hörecker, Scharzhofberg, Oberemmel Hütte, Ockfen Bockstein, Saarburg Rausch, Serrig, and Wiltinger Braune Kuppe. Ruwer: Eitelsbach Karthäuserhofberg, Kasel Nies'chen and Kehrnagel, Maximin Grünhaus Abtsberg and Herrenberg.

> **NOTABLE PRODUCERS** Mosel: Schloss Lieser, Fritz Haag, Reichsgraf von Kesselstatt, Witwe Dr. Thanisch, Erben, Dr. Loosen, Markus Molitor, and Joh. Joseph Prüm. Saar: von Othegraven, von Hövel, Van Volxem, Egon Müller zu Scharzhof, Le Gallais, Reichsgraf von Kesselstatt, Forstmeister Geltz-Zilliken, Dr. Wagner, and Schloss Saarstein. Ruwer: Karthäuserhof and C. von Schubert'sche Schlosskellerei.

RHEINGAU

This wine region of 7,400 acres (3,000 ha) has a worldwide reputation for the quality of its Rieslings (both dry and sweet) and its Pinot Noirs.

> **GRAPE VARIETIES** Riesling (78 percent) for whites; Spätburgunder (Pinot Noir) for reds.

> **SOIL** Marl to a greater or lesser extent, stones with occasional clay-sand, and clay to the east of the region; sandstone, clay-schist, and quartz to the west.

> **STYLE** In the best years, these Rieslings are elegant when young, acquiring complexity and superb balance as they age. They are some of the finest wines in the world. The reds, such as the Spätburgunders, offer aromas of cherries, quince jelly, dried apricots, and cinnamon. They are generally excellent for laying down.

> **TOP VINEYARDS** Assmannshausen Höllenberg, Hallgarten (Hendelberg, Jungfer), Hattenheim Steinberg, Hochheim Hölle, Johannisberg Hölle, Schloss Johannisberg, Lorch Kapellenberg, Kiedrich (Gräfenberg, Turmberg), Rauenthal (Baiken, Nonnenberg), Rüdesheim (Berg Kaisersteinfels, Berg Roseneck, Berg Rottland, Berg Schlossberg), Jesuitengarten Schloss Vollrads, and Winkel Jesuitengarten.

> **NOTABLE PRODUCERS** Staatsweingüter Domaine Assmannshausen, August Eser, J.B. Becker, Georg Breuer, Joachim Flick, August Kesseler, Hessische Kloster Eberbach, Franz Künstler, Johannishof-Johannes Eser, Graf von Kanitz, Josef Leitz, Robert König, Fürst Löwenstein, Peter Jakob Kühn, Querbach, Balthasar Ress, Schloss Johannisberg, and Robert Weil.

Schloss Johannisberg

This Rheingau estate is a jewel among German wineries, with an exceptional location on a hill overlooking the Rhine. No more than 86 acres (35 ha) are turned over to the cultivation of Riesling. Depending on the vintage and the quality (kabinett, spätlese, auslese, etc.), these wines display fruit aromas (oranges, lemons, grapefruit, apples, peaches) of great complexity with notes of hazelnut, almonds, and spices (cinnamon, coriander). Their herbaceous side is represented by angelica, hay, and mint. Fine structure affords a nice balance between fruit, crispness, and body. Laying down is generally limited to about 15 years for dry wines, but at least 30 years for sweet wines. Bottles traditionally carry colored foils according to their level of quality: red (rotlack) for kabinett, green (grünlack) for spätlese, rosé (rosalack) for auslese, silver (silberlack) for Erstes Gewächs VDP, yellow (rosa-goldlack) for beerenauslese, and gold (goldlack) for trockenbeerenauslese.

NAHE

The Nahe River meets the Rhine at Bingen, and the wine region that surrounds it covers more than 9,900 acres (4,000 ha), mainly producing whites. Red varieties are making more of an appearance, but they are mainly used to make rosé (*weissherbst*).

> **GRAPE VARIETIES** Riesling, Müller-Thurgau, Sylvaner, and Grauburgunder (Pinot Gris) for whites; Dornfelder and Spätburgunder for reds.

> **SOIL** Stony terraces, sandstone, clay, and schist soils.

> **STYLE** Reminiscent of some Mosel and Rheingau whites, these Rieslings have fruity and mineral notes and are generally wines to lay down. The fruity and spicy rosés are at their best when young. The reds, especially the Pinot Noirs, offer a wide range of red and black fruits, with notes of forest floor and spices. The wines have great potential for laying down.

> **TOP VINEYARDS** Bad Kreuznach (Brückes, Kahlenberg), Dorsheim (Pittermännchen, Goldloch), Langenlonsheim Rothenberg, Monzingen (Halenberg), Münster-Sarmsheim (Dautenpflänzer), Niederhausen (Hermannsberg), Schlossböckelheim (Felsenberg), and Traisen Bastei.

> **NOTABLE PRODUCERS** Dr. Crusius, Gutsverwaltung Niederhausen-Schlossböckelheim, Dönnhof, Jung, Schlossgut Diel, Tesch, Kruger-Rumpf, Mathern, Göttelmann, Bürgermeister Schweinhardt, von Racknitz, Prinz zu Salm-Dalberg'sches, and Schäfer-Fröhlich.

RHEINHESSEN

German's largest wine-producing region (64,000 acres/26,000 ha), Rheinhessen is located on the west bank of the Rhine and extends from Bingen in the northwest to near Worms in the south. Cultivation of hybrid grape varieties during the 1970s, coupled with high yields and industrial-scale production of mediocre wines for export, did much damage to the region's image. But these days, Rheinhessen produces a wide range of dry, medium-dry, and sweet wines of often excellent quality. The *Rheinterrassen* (Rhine terraces), which occupy just 10 percent of the eastern part of this region, are the best parcels of land. They also are home to a number of famous estates that produce wines of a quality to match those found in the Rheingau.

> **GRAPE VARIETIES** Müller-Thurgau, Riesling, Sylvaner, and Grauburgunder (Pinot Gris) for whites; Dornfelder, Portugieser, and Spätburgunder (Pinot Noir) for reds.

> **SOIL** Loess and fine sandy marl to the east; quartzite and porphyrite to the west.

> **STYLE** These vary according to grape variety. Müller-Thurgau, for example, offers fruit (apples, apricots, peaches, citrus) with herbaceous aromas (nettles, elderberry blossom, basil) and spices (cumin, mustard, aniseed, coriander).

> **TOP VINEYARDS.** Binger Scharlachberg, Flörsheim-Dalsheim (Bürgel and Hubacker), Nackenheim Rothenberg, Nierstein (Brudersberg, Ölberg, Pettenthal), Westhofen Kirchspiel, and Worms Liebfrauenstift-Kirchenstück.

> **NOTABLE PRODUCERS** Klaus Keller, K. F. Groebe, Gunderloch, Kissinger, Kruger-Rumpf, Kühling-Gillot, Manz, Michael-Pfannebecker, Schales, St. Antony, Wagner-Stempel, and Wittmann.

HESSISCHE BERGSTRASSE

Set at the edge of the Odenwald forest, this little wine region (1,077 acres/436 ha) is separated from Worms only by the width of the river (just 650 feet/200 m at this point). The main part of the growing area starts south of Darmstadt, but frosts are exceptional and rains abundant here. A large proportion of the vineyards belong to the state (Domaine Bergstrasse) or to the village of Bensheim. This region produces mainly white wine: good QbA, a large choice of *prädikatswein* (the old QmP), and Eiswein (ice wine). Top local Rieslings are easily a match for those from the Rheingau, but since they are limited in volume, they are rarely encountered far from their point of origin. Müller-Thurgau has been partly replaced by Pinot Noir and Pinot Gris over the past 10 years.

> **GRAPE VARIETIES** Riesling, Grauburgunder (Pinot Gris), and Müller-Thurgau for whites; Spätburgunder (Pinot Noir) and Dornfelder for reds.

> **SOIL** Sand, clay, limestone, loess, and decomposed granite.

> **STYLE** The Grauburgunder is a generally lively wine with aromas of apples, pears, lemon zest, and dried fruits (almond and hazelnuts), as well as notes of lime blossom, celeriac, and cinnamon.

> **TOP VINEYARDS** Bensheim, Kalkgasse, Heppenheim Centgericht, and Steinkopf.

> **NOTABLE PRODUCERS** Domaine Bergstrasse, Weingut der Stadt Bensheim, and Bergsträsser Winzer eG.

FRANKEN (FRANCONIA)

Franken is a region of dense forests located east of the Rhine, at the heart of Germany. Its vineyards (15,600 acres/6,300 ha) are concentrated in valleys along the Main River and its tributaries, and their exposures are to the south and east. Franken's vineyards spread across three sub-regions: Mainviereck, Maindreieck, and upper Steigerwald. Although the quality of these wines is recognized on the German domestic market, they are less known abroad. More than half are *Fränkisch trocken*, a designation for dry wines with less than 4 g/l of residual sugar content. A small, squat, round bottle called a *Bocksbeutel* is generally used for the best wines from the region.

> **GRAPE VARIETIES** Müller-Thurgau, Sylvaner, and Bacchus for whites; Domina and Spätburgunder (Pinot Noir) for reds.
> **SOIL** Red sandstone, limestone, Upper Triassic gypsum
> **STYLE** The best Franken wines are produced from Sylvaner, Domina, and Spätburgunder grapes. Sylvaner, first planted in Franken 350 years ago, produces white wines of character that are good for laying down. They are fruity (apples, citrus zest, pears, apricots), floral (elderberry blossom, hay), and spicy (cumin, mustard flour), with hints of minerals. Domina produces red wines with aromas of dark fruits (blackcurrants, blackberries, prunes), raspberry jam, spices (cinnamon, cloves), and bitter chocolate.
> **TOP VINEYARDS** Bürgstadt Centgrafenberg, Castell Schlossberg, Escherndorf Lump, Homburger Kallmuth, Iphofen Julius-Echter-Berg, Klingenberg Schlossberg, Randersacker Pfülben, and Würzburg (Innere Leiste and Stein).
> **NOTABLE PRODUCERS** Bickel-Stumpf, Bürgerspital, Fürstlich Castell'sches Domäneamt, Rudolf Fürst, Horst Sauer, Michael Fröhlich, Juliusspital, Fürst Löwenstein, and Schmitt's Kinder.

BADEN

Baden's vineyards cover 37,000 acres (15,000 ha), and stretch for more than 180 miles (300 km) along the Rhine, from Lake Constance in the south to Franken in the north, filling the land between the river and the Black Forest. There are nine sub-regions: Badisches Frankenland (part of the Taubertal), Badische Bergstrasse (located south of Hessische Bergstrasse), Kraichgau (located to the east between Karlsruhe and Pforzheim), Ortenau (from Baden-Baden to south of Offenburg), Breisgau (from south of Offenburg to south of Freiburg), Kaiserstuhl (northwest of Freiburg), Tuniberg (south of Kaiserstuhl and west of Freiburg), Markgräflerland (from south of Freiburg to around Basel), and Bodensee (Lake Constance) in the south. Baden boasts a large number of cooperatives (85 percent of total production) and has a reputation for making wines of great quality. Breisach's Badischer Winzerkeller is renowned as the largest producer in Europe, with a range of 500–600 different wines. There are also a number of beautiful estates with considerable historic pedigrees.

> **GRAPE VARIETIES** Müller-Thurgau, Grauburgunder (Pinot Gris), Riesling, Gutedel and Weissburgunder (Pinot Blanc) for whites; Spätburgunder (Pinot Noir) for reds.
> **SOIL** As many as 15 different kinds of soil.

> **STYLE** Rieslings, especially those from Ortenau, are fruity with enchanting floral notes (hay, elderberry blossom, lime blossom, mint), spices (aniseed, coriander, ginger), and excellent minerality. The Pinot Noirs have dominant aromas of cherries, prunes, and blackcurrants.
> **TOP VINEYARDS** Bodensee: Meersburg Rieschen; Breisgau: Bombach Sommerhalde, Hecklingen Schlossberg, amd Malterdingen Bienenberg; Ortenau: Neuweier Mauerberg, Durbach (Ölberg, Plauelrain, Schloss Grohl, Schlossberg, Schloss Staufenberg), Lauf Gut Alsenhof, Neuweier Schlossberg, and Waldulm Pfarrberg; Kaiserstuhl: Blankenhornsberg Doktorgarten, Burkheimer Feuerberg, Ihringen Winklerberg, Oberbergen Bassgeige, and Oberrotweil Henkenberg; Markgräflerland: Efringen-Kirchen Oelberg and Istein Kirchberg.
> **NOTABLE PRODUCERS** Andreas Laible, Bercher, Engist, Graf Wolff Metternich, Gut Nagelförst, Dr. Heger, Heinrich Männle, Jakob Duijn, Schloss Neuweier, Schwarzer Adler, Salwey, Stigler, and WG Durbach.

Bernhard Huber's Wines (Baden)

Working in the Breisgau district of Baden, this family estate of 74 acres (30 ha) is renowned for the fine quality of its white wines and especially for the reds it produces from Spätburgunder (Pinot Noir). The vines, which are divided among the best parcels around the villages of Malterdingen (Bienenberg), Hecklingen (Schlossberg), and Bombach (Sommerhalde), are tended with the greatest respect for nature. Apart from a Muscat, all the white wines are sweet. Pinot Noir accounts for two-thirds of the total plantings, and the wines crafted from this varietal are either from young vines (junge reben) or old vines (alte reben). The "R" for reserve, which is visible on the labels, signifies that the wines have spent between six and eight months in barrel in the case of whites, and 18 months for reds. The estate also produces sparkling wines of great quality.

PFALZ (PALATINATE)

The Pfalz is a region of 54,000 acres (22,000 ha) extending for about 50 miles (80 km) along a north-south axis to the east of the Rhine River. It is divided into three sectors: Mittelhaardt (Central Haardt), Deutsche Weinstrasse (German wine road), and Südliche Weinstrasse (Southern wine

road). The best vineyards are arranged across hills to the east of the Palatinate Forest. It is renowned for the quality of its white wines, and for its Rieslings in particular. They have real character and minerality, are usually full-bodied, but also have great refinement. Red wine production is limited, but the results are generally excellent.

> **GRAPE VARIETIES** Riesling and Müller-Thurgau for whites; Dornfelder, Portugieser, and Spätburgunder for reds.

> **SOIL** Extremely varied: red sandstone and loess, among others.

> **STYLE** Great Rieslings are wines to lay down, and feature aromas of peaches, apples, nuts, apricots, and pineapple. These wines also have fine notes of elderberry blossom, mint, aniseed, and coriander, and very good minerality.

> **TOP VINEYARDS** Bad Dürkheim Michelsberg, Birkweiler (Kastanienbusch, Mandelberg), Deidesheim Hohenmorgen, Hohenmorgen, Duttweiler, Forst (Jesuitengarten, Kirchenstück, Ungeheuer), Gimmeldingen Mandelgarten, Haardt Bürgergarten "Breumel in den Mauern," Königsbach Idig, Schweigen Kammerberg, and Siebeldingen im Sonnenschein.

> **NOTABLE PRODUCERS** Acham-Magin, Geheimer Rat Dr. von Bassermann-Jordan, Bergdolt, Friedrich Becker, Josef Biffar, Dr. Bürklin-Wolf, A. Christmann, Dr. Deinhard, Gies-Düppel Knipser, Koehler-Ruprecht, Georg Mosbacher, Müller-Catoir, Pfeffingen-Fuhrmann-Eymael, Ökonomierat Rebholz, Reichsrat von Buhl, Georg Siben Erben, and Dr. Wehrheim.

WÜRTTEMBERG

Württemberg's vineyards (28,400 acres/ 11,500 ha) begin near Bad Mergentheim and continue south to the area around Heilbronn. They reach as far as the environs of Remstal and Stuttgart, and extend toward Tübingen and Reutlingen.

> **GRAPE VARIETIES** Riesling and Kerner for whites; Trollinger, Schwarzriesling (Pinot Meunier), Lemberger (or Limberger), and Spätburgunder (Pinot Noir) for reds.

> **SOIL** Extremely varied, from Upper Triassic to limestone, marl, mixed stones, and clay soil.

> **STYLE** Of the reds, Trollinger has aromas of cherries, prunes, bitter almonds, and redcurrants. They also show vegetal elements reminiscent of lentils and beets and a note of wood smoke at the finish.

> **TOP VINEYARDS** Bad Cannstatt Zuckerle, Bönnigheim Sonnenberg, Fellbacher Lämmler, Heilbronn Stiftsberg, Hohenbeilstein Schlosswengert, Kleinbottwar Süssmund, Neipperg Schlossberg, Pfaffenhofen Hohenberg, Schnaiter Altenberg, Schwaigern Ruthe, Stettener Brotwasser, Stettener

Pulvermächer, Untertürkheim (Gips, Herzogenberg), and Verrenberg Verrenberg.

> **NOTABLE PRODUCERS** Aldinger, Graf Adelmann, Ernst Dautel, Drautz-Able, J. Ellwanger, Karl Haidle, Fürst zu Hohenlohe-Öhringen, Schlossgut Hohenbeilstein, Rainer Schnaitmann, Wachtstetter, Staatsweingut Weinsberg, and Wöhrwag.

CENTRAL AND SOUTHEAST EUROPE
TO THE BLACK SEA

Wine-producing regions
- Switzerland
- Austria
- Hungary

0   125 miles (200 km)

N

CENTRAL AND SOUTHEAST EUROPE TO THE BLACK SEA

Vines appeared on the slopes of the Caucasus Mountains many centuries ago, and they spread throughout Central Europe and the Balkan countries. From Switzerland to the Black Sea, the production of white wines now dominates these winegrowing areas, all influenced by a very continental climate.

SWITZERLAND

Relative economic isolation means that Switzerland has retained a very traditional focus for its wine production. It encompasses both top quality and everyday wines, most of them consumed locally.

Fragmented vineyards

Dating back to Roman times, Swiss vineyards were, as in the rest of Europe, developed by the church. Precipitous slopes and detailed searches for the best exposures to the sun explain the extremely small vineyard size—averaging 1 acre (0.4 ha). Historically a white wine country, Switzerland now produces some red wine. Most of the vineyards are located in the French-speaking cantons of Valais, Neuchâtel, Vaud, and Geneva.

Valais

The largest wine-producing region in the country, Valais may also produce the best wines. Located in southern Switzerland, east of Lake Geneva, its 13,250 acres (5,300 ha) follow the Rhône River on what are often very steep slopes. Site elevations rarely exceeding 2,000 ft (600 m) above sea level; but in the Vispertermine, there are plantings at 3,600 ft/1,100 m, among the highest in Europe. Rows of terraces have reshaped the mountain landscape, allowing vines the best possible exposure to the sun. The considerable work necessary to maintain the dry stone walls explains why the vineyards are so small—nestled as they are in mountain hollows with dry microclimates and an ever-present wind that dries the grape clusters. Red and white wines compete here on equal footing, with a slight majority to the whites;

SWITZERLAND STATISTICS

Vineyard area: 37,500 acres (12,000 ha)

Production: 1.1 million cases (1 million hl)

Reds: 52%

Whites: 48%

(Office fédéral de l'agriculture, 2007)

although Valais produces 44 percent of the country's red wines. Dôle is a popular light red; a blend of Pinot Noir and Gamay, it is sometimes vinified as a rosé. The main grape varieties are Fendant and Johannisberg (the local names for Chasselas and Sylvaner) as well as Riesling, Muscat, and Roussanne, also known as Ermitage. There also are local varieties such as Petite-Arvine and Amigne, which produce the most character-rich wines. Reds here are often well structured and mainly from Pinot Noir, Gamay, and Syrah.

Neuchâtel

The vineyards surrounding Lake Neuchâtel extend as far as Berne. Together with those around lakes Biel and Morat, they cover some 2,500 acres (1,000 ha) and form Switzerland's second-largest vineyard area after that of Valais. White wine represents more than 70 percent of the production. The Côte Neuchâteloise

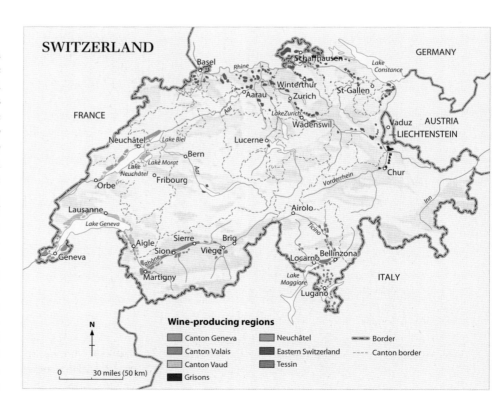

SWITZERLAND

Wine-producing regions

- Canton Geneva
- Canton Valais
- Canton Vaud
- Grisons
- Neuchâtel
- Eastern Switzerland
- Tessin
- Border
- Canton border

0   30 miles (50 km)

> Vineyards near the town of Sion, in the canton of Valais, Switzerland.

extends across 18 miles (30 km) on the northern shore of the lake. With an average altitude between 1,400 and 2,000 ft (430 to 600 m), a cool climate and a drying wind achieve good levels of grape maturity. This is especially so for Pinot Noir, which is vinified into a light rosé called Œil de Perdrix. There are 18 wine-producing villages here, each claiming their own typicity due to *terroir* or the grape varieties used.

The region is best known for its Chasselas wines, usually consumed locally, unfiltered and therefore a little cloudy. Other wines are produced from Sylvaner, Müller–Thurgau, Chardonnay, Riesling, and Doral, a local crossing.

Vaud

This French-speaking canton has an average production of 2.7 million cases (240,000 hl), and that is mostly white wine. Vineyards here grow in terraces along the northern shore of Lake Geneva. The landscape is spectacular, especially in the areas of La Côte and Lavaux, which are classed as UNESCO World Heritage sites.

> ### DID YOU KNOW...?
>
> *There are 20,000 wine producers in Valais, if you count all the members of each winemaking family. This large number is due to the small size of individual vineyards. Consequently, most wines are marketed through cooperatives or négociants. The growers who actually sell their wine in bottle are the ones who own the largest domains. (Source: OIV)*

Chasselas has long been the dominant grape variety here, but there are some good red wines from Gamay, Pinot Noir, or local varieties such as Garanoir and Gamarret. Further north, at the southern extremity of Lake Neuchâtel, are the vineyards of Bonvillars and Côte de l'Orbe, which are among the best in the region.

Geneva

The 2,500 acres (1,000 ha) of vineyards here are situated on a plain at the mouth of the Rhône River, along the Arve River and at the southern end of Lake Geneva. Some Chasselas *crus* such as Mandement have a good reputation, but the traditional practice of blending local grapes with some imported from France causes difficulties for appellations. Red wine production is increasing, mainly from Gamay and Cortaillot, the local name for Pinot Noir.

Ticino

The traditional pergola system of grape growing is becoming rare in this Italian-speaking canton. Also, the character of the reds is similar to their nearby Italian counterparts. Merlot is the main variety, and it thrives on sunny limestone slopes in the sheltered areas of Mendrisiotto, and around Sottoceneri and Bellinzona. Cabernet Sauvignon is also grown in the region, but in more limited quantities. These wines are sometimes blended to produce a "Swiss Bordeaux" that is enjoyed in affluent Italian circles, meaning often high prices.

TRUE OR FALSE?

Switzerland also produces wines in Jura.

FALSE. The Swiss canton of Jura, southeast of Basel and south of Alsace, has virtually no vineyards. But there are some small producers who craft some 4,500 cases (400 hl) of wine. These are sold under the name of the grape variety, and so don't compete with the French AOC of Jura.

German–Swiss vineyards

Most German-speaking cantons, in northern and eastern Switzerland, have very fragmented vineyards. The wines are usually consumed locally. Due to the cool climate and altitude, the grapes in the vineyards around Zurich, Schaffhausen, St. Gallen, and Grisons reach maturity only late in the season thanks to the *foehn*, a southern wind that keeps the grapes dry. Pinot Noir sometimes produces good results in Maienfeld, Grisons, or at Stäfa, on the shores of Lake Zurich.

AUSTRIA

Austria boasts a long tradition of winemaking: its vineyards were established more than 2,000 years ago. And modern Austrian wines are generally of very good quality, even if they are largely unknown outside the country. Production is mostly white wine—Grüner Veltliner is the flagship grape variety. The vineyards are situated in eastern and southern Austria, adjacent to the borders with Hungary, Slovakia, the Czech Republic, and Slovenia.

Lower Austria

Set in the eastern third of the country, and crossed by the Danube River, Lower Austria (Niederösterreich) is the main wine-producing region. It is divided into several wine districts.

WEINVIERTEL. Situated along the Czech and Slovak borders, Weinviertel is an area of some 40,000 acres (16,000 ha) and producing nearly 30 percent of all Austrian wines. Its white wines are best consumed young; they are light, dry, and crisp. There are also noteworthy sparkling and ice wines. Some excellent red wines are produced on the granite soils around the towns of Retz and Falkenstein, close to the Czech border.

AUSTRIA STATISTICS

Area: 110,000 acres (44,000 ha)
Production: 25.5 million cases (2.3 million hl)
Whites: 75%
Reds: 25%

(OIV, 2006)

THERMENREGION. The "thermal region" to the south of Vienna takes its name from nearby hot springs, where a refreshing glass of white wine is most welcome after a good soak. This is mainly a region of fresh, dry, and aromatic whites: Gumpoldskirchen, a blend of two local varieties, Rotgipfler and Zierfandler, was for long one of Austria's most celebrated wines. There are also some powerful red wines made in the Tattendorf sector, based on Blauer Portugieser and Zweigelt.

WACHAU. In the northwest corner of Lower Austria, this area's 3,500 acres (1,400 ha) vineyards are sited on steep volcanic terraces overlooking the Danube River and a spectacular landscape. Good-quality dry whites are the norm here. Grüner Veltliner and Riesling, sometimes blended together, produce powerful wines for long ageing. Schluck, a light and fruity Sylvaner, is also enjoyable.

KREMSTAL AND KAMPTAL. The town of Krems, to the northeast of Wachau, is encircled by volcanic and loess terraces—where Riesling and Grüner Veltliner are grown. They also run alongside the Kamp River, a tributary of the Danube. The Grüners here are similar in character to those of Wachau, and there are some fine Rieslings—sometimes late-harvest, renowned as some of Austria's best.

WAGRAM-TRAISENTAL-CARNUNTUM. Between Krems and Vienna, Wagram (formerly Donauland or "Danube country") is most famous for its white wines made from Grüner Veltliner. Downstream from Vienna, following the course of the Danube, Carnuntum is reputed for its red wines, especially those from Zweigelt. The largest wine-producing domain in Austria is owned by the Capuchin monastery at Klosterneuburg (in Wagram), and is also home to a wine and winemaking school and tasting center.

Burgenland

Along the Hungarian border, on the flat expanse around Lake Neusiedl, is one of Austria's largest vineyard regions (40,000 acres/16,000 ha). It is divided into four sub-zones: Mittelburgenland, Neusiedlersee, Südburgenland, and Neusiedlersee-Hügelland.

> Welschriesling is a white grape variety that is grown in most regions of Austria.

DID YOU KNOW...?

The Wachau region has introduced a classification system based on quality for its dry white wines. It was initiated by Vinea Wachau, an association of small producers. The labels indicate three different levels: the lightest wine is called Steinfeder (11.5% ABV), followed by Federspiel (11.5–12.5% ABV). The richest (the equivalent of a dry spätlese in Germany) is called Smaragd, and must reach a minimum alcohol level of 12.5% ABV. These wines generally come from low-yielding vineyards and late-harvested grapes. When successful, they are superb and age beautifully. The better-known vineyards are mentioned on the label, preceded by the word Ried.

> Harvesting grapes at a Styrian domain.

After a sunny and dry summer, the Neusiedlersee vineyards are bathed in autumn mist rising off the lake. In the Rust area, on the lake's west bank, this encourages the onset of noble rot, and hence the production of Ausbruch, one of the finest sweet wines in the world (*see* p.422). The wines are normally made from Riesling, Welschriesling, Weissburgunder, Müller–Thurgau, or the highly aromatic Muscat Ottonel; although Blaufränkisch makes quality red wine in Mittelburgenland.

TRUE OR FALSE?

Austrian wines are single varietals.

FALSE. While many regions specialize in a particular grape variety, many Austrian white wines are a blend of several varieties, particularly Grüner Veltliner and Riesling.

Styria

Styria (Steiermark) is a vast, rugged region set to the north of the Slovenian border and southwest of Burgenland. Its three sub-regions cover 7,500 acres (3,000 ha). Southern Styria (Südsteiermark) is the largest sub-region and generally produces the best Styrian wines. Many different varieties are cultivated here: Welschriesling, Pinot Blanc, Müller-Thurgau, Riesling, Muskateller, Sauvignon Blanc, Scheurebe, etc. The vineyards are on steep, south-facing slopes at up to 2,000 ft (600 m).

Southeastern Styria (Südoststeiermark) produces mainly light whites, and also some notable wines from Gewurztraminer, Chardonnay (called Morillon), and Sauvignon Blanc. Western Styria (Weststeiermark), between the town of Graz and the Slovenian border, is renowned for Schilcher. This is a slightly tart rosé from Blauer Wildbacher; it's made in very small quantities and is a sought-after local treat, best enjoyed when the wine is young.

Vienna

Some 1,750 acres (700 ha) of vines surround the Austrian capital. Almost all of the wine produced in the region is consumed locally. The wine villages on the edge of the city (Grinzing, Nussdorf...) are full of lively taverns (*heurigen*). There, to the tune of an accordion, winemakers sell their fresh and fruity wines, usually Gemischter Satz, which is a blend of several varieties grown in the same vineyard.

Appellation legislation

Austria has 19 appellations of origin: Kremstal, Kamptal, Wagram, Weinviertel, Wachau, Carnuntum, Traisental, Thermenregion, Weststeiermark, Südsteiermark, Neusiedlersee, Neusiedlersee-Hügelland, Mittelburgenland, Südburgenland, Süd-Oststeiermark, and Wien, plus Niederösterreich, Burgenland, and Styria, these last three being regional appellations.

Austria follows the same rules as the rest of Europe (see also p.98). On the label, a named variety is followed by a quality indication similar to that used in Germany, taking into account both the quality of the wine and the sugar level. Since 1980, all qualitätswein (quality wines) have been strictly tested and carry a registration number for traceability.

HUNGARY

The Romans likely planted the first vines in this region, then called Pannonia. Hungarians, originally a nomadic people who came here from Asia during the 9th and 10th centuries, developed the vineyards across the following centuries, even during Turkish rule. It was during the 18th century that Hungary, by then tightly allied with Austria, started marketing its most famous wine, Tokaj, throughout Europe.

During the country's 50 years of communist rule, the vineyards were managed by cooperatives, with a guaranteed income for the producers. Since the end of the communist era, the free-market economy has forced many smaller producers to give up, and the vineyard area to shrink by more than 30 percent. The vineyards that prosper today are those that have benefited from foreign investment, and those where the cooperatives have successfully adapted to the new economic reality.

HUNGARY STATISTICS

Vineyard area: 212,500 acres (85,000 ha)

Production: 33.3 million cases (3 million hl)

Whites: 70%

Reds: 30%

(OIV, 2006)

Tokaj-Hegyalja: "Wine of kings"

The mountain region of Tokaj covers 10,000 acres (4,000 ha) in the northeast of the country, and it produces the most famous of Hungarian wines. It was highly prized during the time of Louis XIV of France for its sumptuous aromas and refreshing character. As the king of wines (or wine of kings), the appellation of Tokaj (*see* p.422) is known above all for its sweet or semi-sweet wine.

The main grape variety is Furmint, which, in the autumn mists of the Bodrog Valley, consistently develops noble rot. On a par with the best sweet wines in the world, Tokaji is astonishingly long-lived—the best vintages can age for 200 years! Confusingly, there also are some traditional dry wines that bear the Tokaji appellation.

Other regions

EGER. Northeast of Budapest, the Mátraalja-Egri region boasts many cellars run by small producers. The best-known wine in this region is Egri Bikavér, or "Bull's Blood of Eger," a blend of Kékoportó and Cabernet Sauvignon.

LAKE BALATON. Southwest of the capital, in the volcanic soils of the hills surrounding the "Hungarian Sea," are vineyards producing mostly white wines from Olaszrizling (Italian 'Riesling'), Muscat Ottonel, and Szürkebarát (Pinot Gris). The best wines come from the Badacsony district.

SOPRON. By the Austrian border, from hilly vineyards near the town of Sopron, Kékfrankos, Pinot Noir, and Cabernet Sauvignon produce good quality red wines. The southern shore of Fertö Tó, or Austria's Neusiedlersee, is home to some worthy white wines.

VILLÁNY-SIKLÓS. In the far south of the country, near the town of Pécs, this area is renowned for its full, round, red wines based on Cabernet Sauvignon, Merlot, and Kékoportó.

SZEKSZÁRD. The vineyards around the town of Szekszárd are reputed for their red wines, which also can be labeled "Bull's Blood," as in the Eger region. The traditional variety has long been the high-yielding Kadarka, but it is being replaced by Merlot, Cabernet Sauvignon, and Kékoportó. The wine village of Leányvár, with three stories of cellars cut into a hillside is well worth a visit.

> Barrels of wine at the Kovács Borház winery in the village of Hajós, Hungary.

SOUTHEAST EUROPE TO THE BLACK SEA

The fall of the Soviet empire during the early 1990s dramatically changed the wine landscape of the countries downstream along the Danube from Austria, as well as in the former republics of the USSR.

Formerly operated as collective farms, the vineyards of Romania and Slovenia have been partly privatized with the help of capital groups from the West. Those from Bulgaria and former Soviet republics are slow to catch up with modern demand.

Romania

Romania is a large wine producer (575,000 acres/230,000 ha and 133 million cases/12 million hl). For a long time, it was the fifth-largest in Europe, producing mostly whites (60 percent). The loss of its traditional markets in Eastern Europe has led to a significant restructuring of its vineyards—only those with good quality potential are likely to survive with help from the European Union and other Western investors.

First planted along the banks of the Black Sea as many as 3,000 years ago, during the time of the Ancient Greeks, vines then spread across the country and thrived in Transylvania during the Middle Ages, with the arrival of Saxon winemakers. There are as many as 50 different appellations, principally spread across Moldova in the east, Dobrudja in the southeast, Transylvania in the center, and Oltenia on the southern slopes of the Carpathians. The most famous wines are the whites of Cotnari (*see* p.423), in Romanian Moldova.

Bulgaria

During the 1970s, Bulgarian Cabernet Sauvignons competed with Bordeaux on the German, British, and Scandinavian markets. Since the end of communism, the country has seen its production drop dramatically due to the poor consistency and falling quality of its exported wines. It is too early to know whether

> Harvest in a Bulgarian vineyard.

its still recent entry into the European Union will mark the revival of its wine industry.

ANCIENT HISTORY. Bulgaria is one of the oldest wine-producing countries in Europe—the Thracians were making wine here 3,000 years ago, as recorded by Homer in the *Iliad*. For a long time, the wine was released only to the internal market; but toward the end of the communist era, there was a surge in Soviet demand and a partnership with the American Pepsi-Cola company that boosted wine sales in Britain and Germany.

GREAT POTENTIAL, FEW RESOURCES. With a Mediterranean climate tempered by altitude and low-nutrient soils, there is great potential for producing quality wine here. But Bulgaria still lacks infrastructure—so there are fewer than 50 significant wine exporters. The hasty privatization of vineyards during the late 1990s, with parcels of land being restored to their pre-1947 owners, has meant that many plots have been abandoned due to lack of resources. Widespread lack of modern vinification equipment also explains why most bottled wines are pasteurized (which adversely affects their quality). However, large areas have been planted with new vines in recent years, mainly on the initiative of German investors, but another decade may be needed before the results can be judged.

GRAPE VARIETIES. Pamid, Mavrud, Melnik, Cabernet Sauvignon, Merlot, Gamay, and Pinot Noir for reds; Rkatsiteli, Dimiat, Muscat Ottonel, Misket, Chardonnay, Riesling, Gewurztraminer, Aligoté, and Sylvaner for whites.

Cricova, "Treasure" of the Republic of Moldova

The former Soviet republic of Moldova, located between Romania and Ukraine, boasts a unique wine cellar—it's virtually a subterranean town! Cricova's old mines, at a depth of 200–260 ft (60–80 m), have a constant temperature that allows the production of sparkling wines by the traditional method. Placed under the protection of UNESCO, they also store a large number of Moldovan and foreign wines, some of which are very old indeed. A significant tourist destination in Moldova, Cricova even has streets named after grape varieties. About 20–25 ft (6–8 m) wide, their combined length exceeds 60 miles (100 km) over more than 130 acres (53 ha).

> Vineyards in the region of Stajerska in Slovenia.

PRODUCTION AND LEGISLATION. Some 250,000 acres (100,000 ha) of Bulgarian vines yield 10 million cases/900,000 hl of red wine and 6.7 million cases /600,000 hl of white wine, with a large percentage used for distillation. There are 27 local appellations in Bulgaria.

The wine classifications, not yet fully in line with the European Union, include table wines, country wine with an indication of origin and grape variety, wines of controlled geographic origin (DGO), and *Controliran*, a kind of super-DGO.

Ukraine

Crimea, the most "Russian" part of Ukraine, enjoys a Mediterranean climate. Most of the country's vineyards are located here, and this is where "Krim" has been produced for many years, a blended, semi-sweet sparkling wine of average quality. There are also some red wines known as "Ruby." However, the greatest quality wines are found near Sebastopol, at Massandra. The cellars of the Czars there, established in 1894 and miraculously still preserved, hold treasured Black Muscat wines that will soon reach their centennial. Production here is being revived, thanks to the interest it generates among wine lovers in Western Europe.

Slovenia

This former Yugoslav republic is set between Italy, Austria, and Croatia. Its vineyards cover about 75,000 acres (30,000 ha) across 15 wine regions. They face the Adriatic Sea to the west, or are spread through the valleys of the Drava and Sava in the east.

The production is usually of high quality, especially white wines from the region of Podravski, due to an ideal climate at altitude. Slovenian winemakers generally produce some fine dry white wines, as well as ice wine and "late harvest" wine based on Riesling and Pinot Gris.

The best red wines come mainly from the Adriatic coast and the Sava valley. They are made from Merlot, Cabernet Franc, Barbera, and local grape varieties such as Refosk (grown near the Italian border) or Cvicek (which is vinified into a pleasant rosé in the region of Sava).

Georgia

It is likely that this former Soviet republic, along the shores of the Black Sea, is the place from which the grapevine first spread to the rest of Europe in the late Neolithic period. This would explain the wealth of Georgia's native grape varieties—amounting to several hundred.

Unfortunately, the fall of the Soviet system has had disastrous consequences for the 150,000 acres (60,000 ha) of vineyards in this country. On the one hand, a political dispute with Russia has cut off Georgia from its main market; on the other hand, slack controls mean that very many wines are adulterated or tampered with, according to the UN's FAO. Despite the influence of a joint venture with Pernod-Ricard, Georgia struggles to market its Gurdzhaani and Tsinandali, two of the best white wines produced in the region of Rion, in the central part of the country.

Leading wines of Central and Southeast Europe to the Black Sea

Austria and Switzerland produce wines according to the standards of Western Europe. However, except for Slovenia, that's not always the case for former Eastern Bloc countries, whose wine quality remains very mixed.

CHAMOSON GRAND CRU AOC

SWITZERLAND (VALAIS)

Chamoson's vineyards, on steep slopes over the Rhône River, stretch across 1,000 acres (427 ha), and are the largest in Valais. Set within the Valais AOC, Chamoson Grand Cru comprises a wide range of soils and microclimates, where many different varieties thrive. It is also very fragmented, since there are as many as 1,120 vineyard owners. Although Chamoson produces mostly red wines, it owes its reputation to its white wines made from Sylvaner. The harvest is entirely by hand and the appellation rules are extremely strict.

> **GRAPE VARIETIES** Sylvaner (known locally as Johannisberg, since its typicity recalls that of the great wines of the Rhine Valley) and Petite-Arvine for whites; Gamay, Pinot Noir, and Syrah for reds.
> **SOIL** Scree and alluvium, though mainly limestone.
> **STYLE** Sylvaner is vinified as a dry white wine. It is light straw in color with hints of green that turn golden with age. On the palate, there are subtle notes of toasted almonds with a touch of acidity and good minerality. The toasty and fruity notes become more prominent with age. The red wines are fairly simple, except those from Syrah, and are generally well structured.

Color:
Red and white.

Serving temperature:
46 to 50°F (8 to 10°C) for whites;
57 to 63°F (14 to 17°C) for reds.

Ageing potential:
5–6 years, and up to 15 years for the best wines of good vintages.

DÉZALEY GRAND CRU AOC

SWITZERLAND (VAUD)

Nestled in the heart of the Lavaux district, within Vaud canton, this appellation covers only 133 acres (53 ha). It is set entirely within the municipality of Puidoux, and produces only white wines from Chasselas. The vineyards are on a very steep slope, warmed by the sun reflected from Lake Geneva below. The vineyards are planted in terraces, the walls of which also help to reflect light and store heat. With the cold, dry winds slowing the ripening of the grapes and helping Chasselas to preserve its aromas, this microclimate is ideal for bringing fruit to full maturity. Local conditions, carefully observed and managed for years by growers, also give the wines their character, with pronounced aromas of ripe fruit supporting a fresh crispness.

> **GRAPE VARIETY** Chasselas
> **SOIL** Glacial erosion has shaped the Dézaley hillside, leaving behind a moraine with high limestone-clay content, between banks of "pudding" stones.
> **STYLE** Dézaley Grand Cru is characterized by its depth and power. It offers toasted and smoky aromas, notes of almonds and honey, as well as a fruity or floral character, depending on the vintage. It retains good freshness for two to three years, after which its toasted character becomes even more assertive.

Color:
White.

Serving temperature:
46 to 50°F (8 to 10°C).

Ageing potential:
4 to 8 years, and up 10 years in very good vintages.

RUSTER AUSBRUCH DAC

Near the town of Rust, one of the best dessert wines in the world, Ruster Ausbruch, is produced by a method similar to that for Tokaji Aszú (*see below*). Climatic conditions around Lake Neusiedl—hot and dry summers followed by autumn mist from the nearby lake— allow the formation of noble rot with great regularity.

> **GRAPE VARIETIES** Weissburgunder (Pinot Blanc), Welschriesling, Ruländer (Pinot Gris), Muscat Ottonel, Furmint.
> **SOIL** Sandy, on flat or sloping ground by the shores of Lake Neusiedl.

> **STYLE** Sweet wines of great concentration and perfume, with notes of spice and grapey aromas. With age, they take a more pronounced amber color and a more defined spiciness.

Color:	Serving temperature:	Ageing potential:
White.	46 to 54°F (8 to 12°C).	Up to 100 years for the best vintages.

KREMSTAL DAC

The 6,500 acres (2,600 ha) of this appellation extend along the central stretch of the Danube in Austria, near the picturesque town of Krems. Although divided into different zones, with individual geologic and climatic characteristics, the vineyards here have a genuine identity. Producing exclusively white wines from Riesling and Grüner Veltliner, Kremstal became an appellation in its own right in 2007. It is one of the most highly reputed wine regions of Austria, thanks to the strict legislation governing its dry white wines and its rare sweet wines.

> **GRAPE VARIETIES** Riesling and Grüner Veltliner.

> **SOIL** Granite boulders and loess.
> **STYLE** The dry Rieslings are elegant, clean, mineral, and without any botrytis or oak. The dry Grüner Veltliners are fruity and lively without being over-ripe. The region also produces some sweet wines made from grapes that have been affected by botrytis.

Color:	Serving temperature:	Ageing potential:
White.	46 to 54°F (8 to 12°C).	5 to 20 years, depending on the area and vintage.

TOKAJ

The hilly region of Tokaj (Tokaj-Hegyalja) produces sweet, medium-dry, or dry wines, all bearing the appellation Tokaji (meaning "from Tokaj" in Hungarian), which can be confusing for anyone but experts. The most famous wine is made from Aszú (meaning over-ripe) grapes, affected by noble rot and left to shrivel on the vine. This "eszencia" is an exceptionally sweet nectar that runs off naturally from the vats. Tokaji Aszú is therefore always vinified as a sweet wine. After pressing, the wine ferments in barrels for many months. Separately, the pressed Aszú grapes are divided into units of 25 kg called *puttonyos*, and multiples of that volume is added to the must or to the finished wine. The number of *puttonyos* added to each barrel (between three and six) determines the concentration of sugars and wine quality. In lesser years, when noble rot does not affect all the grape clusters, Tokaji Szamorodni ("as is") is produced instead. A dry or medium-dry wine with pronounced oxidation, it is sometimes left to ferment under a film of yeast, like the French *vin jaune* (*see* p.307). There are also some ordinary dry white wines bearing the name Tokaji.

> **GRAPE VARIETIES** Furmint, Muscat Ottonel, Hárslevelü.
> **SOIL** Loess, clay-limestone, and volcanic.
> **STYLE** Eszencia is very low in alcohol, with a sugar concentration above 250 g/l. The sweetness of Tokaji Aszú varies with the amount of Aszú grapes added to the base wine. It is a wine of great delicacy that can age for several generations, taking on darker shades of amber. The quality of Tokaji Szamorodni is uneven, but the best age very well.

Color:	Serving temperature:	Ageing potential:
White.	46 to 50°F (8 to10°C).	Several decades for the best vintages.

Reviving East European wines

CONSIDERABLE ROOM TO MANOEUVRE

For more than 20 years, Jean-François Ragot has traveled extensively throughout Eastern Europe in search of rare gems for his Lyon-based company, Dionis. He pioneered the marketing of Hungarian Tokaj in France, and also has the exclusive distribution rights in France of Grasa de Cotnari from Romania. "Tokaj is already established, even if there are still some problems to resolve in vineyard management. Romania has yet to make an impact, but its potential is enormous," says a very enthusiastic Jean-François Ragot. If he has little trouble sourcing quality grapes for the Tokaj wines that he makes or selects, it is a much more difficult task in Romania. He explains, "They still have a mentality dating back to the Ceausescu era." For a good quality Grasa de Cotnari, he has to visit the area and make very strict grape selections in the vineyard. "Bulgaria will be the next major player out of the former Eastern Bloc countries," he says. As for Slovenia, it is already an established wine country, thanks to its low volume but very high quality wine production.

KARST

SLOVENIA (PRIMORSKY VINORODNI RAJON COASTAL REGION)

In southwestern Slovenia, between the Adriatic coast and the Italian border, the Karst region has given its name to the geologic (karstic) formation of underground rivers flowing through limestone subsoil. Cultivated since Roman times, the long-neglected vineyards here have now found a new life since the entry of Slovenia into the European Union. This area covers 1,400 acres (560 ha) for a production of 1.7 million cases (150,000 hl). The region is renowned for its red wine made from Teran, also known as Refosk, which is similar to the Mondeuse of Savoie (France). This variety produces very dark wines, low in alcohol, and fairly crisp, but very popular in Slovenia. There are also some light rosés and dry white wines.

> **GRAPE VARIETIES** Teran or Refosk, Merlot, and Cabernet Franc for reds and rosés; "Italian Riesling," Sauvignon Blanc, and Pinot Gris for whites.

> **SOIL** Limestone and red clay.

> **STYLE** Red wines are dark, tangy, fruity, and low in alcohol. The rosés are light, and the whites dry and fruity.

Color:	Serving temperature:	Ageing potential:
Red, rosé, and white.	46 to 54°F (8 to 12°C) for whites and rosés; 57 to 63°F (14 to 17°C) for reds.	2 to 10 years for reds; 1 to 3 years for whites and rosés.

GRASA DE COTNARI

ROMANIA

In the northeastern corner of Romania, near the Republic of Moldova, is the small vineyard district of Cotnari. Once very famous for its sweet white wines, it still suffers serious deficiencies from 50 years of communist rule, even if its potential is still there. The grapes are affected by the noble rot that is necessary to produce the best wines; but the strict berry selection that is also essential to this work is not always practiced here, and very different wines can be found under the same appellation.

> **GRAPE VARIETIES** Grasa (similar to the Hungarian Furmint and easily affected by *Botrytis cinerea* or "noble rot"), Feteasca Alba, Francusa, and Tamaioasa Romaneasca.

> **SOIL** Clay-limestone and loess, on often steep hillsides.

> **STYLE** Very uneven. The appellation produces a wide range in quality, from outstanding sweet wines to the very ordinary. The best are characterized by Muscat flavors, taking on spicy notes as they age.

Color:	Serving temperature:	Ageing potential:
White.	46 to 50°F (8 to 10°C).	Depends on quality (more than 20 years for the best).

Strait of
Gibraltar

Rabat

Casablanca

Marrakech

Fès

Meknès

MOROCCO

Oran

Alger

Constantine

ALGERIA

Annaba

Tunis

Sousse

Sfax

TUNISIA

EASTERN MEDITERRANEAN AND NORTH AFRICA

Black Sea

Edirne

MACEDONIA
Thessaloniki   Istanbul
Keşan
Bursa   Ankara   Kızılırmak

THESSALY
GREECE   LIMNOS   TURKEY   Lake Van
Lamia   Malatya

İzmir   Lake Tuz   Tigris
Athens   Konya
Patra   SAMOS   Aydın
Adana   Seyhan
PELOPONNESE   PAROS   Aleppo   Euphrates
RHODES   Nicosia   SYRIA
Mediterranean   Aegean Sea   CYPRUS   Homs
Sea   Iraklio   CRÈTE   LEBANON
Beirut   Damascus
ISRAEL
Tel Aviv-Jaffa
Gaza   Jerusalem
Dead Sea
Suez

EGYPT   Cairo

THE VINEYARDS OF THE EASTERN MEDITERRANEAN AND NORTH AFRICA

The eastern Mediterranean has always been a land of vineyards. The countries with strong Christian traditions, such as Greece and Cyprus, have the most well-established wine culture, although the Lebanon and Israel also produce wines of excellent quality. Some vineyards in North Africa, the origins of which are linked to colonization, also are now achieving high standards.

GREECE

For a long time synonymous with rustic *taverna* wines—particularly Retsina, a white flavored with pine resin—Greek production has improved significantly in the past 20 years.

Ancient roots

The history of wine in Greece can be traced back to the very beginnings of Greek civilization. Elements of the oldest wine press in the world, from more than 3,000 years ago, have been found in Crete. Greece also was the driving force in the spread of wine culture and the planting of vines across the Mediterranean region.

It was from the 13th to the 11th century BC that the development of vineyards hit its peak in the Hellenic world, which included Macedonia. Greek wine production then decreased during the long Ottoman occupation, which ended only shortly before the First World War. However, the Greeks never stopped drinking wine, since its preparation was supervised by the Orthodox Church, whose considerable power was always respected by the Turks.

GREECE STATISTICS

Vineyard area: 172,400 acres (69,760 ha) for wine grapes and 162,450 acres (65,740 ha) for table grapes and raisins

Production: 39 million cases (3,500,000 hl)

White: 60%

Red and rosé: 40%

(Greek Ministry of Economy)

Greek wine today

After stagnating across most of the 20th century, Greek wine production has improved markedly in quality since the country's entry into the European Union. Change has been driven by large companies recognizing market potential. The planting of "international" grape varieties, the training of young Greek oenologists at the best European schools, and a careful study of international demand have resulted, during the past decade, in the production of wines of a high standard.

FRAGMENTED VINEYARDS, MODERN METHODS. About 30 percent of Greek wines are produced and marketed by large producer-merchants, who buy grapes from many small

> In Greece, vines are often grown on pergolas.

DID YOU KNOW...?

Long before its entry into the European Union, Greece was inspired by the French AOC system, going as far as giving French-sounding names to certain appellations, such as Muscat de Patras. Four quality levels were introduced in the 1970s: Epitrapezios Inos (EI: table wines with an indication of the grape variety); Topikoi Oenoi (TO: similar to vins de pays); Onomasià Proeléfsios Anotéras Piotitos (OPAP: the equivalent of the French AOVDQS); and Onomasià Proeléfsios Eleghomeni (OPE: the equivalent of the French AOC). Since 2005, wine names and time spent in barrel can be mentioned (Réserve or Grande Réserve). In most cases, the name of the producer is a label's most prominent feature.

estates and often have wineries in various parts of Greece. The main wine regions are, in order of size, the Peloponnese, Crete, Macedonia and Thrace, Thessaly, and the Aegean islands.

GRAPE VARIETIES. Virgil wrote that it was impossible to list all of the varieties. Today, more than 300 are recognized. For red wine, the main varieties are: Agiorgitiko, Limnio, Halkidiki, Xynomavro, Mandilaria, Mavrodaphne, Grenache, Cabernet Sauvignon, Merlot, and Syrah. For white wine: Chardonnay, Muscat à Petits Grains, Roditis, Assyrtiko, Moschofilero, Sauvignon Blanc, and Muscat of Alexandria.

> Carvings on these barrels at a winery in Patras recall the ancient origins of Greek wine.

The Peloponnese

This peninsula in the southern part of the country is the largest wine region. Out of 148,000 acres (60,000 ha) of vines, 54,000 acres (22,000 ha) produce wine grapes, mainly in the northern peninsula around Patras and Corinth. In terms of appellations (*see* box on previous page), the region produces three OPEs: Muscat of Patras, Muscat Rio of Patras, and Patras Mavrodaphne; and three OPAPs: Mantinia, Nemea, and Patras.

The best-known appellation is Nemea. This name also designates the largest and oldest Greek appellation near the Gulf of Corinth. Nemea produces red wines, mostly from the local grape Agiorgitiko (St. George); but international red grape varieties, such as Syrah, Cabernet Sauvignon, and Merlot, are increasingly being planted in the region.

That said, it is mainly white wines that are produced in the Peloponnese, especially from Moschofilero, a Muscat-style grape that yields dry wines. In the prefecture of Achaia, in the area surrounding Patras, wine production is mostly fortified white wines made from Muscat grapes and fortified reds made from Mavrodaphne. There are also dry rosé wines made from Roditis in the Olympia region.

Macedonia and Thrace

These two regions, with a total of 37,000 acres (15,000 ha) of vines, are located in far northern Greece, bordering Albania, the former Yugoslavia, Bulgaria, and Turkey. They are characterized by rugged terrain and a more continental climate than in the rest of the country, with potentially harsh winters. Production is mainly red wines, particularly from the Xynomavro grape, which is used in the wines of Naoussa, Macedonia's most famous OPAP.

White wines, mainly blends, are found in Thrace and Chalkidiki (or Halkidiki), where the Halkidiki grape, named after the region, is common. Since Thrace does not have an OPE or an OPAP, its wines are primarily known and sold in restaurants under merchants' brand names such as Boutari and Tsantali.

The islands

CRETE. This island has Greece's second largest wine-producing area (approximately 25,000 acres or 10,000 ha). Several thousand years old, the vineyards suffered a relatively late attack of phylloxera in the 1970s, and have gradually been replanted. While, as elsewhere, American rootstock was used, the wine producers were wise enough to graft some native varieties. Crete produces mainly red wines near Heraklion, from the Kotsifali, Mandilaria, and Liatiko grape varieties, and also around Chania, from Romeiko. The most well-known white wines come from the Sitia region in the west.

OTHER ISLANDS. To the north of Crete, the beautiful island of Santorini produces some of Greece's best white wines, mainly from the Assyrtiko grape. The islands of the Aegean Sea are famous for their sweet Muscat wines, especially those from Samos and Lemnos, which are of variable quality. These are either fortified or traditionally produced sweet white wines, meaning grapes that have been dried in the sun.

Retsina

This crisp, white, "resinated" wine is unique to Greece and has an official European allowance for the addition of small amounts of Aleppo pine resin to the must. Its origin dates back to antiquity, when the earthenware amphorae in which wine was transported were sealed with a mixture of plaster and resin, giving the wine a distinct flavor. Relatively cheap, it is served with mezze, in half bottles or jugs. A few rosé retsinas, that are more refined, are produced in the Peloponnese region from the Roditis grape.

CYPRUS

The ancient vineyards of Cyprus used to be spread across the entire island, but they are now concentrated in the southwest—in the Greek part of Cyprus, with very few in the Turkish region.

Production

Approximately 44,000 acres (18,000 ha) of vineyards cover a relatively large area, with 14 appellations. Most wines are served in pitchers and consumed by the Cypriots and tourists. Long ago, the island exported a large part of its production to Russia, but this market is rapidly declining. Furthermore, as a result of entering the European Union, Cyprus is no longer permitted to call its wines "sherry," as it has sometimes done in the past. As well, the European Union has encouraged restructuring vineyards with the planting of good quality grape varieties along slopes, especially at the base of the Troodos Mountains. Since the time of the crusades, Cyprus has been famous for Commandaria, a fortified red wine. The quality varies greatly, but it can be very refined with a fragrant bouquet of incense, when it is matured for several decades in oak casks.

Grape varieties

There are many red and white varieties. Red wines dominate production with Mavron, a local variety of middling quality; but there is also some Cabernet Sauvignon, Grenache, Syrah, and Carignan that yield interesting results. The main variety for white wines is Xynisteri; there is also Lefkas, Sauvignon Blanc, and Chardonnay.

THE LEVANT

The countries of the Levant—Turkey, Lebanon, Syria, and Israel—have a wine tradition dating back to at least ancient Greco-Roman times and probably even earlier among the Canaanites of Palestine and the peoples of the Tigris and Euphrates. However, across the centuries, Arab and then Turkish conquests prevented vines from flourishing except as a privilege granted to Jewish and Christian minorities. It is therefore most common today to find wine production in Lebanon and Israel.

Turkey

More than a thousand different grape varieties can be found in Turkey—this nation is actually the world's fifth-largest producer of grapes. But only a few dozen of these varieties are used to produce wine, and most of the harvest goes to either table grapes or raisins.

Yet wine has always been part of Turkish culture, not only among the Christian (particularly Armenian) and Jewish minorities, but also within the secular Muslim elite, for whom drinking a little wine has always been fashionable. Wine was considered to be more prestigious than beer or raki, two alcoholic beverages that are widely consumed despite the country being predominantly Muslim.

In 2004, for the first time in the country's history, *Hürriyet*, a leading newspaper, presented a selection and tasting of the best Turkish wines from among a hundred samples. The red wines came out on top, with Doluca Öküzgözü from Anatolia, Doluca Villa Neva from the shores of the Aegean, and Doluca Cabernet-Merlot from Thrace.

> In Cappadocia, Turkey, vineyards are exposed to significant variations in temperature with hot, dry summers and cold winters.

Israel

Wine has always been part of Hebrew culture. One of the first modern Jewish settlements even established a vineyard in the sands of Rishon Le Zion, at the end of the 19th century, although production was mainly of a syrupy red wine sold under the Carmel brand. The Israelis did not begin to make better quality wines until the early 1980s, taking advantage of the soil and the fairly cool climate of the Golan Heights. It is here that the majority of Israel's 15,000 acres (6,000 ha) of vines are located, but irrigation also enables good quality red wines to be produced in the country's central region. There are white and red wines, some of which are kosher (*i.e.* they are produced exclusively by observant Jews who steam-sterilize facilities, and use only kosher winemaking products). Many Israeli wines are rather neutral in character, but some have received many favorable reviews from international experts. The country does not have any native grape varieties, and so the wines are made from international varieties such as Chardonnay, Sauvignon Blanc, Cabernet Sauvignon, and Merlot.

Lebanon

This is without doubt the country that produces the best wines in the eastern Mediterranean. Some, particularly those from the Bekaa Valley, are considered by many in the wine world to be exceptionally fine wines. The production of red, rosé, and white wines is shared among approximately 15 vineyard owners in the Christian community, and totals about 889,000 cases (80,000 hl). However, a significant proportion of this wine is distilled for making raki.

There are more than a dozen indigenous grape varieties, though they are often blended with international varieties such as Cabernet Sauvignon, Merlot, Syrah, and Carignan. The best-known and largest estates are Château Musar, Château Ksara, and Château Kefraya. Additionally, there are a dozen small, independent producers.

NORTH AFRICA

Vineyards in three North African countries are essentially due to French colonization and the presence of many Maltese, Spanish, and Italian settlers. Today, plantings are steadily shrinking in Algeria, remain constant in Tunisia, and are tending to increase in Morocco, where a real effort to improve quality has been undertaken in recent years.

Algeria

Until its independence in 1962, Algeria was one of the largest "French" wine-producing regions. High in alcohol and deep in color, but lacking in acidity, these wines were made from southern French grape varieties (Cinsault, Carignan, Grenache) and generously blended into wines from other French regions, including Bordeaux and Burgundy, to give the latter the "muscle" that they sometimes lacked. Since independence, the Algerian industry, which is divided into 12 appellations (Medea, Tlemcen, Mascara, etc.) has been gradually declining in terms of both production and quality.

> Vineyard landscape in Tunisia.

Tunisia

Vines have been grown in Tunisia since Carthaginian times and, during the colonial period, the country had beautiful vineyards that were run mostly by settlers from Italy. Today, grapes for wine production are grown mainly in the north and cover fewer than 25,000 acres (10,000 ha). The most popular wines are dry Muscats from the Kelibia region.

Morocco

Among North African countries, it is Morocco that has made the most effort in recent years to produce good quality wines. But only 25 percent of the 120,000 acres (50,000 ha) of vines there are used to make wine. Production totals nearly 3.3 million cases (300,000 hl), of which about 80 percent is red wine, 18 percent rosé, and only two percent white. There are 14 *appellations d'origine garantie* (AOG) and just one *appellation d'origine contrôlée* (AOC).

Nearly half of the vineyards are concentrated around Meknes, followed by the regions of Khemisset and El Hajeb. The most common grape varieties are Cinsault, Carignan, Alicante Bouschet, and Grenache. Cabernet Sauvignon, Merlot, Mourvèdre, and Syrah have recently been planted in a Franco-Moroccan project managed by the French wine merchant Castel (*see also* box on p.431).

Wine regions of the Eastern Mediterranean and North Africa

Greece produces the most wines here that are known and consumed beyond its borders. The best Turkish, Lebanese, and Moroccan wines are only available in gourmet restaurants in their respective countries.

NAOUSSA, AMYNTEON, GOUMENISSA OPAPs

GREECE (MACEDONIA)

These three appellations are considered to be among the best in Greece. The Naoussa production area is located on the southeastern slopes of Mount Velia; the vineyards of Amynteon and Goumenissa are generally planted at higher altitudes, up to 2,100 feet (650 m). The proximity of the sea and the altitude temper the hot summers, and relatively high rainfall gives the wines a certain finesse.

> **GRAPE VARIETIES** Xynomavro for the Naoussa region; Negosca and Xynomavro for Goumenissa and Amynteon.

> **SOIL** Limestone and clay-limestone hills, sometimes with steep slopes.
> **STYLE** The dry, medium dry, and sweet reds are generally structured and tannic; the rosés are supple and fruity.

Color:	Serving temperature:	Ageing potential:
Red and rosé.	50 to 54°F (10 to 12°C) for rosés; 55 to 61°F (13 to 16°C) for reds.	1 to 2 years for the rosés; 5 to 8 years for the reds.

CÔTES-DE-MELITON OPAP

GREECE (HALKIDIKI)

One of the most popular Greek OPAPs, the tiny appellation of Côtes-de-Meliton (740 acres or 300 ha) lies on slopes overlooking the sea from the center of Halkidiki's three peninsulas. Red and white, the wines are often of exceptional quality and are prized by the best restaurants. They are also among the most expensive in Greece.

> **GRAPE VARIETIES** Limnio, Cabernet Sauvignon, and Cabernet Franc for the reds; Athiri, Roditis, and Assyrtiko for the whites.

> **SOIL** Steep limestone slopes.
> **STYLE** The dry red wines are supple, full-bodied, and very fruity on the palate, developing spicy flavors with age. The dry white wines are rich and full-bodied with toasty and citrus flavors, and good length.

Color:	Serving temperature:	Ageing potential:
Red and white.	50 to 54°F (10 to 12°C) for the whites; 55 to 61°F (13 to 16°C) for the reds.	3 to 8 years for the white wines; 6 to 10 years for the reds.

NEMEA OPAP

GREECE (PELOPONNESE)

The Nemea OPAP is the oldest and largest Greek appellation. It extends over the gentle hills along the Gulf of Corinth and the Saronic Gulf, north of the Peloponnese. Known as the "blood of Hercules," the wines are red. Yet there is name confusion with white wines made from Moschofilero, representing the main production of the same region. *Vin de pays* (TO) wine is also produced under the Corinth and Achaia appellations.

> **GRAPE VARIETIES** Agiorgitiko, supplemented with other varieties (15 to 20 percent).

> **SOIL** Stony limestone hills.
> **STYLE** The wines of Nemea can be dry, medium dry, or sweet, which can be confusing for consumers. The dry, deeply colored reds are not very tannic, but they are powerful with long spicy notes.

Color:	Serving temperature:	Ageing potential:
Red.	59 to 63°F (15 to 17°C).	5 to 10 years.

Delights of Turkish wines

Only a small percentage of Turkey's grapes are used to make wine; and yet an increasing number of wines are of excellent quality. Doluca, a company based in Thrace, produces several million bottles a year from grapes from all over Turkey. Its Doluca Özel Kav Kirmizi, a red wine made from grape varieties grown in the regions of Diyarbakir and Elazig in Kurdistan, won top honors in a tasting organized in 2004 by the Hürriyet newspaper. Sarafin, another notable red wine, comes from western Turkey. Matured in oak barrels, it has won several awards at international competitions. In the Ankara region, Kavaklidere produces a wide range of interesting blends of local and international grape varieties. Its Kavaklidere Bogazkere, a red wine that is matured for 12 months in barrel, was also included in the Hürriyet newspaper selection.

BEKAA VALLEY WINES

Most good quality Lebanese wines are produced in the Zahleh region, at the middle of the Bekaa Valley. The work is led by three main estates: Château Ksara, Château Musar, and Château Kefraya. However, there are a few good smaller properties, including the relative newcomer Château Marsyas. Most producers make all three colors of wine.

> **GRAPE VARIETIES** There are nearly 20 varieties in the Zahleh region, including international varieties such as Cabernet Sauvignon, Merlot, and Syrah for the red and rosé wines; Chardonnay, Sauvignon Blanc, and Muscat for the white wines.

> **SOIL** Predominantly loess.

> **STYLE** Powerful, tannic, fruity red wines with an excellent capacity to improve with age. The rosés are fruity and full-bodied. Some white wines develop great expression over many years, with flavors of spice and menthol.

Color:	Serving temperature:	Ageing potential:
Red, white, and rosé.	*50 to 54°F (10 to 12°C) for the whites and rosés; 59 to 64°F (15 to 18°C) for the reds. (Decant fine reds 30 minutes before serving.)*	*Up to 20 years (Château Musar).*

Rebirth of Meknes

French wine merchant Pierre Castel was the driving force in a restructuring of Moroccan vineyards in the area around Meknes during the mid-1990s. Located between the foothills of the Atlas Mountains to the south and Mount Zerhoun to the north, the vines grow in sandy and clay-limestone soil; the hot climate provides the right conditions for the grapes to thoroughly ripen.

Beni M'Tir, Zerhoune, and Guerrouane are the three "appellations of guaranteed origin," representing 2,030 acres (822 ha) of vines. They are planted with Syrah, Cabernet Sauvignon, and Merlot. The wines are sold primarily under the Halana brand, and are described by the name of the grape variety. They have a pleasant style and go well with Moroccan cuisine.

UNITED STATES

AND CANADA

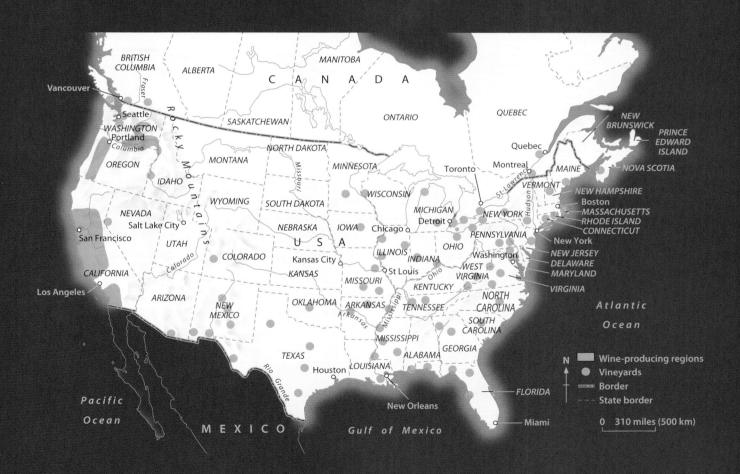

BRITISH
COLUMBIA

ALBERTA

MANITOBA

C A N A D A

Vancouver

Fraser

Seattle

SASKATCHEWAN

ONTARIO

QUEBEC

NEW
BRUNSWICK

WASHINGTON
Portland

Columbia

R
o
c
k
y

M
o
u
n
t
a
i
n
s

NORTH DAKOTA

MONTANA

Missouri

MINNESOTA

Quebec

Montreal

St Lawrence

MAINE

PRINCE
EDWARD
ISLAND

NOVA SCOTIA

OREGON

IDAHO

WYOMING

SOUTH DAKOTA

WISCONSIN

Toronto

VERMONT

Hudson

NEW HAMPSHIRE

Boston

NEVADA

Salt Lake City

NEBRASKA

IOWA

Chicago

MICHIGAN

Detroit

NEW YORK

MASSACHUSETTS
RHODE ISLAND
CONNECTICUT

San Francisco

UTAH

Colorado

COLORADO

Kansas City

ILLINOIS

INDIANA

OHIO

Ohio

PENNSYLVANIA

Washington

WEST
VIRGINIA

New York

NEW JERSEY
DELAWARE
MARYLAND

CALIFORNIA

Los Angeles

ARIZONA

NEW
MEXICO

KANSAS

MISSOURI

St Louis

KENTUCKY

VIRGINIA

OKLAHOMA

ARKANSAS

Arkansas

TENNESSEE

Mississippi

NORTH
CAROLINA

SOUTH
CAROLINA

Atlantic

Ocean

Pacific

Ocean

TEXAS

Rio Grande

Houston

LOUISIANA

New Orleans

MISSISSIPPI

ALABAMA

GEORGIA

FLORIDA

Miami

M E X I C O

Gulf of Mexico

N

Wine-producing regions

Vineyards

Border

State border

0   310 miles (500 km)

UNITED STATES AND CANADA

Wine production in North America is concentrated along the west coast. The size of California's industry alone would make it the fourth-largest producer in the world, if it were an independent country. During the past 30 years, several US wines have developed to match the world's best. Canadian wine production is more modest in scale and concentrated in two provinces: Ontario (in the east) and British Columbia (in the west). In fact, 99 percent of national production takes place in these two regions.

UNITED STATES

The USA is the fourth-largest producer of wine in the world, and it's now the leading wine consumer market. Although wine has been produced here for 300 years, the industry has only really developed since the Second World War. Production is concentrated in four states: California (accounting for about 90 percent of the national total), Washington State, Oregon, and New York State. A young, modern, and dynamic industry, it has achieved a very high level of quality thanks to huge investment and outstanding research. However, the cultural position of wine in America is still very far from that in Europe: consumption per capita per year stands at just over 3 gallons (11.3 liters), only a quarter of French consumption, for example.

UNITED STATES STATISTICS

Vineyard area: 938,550 acres (380,000 ha)

Production: 260 million cases (23,500,000 hl)

Reds and rosés: 55%

Whites: 45%

(Wine Institute & OIV, 2008)

From the Vikings to the modern era

VINLAND, LAND OF THE WILD VINE. We will never know for sure if the Viking Leif Eriksson really did set foot on the North American east coast around 1000 AD, but his description of a country he called "Vinland" is preserved in several medieval manuscripts, and it describes a green landscape dotted with wild vines.

EUROPEAN SETTLEMENT AND AN AGE OF EXPERIMENTATION. From the 16th century, when Europeans first colonized North America, they found several varieties of the *vitis* genus (*vitis labrusca* and *vitis riparia*), but no *vitis vinifera*. Along the east coast, despite a damp climate, many attempts were made to produce wine from grapes of these indigenous varieties. The results had a rather gamey or animal character, sometimes described as

> Napa Valley is the best-known American wine-producing region.

"foxy." Later, European settlers introduced different plantings of their own *vitis vinifera* varieties. Over time, these crossed with local vine strains and resulted in new hybrids up and down the east coast. But all attempts to propagate pure varieties of *vitis vinifera* failed. The cause of the failures, unknown at the time, was a native insect that would later devastate European vineyards, the aphid *phylloxera vastatrix*.

VINEYARD EXPANSION. Despite difficulties, vineyards expanded from the central east coast to the southeast and across the south during the 18th and 19th centuries, starting with numerous hybrid varieties.

> In the USA, harvest work is most often mechanized.

Early west coast development was completely separate. During the 18th century, Spanish Franciscan monks had introduced several varieties of *vitis vinifera* to Mexico and southern California; and the first winery was established near San Diego in 1769. From 1850 onward, California became the scene of remarkable development. Successful plantings of large numbers of European varieties were coupled with a constant stream of migrants from the east coast. The appearance of *phylloxera*, 30 years later, curtailed this expansion only slightly, since the grafting of *vinifera* onto indigenous vine rootstocks had already been discovered in Europe.

FROM PROHIBITION TO THE MODERN ERA. We can only wonder what American winemaking would be like today if national Prohibition had not ruined a booming business. From 1920 to 1933, "the manufacture, sale, or transportation of alcoholic beverages" was banned throughout the country, with the exception of wine for religious sacraments. The result was half a century of stagnation, and a shadow that still hangs

over industry organization. However, a revival started in the 1960s. California wineries increased in number, and alongside high yields for mass production, a very dynamic sector developed. Driven by winemakers focused on quality, this excellent work has expanded beyond California and producer numbers are growing in almost every state.

America's wine market

LEGISLATION. American wine law varies to some extent across the country. Each state sets its own laws regarding the distribution and consumption of alcoholic products. For example, even though Prohibition was repealed in 1933, some places (counties) still maintain a ban on alcohol sales. At the federal level, legislation on wine is governed by the TTB (Alcohol and Tobacco Tax and Trade Bureau). The scope of federal regulation includes approval of labeling, federal taxation, and designation of official production regions–called American Viticultural Areas or AVAs.

AMERICAN VITICULTURAL AREAS (AVAS). To help producers (and consumers) identify a wine's place of production, the government has established a system of certified viticultural areas, AVAs. This constitutes the US appellation system (*see also* p.100). Since recognition of the first AVAs, including the Napa Valley, in 1981, the number of appellations has exploded. Today there are more than 190, and there is a movement to better define more narrow *terroirs*: meaning AVAs within AVAs. With this said, their size is variable—ranging from a single valley to an entire county and sometimes even beyond.

Major wine-producing states

Vineyards exist in most US states, but production is not always significant. With that said, progress in terms of quality is being made everywhere. Three west coast states, California, Oregon, and Washington, produce the vast majority of US wine.

American wine labels

Following the name of the producer, or a producer's brand, the grape variety remains the most common way to designate wines in North America. This approach to the description of a wine was originally the idea of a wine merchant in New York City, Frank Schoonmaker, during the 1930s. It has gradually replaced the former practice of copying the names of famous European production regions such as Chablis, Burgundy, Port, Sherry, or Sauternes. For wines blended from several grape varieties, the use of a proprietary name (or that of a vineyard) is becoming increasingly popular—especially among high-end wines.

CALIFORNIA, WASHINGTON, OREGON

California: other coastal regions/areas

(map)

Seattle
COLUMBIA VALLEY
Spokane
Tacoma
WASHINGTON
Snake
Walla Walla
Yakima
Columbia
Portland
Salem
WILLAMETTE VALLEY
OREGON
Eugene
UMPQUA VALLEY
Roseburg
ROGUE VALLEY
Cascade Range
Coast Ranges
Sierra Nevada
Sacramento
San Joaquin
Santa Rosa
Sacramento
SIERRA NEVADA FOOTHILLS
Oakland
San Francisco
San Jose
Monterey
CENTRAL COAST
CENTRAL VALLEY
Fresno
Paso Robles
CALIFORNIA
San Luis Obispo
Bakersfield
Santa Maria
Santa Ynez
Santa Barbara
Pacific Ocean
Los Angeles
SOUTHERN CALIFORNIA
Temecula
Colorado
San Diego

0   125 miles (200 km)   N

MENDOCINO
POTTER VALLEY
GLENN
Ukiah
ANDERSON VALLEY
CLEAR LAKE
McDOWELL VALLEY
CLEAR LAKE
COLUSA
ALEXANDER VALLEY
DRY CREEK VALLEY
GUENOC VALLEY
SONOMA
KNIGHTS VALLEY
RUSSIAN RIVER VALLEY
Lake Berryessa
YOLO
Santa Rosa
SONOMA COAST
NAPA VALLEY
SONOMA VALLEY
NAPA
Napa
SOLANO
MARIN
LOS CARNEROS
Vallejo
San Pablo Bay
Berkeley
CONTRA COSTA
San Francisco
Oakland
San Mateo
San Francisco Bay
LIVERMORE VALLEY
ALAMEDA
SAN MATEO
San Jose
SANTA CRUZ MOUNTAINS
SANTA CLARA
SANTA CRUZ
SANTA CLARA VALLEY
Santa Cruz
SAN YSIDRO

N

0   30 miles (50 km)

Wine-producing regions
Border
State border
County border

1976: The Judgment of Paris

At the time of America's bicentennial, the British wine merchant Steven Spurrier organized a blind tasting in Paris of some great French and California wines. To everyone's amazement, the California wines won in every category (notably reds from Cabernet Sauvignon, and whites from Chardonnay), beating some of the biggest names from Burgundy and Bordeaux! This now-famous tasting confirmed the quality of California wines to the world. Some felt that the victors would not stand the test of time; but in two "rematches" in 1986 and 2006, with the same vintages from the same producers, the California wines retained their advantage.

California alone produces 90 percent of the national total. In the east, several states have production that deserves consideration, even if their wines are consumed only locally. This is the case for New York, Ohio, and Virginia. These states once cultivated only indigenous grapes, but they have benefited from the introduction of hybrid varieties such as Seyval and Baco, developed in France to resist *phylloxera* and other diseases. To the south, Texas and New Mexico have recently booming industries.

California

According to 2008 figures, there are some 526,000 acres (213,000 ha) of vines producing wine in California. The vineyards are scattered across more than 600 miles (1,000 km) from north to south. In terms of scale, if California were regarded as a single country, it would be the fourth-largest wine-producing region in the world and the biggest outside of Europe.

California's immense geographic area is matched by great climatic diversity, making it possible to develop all types and styles of wine. The most recognized areas are located in the counties of Sonoma and Napa to the north of San Francisco Bay; but great work is also done around Santa Cruz and Monterey, south of San Francisco, and in locations along the coast down toward Los Angeles.

NORTH OF SAN FRANCISCO. In Napa Valley (*see* p.443), the diversity of local conditions merits its division into districts or sub-appellations. Sonoma County is even larger and more complicated. The AVAs to the north and east, such as Alexander Valley and Dry Creek Valley (*see* p.442), are warmer and produce rich wines from Cabernet Sauvignon, Merlot, and Zinfandel. The Russian River Valley (*see* p.442), in the west, and Carneros (*see* p.446), to the south (straddling Sonoma and Napa), have a cooler climate and produce beautiful Chardonnays and Pinot Noirs. Elsewhere along the coast, wine production is less concentrated. Mendocino County to the north, on the Pacific Ocean, has become a center for sparkling wines. Many Champagne producers find conditions here ideal for Pinot Noir and Chardonnay, the grapes that produce the base wines. Lake County, which is further inland and drier, is perfect for Cabernet Sauvignon and Sauvignon Blanc.

CENTRAL AND SOUTHERN COAST. The vineyards of central and southern California stretch from San Francisco to Santa Barbara, with a pocket further south toward San Diego. Monterey County produces Chardonnays and Pinot Noir in very dry, breezy conditions. Halfway between San Francisco and Los Angeles, the region of Paso Robles is very

Mexico

Mexico is the oldest wine-producing country in the Americas: from 1521, early settlers were planting vines. Commercially sustainable viticulture has developed since the 1960s. Mexican vineyards total approximately 123,500 acres (50,000 ha), but only 10 percent are destined for wine production; the rest provide table grapes or go to distillation. The most significant volumes are produced in seven Mexican provinces. The best-known wines come from the north, in Baja California, which accounts for 90 per cent of the country's wine production. This territory is a southern continuation of the US state with the same name, just across the border. Baja's dry climate is very conducive to growing vines, but irrigation is necessary. The varieties planted are the common international ones (Cabernet Sauvignon, Merlot, Malbec, and Syrah for reds; Chardonnay and Sauvignon Blanc for whites); but there are also other varieties such as Zinfandel, Nebbiolo, Barbera, Tempranillo, and Petite Syrah for reds, and Palomino, Colombard, and Chenin Blanc for whites.

> Vineyards and orchards in the Yakima Valley of Washington State.

popular for its Rhône blends (Syrah, Grenache, and Mourvèdre in particular). In one of the most southerly vineyard areas of California, around Santa Barbara and Santa Ynez, the cool ocean air seeps through the mountains, allowing beautiful Pinot Noir and Chardonnay to be produced.

CENTRAL VALLEY AND MASS PRODUCTION. Inland and away from maritime influences, is the vast Central Valley—around the state capital, Sacramento. This hot and dry region produces mainly entry-level wines, except in the areas around Lodi and in the Sierra foothills. There, some of the oldest vineyards in California are capable of producing great wines.

Washington

Anchoring the Pacific Northwest, Washington State is the second-largest wine producer in the country, with 40,000 acres (16,200 ha) of vineyards. Inland valleys (which, in addition to grapes, grow many fruits) are sheltered from the cold, damp weather of the coast by the Cascades Mountains. This protection is complete enough that the skies are largely cloudless and the landscape is semi-desert; so irrigation is drawn from the vast Columbia River system.

The expansion of the wine industry in Washington has been staggering since 1970, and the number of wineries has increased from just a handful to more than 700 today. Officially, 11 AVAs have been defined. The state produces a range of rather fruity white wines (from Chardonnay, Riesling, and Pinot Gris) as well as excellent reds whose style ranges from delicate to powerful, mostly from Bordeaux grape varieties but also from Syrah.

Oregon

Set between Washington and California, the Oregon industry has recently realized its potential for fine wine. The first modern

> Trimming work in the Rogue Valley of southern Oregon.

plantings date from the 1960s, with a few pioneers coming from California in search of cooler conditions to produce Chardonnay and Pinot Noir. Since then, Pinot Noir has carved a place for itself in the Willamette Valley.

Over 40 years, the region has earned a great reputation for its work with this variety, which thrives in the cooler, coastal weather. The same is true for regional white wines (especially Pinot Gris). There are dozens of other varieties planted Oregon, often on an experimental basis.

Total production here is not large (from 20,000 acres), but there are more than 400 active wineries, and as many as 16 approved AVAs.

New York

The state of New York is the third-largest wine producer in the US (including both *vinifera* or hybrid varieties). Plantings stretch between Long Island and the Great Lakes. This is a region where many native North American varieties and hybrids thrive, some of which are tried and tested: Aurora, Cayuga, and Seyval for white wines, and Baco Noir or Catawba for reds. Total production is even more significant when considering the amount of wine (and juice) produced from *vitis labrusca* varieties, such as Concord).

New York State's production areas border the Canadian province of Ontario, and the regions share some climatic similarities, especially around the Niagara-on-the-Lake area (*see next page*). The Finger Lakes district is the largest production area in New York; and its temperate climate, the result of these bodies of water, is conducive to vine cultivation, including *vitis vinifera* varieties such as Riesling. Elsewhere,

the ability of vines to withstand harsh winters is the main factor in selection.

Other wine-producing states

While wine is made in almost all US states, production remains limited and intended for local consumption. In addition, legislation in several states bans wine from being shipped beyond their borders, which hardly encourages development. There are a growing number of exceptions, though, especially Texas and Virginia.

Like the state of New York, Texas and Virginia have districts growing *vitis vinifera*. Texas continues a wine history started by Spanish missionaries from Mexico. It also was a Texan—a botanist called Munson—who helped save the European wine industry from *phylloxera* by shipping native American varieties for grafting during replanting efforts in the 1880s.

There are more than 160 wineries in Texas working about 3,100 acres (1,255 ha) of vineyards. The numbers have been growing at a rapid clip since the beginning of the 21st century, making this the fifth-largest wine-producing state in the country. Most of the vineyards are located in upland areas in the center and west, where the climate is less humid and the nights cooler. Texas has eight AVAs. As for Virginia, it is the second-largest wine-producing state on the east coast. There are six AVAs and several other districts planted with native varieties, hybrids, and *vitis vinifera*.

DID YOU KNOW...?

In the United States, vineyard regions are classified according to a system developed by scientists Maynard Amerine and A. J. Winkler. Their work was based on the research of a 19th-century French scientist, A. P. de Candolle, who found that vines begin to grow each spring after the air temperature averages 50°F (10°C). In 1944, Winkler and Amerine, working at the University of California-Davis, drew up a regional climatic classification based on the total number of degrees (above 50°F) accumulated during the seven months that the vine grows. It is sometimes criticized for its oversimplification, but the system is widely used in reference material on the subject. Thus, Level I regions have less than 2,500 "degree-days" per season; those at Level II, between 2,501 and 3,000 degree-days, those at Level III, between 3,001 and 3,500 degree-days, those at Level IV, between 3,501 and 4,000 degree-days; and those at Level V accumulate more than 4,000 degree-days. As a guide, the average Bordeaux climat is considered to be around Levels II or III.

CANADA

Compared with the USA's wine industry, Canada's work is very modest in scale. Two provinces, Ontario and British Columbia, account for 99 percent of production. A very limited quantity also comes from other provinces, such as Quebec. Wine production on a commercial scale is a recent occurrence here for three main reasons: the difficulty of adapting *vitis vinifera* varieties to a harsh climate; a puritanical attitude that severely controlled (when it did not entirely prohibit) production and consumption of alcohol; and, as a consequence, a delay in the exploration and development of sites suitable for *vitis vinifera* or quality hybrids.

CANADA STATISTICS

Vineyard area: 27,000 acres (10,900 ha)

Production: 8 million cases (720,000 hl)

Whites: 55%

Reds and rosés: 45%

(Canadian Vintners Association & Ministry of Agriculture, 2008)

Recent start and rapid expansion

Modern Canadian viticulture started in Ontario during the 1950s, as a result of experiments by Brights Wines with Riesling and Chardonnay. But it was not until the foundation of Inniskillin Wines in Niagara-on-the-Lake, southern Ontario—in 1974 by Donald Ziraldo and Karl Kaiser—that Canada took its place in world wine production. Using techniques of cultivation and vinification from his native Austria, Kaiser demonstrated the remarkable possibilities for Ontario's production of ice wine, especially from hybrids such as Seyval. Others have followed suit, and ice wine is now a specialty of the region, and widely exported. In 1979, the establishment of Sumac Ridge Winery in the Okanagan Valley marked the starting point for British Columbia's commercial wine industry. Now a quality label, the Vintners Quality Alliance (VQA), brings together the best producers and insists on production from *vitis vinifera* or the finest hybrids (*see* p.102).

Niagara-on-the-Lake and Okanagan Valley

Separated by thousands of miles, these two regions produce almost all of Canada's wines. While Niagara specializes in ice wine, it also produces good quality dry whites from Riesling, Chardonnay, and hybrid grape varieties. In addition, the local market tends to support Canadian white wines over imported ones. With the gradual development of the Okanagan Valley, it's clear that the warmer, drier climate and rugged terrain are capable of producing fine red wines. Overall, the country's production has increased dramatically—there has some 500 wineries, 10 times more than 20 years ago!

Ice wine: Canada's frozen nectar

Ice wine is a rare and very special product, of which Canada is the world's largest source. The grapes are left on the vine long after the leaves fall, and until bitter cold arrives in December or January. As a result of deep freezing, there is a kind of dehydration that causes a high concentration of all components of the berry: sugars, acids, and other solids. The amount of juice available at the time of harvesting is no more than 5 to 10 percent of a normal harvest. These precious grapes are picked at night in temperatures around 14°F (−10°C) in order to ensure that the berries are still frozen for the press. After pressing, the thick and very sweet juice is fermented very slowly for several months, producing a white wine or, more rarely, a red, that is relatively low in alcohol (between 10 and 12% ABV), but very rich in sugar and full of flavor. Ice wine is produced in Quebec and British Columbia, but especially in Ontario, in the Niagara-on-the-Lake region. The technique for creating ice wine was introduced for the first time in 1980 by Karl Kaiser, co-founder of the Inniskillin Winery. The importance of this production to Canada is such that the term "ice wine" has been trademarked.

> In the Okanagan Valley, the vines are sprayed with water to form a layer of ice to protect the plants against frost.

Leading USA and Canada wineries

Although almost every US state produces wine, only four of them—California, Washington, Oregon, and New York—produce any significant volume that is regularly consumed beyond their borders. California, whose most important sub-regions we detail here, accounts for about 90 percent of the national total. As for Canada, its production is small, but growing and improving in quality.

WASHINGTON STATE

The second-largest wine region after California, Washington dominates production in the Pacific Northwest. Commercial winemaking is only 40 years old here, but the rapid expansion of vineyard and winery numbers has been unrelenting. All key growing areas are located inland, 150 miles (250 km) from the coast. The Cascade Mountains shelter them from wet weather that comes from the ocean, which means a sunny, dry climate. Irrigation is needed almost everywhere. You might be surprised to discover that the latitude of this region is equivalent to the median between Bordeaux and Burgundy. The continental conditions produce large temperature variations between summer and winter, and even between day and night. The color and intensity of flavors in the wines are often impressive. Prestigious foreign investors, such as Antinori (Italy) and Loosen (Germany), have been convinced by the potential of this region.

> **PRODUCTION AREAS** (AVAs) Columbia Valley, Horse Heaven Hills, Red Mountain, Wahluke Slope, Walla Walla Valley, Yakima Valley, and others.

> **GRAPE VARIETIES** For red: Merlot, Cabernet Sauvignon, Syrah, Malbec, and others; for white: Chardonnay, Riesling, Sauvignon Blanc, Sémillon, Pinot Gris, and others.

> **SOIL** Loess and sandy, alluvial soil on a bed of volcanic basalt.

> **STYLE** Reds and whites are produced in equal numbers, and both generally display great intensity of flavor. Some may achieve considerable power or finesse (or both).

> **NOTABLE PRODUCERS** Barnard Griffin, Cayuse, Château Ste Michelle, Columbia Crest, DeLille, L'Ecole No41, Hogue Cellars, K Vintners, Leonetti, Milbrandt Vineyards, Quilceda Creek, Andrew Will, and Woodward Canyon.

OREGON

The fourth-largest wine-producing state in America, Oregon is a region of very small producers. Its composition is a reflection of its topography, with numerous valleys divided into artisanal plots. That scale, and the fact that it works with a cooler, wetter climate than its two neighbors, California and Washington, explains why Oregon has developed more slowly. The exact location of plots is often crucial in bringing the grapes to maturity. Despite the cool climate, summer drought is common in inland valleys. Oregon has established it reputation largely with Pinot Noir. In fact, the Burgundy *maison* Drouhin has established an estate here in the Willamette Valley.

> **PRODUCTION AREAS** (AVAs) Applegate Valley, Rogue Valley, Snake River Valley, Umpqua Valley, Willamette Valley (with six sub-AVAs), as well as several appellations that extend into Washington (including Walla Walla Valley).

> **GRAPE VARIETIES** For red: Pinot Noir and Syrah; for white: Chardonnay, Pinot Gris, and Riesling.

> **SOIL** Mixed sedimentary or fractured volcanic basalt.

> **STYLE** These wines reflect their cool climate. Both whites and reds tend toward finesse rather than power.

> **NOTABLE PRODUCERS** Adelsheim, Amity, Argyle, Beaux Frères, Brick House, Cristom, Domaine Drouhin, Domaine Serene, Eyrie Vineyards, King Estate, Lemelson.

MENDOCINO COUNTY AND LAKE COUNTY

In addition to Anderson Valley, several AVAs cover this vast stretch of northern California. But they sometimes overlap, so that they are not easily differentiated. In Mendocino, the climate varies from maritime to almost continental over the course of short distance. On the Winkler scale, this climate is generally part of Level III (*see box* p.438). The best vineyards are located on hillsides. The upper part of Lake County is in Level II, that is to say that the climate is much cooler because of the altitude; the lower part, such as Guenoc Valley, enjoys a climate comparable to Mendocino.

> **GRAPE VARIETIES** For red: Pinot Noir, Cabernet Sauvignon, Merlot, and Zinfandel; for white: Chardonnay and Sauvignon Blanc.

> **SOIL** Highly variable. Sometimes volcanic, sometimes schist, as well as alluvial red clay.

> **STYLE** As variable as the exposures and soils, ranging from fresh to powerful.

> **NOTABLE PRODUCERS** Fetzer, Kendall-Jackson, Navarro, McDowell Valley Vineyards, Parducci, and Scharffenberger.

Three Mendocino County estates

• **Fetzer (Mendocino).** With its base and main vineyards in Mendocino, Fetzer is a pioneer of large-scale organic viticulture for the country. It was part of a large corporate spirits group (Brown-Forman) until early 2011, but is now part of Chile's Concho y Toro wine group.

• **Kendall-Jackson (Anderson Valley).** Like many large producers in California, "K-J" has vineyards in several regions and produces a wide range of wines. Its vineyards in Lake County are the historic home of this company, founded in 1974 by Jess Jackson, a former lawyer from San Francisco. Its wines are well made, highly consistent, and have a very accessible style.

• **Roederer Estate (Anderson Valley).** Working here since 1982, this fine Champagne house focuses on the production of sparkling wines made from Pinot Noir and Chardonnay grown exclusively in its own vineyards. Its sparkling wines are among the finest in the United States.

ANDERSON VALLEY

Located in Mendocino County, about 100 miles/160 km north of San Francisco, this narrow valley (rarely more than a mile wide) is sandwiched between two mountain ranges. This produces significant climatic differences between the growing areas at the bottom of the valley (which are cooler and misty), and those at higher altitudes (above the line of mist and sunnier). Visitors to the bottom of the valley would never suspect that red grapes could reach such an excellent level of maturity above them.

> **GRAPE VARIETIES** For red: primarily Pinot Noir; for white: mainly Chardonnay, Gewurztraminer, and Riesling

> **SOIL** Alluvial, clay and gravel soil in the valley; less fertile and more acidic soils on the hillsides.

> **STYLE** Quite fine and fresh, just like the climate; but the precise location of the vineyard may result in large variations in style.

> **NOTABLE PRODUCERS** Greenwood Ridge, Kendall-Jackson, Navarro, Roederer Estate, and Scharffenberger (sparkling wines).

RUSSIAN RIVER VALLEY

This beautiful valley runs east to west, and lies southwest of the fabulous tourist town of Healdsburg. As a result of its orientation to the Pacific, the climate is fresh and cool, especially at the western end, where it is often misty. The area is well suited to Chardonnay and Pinot Noir, which are used to produce high quality sparkling or still wines. Total plantings are about 15,000 acres (6,000 ha), but they are expanding.

> **GRAPE VARIETIES** For red: Pinot Noir (30 percent of plantings), Zinfandel, Merlot, and Cabernet Sauvignon; for white: Chardonnay (40 percent of plantings) and Sauvignon Blanc.
> **SOIL** In general, they are Franciscan (a mixture of sandstone and schist) and well drained. But there are variations in certain areas, such as Chalk Hill, where they are sandy and lighter.
> **STYLE** The cool climate enables producers to make fine and intense Chardonnay, as well as notable Pinot Noirs.
> **NOTABLE PRODUCERS** DeLoach, Ferrari-Carano, Gary Farrell, Hartford Family, Iron Horse, J Vineyards, Kistler, Marimar Estate, Rocchioli, Sonoma-Cutrer, and Williams Selyem.

ALEXANDER VALLEY

Located in northern Sonoma County, with the town of Healdsburg at its southern tip, Alexander Valley lies east of Russian River and runs parallel to the coast. The vineyard (just over 15,000 acres/ 6,000 ha) lies between the coastal zone and the Mayacamas Mountains, which separate Napa from Sonoma. The climate is warmer and more diverse than the Russian River Valley. Almost all key varieties can be matured here, and the range is wide. The neighboring Dry Creek Valley hosts some of the oldest and most sought-after Zinfandel vines in the state of California.

> **GRAPE VARIETIES** For red: Cabernet Sauvignon, Zinfandel, and Merlot; for white: Chardonnay, Sauvignon Blanc, and Viognier.
> **SOIL** Alluvium with a variable amount of gravel, depending on the area; the hillsides have very diverse soils.
> **STYLE** Given the diversity of local climates and grape varieties, it is difficult to identify a dominant style for this region. Cabernet Sauvignon dominates Alexander Valley, but Dry Creek is famous for its Zinfandels, often produced from very old vines.
> **NOTABLE PRODUCERS** Clos du Bois, Coppola, Gallo Family, Hanna, Jordan, Ridge (Lytton Springs & Geyserville), Rodney Strong, Seghesio, Silver Oak, Simi, Trentadue, and Verité.

Two Sonoma County estates

• **Seghesio (Alexander Valley).** This family business could by itself tell the history of Sonoma County wine. The Seghesios came from Italy during the 19th century, and initially practiced cooperative and mixed farming before becoming specialists in wine production. The current generation has changed its focus by concentrating on the production of wines from their own vineyards. Some of them, such as the concentrated and very juicy Zinfandels, are among the best in Sonoma County.

• **Sonoma-Cutrer (Russian River).** Specializing in two grape varieties—Chardonnay and Pinot Noir—this estate has long been responsible for one of the best California Chardonnays, a wine called "Les Pierres." All its wines are capable of great longevity.

SONOMA VALLEY

CALIFORNIA (SONOMA COUNTY)

Sonoma Valley is located north of San Francisco Bay and west of Napa. Its topography is very diverse. Unlike Napa, which is almost entirely dedicated to viticulture, Sonoma is fragmented with vineyards alongside other forms of agriculture. Yet its wine production began in the middle of the 19th century (before the first plantings in Napa). The sub-region of Sonoma Mountain is interesting because of the cool air at night and sunshine by day that results from its altitude.

> **GRAPE VARIETIES** For red: Cabernet Sauvignon, Merlot, Pinot Noir, Syrah, and certainly Zinfandel; for white: Chardonnay, Sauvignon Blanc, and Sémillon.

> **SOIL** In the valley, Franciscan soils, a mixture of sandstone, schist, and stones that have come down from the mountains; volcanic soils or metamorphic rocks in the hills.

> **STYLE** The Cabernets and Zinfandels from Sonoma Mountain combine power and finesse. Styles in the valley are more variable and depend on their proximity to or distance from San Francisco Bay.

> **NOTABLE PRODUCERS** Cline, Gundlach Bundschu, Hanzell, Kenwood, Matanzas Creek, and Ravenswood.

NAPA VALLEY

CALIFORNIA (NAPA COUNTY)

While Napa accounts for only four percent of the wine produced in California, this valley—37 miles (60 km) long and no more than four miles (6 km) wide—is for many a symbol in itself of California wine. It is separated from Sonoma to the west by the Mayacamas Mountains. The only access to the effects of the ocean lies at its southern end, where it opens onto San Francisco Bay. This creates differences in climate between the south (which is cool) and the north end of the valley around Calistoga (which is very warm). Napa is fully enclosed by mountains to the west and east. South of Napa, the Carneros region (*see* p.446), which has

its own AVA, extends into Sonoma Valley. Note that Napa Valley encompasses many much smaller AVAs, such as Calistoga, Rutherford, Stag's Leap, Mount Veeder, Howell Mountain, and Oakville. Though if their name appears on the label, it must be overtly associated with Napa.

> **GRAPE VARIETIES** For red: Cabernet Sauvignon, Merlot, Cabernet Franc, Zinfandel, and Sangiovese; for white: Chardonnay and Sauvignon Blanc.

> **SOIL** More than 30 soil types have been identified: alluvium with varying gravel content in the valley; alluvial clays and stony, sometimes volcanic, soils on hillsides and in the northern valley.

> **STYLE** A very full body and rich flavors are the benchmark for Cabernet Sauvignon or Merlot from Napa; though this is of course dependent on the location of the vineyard, the diversity of grape varieties, and the choices of producer.

> **NOTABLE PRODUCERS** Beringer, Cakebread, Caymus, Château Montelena, Clos Pegase, Clos du Val, Corison, Diamond Creek, Freemark Abbey, Harlan, Heitz, Hess Collection, Joseph Phelps, Newton, Opus One, Robert Mondavi, Rubicon, Schramsberg (sparkling), Shafer, Stag's Leap Wine Cellars, and Storybook Mountain.

Selected Napa Valley wineries

- **Robert Mondavi.** Robert Mondavi died in 2008, but the winery that bears his name remains a tribute to the man who has probably done more than anyone else to make Napa one of the best wine regions in the world (see also pp.444-5). The specialties of the estate are Cabernet Sauvignons and a very good Sauvignon Blanc called "Fumé Blanc."

- **Clos du Val.** This estate, established by businessman John Goelet during the 1970s, has followed the philosophy of its director, Frenchman Bernard Portet, since its inception. The wines are often lower in alcohol and lighter in extract than the typical Napa style, but age well.

- **Diamond Creek.** This is one of the pioneers of vineyard block-based vinification (which involves producing wines separately from the grapes in each plot). The wines thus bear the names of their parent sites: Red Rock Terrace, Gravelly Meadow, Winery Lake, and Volcanic Hill. Wines of great intensity and power.

- **Joseph Phelps.** This estate is a pioneer in producing Rhône varieties: Syrah, Grenache, Mourvèdre, and Viognier. Its Cabernet Backus and Bordeaux blend Insignia rank it as one of the top producers in Napa.

1. Opus One winery in Oakville, Napa Valley, California.
2. Robert Mondavi, who died in May 2008.
3. Opus One label, "signed" by Baron Philippe de Rothschild and Robert Mondavi.
4. Oak barrels in the enormous Opus One cellars.

2005
OPUS ONE

Opus One, exceptional California wine

It is now generally accepted that the land to the north of San Francisco, particularly in the Napa Valley, has remarkable *terroirs* for wine production. For decades, many wines produced here have achieved exceptional quality. And this has been confirmed by several blind tastings, the most famous being in 1976, known ever since as the "Judgment of Paris" (see p.436).

OPUS ONE

Opus One is one of the contemporary legends of Californian wine production, and considered one of the best New World wines in general. It is the product of a magnificent California *terroir* and an alliance of two personalities with strong convictions: the Bordeaux Baron

Philippe de Rothschild and the American Robert Mondavi.

A FRENCH BARON AND AN AMERICAN WINEMAKER

Philippe de Rothschild will be long remembered as the head of Château Mouton-Rothschild. He used his talent and tenacity to ensure that its wine, originally classified as Second Cru, was raised to Premier Cru status in 1973, the only change in the classification of Bordeaux wines since 1855. His daughter, Baroness Philippine de Rothschild, took over with the same enthusiasm. For his part, Robert Mondavi had been the leader of California wineries since the mid-1960s. He had proved that it was possible to make great wines in the

region, given sufficient determination. He was both obstinate and modest and never gave up on what he called his "mission." His sons also followed this same path. In 1970, these two men met in Hawaii, and they quickly understood each other. So in 1978, Robert Mondavi went to see the baron, and both men agreed to create a vineyard together in California. In 1979, the cellar master of Mouton went to the Napa Valley and started "creating" a new wine using the methods from Château Mouton-Rothschild.

BIRTH OF AN ESTATE

The project was officially announced in 1980, to general amazement. In 1983, sites were chosen in Napa Valley that met

4

the requirements of both parties. They then thought about a name that would be easy to remember and pronounce on both sides of the Atlantic. The baron, who was a great music lover, suggested "Opus" and, since this was the first wine of its kind, the name "Opus One" was finally settled on.

A STAR IS BORN

In 1984, two vintages were presented to the public: the 1979 and the 1980. They were an immediate success and were critically acclaimed by the press and by trade experts. Of course, when two such talents work together in a high quality *terroir*, some wonderful bottles of wine are only to be expected. Since 1991, spectacular new wine cellars have been built to produce and house the wine. These facilities meet a single criterion: the very best storage for quality wine of this kind.

BORDEAUX VARIETIES

As always, it begins with the vine. The majority grape is Cabernet Sauvignon, which produces great results in Napa. Cabernet Franc and Merlot are also represented, and have recently been rounded off with some Petit Verdot and Malbec. All of these varieties originate in Bordeaux and are ultimately blended in varying proportions depending on the vintage. The harvests are handled gently, and are sometimes even carried out at night to take advantage of the cool temperatures. Upon arrival at the estate, the grapes are carefully sorted and all traces of rot or leaves are manually removed from the grapes.

CAREFUL PRODUCTION

After fermentation, in order to maximize extraction of color and flavor material, the maceration period can last for more than 40 days. The wine is then put into

new French oak barrels where it will spend 17 to 20 months. All of these processes are traditional and lightly handled. For example, when it comes to clarifying the wine, filtration is not used. Instead, the old method of egg white fining is employed: mixed with wine, the egg whites coagulate and carry all fine particles still in suspension to the bottom of the barrel.

WINE FOR AGEING

After three decades of vintages, all successful, Opus One has proven its ability to age. Its development in bottle lasts several years, and its peak can be reached after 20 to 30 years. It's worth decanting this wine two hours before serving. Served at 61°F (16°C), it goes perfectly with red meats and game birds. Rich, dense, and full of flavor, the palate has fine, very ripe tannins, while retaining harmony and genuine nobility.

CARNEROS

Carneros is the area overlapping the southern ends of Napa Valley and Sonoma. It occupies the southern foothills of the Mayacamas Mountains, which separate these two valleys. The climate is much cooler than in most of Napa or Sonoma, because it is entirely open to the effect of the ocean via San Francisco Bay. Located in the main corridor that conveys maritime airflows to the east, Carneros is also a very windy area. These conditions have made it a fairly well-defined AVA,

and very conducive to producing wines whose character is based mainly on freshness, including white and sparkling wines. Many of the finest Chardonnays come from Carneros.

> **GRAPE VARIETIES** For red: Pinot Noir as well as Merlot, and Syrah; for white: Chardonnay.

> **SOIL** Very shallow, and not particularly fertile. A hard clay subsoil on limestone bedrock. In some places, there are sedimentary pockets rich in manganese.

> **STYLE** The wines are fine and sometimes quite lively. The Chardonnays here have a style that is distinct from those produced elsewhere in California. Fine Pinot Noirs are also produced here.

> **NOTABLE PRODUCERS** For sparkling wines: Domaine Carneros (Taittinger) and Gloria Ferrer (Freixenet); for still wines: Acacia, Buena Vista, Cuvaison, Cline, Saintsbury, and Schug. Note: several good producers located elsewhere include Carneros wines in their line.

Selected Carneros wineries

• **Buena Vista.** This winery was one of the first in California, established in 1857 by Agoston Haraszthy, a Hungarian immigrant. After a bleak period, Buena Vista was re-created in 1979. In recent years, the wines have regained the level required for an estate with such a venerable reputation.

• **Cline Cellars.** In Carneros, which focuses mainly on Chardonnay and Pinot Noir, Cline (based in Sonoma) is an atypical producer. It's known primarily for its pioneering work with Mediterranean grape varieties (Mourvèdre, Barbera, and Carignan), and for wonderful Zinfandel wines.

• **Gloria Ferrer.** This estate, which is owned by the Catalan cava producer Freixenet, is known for its sparkling wines. They are rich but fresh, and among the finest in California. It also produces a range of still wines.

• **Schug.** Originally from Germany, Walter Schug gained professional experiences with well-known California producers (Gallo, Joseph Phelps) and then chose to specialize in artisan wines, produced in a cool climat. His lively and elegant Chardonnays are typical of the style of Carneros.

SANTA CRUZ MOUNTAINS

This mountainous region south of San Francisco can be spectacular. Bisected by the San Andreas Fault (which threatens the entire California coast with earthquakes), it appears to be perched between two worlds: the Pacific is on one side, and on the other is one of the biggest high-tech centers in the world, Silicon Valley. Local *climats* depend on the altitude and aspect of each vineyard, but overall it is generally cooler than Napa or Sonoma. Most of the vineyards are located above

the line of sea mist, which, coupled with cool nights due to altitude, leads to a relatively prolonged ripening of the grapes.

> **GRAPE VARIETIES** For red: Cabernet Sauvignon, Pinot Noir, Merlot, Zinfandel, and Syrah; for white: Chardonnay, Marsanne, and Roussanne.

> **SOIL** Mainly schist, formed by the decomposition of bedrock. The soils are very thin and infertile. They are specific to this region.

> **STYLE** This depends largely on the altitude and exposure of the vines. Some estates, such as Ridge, are among the highest vineyards in California. The alcohol content is lower than for wines from Napa, further north.

> **NOTABLE PRODUCERS** Ahlgren, Bargetto, Bonny Doon, David Bruce, Mount Eden, and Ridge.

Two Santa Cruz estates

- **Bonny Doon.** Few characters in the wine world are as original as Randall Grahm. Philosophical or humorous references abound in the names he gives his wines, and that is just the tip of the iceberg! He has been one of the pioneers of varietal diversification, first using Rhône varieties and then switching to Italian varieties in response to a saturation of Cabernet and Chardonnay. Consequently, the style of its wines mirrors some of those produced in Italy or the Rhône.

- **Ridge.** With its historic base in Montebello, at the top of a mountain, Ridge Vineyards is one of the best wine producers in California and the world. Its Montebello 1973 vintage (a Bordeaux blend) triumphed at the last "rematch" of the "Judgment of Paris," after finishing third in the first version in 1976 (see box p.436). Ridge wines are often noted for their very reasonable level of alcohol and their ability to age well. This winery, which dates from the 19th century, owes its success to Paul Draper (see also p.31), who has been its chief winemaker for 40 years.

> Vineyards in Monterey County.

MONTEREY

CALIFORNIA (CENTRAL COAST)

The Monterey region is a southern extension of the Santa Cruz area. Its climate is cool, and largely influenced by the ocean and nearly constant winds. It includes some smaller AVAs, such as Carmel Valley and Arroyo Seco. At the center of the region, much of the substantial production of the Salinas Valley is used to make entry-level wines for the broader wine industry. But sheltered areas and those at altitude, like Arroyo, Chalone (an appellation consisting of a single producer!), or the Santa Lucia Highlands, are capable of excellent work with Chardonnay and Pinot Noir.

> **GRAPE VARIETIES** For red: Pinot Noir; for white: Chardonnay, Riesling, Sauvignon Blanc, and Gewurztraminer.

> **SOIL** There are light soils of alluvium in the valley, and more complex soils often consisting of limestone in the hills, such as the Santa Lucia Highlands.

> **STYLE** Interesting, lively, and fresh wines, which have a great deal of flavor, come from higher altitude areas.

> **NOTABLE PRODUCERS** Chalone, Hahn, J Lohr, Jekel, Lockwood, and Morgan.

PASO ROBLES TO SANTA YNEZ

This region, stretching from Monterey in the north to Santa Barbara in the south, includes some very promising AVAs. Most of them are only recently established, but plantings are increasing. Not only is land much less expensive than in Napa, but the climate is more varied, and indeed sometimes cooler. Vineyards are generally located in valleys at low altitude and open to the Pacific. Local climatic conditions permit a wide range of grape varieties to be grown.

> **GRAPE VARIETIES** For red: Pinot Noir, Syrah, Mourvèdre, and Grenache; for white: Chardonnay, Marsanne, Viognier, Sauvignon Blanc, and Pinot Blanc.

> **SOIL** Ancient seabeds with varying limestone content and rather neutral (pH 7). Also clay soil, sandy soil, and alluvium.

> **STYLE** Paso Robles specializes in Rhône grape varieties (Syrah, Grenache, Mourvèdre, and so on). In Santa Ynez and Santa Maria, where the *climat* is similar to Burgundy, some very fine Chardonnays are produced without heaviness of any kind.

> **NOTABLE PRODUCERS** Alban, Au Bon Climat, Byron, Edna Valley Vineyards, Fess Parker, Firestone, Qupé, Sanford, and Tablas Creek.

Two Central Coast estates

• **Au Bon Climat (Solvang).** The name of this estate clearly indicates inspiration from Burgundy. Indeed, Jim Clendenen, its owner, is one of the staunchest defenders of the concept of terroir in California. Au Bon Climat is a specialist in Pinot Noir and Chardonnay from vineyards in cool areas, including its own vineyard at Bien Nacido in the Santa Maria AVA.

• **Tablas Creek (Paso Robles).** Tablas Creek is a joint venture between the Perrin family, owners of the famous Château de Beaucastel in Châteauneuf-du-Pape, and its import partner in the United States, Robert Haas. In a beautiful region of undulating terrain, it sits behind the hill that shelters it from the ocean and along a stream that gives it its name. The *climat* is conducive to Rhône grape varieties, which this estate has made its particular specialty.

LODI, SIERRA FOOTHILLS, EL DORADO, AND THE REST OF CENTRAL VALLEY

Central Valley extends 400 miles (640 km) from the foothills of Mt Shasta in the north to Bakersfield (around 60 miles/100 km from Los Angeles) in the south. In terms of volume, it is by far the most productive region in California. It is there that future wine giants settled from the 1920s onward, including Gallo (still under family control), which became the largest wine producer in the world. But aside from this industrial-scale production, there has been development of smaller sub-regions in certain parts of the mountains and hills surrounding the valley. The vineyards of Lodi, the Sierra Foothills, and El Dorado, which have their own AVAs, can produce quality wines from some of the oldest vineyards on the continent, mainly Zinfandel.

> **GRAPE VARIETIES** For red: Zinfandel, Syrah, Cabernet Sauvignon, and Sangiovese; for white: Chardonnay, Chenin Blanc, and Sauvignon Blanc.

> **SOIL** Alluvium, or at times sandy, soils in the valley; rather varied and volcanic soils on the slopes.

> **STYLE** A sharp contrast exists between the wines of the valley, which are generally ordinary, and less numerous pockets of vineyards at altitude, which are often concentrated and fine.

> **NOTABLE PRODUCERS** Amador, Gallo, Michael David, and Terre Rouge.

OKANAGAN VALLEY

British Columbia now has about 9,100 acres (3,684 ha) of vineyards and is the second-largest wine-producing region of Canada, after Ontario and the Niagara-on-the-Lake region. Okanagan Valley is located inland, about 185 miles (300 km) east of Vancouver. In terms of climate, it forms a northern extension of the wine regions of Washington State, just over the border. The southern part of this long valley is semi-desert because the Cascade Mountains shield it from the westerly winds that bring rain off the Pacific. Okanagan Lake, which occupies much of the valley, helps protect the vines from the winter cold. The surrounding mountains cause a very wide temperature variation between day and night.

> **GRAPE VARIETIES** For red: Merlot, Cabernet Sauvignon, Cabernet Franc, Gamay, and Pinot Noir; for white: Chardonnay and Sauvignon Blanc.

> **SOIL** Alluvial deposits produced by glaciers on a very complex background of basalt, limestone, granite, and gneiss.

> **STYLE** Given the temperature range in this region, the wines found here are firm but not heavy. The recent history of the Okanagan Valley and the many grape varieties mean that the wine styles are quite varied.

> **NOTABLE PRODUCERS** Blue Mountain, Cedar Creek, Jackson-Triggs, Mission Hill, Osoyoos Larose (partnered with Château Gruaud-Larose in Bordeaux), Quail's Gate, Sandhill, and Sumac Ridge.

NIAGARA PENINSULA

It may seem surprising that this area, located along the shores of Lake Ontario, has become the largest wine-producing region in Canada, consisting of 13,600 acres (about 5,500 ha) of vineyards. It can be better understood when we know it is crossed by the 45th parallel; in other words, it is at the same latitude as Bordeaux. The influence of the huge mass of water formed by nearby lakes, and to a lesser degree by the Niagara River, means that some varieties can ripen well in a climate that would otherwise be much harsher. While this peninsula is the largest producer of ice wines in the world, it also produces a number of dry wines, particularly from Riesling as well as a few lighter reds. The region is comparable in size to Napa Valley, and it has established many sub-appellations governed by the Vintners Quality Alliance (VQA).

> **GRAPE VARIETIES** For red: Pinot Noir and Syrah; for white: Seyval, Vidal, Riesling, and Chardonnay.

> **SOIL** Ancient glacier alluvium, with limestone in the hills.

> **STYLE** There is definitely a big difference between the dry wines, which are rather light, and the ice wines, which are very concentrated in both sugar and acidity.

> **NOTABLE PRODUCERS** Cave Spring, Clos Jordanne, Henry of Pelham, Inniskillin, Pillitterri, and Vineland.

Osoyoos Larose

A FRANCO-CANADIAN JOINT VENTURE

Based in the Okanagan Valley of British Columbia, Osoyoos Larose is a joint venture between Château Gruaud-Larose (a St-Julien second growth estate) and the Inniskillin winery. It produces blended wines inspired by Bordeaux (Merlot, Cabernet Franc, Cabernet Sauvignon, Malbec, and Petit Verdot). The tiny property, whose vineyards overlook Lake Osoyoos, boasts French expertise: selected vines from a nursery near Bordeaux, French oak barrels, and the assistance of consultant winemakers Michel Rolland and Alain Sutra.

CHILE

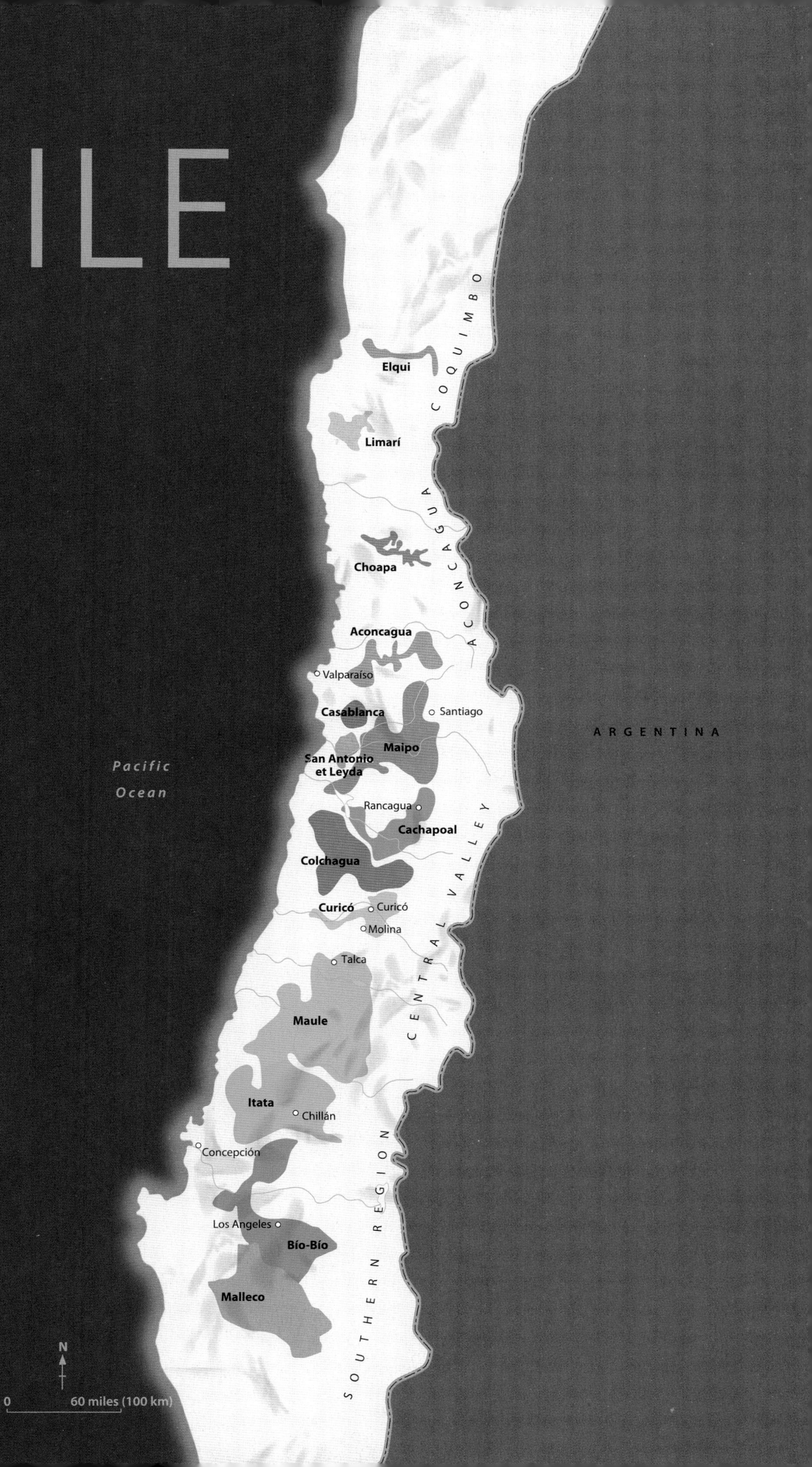

Pacific
Ocean

ARGENTINA

Elqui

Limarí

Choapa

Aconcagua

Valparaíso

Casablanca

Santiago

Maipo

San Antonio
et Leyda

Rancagua

Cachapoal

Colchagua

Curicó

Curicó

Molina

Talca

Maule

Itata

Chillán

Concepción

Los Angeles

Bío-Bío

Malleco

COQUIMBO

ACONCAGUA

CENTRAL VALLEY

SOUTHERN REGION

N

0   60 miles (100 km)

CHILE

Many of us are familiar with Chile's well-made, single-variety wines: straightforward and very good value for money. But during the past 10 years, the best have broken through to a higher level. The reds are gaining depth and intensity, the whites finesse and freshness. Chile is no longer just a producer of good wines; it also now produces some great wines.

Five centuries of winemaking

At the end of the 1970s, Spain's Miguel Torres was one of the first foreigners to try his luck in Chile, aquiring a small winery in Curicó, in the Chilean Central Valley. He instigated what has become a remarkable economic success. Four centuries earlier, it was another Spaniard, Brother Francisco de Carabantes, who planted the first Chilean vines; and from the 18th century onward, Chile was a significant wine exporter.

By the 19th century, French grape varieties were being planted in Chile, and the wine industry had become dynamic and modern. In the early 1950s, the region faced a crisis of overproduction, resulting in a massive uprooting of vines. Popularity on the international scene returned a quarter of a century later.

The Chilean wine miracle can be explained by a happy combination of its particularly suitable vine-growing environment, its low production costs, and the dynamism of it producers. Historic estates, investors from abroad, and a new generation of wineries are all increasingly focused on exploring the specificity of Chilean *terroirs*.

CHILE STATISTICS

Vineyard area: 317,500 acres (127,000 ha)

Production: 91 million cases (8.2 million hl)

Reds: 70%

Whites: 30%

(Ministry of Agriculture, OIV [International Office of Vines and Wine] 2008)

Between mountains and the sea

VINEYARD EXPANSION. Chile occupies a long, narrow strip of land extending over 2,670 miles (4,300 km) from north to south. It is bordered to the west by the Pacific, and to the east by the Andean Cordillera. Also, there is desert to the north and glaciers to the south. The wine-producing area is concentrated in the Central Valley, a large sector around the capital, Santiago; but it also extends as far as Limarí and Elqui in the north and to Bío Bío in the south. In past years, vines were planted mainly on the plains lying between the coastal mountain chains and the Andean Cordillera—on fertile, easily cultivated land. Producers are now going further afield to plant on new land with good potential, such as on the western slopes of Andean foothills, or in the cooler regions close to the Pacific Ocean. Fertile for the most part, the soil is a light mix of sand, clay, and limestone; it is granitic and poorer on the slopes of the Andes.

IDEAL CLIMATE FOR VINES. Chile has an almost ideal climatic situation for ripening grapes. Warm, Mediterranean-style weather of constant sunshine and low rainfall is balanced by cool influences from the west (notably the Humboldt Current that flows

Ungrafted vines

Ever since phylloxera invaded the world's vineyards, ungrafted (franc de pied) vines have been a rarity. Most vines are now grafted onto rootstocks of American origin, which have a natural resistance to the phylloxera aphid. However, Chile is an exception. This can no doubt be explained by its geographic isolation, but perhaps also by the significant presence of copper in the soil, or by the practice of flooding the vineyards to irrigate them. It is certainly so because of the vigilance of authorities here, who strictly control the importation of all plant matter.

> Cellar on the Errazuriz estate in the Aconcagua Valley.

> Workers among the vines at the Casa Lapostolle estate, in the Colchagua Valley.

along the coast). Also, nocturnal air from the Andes in the east creates wide temperature variations. A lack of water in summer, when the Central Valley becomes semi-desert, is the only natural deficiency. Irrigation is therefore indispensible in most of the wine-producing areas.

Varieties and styles

The alternating heat of the sun and the cool of the nights is one of the keys to understanding the style of Chilean wines: rounded and supple with a bright and intense fruitiness that is rarely heavy or oppressive. Chile is a country of principally red wines (75 percent of production), despite a marked increase in the planting of white grapes. Of the 50 or so varieties now planted (including both reds and whites), just seven make up 85 percent of the total area. Some grape varieties, such as País (37,500 acres/15,000 ha) or Muscat of Alexandria, are legacies from the Spanish colonial past; but current trends are more than ever skewed toward the big, international grape varieties.

RED GRAPE VARIETIES. Cabernet Sauvignon, which is grown on a total of 100,000 acres (40,000 ha), produces solid wines with supple tannins, marked by notes of black fruit, spices, and menthol. Two other Bordeaux varieties, Merlot and Carmenère, are grown on 32,500 acres (13,000ha) and 183,250 acres (73,300 ha), respectively. The wines are rounded and velvety, sometimes with marked herbaceous notes. Worthy of mention is new interest in Syrah, Pinot Noir, and Malbec, which are fast gaining ground.

WHITE GRAPE VARIETIES. Most of the white wines for export come from two grape varieties: Chardonnay and Sauvignon Blanc. The first, which is grown on 21,750 acres (8,700 ha), produces supple, rounded, aromatic wines, with more or less pronounced yellow fruit notes. The second has made tremendous progress and is at the point of passing Chardonnay production in numbers; although it seems that a significant proportion is comprised of related varieties (Sauvignon Vert or Sauvignonasse). In the cooler areas, Sauvignon Blanc produces pleasant, balanced wines, sometimes with dominant herbaceous notes.

Wine regions

Chilean vineyards are divided into four large growing areas, from north to south: Coquimbo, Aconcagua, Central Valley, and the Southern Region. Each is then divided into sub-regions that correspond, for the most part, to valleys running from east to west. Coquimbo, the most northern region, is subdivided into Elqui, growing grapes destined to make Pisco, the local brandy, and Limarí, which is potentially more promising, though more sparsely planted. Further south, Aconcagua is now enjoying popularity, thanks to the cool Casablanca and San Antonio valleys, which produce the most convincing of Chilean whites. The vineyards of the Central Valley run from Santiago as far as the Maule Valley in the south. As the heart of the Chilean wine industry, this is where the bulk of production takes place. It is home to most of the great Chilean wine producers, many of whom are installed in the Maipo and Colchagua valleys. The Southern Region, which includes the Itata and Bío Bío zones, has long been where the traditional varieties such as País are made; but some promising white wines have recently emerged from this sunny, but cool, climate.

Carmenère rediscovered

Argentina has Malbec, Uruguay has Tannat, but Chile long lacked its own "signature" grape variety. This was remedied when two French scientists, Jean-Michel Boursiquot and Claude Valat, formally identified certain Chilean Merlot vines as being a type of Carmenère. A native of Bordeaux, this grape variety from the Cabernet family was ousted from the Gironde region after the phylloxera crisis. Planted in Chile during the 19th century, it has now been reborn under its original name. It produces wines with depth, offering seductive aromas of ripe fruit and licorice, as well as an herbaceous accent (sweet peppers and damp undergrowth).

Key Chilean regions and wines

For a long time, Chilean wine producers concentrated on the production of single-variety wines that were reliable and consistent, and often made by blending wine from more than one region. Today, more wines come from limited geographic zones, from specific valleys (the name of which appears on the label) and sometimes from individual plots.

MAIPO VALLEY

Maipo is the most famous name in Chilean wine. This valley extends from the Andes to the Coastal Cordillera, with Santiago virtually at its center. During the 19th century, the proximity of the capital encouraged the creation of vast estates, funded by rich Santiago families. These wine companies, such as Santa Rita and Concha y Toro, have become giant businesses. The vineyards cover 16,000 acres (10,000 ha) and grow predominantly red grape varieties from Bordeaux (Cabernet Sauvignon, Merlot, and Carmenère). The climate is Mediterranean: hot and dry, with sparse rain falling mainly during the winter months. The region is also divided into several zones. Alto Maipo, the highest, is subject to the influence of the Andes. The vineyards on these slopes benefit from wide temperature variation and produce structured red wines. Central Maipo and Pacific Maipo, to the south and southwest of Santiago, experience higher temperatures and produce more supple, fruity, and ripe wines on fertile soil.

> **GRAPE VARIETIES** Cabernet Sauvignon, Merlot, Carmenère, and Syrah for red wines; Chardonnay and Sauvignon Blanc for whites.

> **SOIL** Alluvial (clay-and-limestone) and granite.

CENTRAL VALLEY

> **STYLE** Maipo is known for the quality of its Cabernet Sauvignon. The wines have powerful aromas of well-ripened fruit, spices, menthol, or eucalyptus. Ample structure and firm tannins are found in certain very concentrated wines like the Cru Almaviva (*see* below). Other red grape varieties yield fruity wines, ripe and rather supple. In terms of white wine, some of the Chardonnays grab attention with their fruity, very pleasant, roundness.

> **NOTABLE PRODUCERS** Almaviva, Concha y Toro, Cousino Macul, Santa Alicia, Santa Carolina, Santa Rita, Undurraga, Vinedo Chadwick.

Almaviva, a Chilean grand cru

In 1997, Concha y Toro—an historic estate here, founded in the Maipo Valley in 1883—partnered with the Bordeaux wine group Baron Philippe de Rothschild with the stated intention of producing a "great" Chilean wine. Vintage after vintage, the international press have been persuaded by this impressive cuvée, which combines the ample fruitiness typical of Chilean wines with the refinement of the great wines of Bordeaux. In just over 10 years, the gamble has paid off and Almaviva is now a member of the close-knit circle of the greatest New World wines. This Bordeaux blend, predominantly Cabernet Sauvignon, comes from a 212-acre (85-ha) vineyard in Puente Alto, about 20 miles (30 km) south of Santiago. Produced in a very modern winery, it is subject to long and careful maturation (17 to 18 months) in new oak casks. On the palate, it is a wine of great depth. It is complex, concentrated, warm, and fruity. Modern and seductive, it has a clearly defined structure that makes it good for laying down.

Von Siebenthal

Carabantes 2007
Viña von Siebenthal   Syrah Chile
Limited edition
20892 bottles
PRODUCED & BOTTLED BY VIÑA von SIEBENTHAL S.A.
Panquehue, Aconcagua Valley, Chile
14,5% Vol.   Hand picked - Unfiltered   750 ml
Denominación de origen Panquehue Aconcagua Valley - Chile
www.vinavonsiebenthal.com

With just 50 acres (20 ha) of vines, this estate is tiny compared with those of many hundreds or even thousands of acres that are the norm in Chile. Based in the beautiful Aconcagua Valley, Von Siebenthal is one of the small, independent estates that, over the past 10 years, have greatly increased the stylistic range of Chilean wines. With a real passion for wine, former Swiss lawyer Mauro von Siebenthal acquired a few plots of land at Panquehue, halfway between the Andes and the Pacific Ocean. Paying careful attention to the characteristics of individual varieties, he matched grapes to soil—planting Cabernet Franc and Merlot in clay-limestone, and Cabernet Sauvignon, Syrah, Carmenère, and Petit Verdot along the stony slopes. The result is a limited but delightful range of wines, dominated by a pure Carmenère (Carmenère Reserva), which is succulent and spicy, as well as an exuberant and delightfully perfumed Syrah (Carabantes).

COLCHAGUA VALLEY

In the Central Valley, the Rapel district is divided into two zones, Cachapoal in the north and Colchagua in the south. The latter has witnessed significant vineyard expansion during the past decade, and they now cover 57,500 acres (23,000 ha) —95 percent of which is planted with red varieties. Colchagua enjoys a hot climate that is tempered from the west by the fresh breezes from the ocean. Originally planted in the valleys and foothills, vineyards have now reached the mountain slopes (as high as 3,350 ft/1,000 m). Bordeaux grape varieties have generally proven their worth in Colchagua, giving rise to some of the greatest Chilean *cuvées* (Clos Apalta, Montes Alpha); but Syrah and Malbec are also promising.

> **GRAPE VARIETIES** Cabernet Sauvignon, Merlot, Carmenère, and Syrah for red wines; Chardonnay for white wines.
> **SOIL** Sedimentary (clay and limestone) and granitic.
> **STYLE** Colchagua is well known for its pleasant, ripe, and fleshy red wines. Cabernet Sauvignon, the dominant variety, produces full-bodied wines that are certainly capable of ageing. But the region possesses other specialties, such as concentrated and succulent Merlots, and Malbecs sourced from very old vines, which result in particularly intense and structured wines. The white wines (especially the Chardonnays) are fairly rounded, simple, and warm.

> **NOTABLE PRODUCERS** Casa Lapostolle, Casa Silva, Errazuriz, Guelbenzu, El Araucano (Lurton), Los Vascos, Luis Felipe Edwards, Santa Helena, Siegel, Viña Montes, Viu Manent.

CASABLANCA VALLEY

This area has only recently started producing wine; 25 years ago there were no vineyards at all in Casablanca. Development has coincided with the drive to exploit more temperate zones that are capable of producing fresh, fine, and well-balanced white wines. The growing area here now extends over 10,000 acres (4,000 ha), close to the coast between Santiago and the port of Valparaiso. The vineyards are strongly influenced by the Pacific Ocean, thanks to which they are enveloped in morning mist. However, spring frosts, which are an exception elsewhere, prove to be a real menace here. Irrigation is essential, and the cost of drilling wells is one of the reasons why a brake has been put on some new development. Vineyards extend over the Coastal Cordillera, in terraces along the slopes.

> **GRAPE VARIETIES** Pinot Noir, Merlot, and Carmenère for reds; Chardonnay and Sauvignon Blanc for whites.
> **SOIL** Sand, limestone, and granite.

> **STYLE** Casablanca specializes in dry white wines made from Chardonnay and Sauvignon Blanc. The style is elegant and fresh, with fruity and sometimes herbaceous notes for the Sauvignon Blancs. Red grape varieties are in the minority, but Pinot Noir has recently broken through with a style that is fairly full-bodied and fruity, but not lacking in freshness.
> **NOTABLE PRODUCERS** Concha y Toro, Cono Sur, Loma Larga, Quintay, Santa Rita, Veramonte.

ARGENTINA, BRAZIL, AND URUGUAY

VENEZUELA

COLOMBIA

ECUADOR

PERU

Amazon

Madeira

B R A Z I L

**Vale
São Francisco**

São Francisco

BOLIVIA

Brasília

*Pacific
Ocean*

PARAGUAY

Parana

Rio de Janeiro

São Paulo

*Atlantic
Ocean*

Salta

Salta

Salta

Catamarca

Salado

**Vale Do Rio
Do Peixe**

— Planalto
Serrano

**Vale Dos
Vinhedos**

— Serra
Gaúcha

La Rioja
San Juan

Mendoza

Fronteira

— Serras Do
Sudeste

URUGUAY

Mendoza

Buenos Aires

Montevideo

CHILE

San Rafael

A R G E N T I N A

— Río de la Plata

La Pampa
Río Negro

Neuquén

Negro

Deseado

Wine-producing regions

Brazil

Argentina

Uruguay

N

0   620 miles (1,000 km)

ARGENTINA, BRAZIL, AND URUGUAY

During the past 15 years, the wine industry in South America has undergone significant change. Argentina has been successful in securing a place for its wines on the international market, while Brazil and Uruguay are making every effort to modernize and develop high quality production.

ARGENTINA

The profile or perception of a wine-producing country can change radically in the space of a generation, as Argentina has demonstrated. Right up to the end of the 1980s, Argentina was still producing vast quantities of wine lacking in any real appeal. Now, the industry there is producing red wines of great intensity, and Mendoza has become a world-renowned region—unique in part for the altitude at which some of its many vineyards are planted.

Rapid modernization

In 1990, Argentina looked with envy at the success of its neighbor Chile. The two countries had long followed parallel paths, from the very first vine plantings in the mid-16th century, right up to the 1970s, when they both experienced an overproduction crisis linked to a big drop in local wine consumption.

While Chile turned to exporting as a solution, Argentina remained embroiled in economic problems. Then—following the example of many regions and producers before them, such as

ARGENTINA STATISTICS

Vineyard area: 563,000 acres (228,000 ha)
Production: 163 million cases (14.7 million hl)
Reds: 56%
Whites: 43%
Rosés: 1%

OIV (National Institute of Vine and Wine Cultivation) 2008.

the French company Moët & Chandon—this South American wine giant finally woke up. Traditional cellars were renovated and new estates appeared, thanks to both local and foreign initiative. Vineyard area was reduced and the mix of grape varieties completely modified. The wines produced became more focused and fruitier, in response to more demanding global and even local markets. Argentines consume 75 percent of the wine they produce, but exports have more than doubled in the past five years.

Latin American leader

Argentina is big country, covering more than a million square miles (2.7 million sq km). It cultivates 527,000 acres (211,000 ha) of vines, which are concentrated in the eastern foothills of the Andean Cordillera. This is a relatively narrow fringe of land, running across 900 miles (1,500 km) from Salta in the north as far as Patagonian vineyards in the south. In Mendoza, the main wine-producing region, the vines stretch farther than the eye can see over high plateaus and on sloping foothills.

VINEYARDS WITH ALTITUDE. Argentina's main advantage can be summed up in a single word: elevation. The vineyards are sited at an average of 2,950 ft (900 m) above sea level, and

> Vines at the Esteco winery in Salta province, Argentina.

> The Zuccardi family winery in Mendoza produces a wide range of wines, both red and white.

even reach 9,800 ft (3,000 m) at Salta in the north. Around Mendoza, most are planted at an average of between 1,900 and 3,600 ft (600 and 1,100 m). These altitudes present cool nights, but during the day the temperature range hovers around 68°F (20°C), allowing the grapes to retain all their aromatic potential without being "burned" by the sun. Thanks to this healthy, dry environment, the fruit ripens well. Argentina's vineyards also are protected against many ailments—including phylloxera, which, although not quite absent, is far from virulent.

Climate and soil

With the exception of some areas in the south, arid conditions are the dominant norm here. Rainfall very often amounts to less than 10 in (250 mm) per year, and is concentrated during the seasonal vine growth phase. Temperatures are moderate, but can reach 104°F (40°C) in the summer. Winters can be cold, and spring frosts are relatively frequent. The same is true of hailstorms, which can be quite dramatic. Vineyards are irrigated with water thawed from mountain snow, and drip irrigation has now largely replaced the old method—where the rows were flooded. Soil is mostly poor in nutritional quality, and alluvial, with a significant amount of sand on a gravelly, limestone, or clay substratum.

Eclectic mix of grapes

Argentina has grown vines for more than 450 years. The origin of the 116 varieties now planted—essentially Spanish, Italian, Portuguese, and French—is a reflection of the different waves of European immigration since the 16th century. While a few varieties are dominant, this abundance of grapes stands in sharp contrast to the simplicity of the grape mix in Chile (see p.453) and gives Argentina's producers a great many options. Pink-skinned, traditional grape varieties, such as Criolla, Cereza, and Moscatel Rosada, are still grown in 29 percent of the vineyards; but they are gradually being replaced, particularly by red varieties.
RED VARIETIES. Malbec, introduced in 1868 by French agronomist Michel Pouget, has become the emblematic grape

variety of Argentina. It is planted on fully one quarter of the 250,000 acres (100,000 ha) now growing red grape varieties, and it produces a good number of the best wines: opulent, powerful, and ripe in style. Bonarda, originally from Lombardy, is valued for its colorful, supple, and fruity wines. Cabernet Sauvignon produces full-bodied, well-structured wines with generous aromas and capable of ageing. Syrah is very much in vogue, followed by Merlot and Tempranillo.
WHITE VARIETIES. Apart from Pedro Giménez, which is still planted more than any other white, two varieties stand out—each in a very different style: Torrontés, a local grape variety that is back in favor thanks to its supple, tender, and aromatic wines, with notes of flowers and fresh grapes; and Chardonnay, which produces powerful, often warm, wines with exuberant aromas of yellow fruit and spices. Planted at high altitude, Sauvignon Blanc is also arousing a certain amount of interest.

Wine-producing regions

Among three small wine regions in the north—Salta, Jujuy, and Catamarca—only the first produces wines worthy of broad interest (see p.462). Further south, La Rioja province specializes in white wines made from Torrontés Riojano and Muscat of Alexandria, but not many of these are exported. With more than 100,000 acres (40,000 ha) of vineyards, San Juan, between La Rioja and Mendoza, is the second-largest wine-producing region in Argentina. Most of the vines are grown in small, irrigated valleys that are subject to a very hot and dry climate. Producing mainly dry white wines and rosés, as well as fortified wines, San Juan is slowly converting to the production of red wines.

The Mendoza region is the powerhouse of Argentina's wine industry, producing most of the best red wines (see p.463). In Patagonia, in the far south of the country, the Río Negro and Neuquén regions (totaling just under 10,000 acres/4,000 ha) are influenced by the Atlantic Ocean. The cooler and damper climate, and the limestone soils, form the basis for livelier, very intense wines produced from Malbec, Merlot, and Torrontés. Some zones, like the high valley of Río Negro, are currently attracting investors.

BRAZIL

With almost 216,000 acres (88,000 ha) planted to vines (as of 2006), Brazil is the third-largest wine producer in South America, behind Argentina and Chile. There were a few tentative attempts at planting vines during the 16th century, but Brazil had to wait until the beginning of the 20th century before achieving significant production. And it took until 1970 to see the first high quality wines, with the arrival of big groups such as Moët and Chandon or Martini & Rossi.

Wine-producing regions

Except for vineyards in the Vale do São Francisco, in the far northeast, most Brazilian wines are produced in the extreme south, in the states of Santa Catarina and Rio Grande do Sul. The latter is by far Brazil's largest and most interesting winemaking region, covering 95,000 acres (38,000 ha). Its vineyards are concentrated in two sub-regions: Serra Gaúcha and Campanha.

Serra Gaúcha produces the bulk of Brazilian wines, and it includes the Vale dos Vinhedos, the country's only appellation

BRAZIL STATISTICS

Vineyard area: 217,000 acres (88,000 ha)
Production: 40 million cases (3.6 million hl)
Reds: 80%
Whites: 18%
Rosés: 2%

(Uvibra, Ibravin, 2008)

of origin. The damp climate (207 in/1,750 mm rainfall per year) and the heavy, badly drained soil impose a limit on the production of quality wines. The Campanha sub-region, along the Uruguayan border, benefits from more favorable conditions with a reasonable amount of rainfall and sandy, well-drained soil.

Varieties and wines

The particularly damp climate, especially in Serra Gaúcha, favors the cultivation of hybrid grape varieties that are resistant to disease, so they are grown in substantial quantities. The most important development, though, is the planting of *Vitis vinifera* varieties in the Campanha region, including Cabernet Sauvignon, Merlot, Tannat, Chardonnay, Sauvignon Blanc, and Pinot Grigio.

While Brazil has acquired some reputation thanks to its sparkling wines, made either traditionally or by the sealed tank method (*see box* p.71), the greatest part of its production is made up of dry red wines. These can be very appealing, in a fresh style that is fairly light in alcohol, when the grapes have ripened particularly well.

NOTABLE PRODUCERS. Dal Pizzol, Don Laurindo, Miolo, Mioranza, Pizzato, Salton.

> Hand harvesting at the Vale dos Vinhedos estate in Brazil.

URUGUAY

As perhaps the largest per-capita wine market on the South American continent, Uruguay has a well-established winemaking tradition, which dates back to the 18th century. It is the fourth-largest wine producer in South America in terms of volume, and it consumes most of the wine it produces. However, the quality achieved by its best red wines has opened the doors to the export market, mainly Brazil.

> Vines trained at Royat (Uruguay).

Wine-producing regions

The Uruguayan climate is maritime with plenty of sunshine, regular rainfall (40 in /1,000 mm per year), and cool nights. The conditions are ideal for the vines as long as vigorous foliage growth is controlled—it can sometimes be excessive due to the humidity and the very fertile nature of the clay-based soils.

The vineyards, which cover 21,250 acres (8,500 ha), are owned and managed by 2,400 growers. They sell their grapes to the country's 272 producers, just over 10 percent of whom export a part of their production. The large wine-producing regions of Canelones, Montevideo, Colonia, and San José all lie along the south coast, near the capital. But some small vineyards are also set along the left bank of the Río de la Plata as well as in the center and north of the country, close to the Brazilian border.

Varieties and wines

Though almost 70 grape varieties are grown in Uruguay, only a few varieties are widely cultivated. Tannat is planted in almost a quarter of the vineyards and produces the most highly prized reds. They are made in a firm style, and also yield some interesting rosés. The significant presence of this little-known variety, originally from the southwest of France, is due to Basque immigrants in the 19th century. After Tannat, Merlot, Cabernet Sauvignon, and Cabernet Franc are the most cultivated red grape varieties, and are made into red or rosé. Among the white varieties, Ugni Blanc is by far the most widely grown; but the best white wines, still or sparkling, come from Sauvignon Blanc, Chardonnay, Viognier, or Muscat. The wines are marketed in two categories: VCP (*Viño de calidad preferente* [quality wine]) and VC (*Viño común* [table wine]). These mainly relate to the red wines made from Tannat, sometimes blended with Merlot, Cabernet Sauvignon or Cabernet Franc. The best have an austere but seductive profile with firm tannins, a great deal of freshness, and modest alcohol content. This brings them more in line with European expectations than the more powerful wines of Argentina.

Other Latin American countries

Even though production remains modest, most larger South American countries have maintained a winemaking industry from origins dating back to the Spanish colonization of the 16th century. Ecuador, Columbia, Paraguay, Venezuela, and Bolivia together have a total of several thousand acres of vines. Many of them are planted at altitude (as much as 9,200 ft /2,800 m in Bolivia), in a damp, sub-tropical, or equatorial climate. The wines, both dry and sweet, or wine-based alcohols such as Pisco, are the product of hybrids, traditional grape varieties (Criolla), or varieties of Vitis vinifera.

Peru's production of wine has increased considerably in the past 10 years. While the greater part of it is converted into brandy, Peru also makes dry wines that are rapidly improving in quality. The vineyards are concentrated in the coastal province of Ita, which includes the Tacama zone, located 45 miles (70 km) inland. In this semi-desert region, refreshed by the cool air from the Pacific, the vines are planted on poor soil and are irrigated with water from the Andean Cordillera. The Tacama estate, one of the oldest in Peru, has been working with French oenological services and experts since the 1960s and makes good quality wines from the Tannat, Malbec, Petit Verdot, Sauvignon Blanc, Chardonnay, Chenin Blanc, and Albilla grape varieties.

Key wine regions of Argentina, Brazil, and Uruguay

Of Argentina's regions, only Mendoza and, to a lesser extent, Salta (including Cafayate) have any real reputation. Uruguay is known for red wines made from Tannat, but from no specific region. Brazil is slowly emerging from obscurity, thanks to a few model producers.

SALTA

Among the small wine-producing regions in northern Argentina, only Salta (5,250 acres/2,100 ha) has succeeded in creating a name for itself. This is thanks to the quality of its dry white wines from the dominant grape variety Torrontés

Riojano (a cross, perhaps, between Muscat of Alexandria and Criolla Chica). The most renowned district is in the Calchaquíes Valley, near the town of Cafayate, where vines are perched at an altitude of almost 4,900 ft (1,500 m). Some are planted as high as 9,800 ft (3,000 m), making Calchaquíes the highest vineyard area in the world. The sandy soil and the continental climate are similar to those of Mendoza. The very wide temperature range means that the white grapes ripen while retaining a sufficient amount of acidity. Apart from Torrontés, a few red grape varieties, including Cabernet Sauvignon, Malbec, and Tannat, also produce good results.

> **GRAPE VARIETIES** Cabernet Sauvignon, Malbec, and Tannat for reds; Torrontés Riojano, Chardonnay, and Chenin Blanc for whites.

> **SOIL** Sandy.

> **STYLE** White wines made from Torrontés have a distinct personality, with exuberant or very vivid aromas of fresh grapes (similar to Muscat), flowers, citrus fruits, and spices. On the palate they are supple and mouth-filling, with an alcohol content that can be quite high. Most of them are dry, but some retain a certain amount of residual sugar, which reinforces a typical sense of roundness of this grape variety. They are wines for drinking young, and always between 46 and 50°F (8 and 10°C). The reds are perfumed and intense, with a fruity quality that is typical of most good red Argentine wines.

> **NOTABLE PRODUCERS** La Esperanza Estate, Etchart, Colomé, Trapiche, O. Fournier, Terrazas de los Andes.

François Lurton

Coming from a large wine family in the Bordeaux region, Jacques and François Lurton started a global business in 1988. The idea was to choose the best terroirs in the world and produce wines there representing good value. The two brothers arrived in Argentina in 1992, at a time when few people had recognized the potential of the high-altitude vineyards in Mendoza. Three years later, they bought their first plot at Vista Flores, in the Uco Valley. It was at an altitude of 3,600 ft (1,100 m) on poor quality but healthy and well-drained soil, where vines had never been planted before. Today, with a holding of 500 acres (200 ha), Argentina is at the heart of the Lurton empire, and now the property of François since his brother's departure. He produces a very reliable line that is impeccably made, from fruity and intense wines at entry level, under the Tierra de la Luna label, to the particularly fine Chacayes, an ambitious cuvée based on Malbec grown in the best plots of the estate.

MENDOZA

Three-quarters of Argentina's vineyards are concentrated in Mendoza. They cover 390,000 acres (156,000 ha), situated mostly to the south and east of the city of the same name. The vines are planted at altitudes between 1,640 and 5,775 ft (500 and 1,700 m), spread over 185 miles (300 km) from north to south. The climate is continental: hot and dry in summer, with a wide temperature variation linked to the altitude, and severe winters. The lower regions—San Rafael to the south, San Martin to the east, and Lavalle to the north—produce everyday wines, white and rosé, from traditional grape varieties. Most of the quality wines come from two sectors: the Central Valley, along each side of the Mendoza River, to the south and southwest of the city of Mendoza; and the Uco Valley, situated more to the south and extending over a distance of nearly 50 miles (80 km).

> **GRAPE VARIETIES** Malbec, Bonarda, Cabernet Sauvignon, Syrah, Merlot, and Tempranillo for red wines; Pedro Giménez, Torrontés, Chardonnay, Muscat of Alexandria, Chenin Blanc, Ugni Blanc, and Sauvignon Blanc for whites.
> **SOIL** Poor, sandy, with gravelly pockets in the Central Valley; thin, mixed sand and alluvium with some limestone zones in the higher reaches of the Uco Valley.
> **STYLE** With warm aromas of very ripe fruit, spices, and licorice, the red wines made from Malbec are fleshy and soft. Tannins are more or less powerful according to the level of concentration. The high quality *cuvées* can be aged for five to 10 years. Cabernet Sauvignon offers intense aromas of very ripe black and red fruit, with herbaceous accents (sometimes mentholated) and a generous palate with usually supple tannins. The Chardonnays are pleasant, perfumed, and often warm.

> **NOTABLE PRODUCERS** Alta Vista, Altos Las Hormigas, Fabre Montmayou, Catena Zapata, Cheval des Andes, Clos de Los Siete, Don Cristobal, Etchart, Familia Zuccardi, François Lurton, Monteviejo, Norton, O. Fournier, Terrazas de los Andes, Trapiche.

Miolo, the Brazilian avant-garde

Italian immigrant Guiseppe Miolo established his estate in 1897, near the town of Bento Gonçalves in the Vinhedos Valley. For three generations, his descendants were content to just sell their grapes—until an overproduction crisis drove them to begin making their own wine in the 1990s. A pioneer of planting quality grape varieties and using expert advisors, Miolo set the bar high and was proof of Brazil's potential to produce fine wines. Today, it is one of the country's largest wine businesses, represented in five production regions and offering a very wide range of wines. The Quinta do Seival cuvée, from a vineyard in the Campanha region, has done much to establish the reputation of Miolo outside Brazil. But the winery also produces some very attractive cuvées based on Cabernet, as well as sparkling white wines with a great deal of finesse.

TANNAT

Uruguay's wine industry is firmly linked with the dominant red grape variety grown there, Tannat (or Harriague). This variety is grown across 20 percent of the country's vineyards, planted especially in the two main production regions: Canelones and Montevideo in the south. It adapts well to the rich soil and damp, but mild climate of these coastal zones. Sometimes made into rosé, Tannat is known mainly for its structured red wines. The best have seduced importers in search of more unusual "niche" wines in a different style from those of Chile or Argentina.

> **GRAPE VARIETY** Tannat, sometimes blended with Cabernet Sauvignon, Merlot, or Cabernet Franc.
> **SOIL** Clay and sand.
> **STYLE** Following in the footsteps of Madiran (*see* p.339), Uruguayan Tannat produces deeply colored wines with notes of black fruit, licorice, spices, and sometimes damp undergrowth or menthol. Quite austere on the palate when young, with firm tannins, a great deal of freshness, and a modest alcohol level, the wines are closer to European standards than the powerful wines of neighboring

Argentina, for example. Matured in cask or blended with other grape varieties (Merlot, Cabernet Franc), they show a great degree of suppleness. Their rich tannins and acidity make them wines to lay down (10 years). When matured, they can develop a seductive bouquet marked by tobacco, spices, and damp undergrowth.

> **NOTABLE PRODUCERS** Bouza, Carrau, Castillo Viejo, De Lucca, Juanico, Marichal, Leda, Pisano, Pizzorno, Stagniari.

Coastal region
- Stellenbosch
- Franschhoek
- Tulbagh
- Paarl-Wellington
- Constantia
- Swartland
- Durbanville

Breede River Valley
- Worcester
- Robertson

Olifants River

Districts not attached to a region
- Hermanus, Overberg Walker Bay
- Klein Karoo

Lutzville
Vredendal
Lamberts Bay
Clanwilliam
Elands Bay
Citrusdal
Olifants

Beaufort West
Sutherland

WESTERN CAPE

Berg Piketberg
Moorreesburgg
Tulbagh
Yzerfontein
Malmesbury
Wolseley Ceres
De Doorns
Matjiesfontein
Laingsburg
Prince Albert
Ladismith
Calitzdorp
Oudtshoorn
Wellington
Worcester
Montagu
Paarl Robertson Ashton
Barrydale
George
Cape Town Franschhoek Bonnievale
Stellenbosch Villiersdorp Swellendam
Strand Riviersonderend
Riversdale
Heidelberg Mosselbaai
Brée
Kleinmond Caledon
Hermanus
Bredasdorp
Cape of Good Hope
False Bay
Atlantic Ocean
Walker Bay
0   30 miles (50 km)
Cape Agulhas

SOUTH AFRICA

SOUTH AFRICA

South Africa's wines enjoy worldwide success due to their balance between quality and price, and also because of the simply excellent standard of the finest among them. After a long period of political and economic isolation, South Africa had to demonstrate real dynamism in order to re-launch its wines on the world market. In their turn, foreign investors, notably those from Bordeaux, were quick to grasp the country's potential quality.

Long history

The first plantings in the Cape region date from the settlement of Dutch colonies during the 17th century, when this maritime province was a way station for ships en route to Asia. Jan Van Riebeeck, the first regional governor, arrived on the Cape in 1652 tasked with exploiting the province's lands and establishing the first vineyards. Reinforced by the arrival of 200 French Huguenot families between 1688 and 1690, South African viticulture prospered thereafter thanks to its principal customer, Great Britain. But the appearance of phylloxera in 1886 led to a long period of crisis, aggravated by conflicts between the British and the Afrikaners.

In the 20th century, serious problems of overproduction led to the Kooperatiewe Wijnbouwers Vereniging (KWV, the Cooperative Winemakers Society) being granted, in 1940, almost total control over the South African wine industry. During the period of apartheid, the country's political and economic isolation left South Africa without the benefit of the enormous progress that took place in the wine world during the 1980s. The abolition of the regime in 1991 finally opened the country to the wider world, and producers turned successfully to exporting.

SOUTH AFRICA STATISTICS

Vineyard area: 252,000 acres (102,000 ha)

Production: 114 million cases (10,261,000 hl)

Whites: 56%

Reds: 44%

(WOSA, SAWIS, OIV, 2007)

Geography

The Republic of South Africa is situated at the southernmost point of the African continent, at a latitude of about 35° south. The climate is generally hot and dry, but coastal regions are tempered by the cold Benguela Current, which moves along the southwestern coast. The country's 252,000 acres (102,000 ha) of vineyards are largely situated in this coastal region, and it is rare to find a vineyard more than 60 miles (100 km) from the sea. There are two very different seasons: a hot and dry Mediterranean summer, followed by a moderately warm and humid winter season from May to September. Rainfall varies from one region to another, but it also follows the seasons within the same region, making irrigation essential to viticulture in many areas.

Grape varieties

Like other New World countries, South Africa has learned to adapt its wines to market forces. Production was formerly dominated by white wine, with a significant amount being earmarked for distillation; but over the past two decades, red wine has gained significant ground. It is made chiefly from Cabernet Sauvignon, Syrah, Merlot, and Pinotage (a Cinsaut/ Pinot Noir cross developed in South Africa in 1925) grapes; but Pinot Noir and Cabernet Franc are making significant progress.

Wine regions and districts

Olifants River is the most northerly wine-producing region, and its winelands extend throughout the Olifants River Valley, which borders the Atlantic. Its output remains largely oriented toward bulk production destined for distilling.

Swartland and Tulbagh lie further south; and the Worcester region, adjoining Tulbagh to the southeast, is responsible for 27 percent of national

> Harvesting grapes at a Paarl district farm in South Africa.

> Vines on the Groot Constantia estate.

wine production. Robertson lies inland to the east, bordering Worcester at its western part; irrigation is essential in this hot, dry climate. White grape varieties flourish in these chalk-rich soils, but in recent years real progress has been made in red wine production. Due to a hot, extremely dry climate, the vast, east-west Klein Karoo region contributes only three percent of national wine output, but it manages to produce good fortified wines.

Turning toward Cape Town, between Swartland to the north and Worcester to the east, the Paarl district is home to 13 percent of the nation's wine. A long-term producer of fortified wines, it now offers dry white wines and quality reds. The little Franschhoek vineyard area lies southeast of Paarl.

Stellenbosch, although it produces only eight percent of the country's output, is the best-known South African wine district. It starts west of Franschhoek and south of Paarl, descending to the ocean at False Bay and extending toward Cape Town to the west. Surrounded by mountains, its topography is varied. It enjoys a moderate climate and an almost ideal level of rainfall, concentrated in the winter months. Many of the best red wines from this country come from the granite soil of its mountain flanks.

Some vineyards in the small Tygerberg region northwest of Stellenbosch are planted on slopes perched along the side of the Dortsberg Mountains, which are cooled by winds blowing from the Atlantic Ocean. Further south, behind Table Mountain, which separates it from Cape Town, the small historic vineyards of Constantia constitute a "ward," a designation roughly equivalent to a European appellation. Even further south, along the coast toward the east, Walker Bay and Elim have the country's coolest growing climates, favorable to white grape varieties as well as Pinot Noir.

Wine of Origin: Hierarchy of appellations

To understand the structure of South African wine, it's necessary to grasp the hierarchy of regional and local appellations. The introduction of the Wine of Origin system in 1973 established three classifications: region, district, and ward, going from the largest to the smallest areas (see also p.103). At present, there are five official regions: Breede River Valley, Cape South Coast, Coastal Region, Klein Karoo, and Olifants River. In general, a region includes several districts and a district several wards. However, a ward may sometimes be included in a region without being attached to the intermediate category of district. This is the case with the Constantia ward, which is listed under the Coastal Region. Some wards, such as Cederberg or Ceres, do not as yet form part of an official region or district. The country's best-known appellations, most of which are mentioned in these pages, are generally from districts and sometimes from wards (Stellenbosch, Franschhoek, Constantia). The great majority of quality wines that are exported come from the Coastal Region, which includes many districts, e.g. Paarl, Stellenbosch, and Tygerberg.

Leading South African regions and wines

The best-known regions or districts are those that produce and export the finest wines, led by Stellenbosch. However, the key factor in South African wine production today is the exploration of new regions with cooler climates that are capable of producing even finer wines.

CONSTANTIA

The ward of Constantia is situated on the southeastern slopes of mountains separating the city of Cape Town from False Bay. Although it is quite small, encompassing seven wine domains and around 1,236 acres (500 ha) of vines, it certainly deserves its reputation, as this was where the country's first vineyards were established. The Constantia estate was founded in 1685, taking its name from the daughter of the commissioner of the Dutch Cape Colony, by Simon Van der Stel (who also gave his name to Stellenbosch). In the 18th century, this large property had 1,800 acres (750 ha) of vines under cultivation. It was later subdivided and now several family enterprises work different plots. The relatively cool climate is influenced both by cold air coming from the mountains and by the "Cape Doctor," a wind blowing from the ocean. This is all very suitable for Bordeaux grape varieties, especially Sauvignon Blanc, a local specialty. Irrigation is unnecessary as the annual rainfall is around 39 inches (1,000 mm).

> **GRAPE VARIETIES** Sauvignon Blanc for white wines; Cabernet Sauvignon and Merlot for reds.

> **SOIL** Ancient, dating from the Precambrian era. Slopes are more or less steep, depending on the altitude, along the southern side of Table Mountain.

> **STYLE** The relatively cool climate and the small size of this ward give the white wines produced from Sauvignon Blanc grapes a distinctive style, full of freshness. The reds may be somewhat "vegetal."

> **NOTABLE PRODUCERS** Steenberg, Buitenverwachtig, Groot Constantia, Klein Constantia, Constantia Glen.

STELLENBOSCH

Of all South African wine appellations, Stellenbosch (which is a district) is the best known outside the country; but it is also the most densely planted. This additionally means it has the greatest concentration of top producers in South Africa. The town of the same name, whose architecture is a microcosm of the Cape Dutch style, is home to a viticulture and oenology school and a highly regarded research center, both at the local university. Given Stellenbosch's diversity of topography and climate, it is difficult to restrict its wines to a single style, all the more so since many grape varieties, both red and white, are cultivated. The wines also differ in relation to the altitude and/or proximity to the ocean.

> **GRAPE VARIETIES** White: Chenin Blanc, Chardonnay, Sauvignon Blanc, Semillon; red: Cabernet Sauvignon, Shiraz, Merlot, Pinotage.

> **SOIL** Varied, with an ancient foundation, since the Cape region is one of the world's oldest geologic structures. The soil ranges from light and sandy to granitic on the mountain foothills, and the topography is often very rugged.

> **STYLE** Stellenbosch's international fame flows from fine, full-bodied Cabernet Sauvignons and blends associated with this grape, although some of the best reds also come from Syrah and Pinotage. The whites are generally rich and aromatic.

> **NOTABLE PRODUCERS** Beyerskloof, Cordoba, De Trafford, Ernie Els, Ingwé, Grangehurst, Kaapzicht, Kanonkop, Meerlust, Morgenster, Raats Family, Rudera, Rupert & Rothschild, Rustenburg, Rust en Vrede, Thelema, Tokara, Waterford, Uitkyk, Vergelegen.

OVERBERG, WALKER BAY, CAPE AGULHAS

During recent years, there has been a significant shift toward production in cooler climates, as in other New World countries. The objective is three-fold: to limit the relatively high alcohol levels that result from a hot climate, to conserve the natural acidity of the grapes, and to cultivate varieties that prosper only in cool climates. Obviously these three factors are interconnected, and this is why plantings are increasingly being developed in high-altitude zones as well as in areas near oceans—the Atlantic meets the Indian Ocean at Cape Agulhas, the southernmost point of the African continent—where the air is cooler, especially at night. Notable among the districts here are Overberg, Walker Bay, and Cape Agulhas, all of which belong to the Cape South Coast region, extending along the coast southeast of Stellenbosch and False Bay.

> **GRAPE VARIETIES** White: Sauvignon Blanc, Chardonnay; red: Pinot Noir.

> **SOIL** Ancient, essentially from the Precambrian era.

> **STYLE** In this appreciably cooler southern area, the wines (largely white) are lively and fresh.

> **NOTABLE PRODUCERS** Agulhas Wines, Bouchard Finlayson, Hamilton Russell, Lomond, Newton Johnson, Raka.

PAARL AND FRANSCHHOEK

Part of the very large Coastal Region, Paarl extends north of Stellenbosch, and its distance from the ocean means that it has a rather warmer climate. For this reason, Paarl specialized for many years in port-type fortified wines, which were appreciated by the home market. Today production is much more diversified, thanks largely to magnificent wines made from Syrah and other Rhône grape varieties. The Franschhoek valley district extends to the southeast and is separated from Stellenbosch by the Simonsberg Mountains. It owes its name ("French corner") to the arrival in the 17th century of Huguenot refugees fleeing religious persecution in France. The names of some farms still testify to this French origin: La Motte, Grande Provence, Mont Rochelle, Chamonix, Cabrière, etc.

> **GRAPE VARIETIES** White: Chenin Blanc, Chardonnay, Sauvignon Blanc, Colombard; red: Cabernet Sauvignon, Shiraz, Merlot, Pinotage, Cinsaut.

> **SOIL** Granite soil at the foot of the mountains, sand and clay elsewhere in the region.

> **STYLE** The wines are often heartier than their Stellenbosch neighbors, but this generalization should be qualified by a given site's geographic situation and its altitude.

> **NOTABLE PRODUCERS** Glen Carlou, Boekenhoutskloof, Fairview, Nederburg, Porcupine Ridge, Veenwouden.

The Wine of Constantia

Historically, the Constantia estate was famous for a dessert wine called Vin de Constance, made from late-harvested Muscat varieties. Despite the subdivision of this property into two parts (Groot and Klein), the wine gained a worldwide reputation during the 18th and 19th centuries, to the extent that it became one of the most expensive and most sought-after wines in the world. However, production was halted in the late 19th century when South African vineyards were devastated by phylloxera, and for over a century Vin de Constance ceased to exist.

It was revived thanks to the work of the Jooste family, who bought Klein Constantia in 1980. From the start, they had a clear vision: to re-create a great dessert wine, working with original grape varieties but with the benefit of modern science. Sold in a bottle that is a copy of an ancient flagon, today's Vin de Constance from Klein Constantia has undoubtedly achieved its objective: once again it is one of the world's great dessert wines, alongside the best Tokajs from Hungary, the sweet wines from Austria's Burgenland, and Sauternes from Bordeaux.

AUSTRALIA

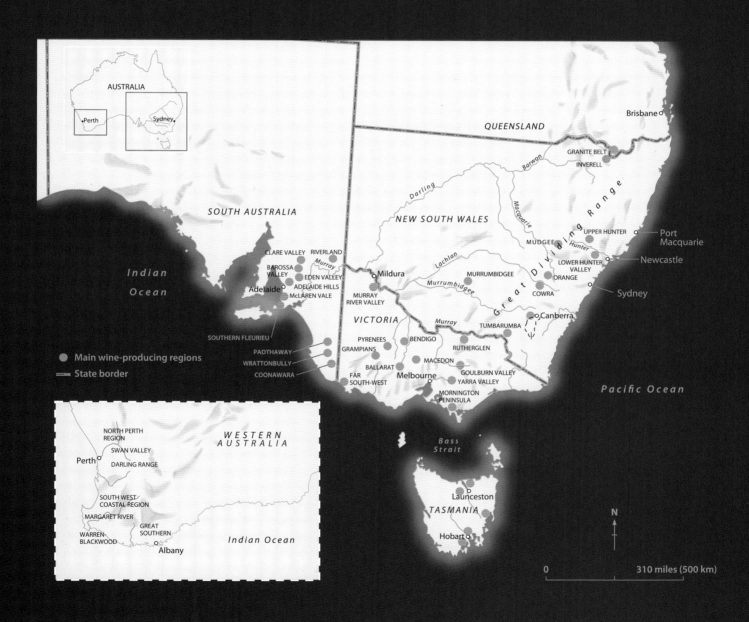

AUSTRALIA

Perth •

Sydney •

QUEENSLAND

Brisbane ○

SOUTH AUSTRALIA

NEW SOUTH WALES

Barwon

GRANITE BELT

INVERELL

Darling

Macquarie

Indian Ocean

CLARE VALLEY   RIVERLAND

MUDGEE

UPPER HUNTER

Port Macquarie

Hunter

Murray

BAROSSA VALLEY

EDEN VALLEY

ADELAIDE HILLS

McLAREN VALE

Adelaide

Mildura ○

Lachlan

MURRUMBIDGEE

LOWER HUNTER VALLEY

Newcastle

ORANGE

Murrumbidgee

COWRA

Great Dividing Range

Sydney

MURRAY RIVER VALLEY

SOUTHERN FLEURIEU

VICTORIA

Murray

TUMBARUMBA

Canberra ○

PADTHAWAY

WRATTONBULLY

COONAWARA

PYRENEES

GRAMPIANS

BENDIGO

MACEDON

RUTHERGLEN

BALLARAT

FAR SOUTH-WEST

Melbourne ○

GOULBURN VALLEY

YARRA VALLEY

MORNINGTON PENINSULA

Pacific Ocean

● Main wine-producing regions

State border

Bass Strait

Launceston

TASMANIA

N

Hobart ○

NORTH PERTH REGION

SWAN VALLEY

Perth ○

DARLING RANGE

WESTERN AUSTRALIA

SOUTH WEST COASTAL REGION

MARGARET RIVER

GREAT SOUTHERN

WARREN-BLACKWOOD

Albany ○

Indian Ocean

0   310 miles (500 km)

AUSTRALIA

Over the past two decades, Australia's vineyard acreage has almost tripled and Australian wines are now known worldwide. Australian success can be credited to producer dynamism, their organization, and their skill in developing wines to suit consumer taste. But Australia also produces great wines that owe their character to the terroir and to an impressive reserve of old vines.

Early beginnings and modern progress

VINES FROM EUROPE. Between 1820 and 1850, viticulture became a significant agricultural activity in southeastern Australia—the region surrounding the developing townships of Sydney, Melbourne, and Adelaide. Throughout the 19th century, there were many private initiatives to import grape varieties from the Old World as immigrants, explorers, and farmers arrived from Europe with a few cuttings of *vitis vinifera*.

PRODUCTION FOR THE UK MARKET. Until the outbreak of phylloxera in 1877, the state of Victoria was the country's chief production center. Thereafter the output from another state, New South Wales, grew considerably thanks to the production of fortified wines largely destined for the English market, and due to the development of irrigation systems in the Murray Valley.

> **AUSTRALIA STATISTICS**
>
> **Vineyard area:** 417,600 acres (169,000 ha)
>
> **Production:** 133 million cases (12,000,000 hl)
>
> **Reds:** 54%
>
> **Whites:** 46%
>
> (Australian Government – AWBC – OIV, 2008)

By 1930, 75 percent of the country's wine output came from this region, and exports flourished thanks to opportunities offered in Commonwealth outlets. In terms of the volume of wine exported to the UK market, Australia had already outstripped France by 1927, and France did not recapture a lead until 2005. During the postwar period, the viticultural industry really began to evolve. The demand for dry wines, especially whites, increased; and producers developed new techniques of vinification, notably the introduction of stainless steel tanks and temperature control systems.

GROWING HOME MARKET AND QUALITY WINES. Production exploded during the 1980s, chiefly driven by growth of the home market. Faced with new demand, winemakers expanded their output (some of it from unpromising sites), and sales of wine in bulk and in boxes accounted for 80 percent of production during this period. Over the past 25 years, wine quality has made great progress due to rapid diffusion of technical progress and a better choice of grape varieties. The wine industry has focused, with great commercial success, on providing reliable, well-made, good-value wines, rapidly enabling Australian wines to conquer export

> Drought has struck some vineyard areas, prompting the search for cooler climes.

Water problems

In this enormous and arid continent, wine production (like most of the population) is concentrated in the southern and coastal regions, especially in the southeast. Although winter and spring can be rainy, the summers are particularly hot and dry, especially in some parts of western and southern Australia. Lack of water remains a primary concern in many regions, and irrigation is essential.

The Riverland area, bordering the states of Victoria and South Australia, produces nearly 50 percent of Australia's wine thanks to irrigation, which has transformed a semi-desert region into a sea of vines. However, the limitations of this system are evident, with repeated droughts and the gradual drying-up of the Murray River.

> Vines at the Oliverhill winery in McLaren Vale, South Australia.

markets. Alongside standardized production, a growing number of small, independent estates are securing a strong regional identity for their wines. Today, Australia is the world's sixth-largest wine producer and the fourth-largest exporter.

Climate and grape varieties

Australia benefits from almost ideal conditions for wine production: plenty of sunshine, low humidity, maritime influences, and local mountain ranges. While Australians originally regarded climate as the essential factor in a vineyard's potential, today the question of soils, orientation, and altitude of plots is taken into account.

The majority of white wines are made using Chardonnay grapes, ahead of Sémillon, Colombard, Sauvignon Blanc, and Riesling. Shiraz (Syrah) remains the great national grape variety for red wines. Introduced during the 19th century, it produces several of the country's most successful wines, either as a single grape variety or blended with Cabernet; increasingly it may also be blended with Grenache or Mourvèdre (Mataro). Cabernet Sauvignon, Merlot, Pinot Noir, and Grenache have also gained ground. Beyond these varieties, a certain amount of diversification is in progress: Verdelho, Viognier, and Marsanne being used for white wine; while Mourvèdre, Sangiovese, Barbera, Cabernet Franc, and Petit Verdot are used in reds.

Formerly, each producer tried to grow a wide range of grape varieties whatever the local climate; but now there is increasing specialization, especially in relation to regional conditions. Examples include Riesling in the Clare Valley, Cabernet Sauvignon at Coonawarra or Margaret River, Shiraz in the Barossa Valley, etc.

Moving to appellations

Australian (and now many) consumers rely chiefly on the grape variety and the brand. Until recently, the geographic origin of the wine was a far less important indicator—but that is changing. Following initial efforts in the 1960s, labeling regulations were established in early 1990s under the Label Integrity Program. A particular grape variety may not be cited on a label unless at least 85 percent of the wine is made from it. If several varieties are named on the label, they must be listed in decreasing order of importance (see also p.103). The geographic origin

Cool climate quest

Faced with the troubles of drought, Australian growers have spent 20 years assiduously searching for cooler climates more favorable to the production of fine wines. During this period, Tasmania and the coastal regions in the extreme south of the country, both in the state of Victoria and in Western Australia, have seen rapid expansion of their vine plantings.

> Cathcart Ridge estate in the state of Victoria.

of the grapes also may be specified. South Eastern Australia is the country's largest "geographical indication" or GI, a categorization created in response to European Union law that states, when labeled with the grape variety from which they are made, imported wines must also bear the name of an officially recognized geographic area of origin. This GI (geographical indication) applies to blended wines where the grapes come from several eastern states (New South Wales, Victoria, Queensland, and South Australia). The next categorization relates to a single state (Victoria, for example). Below that there are some 60 regions or sub-regions. For some of them, such as Coonawarra, boundary disputes have led to prolonged legal battles.

New South Wales

The state of New South Wales, in southeast Australia, is the oldest and one of the largest production areas in the country. It continues to expand, with output growing year on year. The flagship zone is Hunter Valley, 125 miles (200 km) north of Sydney (*see* p.476), famous for its Shiraz and Sémillon wines. Southwest of Hunter Valley, the Mudgee region (*see* p.476)

DID YOU KNOW...?

Like many countries where wine appreciation is a relatively recent development, Australia places a lot of emphasis on wine challenges and competitions. These shows are very professionally organized and make a good promotional platform for the winning wines. They may be national or regional, confined to wines from certain grape varieties, or simply encompass all wine categories.

benefits from a drier, warmer climate than its coastal neighbor. Further south, the small Orange region has recently received investment from major groups, attracted by the potential of the cool slopes of Mount Canobolas. Further inland, toward the west, the large Murrumbidgee Irrigation Area produces everyday wines, chiefly from Sémillon and Trebbiano (Ugni Blanc) grapes. Finally, in the southeast of the state, and in addition to Canberra District's flourishing boutique wineries, mention should be made of the potential of the Tumbarumba region, which benefits from the altitude of the Snowy Mountains.

Victoria

South of New South Wales, the state of Victoria is responsible for 17 percent of the country's wine production, spread over a multitude of very different zones and regions.

North East Victoria's particularly hot climate is ideal for Rutherglen's splendid Muscat- or Muscadelle-based dessert wines. Further south, the high-altitude vineyards of King Valley have the advantage of a cool climate and are planted mostly with Riesling, Chardonnay, and Cabernet Sauvignon. In the southeast of the state, the Gippsland zone's vast acreage is sparsely planted as yet, but growing strongly.

In the most southerly regions of Victoria, which benefit from oceanic influences, Pinot Noir and Chardonnay produce rather elegant wines. The area around Port Philip Bay, west of Gippsland, sees similar conditions and is home to several famous regions, such as Mornington (*see* p.478) and Yarra Valley (*see* p.477). Further north, Central Victoria includes the Bendigo region as well as that of Goulburn Valley, which is chiefly devoted to Shiraz (Syrah) and Cabernet Sauvignon. Nearly 80 percent of the grapes grown in the state come from the North West Victoria zone, where the heat can be crushing and irrigation is indispensable. Muscat Gordo Blanco and Sultana grapes are still strongly represented, although their share of the crop is diminishing. In the south of Western Victoria, the climate is cooler and the Grampians region chiefly produces sparkling wines, although the Riesling and Shiraz table wines show promise.

Tasmania

Tasmania is a large island south of Victoria. Until recently, its cool, windy climate was considered suitable only for the production of sparkling wines. But over the past few years (and probably thanks to climate change that has led to rising temperatures) very good still white wines have been made here, as well as promising Pinot Noirs.

South Australia

The state of South Australia produces 46 percent of the country's wine output. It is largely due to huge volumes of everyday wines made in the Riverland area along the Murray River Valley. However, its true riches are found in the coastal zones that benefit from the cool ocean winds.

In the southeast, several regions of the Limestone Coast zone, such as Padthaway and Wrattonbully, are on the rise; but they are far from reaching the fame of Coonawarra (*see* p.481). Running north along the coast, the zones of Fleurieu, Barossa, and Mount Lofty Ranges are backed by a north-south chain of mountains and are home to several remarkable sites. These include the hills of McLaren Vale (*see* p.480), where a Mediterranean climate produces fine red wines from Shiraz and Cabernet Sauvignon grapes. Further north, the Barossa

Valley (*see* p.479) is the stronghold of old Shiraz vines that yield robust, full-bodied wines in a hot climate. Like the Cabernet wines of the Medoc (France), they constitute a kind of stylistic reference point for Australian Shiraz. Bordering Barossa to the east, Eden Valley (*see* p.480) is better known for its Rieslings. Further north, in the Mount Lofty Ranges zone, the coastal influences diminish and the climate becomes more continental. Still further north, Riesling and Cabernet Sauvignon offer good results in Clare Valley (*see also* p.478), where the altitude makes for a cooler climate.

Western Australia

This state produces only three percent of the nation's wine, although the volume has doubled since 1997. It is testament to the dynamism of the region, where many sites are being prospected. The climate is varied, ranging from scorching northwestern regions, such as Swan Valley, to the more temperate regions of Margaret River and the appreciably cooler Great Southern region. Margaret River (*see also* p.481) is a very trendy region, and some big companies have recently established themselves there. Further east along the coast, Great Southern (*see* p. 481) is one of the great future hopes for cool-climate grape varieties such as Riesling, Chardonnay, and Pinot Noir. Among other regions of note, Pemberton, situated between Margaret River and Great Southern, stands out for its promising Chardonnays, while Geographe, which extends along the west coast above Margaret River, produces elegant Cabernet Sauvignon and Shiraz wines.

> In the cellar at Campbells Winery in Rutherglen, Victoria.

Leading Australian regions and wines

Precise geographic origins of wines destined for mass consumption are not usually indicated. Most of these wines are made from grapes harvested in several regions. Technology has permitted this kind of industrial production, and the result is a remarkable standard of reliability. But Australia also has identified many clearly defined regions that are winning a reputation as distinctive indicators of wine character.

HUNTER VALLEY

North of Sydney and upstream from the port of Newcastle, the Hunter Valley zone sprawls along the river of the same name. It includes Upper Hunter in the north and Lower Hunter in the south, each considered separate regions, although linked by the river. At first glance, the hot and humid climate makes it an unlikely location for the development of great wines. Nevertheless, Hunter Valley is to some extent the cradle of Australian viticulture and remarkable wines are produced there. These include Sémillons for laying down; they are some of the country's most distinctive wines.

> **GRAPE VARIETIES** White: Sémillon, Chardonnay; red: Cabernet Sauvignon, Shiraz.

> **SOIL** Sandy, well-drained alluvial flats.

> **STYLE** Hunter Valley's great Sémillons are among Australia's best dry white wines. Usually fermented in vats, they have remarkable ageing characteristics. A good mature Sémillon has a honeyed bouquet with notes of exotic fruit and an intense smoky, mineral background. The Chardonnays are generally more concentrated and rounder, while the Shiraz style is varied, ranging from round and powerful to relatively fresh and tannic.

> **NOTABLE PRODUCERS** Brokenwood, De Bortoli, Evans Family, Mount View Estate, Rothbury Ridge, Tyrell's, Wyndham Estate.

MUDGEE

Its Aboriginal name meaning "nest of hills," Mudgee is separated from Hunter Valley by the Great Dividing Range, the chain of mountains on its eastern border. It has a hot, dry climate, so irrigation is necessary. The region does not enjoy the same reputation as its neighbor, but much of its harvest is sold to the big Hunter Valley producers.

> **GRAPE VARIETIES** White: Chardonnay, Pinot Gris, Viognier; red: Cabernet Sauvignon, Merlot, Shiraz.

> **SOIL** Sandy loam and clay.

> **STYLE** The most interesting wines are made with Cabernet Sauvignon, sometimes blended with Merlot or Shiraz. They show a rich, warming style with aromas of overripe fruits and cacao with eucalyptus notes. The Shiraz wines are of the same caliber. Chardonnay has long been established here and produces heavy, aromatic wines with good ageing potential—like the Sémillon wines made in a style similar to that of Hunter Valley.

> **NOTABLE PRODUCERS** Huntington Estate, Miramar, Poet's Corner.

HEATHCOTE

This small wine region is situated at the center of Victoria, between the Goulburn Valley and Bendigo. Although the earliest vine plantings in the area date back to the 1860s, it was not until the 1970s that winemakers took a close look at the region's potential. They remain few in number, but they are often highly reputed and their wines are sought after. The growing area covers less that 4,900 acres (2,000 ha) on moderately elevated slopes (490–1,150 ft/ 150–350 m). The climate, influenced by the chain of the Mount Camel Range, is cooler, more humid, and windier than surrounding regions. Local production is dominated by red grape varieties, especially Shiraz followed by Cabernet Sauvignon.

> **GRAPE VARIETIES** Red: Cabernet Sauvignon, Merlot, Shiraz.

> **SOIL** Weathered earth (Cambrian greenstone) over chalk and red clay.

> **STYLE** Shiraz expresses itself in a particularly intense way (soft fruits, cherries, prunes); it is powerful and concentrated with supple tannins and, sometimes, menthol notes that bring a touch of freshness. Cabernet Sauvignon, sometimes blended with Merlot, also makes rich, generous wines with mint or eucalyptus notes.

> **NOTABLE PRODUCERS** Coliban Valley Wines, Heathcote Estate, Jasper Hill, M. Chapoutier.

YARRA VALLEY

Situated less than one hour's drive east of Melbourne, Yarra Valley is Victoria's best-known wine region. With altitudes ranging from 160–1,300 ft (50–400 m), and steep slopes in places, the valley's topography is fairly complex. But the style of its wines is also influenced by the cool, humid climate. Yarra is noted for producing some of Australia's best sparkling wines, and for good Chardonnays and Pinot Noirs.

> **GRAPE VARIETIES** White: Chardonnay, Sauvignon Blanc; red: Pinot Noir, followed by Cabernet Sauvignon and Shiraz.

> **SOIL** Sandy clay-loams in the north, red volcanic soil in the south.

> **STYLE** The best sparkling wines are made by the traditional method and are full of finesse and freshness. The Chardonnays are generally well balanced, perhaps less exuberant than others, but fresh and aromatic (nutty, fig or white peach flavors). The best red wines are made from Pinot Noir, with lots of fruit (cherries), spices, and vivacity; or from Shiraz in a fruity, often juicy style.

> **NOTABLE PRODUCERS** Coldstream Hills, De Bortoli, Domaine Chandon, Giant Steps, TarraWarra, Yarra Yering, Yeringberg, Yering Station.

Giaconda – a small, high quality estate

During the 1970s, Rick Kinzbrunner, a mechanical engineer by training, decided to make a career in wine. For 10 years, he traveled the world honing his skills at the University of California-Davis, at Stag's Leap and at other wineries in the Napa and Sonoma valleys, and at the Bordeaux properties of the Moueix family, co-owners of Petrus, before becoming assistant winemaker at an Australian estate (Brown Brothers Milawa). In 1982, he planted his first vines in Beechworth, a little regarded region in northeast Victoria, producing his first wine in 1986. Despite its minuscule acreage, Giaconda has become one of Australia's most famous names, and its wines fetch astronomical prices. From a pocket-sized vineyard (15 acres/6 ha), this artisan winemaker draws powerful, complex wines—the result of the most natural vinification possible (local yeasts and no filtration), and of particularly careful viticulture. His Chardonnays (Nantua) and Shiraz (Warmer Vineyard) show a rich, powerful style and are among the best Australia has to offer.

MORNINGTON PENINSULA

Located at Victoria's southernmost point, the Mornington Peninsula is one of those regions recently prospected by winegrowers in search of cooler climes. Surrounded by the sea and swept by winds, it enjoys plenty of sunshine and moderate temperatures, and there is no water problem for the vines. A small group of producers have rapidly exploited this fortunate spot to produce fine, fresh wines made from varieties that adapt well to such conditions, notably Chardonnay and Pinot Noir.

> **GRAPE VARIETIES** White: Chardonnay, Pinot Gris, Viognier; red: Cabernet Franc, Cabernet Sauvignon, Merlot, Pinot Noir.
> **SOIL** Compacted, well-drained sandy, clay, and red soils of volcanic origin.
> **STYLE** The Chardonnay produces lively, aromatic wines (citrus and nutty flavors). The Pinot Gris also has recently become much sought-after. As for the red wines, the Pinots Noirs are fresh and fruity (cherries) and are best consumed while young. The Bordeaux varieties are grown in the warmest sectors, such as the Moorooduc Valley, and make relatively light, low-tannin wines.
> **NOTABLE PRODUCERS** Dromana, Kooyong, Montalto, Moorooduc, Paringa, Stonier, Ten Minutes by Tractor, T'Gallant, Yabby Lake.

TASMANIA

The quest for cooler climates than those of Australia's large production zones, which have suffered from global warming and drought, is vividly illustrated in the case of Tasmania. This huge island, just below Australia's southeasternmost point, now harbors a growing number of mostly small-scale producers. The vineyards are all situated on the northern or southeastern sides of the island, where the cool (and sometimes very windy) climate favors the cultivation of white grape varieties and Pinot Noir, as well as the production of sparkling wines. (The latitude is identical to that of New Zealand's South Island.)

> **GRAPE VARIETIES** White: Chardonnay, Riesling, Sauvignon Blanc, Sémillon; red: Cabernet Franc, Cabernet Sauvignon, Gamay, Pinot Noir.
> **SOIL** Ancient compacted sandstone and shale; river alluvials and rich volcanic earth in some places.

> **STYLE** Products of a cool climate, most of Tasmania's wines possess great natural freshness. At their peak, the sparkling wines (most frequently Chardonnay and Pinot Noir) offer plenty of vivacity and aromatic finesse. The Rieslings can be sharp and need to be cellared for some time, while the good Sauvignon Blancs are particularly aromatic and firm, close in style to those from Marlborough (see p.486). The Pinot Noirs are aromatic (fresh berry fruits, spices) and well structured.
> **NOTABLE PRODUCERS** Bay of Fires, Freycinet, Jansz (sparkling wines), Meadowbank, Pipers Brook, Pirie, Tamar Ridge.

CLARE VALLEY

Situated in the northern Mount Lofty Ranges, the Clare Valley's undulating landscape makes it one of Australia's most attractive wine-producing regions. The days are warm to hot and the nights are cool, but local orientation and the altitude within the valley play an important role. Towards the end of the 1990s, local winemakers were the first to adopt the screwcap wine closure. The Clare Valley is particularly renowned for its Rieslings, but red grape varieties (chiefly Cabernet Sauvignon and Shiraz) are also successful.

> **GRAPE VARIETIES** White: Riesling, Sémillon; red: Cabernet Sauvignon, Grenache, Malbec, Shiraz.
> **SOIL** Red topsoil over limestone; fertile alluvial soil in the north, sandy loams with degraded quartz to the west.
> **STYLE** Clare Valley's Riesling is a firm, dry wine with fine natural acidity and juicy citrus and mineral aromas; when young it is rather austere, but it has long cellaring potential. In addition to intense white wines, the region also offers well-structured, fruity Shiraz (red berries, spices) and Cabernet Sauvignons that, at their best, are famous for their aromatic complexity (dark berries, menthol, cigar box), balance, and longevity.
> **NOTABLE PRODUCERS** Grosset, Jim Barry, Kilikanoon, Leasingham, Mitchell, Mount Horrocks, Tim Adams.

BAROSSA VALLEY

The Barossa Valley is less than 30 miles (50 km) northeast of Adelaide and is the country's most famous wine-producing region. Viticulture dates back to the wave of emigration from Silesia during the 19th century, the influence of which is still evident. Today, it is Australia's leading quality winemaking region and home to producers of varying sizes, ranging from such giants of Australian wine production as Penfolds to many highly regard smaller estates. Century-old Shiraz vines and some Grenache and Mourvèdre sit alongside more recent plantings, notably of Cabernet Sauvignon, Chardonnay, and Riesling. The climate is warm and dry, and the wines exemplify this characteristic.

> **GRAPE VARIETIES** White: Chardonnay, Riesling, Sémillon; red: Cabernet Sauvignon, Grenache, Merlot, Mourvèdre, Shiraz.

> **SOIL** Clay-loam and sandy soil.

> **STYLE** Powerful, ripe, exuberant reds. They have great depth when made with grapes from old vines. They also have good ageing potential. The Shiraz in particular can achieve rare amplitude, with plenty of fruit. The whites tend to be soft and rounded, although some Rieslings from grapes grown at higher altitude display finesse and elegance. Excellent port-style fortified wines are also produced.

> **NOTABLE PRODUCERS** Charles Melton, Glaetzer, Kaesler, Penfolds, Peter Lehmann, Rockford, St. Hallett, Seppelt, Torbreck, Turkey Flat, Wolf Blass, Yalumba.

Penfolds Grange, Australia's first icon wine

As for so many great wines, the story of Penfolds Grange, formerly known as Grange Hermitage, is something of a miracle. Max Schubert, the creator of this Barossa Valley hallmark, initially developed it in secret, without telling his employers. He called it "Bin 95," and the work followed a 1950 visit to Bordeaux where he had the opportunity to taste some magnificently aromatic 40-year-old wines. His revelation about the ageing potential of certain wines convinced Schubert that he could improve on the still-mediocre Australian wines of that time. He decided to develop a wine that would mature well while retaining its Australian character.

Schubert used Shiraz (Syrah), which is also used in the great wines of Côte-Rôtie and Hermitage (see pp.326 and 328). The reaction of the Penfolds directors to the first vintages was so negative that the experiment was nearly terminated. However, Grange needed time to reveal the richness of its flavors and for public opinion to accept an innovative, unfamiliar taste. The pioneering Schubert was right, for Grange has become the uncontested king of Australian wines and today commands peak prices at auction. The name comes from Grange Cottage, the original farm of the Penfolds' founder, near Adelaide.

EDEN VALLEY

At an altitude of 1,200–1,650 ft (370–500 m), Eden Valley enjoys a cooler climate than its famous neighbor. This wooded region is noted for its white wines, with a long tradition in Riesling started by German immigrants during the 19th century. Chardonnay is also cultivated and offers supple, intense wines. In terms of reds, Eden Valley remains largely loyal to Shiraz, which is the basis for Henschke's Hill of Grace.

> **GRAPE VARIETIES** White: Chardonnay, Riesling; red: Cabernet Sauvignon, Shiraz.
> **SOIL** Loamy sand, clay, and silt, sometimes mixed with ironstone gravels and quartz.
> **STYLE** The Rieslings are firm, lively, and aromatic (citrus and flinty notes), with excellent cellaring potential. Shiraz wines have a generous bouquet of candied fruits, spices, and sometimes kirsch or eucalyptus; they are warming on the palate, with a supple, silky structure. The best combine depth and a long finish with good ageing potential, although they are delightful when young.
> **NOTABLE PRODUCERS** Heggies, Henschke, Mountadam, Pewsey Vale.

ADELAIDE HILLS

Adelaide Hills is a wine region situated east of the city of Adelaide and north of the McLaren Vale. Its distinction is one of the coolest climates in South Australia, thanks to its proximity to the sea and its altitude, which peaks at above 1,970 ft (600 m). This makes it highly suitable for white grape varieties, which are especially dominant in the southern sites of two famous sub-regions: Lenswood and Piccadilly. In the warmer northern sites, Cabernet Sauvignon, sometimes blended with Merlot, achieves a good level of maturity.

> **GRAPE VARIETIES** White: Chardonnay, Riesling, Sauvignon Blanc; red: Cabernet Sauvignon, Merlot, Pinot Noir.
> **SOIL** Sandy loams and clay subsoils.
> **STYLE** Adelaide Hills offers some of Australia's best Sauvignon Blancs. They have a lively, fragrant style (aromas of green fruits, citrus, sometimes exotic fruits), and should be consumed young. The Chardonnays are often used as the basis for sparkling wines, blended with Pinot Noir, which is also widely planted.
> **NOTABLE PRODUCERS** Knappstein, Lenswood, Nepenthe, Petaluma, Shaw & Smith.

MCLAREN VALE

Largely open to the ocean and bordered to the east by the Mount Lofty Ranges, McLaren Vale is a small region but one with a longstanding winemaking tradition. Its gently undulating green landscape and its Mediterranean climate have attracted many independent winemakers, often of a high standard. Although there is plenty of sunshine everywhere, local conditions vary significantly depending on aspect, altitude, and the degree of exposure to maritime influences.

> **GRAPE VARIETIES** White: Chardonnay, Sauvignon Blanc; red: Cabernet Sauvignon, Grenache, Shiraz.
> **SOIL** Sandy alluvials, loam, and silt.
> **STYLE** McLaren Vale is known primarily for its instantly seductive, rich, full-bodied red wines with exuberant fruity flavors. The Cabernet Sauvignons evoke ripe dark fruits with spicy, chocolaty notes and rounded tannins. The Shiraz is dark with warming accents, concentrated fruit, and a generous level of alcohol. Grenache from old vines is sometimes blended with Shiraz to make particularly deep, smooth wines with aromas of candied fruit or kirsch.

> **NOTABLE PRODUCERS** Clarendon Hills, D'Arenberg, Gemtree, Hardy's Reynella, Mitolo, Wirra Wirra.

COONAWARRA

At the extreme southeast corner of South Australia, this region is one of the temples of great Australian Cabernet Sauvignon. Situated 37 miles (60 km) inland, swept by western winds and cooled by Antarctic currents, it enjoys a temperate maritime climate. Uniquely in Australia, its boundaries are defined—after a long legal battle—by a specific kind of soil called "terra rossa," composed of a thin layer of reddish earth over a thick bed of limestone. This formation encompasses a narrow strip of vineyards 1.2 miles (2 km) wide by about 9 miles (15 km) long, running north to south. Coonawarra made its reputation with the first plantings of Cabernet Sauvignon in the 1960s, eclipsing Shiraz—although this is still grown, as are Chardonnay and Riesling.

> **GRAPE VARIETIES** White: Chardonnay, Riesling; red: Cabernet Sauvignon, Merlot, Shiraz.

> **SOIL** Friable red clays ("terra rossa") over limestone.

> **STYLE** Cabernet Sauvignon makes intense wines distinguished by flavors of black fruits (blackcurrant, prunes, etc.) with spicy or smoky overtones; they are more structured than most Australian Cabernets, and fresher, with relatively firm tannins. These wines usually have good cellaring potential. The Shiraz shows a similar register, with a more marked fruitiness and freshness than wines from warmer regions.

> **NOTABLE PRODUCERS** Katnook, Parker, Wynns, Zema.

MARGARET RIVER

About 165 miles (270 km) south of Perth, this region was hardly planted before the 1980s; but its reputation has grown and grown ever since its potential was highlighted by pioneering estates including Cape Mentelle and Cullen. The climate is Mediterranean—hot and dry—but more tempered and more humid than inland zones, thanks to the ocean that buffers it on three sides. The highly permeable gravelly, sandy soil is excellent for the Cabernet Sauvignon that has given the region its distinction.

> **GRAPE VARIETIES** White: Chardonnay, Sauvignon Blanc, Sémillon; red: Cabernet Sauvignon, Merlot, Shiraz.

> **SOIL** Sandy and gravelly.

> **STYLE** Cabernet Sauvignon, sometimes blended with Merlot, produces particularly distinguished, ripe, and elegant wines, most of which display (with maturity) a refinement and complexity approaching that of top Bordeaux wines. As for the white wines, the Sauvignon Blanc, usually blended with Sémillon, produces soft, well-balanced wines, often with herbaceous aromas.

> **NOTABLE PRODUCERS** Cape Mentelle, Cullen, Gralyn, Juniper Estate, Leeuwin, Moss Wood, Pierro, Vasse Felix, Voyager.

GREAT SOUTHERN

This vast wine-producing region, with its numerous sub-regions (Albany, Denmark, Frankland River, Mount Barker, and Porongorup), is both Australia's most extensive and most recent wine region, as well as the one least under cultivation. It encompasses a good part of the country's southwest, and is the coolest part of Western Australia. Because of its proximity to the ocean and its southern aspect, the nights are very cool. But the days are sunny; rainfall is lower than at Margaret River, for example. Two sub-regions, Denmark and Albany, are open to strong maritime influences. Many winemakers based elsewhere in Western Australia buy grapes from Great Southern (although 20 years ago, apples were the major crop).

> **GRAPE VARIETIES** White: Chardonnay, Riesling, Sauvignon Blanc, Sémillon; red: Cabernet Sauvignon, Pinot Noir, Shiraz.

> **SOIL** Impoverished gravelly, sandy loams; loams deriving from gneiss or granite bedrocks; rich loams in the Denmark sector.

> **STYLE** The most successful red wines are made with Cabernet Sauvignon, in—for Australia—an unusually firm and structured style; Shiraz produces very fruity, well-balanced wines. In whites, Riesling offers plenty of vigor and intense citrus flavors, while Chardonnay makes fresh and sometimes structured wines.

> **NOTABLE PRODUCERS** Alkoomi, Chatsfield, Howard Park, Mount Trio, Plantagenet, West Cape Howe.

NEW ZEALAND

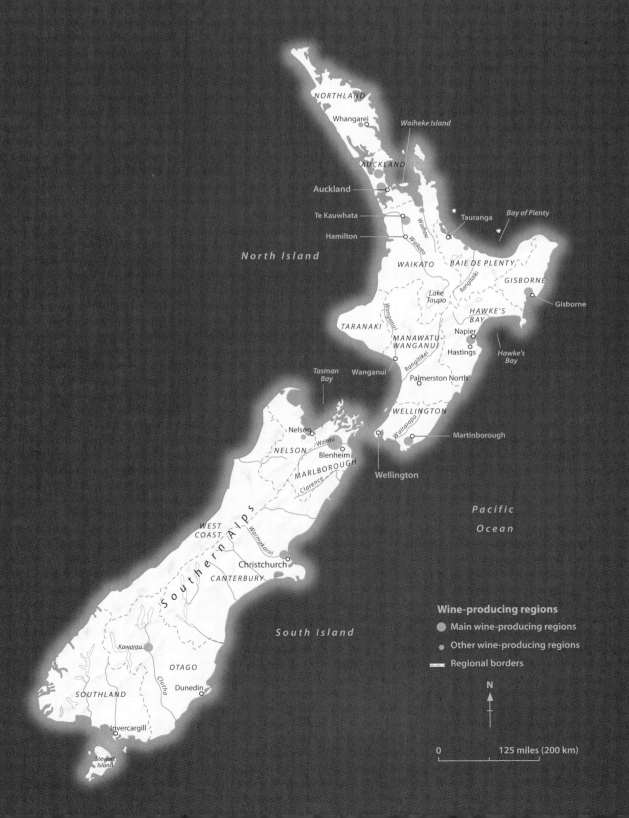

NORTHLAND

Whangarei

Waiheke Island

AUCKLAND

Auckland

Te Kauwhata

Waihou

Tauranga

Bay of Plenty

Hamilton

Waikato

North Island

WAIKATO

BAIE DE PLENTY

Rangitaiki

GISBORNE

Lake Taupo

Gisborne

Wanganui

HAWKE'S BAY

Napier

TARANAKI

MANAWATU WANGANUI

Hastings

Hawke's Bay

Rangitikei

Tasman Bay

Wanganui

Palmerston North

Nelson

Wairau

WELLINGTON

Wairarapa

Martinborough

NELSON

Blenheim

MARLBOROUGH

Wellington

Clarence

Pacific Ocean

West Coast

Waimakariri

Christchurch

CANTERBURY

Southern Alps

South Island

Kawarau

OTAGO

SOUTHLAND

Clutha

Dunedin

Invercargill

Stewart Island

Wine-producing regions

● Main wine-producing regions

● Other wine-producing regions

⌁ Regional borders

N

0   125 miles (200 km)

NEW ZEALAND

Despite relatively small production, this island nation at the end of the world has managed to penetrate the global market with wines of remarkable flavor and freshness. Whether Sauvignon Blanc (the most popular variety), Chardonnay, or Pinot Noir, New Zealand wines occupy a special place in the New World.

Rapid change

The astonishing success of New Zealand wine today had a slow start. Since the establishment of the first vineyards in 1819, the industry has had to overcome vine diseases, which are virulent in such a humid climate, along with puritanical and prohibitionist attitudes that long prohibited, restricted, or supervised the sale and distribution of alcohol. The real turning point was in the 1970s, with the introduction of varieties of *Vitis vinifera* in place of American hybrids, the development of new regions like Marlborough, and the gradual shift of production, once dominated by sweet wines, toward dry wines.

After a realignment in 1986, during which a quarter of old vineyards disappeared, change has continued with expanded plantings of grape varieties such as Chardonnay and Sauvignon Blanc. These permitted the emergence of a fresh style of wine, full of flavor and technically well produced—and this has enhanced the country's reputation. Since 1999, production has quadrupled and been supported by export growth of 550 percent, and by a significant increase in domestic consumption.

NEW ZEALAND STATISTICS

Vineyard area: 71,660 acres (29,000 ha)

Production: 22 million cases (2,000,000 hl)

Whites: 75%

Reds: 25%

(New Zealand Winegrowers, OIV, 2008)

Climate

The country consists of two parts, North Island and South Island, extending over 930 miles (1,500 km) from north to south. A maritime climate is subject to the influence of moist westerly winds as well as cold southerly winds blowing from the Antarctic. It is more temperate (cooler) and much more humid, especially on the west coast, than its neighbor Australia. The northernmost regions, which saw the very first vineyard plantings, have a semi-tropical (warm and rather humid) climate. South Island, which is closer to Antarctica, has a cooler but sunny climate—perfect for producing lively and aromatic wines.

> Vineyard landscape in the region of Hawke's Bay on North Island.

> Vines are sometimes protected by nets to prevent birds from pecking the berries.

Soils

Most soils are heavy, such as clay, and impermeable. Combined with the damp climate, this leads vines to develop big leafy expanses and suffer greater exposure to diseases as well as the development of vegetal flavors in a number of wines. However, in some well-drained gravelly areas, such as Marlborough and Hawke's Bay, irrigation may be necessary.

Wine regions

NORTH ISLAND. This area long accounted for the bulk of New Zealand wine production, but it has declined due to the sustained growth of cooler and drier vineyards on South Island. That said, it contains seven of the 11 wine regions in the country. At the northern tip, small parts of Northland and Auckland produce red wines from Bordeaux grape varieties, including magnificent wines from tiny Waiheke Island. The regions of Waikato and Bay of Plenty have been recently converted to Sauvignon Blanc. On the east coast, Gisborne, the third-largest region in terms of volume, is the home of powerful Chardonnays; but there are also some splendid Gewurztraminers. Hawke's Bay, further south on the coast, has a fairly wide range of good quality red and white wines (*see* p.486). The vineyards of the Wellington region are located in the Wairarapa district, which includes the sub-region of Martinborough. It enjoys a reputation disproportionate to its small area (less than 2,200 acres or 900 ha), which has doubled in five years thanks to its Sauvignon Blanc and Pinot Noir in particular.

SOUTH ISLAND. Marlborough, at the north end of the island, produces more than half of New Zealand's wines. It is the epicenter of the country's wine production and the home of the best Sauvignon Blancs (*see* p.486). Nelson, in the northwest, has not escaped the enthusiasm for this grape variety, which covers 50 percent of its vineyards. Canterbury, with the valley of Waipara (*see details* p.487), is also booming, and produces pleasant Riesling, Chardonnay, and Pinot Noir. In the extreme south, the continental and mountain climate in Otago (*see* p.487) has long deterred producers, but it is an area full of promise, where some excellent Pinot Noir is already produced.

Grape varieties and wine styles

Of all the New World countries, New Zealand has the coolest climate; and its current grape varieties are well suited to these conditions. Since the 1990s, German grape varieties have almost disappeared (with the notable exception of Riesling) to be replaced by Sauvignon Blanc, Chardonnay, and, more recently, Pinot Noir. Together, they occupy more than 80 percent of total vineyard area.

WHITE GRAPE VARIETIES. About 75 percent of the wines produced in New Zealand are white. With 34,600 acres (14,000 ha) planted in 2008, Sauvignon Blanc is the leading grape. It is very often vinified in stainless steel tanks, and is the archetypal New Zealand white wine: fresh, lively, with exuberant flavors, and intended to be consumed young. Chardonnay, although a distant second in terms of planted area, has consolidated its position. It produces wines of great intensity, which can be matured in wood in some cases. Fermented as sparkling wine, often blended with Pinot Noir, it can produce wines of real finesse; and the best of these can compete with good Champagne. Pinot Gris, Riesling, and Gewurztraminer are increasingly produced in the cool regions of Marlborough, Waipara, and Otago. Mainly produced as dry wines, they also provide some very beautiful and rare dessert wines.

RED GRAPE VARIETIES. Only Cabernet Sauvignon has survived from the nation's original plantings (in 1832), but its difficulty in achieving a regularly high level of maturity explains its decline. It has now been widely superseded by Merlot and especially by Pinot Noir—now growing some 10,300 acres (4,200 ha) on South Island. While there are some benchmark wines made from Cabernet and Merlot, produced in an elegant style and close to Bordeaux standards with even ageing capacity, the best red wines come from Pinot Noir. They show an amazing freshness, intensity, and purity of flavor.

Leading New Zealand regions and wines

The Kiwi system of wine nomenclature is based on the grape variety, generally accompanied by the region, sometimes the sub-region, on the label. Yet apart from Marlborough, which has a worldwide reputation, it is the producer's name that indicates the most about the wine.

HAWKE'S BAY

Hawke's Bay is the second-most planted area (12,108 acres or 4,900 ha) in New Zealand. It's located along the east coast of North Island, and the landscape consists of a chain of coastal mountains, protecting the vineyards from westerly winds, and a very fertile coastal plain. Hawke's Bay has excellent sunshine and reasonable rainfall of about 35 inches (890 mm) per year. White and red grape varieties are equally planted. Among whites, Sauvignon Blanc is second only to Chardonnay in terms of area. The region is particularly noted for producing fine red wines from Merlot and Cabernet Sauvignon planted on warm, gravelly soils.

> **GRAPE VARIETIES** Chardonnay, Sauvignon Blanc, and Pinot Gris for whites; Merlot, Cabernet Sauvignon, Syrah, and Pinot Noir for reds.

> **SOIL** Varies between rich alluvial soil and poor soils consisting of deep gravel.

> **STYLE** Hawke's Bay is famous for its red wines made from Merlot and Cabernet. They are elegant and structured. Firm tannins are often softened by being matured in wood, and they have good potential for improving with age. The Pinot Noirs and Syrahs are very popular, both fruity and juicy, and should be consumed while they are young. The Sauvignon Blancs and Chardonnays (among the best in the country) are richer and fuller than those of South Island, and some allow the wine to be made in barrel.

> **NOTABLE PRODUCERS** Bilancia, Craggy Range, Esk Valley, Mills Reef, Sacred Hill, Te Mata, Te Awa, and Trinity Hill.

MARLBOROUGH

Vineyard planting in this region, on the northeastern tip of South Island, started in 1973. Since then, Marlborough has become both the largest wine area in the country, covering 39,290 acres (15,900 ha), and the most famous. The region includes the long and wide Wairau Valley and its tributaries. Further south, it also includes the Awatere Valley. Apart from frosts in the spring, the weather is an ideal combination of very sunny days and cool nights. Marlborough has developed a global reputation for New Zealand Sauvignon Blanc. Covering 28,900 acres (11,700 ha), it occupies most plantings. But Marlborough also produces good Pinot Noirs and Chardonnays, and some fine Rieslings.

> **GRAPE VARIETIES** Sauvignon Blanc, Chardonnay, Pinot Gris, and Riesling for whites; Pinot Noir for reds.

> **SOIL** Alluvial and gravelly soil. Well drained and rather poor in the north, richer and more impermeable to the south.

> **STYLE** Independent of grape variety, all wines here are characterized by intense flavor and freshness. The Sauvignon Blancs are crisp and fragrant with hints of citrus, green fruit, or fresh grass. They have a bracing sharpness, and sometimes a beautiful volume that gives them great presence on the palate. The best Chardonnays are well balanced and fresh, capable of reaching heights of elegance and intensity. The Pinot Noirs, which should be consumed young, are fruity with a pleasing liveliness.

> **NOTABLE PRODUCERS** Cloudy Bay, Delta, Fromm, Herzog, Jackson Estate, Kim Crawford, Staete Landt, TerraVin, Tohu Wines, Villa Maria, and Wairau River.

CANTERBURY/WAIPARA

South of Marlborough on the east coast of South Island, this region has seen vineyard plantings triple (4,200 acres or 1,700 ha) in five years. It consists of two sub-regions (whose names appear on the labels): the Canterbury area, consisting of a large plain surrounding the city of Christchurch; and the hills of Waipara, located about 30 miles (48 km) north of the city. The combination of a cool climate, wind, sun, and little rain, plus light and poor soil is ideal for grape varieties such as Sauvignon Blanc, Riesling, and Pinot Noir. They dominate production, particularly in Waipara, where the current boom has been spectacular.

> **GRAPE VARIETIES** Riesling, Sauvignon Blanc, Pinot Gris, and Chardonnay for whites; Pinot Noir for reds.

> **SOIL** In the south, alluvium, silt, and gravel; to the north, clay, silt, and limestone.

> **STYLE** Many of the wines produced in the region are Rieslings. They are firm, slightly sharp, and straightforward, with mineral (flint) and lemony notes. The best are outstanding. Another regional specialty is Pinot Noir that offers, when properly ripened, fruity, spicy, spirited, fresh, and sometimes very pure wines. It also produces lively and scented Sauvignon Blancs and structured Chardonnays.

> **NOTABLE PRODUCERS** Mountford, Pegasus Bay, Waipara Hills, and Waipara West.

CENTRAL OTAGO

Central Otago is the southernmost vineyard region in the world, and also the only inland vineyard region on South Island. This mountainous area, which produces only five percent of New Zealand wine, has become one of the most attractive in recent years because of the quality of its Pinot Noir (80 percent of production). Its planted area has tripled since 2002, and the number of wineries here has increased fourfold. Vines are planted along valley bottoms and on hillsides with varying exposures. Altitude rarely exceeds 980 feet (300 m) due to the risk of frost. The climate is continental with short, dry, and very sunny summers, plus a wide variation in temperature between day and night. While the growing season is shorter than elsewhere, the exceptionally intense sunshine provides ideal conditions for maturing Pinot Noir.

> **GRAPE VARIETIES** Pinot Gris, Chardonnay, Riesling, and Sauvignon Blanc for whites; Pinot Noir for reds.

> **SOIL** Loess mixed with gravel on a base of schist. There are limestone pockets in the northeast (Waitaki Valley).

> **STYLE** While there are several styles of Pinot Noir from Otago, the wines often present a rich nose (very ripe red fruit), with spicy and toasty notes that vary in power depending on the type and length of ageing. On the palate, they are generous and concentrated wines that impress with their intense fruit flavors. Most are low in tannin but have a fresh structure that gives them a lot of presence and life. Very pleasing when young, the more concentrated may be kept for five to 10 years. The whites are mostly crisp and fragrant.

> **NOTABLE PRODUCERS** Amisfield, Chard Farm, Felton Road, Mount Edward, Maude, Mt Difficulty, Olssens, Quartz Reef, and Rockburn.

Cloudy Bay, Kiwi icon wine

Cloudy Bay is the waterfront at the mouth of the Wairau River in Marlborough. It is also the name of the most famous vineyard in New Zealand, founded by David Hohnen and Kevin Judd from the Australian Cape Mentelle estate. Established in 1985, with a very evocative label featuring a drawing of the surrounding mountains, it has largely driven the popularity of Sauvignon Blanc and its region, Marlborough. It is a wine with great freshness and perfume, and it has become a national and international standard. As it has developed through the years, the wine has gained in finesse and elegance while retaining its exuberant aromas (citrus, green and exotic fruits, and fresh herbs) and its bracing sharpness—all the hallmark of good New Zealand Sauvignon Blancs. Since its inception, the estate has grown dramatically and it has expanded production. It now makes one of the country's finest and most vibrant Chardonnays, vinified in oak barrels, and a pure and refreshing Pinot Noir, as well as a sparkling wine (Pelorus) with impressive finesse.

JAPAN, CHINA, AND INDIA

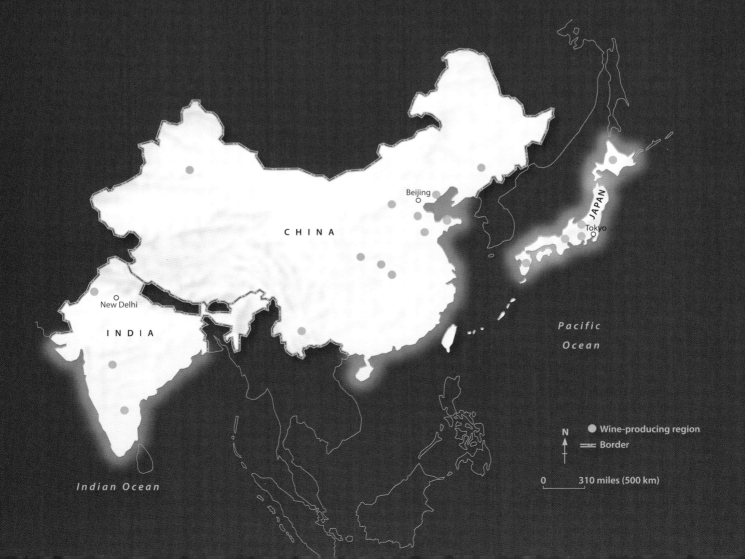

Beijing

CHINA

JAPAN

Tokyo

New Delhi

INDIA

Pacific
Ocean

● Wine-producing region
N ⊟ Border

Indian Ocean

0   310 miles (500 km)

JAPAN, CHINA, AND INDIA

Wine consumption in Asia has risen sharply in recent decades, but only a handful of countries have a significant wine industry. While Japanese and Indian vineyards are small scale, those of China are growing at an impressive rate.

JAPAN

The vine has been cultivated in Japan since the 8th century, but there is little evidence of wine consumption prior to the arrival of Portuguese missionaries during the 16th century. Some 300 years later, in the Yamanashi region, Yamada Hironori and Takuna Norihisa established the first modern wine estate. However, the current craze for wine really dates to the 1980s.

Vineyard landscape

Only 10 per cent of Japan's 50,000 acres (20,000 ha) of vineyards are intended for the production of wine. Vineyards are cultivated on almost all the islands, but in terms of surface area, the majority are concentrated on the main island, Honshu—especially in the Yamanashi and Nagano regions (40 percent of production), which lie west of Tokyo. A very wet climate, subject to monsoons and typhoons, as well as rich and acidic soils, represents far from ideal conditions for producing quality grapes. But wine producers have responded with their cultivation methods and the use of suitable varieties.

GRAPE VARIETIES. Hybrids like the Kyoho, the Campbell Early, Muscat Bailey A, and Delaware sit alongside imported varieties (Cabernet, Merlot, Müller-Thurgau, and Chardonnay). But the most prominent wines are made from a local variety of *vitis vinifera*, the Koshu. At Yamanashi, near Mount Fuji, this pink-skinned variety is capable of producing pleasant, light, and elegant white wines. Some of the best wines come from the well-drained hillsides of Katsunuma, where legend has it that the first Koshu vines were planted in the 8th century by Buddhist monks from China.

> *Japan is the most sophisticated wine market in Asia. While most wine is imported, there is a small amount of local production from wineries that have learned to cope with a challenging natural environment.*

Bordeaux in Katsunuma

Bernard Magrez, who owns 35 vineyards in France and worldwide, has partnered with Japanese Koshu specialist Yuji Aruga, based in Katsunuma. The wine, which is called Magrez Aruga, is a very pleasant example of this native Japanese grape variety, with a fresh, aromatic, and clean style.

NOTABLE PRODUCERS. Lumière, Manns, Magrez-Aruga, Château Mercian, Sapporo, Shizen, Suntory.

CHINA

About 15 years ago, the per capita consumption of wine in China was almost zero; today that figure is almost half a liter per year. Of course, that's very low in terms of Western consumer patterns, but it represents a significant change in a country that has remained culturally impervious to wine for centuries. It also conceals a huge market!

The recent and rapid Westernization of Chinese cities largely explains this development, as can be seen by a significant increase in wine imports. But there also has been a dramatic increase in Chinese wine production. Although it is difficult to obtain reliable statistics

> Harvesting near the city of Turpan, in Xinjiang province, China.

> Harvesting grapes
on the Grover estate,
north of Bangalore, in
Karnataka state, India.

Some independent and smaller producers also produce pleasant wines; for example, Grace Vineyard, located in Shanxi, draws its inspiration from Bordeaux (Cabernet Sauvignon, Cabernet Franc, and Merlot) and Burgundy (Chardonnay) to produce some very appealing wines.

NOTABLE PRODUCERS. Catai, Changyu, Château Junding, Dragon's Hollow, Grace Vineyard, Great Wall, Huadong, Jade Valley, and Silver Heights.

INDIA

While ancient texts offer evidence that India was producing wine as early as the 4th century BC, religious taboos have long made wine, like other alcoholic beverages, a marginal or suspect drink. With that said, it has been tolerated during different periods of Indian history.

on vineyards, they have more than doubled in 10 years, and amount to 1.2 million acres (470,000 ha) in 2008 according to the OIV. Taking into account the significant production of table grapes, we can nevertheless rank China among the world's top 10 wine producers.

Vineyard landscape

China is a huge country with dramatic climatic and topographic differences, but the main wine regions are Shandong, Hebei, Henan, Liaoning, and Xinjiang provinces. The well-exposed slopes of the Shandong peninsula, and specifically at Yantai, have good potential due to the maritime influences that moderate any excesses of climate.

GRAPE VARIETIES. Varieties imported by missionaries during the early 19th century, such as Welschriesling and Black Hamburg, and local grape varieties, such as Longyan, still dominate; but international grape varieties such as Cabernet Sauvignon, Merlot, and Chardonnay are making rapid progress.

Wines standards

Production is concentrated in the hands of three companies: Changyu, Dynasty, and Great Wall; and some have benefited from joint ventures with foreign partners. This transfer of knowledge is having an impact. Chinese wines, which had been produced using unorthodox procedures only a short time ago, have cleaned up their act and moved closer to international standards of wine production.

SPECTACULAR PROGRESS. The recent Westernization of urban middle and upper classes has changed the perception of wine in India. A new market has grown dramatically here over the past 10 years. Taxes on imports of foreign wines, and concessions granted to local producers, have meant that domestic production has doubled in recent years. Vineyards cover 155,000 acres (63,000 ha), but only a few thousand are dedicated to wine production.

Key players

With 40 estates as of 2007, the state of Maharashtra is the country's leading wine region. Two of the three key Indian producers are based there: Château Indage, a true pioneer, which successfully launched its production of sparkling wines in 1982; and Sula Vineyards, established in 1997 by Rajeev Samant, in the Nasik region north of Mumbai. The latter has demonstrated that a hot, humid, tropical climate is not inconsistent with the production of fine wines, including a fresh Sauvignon Blanc that is full of flavor.

The same conditions exist in the state of Karnataka, the second-most important region for Indian production. The Kanwal Grover estate, which was established in 1988 in the hills above Bangalore, is now India's leading exporter. It produces good wines including a dry red (La Réserve), which regularly wins critical acclaim. The wine is a blend of Cabernet Sauvignon and Syrah, the two most popular red grape varieties in India.

NOTABLE PRODUCERS. Château Indage, Sula Vineyards, and Grover Vineyards.

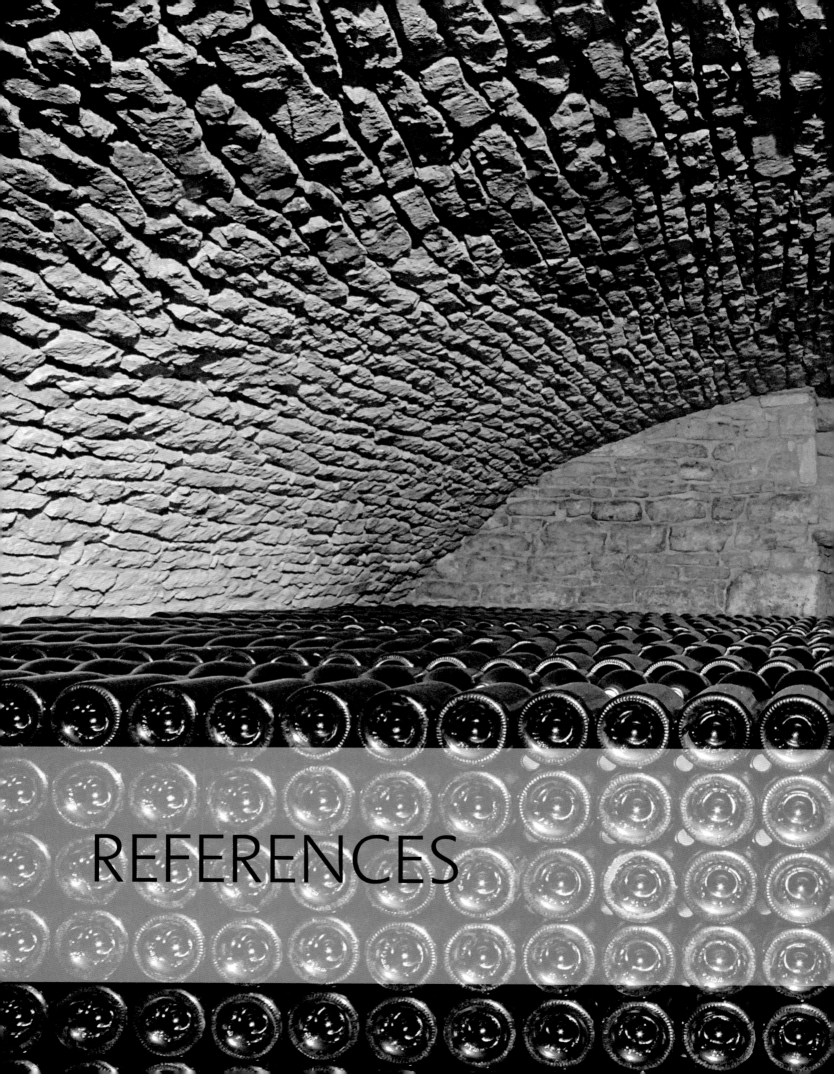

REFERENCES

Glossary

This glossary defines terms from the world of wine—with the exception of vocabulary devoted to tasting, which is covered in "Describing Wine" on pp.228–35. The origins of foreign words are indicated with the following abbreviations: Fr = French; Ger = German; It = Italian; Po = Portuguese; Sp = Spanish.

Words featured as entries in the glossary are marked with an asterisk (*).

 A

ABBOCCATO (It) A slightly sweet wine.

ACETIC ACID This acid is found in small quantities in every wine; when quantities grow too large, the wine turns to vinegar.

ACIDITY Wine contains several organic acids (tartaric*, malic*, citric*, lactic*, etc.). Acidity plays an important role in tasting. It augments and partially masks the sweet* elements of a wine (sugar, alcohol, glycerin). Also, in conjunction with tannins*, it creates a synergy that enhances the sensation of crispness or even astringency. Excessive or injudicious acidity can turn a sensation of liveliness into something acrid. By contrast, a lack of acidity, or an imbalance where the acidity is swamped by the wine's sweetness, leads to slackness or heaviness. When acidity is discreetly forthcoming, it creates freshness; when more diffident, it creates suppleness.

ADEGA (Po) A wine cellar or winemaking estate in Portugal.

AGEING The evolution of a wine's components over time.

ALCOHOL Ethyl alcohol, one of the principal ingredients of wine, is produced during alcoholic fermentation*: an enzymatic metabolism by yeasts* transforms sugars in grape juice into alcohol, carbon dioxide, and heat. The alcoholic content* of wine can vary from less than 7% to more than 15% by volume, depending on the natural sugar content of the must* and any added sugar. Contents higher than 15% by volume are usually indicative of fortified wines. It should be remembered that obtaining one percentage point of alcohol requires 17 grams of sugar per liter (or 1.7% concentration) for white wines and 18g (1.8%) for red wines. *See also* CHAPTALIZATION*.

ALCOHOL BY VOLUME *See* ALCOHOLIC CONTENT.

ALCOHOLIC CONTENT The amount of alcohol in a wine is calculated as the volume of ethyl alcohol in the liquid (expressed as % by volume [ABV]).

ALCOHOLIC FERMENTATION The primary stage of winemaking: grape juice becomes wine when the sugars contained in the must* are transformed into alcohol, carbon dioxide, and heat by the action of yeast*.

AMABILE (It) A slightly sweeter style of wine than *abboccato**.

AMONTILLADO (Sp) Sherry that develops a stage beyond *fino*. It displays an amber color, substantial body, and hazelnut characters.

AMPELOGRAPHY The field of botany associated with the identification and classification of grapevines.

ANTHOCYANINS Pigments in grapes that are the source of color in red wines. The violet coloration of many young red wines is almost exclusively due to mildly reactive anthocyanin molecules (phenolic compounds) that go on to combine with tannins* (which are also phenolic ingredients) as the wine ages. This leads to a ruby red color, then more brick, then eventually brown.

APPELLATION D'ORIGINE CONTRÔLÉE (AOC) (Fr) A French term meaning "controlled designation of origin." It is used for wines made in specific regions and from particular grape varieties* that are strictly defined in regulations laid down by the INAO*. These wines all qualify for the European "quality wines produced in specified regions" designation. AOC wines must conform to exacting regulations not only with respect to their area of production and their grape variety*, but also minimum sugar content to be obtained in their must*, their alcoholic content*, their yield per hectare, the pruning of their vines, and their method of cultivation and vinification. AOC wines are finally subject to a tasting inspection before they are released to the market.

APPELLATION D'ORIGINE PROTÉGÉE (AOP) (Fr) A French term corresponding to the new European designation for "quality wines produced in specified regions" (PDO—protected designation of origin—in English) to be used in the various countries of the EU.

APPELLATION D'ORIGINE VIN DÉLIMITÉ DE QUALITÉ SUPERIEURE (AOVDQS), (Fr) A wine produced in a specified region to lower qualification requirements than AOC. New European regulations mean that the AOVDQS designation is due to be abolished from the 2011 vintage.

AROMAS A term designating the olfactory characters of a wine. In other words, the sensations perceived more in the nose than in the mouth. A distinction is drawn between aromas resulting from grape variety, from fermentation, and from the maturation period after fermentation.

AUSBRUCH (Ger) An Austrian wine category, sweeter than a Beerenauslese* but less sweet than a Trockenbeerenauslese*.

AUSLESE (Ger) A German wine made with late-harvested grapes, often botrytized but always containing a considerable concentration of sugar. Auslesen may be made dry or sweet.

 B

BAG IN BOX (WINEBOX) A soft bag with a tap, enclosed in cardboard packaging. Often used for the sale and storage (for up to nine months after opening) of wine in bulk. Often three liters in capacity.

BAN DES VENDANGES (Fr) Historically, the official date (*ban*) when harvesting (*vendange*) began in a region. The modern term refers to the date after which chaptalization* is authorized; this is proposed by the INAO* in conjunction with the appellation's executive syndicate and decided by the prefect of the region.

BARREL A cask of a size that varies from region to region; in Burgundy, a barrel contains just over 60 gallons (228 liters), while a Bordeaux barrel (barrique) contains 59 gallons (225 liters). A barrel in Touraine-Anjou contains just over 61 gallons (232 liters).

BARRICA (Sp) Spanish barrel containing approximately 59 gallons (225 liters).

BATONNAGE (Fr) *Batonnage* is the process of stirring the fine lees* that have settled at the bottom of a barrel* or vat* of wine after fermentation. It is performed to obtain more complexity, suppleness, and more body.

BEERENAUSLESE (Ger) An Austrian or German wine made with late-harvested, often botrytized, grapes with high sugar content.

BEREICH (Ger) A German winegrowing region.

BITTERNESS One of the four components of physiological taste.

BLANC DE BLANCS (Fr) A white wine made exclusively with white grapes.

BLANC DE NOIRS (Fr) A white wine made with red or black grapes.

BLENDING The mixing of several wines. The aim of a blend is to produce something better than each element on its own.

BLUSH A US term for a rosé wine.

BODEGA (Sp) The Spanish equivalent of a wine cellar. Also used to mean a winery.

BORDEAUX MIXTURE A vineyard fungicide made from copper (II) sulfate and hydrated lime. It was developed by P.M.A. Millardet during the 19th century to combat mildew*. It is now being increasingly replaced with synthetic copper compounds.

BOTRYTIS Rot caused by the fungus *Botrytis cinerea* . Its growth is promoted by humidity.

BOTRYTIS CINEREA A necrotrophic fungus that attacks grapes. A small amount of botrytis, known as "gray mold" encourages fermentation agents during *cuvaison**, the period when the seeds, skin, and stalks are left to macerate in the wine. Larger degrees of botrytis will compromise the harvest (more than 10 or 15 percent for red wines, 20 percent for whites). Excessive botrytis,

under certain atmospheric conditions, can lead to the famed "noble rot*." This concentrates the juice in the grapes to a special kind of over-maturity*. Such botrytized grapes produce famous sweet* wines such as Sauternes from France and Tokaj from Hungary.

BOTTLING As the name might suggest, this is the transfer of wine into bottles. Only French AOC* wines may bear the terms *mis en bouteille au château* or *mise d'origine* (estate-bottled); although French country wine (VDP/IGP) may be labeled *mis en bouteilles à la propriété or au domaine* (bottled on the premises). AOC wines that are labeled *mis en bouteille dans la région de production* must be bottled somewhere in the region of their own appellation.

BOUQUET A fairly complex mixture of agreeable aromas* in a wine. Sensed through the nose (rather than the mouth). *See* AROMAS*.

BRANCO (Po) White.

BRANDED WINE Generally wine intended for broad commercial distribution and produced with a consistent flavor and style. Wines in this category may be either: a mix of various basic table wines* topped off with a dash of a superior grape variety to improve it; a judiciously balanced blend of different wines, which, though subordinating their appellation in favor of the brand, will suit the tastes of most consumers; or indeed blends of large volumes of wine with regional or village appellations that are connected with the brand but take a back seat to it.

BREATHING Leaving wine in contact with the air to release aromatic compounds.

BRUT (Fr) A term indicating a very low sugar content in sparkling* wines (from 0 to 15 grams per liter); *brut zéro* and *brut intégral* are completely unsweetened.

BUDDING Point in the vine's growth cycle during which new buds swell and open.

CAP A term for the floating mass of solids (skins, pulp, seeds, and stems) that are forced to the surface of the must* during red wine fermentation by the release of carbon dioxide. It is important that maceration* is encouraged to optimize the extraction of colors and aromas* from the cap. For this reason, many production methods agitate, stir, dip, and squeeze this cap in order to

increase the interaction of the solid material with the liquid, *i.e.* the wine.

CAPSULE (Fr) Another term for the foil* covering the closure (or cork) of a wine bottle.

CARBONATED A term describing an effervescent* wine produced in a closed vat through the mechanical addition of carbon dioxide—in place of secondary fermentation by yeast*, as would happen in the traditional or Champagne method. High quality wines generally are not carbonated.

CARBONIC MACERATION A method of vinification* whereby red wine grapes are placed in vats* without being pressed. The vat is then sealed and saturated with carbon dioxide, which starts intracellular fermentation or transformation of sugars into alcohol* within berries. This first phase, which may last a matter of hours or days, takes place at relatively high temperatures (between 86 and 90°F/30 and 32°C). The press wine* and the free-run wine* are then subjected to separate secondary fermentations at lower temperatures (68°F/20°C) for a relatively short period. This method allows the production of a press wine of superior quality to what is typical, and the procedure has proved successful with Gamay wines that are marketed young, such as *Beaujolais nouveau*.

CAUDALIE *See* "Describing Wine," p.230.

CAVA (Sp) Generic term for Spanish sparkling wines made using traditional methods*.

CELLAR MASTER Person charged with directing the various operations carried out at a winery, from vinification* to maturing*.

CENTRIFUGATION A process to clarify* musts* or wines using centrifugal force to eliminate heavy particles or cloudiness. The procedure can used when "racking" musts, clarifying wine, and removing deposits of finings*.

CEP The wood section, more than a year old, at the foot of a vine.

CHAPTALIZATION A process first advocated by the chemist J.A. Chaptal, chaptalization consists of adding sugar (cane, beet, or rectified; or concentrated must*) to grape juice that is insufficiently rich before fermentation. The result obtains a higher alcoholic content* in the wine. Strictly forbidden in a number of countries, the technique is usually very closely regulated in the countries that allow it.

CHARMAT (Fr) A production method for sparkling* wines in which sugar and yeasts* are added to start secondary fermentation* in closed stainless steel or enameled tanks.

CHÂTEAU (Fr) Literally a "castle," but generally a wine-producing estate. There is not always a building that corresponds to the estate *château* mentioned. Many more *châteaux* are listed on wine labels than are actually found in any given area.

CITRIC ACID An acid plentiful in fruit and citrus fruits in particular, but also found in grapes, if only in minute quantities. White grapes contain larger amounts, particularly those affected by the famous "noble rot*."

CLAIRET (Fr) A light Bordeaux red or rosé made by the *saignée** (vat "bleeding") method.

CLARIFICATION A series of operations intended to obtain transparency in a wine. Various procedures may be employed, including centrifugation*, filtration*, and fining*. Clarification must be completed by physical, chemical, and microbiological stabilization of the wine to prevent the later formation of haziness or deposits*.

CLASSICO (It) Wine from the historic heart of a wine region.

CLAVELIN Traditional bottle for Jura wines, especially *vin jaune** ("yellow wine"). Its volume of 21 fl oz (620 ml) represents the sole remains of the wine's original 34 fl oz (1 liter), after considerable evaporation during six years of barrel ageing. This wine matures under a layer of yeasts and is not subject to topping*.

CLIMAT (Fr) In Burgundy, this term refers not only to the atmospheric conditions prevailing in the region (climate), but also to specific divisions within each village or commune. Some *climats* have first growth qualities, while others have remained unclassified. The latter may nonetheless appear on wine labels under the communal appellation, except where this may be confused with an official *premier cru* (first growth) wine.

CLONAL SELECTION The use of exactly identical plants for their resistance to diseases, growing characteristics, or yield.

CLONE A single genetic variant of a vine sub-species, created by asexual reproduction (cuttings and grafts*). *See* CLONAL SELECTION.

CLOS (Fr) A walled vineyard. The term is reserved for those wines to which it applies—the wine must come exclusively from vines within the *clos*. If the designation is of historic standing, the wine may continue to bear the name even if the walls have disappeared over the centuries.

CLOSURE Cylinder of natural cork, a cylinder of plastic, or an aluminum screwcap—used to seal bottles hermetically. The quality of natural cork can vary, and closures of lower quality are sealed with cork paste.

COLORANTS Phenolic compounds made up of anthocyanins*, tannins*, and anthocyanin or tannin polymers. The color of young red wine is a result of free anthocyanins; during ageing*, the anthocyanins bond with tannins and precipitate to lend the wine a ruby and then brick red color.

COMPLANTATION This is the practice of inter-planting different grape varieties at the same site.

COPPER SULFATE One ingredient of powdered Bordeaux mixture*, with which vines are treated for cryptogamic* diseases. Bordeaux mixture now refers to a large number of synthetic products that contain no copper sulfate.

CORKED Said of a wine tainted by the odor of cardboard or damp cork; the wine is usually undrinkable. This irreversible phenomenon is the result of several specific molds growing in poorly processed natural cork.

COULURE (Fr) Failure to pollinate the ovaries of grape flowers. It is caused by unfavorable climatic conditions such as cold, rain, or the premature arrival of spring. *Coulure* hampers the redistribution of sugars within the plant; the flowers and the grapes wither and develop either inconsistently or not at all.

COUPAGE (Fr) Blending*.

CRÉMANT A sparkling wine made using the traditional method* but often with less pressure than Champagne (2.5 to 3 bar instead of 5).

CRIANZA (Sp) Designation for Spanish wines that have been barrel-aged for a minimum period; con *crianza means* aged. *See also* SIN CRIANZA.

CROSS The offspring of two varieties of *Vitis vinifera*; the best known is Müller-Thurgau, which is very popular in Germany. *See also* HYBRID.

CRU (Fr) This term generally indicates a specific area recognized for the characteristics of its wine. Similar to the way that *climat** is used in Burgundy. In Bordeaux, however, it refers to a particular winemaking estate, and thus necessarily to the selection of varieties and human expertise as much as to any site. The totality of a *cru* is everything that goes to make up the estate* or *château**. In Champagne, an *échelle des crus** ("ladder of growths") is used to determine grape pricing, and each area is allotted a percentage based on the 100 percent *crus* that are considered the best. Various designations such as *grand cru*, *premier cru*, and *cru classé* are attached to certain sub-appellations, and these are defined by restrictions to the manner of production (in the case of *grand cru* and *premier cru*) or by classifications set out by the French ministry of agriculture. Such classifications have been laid down for Médoc, Pessac-Léognan, Sauternes, and St-Émilion wines.

CRU BOURGEOIS (Fr) Bordeaux wines of lesser renown than the *grands crus*.

CRUSHING Post-harvest procedure, carried out just before fermentation*, whereby grape berries are burst to release their juice.

CRYPTOGAMIC DISEASES Vine ailments carried by spores. The best-known include oidium*, mildew*, black rot, excoriosis (dead-arm disease), brettanomyces, and botrytis*.

CUBITAINER (WINE BOX) (Fr) A plastic container protected by a cardboard box, currently used to sell unbottled wine to individual purchasers. Volume may vary between one-and-a-half and nine gallons (5 to 33 liters). As its walls are slightly porous to the air, a cubitainer is only suitable for temporary storage of wine.

CUVAISON (also known as CUVAGE) (Fr) The phase of winemaking that includes leaving the musts* from the harvest to ferment, pumping the grape juice over the cap* (in the case of red winemaking), and running off the resultant young wine. See DÉCUVAISON.

CUVÉE (Fr) A term indicating a specific wine, which may or may not be a blend*. In Champagne, a *cuvée* is a wine made with grape juice from the first pressing.

 D

DECANTING A procedure to separate sediment* from clear liquid. A fine wine or a vintage port is decanted by allowing it to flow slowly from its original bottle into a carafe or decanter—leaving the sediment* behind.

DECLASSIFICATION Downgrading a wine from its original appellation. This may be at the request of the producer, or by decree from government inspectors in consultation with experts. Such a decision is made if significant changes are made to the wine; in other cases, a producer may fall back on a more general appellation than the one entitled for commercial or other reasons. This is known in France as *repli*.

DÉCUVAISON (or DÉCUVAGE) (Fr) A term for the process at the end of alcoholic fermentation*, when white wines are transferred into other containers. For red wines, which have often undergone fermentation in the presence of grape skins, seeds, and sometimes stems, the procedure is more complex: first the wine is run off by tapping the lowest part of the vat (thus obtaining so-called "free-run wine*"); then the upper portion, which is less fluid, is taken to the press to obtain press wine*. The solid material left after this pressing is known as marc*.

DÉGORGEMENT (Fr) An important and delicate phase in sparkling wine production when the deposits of yeast* that have accumulated in the bottle during secondary fermentation are removed. Called disgorgement in English.

DEMI-SEC (Fr) A category of sparkling* wine conventionally containing between 33 and 50 g/l (3.3 to 5%) of sucrose. This equates 7 to 10 percent of the total fluid (*see* DOSAGE) that is added after the removal of the yeast (*see* DÉGORGEMENT).

DEPOSIT (*also* SEDIMENT) Solid particles found in wine. In white wines, these often are neutrally colored flakes or crystals of tartaric acid*; in red wines, they are principally tannins* and pigments*.

DESSERT WINE This category includes fortified wines*, and unfortified wines that may be sweet* very sweet*, or naturally sweet*. These wines may be consumed as an aperitif or at the beginning of a meal, but their most common service is with the dessert.

DESTALKING Procedure to separate grapes from their stems and stalks, whose peduncles contain oils and tannins* that tend to make the wine bitter and sharply pungent.

DESTEMMING *See* DESTALKING.

DO (Sp) The *denominación de origen* is a denomination for Spanish wines of certified origin.

DOC (It) Italy's *denominazione di origine controllata* corresponds to France's AOC* classification.

DOC (Po) Portugal's *denominação de origem controlada* corresponds to France's AOC* classification.

DOC (Sp) The *denominación de origen calificada* denotes a Spanish wine of superior quality.

DOCG (It) Italy's *denominazione di origine controllata e garantita* is a mark of quality superior to the DOC, and indicates that the wine has been tasted and approved.

DOSAGE After the yeast* is removed from sparkling* wine, a sugary liquid known as *liqueur d'expédition** is added; the sugar content may vary, depending on whether the wine is to be *brut** (a maximum of 15 grams per liter or 1.5% residual sugar [RS]), *extra dry** (12 to 20 g/l or 2% RS), *sec* (17 to 35 g/l or 3.5% RS), or *doux* (more than 50 g per liter or 5% RS).

DRY A wine with no perceptible sweetness. In actual fact, the residual sugar content* may not exceed 9 grams per liter (0.9%). For effervescent* wines, this content may rise to between 15 and 35 g/l (3.5%).

ÉCHELLE DES CRUS (Fr) ("Ladder of growths") Classification used by villages in Champagne to determine the price of grapes. The best growths are rated 100 percent, others may drop as low as 70 percent.

EDELZWICKER Word used in Alsace-Lorraine (France) to denote blended* wines made with various grape varieties.

EFFERVESCENT Denoting a sparkling* wine. A bottle that contains carbon dioxide under pressure, which is released to create bubbles when the bottle is opened. The term "effervescent" will be the official replacement for the traditional French term *mousseux** ("frothy"). Effervescent wines can be made using a number of methods, including:

- secondary bottle fermentation, for Champagne and sparkling* wines from traditional appellations;

- fermentation in sealed vats under pressure, for branded products with no appellation;

- injection of carbon dioxide by industrial method, for extremely cheap products. See CARBONATED.

One intermediary process between the first two above involves bottle fermentation followed by yeast removal by filtration* under pressure, instead of traditional *dégorgement**. Effervescent wines with a pressure of less than 2.5 bar are not considered *mousseux**. Also, the term *méthode champenoise** is reserved for Champagne wines.

EISWEIN (Ger) Wine made in Austria, Germany, and even Canada, with bunches of late-harvested grapes that have frozen on the vine.

EN PRIMEUR (Fr) A means of purchasing fine Bordeaux wines, generally five or six months after the grape harvest. The wines are kept at the estates until they are bottled some two or three years later. Also called wine futures.

ENCEPAGEMENT (Fr) ("grape selection") Term describing a composition of different grape varieties*; this may refer to a wine, a single estate, or a region. A single variety may be used for many wines, the use of several varieties can mean more complexity and nuance. Chardonnay is used in Champagne for its finesse and lightness, while Pinot Noir and Pinot Meunier bring body and roundness to the final wines. In regions such as Alsace-Lorraine, planting a wide range of grape varieties produces a varied palette of wines.

ESTATE A legal and geographical entity belonging to a winery. An estate is thus the vineyard, the buildings, and the equipment used to cultivate vines and make wine. Also known as a domain.

EXCISE LABEL Government seal on a wine bottle (marked CRD in France) indicating that the wine may be transported and sold legally.

EXCISE RECEIPT Government document that accompanies alcoholic drinks during shipment. Such documents are not required where tax stamps are used; and some producers and merchants have excise registration supported only by stamps. Other producers and wine merchants use an excise capsule placed over the mouth of each bottle.

EXTRA DRY Term designating an effervescent* wine with a very low dosage* of residual sugar* (from 2 to 20 g/l, or up to 2%). A very dry wine.

FERMENTATION See ALCOHOLIC FERMENTATION, MALOLACTIC FERMENTATION.

FILTRATION A clarification procedure using a physical barrier to trap particles that cloud the wine; this may consist of a layer of *kieselguhr* (diatomaceous earth), cellulose-based plates, or synthetic membranes.

FINING A wine clarification* procedure used before bottling. The method introduces a colloid into the wine that adheres to any residues in suspension (a process known as flocculation) before precipitating to the bottom under the influence of gravity. A number of products are used, including beaten egg whites, isinglass, casein, and bentonite (a clay). The wine is then extracted and usually filtered before bottling.

FLOWERING Phase in the vine's life cycle when pollination is possible. That in turn leads to the formation of grape berries.

FOIL A capsule* or sleeve that surrounds the neck and opening of a bottle. Originally an alloy of tin, the "foil" is now just as likely to be plastic.

FOUDRE (Fr) A very large vat, with a capacity ranging from 1,320 to 4,000 gallons (50 to 150 hl).

FREE-RUN WINE Wine that runs freely after *cuvaison*, in contrast to press wine*, which results from pressing the *marc* after *décuvaison*.

GENERIC In the widest sense, this refers to characteristics relating to any genre of items or products; when referring to appellations of origin, a distinction is generally made between "generic appellations" and more specific "regional appellations."

GLYCEROL or **GLYCERINE** The third key ingredient of wine after water and alcohol*. The presence of "legs" on the walls of a wine glass is usually attributed to the presence of glycerol.

GRAFTING After the phylloxera* crisis of the 19th century, Europe was obliged to use American vines (*Vitis labrusca*, *Vitis riparia*, *Vitis rupestris*) as rootstock since the latter's roots were resistant to this infestation. The European vine (*Vitis vinifera*) thus largely now exists as just a graft or scion.

GRAN RESERVA (Sp) Spanish red wines from the best vintages, aged for two years in barrel* and three years in bottle.

GRAND VIN (Fr) A term for the premier blended wine from the best vineyards of a Bordeaux *grand cru* estate.

GRAPE VARIETY A variant of the species *Vitis vinifera* (or *labrusca*, *riparia*, *rupestris*). There are several thousand different grape varieties scattered across the world.

GRAVES (Fr) A sub-region of Bordeaux. Also a geographic term indicating areas or specific vineyards with gravel soils. Such a composition often produces wines of great quality.

GREEN HARVEST A practice whereby some grape clusters are removed during the summer (when they are still green), so that the remaining fruit harvested in the fall will be of better quality.

HAIL A significant vineyard hazard; hail spoils bunches of grapes by breaking stalks and bursting individual grapes anywhere near maturity*. Such damage is usually followed by rot and mold.

HYBRID The offspring of two different species of vine. After the phylloxera* crisis, cross-breeding American and European vine species resulted in hybrids that are resistant to phylloxera but produce wines of mediocre quality. *See also* CROSS.

INAO (Fr) France's *Institut national de l'origine et de la qualité* is a public body founded on July 30, 1935, to monitor and delimit the production conditions of French quality wines from specified regions.

INDICATION GEOGRAPHIQUE PROTEGÉE (Fr) "Indication of protected geographic origin" is the official designation (replacing *vin de pays*) for country wine from France or other EU countries. See VIN DE PAYS.

IPR (Po) *Indicação de proveniencia regulamentada*, the second-tier appellation of origin in Portugal.

JOVEN (Sp) Young.

KABINETT (Ger) Dry white German wines (Prädikatswein, formerly QmP) that are never chaptalized.

LACTIC ACID A soft acid produced by a wine's malolactic fermentation*.

LEES A mixture of impurities, dead yeast cells, tartaric deposits, and residual matter from harvest, the lees form as a muddy sediment at the bottom of a barrel. The lees are usually removed when the wine is racked.

LEES, ON THE Said of wines (Muscadet, for example) that are aged in contact with lees and theoretically bottled before racking*.

LENGTH See "Describing wine," p.232.

LIQUEUR DE TIRAGE (Fr) Cane sugar syrup added to a base wine to start secondary fermentation. Once fermented by yeast, this sugar produces up to 1.5% more alcohol, as well as carbon dioxide to create effervescence. Approximately 25 g/l (2.5% concentration) is needed to make *mousseux* wines. Some semi-sparkling wines receive only half this amount.

LIQUEUR D'EXPEDITION (Fr) Sugar-based syrup introduced to Champagne or other sparkling* wines after the removal of yeast sediment*. This practice regulates sweetness to produce *extra dry*, *brut*, *sec*, and *demi-sec* wines. It also adds stabilizers, if necessary, including citric acid* and sulfur dioxide*.

LIQUEUR WINE A wine with an elevated alcoholic content*, either natural or added, and a high content of unfermented sugar.

MACERATION A phase for vinification* for red wines, and sometimes rosés, whereby grape solids (skins and stems) are left in contact the must* before or during alcoholic fermentation* in order to extract color, aromas*, tannins*, and other substances. Maceration is a principal area of concern for winemakers, and many technical procedures intended to improve the vinification of red wine revolve around it. See *also* CARBONIC MACERATION.

MADERIZED Referring to a wine that tastes reminiscent of Madeira; most often said of long-aged white wines subject to oxidation*. It can be recognized by the dark amber color it engenders.

MALIC ACID A strong acid, and an unstable compound found in large quantities in young grapes, but which becomes less concentrated as the grapes ripen. It is recognizable by its sour, green apple taste. Once alcoholic fermentation* is complete, another process converts malic acid to lactic acid*. See below.

MALOLACTIC FERMENTATION Chemical conversion that follows alcoholic fermentation*. Malic acid* (which is reminiscent of green apples) is transformed into lactic acid* (which is reminiscent of yogurt) and carbon dioxide under the influence of certain bacteria. Since lactic acid has a less pungent flavor than malic acid, the wine becomes more supple.

MARC (Fr) After pressing grapes, a so-called *gâteau* (or "cake") of the solid elements remains. This is known as *marc* (or pomace). It can be distilled to make a brandy of the same name.

MAS (Fr) Term sometimes used in southern France to describe the wine estate of an autonomous producer or one with independent means of production.

MASSAL SELECTION Intentional planting of various vine clones (or replanting from a heterogeneous mix) to preserve diversity and quality within a particular parcel of land.

MATURATION A seasonal period in the life cycle of the vine between the onset of fruit ripening and full maturity*, during which grape berries do not grow very much; instead, sugars are accumulated and acids reduced. Physiological maturity is reached once these two processes have stabilized, and grapes passing beyond this stage reach over-maturity*, *passerillage** (drying), or even the noble rot* sought for some wines.

MATURING (WINE) The various procedures between removal of wine from vats* and final bottling*.

MATURITY A physiological stage of the vine's lifecycle. *See* MATURATION.

MEDIUM-SWEET A term applied to a range of sweetness (12 to 45 g/l or up to 4.5% residual sugar) in white wines. A stage between dry* and sweet*.

MERCAPTAN A term derived from a contraction of *mercurium captans*, which denotes a compound arising from the interaction of alcohol and hydrogen sulfide. A faulty condition revealed by very strong and unpleasant odor, reminiscent of rotten eggs.

MERCHANT A buyer and distributor of wine. A merchant-grower will also take over some aspects of the wine's production, notably blending*, clarification*, and bottling*. In the Champagne region, a merchant known as a *négociant-manipulant* is responsible for purchasing grapes, must* or base wine and converting it into Champagne.

MÉTHODE CHAMPENOISE (Fr) ("Champagne method") A production method for effervescent* wines with the unique feature that carbonation is effected in bottle. Originally used to make Champagne (after which it is named), but it is also used in other winemaking areas, where it is known as the *méthode traditionnelle**.

MÉTHODE RURALE (Fr) ("rural method") A production method for semi-sparkling wines, which involves bottling before alcoholic fermentation* is completed.

MÉTHODE TRADITIONNELLE (Fr) ("traditional method") A used to describe the use of *méthode champenoise** to make sparkling wines outside the Champagne region. In Italy, this is known as *metodo tradizionale* or *metodo classico*.

MICROCLIMATE In the context of viticulture, this term denotes a collection of climatic conditions in a small area. They often differ from the general climate of the surrounding region, thus creating an advantageous location for a vineyard or estate.

MILDEW A fungal condition of North American origin that attacks the green parts of vines. It was once fought with a mixture of copper (II) sulfate and hydrated lime (Bordeaux mixture*), but there are now effective synthetic products.

MISTELLE (FORTIFIED WINE) Known as *mistelle* in French, *sifone* in Italian, and *mistela*

in Spanish, this is a blend obtained by the addition of neutral alcohol* to grape juice before any fermentation*.

MUST Grape juice obtained by crushing or pressing, and before it is fermented into wine.

MUTAGE A procedure that halts alcoholic fermentation* through the introduction of neutral alcohol*; this is an essential stage in the production of port and naturally sweet wines*.

N-O

NATURALLY SWEET WINE *See* VIN DOUX NATUREL.

NECK LABEL Label placed near the bottom of the neck of a bottle, often indicating just the vintage of the wine.

NOBLE (Fr) A term applied to classic, high quality grape varieties* and superior wines to distinguish them from table wines made from ordinary varieties and the hybrids* that flourished after the phylloxera* crisis.

NOBLE ROT When climatic conditions at the end of summer offer a combination of alternating sun and rain or mist, grape berries may be affected by a particular decay caused by the mold known as *Botrytis cinerea**. This fungus can "rot" grapes to concentrate and alter their juice for the production of great sweet wines.

NOUVEAU (Fr) "New" wines intended for consumption as soon as possible after harvest. The best-known example is Beaujolais nouveau, which comes to market in mid-November.

NUIT (VIN D'UNE) (Fr) Literally a "wine of one night;" a deep rosé wine obtained from maceration* of very short duration (between 12 and 24 hours).

OIDIUM A vine disease of North American origin caused by a microscopic fungus that attacks the flowers, leaves, and grape berries; the berries dry out and a whitish powder covers the vine. It can be remedied by application of sulfur.

ORGANOLEPTIC A term referring to sensory properties such as the aroma*, color, and flavor of a wine.

OVER-MATURITY The physiological state following that of normal maturity* for grape berries. It may reveal itself either through the appearance of noble rot* or through *passerillage**. Over-maturity of white grapes can produce sweet* and very sweet* wines.

OXIDATION Direct contact between wine and air; this may alter its color, aroma*, and flavor.

P

PASSERILLAGE (Fr) Over-maturity* causing grape berries to dry out, shrivel, and increase their sugar content. This is how so-called "straw wines*," some Muscats, and sweet Jurançon wines are made. These should not be confused with liqueur wines*.

PASSETOUTGRAIN A wine made in Burgundy from a pre-fermentation vat mixture of Gamay Noir and Pinot Noir grapes; the latter must make up at least one third of the blend.

PASSITO (It) An Italian wine made from dried grapes.

PERLANT (Fr) Term relating to slightly effervescent* wines. In France, the term *perlant* is applied to wines that are less effervescent than *pétillant** wines.

PÉTILLANT (Fr) A category of effervescent* wine made using the secondary fermentation in bottle method (*méthode traditionnelle**), but resulting in a pressure less than half that of traditional sparkling wines. *Pétillant* wines of this kind are traditional in regions such as the Loire Valley—Montlouis and Vouvray, in particular.

PHYLLOXERA An aphid that attacks vines and their roots. It was accidentally exported from the United States and ravaged Europe's vineyards between 1860 and 1880.

PIGEAGE (Fr) Production method used for red wine*. It involves regularly submerging the cap* of marc* that accumulates on the surface of fermenting wine. *Pigeage* enriches the must* through contact with the grape skins, and promotes the extraction of the anthocyanins* and tannins* responsible for the wine's color. The procedure also reduces the risk of spoilage that may result from the cap being exposed to the air for too long. Once carried out by hand (or indeed foot), pigeage is now a mechanical process that takes place in specially equipped vats*.

PIGMENTS Vegetable material causing coloration. In the case of grapes, pigments are almost exclusively anthocyanins*.

POLYPHENOLS A range of compounds including tannins*, anthocyanins*, and phenolic acids*. Their combination determines the aromas*, color, and structure of a wine.

PRE-FERMENTATION MACERATION

In white winemaking, pressing* takes place before fermentation*. However, there are many aromatic compounds trapped in the grape skins, so pre-fermentation maceration consists of leaving the juice in contact with the grape skins for a few hours to draw out those characters before pressing.

PRESS WINE Red wine* obtained by pressing* any solid matter remaining after fermentation and after the free-run wine* has been collected. *See also* DÉCUVAISON.

PRESSING

1. The act of squeezing grapes in a press to extract their liquid.
2. The product obtained by such a procedure. There are essentially two methods of pressing: with white wines and rosés, fresh grapes are pressed before fermentation and the resultant liquid is known as must* or juice; with red wines, pressing takes places after fermentation using the marc* obtained during *cuvaison**.

PRUNING Annual or semi-annual elimination of excess growth. Good practice leaves just one or two well-situated branches to provide the buds that will, in turn, produce fruit clusters. (Clusters of grapes grow on buds or "eyes" that form on wood from previous years.) *Gobelet* or bush pruning makes the vine hardier against the vagaries of a hot climate (wind, drought). *Guyot* pruning (single or double) leaves just a branch or two from the existing vine trunk and is better suited to more temperate climes.

PUMPING OVER A technique in red winemaking whereby the fermenting must* is pumped from the base of the vat* over the top of the cap* of marc* to aid the extraction of phenolic compounds.

Q-R

QBA (*Qualitätswein bestimmter Anbaugebiete*) Category of German quality wines that have been produced in one of 13 official regions. May be subject to chaptalization*.

QMP (*Qualitätswein mit Prädikat*) Designation for German wines of higher quality than QBA*. Includes indication of one of six levels

of ripeness. These wines may not be subject to chaptalization*.

QUINTA (Po) The Portuguese term for a wine estate. A quinta's wines may originate from vineyards other than those named.

RACKING A procedure whereby wine is separated from its lees* and poured into another container.

RAMEAU (Fr) A vine shoot that has grown during the current year.

RANCIO (Fr & Sp) A character (reminiscent of prunes) caused by leaving air in a vat* or barrel* of fortified wine. Rancio is the direct result of oxidation*.

RATAFIA (Fr) An aperitif liqueur made in Champagne and Burgundy by adding approximately one part marc* brandy to two parts fresh grape juice.

RECIOTO (It) A type of wine made in Italy with grapes that have been suspended or left to dry for a certain period. They are thus extremely concentrated, and produce a sweet dessert wine*.

RECOLTANT-MANIPULANT (Fr) A specific term in Champagne for a producer who makes wine from his own grapes.

RED (WINE) A wine produced by maceration of must* with red or black grape skins to extract their color, as well as aromas* and tannins*. The grapes are most often destemmed*. Maceration* may last from a few days to several weeks, and the color obtained is dependent on genetic factors (grape variety*), climatic conditions, characteristics of the soil—and winemaking techniques such as the frequency of pumping over, temperature control, etc..

REDUCTION A chemical state that is the opposite or inverse of oxidation*. Wine reduction is caused by prolonged deprivation of oxygen. This presents no danger for wine storage*, quite the contrary. But it does promote the temporary formation of slightly fetid, gamey odors and various hints of sulfur, to the greater or lesser detriment of the wine's bouquet*. These drawbacks can easily be addressed by allowing the wine to breathe* before drinking.

RE-FERMENTATION A faulty re-initiation of alcoholic fermentation*. This phenomenon may occur in poorly stabilized wines containing residual sugar*.

RESERVA (Sp) Red wines matured at a *bodega** for a period of three years, of which at least one is in barrel*. For white wines and rosés, this storage period is reduced to two years, of which at least six months must be in barrel.

RESERVE WINE The portion of production held back by wineries for use in later blends*. The final wine is identified with a specific vintage. In Champagne, reserve wines are used to make non-vintage wines. Additionally, producers may use the term reserve simply for their high-end wines.

RESIDUAL SUGAR The amount (grams or percentage) of sugar remaining in the wine after alcoholic fermentation*.

RIDDLING A procedure applied to Champagne-style sparkling* wines, whereby the sediment of spent yeast* is encouraged to settle against the bottom of the bottle closure* before being removed.

RIMAGE (Fr) A vintage Banyuls wine that is bottled quickly to avoid oxidation and preserve the wine's fruit character and freshness. The word means "age of the grape" in Catalan.

RISERVA (It) Italian DOC* or DOCG* wines that have been aged for official minimum periods in barrel* and in bottle.

ROASTED A term sometimes applied to very sweet* wines with aromas* of grapes affected by noble rot*.

ROOM TEMPERATURE Back in the days when cellars were cold and meals were eaten in rooms that were not continually heated, wines were served at a "room temperature" that rarely exceeded 64°F (18°C). Today, when "room temperature" often means 70°F (21°C) or more, it's advisable to serve even red wine as slightly "cool."

ROOTSTOCK The underground portion of a vine that has been grafted. Most European vines have been grafted onto phylloxera-resistant North American rootstock since the late 19th century.

ROSADO (Sp) / **ROSATO** (It) Rosé.

ROSÉ (WINE) A wine with a more or less obvious pink color. It's obtained either by directly pressing* red grapes, by pressing crushed red grapes after several hours of cold maceration*, or by very brief, partial maceration before applying

the wine press. Macerated rosés have more intense fruit flavors than directly pressed wines, but lack their finesse.

RUNNING-OFF Part of the vinification* procedure for red wine* during which "free-run*" wine is removed from the bottom of the vat*, leaving the marc* behind.

S

SABLE (VIN DE) (Fr) Literally "sand wine," or wine made from vines growing in sandy soil near the sea.

SAIGNÉE (Fr) ("Bleeding the vats"). A procedure during which a fraction of the must is drawn off or "bled" from a vat* of red wine*— early in its production. Clairet* wine and some rosés* are made this way. It's also a method to concentrate red wines.

SECO (Sp and Po) / **SECCO** (It) Dry.

SECOND WINE A selection or blend* not considered good enough for use in a producer's best wine or *grand vin**. At good estates, the second wine often represents excellent value.

SEDIMENT A small fraction of the must* or wine containing a high concentration of vegetal and organic debris. *See also* RACKING.

SÉLECTION DE GRAINS NOBLES (SGN) (Fr) "Selection of noble grape berries"—a term used in France to denote wines made with botrytized* or dried grapes.

SIN CRIANZA (Sp) Wines that have spent no time in barrel*, or too little time to bear the designation *crianza**.

SINGLE-VARIETY (WINE) A wine made from only one grape variety*. A French single-variety wine must be 100 percent from the variety in question; but in many other countries there are regulated tolerances (75 or 85 percent), or indeed no regulation at all. *See also* VARIETAL (WINE).

SOLAR (Po) A *château* or estate in Portugal.

SOLERA (Sp) A system of fractional blending used in Jerez (Spain), whereby several harvests are aged in a tiered succession of barrels* that create a consistent blend or house style.

SPARKLING There are several methods to produce effervescent* wine: the *méthode*

*traditionnelle** (also known as *méthode champenoise**); the *méthode rurale** (used in Gaillac and Die (both in France) among other regions), where effervescence is the result of arrested secondary fermentation in bottle; and the Charmat* (closed vat) method, where effervescence is developed in a vat* to avoid the necessity of bottle-by-bottle riddling* and dégorgement (disgorgement)*.

SPÄTLESE (Ger) A QMP* designation for late-harvested German wine.

SPUMANTE (It) An effervescent Italian wine.

STABILIZATION Wines are stabilized during production to prevent in-bottle precipitation of deposits, harmful chemical reactions, and the growth of microorganisms that may arise in the course of transportation and storage*.

STEM The "skeleton" of a bunch of grapes. Stems are made of woody tissue rich in phenolic compounds, which have a tendency to yield herbaceous flavors.

STILL (WINE) The opposite of effervescent*. The term refers to wines with no discernible carbon dioxide content.

STORAGE Wine is a relatively delicate product, and it may develop unfavorably if not stored correctly. Commonly observed guidelines are intended to protect wine from the action of microbes, particularly acidic bacteria, and against physical and chemical changes that result from exposure to air and heat. Once bottled, the storage period of a wine can of course vary according to the characteristics of the cellar and the wine itself.

STRAW WINE A sweet* wine made from dried grapes. These grapes were traditionally laid on beds of straw or hung up to dehydrate; and their sugars concentrated in greater proportions than their acid content. Principally produced in France, in Jura or Côtes du Rhône, and with an alcoholic content of more than 14% by volume, these wines can be cellared for great lengths of time.

SULFITING A strictly regulated procedure whereby sulfur dioxide* is added to a wine to assure its microbial and chemical stability.

SULFUR DIOXIDE (SO_2) Winemakers have adapted sulfur dioxide for a number of uses since time immemorial: it stops premature fermentation* of harvested grapes, inhibits action by various kinds of yeasts*, eliminates microbes and bacteria, protects against oxidation*, acts as a solvent, and can check malolactic fermentation*; it has proved itself a useful ally for sweet* white wines with a tendency toward (faulty) secondary fermentation in bottle.

SUPERIORE (It) Term for an Italian wine with a higher-than-typical alcohol level (or having undergone a longer period of ageing) than a standard DOC* wine.

SWEET Designation for wine with a sugar content of more than 45 g per liter (or 4.5%).

T

TABLE WINE A wine with no geographic indication of origin or particular quality classification—intended for everyday drinking.

TAFELWEIN (Ger) German table wine.

TANNIN or **TANNINS** The stems*, skins, and seeds of a grape cluster contain chemical compounds (tannins) that are released by pressing and maceration*. These organic chemicals provide the wine's aromas* and flavors, and determine its capacity for ageing.

TARTARIC ACID The most refined acid and the most acidic component of a wine; rarely encountered in the plant kingdom. Its presence in grape berries gradually diminishes with the onset of ripening, and then varies according to climatic conditions.

TARTRATES White crystalline substances that form on the walls of wine vats*, barrels*, and sometimes at the bottom of bottles. They are harmless salts of tartaric acid* and have no taste.

TASTEVIN (Fr) A traditional cellar instrument taking the form of a small, shallow, metallic cup. Used to observe the clarity and color of a wine, characteristics that are assessed to determine the wine's later treatment. Its use in actually tasting cellared wine from barrels* was originally a secondary function.

TASTING NOTE A systematically documented impression of a wine by a taster. Such notes generally list (in order) visual, olfactory, gustatory, and tactile sensations.

TENUTA (It) Italian wine estate.

TERROIR (Fr) The composite impact of soils, topography, climate, and even cultural practices—all of which determine the final character of a wine.

THINNING Cutting back spring or summer growth so that nutrients necessary to ripen grapes are not lost to unnecessary shoot or leaf development. Too little thinning early in the season many lead to *coulure** and the loss of the harvest.

TINTO (Sp and Po) Red.

TONNEAU Term for a specific type of barrel*. In Bordeaux, the tonneau is a unit of volume equivalent to four standard barrels, or about 240 gallons (900 liters).

TOPPING (or TOPPING UP) A procedure through which wine containers are monitored and refilled so that the wine is not left in (adverse) contact with the air.

TRELLISING Modern vineyards are generally trellised, *i.e.* vines are attached to a structure consisting of stakes and parallel wires.

TRIES or **TRIS** (Fr) This term refers to the succession of very selective harvests used to gather dried or botrytized *grapes.

TROCKEN (Ger) Dry.

TROCKENBEERENAUSLESE (Ger) A very sweet German *Prädikatswein* (QMP*), the highest quality level in this category.

V

VARIETAL (WINE) A wine made from only one grape variety. A French varietal wine must be 100 percent from the variety in question; but in many other countries there are regulated tolerances (75%, 85%), or indeed no regulation at all. *See also* SINGLE-VARIETY (WINE).

VAT Vats are winemaking receptacles whose capacity may vary between a couple or hundred and several thousand gallons. They are used for vinification*, maturation*, and storage* of wine. A number of materials are used in their construction, including wood, stone, concrete, galvanized steel, stainless steel, fiberglass, and plastic. Vats used for vinification may be equipped with various fixtures to carry out *pigeage** (the submersion of the cap* of grape skins) or *remontage** (pumping of wine over the cap) automatically.

VDN *See* VIN DOUX NATUREL.

VECCHIO (It) An Italian wine that has been aged for longer than average in barrel* or in bottle.

VERAISON (Fr) The onset of ripening, or the stage of grape cluster development during which the berries begin to change color.

VERY SWEET A wine produced with extremely rich must* or a liqueur wine* that has been concentrated by heating; also wine from *mutage** of must with neutral alcohol and without fermentation (naturally sweet* wine).

VIGNA (It) Vineyard.

VIGNETO (It) Winemaker.

VIN DE PAYS (Fr) Former name for wine produced according to regulated choice of grape variety*, maturity*, and quality. Sold with limited indication of its area of origin. European regulations now provide that such wines are part of the "table wines with geographical indication" category and may not be blended with wines from other areas. *See* INDICATION GEOGRAPHIQUE PROTEGÉE.

VIN DOUX NATUREL (Fr) Naturally sweet wine whose initial sugar content is no less than 252 grams per liter (25%). The alcoholic fermentation* of the wine is halted through the addition of neutral spirit alcohol.

VIN GRIS (Fr) "Gray wine" is a rosé produced when the pulp and red grape skins come into only brief contact with the must. The slightly pink juice that is run off is then fermented.

VIN JAUNE (Fr) "Yellow wine," or a white wine from Jura, France, matured in barrel* under a film of yeast*.

VIN SANTO (It) An Italian *passito** wine.

VINE SHOOT The new stems created by the vine each year. Shoots are the year's new growth and not the older wood of the canes or trunk.

VINIFICATION The stages of winemaking between grape-picking and the end of alcoholic fermentation*.

VINO DE CRIANZA (Sp) A quality wine that must be aged, if red, for two years, or for just one year if white or rosé (of which six months must be in barrel*) before sale.

VINTAGE The year of the harvest from which a wine originates. The character of any vintage is a function of many climatic factors, and they determine much of the quality of the wine and its potential for ageing. Differences between vintages are such that a producer may blend wines from different years to obtain a more balanced wine. Multi-vintage blends (non-vintage wines) are the norm in Champagne.

VITIS LABRUSCA A North American species of grape vine.

VITIS VINIFERA The European species of grape vine.

 W-Z

WEEDING Vineyards are weeded to eliminate (plant) competition for water and nutrients during the vine-growing season.

WHITE (WINE) A wine made from white grapes (or red grapes with white juice) after immediate extraction of the juice or must* from the skins, followed by alcoholic fermentation*. *See also* VINIFICATION.

WINERY A place where wine is made and/or matured in barrels* or vats*.

YEAST Microscopic single-celled fungi found naturally on grape skins (and such yeasts are known as indigenous yeasts). Yeasts multiply in grape juice and drive alcoholic fermentation*.

Research has enabled laboratory cultivation of the most appropriate yeasts for certain kinds of fermentation, and even dried yeast can now be used to make wine.

YIELD The weight of grapes, or equivalent volume in wine, harvested per acre or hectare of vineyard. In Europe, this is a regulated maximum figure for quality wines from a specified region, and is expressed in kilograms of grapes or hectoliters of wine per hectare. In the latter case, the lees* and sediment* are included. In France, the yield of any particular harvest may be reduced by order of the national wine authorities in response to variance in the weather. Depending on the quality of the harvest, the authorities also can set a temporary upper limit for the yield, which will always be lower than the absolute limit prescribed by the definition of each appellation.

Index

Figures in italics indicate captions; main references to AOCs are indicated in bold type.

Index of grape varieties

Red and rosé grape varieties

A-C

Agiorgitiko 427, 430
Aglianico 358, 371
Aglianico Rosato 371
Aleatico 41
Alfrocheiro 398
Alicante Bouschet 399, 429
Alvarelhao 397, 398
Amaral 397
Aragonês 394, 398, 399
Auxerrois 155
Baco 436
Baco Noir 438
Baga 393, 395, 398
Barbera 38, 358, 362, 364, 420, 437, 446, 473
Bastardo 398
Black Hamburg 491
Black Muscat 420
Blauerportugieser 404, 416
Blaufränkisch (Lemberger in Germany) 38, 417
Bombino Nero 371
Bonarda 358, 459, 463
Borraçal 397
Brachetto 358
Brancellaon 380
Braucol (Fer Servadou) 338
Cabernet Cubin 404
Cabernet Franc 29, 33, 34, 36, *36*, **36–37**, 44, 95, 147, 154, 155, 156, 160, 161, 162, 246, 252–56, 259, 261, 263, 266–70, 313, 314, 318, 319, 320, 336–39, 356, 365, 368, 369, 423, 430, 443, 445, 449, 463, 466, 473, 478, 491
Cabernet Sauvignon 23, 31–34, *36*, **36**, 37, *44*, **44**, 87, 95, 147, 155, 161, 206, 217, 218, 221, 245, 246, *247*, 252–57, *258*, 259, 260, 261, 263, 266–70, 319, 320, 335, 336, 337, 339, 348, 350, 356, 362, 365, 368, 369, 371, 372, 382, 383, 384, 386–89, 393, 394, 395, 398, 399, 404, 415, 418, 419, 427–31, 436, 437, 440–43, 445–49, 453, 454, 455, 459–63, 466, 468, 469, 473–81, 486, 490, 491
Caiño Tinto 380
Calabrese 372
Calitor 332
Callet 389
Camarate 398
Camarèse 326
Campbell Early 490
Canaiolo Nero 367
Cannonau 358, 372
Cappuccio 373
Carignan 38, 147, 154, 155, 156, 157, 325, 326, 329, 332, 333, 340–46, 348, 349, 350, 428, 429, 446
Cariñena 378, 386, 387
Carmenère 39, 384, 453, 454, 455

Castelao (Periquita) 294, 395, 398
Catawba 438
Cereza 459
Cinsaut (Cinsault) 39, 156, 325, 326, 329, 330, 332, 333, 337, 340–43, 346, 348, 349, 350, 429, 469
Clairette Rosé 326
Cortaillot (Pinot Noir) 415
Corvina Veronese 362, 364
Counoise 326, 330, 350
Criolla 459
Croatina 362
Cvicek 420

D-F

Dolcetto 358, 360
Domina 404, 406, 410
Dornfelder 404, 406–9, 411
Duras 338
Dureza 325
Espadeiro 380, 397
Fer Servadou (Pinenc, Mansois) 335–39
Fogoneu 389

G-I

Gaglioppo 371
Gamarret 415
Gamay 33, *36*, **37**, 69, 95, 147, 154, 206, 217, 274, 275, 276, 280, 293, 294, 295, 307, 311, 314, 337, 338, 358, 414, 415, 419, 421, 449
Gamay de Bouze 314
Gamay de Chaudenay 314
Gamay Noir 311, 314
Garanoir 415
Garnacha 381, 382, 383, 386–89
Graciano 383
Grenache 23, 31, *37*, **37**, 147, 154–57, 163, 325, 332, 333, 340–44, 346–51, 358, 387, 427, 428, 429, 437, 443, 448, 473, 478, 479, 480
Grenache Gris 161, 326
Grenache Noir 161, 326, 329–33, 341, 342, 344, 345
Gris Meunier 314
Grolleau 39
Halkidiki 427
Hondarribi Beltza 380

J-L

Jaen 398
Kadarka 39
Kékfrankos 418
Kékoportó 418
Kotsifali 427
Kyoho 490
Lambrusco 39, 358
Lambrusco di Sorbara 366
Lambrusco Grasparossa 366

Lambrusco Salamino 366
Lemberger (Limberger) 411
Limnio 427, 430
Lladoner 342, 344
Loureiro 380

M-O

Maccabeu 161
Malbec 39, 155, 246, 252, 253, 254, 256, 257, 260, 263, 266, 267, 269, 335, 336, 337, 382, 384, 437, 440, 445, 449, 453, 459, 461, 462, 463, 478
Malvasia del Chianti 367
Mandilaria 427
Manto Negro 389
Mataro 23
Mavrodaphne 427
Mavron 428
Mavrud 419
Mazuelo 383, 386
Melnik 419
Mencia 378, 380, 381, 382
Merille 336
Merlot 23, 33, 34, 36, *37*, **37**, 44, 95, 147, 154, 155, 157, 161, 162, 218, 246, 252–57, 259, 260, 261, 263, 266–70, 336, 337, 354, 362, 365, 372, 382, 383, 384, 386–89, 398, 418, 419, 420, 423, 427, 429, 431, 436, 437, 440–43, 446, 453, 454, 455, 459, 460, 461, 463, 466, 468, 469, 473, 476–81, 485, 486, 490, 491
Molinara 362, 364
Monastrell 387, 388, 389
Mondeuse 38, 39, 154, 311
Montepulciano 39, 358, 370
Moreto 399
Moscatel Rosada 459
Mourvèdre 23, 37, 39, 147, 155, 157, 325, 326, 330–33, 340–44, 346, 348, 349, 350, 388, 429, 437, 443, 446, 448, 473, 479
Muscardin 326, 330
Muscat Bailey A 490
Nebbiolo *37*, **37**, 147, 155, 358, 360, 361, 437
Negosca 430
Negrara Trentina 362, 364
Négrette 39, 157, 335, 337, 338
Nerello Mantellato 373
Nerello Mascalese 372, 373
Nero d'Avola 358, 372
Niellucio 39, 347, 350, 351

P-R

Padeiro 397
País 453
Pamid 419
Pedral 397
Periquita 399
Petit Verdot 39, *39*, 147, 246, 252–57, 259, 260, 445, 449, 461, 473

Acknowledgments

The Editor would like to thank all those who opened their doors to our photographer:

Bouchard Père & Fils, Château de Beaune, 21200 Beaune
Champagne Gosset 69, rue Jules Blondeau, 51160 Ay
Champagne Krug 5, rue Coquebert, 51100 Reims
Champagne Louis Roederer 21, boulevard Lundy, 51100 Reims
Château Climens 33720 Barsac
Château d'Yquem 33210 Sauternes
Château Lascombes 1, cours de Verdun, 33460 Margaux
Château Latour Saint-Lambert 33250 Pauillac
Château Le Bon Pasteur "Maillet," 33500 Pomerol
Château Moncontour 37210 Vouvray
Château de Pommard 15, rue Marrey Monge, 21630 Pommard
Domaine de la Charmoise, Henry et Jean-Sébastien Marionnet, 41230 Soings-en Sologne
Domaine de la Coulée de Serrant, Château de la Roche aux Moines, 49170 Savennières
Domaine Jean-Maurice Raffault 74, rue du Bourg, 37420 Savigny-en-Véron
Domaine Marcel Deiss 15, route du Vin, 68750 Bergheim
Domaine Michel Juillot 59, Grande Rue, 71640 Mercurey
Domaine de La Romanée-Conti 1, rue Derrière-le-Four, 21700 Vosne-Romanée
Domaines Denis Dubourdieu Château Reynon, 33410 Beguey
Domaines Hugel & Fils 3, rue de la Première Armée, 68340 Riquewihr
Domaines Schlumberger 100, rue Théodore Deck, 68501 Guebwiller
Maison Trimbach 15, route de Bergheim, 68150 Ribeauvillé

and Château Lynch-Bages, Château Rayas, Opus One, Ridge Wineyards,
Vignobles Joseph Mellot à Sancerre, le site www.VotreCave.com

and Tonnellerie Vincent Darnajou, Lieu-dit Goujon, 33570 Montagne

The Editor would like to thank the following people for their help :

David Allan (for his collection of corkscrews), Antoine Caron, Etienne Hunyady, Éric Inglessis
(for his collection of labels), Yann Lioux (South World Wines), Alain Marnat,
Christophe Vidal (Cave de Tolbiac 45, rue de Tolbiac, 75013 Paris) et
La Vaissellerie, 85, rue de Rennes, 75006 Paris.

Picture acknowledgments

16 Ph. © Erich Lessing/AKG, 17 Ph. Coll. Archives Larbor, 18 t l Ph. Coll. Archives Larbor, 18 m l Ph. © Heritage Images/Leemage, 18 m r Ph. Coll. Archives Larbor, 18 b Ph. Coll. Archives Larbor, 19 t l Ph. Coll. Archives Larbor, 19 t r Ph. Coll. Archives Larbor, 19 b l Ph. © Photo Josse/Leemage, 19 b r Ph. Coll. Archives Larbor, 20 Ph. © Hervé Lewandowski/RMN, 21 Ph. © Adoc-photos, 22 Ph. © K.J. Historical/Corbis, 23 t Ph. © Library of Congress, Washington, 23 b Ph. © Alamy/Photo12.com, 28 Ph. © Philippe S. Giraud/Terres du Sud/Sygma/Corbis, 30 t l Ph. © J.L. Barde/Scope, 30 m l Ph. © Domaines Denis Dubourdieu, 30 m r Ph. © P. Othoniel/JDD/Gamma/Eyedea Presse, 31 t r Ph. © Charles O'Rear/Corbis, 31 m r Ph. © Josep Lago/AFP, 31 m l Ph. © Ridge Wineyards, 34 Ph. © J. Guillard/Scope, 36 b r Ph. © Jack K. Clark/AgStock Images/Corbis, 37 b l Ph. © J. Guillard/Scope, 37 b r Ph. © S. Matthews/Scope, 38 t Ph. © Alamy/Photo12.com, 38 m Ph. © J. Guillard/Scope, 39 b l Ph. © Alamy/Photo12.com, 39 b m Ph. © Alamy/Photo12.com, 40 b l Ph. © David Gubernick/AgStock Images/Corbis, 40 b m Ph. © J. Guillard/Scope, 40 b r Ph. © J. Guillard/Scope, 41 b l Ph. © J. Guillard/Scope, 41 b m Ph. © J. L. Barde/Scope, 41 b r Ph. © Martin Rugner/Age Fotostock/Hoa-Qui/Eyedea Presse, 42 t Ph. © Alamy/Photo12.com, 44 Ph. © P. Roy/Hemis.fr, 45 t Ph. © J. Guillard/Scope, 45 b Ph. © John Frumm/Hemis.fr, 48 r Ph © Catherine Corbeau-Mellot (Vignobles Joseph Mellot, Sancerre), 55 Ph. © P. Roy/Hoa-Qui/Eyedea Presse, 59 t Ph © Dom. de la Coulée de Serrant, 72 Ph. © Marc Volk/fstop/Corbis, 74 Porto Sandeman. Ph. © D. Bartruff/Encyclopedia/Corbis, 75 t l Ph. © Alamy/Photo12.com, 75 Ph. © Alamy/Photo12.com, 75 Ph. © J.L. Barde/Scope, 96 Ph. © Emilio Suetone/Hemis.fr, 97 Ph. © Alamy/Photo12.com, 98 Ph; © J. Guillard/Scope, 100 Ph. © Alamy/Photo12.com, 101 Ph. © Alamy/Photo12.com, 102 Ph. © S. Matthews/Scope, 103 Ph. © Alamy/Photo12.com, 116 t l Ph. © Hulton Archive/Getty Images, 116 t r Ph. © Costa/Leemage, 125 Ph. © Derrick Ceyrac/AFP, 126 Ph. © Jeff Pachoud/AFP, 127 Ph. © Michael John Kielty/Corbis, 128 l Ph. © Château Lynch-Bages, 129 t Ph. © J. Guillard/Scope, 129 m r Ph. © Scope, 130 Ph. © Getty Images/AFP, 131 Ph. © Jeff Pachoud/AFP, 134 Ph © VotreCave.com, 136 Ph. © J. Guillard/Scope, 137 Ph. © J.L. Barde/Scope, 141 b r Château l'Angélus barrel cellar, Saint-Emilion. Ph. © P. Roy/Hemis.fr, 142 Ph. © Masterfile-Royalty Free, 143 Ph. © J. Guillard/Scope, 147 Ph. © F. Cateloy/Hoa-Qui/Eyedea Presse, 151 Ph. © Philippe Petit/Paris-Match/Scoop, 152 Ph. © Ryman Cabannes/Corbis, 162 t r Ph. © J.L. Barde/Scope, 163 b r Ph. © Château Rayas, 163 t l Ph. © J. L. Barde/Scope, 163 t r Ph. © J. Guillard/Scope, 163 m l Ph. © J. Guillard/Scope, 169 Ph. © Redcover.com/Getty Images, 170 Ph. © Mallet/Photocuisine/Corbis, 171 Ph. © D. Japy, 173 t Ph. © P. Roy/Hemis.fr, 173 b Ph. © J.-D. Sudres/Hemis.fr, 188–189 b Ph. © Larousse/Diaf Studiaphot/Hervé Geyssels, 195 Ph. © D. Japy, 196 Ph. © B. Hechler/Fotolia.com, 197 Ph. © J.C. Cuvelier/Fotolia.com, 198–201 l and t r Ph. © D. Japy, 204 Ph. © Sébastien Montier/Fotolia.com, 208 Ph. © Alamy/Photo12.com, 214 Ph. © D. Japy, 226 Ph. © James Jackson/Alamy, 242 Clos de Vougeot. Ph. © C. Boisvieux/Hoa-Qui/Eyedea Presse, 244 Château de Monbadon et son vignoble, AOC Côtes de Castillon. Ph. © P. Roy/Hemis.fr, 252 Ph. © P. Roy/Hemis.fr, 253 Ph. © J.L. Barbe/scope, 254 m Ph. © J.-D. Sudres/Hemis.fr, 255 Cos d'Estournel, Saint-Estèphe. Ph. © Alamy/Photo12.com, 256 t Château Pichon-Longueville. Ph. © A. Chicurel/Hemis.fr, 257 Ph. © P. Roy/Hemis.fr, 260 t Ph. © P. Roy/Hemis.fr, 261 Ph. © P. Roy/Hemis.fr, 263 Ph. © Ph. Roy/Hemis.fr, 267 b Ph. © P. Roy/Hemis.fr, 268 t Ph. © P. Jacques/Hemis.fr, 268 m Ph. © Alamy/Photo12.com, 270 Ph. © P. Roy/Hemis.fr, 272 Ph. © S. Grandadam/Hoa-Qui/Eyedea Presse, 273 Ph. © F. Jalain/Explorer/Hoa-Qui/Eyedea Presse, 275 Ph. © H. Hughes/Hemis.fr, 280 t Ph. © Alamy/Photo12.com, 280 Maison Deliance, Dracy-le-Fort. Ph. © J.L. Barde/Scope, 281 Ph. © J. Guillard/Scope, 282 Ph. © Alamy/Photo12.com, 283 Ph. © Alamy/Photo12.com, 285 t Domaine du Château Gris, Nuits-Saint-Georges. Ph. © C. Boisvieux/Hoa-Qui/Eyedea Presse, 285 b Ph. © Alamy/Photo12.com, 286 Ph. © J. Guillard/Scope, 287 Ph. © Alamy/Photo12.com, 290 t Château de Meursault. Ph. © Alamy/ Photo12.com, 290 b Ph. © Alamy/Photo12.com, 292 Château de Rully. Ph. © Alamy/Photo12.com, 294 t Ph. © H. Hughes/Hemis.fr, 294 b Ph. © J.L. Barde/Scope, 306 Château d'Arlay. Ph. © J. Guillard/Scope, 310 Domaine Macle, Château-Chalon. Ph. © J. Guillard/Scope, 314 Ph. © M. Guillard/Scope, 316 b Ph. © M. Rougemont/Top/Eyedea Presse, 318 Ph. © P. Blondel/Scope, 319 Ph. © P. Body/Hemis.fr, 321 Ph. © M. Plassart/Scope, 322 Ph. © J. Guillard/Scope, 324 Ph. © E. Labadie, 325 Ph. © J. Guillard/Scope, 326 Ph. © J. Guillard/Scope, 328 Ph. © E. Labadie, 329 Domaine Auguste Clape, Cornas. Ph. © J. Guillard/Scope, 330 Ph. © B. Rieger/Hemis.fr, 332 Ph. © J.-D. Sudres/Top/Eyedea Presse, 334 Ph. © J.L. Barde/Scope, 336 t Clos Uroulat. Ph. © J.L. Barde/Scope, 337 Ph. © Jean-Loius Pieux avec Création, 338 Buzet Cooperative Ph. © J.L. Barde/Scope, 339 Xavier Martin tasting, Irouleguy. Ph. © J. L. Barde/Scope, 340 Ph. © Chris Hellier/Corbis, 342 Abbaye de Lagrasse. Ph. © R. Nourry/Scope, 344 Ph. © Dom. La Coume du Roy, 345 Ph. © Owen Franken/Corbis, 347 Ph. © J. Guillard/Scope, 348 Ph. © C. Moirenc/Hemis.fr, 349 Domaine Ott, Domaine de Trevallon, Château Sainte Roseline and Château d'Esclans. Ph. © J. Guillard/Scope, 350 Ph. © C. Goupi/Scope, 351 Domaine Torracia, Lecci. Ph. © Colonel Mario/Scope, 352 Ph. © Alamy/Photo12.com, 354 Ph. © Cuboimages/Leemage, 355 Ph. © Guenter Rossenbach/Corbis, 357 t Ph. © R. Mattes/Hemis.fr, 357 b DR, 358 Ph. © Alamy/Photo12.com, 359 Ph. © Stefano Amantini/Atlantide Phototravel/Corbis, 360 t Ph. © C. Vaisse/Hoa-qui/Eyedea Presse, 360 m Ph. © Alamy/Photo12.com, 361 b Ph. © Pierrick Bourgault, 362 Ph. © Alamy/Photo12.com, 365 Ph. © Cuboimages/Leemage, 366 Ph. © Stefano Amantini/Atlantide Phototravel/Corbis, 367 Ph. © Alamy/Photo12.com, 368 and 369 r Ph. © Etienne Hunyady, 369 l Mario Incisa della Rochetta. Ph. © Farabola/Leemage, 371 Ph. © Pierrick Bourgault, 372 Ph. © P. Renault/Hemis.fr, 374 Ph. © Jose Barea/Tmn/Hoa-Qui/Eyedea Presse, 376 Ph. © Alamy/Photo12.com, 377 Ph. © Alamy/Photo12.com, 378 Ph. © Alamy/Photo12.com, 379 Ph. © Alamy/Photo12.com, 380 t Ph. © Alamy/Photo12.com, 380 b Ph. © Alamy/Photo12.com, 381 Ph. © Alamy/Photo12.com, 382 Ph. © Alamy/Photo12.com, 383 Ph. © Alamy/Photo12.com, 384 t l Ph. © J. Guillard/Scope, 384 t r Ph. © Charles O'Rear/Corbis, 385 t l Ph. © J. Guillard/Scope, 385 t r Ph. © J. Guillard/Scope, 386 Ph. © Alamy/Photo12.com, 388 Ph. © J.L. Barde/Scope, 389 Ph. © Alamy/Photo12.com, 390 Ph. © Alamy/Photo12.com, 392 Ph. © Alamy/Photo12.com, 393 Ph. © J. Guillard/Scope, 394 Ph. © Alamy/Photo12.com, 395 Ph. © J. Guillard/Scope, 396 t Ph. © Alamy/Photo12.com, 396 b Ph. © Alamy/Photo12.com, 397 t Ph. © Alamy/Photo12.com, 398 Ph. © G. Monica/White Star/age Fotostock, 399 t Ph. © R. Mattes/Hemis.fr, 400 Ph. © Alamy/Photo12.com, 402 Ph. © Alamy/Photo12.com, 403 Ph. © Alamy/Photo12.com, 404 t Ph. © M. Rugnier/Age Fotostock/Hoa-Qui/Eyedea Presse, 404 m Ph. © Alamy/Photo12.com, 405 Ph. © Imagebroker/Hemis.fr, 406 t Ph. © Alamy/Photo12.com, 406 b Ph. © Alamy/Photo12.com, 407 Ph. © Alamy/Photo12.com, 408 t Ph. © Doug Pearson/JAI/Corbis, 409 t Ph. © J. Guillard/Scope, 409 b Ph. © Alamy/Photo12.com, 410 Ph. © Alamy/Photo12.com, 411 Ph. © Alamy/Photo12.com, 412 Ph. © J. Guillard/Scope, 415 Ph. © J. Guillard/Scope, 416 Ph. © J. Guillard/Scope, 417 Ph. © Alamy/Photo12.com, 418 Ph. © Alamy/Photo12.com, 419 Ph. © Anthony Blake/Age Fotostock, 420 Ph. © Richard Nebesky/Lonely Planet Images, 421 Ph. © G. Rigoulet/Hemis.fr, 422 Ph. © J. - D. Sudres/Top/Eyedea Presse, 423 Ph. © Alamy/Photo12.com, 424 Ph. © John Sims/age Fotostock, 426 Ph. © P. De Wilde/Hoa-Qui/Eyedea Presse, 427 Ph. © Yiergos Ventouris-IML/Hemis.fr, 428 Ph. © M. Dozier/Hemis.fr, 429 Ph. © C. Bowman/Scope, 430 Ph. © Alamy/Photo12.com, 431 m Ph. © Alamy/Photo12.com, 432 Ph. © Alamy/Photo12.com, 434 Ph. © Alamy/Photo12.com, 435 Ph. © Alamy/Photo12.com, 437 Ph. © Alamy/Photo12.com, 438 Ph. © Alamy/Photo12.com, 439 Ph. © Alamy/Photo12.com, 440 Ph. © Alamy/Photo12.com, 441 m Ph. © Fetzer Vineyards, 441 Ph. © Alamy/Photo12.com, 442 Ph. © Alamy/Photo12.com, 443 t Ph. © Alamy/Photo12.com, 443 b Ph. © Clos du Val Winery, 444 t Ph. © Opus One Winery, 444 m Ph. © El Kashi/Corbis, 447 Ph. © David Gubernick/Corbis, 448 Ph. © Alamy/Photo12.com, 449 Ph. © B. Rondel/Corbis, 450 Ph. © Kordcom Kordcom/Age fotostock/Photolibrary.com, 452 Ph. © Kactus/Scope, 453 Ph. © S. Matthews/Scope, 454 t Ph. © S. Matthews/Scope, 455 m r Ph. © Kactus/Scope, 456 Ph. © Eduardo Longoni/Corbis, 458 Ph. © C. Heeb/Hemis.fr, 459 Ph. © Eduardo Longoni/Corbis, 460 Ph. © Jefferson Bernardes/Getty Images, 461 Ph. © Alamy/Photo12.com, 462 t Ph. © C. Heeb/Hemis.fr, 462 m Ph. © Alamy/Photo12.com, 462 b Ph. © Michael Lewis/Corbis, 463 Catena Zapata Winery. Ph. © Michael Lewis/Corbis, 464 Ph. © Alamy/Photo12.com, 466 Ph. © Alamy/Photo12.com, 467 Ph. © Alamy/Photo12.com, 468 t Ph. © Alamy/Photo12.com, 468 b Ph. © P. Narayan/Age Fotostock/Hoa-Qui/Eyedea Presse, 469 Ph. © C. Heeb/Hemis.fr, 470 Ph. © Andrew Watson/Ticket/Photolibrary.com, 472 Ph. © Russell Mountford/Lonely Planet Images, 473 Ph. © Neale Clarke/Robert Harding World Imagery/Corbis, 474 Ph. © Shoot/Age fotostock/Hoa-Qui/Eyedea Presse, 475 Ph. © J. Du Cange/Top/Eyedea Presse, 476 t Ph. © Alamy/Photo12.com, 476 m Ph. © J.L. Barde/Scope, 477 Domaine Chandon, Yarra Valley. Ph. © E. Valentin/Hoa-Qui/Eyedea Presse, 478 Ph. © D. Dutay/Scope, 479 Ph. © B. Gardel/Hemis.fr, 480 Ph. © Alamy/Photo12.com, 481 Ph. © Alamy/Photo12.com, 482 Ph. © Nick Servian/Scope, 484 Ph. © Alamy/Photo12.com, 485 Ph. © Alamy/Photo12.com, 486 t Ph. © Alamy/Photo12.com, 486 b Ph. © Nick Servian/Scope, 488 Ph. © Tony McNicol/Alamy, 490 Ph. © Morales/Age Fotostock, 491 Ph. © Indranil Mukherjee/AFP

Ph. Olivier Ploton © Archives Larousse: 1, 4, 7, 12–13, 14 (Château Reynon), 27, 32, 35, 36 l and m, 37 m, 39 r, 42 b, 43, 46, 48 l and m, 49–54, 56–58, 59 b, 60–61, 62–63, 67–71, 76–81, 82–83 (Tonnellerie Darnajou), 84–89, 90–91 (Bouchard Père & Fils), 92, 94–95, 104–108, 118 (Cave Tolbiac), 120–121, 124 (Cave de Tolbiac), 128 r (Château de Pommard), 129 l, 132 (Château d'Yquem), 135 (Bouchard Père & Fils), 140, 141 (except b r), 142 r, 146 (Bouchard Père & Fils), 150 (Château Latour), 154–161, 164 l, 166–167 (Cave Tolbiac), 172, 177, 181, 186, 189 t, 190 (collection of old corkscrews, coll. David Allan, Paris), 191, 192–194, 195 b, 201 b r, 203–207, 209–213, 217 (Cave Tolbiac), 218–219, 228, 233, 236–237, 241, 247–249, 258–259, 264–266, 267 t, 276, 277 (Bouchard Père & Fils), 279, 288–289, 296, 298–299 (Maison Louis Roederer), 300–305, 308 b, 313, 316 t, 320, 336 b, 479 b, 492–493 (Dom. Michel Juillot).